Lecture Notes in Computer Science　　9944

Commenced Publication in 1973
Founding and Former Series Editors:
Gerhard Goos, Juris Hartmanis, and Jan van Leeuwen

More information about this series at http://www.springer.com/series/7411

Parosh Aziz Abdulla · Carole Delporte-Gallet (Eds.)

Networked Systems

4th International Conference, NETYS 2016
Marrakech, Morocco, May 18–20, 2016
Revised Selected Papers

Editors
Parosh Aziz Abdulla
Uppsala University
Uppsala
Sweden

Carole Delporte-Gallet
Université Paris Diderot
Paris
France

ISSN 0302-9743   ISSN 1611-3349   (electronic)
Lecture Notes in Computer Science
ISBN 978-3-319-46139-7   ISBN 978-3-319-46140-3   (eBook)
DOI 10.1007/978-3-319-46140-3

Library of Congress Control Number: 2016950896

LNCS Sublibrary: SL5 – Computer Communication Networks and Telecommunications

Printed on acid-free paper

This Springer imprint is published by Springer Nature
The registered company is Springer International Publishing AG
The registered company address is: Gewerbestrasse 11, 6330 Cham, Switzerland

Preface

NETYS 2016 received 121 submissions. The reviewing process was undertaken by a Program Committee of 31 international experts in the areas of networking, distributed computing, security, formal methods, and verification. This process led to the definition of a strong scientific program. The Program Committee accepted 22 regular papers and 11 short papers. In addition, 19 papers were selected for poster presentation. Besides these high-quality contributions, the program of NETYS 2016 included keynote talks by three world-renowned researchers:

Joost-Pieter Katoen (RWTH Aachen University, Germany),
Andreas Podelski (University of Freiburg, Germany), and
Luis Rodrigues (Universidade de Lisboa, Portugal).

We warmly thank all the authors for their great contributions, all the Program Committee members for their hard work and their commitment, all the external reviewers for their valuable help, and the three keynote speakers to whom we are deeply grateful for their support. Special thanks to the two conference general chairs, Mohammed Erradi (ENSIAS, Rabat, Morocco), and Rachid Guerraoui (EPFL, Lausanne, Switzerland), for their invaluable guidance and tremendous help.

June 2016   Parosh Aziz Abdulla
                                                                          Carole Delporte-Gallet

Organization

Program Committee

Parosh Aziz Abdulla	Uppsala University, Sweden
Mohamed Faouzi Atig	Uppsala University, Sweden
Slimane Bah	Ecole Mohammadia d'Ingénieurs - Mohammed V University, Morocco
Gregor Bochmann	University of Ottawa, Canada
Silvia Bonomi	Sapienza Università di Roma, Italy
Ahmed Bouajjani	LIAFA, University Paris Diderot, France
Carole Delporte-Gallet	University Paris Diderot, France
Stéphane Devismes	VERIMAG UMR 5104, France
Mohamed El Kamili	LiM, FSDM, USMBA, Fès, Morocco
Mohammed El Koutbi	ENSIAS, Morocco
Michael Emmi	IMDEA Software Institute, Spain
Javier Esparza	Technische Universität München, Germany
Panagiota Fatourou	University of Crete & FORTH ICS, Greece
Hugues Fauconnier	LIAFA, France
Bernd Freisleben	University of Marburg, Germany
Maurice Herlihy	Brown University, USA
Zahi Jarir	Cadi Ayyad University, Marrakech, Morocco
Mohamed Jmaiel	ReDCAD, ENIS, Tunisia
Anne-Marie Kermarrec	Inria, France
Akash Lal	Microsoft Research, India
Roland Meyer	University of Kaiserslautern, Germany
Ouzzif Mohammed	ESTC, Morocco
Madhavan Mukund	Chennai Mathematical Institute, India
Madan Musuvathi	Microsoft Research, USA
Guevara Noubir	Northeastern University, USA
Franck Petit	LiP6 CNRS-INRIA UPMC Sorbonne Universités, France
Michel Raynal	IRISA, France
Ahmed Rezine	Linköping University, Sweden
Liuba Shrira	Brandeis University, USA
Serdar Tasiran	Koc University, Turkey
Viktor Vafeiadis	MPI-SWS, Germany

Contents

Abstracts of Posters

Nonrepudiation Protocols
Without a Trusted Party

Muqeet Ali[(✉)], Rezwana Reaz, and Mohamed G. Gouda

Department of Computer Science, University of Texas at Austin,
Austin, TX 78712, USA
{muqeet,rezwana,gouda}@cs.utexas.edu

Abstract. A nonrepudiation protocol from party S to party R performs two tasks. First, the protocol enables party S to send to party R some text x along with sufficient evidence (that can convince a judge) that x was indeed sent by S. Second, the protocol enables party R to receive text x from S and to send to S sufficient evidence (that can convince a judge) that x was indeed received by R. Almost every published nonrepudiation protocol from party S to party R involves three parties: the two original parties S and R, and a third party that is often called a trusted party. A well-known nonrepudiation protocol that does not involve a third party is based on an assumption that party S knows an upper bound on the computing power of party R. This assumption does not seem reasonable especially since by violating this assumption, party R can manipulate the nonrepudiation protocol so that R obtains all its needed evidence without supplying party S with all its needed evidence. In this paper, we show that nonrepudiation protocols that do not involve a third party can be designed under reasonable assumptions. Moreover, we identify necessary and sufficient (reasonable) assumptions under which these protocols can be designed. Finally, we present the first ever ℓ-nonrepudiation protocol that involves ℓ parties (none of which is trusted), where $\ell \geq 2$.

1 Introduction

A nonrepudiation protocol from party S to party R performs two tasks. First, the protocol enables party S to send to party R some text along with sufficient evidence (that can convince a judge) that the text was indeed sent by S to R. Second, the protocol enables party R to receive the sent text from S and to send to S sufficient evidence (that can convince a judge) that the text was indeed received by R from S.

Each nonrepudiation protocol is also required to fulfill the following opportunism requirement. During any execution of the nonrepudiation protocol from S to R, once a party (S or R, respectively) recognizes that it has already collected all its needed evidence, then this party concludes that it gains nothing by continuing to execute the protocol and so it terminates. The other party (R or S, respectively) continues to execute the protocol with the hope that it will eventually collect all its needed evidence.

© Springer International Publishing AG 2016
P.A. Abdulla and C. Delporte-Gallet (Eds.): NETYS 2016, LNCS 9944, pp. 1–15, 2016.
DOI: 10.1007/978-3-319-46140-3_1

The opportunism requirement which is satisfied by each party in a nonrepudiation protocol can be thought of as a failure of that party. It is important to contrast this failure model with the failure model used in the celebrated paper of Cleve [6]. Recall that Cleve's paper states an impossibility result regarding agreement on random bits chosen by two processes provided that one of the processes is faulty. In Cleve's paper the faulty process can fail at any time during the execution of the protocol. Therefore, Cleve's impossibility result is not applicable in our case, as in our model, failures occur only as dictated by the opportunism requirement.

The intuitive reasoning behind our failure model is that parties do not wish to stop executing the protocol (and thus fail) before collecting their needed evidence. Once a party recognizes that it has already collected all its needed evidence, this party decides to stop executing the protocol (i.e., fail) because it gains nothing by continuing to execute the protocol.

The opportunism requirement, that needs to be fulfilled by each nonrepudiation protocol, makes the task of designing nonrepudiation protocols very hard. This is because once a party in a nonrepudiation protocol terminates (because it has recognized that it has already collected all its needed evidence), then from where will the other party continue to receive its needed evidence?

The standard answer to this question is to assume that a nonrepudiation protocol from party S to party R involves three parties: the two original parties S and R and a third party T, which is often referred to as a trusted party. Note that the objective of each original party is to collect its own evidence, whereas the objective of the third party is to help the two original parties collect their respective evidence. Therefore, the opportunism requirement for the third party T can be stated as follows. Once T recognizes that the two original parties have already collected their evidence (or are guaranteed to collect their evidence soon), T terminates.

An execution of a nonrepudiation protocol from party S to party R that involves the three parties S, R, and T can proceed in three steps as follows:

1. Party S sends some text to party T which forwards it to party R.
2. Party T computes sufficient evidence to establish that S has sent the text to R then T forwards this evidence to R.
3. Party T computes sufficient evidence to establish that R has received the text from S then T forwards this evidence to S.

Most nonrepudiation protocols that have been published in the literature involve three parties: the two original parties and a third party [10]. A nonrepudiation protocol that does not involve a third party was published in [12]. We refer to this protocol as the MR protocol in reference to its two authors Markowitch and Roggeman. Unfortunately, the correctness of this protocol is questionable as discussed next.

In the MR protocol, party S first sends to party R the text encrypted using a symmetric key SK that only S knows. Then party S sends to party R an arbitrary number of random numbers, each of which looks like, but in fact is quite different from, the symmetric key SK. Finally, party S sends to party R

the symmetric key SK. After R receives each of these messages from S, R sends to S an ack message that acknowledges receiving the message from S.

The evidence that R needs to collect is the first message (containing the text encrypted using SK) and the last message (containing SK). The evidence that S needs to collect is the acknowledgements of R receiving the first and last messages.

In the MR protocol, when party R receives the i-th message from S, where i is at least 2, R recognizes that the message content is either a random number or the symmetric key SK. Thus, R can use the message content in an attempt to decrypt the encrypted text (which R has received in the first message). If this attempt fails, then R recognizes that the message content is a random number and proceeds to send an ack message to S. If this attempt succeeds, then R recognizes that the message content is the symmetric key SK and terminates right away (in order to fulfill the opportunism requirement) without sending the expected ack message to S. In this case, R succeeds in collecting all the evidence that it needs while S fails in collecting all the evidence that it needs.

To prevent this problematic scenario, the designers of the MR protocol adopted the following three assumptions: (1) there is a lower bound lb on the time needed by R to decrypt the encrypted text, (2) S knows an upper bound ub on the round trip delay from S to R and back to S, and (3) lb is larger than ub. Based on these assumptions, if party S sends a random number to party R and does not receive back the expected ack message for at least ub time units, then S recognizes that R has tried to cheat (but failed) by attempting to decrypt the encrypted text using the received random number. In this case, party S aborts executing the protocol and both S and R fail to collect all their needed evidence. Now, if party S sends a random number to party R and receives back the expected ack message within ub time units, then both parties continue to execute the protocol.

Unfortunately, party R can secretly decrease the value of lb, for example by employing a super computer to decrypt the encrypted text, such that assumption (3) above is violated. By violating assumption (3), the attempts of R to cheat can go undetected by party S and the MR protocol can end up in a compromised state where party R has terminated after collecting all its needed evidence but party S is still waiting to collect its needed evidence that will never arrive. This problematic scenario calls into question the correctness of the MR protocol.

In this paper, we discuss how to design nonrepudiation protocols that do not involve a trusted party. We make the following five contributions:

1. We first state the round-trip assumption as follows: Party R knows an upper bound on the round trip delay from R to S and back to R. Then we show that adopting this assumption is both necessary and sufficient for designing nonrepudiation protocols from S to R that do not involve a third trusted party and where no sent message is lost.
2. Our sufficiency proof in 1 consists of designing the first (provably correct) nonrepudiation protocol from S to R that does not involve a third party and where no sent message is lost.

3. We state the bounded-loss assumption as follows: Party R knows an upper bound on the number of messages that can be lost during any execution of the protocol. Then we show that adopting both the round-trip assumption and the bounded-loss assumption is both necessary and sufficient in designing nonrepudiation protocols from S to R that do not involve a third trusted party and where every sent message may be lost.
4. Our sufficiency proof in 3 consists of designing the first (provably correct) nonrepudiation protocol from S to R that does not involve a third party and where every sent message may be lost.
5. We extend the nonrepudiation protocol in 2 that involves only two parties, S and R, into an ℓ-nonrepudiation protocol that involves ℓ parties (none of which is trusted), where $\ell \geq 2$.

The proofs of all the theorems that appear in this paper are described in the technical report [1]

2   Related Work

The most cited nonrepudiation protocol was published by Zhou and Gollmann in 1996 [15]. This protocol involves three parties S, R, and a trusted third party T. It turns out that each execution of this protocol requires the active participation of all three parties S, R, and T. A year later, Zhou and Gollmann published a second version [16] of their protocol, where each execution requires the active participation of parties S and R, but does not necessarily require the participation of party T. (Thus, some executions of this second version requires the participation of T and some don't.)

Later, Kremer and Markowitch generalized nonrepudiation protocols that are from a party S to a party R into protocols that are from a party S to several parties $R1, \cdots, R.n$. They referred to the generalized protocols as multiparty protocols, and published the first two multiparty protocols [9,11].

Most nonrepudiation protocols involve the services of a third party for successful completion of the protocol [8,9,11,15,16]. There are protocols which involve a third party in every execution of the protocol from party S to party R [9,15]. These protocols are said to have on-line third party. The involvement of third party in every execution can become a bottleneck therefore protocols were proposed to limit the involvement of third party [8,11,16]. In such protocols, the third party is not involved in every execution of the protocol. Such protocols are said to have an off-line third party, and are known as optimistic nonrepudiation protocols. Nonrepudiation has also found a number of applications [14,17].

The problem of designing nonrepudiation protocols is similar to the problem of designing contract signing protocols. However, in contract signing protocols the contract C to be signed is known to all parties before the execution of contract signing protocol begins, while in nonrepudiation protocols the text x is only known to party S before the execution of the nonrepudiation protocol begins. Most contract signing protocols do make use of a trusted third party. See for example [2,3]. However, the trusted third party in some of the published contract signing protocols is rather weak [4,13]. For example, the trusted third party in Rabin's protocol [13] does not receive any messages from either of the two parties S or R. Rather, Rabin's third party periodically generates random numbers and sends them to the original parties S and R.

Some published contract signing protocols do not employ a trusted third party. See for example [5,7]. However, the opportunism requirement that is fulfilled by these protocols is weaker than our opportunism requirement. Thus, in each of these protocols, a party (S or R) may continue to execute the contract signing protocol even after this party recognizes that it has collected all its needed evidence with the hope that the cost of processing its collected evidence can be reduced dramatically.

3 Nonrepudiation Protocols

In this section, we present our specification of a nonrepudiation protocol that does not involve a third party. A nonrepudiation protocol from party S to party R that does not involve a third party is a communication protocol between parties S and R that fulfills the following requirements.

(a) **Message Loss:** During each execution of the protocol, each message that is sent by either party (S or R, respectively) is eventually received by the other party (R or S, respectively).

(b) **Message Alternation:** During any execution of the protocol, the two parties S and R exchange a sequence of messages. First, party S sends msg.1 to party R. Then when party R receives msg.1, it sends back msg.2 to party S, and so on. At the end when R receives msg.$(r - 1)$, where r is an even integer whose value is at least 2, R sends back msg.r to S. This exchange of messages can be represented as follows:

$$S \rightarrow R: \text{msg.1}$$
$$S \leftarrow R: \text{msg.2}$$
$$\cdots$$
$$S \rightarrow R: \text{msg.}(r - 1)$$
$$S \leftarrow R: \text{msg.}r$$

(c) **Message Signatures:** Party S has a private key that only S knows and the corresponding public key that all parties know. Party S uses its private key to sign every message before sending this message to R so that S can't later repudiate that it has generated this message. Similarly, Party R has a private key that only R knows and the corresponding public key that all parties know. Party R uses its private key to sign every message before sending this message to S so that R can't later repudiate that it has generated this message.

(d) **Collected Evidence:** Both parties S and R collect evidence during execution of the protocol. The evidence collected by party S is a subset of those messages received by party S (from party R). Similarly, the evidence collected by party R is a subset of those messages received by party R (from party S).

(e) **Guaranteed Termination:** Every execution of the protocol is guaranteed to terminate in a finite time.

(f) **Termination Requirement:** Party S terminates only after S sends some text to R and only after S receives from R sufficient evidence to establish that R has indeed received the sent text from S. Similarly, party R terminates only after R receives from S both the sent text and sufficient evidence to establish that S has indeed sent this text to R.

(g) **Opportunism Requirement:** If during any execution of the protocol, party S recognizes that it has already sent some text to R and has later received from R sufficient evidence to establish that R has indeed received this text, then S terminates. Similarly, if during any execution of the protocol, party R recognizes that it has received from S some text and sufficient evidence to establish that S has indeed sent this text, then R terminates.

(h) **Judge:** Anytime after execution of the nonrepudiation protocol terminates, each of the two parties, S or R, can submit its collected evidence to a judge that can decide whether the submitted evidence is valid and should be accepted or it is invalid and should be rejected. The decision of the judge is final and legally binding on both S and R. To help the judge make the right decision, we assume that the judge knows the public keys of S and R. We also assume that the judge has a public key (that both S and R know) and a corresponding private key (that only the judge knows). (Note that the role of the judge is different than that of a trusted third party. The trusted third party is used to generate and distribute the needed evidence to the two parties, S and R. Therefore, the trusted third party is directly involved during the execution of the nonrepudiation protocol. The judge, however, is not directly involved during the execution of the protocol, and it never generates nor distributes any part of the needed evidence to either party. The judge only verifies the submitted evidence after it has already been collected during execution of the protocol. In fact every nonrepudiation protocol that has been published in the past has both a trusted third party and a judge)

The opportunism requirement needs some explanation. Once party S recognizes that it has already collected sufficient evidence to establish that party R has indeed received the text from S, S concludes that it gains nothing by continuing to participate in executing the protocol and so S terminates. (In this case, only R may gain by continuing to participate in executing the protocol.)

Similarly, once party R recognizes that it has already collected sufficient evidence to establish that party S has indeed sent the text to R, R concludes that it gains nothing by continuing to participate in executing the protocol and so R terminates.

Next, we state a condition, named the round-trip assumption and show in the next section that adopting this assumption is both necessary and sufficient to design nonrepudiation protocols from party S to party R that do not involve a third party.

Round-Trip Assumption: Party R knows an upper bound t (in time units) on the round trip delay from R to S and back to R.

4 Necessary and Sufficient Conditions for Nonrepudiation Protocols

We prove that it is necessary to adopt the round-trip assumption when designing nonrepudiation protocols from party S to party R that do not involve a third party.

Theorem 1. *In designing a nonrepudiation protocol from party S to party R, that does not involve a third party, it is necessary to adopt the round-trip assumption. (The proof of this theorem is omitted due to lack of space.)*

Next, we prove that it is sufficient to adopt the round-trip assumption in order to design a nonrepudiation protocol from party S to party R that does not involve a third party.

Theorem 2. *It is sufficient to adopt the round-trip assumption in order to design a nonrepudiation protocol from party S to party R that does not involve a third party.*

Proof. We present a design of a nonrepudiation protocol from party S to party R that does not involve a third party and show that correctness of this protocol is based on adopting the round-trip assumption. Our presentation of this protocol consists of four steps. In each step, we start with a version of the protocol then show that this version is incorrect (by showing that it violates one of the requirements in Sect. 3). We then proceed to modify this protocol version in an attempt to make it correct. After four steps, we end up with a correct nonrepudiation protocol (that satisfies all eight requirements in Sect. 3).

First Protocol Version: In this protocol version, party S sends a txt message to party R which replies by sending back an ack message. The exchange of messages in this protocol version can be represented as follows.

$$S \rightarrow R: \text{txt}$$
$$S \leftarrow R: \text{ack}$$

The txt message contains: (1) the message sender S and receiver R, (2) the text that S needs to send to R, and (3) signature of the message using the private key of the message sender S. Similarly, the ack message contains: (1) the message sender R and receiver S, (2) the text that S needs to send to R, and (3) signature of the message using the private key of the message sender R.

The txt message is the evidence that R needs to collect and can later present to the judge to get the judge to declare that the text in the message was indeed sent by S to R. Similarly, the ack message is the evidence that S needs to collect and can later present to the judge to get the judge to declare that the text in the message was indeed received by R from S.

This protocol version is incorrect for the following reason. When R receives the txt message, it recognizes that it has already collected sufficient evidence to establish that S has indeed sent the text to R and so R terminates, by the opportunism requirement, before it sends the ack message to S. Party S ends up waiting indefinitely for the ack message that will never arrive violating the guaranteed termination requirement.

To make this protocol version correct, we need to devise a technique by which R does not recognize that it has collected sufficient evidence to establish that S has indeed sent the text to R, even after R has collected such evidence.

Second Protocol Version: In this protocol version, party S sends n txt messages to party R, where n is a positive integer selected at random by S and is kept as a secret from R. The exchange of messages in this protocol version can be represented as follows.

$$S \rightarrow R: \text{txt.1}$$
$$S \leftarrow R: \text{ack.1}$$
$$\cdots$$
$$S \rightarrow R: \text{txt.}n$$
$$S \leftarrow R: \text{ack.}n$$

Each txt.i message contains: (1) the message sender S and receiver R, (2) the text that S needs to send to R, (3) the sequence number of the message i, and (4) signature of the message using the private key of the message sender S. Similarly, each ack.i message contains: (1) the message sender R and receiver S, (2) the text that S needs to send to R, (3) the sequence number of the message i, and (4) signature of the message using the private key of the message sender R.

The txt.n message is the evidence that R needs to collect and can later present to the judge to get the judge to declare that the text in the message was indeed sent by S to R. Similarly, the ack.n message is the evidence that S needs to collect and can later present to the judge to get the judge to declare that the text in the message was indeed received by R from S.

When R receives the txt.n message from S, then (because R does not know the value of n) R does not recognize that it has just received sufficient evidence to establish that S has indeed sent the text to R. Thus, R does not terminate and instead proceeds to send the ack.n message to S.

When S receives the ack.n message from R, then (because S knows the value of n) S recognizes that it has just received sufficient evidence to establish that R

has received the text sent from S to R. Thus, by the opportunism requirement, S terminates and R ends up waiting indefinitely for the txt.$(n+1)$ message that will never arrive violating the guaranteed termination requirement.

This protocol version is incorrect. To make it correct, we need to devise a technique by which party R recognizes, after S terminates, that R has already collected sufficient evidence to establish that S has indeed sent the text to R.

Third Protocol Version: This protocol version is designed by modifying the second protocol version (discussed above) taking into account the adopted round-trip assumption, namely that R knows an upper bound t (in time units) on the round trip delay from R to S and back to R.

The exchange of messages in the third protocol version is the same as that in the second protocol version. However, in the third protocol version, every time R sends an ack.i message to S, R activates a time-out to expire after t time units.

If R receives the next txt.$(i+1)$ before the activated time-out expires, then R cancels the timeout. If the activated time-out expires before R receives the next txt.$(i+1)$ message, then R recognizes that the last received txt.i message is in fact the txt.n message and so R recognizes that it has already collected sufficient evidence to establish that S has already sent the text to R and so R terminates (by the opportunism requirement). Execution of this protocol version can be represented as follows:

$$S \rightarrow R: \text{txt}.1$$
$$S \leftarrow R: \text{ack}.1;\ R\text{ activates time-out}$$
$$S \rightarrow R: \text{txt}.2;\ R\text{ cancels time-out}$$
$$\cdots$$
$$S \rightarrow R: \text{txt}.n;\ R\text{ cancels time-out}$$
$$S \leftarrow R: \text{ack}.n;\ R\text{ activates time-out};\ S\text{ terminates}$$
$$\text{time-out expires};\ R\text{ terminates}$$

This protocol version still has a problem. After execution of the protocol terminates, party R may decide to submit its collected evidence, namely the txt.n message, to the judge so that the judge can certify that S has indeed sent the text in the txt.n message. The judge can make this certification if it observes that the sequence number of the txt.n message equals the random integer n that S selected when execution of the protocol started. Unfortunately, the value of n is not included in the txt.n message.

Similarly, after execution of the protocol terminates, party S may decide to submit its collected evidence, namely the ack.n message, to the judge so that the judge can certify that R has indeed received the text in the ack.n message. The judge can make this certification if it observes that the sequence number of the ack.n message equals the random integer n that S selected when execution of the protocol started. Unfortunately, the value of n is not included in the ack.n message.

To solve these two problems, we need to devise a technique by which the value of n is included in every txt.i message and every ack.i message such that the following two conditions hold. First, the judge can extract the value of n from any txt.i or ack.i message. Second, party R can't extract the value of n from any txt.i message nor from any ack.i message.

Fourth Protocol Version: In this protocol version, two more fields are added to each txt.i message and each ack.i message. The first field stores the encryption of n using a symmetric key KE that is generated by party S and is kept as a secret from party R. The second field stores the encryption of the symmetric key KE using the public key of the judge.

These two fields are computed by party S when execution of the protocol starts and are included in every txt.i message before this message is sent from S to R. When party R receives a txt.i message from party S, party R copies these two fields from the received txt.i message into the next ack.i message before this message is sent from R to S.

After execution of this protocol version terminates, party S can submit its collected evidence, namely the last ack.i message that S has received from R, to the judge so that the judge can examine the ack.i message and certify that R has received the text in this message from S. The judge makes this certification by checking, among other things, that the sequence number i of the ack.i message is greater than or equal to n. The judge then forwards its certification to party S.

Similarly, after execution of this protocol version terminates, party R can submit its collected evidence, namely the last txt.i message that R has received from S, to the judge so that the judge can examine the txt.i message and certify that S has sent the text in this message to R. The judge makes this certification by checking, among other things, that the sequence number i of the txt.i message is greater than or equal to n. The judge then forwards its certification to party R.

Note that the judge can certify at most one ack.i message from party S, and at most one txt.i message from party R. This restriction forces S to send to the judge only the last ack.i message that S has received from R. This restriction also forces R to send to the judge only the last txt.i message that R has received from S. □

5   Nonrepudiation Protocols with Message Loss

In the remainder of this paper, we consider a richer class of nonrepudiation protocols where sent messages may be lost before they are received. Each protocol in this class is required to fulfill the following requirements.

(a) **Message Loss:** During each execution of the protocol, each message that is sent by either party (S or R, respectively) can be lost before it is received by the other party (R or S, respectively).

(b) **Message Alternation:** During any execution of the protocol where no sent message is lost, the two parties S and R exchange a sequence of messages.

First, party S sends msg.1 to party R. Then when party R receives msg.1, it sends back msg.2 to party S, and so on. At the end when R receives msg.$(r-1)$, where r is an even integer whose value is at least 2, R sends back msg.r to S. This exchange of messages can be represented as follows:

$$S \rightarrow R: \text{msg.1}$$
$$S \leftarrow R: \text{msg.2}$$
$$\cdots$$
$$S \rightarrow R: \text{msg.}(r-1)$$
$$S \leftarrow R: \text{msg.}r$$

(c) **Message Signatures:** This requirement is the same as the message signature requirement in Sect. 3.

(d) **Collected Evidence:** This requirement is the same as the collected evidence requirement in Sect. 3.

(e) **Guaranteed Termination:** This requirement is the same as the guaranteed termination requirement in Sect. 3.

(f) **Termination Requirement:** This requirement is the same as the termination requirement in Sect. 3.

(g) **Opportunism Requirement:** This requirement is the same as the opportunism requirement in Sect. 3.

(h) **Judge:** This requirement is the same as the requirement of the judge in Sect. 3.

Next, we state a condition, named the bounded-loss assumption. We then show in the next section that adopting this assumption along with the round-trip assumption (stated in Sect. 3) is both necessary and sufficient to design nonrepudiation protocols from party S to Party R that do not involve a third party and where sent messages can be lost.

Bounded-Loss Assumption: Party R knows an upper bound K on the number of messages that can be lost during any execution of the nonrepudiation protocols.

6   Necessary and Sufficient Conditions for Nonrepudiation Protocols with Message Loss

We prove that it is necessary to adopt both the round-trip assumption and the bounded-loss assumption when designing nonrepudiation protocols from party S to party R that do not involve a third party and where sent messages may be lost.

Theorem 3. *In designing a nonrepudiation protocol from party S to party R that does not involve a third party and where sent messages may be lost, it is necessary to adopt the round-trip assumption. (The proof of this theorem is omitted due to lack of space.)*

Theorem 4. *In designing a nonrepudiation protocol from party S to party R that does not involve a third party and where sent messages may be lost, it is necessary to adopt the bounded-loss assumption. (The proof of this theorem is omitted due to lack of space)*

Next, we prove that it is sufficient to adopt both the round-trip assumption and the bounded-loss assumption in order to design a nonrepudiation protocol from party S to party R that does not involve a third party and where sent messages may be lost.

Theorem 5. *It is sufficient to adopt both the round-trip assumption and the bounded-loss assumption in order to design a nonrepudiation protocol from party S to party R that does not involve a third party and where sent messages may be lost.*

Proof. In our proof of Theorem 2, we adopted the round-trip assumption in order to design a nonrepudiation protocol, which we refer to in this proof as protocol P, from party S to party R that does not involve a third party and where no sent message is ever lost. In the current proof, we adopt the bounded-loss assumption in order to modify protocol P into protocol Q, which is a nonrepudiation protocol from party S to party R that does not involve a third party and where sent messages may be lost.

In protocol P, every time party R sends an ack.i message to party S, R activates a time-out to expire after t time units, where (by the round-trip assumption) t is an upper bound on the round trip delay from R to S and back to R. Because no sent message is ever lost in protocol P, then if the activated time-out expires before R receives the next txt.$(i+1)$ message from S, R concludes that S has already terminated, the next txt.$(i+1)$ message will never arrive, and R has already collected sufficient evidence to establish that S has sent the text to R. In this case, R also terminates fulfilling the opportunism requirement.

In protocol Q, every time party R sends an ack.i message to party S, R activates a time-out to expire after t time units. However, because every sent message in protocol Q may be lost, if the activated time-out expires before R receives the next txt.$(i+1)$ message from S, then R concludes that either the ack.i message or the txt.$(i+1)$ message is lost, and in this case R sends the ack.i message once more to S and activates a new time-out to expire after t time units, and the cycle repeats.

By the bounded-loss assumption, R knows an upper bound K on the number of messages that can be lost during any execution of protocol Q. Therefore, the cycle of R sending an ack.i message then the activated time-out expiring after t time units can be repeated at most K times.

If the activated time-out expires for the $(K+1)$-th time, then R concludes that S has already terminated, the next txt.$(i+1)$ message will never arrive, and R has already collected sufficient evidence to establish that S has sent the text to R. In this case, R terminates fulfilling the opportunism requirement. $\square$

7 An ℓ-Nonrepudiation Protocol

In the Proof of Theorem 2, we presented a nonrepudiation protocol from party S to party R that does not involve a trusted party and where no sent message is lost. In this section, we discuss how to extend this protocol to a nonrepudiation protocol that involves ℓ parties, namely $P1, \cdots, P\ell$, and satisfies three conditions: (1) $\ell \geq 2$, (2) none of the involved parties in the protocol is a trusted party, and (3) no sent message during any execution of the protocol is lost. We refer to this extended protocol as an ℓ-nonrepudiation protocol.

The objectives of an ℓ-nonrepudiation protocol are as follows. For each two parties in the protocol, say Pi and Pj, the protocol achieves two objectives:

1. One of the two parties, say Pi, is enabled to send the text to the other party Pj and to receive from Pj sufficient evidence that can convince a judge that Pj has indeed received the text from Pi.
2. The other party Pj is enabled to receive the text from Pi and to receive sufficient evidence from Pi that can convince a judge that Pi has indeed sent the text to Pj.

Therefore, each party Pi ends up collecting sufficient evidence from every other party Pj indicating that either Pj has indeed received the text from Pi or Pj has indeed sent the text to Pi.

Before we describe our ℓ-nonrepudiation protocol, as an extension of the 2-nonrepudiation protocol in the proof of Theorem 2, we need to introduce two useful concepts: parent and child of a party Pi. Each of the parties $P1, \cdots, P(i-1)$ is called a parent of party Pi. Also each of the parties $P(i+1), \cdots, P\ell$ is called a child of party Pi. Note that party $P1$ has no parents and parent $P\ell$ has no children. Note also that the number of parents plus the number of children for each party is $(\ell - 1)$.

Execution of our ℓ-nonrepudiation protocol proceeds as follows:

1. Party $P1$ starts by sending a txt.1 message to each one of its children.
2. When a party Pi, where $i \neq 1$ and $i \neq \ell$, receives a txt.1 message from each one of its parents, party Pi sends a txt.1 message to each one of its children.
3. When party $P\ell$ receives a txt.1 message from each one of its parents, party $P\ell$ sends back an ack.1 message to each one of its parents.
4. When a party Pi, where $i \neq 1$ and $i \neq \ell$, receives an ack.1 message from each one of its children, party Pi sends an ack.1 message to each one of its parents.
5. When party $P1$ receives an ack.1 message from each one of its children, party $P1$ sends a txt.2 message to each one of its children, and the cycle consisting of Steps 2, 3, 4, and 5 is repeated n times until $P1$ receives an ack.n message from each one of its children. In this case, party $P1$ collects as evidence the ack.n messages that $P1$ has received from all its children, then $P1$ terminates.

6. Each party Pi, where $i \neq 1$, waits to receive a txt.$(n+1)$ message (that will never arrive) from each one of its parents, then times out after $(i-1)*T$ time units, collects as evidence the txt.n messages that Pi has received from all its parents and the ack.n messages that Pi has received from all its children, then Pi terminates.

Note that T is an upper bound on the round trip delay from any party Pi to any other party Pj and back to Pi. It is assumed that each party, other than $P1$, knows this upper bound T.

8   Concluding Remarks

In this paper, we address several problems concerning the design of nonrepudiation protocols from a party S to a party R that do not involve a trusted third party. In such a protocol, S sends to R some text x along with sufficient evidence to establish that S is the party that sent x to R, and R sends to S sufficient evidence that R is the party that received x from S.

Designing such a protocol is not an easy task because the protocol is required to fulfill the following opportunism requirement. During any execution of the protocol, once a party recognizes that it has received its sufficient evidence from the other party, this party terminates right away without sending any message to the other party. In this case, the other party needs to obtain its evidence without the help of the first party. (To fulfill this opportunism requirement, most published nonrepudiation protocols involve a trusted third party T so that when one of the two original parties recognizes that it has already received its sufficient evidence and terminates, the other party can still receive its evidence from T.)

Our main result in this paper is the identification of two simple conditions that are both necessary and sufficient for designing nonrepudiation protocols that do not involve a trusted third party.

In proving that these two conditions are sufficient for designing nonrepudiation protocols, we presented an elegant nonrepudiation protocol that is based on the following novel idea. By the time party S recognizes that it has received its evidence, party S has already sent to R its evidence, but R has not yet recognized that it has received all its evidence. In this case, S terminates as dictated by the opportunism requirement but R continues to wait for the rest of its evidence from S. Eventually R times-out and recognizes that S will not send any more evidence. This can only mean that party S has terminated after it has already sent all the evidence to R. Thus, R terminates as dictated by the opportunism requirement.

Acknowledgement. Research of Mohamed Gouda is supported in part by the NSF award #1440035.

References

1. Ali, M., Reaz, R., Gouda, M.: Nonrepudiation protocols without a trusted party. University of Texas at Austin, Department of Computer Science. TR-16-02 (regular tech. report) (2016)
2. Asokan, N., Schunter, M., Waidner, M.: Optimistic protocols for fair exchange. In: Proceedings of the 4th ACM Conference on Computer and Communications Security, CCS 1997, pp. 7–17. ACM, New York (1997)
3. Baum-Waidner, B.: Optimistic asynchronous multi-party contract signing with reduced number of rounds. In: Orejas, F., Spirakis, P.G., van Leeuwen, J. (eds.) ICALP 2001. LNCS, vol. 2076, pp. 898–911. Springer, Heidelberg (2001)
4. Ben-Or, M., Goldreich, O., Micali, S., Rivest, R.L.: A fair protocol for signing contracts (extended abstract). In: Brauer, W. (ed.) ICALP 1985. LNCS, vol. 194, pp. 43–52. Springer, Heidelberg (1985)
5. Boneh, D., Naor, M.: Timed commitments. In: Bellare, M. (ed.) CRYPTO 2000. LNCS, vol. 1880, pp. 236–254. Springer, Heidelberg (2000)
6. Cleve, R.: Limits on the security of coin flips when half the processors are faulty. In: Proceedings of the Eighteenth Annual ACM Symposium on Theory of Computing, STOC 1986, pp. 364–369. ACM, New York (1986)
7. Even, S., Goldreich, O., Lempel, A.: A randomized protocol for signing contracts. Commun. ACM 28(6), 637–647 (1985)
8. Hernandez-Ardieta, J.L., Gonzalez-Tablas, A.I., Alvarez, B.R.: An optimistic fair exchange protocol based on signature policies. Comput. Secur. 27(7), 309–322 (2008)
9. Kremer, S., Markowitch, O.: A multi-party non-repudiation protocol. In: Qing, S., Eloff, J.H.P. (eds.) Information Security for Global Information Infrastructures. IFIP, vol. 47, pp. 271–280. Springer, New York (2000)
10. Kremer, S., Markowitch, O., Zhou, J.: An intensive survey of fair non-repudiation protocols. Comput. Commun. 25(17), 1606–1621 (2002)
11. Markowitch, O., Kremer, S.: A multi-party optimistic non-repudiation protocol. In: Won, D. (ed.) ICISC 2000. LNCS, vol. 2015, p. 109. Springer, Heidelberg (2001)
12. Markowitch, O., Roggeman, Y.: Probabilistic non-repudiation without trusted third party. In: Second Conference on Security in Communication Networks, Amalfi, Italy (1999)
13. Rabin, M.O.: Transaction protection by beacons. J. Comput. Syst. Sci. 27(2), 256–267 (1983)
14. Xiao, Z., Xiao, Y., Du, D.C.: Non-repudiation in neighborhood area networks for smart grid. IEEE Commun. Mag. 51(1), 18–26 (2013)
15. Zhou, J., Gollman, D.: A fair non-repudiation protocol. In: 1996 IEEE Symposium on Security and Privacy, pp. 55–61. IEEE Computer Society (1996)
16. Zhou, J., Gollmann, D.: An efficient non-repudiation protocol. In: 10th Proceedings of Computer Security Foundations Workshopp, pp. 126–132. IEEE (1997)
17. Zhou, J., Lam, K.Y.: Undeniable billing in mobile communication. In: Proceedings of the 4th Annual ACM/IEEE International Conference on Mobile Computing and Networking, pp. 284–290. ACM (1998)

Exploiting Concurrency in Domain-Specific Data Structures: A Concurrent Order Book and Workload Generator for Online Trading

Raphaël P. Barazzutti[✉], Yaroslav Hayduk, Pascal Felber,
and Etienne Rivière

University of Neuchâtel, Neuchâtel, Switzerland
{raphael.barazzutti,yaroslav.hayduk,pascal.felber,
etienne.riviere}@unine.ch

Abstract. Concurrent programming is essential to exploit parallel processing capabilities of modern multi-core CPUs. While there exist many languages and tools to simplify the development of concurrent programs, they are not always readily applicable to domain-specific problems that rely on complex shared data structures associated with various semantics (e.g., priorities or consistency). In this paper, we explore such a domain-specific application from the financial field, where a data structure—an *order book*—is used to store and match orders from buyers and sellers arriving at a high rate. This application has interesting characteristics as it exhibits some clear potential for parallelism, but at the same time it is relatively complex and must meet some strict guarantees, notably w.r.t. the ordering of operations. We first present an accurate yet slightly simplified description of the order book problem and describe the challenges in parallelizing it. We then introduce several approaches for introducing concurrency in the shared data structure, in increasing order of sophistication starting from lock-based techniques to partially lock-free designs. We propose a comprehensive workload generator for constructing histories of orders according to realistic models from the financial domain. We finally perform an evaluation and comparison of the different concurrent designs.

1 Introduction

Stock exchanges provide fully automated order matching platforms to their clients. For each security available on the market, a stock exchange broker maintains a structure called an *order book*, that agglomerates orders received from clients (see Fig. 1). Orders can be of two kinds. *Bid* orders offer to buy a given security at a target (maximal) price, while *ask* orders propose to sell it, also at a target (minimal) price. A *matching engine* is in charge of comparing incoming bid and ask orders, triggering trade operations when a match exists.

With the advent of high-frequency trading, clients expect very low latencies from order matching platforms. The offered latency is actually a key commercial argument for stock exchange services [1]. Brokers and traders expect the latencies

© Springer International Publishing AG 2016
P.A. Abdulla and C. Delporte-Gallet (Eds.): NETYS 2016, LNCS 9944, pp. 16–31, 2016.
DOI: 10.1007/978-3-319-46140-3_2

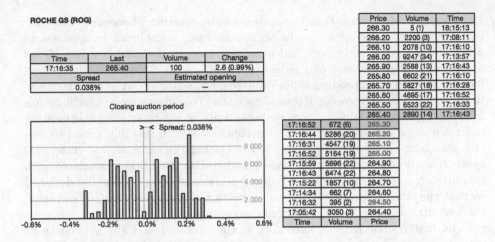

Fig. 1. An order book, as seen on real trading platform.

to be in the order of a few milliseconds. This means that the stock exchange matching service needs to have internal latencies that are at least one order of magnitude lower. To achieve such low latencies, designers of brokers started using new communication mechanisms [2] to gain advantages of a few milliseconds to even microseconds, sometimes resorting to dedicated hardware and custom algorithms running on FPGAs [3].

Instead of concentrating on communication mechanisms, we focus in this paper on the effectiveness of the matching engine in order to minimize service latency and maximize throughput. The matching engine improvements are largely independent from those of communication mechanisms: as an incoming order must be processed by the matching engine before a response can be sent to the clients, a reduced matching time will improve end-to-end latency. State-of-the art matching engines thus far work sequentially [4], which means that, despite the system capacity to receive multiple orders concurrently, the processing of orders is handled one after the other. There is a great potential for obtaining performance gains for the matching operation, by taking advantage of the parallel processing capabilities of modern multi-core CPUs. We investigate in this paper the support of concurrent order processing, and explore different design strategies to introduce parallelism in the non-trivial data structure that is the order book, starting from basic lock-based techniques to more sophisticated partially lock-free algorithms. The primary objective of this study is to demonstrate how one can turn a sequential data structure into a concurrent one by carefully combining different synchronization mechanisms and reasoning about concurrency under domain-specific constraints.

Order matching has interesting characteristics as it exhibits some clear potential for parallelism: there are multiple clients and two types of orders, and matching takes place only at the frontier between the two. At the same time, it is not trivial and presents a number of challenges that must be carefully addressed.

First, we need to ensure that the output of the matching process in the concurrent case is the same as in the sequential case, notably when it comes to processing orders exactly once and according to arrival rank,[1] because clients are paying customers and real money is being traded. Second, as the system handles a variety of messages types (add/remove, sell/buy), it is not clear how to safely capture all message interactions in the concurrent case. Lastly, to fulfil an order, the matching engine can potentially access more than one existing order already stored in the book. In the concurrent case this might lead to several matching operations simultaneously accessing the same shared state, and special care needs to be taken to avoid possible data corruption associated with concurrency hazards. As such, the implementation need to be carefully designed so that the synchronization costs and algorithmic complexity do not outweigh the benefits associated with concurrent processing.

The first contribution of this work is the proposal and the evaluation of domain-specific strategies for processing orders concurrently in the order book. Specifically, the concurrent strategies we explore include: (1) a baseline thread-safe design based on a single global lock; (2) a fine-grained design for locking parts of the order book; and (3) several variants of partially lock-free designs, which trade runtime performance for weaker consistency guarantees. The second contribution of this work is the implementation of a synthetic workload generator that complies with widely-accepted models [5,6]. We further use this workload generator to assess the effectiveness of our concurrent matching algorithms.

2   Online Trading and the Order Book

We first describe the principle and guarantees for trading operations. We start by defining some domain-specific terms. An **order** is an investor's instruction to a broker to buy (*bid*) or sell (*ask*) securities. There are two types of orders: *limit* and *market* orders. A **limit order** specifies a maximum purchase price or minimum selling price. A **market order** does not specify a price and will be immediately matched with outstanding orders, at the best available price for this security. The **volume** indicates the amount of securities in an order as an integer value. The **order book** is a data structure for storing unfulfilled limit orders sent for a particular security. It features two queues, one for **asks** and one for **bids** orders. Orders stored in the book can be cancelled with a specific command. Finally, the **top of the book** consists of the ask with the lowest price and the bid with the highest price, and the difference between these two prices is the **spread**.

An order book maintains two separate queues, one for *bid* orders, and one for *ask* orders. Both data structures are organized in a way that facilitates the fast extraction of the best order as well as the quick insertion of new orders. In each of the queues, orders with the same price are aggregated, i.e., queues are

---

[1] To avoid possible confusion with the word "order" used to designate trading requests and for prioritizing operations (arrival and processing order), we will only use it in the former sense and resort to alternative expressions for the latter.

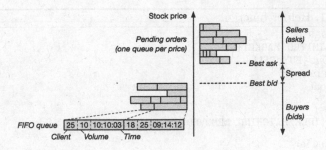

Fig. 2. Internal structure of the order book.

organized as maps, where keys represent prices (with a granularity going up to the cent) and values are pending limit orders for a particular price. Pending orders for a particular price are sorted according to arrival rank and, thus, upon arrival are stored in a first-in first-out (FIFO) queue (Fig. 2).

Matching occurs only during order processing, when an incoming ask order satisfies some bid(s) or, vice versa, an incoming bid can be satisfied by some ask(s). When a match occurs, the associated existing orders are removed from the book. The priority of matching is driven by price, i.e., lowest selling prices (resp., highest) are sold (bought) first. If multiple orders have the same price, they are matched according to arrival time starting with the oldest. If there are no pending order to process, the system is in a *stable* state where the spread is positive and the two types of orders do not overlap.

To fulfil an order, the matching engine can "consume" more than one order on the other side of the book. This happens when an incoming order matches the best order on the opposite side of the order book, but it is not completely fulfilled and continues to match the next best order. This aggregation process stops once the incoming order has been filled completely, or when there are no more orders that can be consumed given the price and volume constraints. The remaining part of the incoming order is then added to the order book. Similarly, when the already existing order in the order book cannot be fully matched with the incoming order, the partially-matched order remains in the book with its volume decreased by the volume subsumed by the transactions.

The pseudo-code for the baseline sequential matching algorithm is shown in Algorithms 1 and 2. Sell and buy orders are stored it two separate *heaps*, each holding FIFO queues with orders of identical price sorted according to their arrival time. Queues are sorted by increasing price in the asks heap, and by decreasing price in the bids heap. The algorithm matches incoming orders against existing ones from the opposite heap, possibly adding them to the book if they are not completely fulfilled. To keep the pseudo-code as simple as possible, we assume that the heap at other side of the book is not empty when inserting an order and we do not explicitly handle the creation and removal of the queues in the heaps. This code is used as a basis for the concurrent variants presented in Sect. 3.

Algorithm 1. Helper functions.

```
 1: Type ORDER is:
 2:    type: {LIMITED, MARKET}                        ▷ Limited or market price?
 3:    operation: {BUY, SELL}                                    ▷ Buy or sell?
 4:    volume: integer                               ▷ How many securities?
 5:    price: float                                       ▷ At what price?
       ...
 6:    id: integer                    ▷ Timestamp (for concurrent algorithms)
 7:    status: {IDLE, MATCHING, REMOVED}     ▷ Status (for concurrent algorithms)

 8: Type BOOK is:
 9:    asks: heap of FIFO queues (orders of same price)  ▷ Sorted by increasing price
10:    bids: heap of FIFO queues (orders of same price)  ▷ Sorted by decreasing price
       ...

11: function CAN_MATCH(node, order)   ▷ Can incoming order match node in book?
12:    if order.operation = node.operation then      ▷ Need order of opposite type
13:        return false
14:    if order.type = MARKET then                   ▷ Market orders always match
15:        return true
16:    if order.operation = SELL then
17:        return order.price ≤ node.price
18:    else
19:        return order.price ≥ node.price
```

Algorithm 2. Sequential order insertion (single-threaded).

```
 1: function HANDLE_ORDER_SEQ(order)
 2:    sell ← (order.operation = SELL)
 3:    while order.volume > 0 do
 4:        q ← TOP(sell ? book.bids : book.asks)   ▷ Non-empty top queue on other side
 5:        n ← FIRST(q)                                ▷ Top order in the queue
 6:        if ¬CAN_MATCH(n, order) then
 7:            q ← GET(sell ? book.asks : book.bids, order.price)   ▷ Queue at price
 8:            PUSH(q, order)                 ▷ Store order in book (append to queue)
 9:            break
10:        if n.volume > order.volume then
11:            n.volume ← n.volume − order.volume
12:            break
13:        order.volume ← order.volume − n.volume
14:        POP(q)                            ▷ Remove top order from other heap
15:    return SUCCESS
```

3   A Concurrent Order Book

We now describe different strategies for supporting concurrency in the order book. This data structure is interesting because it is non-trivial and the matching operation may be time-consuming (e.g., when an incoming order matches and "consumes" many existing orders from the book). Hence, taking advantage of the parallel processing capabilities of recent multi-core architectures is obviously desirable.

It is, however, not easy to perform concurrent operations on the order book while at the same time preserving consistency. Some synchronization is necessary for correctness, but too much synchronization may hamper performance. We will start by discussing simple synchronization techniques and gradually move to more sophisticated strategies that achieve higher levels of concurrency.

In all concurrent approaches discussed below, requests to the order book are handled and processed by a pool of threads. As we would like the order book to yield the same output in a concurrent execution as when processing operations one at a time, we need to process requests in the same sequence as they have been received. We therefore insert incoming requests in a FIFO queue[2] and assign to each request a unique, monotonously increasing timestamp that we use to sort operations (see Algorithm 3, lines 1–8). We will discuss later scenarios where we can process some requests in a different sequence while still preserving the linearizability of the order book operations.

Before discussing our strategies for handling concurrent operations, let us first consider some observations about the specific properties of the order book. First, matching always occur at the top of the book. Therefore, the matching operation has interesting locality properties, and it will not conflict, for instance, with operations that are "far enough" from the top of the book. Second, an order that is matched upon insertion only needs to be inserted in the book if it is not fully matched. We can thus identify two interesting common cases: (1) an order is not inserted at the top of the book and hence no matching occurs, and (2) an order inserted at the top of the book is fully subsumed by existing orders and therefore does not need to be inserted in the book.

Finally, there are several scenarios where we can straightforwardly determine that two concurrent limit orders do not conflict. For instance, insertions of an ask and a bid can take place concurrently if there is no price overlap between them, i.e., the ask has a higher price than the sell, as they cannot both yield a match. As another example, insertions of two limit asks or two limit bids can take place concurrently if they have different prices (i.e., they are in different queues) and they do not both yield a match. These observations will be instrumental for the design of advanced concurrency strategies.

3.1   Coarse-Grained Locking

We first consider the trivial approach of using a single lock (SGL) to serialize accesses to the shared data structure. To simplify the presentation of concurrent algorithms, we assume that threads from the pool repeatedly execute the function THREAD_PROCESS to process one order from the incoming queue, and the result of this function is then returned to the corresponding client. The basic operating principle of the coarse-grained approach is shown in Algorithm 3, lines 9–14. Threads from the pool acquire the main lock, process the next order

---

[2] We assume that this queue is thread-safe as processing threads may dequeue orders concurrently with one another and with the (unique) thread that enqueues incoming orders.

from the queue, and release the lock before the response is sent back to the client. Hence, the processing of orders is completely serialized and no parallelism takes place for this operation. The main advantage of this approach is its simplicity, which also makes the algorithm easy to prove correct. It will serve as a baseline for the rest of the paper.

Algorithm 3. Coarse-grained locking and common functions.

1: **Variables:**
2:     *incoming*: FIFO queue (orders)   ▷ Thread-safe queue for incoming orders
3:     *ts*: integer   ▷ Timestamp for incoming orders (initially 0)
4:     *sgl*: lock   ▷ Single global lock (initially unlocked)
      ...

5: **upon** RECEIVE(*order*):   ▷ Reception of an order from a client (single thread)
6:     *order.id* ← *ts*   ▷ Assign unique timestamp
7:     PUSH(*incoming*, *order*)   ▷ Append order to queue
8:     *ts* ← *ts* + 1

9: **function** THREAD_PROCESS^{SGL} ▷ Processing of an order by a thread
10:     *order* ← POP(*incoming*)   ▷ Take next order from queue
11:     LOCK(*sgl*)   ▷ Serialize processing
12:     *r* ← HANDLE_ORDER_SEQ(*order*)   ▷ Use sequential algorithm
13:     UNLOCK(*sgl*)
14:     **return** *r*

3.2 Two-Level Fine-Grained Locking

We now explore opportunities for finer-grained locking to increase the level of concurrency. We start from the observation that two threads accessing limit orders from the book with different prices, i.e., located in different queues in the heaps, can do so concurrently without conflicts. Therefore, it is only necessary to control access to the queues that are accessed by both threads.

The principle of the two-level locking strategy is shown in Algorithm 4. As before, threads first attempt to acquire the main lock (line 3). Once a given thread acquires the main lock, it traverses the queues in the opposite heap of the book in sequence, starting from the top, and locks each visited queue individually (lines 7–12). This process stops as soon as the accumulated volume of orders in already traversed queues reaches the volume of the incoming order. In case of a limit buy or ask order, the process also stops whenever visiting a queue at a price that is higher, respectively lower, than the price of the incoming order. Finally, if the incoming order has not been fully matched, it needs to be inserted in the book and we also lock the queue associated with the price of the incoming order (lines 13–15). The algorithm then releases the main lock (line 16). It can now safely perform the actual matching operations on the previously locked queues, including the optional insertion of the incoming order in the book if some unmatched volume remains, and release the individual locks as soon as they are

---

Algorithm 4. Fine-grained locking.

1: **function** THREAD_PROCESS^{FGL} ▷ Processing of an order by a thread
2:　　$order \leftarrow$ POP($incoming$)   ▷ Take next order from queue
3:　　LOCK(sgl)   ▷ Serialize traversal of heap
4:　　$sell \leftarrow (order.operation =$ SELL$)$
5:　　$v \leftarrow order.volume$
6:　　$q \leftarrow$ TOP($sell$? $book.bids$: $book.asks$)   ▷ Top queue at other side
7:　　**while** $v > 0$ **do**
8:　　　　**if** ¬CAN_MATCH(FIRST(q), $order$) **then**
9:　　　　　　**break**
10:　　　　LOCK(q)   ▷ Acquire lock on queue
11:　　　　$v \leftarrow v -$ VOLUME(q)   ▷ Subtract volume of all orders in queue
12:　　　　$q \leftarrow$ NEXT(q)   ▷ Next queue from heap
13:　　**if** $(v > 0)$ **then**
14:　　　　$q \leftarrow$ GET($sell$? $book.asks$: $book.bids$, $order.price$)   ▷ Queue at price
15:　　　　LOCK(q)   ▷ Acquire lock on queue
16:　　UNLOCK(sgl)
17:　　$r \leftarrow$ HANDLE_ORDER_SEQ^{FGL}($order$)   ▷ Use sequential algorithm
18:　　**return** r
　　function HANDLE_ORDER_SEQ^{FGL} ≡ HANDLE_ORDER_SEQ^{SGL} ▷ Algorithm 2
　　... UNLOCK(q) ...   ▷ All locks released once no longer needed (before line 15)

---

no longer needed. To that end, we simply reuse the sequential algorithms with the addition of lock release, which happen right before line 15 in Algorithm 2 or whenever a queue becomes empty.[3]

This approach provides higher concurrency than coarse-grained locking because the algorithm holds the main lock for a shorter duration, when determining which queues from the book will be accessed. To ensure consistency, it uses a second level of locks for concurrency control at the level of individual queues. Therefore, multiple orders can execute concurrently if they operate in different parts of the order book, but they are serialized if the sets of queues they access overlap.

3.3 Toward Lock-Free Algorithms

The final stage in our quest for concurrency is to try to reduce the dependencies on locks, whether coarse- or fine-grained, as they introduce a serial bottleneck and may hamper progress. In particular, a thread that is slow, faulty, or preempted by the OS scheduler while holding a lock may prevent other threads from moving forward.

Our objective is thus to substitute locking operations by lock-free alternatives. To that end, we first need to remove the locks protecting the queues and permit threads to enqueue and dequeue orders concurrently. We do so by replacing the queues in Algorithm 1, lines 9–10, by a concurrent heap structure for

---

[3] Some implementation details, such as avoiding a second traversal of the heap by keeping track of locked queues, are omitted for simplicity.

backing the order book. Specifically, we use a concurrent map,[4] which imposes a custom sorting of the orders it contains. First, orders are sorted according to prices, and then, according to the timestamp.

To handle concurrent accesses explicitly, we also add in the order object an additional status flag that we use to indicate whether the order is being processed or has been removed by some thread. We modify this flag in a lock-free manner using an atomic compare-and-set (CAS) operation.

The *order.status* flag (Algorithm 1, line 7) can be in one of three states: IDLE indicates that the order is not being processed by any thread; MATCHING specifies that some thread is processing the order; and REMOVED means that the order, although still present in the order book, has been logically deleted.

We have developed three variants of the concurrent, almost[5] lock-free algorithm, with each having different guarantees. The first algorithm, which we call LF-GREEDY, provides the least guarantees in terms of the sequence in which orders are processed. The second algorithm, LF-PRIORITY, prevents an incoming order from consuming new orders that have arrived later. The last algorithm, LF-FIFO, additionally prevents incoming orders arriving later from stealing existing orders from incoming orders arriving earlier.

For the sake of simplicity, the pseudo-code as presented further does not show the handling of market orders. Instead it only considers the more general case of limit orders. In the case of market orders, if there is no or only a partial match, the unmatched orders are returned back to the issuer. We furthermore omit obvious implementation-specific details, e.g., an incoming order is naturally matched against the opposite side of the order book.

The LF-Greedy Algorithm. The LF-GREEDY algorithm (see Algorithm 5, omitting text within square brackets) works as follows. After the incoming order *order* has been received and scheduled for processing, the worker thread obtains the best order n from the order book's heap. Orders in our lock-free algorithms can be marked as MATCHING to indicate that they are being processed, or as REMOVED when logically deleted but still physically present in the order book. As such, the thread first checks if n has been marked as removed (line 5). If so, it removes n from the order book (line 6) and continues to another iteration of the algorithm. Otherwise, we know that n has not been removed, and we need to check whether some other thread has already started processing n, in which case we wait until the processing has finished by polling the *n.status* flag (line 8). Thereafter, we attempt to change the status of n from IDLE to MATCHING using CAS (line 9). If the CAS operation succeeds, then we know that the order was indeed idle (note that it could have been removed in the meantime, or taken over for matching by another thread) and the thread has successfully taken exclusive

---

[4] `java.util.concurrent.ConcurrentSkipListMap`.

[5] While the algorithms do not use explicit locks, they are not completely "lock-free" as in some situations a thread may be blocked waiting for the status flag to be updated by another thread. Techniques based on "helping" could be used to avoid such situations, at the price of increased complexity in the algorithms. We therefore slightly abuse the word "lock-free" in the rest of the paper.

Algorithm 5. Greedy [and priority] order insertion algorithm.

```
 1: function THREAD_PROCESS^GREEDY/PRIORITY        ▷ Processing of an order by a thread
 2:    order ← POP(incoming)
 3:    while order.volume > 0 do
 4:       n ← 1ˢᵗ node from heap [ such that n.id < order.id ]
 5:       if n.status = REMOVED then                        ▷ Order logically removed?
 6:          heap ← heap \ {n}                              ▷ Yes: remove order from book
 7:          continue
 8:       wait until n.status ≠ MATCHING                    ▷ Avoid useless CAS
 9:       if ¬CAS(n.status, IDLE, MATCHING) then            ▷ Take ownership of node
10:          continue
11:       if ¬CAN_MATCH(n, order) then                      ▷ Can we match order?
12:          heap ← heap ∪ {order}                          ▷ No: store order in book
13:          n.status ← IDLE
14:          break
15:       if n.volume > order.volume then                   ▷ Order fully satisfied
16:          n.volume ← n.volume − order.volume
17:          n.status ← IDLE
18:          break
19:       order.volume ← order.volume − n.volume            ▷ Node fully consumed
20:       n.status ← REMOVED
21:    return SUCCESS
```

ownership over it. If the CAS operation fails, then some other thread must have just changed the order's status to either MATCHING or REMOVED and we continue to another iteration of the algorithm.

After taking ownership of n, we need to check if the price of the incoming order $order$ could be matched with the price of n. If not, we store $order$ in the order book and release n by setting its status to IDLE (line 13), effectively finishing the matching process of the incoming order. Otherwise, if the prices of n and $order$ can be matched, we check if the incoming order $order$ could fully consume n. If so, we decrease the incoming order's volume (line 19) and mark n as REMOVED. Note, that we do not physically remove n from the $heap$ at this step; instead, we rely on other threads' help for removing it lazily (lines 5 and 6). If the volume of n is larger than $order$ can consume, we decrease it and unlock n (line 17). This implies that the outstanding volume of n remains in the order book and can be consumed by other threads.

If the incoming order has a large volume, it can potentially consume multiple orders from the book. In this version of the algorithm we do not enforce any restrictions on which existing orders can be consumed by the incoming order, i.e., concurrent threads might consume existing orders that are interleaved in the heap.

The LF-Priority Algorithm. The LF-PRIORITY algorithm provides more guarantees in terms of sequence in which incoming orders consume existing orders stored in the book. Specifically, when matching an incoming order $order$ with the content of the book, we want to only consider existing orders that have been received strictly before *order* has been received. To that end, we rely on the timestamp *order.id* assigned to each order upon arrival (Algorithm 3, lines 6). We then modify Algorithm 5 by adding an extra condition (line 4 between square brackets), which restricts *order* to only process orders from the order book having a smaller timestamp. This condition can be supported straightforwardly in our implementation because of the key we use to store orders in the concurrent heap. Indeed, we use the same concurrent map as before and, when retrieving the best order, we apply an extra filter condition to select orders having keys with timestamps that are smaller than the currently processed order.

The LF-FIFO Algorithm. To introduce the LF-FIFO algorithm, we first informally discuss where LF-PRIORITY is lacking and how its shortcomings can be addressed. In Algorithm 5, if the thread processing an order is delayed (e.g., preempted by the OS scheduler), an order arriving later might consume the best outstanding orders in the book. This is a problem if one needs to enforce that orders arriving first are given precedence over orders arriving later. Furthermore, concurrent orders may consume interleaved orders from the book, i.e., an incoming order may be matched against a set of existing orders that does not represent a continuous sequence in the book, hence breaking atomicity. The main idea of LF-FIFO is therefore to prevent threads from consuming orders from the book before the processing of incoming orders received earlier has finished.

To provide these stricter guarantees, we employ ideas from the hand-over-hand locking [7] technique. The principle is that, when traversing a list, the lock for the next node needs to be obtained while still holding the lock of the current node. That way, threads cannot overtake one another. The pseudo-code of the LF-FIFO is show in Algorithm 6. A thread processing an incoming order *order*, which would consume multiple existing orders, first performs a CAS on the first best order (line 12), marking it as removed in the end (line 26). Then it saves the first best order in a local variable (line 28) and continues to another iteration, during which it select the second best node (line 5) and perform a CAS to atomically change its status to MATCHING. Upon success and only then do we physically remove the first best node from the heap (line 15).

The process describing order removals is distinctly different from that which was presented in prior algorithms. In LF-GREEDY and LF-PRIORITY algorithms, when an arbitrary thread detects that an order has been marked as REMOVED (Algorithm 5, line 5), it helps by removing that order (i.e., lazy removal with helping). In contrast, instead of assisting in the removal of *n* from the heap, the LF-FIFO algorithm restarts from the beginning (line 9), relying on the thread that has marked *n* as REMOVED to also physically remove it from the heap (lines 15 and 30). Therefore, the LF-FIFO algorithms provides weaker progress guarantees but better fairness between threads.

Algorithm 6. Order insertion algorithm with FIFO properties.

```
1:  function THREAD_PROCESS^FIFO                    ▷ Processing of an order by a thread
2:      order ← POP(incoming)
3:      p ← ⊥                                    ▷ Previous node fully matched by thread
4:      while order.volume > 0 do
5:          n ← 1^st node n ≠ p from heap such that n.id < order.id
6:          if n = ⊥ then                              ▷ Any matching order in book?
7:              heap ← heap ∪ {order}                     ▷ No: store order in book
8:              break
9:          if n.status = REMOVED then                   ▷ Order logically removed?
10:             continue                          ▷ Yes: wait until physically removed
11:         wait until n.status ≠ MATCHING                    ▷ Avoid useless CAS
12:         if ¬CAS(n.status, IDLE, MATCHING) then        ▷ Take ownership of node
13:             continue
14:         if p ≠ ⊥ then
15:             heap ← heap \ {p}                               ▷ Delayed removal
16:             p ← ⊥
17:         if ¬CAN_MATCH(n, order) then                    ▷ Can we match order?
18:             heap ← heap ∪ {order}                     ▷ No: store order in book
19:             n.status ← IDLE
20:             break
21:         if n.volume > order.volume then                 ▷ Order fully satisfied
22:             n.volume ← n.volume − order.volume
23:             n.status ← IDLE
24:             break
25:         order.volume ← order.volume − n.volume         ▷ Node fully consumed
26:         n.status ← REMOVED
27:         n.id ← order.id                          ▷ Prioritize concurrent insertions
28:         p ← n                              ▷ Keep in book (to avoid being overtaken)
29:     if p ≠ ⊥ then
30:         heap ← heap \ {p}                          ▷ Remove last consumed order
31:     return SUCCESS
```

4   Generating Workloads

Besides algorithms for exploiting concurrency in the order book operation, we contribute in this section a workload generator that allows evaluating the throughput of the matching operation under realistic workload assumptions.

The sensitive nature of financial data and the strict rights of disclosures signed between clients of stock quote operators typically prevent from using real datasets and call instead for appropriate models for synthetic data generation. Models emerged in economics and econophysics (i.e., physicists' approaches to tackle problems in economics) such as the ones by Maslov [5], Bartolozzi [8] and Bak et al. [9]. These models allow understanding the properties of the order book in terms of the total volume of securities available or requested at each price point in the bid and ask queues. This aggregated information is enough for the targeted users of these models, who are interested in modelling and implementing investment strategies based on the total volume of securities at each price point, independently from their origin or destination. The distribution of individual order sizes has been studied separately, and shown to follow a power law by several authors [6,10,11]. Some models that consider individual orders nonetheless use a unit order size rather than a distribution in the interest of simplicity [5,12].

We implement a variation of the model proposed by Maslov [5], which uses simple rules and which output has been shown to compare well with the behaviour of a real limit order-driven market. The original model assumes however, similarly to [12], that all orders have the same volume of one single security. This simplification is problematic for testing a matching engine, in particular for testing its behaviour and performance in the presence of partially matched orders. We therefore extend the model by allowing orders to feature arbitrary volumes and assign volumes following a power law distribution based on findings made by Maslov and Mills in [6]. We note that another limitation of this model is that it does not consider changes to existing orders stored in the order book, unlike for instance the Bak-Paczuski-Shubik model [9]. We choose not to address this limitation as it does not fundamentally limit the representativeness of the behaviour of clients using the order book for what concerns the matching algorithm itself. The expiry mechanism for existing orders proposed by the model, along with new insertions is indeed enough to model dynamics.

We now proceed to detailing the model itself. An average price p is fixed at the beginning of the generation, which starts by the generation of one bid and one ask limit order. Thereafter, orders are generated by first deciding on their operation (bid or ask), with equal priority. Each order is a *limit* order with priority q_{lo}, and a *market* order otherwise. The price attached to a limit order is generated based on the base price b of the best available order on the other side of the order book: the cheapest ask for a bid, and the largest bid for an ask. A random variation Δ, generated randomly in $\{1, 2, ..., \Delta_{max}\}$ is applied: the price for the order is set to $p(t) + \Delta$ for a bid, or to $p(t) - \Delta$ for an ask. The volume v for each order is generated according to the power law identified in [6]. For market orders, $P[v] \propto v^{-1-\mu_{\text{market}}}$ where $\mu_{\text{market}} = 1.4$. For limit orders, $P[v] \propto \frac{1}{v} e^{-\frac{(A-\ln(v))^2}{B}}$, where $A = 7$ and $B = 4$. These values for μ_{market}, A and B are the ones suggested in the original paper [6], as are the values we use for the other parameters: $q_{lo} = \frac{1}{2}$, and $\Delta = 4$. We use an initial price of $p = 1,000$.

In order to prevent limit orders staying indefinitely in the order book, an expiry mechanism removes unmatched limit orders from the order book after λ_{max} time steps. The expiry mechanism prevents the accumulation of limit orders having prices that differ significantly from the current market price. In the real market, this operation is performed by either traders or by the stock exchange itself. For instance, the New York Stock Exchange purges all unmatched orders at the end of the day. Maslov indicates that for any reasonably large value of the cut-off parameter λ_{max}, the model produces the same scaling properties of price fluctuations. We use $\lambda_{max} = 1,000$ as in the original paper.

5   Evaluation

We experiment on two different architectures. The first is an Intel i7-5960X Haswell CPU (8 cores, 16 hardware threads with hyperthreading enabled) with 32 GB of RAM. The second is an IBM POWER8 S822 server (10 cores, 80 hardware threads) with 32 GB of RAM. We run our experiments in OpenJDK's Runtime Environment, build 1.8.0_40, with default options.

For all concurrent order book implementations considered, we process 100,000 orders in total. We vary the thread count from 1 to the maximum number of threads supported by each architecture. We run all experiments 10 times and present the average. The orders are generated offline using the model from Sect. 4, kept in memory and replayed directly to each of the order book implementations. For each of the experiments performed, we also plot the obtained speedup related to the baseline sequential matching engine running with a single thread.

For all the tests, we observe that the lock-free approaches outperform fine-grained locking. The latter approach does not scale beyond 4 threads for the Haswell architecture and 8 threads for POWER8. When more threads are used, however, its performance does not degrade significantly and remains relatively constant. In contrast, when looking at the lock-free approaches, we see that they scale almost linearly. Also, we see that the more guarantees in terms of the sequence in which orders are processed a lock-free algorithm provides, the slower it performs. The variations in performance are, however, minimal.

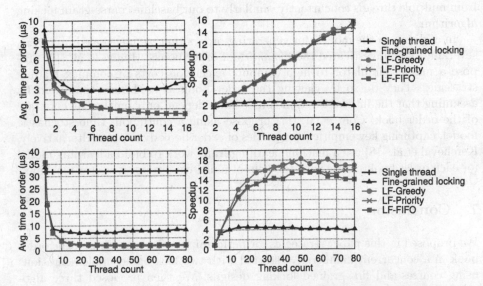

Fig. 3. Order processing time (average over 100,000) and speedup for different order book implementations on the Intel Haswell (top) and IBM POWER8 (bottom) architectures.

6 Related Work

Strategies for optimizing the operation of matching platforms can be broadly divided into two categories: the reduction of latency and optimizations related to order processing. To achieve ultra-low latencies, high-frequency trading servers are typically housed in the same building as the matching engine servers [2]. Additionally, novel communication technologies, such as microwaves, are gaining popularity as they promise to convey orders faster than fibre optic [13].

Significant effort was also spent towards efficient middleware systems for order handling, besides the matching operation itself. *LMAX Disruptor* [14] is an integrated trading system running on the JVM. It implements the reception and pre-processing of orders. It stores the received orders in a queue with ordering guarantees similar to the *incoming* queue used in our algorithms. Disruptor features a simple single-threaded matching engine that fetches and process orders from the queue sequentially, but it also allows the implementation of more sophisticated matching or order processing engines including those using multiple-threads implementation. It is therefore complementary to our study, which concentrates on the internal of the matching engine.

Although, to the best of our knowledge, there does not exist concurrent lock-free implementations of matching engines, substantial effort has been dedicated to developing efficient single-threaded implementations. For instance, Shetty et al. [15] propose such an implementation for the .NET platform. The authors detail the steps required for locking the order book when accessing it from multiple threads concurrently, similarly to our baseline coarse-grain locking algorithm.

In addition to the models for generating orders that we mentioned in Sect. 4, several authors investigated the *dynamics* of order books. Huang et al. [16] propose a market simulator to help compute execution costs of complex trading strategies. They do so by viewing the order book as a Markov chain and by assuming that the intensities of the order flows depend only on the current state of the order book. Cont et al. [17] propose using a continuous-time stochastic model, capturing key empirical properties of order book dynamics. Alternatively, Kercheval et al. [18] use a machine learning framework to build a learning model for each order book metric with the help of multi-class support vector machines.

7 Conclusion

We proposed in this paper strategies for performing order matching in the order book in a concurrent manner. We started with two lock-based implementations using coarse- and fine-grained locking designs. We then proposed three algorithms that do not use explicit locks and provide different guarantees in terms of the sequence of order processing. We also contributed a workload generator that allows us to evaluate the throughput of order matching under realistic workload assumptions. Experimental results suggest that, although the fine-grained approach scales only up to a few cores, by carefully substituting locking operations by lock-free alternatives, we can achieve high performance and good scalability. Future work might target combining our concurrent matching engine with *LMAX Disruptor*, forming a cohesive framework where both, order dispatch and matching, are executed in an almost lock-free manner.

References

1. Ende, B., Uhle, T., Weber, M.C.: The impact of a millisecond: measuring latency effects in securities trading. In: Wirtschaftsinformatik Proceedings, Paper 116 (2011)
2. WIRED: Raging bulls: how wall street got addicted to light-speed trading (2012). http://www.wired.com/2012/08/ff_wallstreet_trading/2/
3. Leber, C., Geib, B., Litz, H.: High frequency trading acceleration using FPGAs. In: International Conference on Field Programmable Logic and Applications, FPL (2011)
4. Preis, T.: Ökonophysik - Die Physik des Finanzmarktes. Springer, Wiesbaden (2011)
5. Maslov, S.: Simple model of a limit order-driven market. Phys. A Stat. Mech. Appl. **278**(3), 571–578 (2000)
6. Maslov, S., Mills, M.: Price fluctuations from the order book perspective - empirical facts and a simple model. Phys. A Stat. Mech. Appl. **299**(1), 234–246 (2001)
7. Lea, D.: Concurrent Programming in Java: Design Principles and Patterns. Addison-Wesley, Boston (1996)
8. Bartolozzi, M.: Price variations in a stock market with many agents. Eur. Phys. J. B **78**(2), 265–273 (2010)
9. Bak, P., Paczuski, M., Shubik, M.: Price variations in a stock market with many agents. Phys. A Stat. Mech. Appl. **246**(3–4), 430–453 (1997)
10. Gabaix, X.: Power laws in economics and finance, Technical report. National Bureau of Economic Research (2008)
11. Bouchaud, J.-P., Mézard, M., Potters, M.: Statistical properties of stock order books: empirical results and models. Quant. Finan. **2**(4), 251–256 (2002)
12. Khanna, K., Smith, M., Wu, D., Zhang, T.: Reconstructing the order book, Technical report. Stanford University (2009)
13. Singla, A., Chandrasekaran, B., Godfrey, P.B., Maggs, B.: The internet at the speed of light. In: 13th ACM Workshop on Hot Topics in Networks, HotNets (2014)
14. Thompson, M., Farley, D., Barker, M., Gee, P., Stewart, A.: Disruptor: high performance alternative to bounded queues for exchanging data between concurrent threads. White paper (2011). http://disruptor.googlecode.com/files/Disruptor-1.0.pdf
15. Shetty, Y., Jayaswal, S.: The order-matching engine. In: Practical .NET for Financial Markets. Apress, pp. 41–103 (2006)
16. Huang, W., Lehalle, C.-A., Rosenbaum, M.: Simulating, analyzing order book data: the queue-reactive model. J. Am. Stat. Assoc. **110**(509), 107–122 (2013)
17. Cont, R., Stoikov, S., Talreja, R.: A stochastic model for order book dynamics. J. Am. Stat. Assoc. **58**(3), 549–563 (2010)
18. Kercheval, A.N., Zhang, Y.: Modelling high-frequency limit order book dynamics with support vector machines. Quant. Financ. **15**(8), 1315–1329 (2015)

Fault Tolerant P2P RIA Crawling

Khaled Ben Hafaiedh[✉], Gregor von Bochmann, Guy-Vincent Jourdan,
and Iosif Viorel Onut

EECS, University of Ottawa, Ottawa, ON, Canada
hafaiedh.khaled@uottawa.ca, {bochmann,gvj}@eecs.uottawa.ca,
vioonut@ca.ibm.com
http://ssrg.site.uottawa.ca/

Abstract. Rich Internet Applications (RIAs) have been widely used in
the web over the last decade as they were found to be responsive and
user friendly compared to traditional web applications. Distributed RIA
crawling has been introduced with the aim of decreasing the crawling
time due to the large size of RIAs. However, the current RIA crawling
systems do not allow for tolerance to failures that occur in one of their
components. In this paper, we address the resilience problem when crawling RIAs in a distributed environment and we introduce an efficient RIA
crawling system that is fault tolerant. Our approach is to partition the
RIA model that results from the crawling over several storage devices
in a peer-to-peer (P2P) network. This makes the distributed data structure invulnerable to the single point of failure. We introduce three data
recovery mechanisms for crawling RIAs in an unreliable environment:
The Retry, the Redundancy and the Combined mechanisms. We evaluate the performance of the recovery mechanisms and their impact on the
crawling performance through analytical reasoning.

Keywords: Fault tolerance · Data recovery · Rich internet applications · Web crawling · Distributed RIA crawling · P2P Networks

1 Introduction

In a traditional web application, each web page is identified by its URL. The
basic function of a crawler in traditional web applications consists of downloading
a given set of URLs, extracting all hyperlinks contained in the pages that follow
from loading these URLs, and iteratively downloading the web pages that follow
from these hyperlinks. Distributed traditional web crawling has been introduced
to reduce the crawling time by distributing the work among multiple crawlers. In
a concurrent environment, each crawler explores only a subset of the state space
by contacting one or more units that are responsible for storing the application
URLs and coordinating the exploration task among crawlers, called controllers.
In a centralized distributed system, the single controller is responsible for storing a list of the newly discovered URLs and gives the instruction of loading each
unexplored URL to an idle crawler [6]. However, this system has a single point

© Springer International Publishing AG 2016
P.A. Abdulla and C. Delporte-Gallet (Eds.): NETYS 2016, LNCS 9944, pp. 32–47, 2016.
DOI: 10.1007/978-3-319-46140-3_3

of failure. P2P traditional crawling systems have been introduced to avoid the single point of failure and to continue the crawling task in case of a node failure, possibly at a reduced level, rather than failing completely. In this system, the URLs are partitioned over several controllers in which each controller is responsible for a set of URLs. Crawlers can find locally the identifiers of a database by mapping the hash of each discovered URL information using the Distributed Hash Table (DHT) [11], i.e. each URL is associated to a single controller in the DHT. P2P systems [4] have been used in traditional web crawling and are well-known for their decentralization and scalability.

As the web has evolved towards dynamic content, modern web technologies allowed for interactive and more responsive applications, called Rich Internet Applications (RIAs), which combine client-side scripting with new features such as AJAX (Asynchronous JavaScript and XML) [13]. In a RIA, JavaScript functions allow the client to modify the currently displayed page and to execute JavaScript events in response to user input asynchronously, without having the user to wait for a response from the server. A RIA model [15] is composed of states and transitions, where states describe the distinct pages (DOM instances) and transitions illustrate the possible ways to move from one page to another by triggering a JavaScript event at the user interface.

The triple *(SourceState, event, DestinationState)* describes a transition in a RIA model where *event* refers to the triggered JavaScript event, *SourceState* refers to the page where the event is triggered and *DestinationState* refers to the next page that follows from triggering the event. The status of a RIA transition can take the following values: *free, assigned* or *executed*. A *free* transition refers to the initial status of the transition where the destination state is not known. An *assigned* transition refers to a transition that has been assigned to a crawler, and an *executed* transition is a transition that has been explored, i.e. the destination state is known. The task of crawling a RIA application consists of finding all the RIA states, starting from the original application URL. In order to ensure that all states have been identified, the crawler has to explore all transitions as it is not possible to know a priori whether the execution of a transition will lead to an already explored state or not [15]. This introduces new challenges to automate the crawling of RIAs as they result in a large number of states derived from each single URL. In RIA crawling, a Reset consists of returning to the original page by loading the RIA URL, called *SeedURL*. Efficiency of crawling a RIA is to find all RIA states as quickly as possible by minimizing the number of events executed and Resets [15]. The greedy strategy has been suggested by Peng et al. [16] for crawling RIAs due to its simplicity. The basic greedy strategy with a single crawler consists of exploring an event from the crawler's current state if there is any unexplored event. Otherwise, the crawler executes an unexplored event from another state by either performing a Reset, i.e. returning to the initial state and retracing the steps that lead to this state [15], or by using a shortest path algorithm [1] to find the closest state with a free event without performing a Reset.

A distributed decentralized scheme for crawling large-scale RIAs was recently introduced by Ben Hafaiedh et al. [19]. It is based on the greedy strategy and consists of partitioning the search space among several controllers over a chordal ring [5]. In this system, RIA states are partitioned over several controllers in which each controller is responsible for only a subset of states. Crawlers can find locally the identifiers of a controller by searching for the controller responsible for a given state by means of the state identifier, i.e. by mapping the hash of each discovered state information using the Distributed Hash Table (DHT), which allows for avoiding the single point of failure. In this system, the RIA crawling performs as follows, as introduced in Fig. 1: The controller responsible for storing the information about a state (Current Controller) is contacted when a crawler reaches a new state by sending a search message, called *StateInfo* message. The *StateInfo* message consists of the information about the newly reached state along with all transitions on this state. Initially, the status of each transition is *free* and the destination state of the transition is not known by the controller. For each *StateInfo* message sent, the controller returns in response a new event to be executed on this state by sending a message, called *ExecuteEvent* message. However, if there is no event to be executed on the current state of a visiting crawler, the controller associated with this state may look for another state with a free event among all the states it is responsible for. Upon sending an *ExecuteEvent* message, the controller updates the status of the transition to *assigned*. The crawler then executes the assigned transition and sends the result of the execution back to the visited controller by means of an *AckJob* message. Upon receiving an *AckJob* message, the controller updates the destination state of the transition and changes the status of the transition to *executed*. The controller responsible for storing the information about the newly reached state (Next Controller) is then contacted by the crawler.

However, this system is not fault tolerant, i.e. lost states and transitions are not recovered when failures occur at the crawlers and controllers. In this paper, we address the resilience problem when using the proposed P2P RIA crawling system introduced by Ben Hafaiedh et al. [19] when controllers and crawlers are vulnerable to node failures, and we show how to make the P2P crawling system fault tolerant. Moreover, we introduce three recovery mechanisms for crawling RIAs in a faulty environment: The Retry, the Redundancy and the Combined mechanisms. Notice that the proposed RIA fault tolerance handling could be applied to any structured overlay network. However, the network recovery may depend on the structured overlay applied. The rest of this paper is organized as follows: The related work is described in Sect. 2. Section 3 introduces the fault tolerant P2P RIA crawling. Section 4 introduces the data recovery mechanisms. Section 5 evaluates the performance of the data recovery mechanisms and their impact on the crawling performance. A conclusion is provided in the end of the paper with some future directions for improvements.

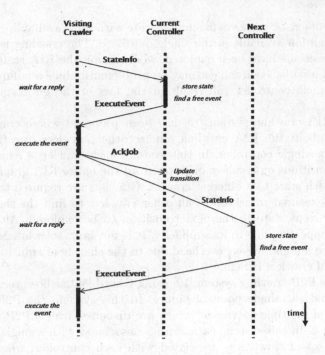

Fig. 1. The P2P RIA crawling introduced by Ben Hafaiedh et al. [19] during the exploration phase.

2   Related Work

In traditional web crawling, increasing the crawling throughput has been achieved by using multiple crawlers in parallel and partitioning the URL space such that each crawler is associated with a different subset of URLs. The coordination may be achieved either through a central coordination process [9] that is responsible for coordinating the crawling task, or through a structured peer-to-peer network in order to assign different subsets of URLs to different crawlers [11]. Various decentralized architectures using DHTs have been proposed over different structured topologies in traditional web crawling such as Chord [5], CAN [2], Tapestry [12] and Pastry [3], which are well known for their scalability and low latency. However, their performance may degrade when nodes are joining, leaving or failing, due to their tightly controlled topologies. This requires some resilience mechanisms on top of each of these architectures.

In RIA crawling, a distributed centralized crawling scheme [17] with the greedy strategy has been introduced, allowing each crawler to explore only a subset of a RIA simultaneously. In this system, all states are maintained by a single entity, called a controller, which is responsible for storing information about the new discovered states including the available events on each state. The crawler retrieves the required graph information by communicating with the single controller, and executes a single available event from its current state if such an event exists, or moves to another state with some available events based on the information available in the single database. The crawling is completed when all transitions have been explored. Maintaining the RIA states within a single unit in a faulty environment may be problematic since a failure occurring within the single controller will result in the loss of the entire graph under exploration.

A P2P RIA crawling system [18] has been proposed where crawlers share information about the RIA crawling among other crawlers directly, without relying on the single controller. In this system, each crawler is responsible for exploring transitions on a subset of states from the entire RIA graph model by associating each state to a different crawler. Crawlers are required to broadcast every newly executed transition to all other crawlers to find the shortest path from their current state to the next transition to be explored. Although this approach is appealing due to its simplicity, it is not fault tolerant. Moreover, it may introduce a high message overhead due to the sharing of transitions in case the number of crawlers is high.

A scalable P2P crawling system [19] using Chord [5] has been recently introduced to avoid the single point of failure. In this system, the P2P structure is composed of multiple controllers which are dispersed over a P2P network as shown in Fig. 2. In this system, each state is associated with a single controller. Moreover, a set of crawlers is associated with each controller, where crawlers are not part of the P2P network. Notice that both crawlers and controllers are independent processes running on different computers.

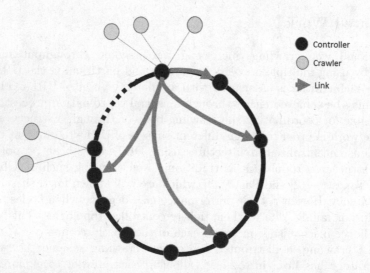

● Controller
○ Crawler
▶ Link

Fig. 2. Distribution of states and crawlers among controllers: each state is associated with one controller, and each crawler gets access to all controllers through a single controller it is associated with.

In this system, controllers maintain the topology of the P2P RIA crawling system and are responsible for storing information about the RIA crawling. If a controller fails, the connectivity of the overlay network is affected and some controllers become unreachable from other controllers. Since a P2P network is a continuously evolving system, it is required to continuously repair the overlay to ensure that the P2P structure remains connected and supports efficient look-ups. The maintenance of the P2P network consists of maintaining its topology as controllers join and leave the network and repairing the overlay network when failures occur among controllers independently of the RIA crawling.

There are mainly two different approaches for maintaining a structured P2P network when failures occur: The active and the passive approaches. In the active approach, a node may choose to detect failures only when it actually needs to contact a neighbor. A node n_x may perform actively the repair operation upon detecting the disappearance of another node n_y in the network, i.e. the node n_x trying to reach n_y becomes aware that n_y is not responsive. Node n_x then runs a failure recovery protocol immediately to recover from the failure of n_y using $ID(n_y)$. One drawback of the active approach is that only the routing table of some neighboring nodes are updated when a node n_y fails. The passive approach solves theses inaccuracies by running periodically a repair protocol by all nodes to maintain their routing tables up-to-date, called the *idealization protocol* [8]. The *idealization protocol* runs periodically by every single controller in the network where each controller attempts to update its routing information. Liben-Nowell et al. [8] suggests to use the passive approach for detecting failures to avoid the risk that all of a node neighbors fail before it notices any of the failures. In this paper, we use the passive approach for maintaining the structured overlay network.

The structured P2P overlay network allows for partial resilience only, i.e. avoiding the single point of failure allows the non-faulty crawlers and controllers to resume the crawling task in case of a node failure, after the reestablishment of the overlay network, rather than failing completely. However, this system is not fully resilient since lost states and transitions are not recovered after the network recovery.

3   Fault Tolerant RIA Crawling

In the fault tolerant P2P RIA crawling system we propose, crawlers and controllers must achieve two goals in parallel: Maintaining the P2P network and performing the Fault Tolerant RIA crawling using a data recovery mechanism.

3.1   Assumptions

- The unreliable P2P network is composed of a set of controllers, and a set of crawlers is associated with each of these controllers where both crawlers and controllers are vulnerable to Fail-stop failures, i.e. they may fail but without causing harm to the system. We also assume a perfect failure detection and reliable message delivery which allows nodes to correctly decide whether another node has crashed or not.

– Crawlers can be unreliable as they are only responsible for executing an assigned job, i.e. they do not store any relevant information about the state of the RIA. Therefore, a failed crawler may simply disappear or leave the system without being detected, assuming that some other non-faulty crawlers will remain crawling the RIA. However, for the RIA crawling to progress, there must be at least one non-faulty crawler that is able to achieve the RIA crawling in a finite amount of time.

3.2   Protocol Description

A major problem we address in this section is to make the proposed P2P RIA crawling system introduced by Ben Hafaiedh et al. [19] resilient to node failures, i.e. to allow the system to achieve the RIA crawling when controllers and crawlers may fail. The fault-tolerant crawling system is required to discover all states of a RIA despite failures, so that the entire RIA graph is explored. In the P2P crawling system, controllers are responsible for storing part of the discovered states. If a controller fails, the set of states maintained by the controller is lost. For the P2P crawling system to be resilient, controllers are required to apply a data recovery mechanism so that lost states and their transitions can be eventually recovered after the reestablishment of the overlay network. For the data recovery to be consistent, i.e. all lost states can be recovered when failures occur, each newly reached state by a crawler must be always stored by the controller the new state is associated with before the transition leading to the state is assumed to be executed. If a new state is not stored by the controller it is associated with, the controller performing a data recovery will not be aware of the state and the data recovery becomes inconsistent if the state is lost. As a consequence, the state becomes unreachable by crawlers and the RIA graph cannot be fully explored.

In Fig. 1, an acknowledgment for an assigned transition was sent by a crawler informing the controller responsible for the transition about the destination state that follows from the transition execution. However, in a faulty environment, a crawler may fail after having sent the result of a transition execution to the previous controller and before contacting the next controller. As a consequence, the destination state of the executed transition may never be known by the next controller and data recovery of the state cannot be performed. For the P2P crawling system to be resilient, every newly discovered state must be stored by the next controller before the executed transition is acknowledged to the previous controller. Therefore, we introduce a change to the P2P crawling described in Fig. 1 to make it fault tolerant, as shown in Fig. 3: When the next controller responsible for a newly reached state by a crawler is contacted, the controller stores the newly discovered state and forwards the result of the transition execution, i.e. an *AckJob* message, to the previous controller. As a consequence, the controller responsible for the transition can only update the destination state of the transition after the newly reached state is stored by the next controller. Moreover, the fault-tolerant P2P system requires each assigned transition by a controller to be acknowledged

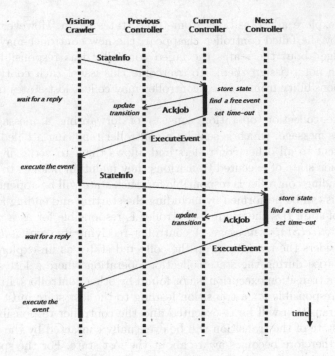

Fig. 3. The fault tolerant P2P RIA crawling during the exploration phase.

before a given time-out. When the time-out expires due to a failure, the transition is reassigned by the controller to another crawler at a later time.

4 Data Recovery Mechanisms

The data recovery mechanisms allow for either recovering lost states a failed controller was responsible for, reassigning all transitions on the recovered states to other crawlers and rebuilding the RIA graph model, or for making back-up copies of the RIA information on neighboring controllers when a newly reached state or an executed transition is known by a controller so that crawlers can resume crawling from where a failed controller has stopped. We introduce three data recovery mechanisms to achieve the RIA crawling task properly despite node failures, as follows:

4.1 Retry Strategy

The Retry strategy [10] consists of replaying any erroneous task execution, hoping that the same failure will not occur in subsequent retries. The Retry strategy may be applied to the P2P RIA crawling system by re-executing all lost jobs a failed controller was responsible for. When a controller becomes responsible for the set of states a faulty controller was responsible for, the controller allows crawlers to explore all transitions from these states again. However, since all states held by the failed controller disappear, the new controller may not have the knowledge about the states the failed controller was responsible for and therefore can not reassign them. To overcome this issue, each controller that inherits responsibility from a failed controller may collect lost states from other controllers.

The state collection operation consists of forwarding a message, called *CollectStates* message, which is sent by a controller replacing a failed one. The message is sent to all other controllers and allows them to verify if the ID of any destination state of executed transitions they maintain belongs to the set of states the sending controller is responsible for; such state will be appended to the message. This can be performed by including the starting and ending keys defining the set of state IDs the sending controller is responsible for as a parameter within the *CollectStates* message. A controller receiving its own *CollectStates* message considers the transitions on the collected states as un-explored. A situation may arise during the state collection operation where a lost state that follows from a transition execution is not found by other controllers. In this case, a controller responsible for a transition leading to the lost state must have also failed. The transition will be re-executed and the controller responsible for the destination state of the transition will be eventually contacted by the executing crawler and therefore becomes aware about the lost state. For the special case where the initial state can be lost, a transition leading to the initial state may not exists in a RIA. As a consequence, the *CollectStates* message may not be able to recover the initial state. To overcome this issue, a controller that inherits responsibility from a failed controller always assumes that the initial state is lost and asks a visiting crawler to load the *SeedURL* again in order to reach the initial state. The controller responsible for the initial state is then contacted by the crawler and becomes aware about the initial state.

4.2   Redundancy Strategy

The Redundancy strategy is a strategy based on Redundant Storage [10] and consists of maintaining back-up copies of the set of states that are associated with each controller, along with the set of transitions on each of these states and their status, on the successors of each controller. The main feature of this strategy is that states that were associated with a failed controller and their transitions can be recovered from neighboring controllers, which allows for reestablishing the situation that was before the failure i.e. the new controller can start from where the failed controller has stopped. This strategy consists of immediately propagating an update from each controller to its r back-up controllers in the overlay network when a new relevant information is received, where r is the number of back-up controllers that are associated with each controller, i.e. a newly discovered state or a newly executed transition becomes available to the controller. When a newly reached state is stored by a controller, the controller updates its back-up controllers with the new state before sending an acknowledgment to the previous controller. This ensures that every discovered state becomes available to the back-up controllers before the transition is acknowledged. Note that the controller responsible for the new state must receive an acknowledgment of reception from all back-up controllers before sending the acknowledgment. On the other hand, each executed transition that becomes available to the previous controller is also updated among back-up controllers before the result of the transition is locally acknowledged to the previous controller.

4.3   Combined Strategy

One drawback of the Redundancy strategy is that an update is required for each newly executed transition received by a controller. This may be problematic in RIA crawling since controllers may become overloaded. The Combined strategy overcomes this issue by periodically copying the executed transitions a controller maintains so that if the controller fails, a portion of the executed transitions remains available to the back-up controller; and the lost transitions that have not been copied have to be re-executed again. The advantage of using the Combined strategy is that all executed transitions maintained by a controller are copied one time at the end of each update period rather than copying every newly executed transition, as introduced by the Redundancy strategy. Note that the state collection operation used by the Retry strategy is required by the Combined strategy since not all states are recovered when a failure occurs.

5   Evaluation

We compare the efficiency of the Retry, the Redundancy and the Combined strategies in terms of the overhead they introduce during the exploration phase as controllers fail. We use the following notation: t_t is the average time required for executing a new transition, T is the total crawling time with normal operation, c is the average communication delay of a direct message between two nodes, n is the number of controllers and λ_f is the average failure rate of a node in the P2P overlay network, which is of the order of 1 failure per hour per node. Moreover, since the recovery of the overlay network is performed in parallel and is independent of the RIA crawling, we ignore the delay introduced by running the *idealization protocol* and we assume that queries are resolved with the ideal number of messages after a short period of time after the failure of a controller. We also assume that there are no simultaneous failures of successive controllers, which means that only one back-up copy is maintained by each controller, i.e. r is equal to 1. Notice that this simplified model may be extended to allow simultaneous failures among controllers, with the condition that r back-up copies must be maintained by each controller to allow r simultaneous correlated failures, where $r < n$.

We performed a simulation study on experimental data-sets in a real execution environment, and measurements from the simulation results are used as parameters in the following analytical evaluation. One of the tested real large-scale applications we consider in this study is the Bebop[1] RIA. It consists of 5,082 states and 468,971 transitions with a reset cost that is equivalent to 3 transition executions. The average communication delay c is 1 ms. For a crawling system composed of 100 controllers and 1000 crawlers, the average transition execution delay t_t is 0.3 ms. The delay introduced by each data recovery mechanism, when a controller fails, is described in the following.

5.1 Retry Strategy

When a controller fails, all states associated with the controller are lost and all transitions from these states have to be re-executed. Since states are randomly distributed among controllers, the fraction of transitions to be re-executed when a controller fails is of the order of $1/n$. Assuming that a controller fails in the middle of the total crawling period T, the delay introduced by the failure of a controller is equivalent to $\lambda_f.T/(2.n)$. Additionally, the state collection operation results in a delay of $c.(n-1)$ units of time before the message is received back by the neighbor responsible for the recovered states, which is very small compared to the first delay and could be neglected. Therefore, the overhead of the Retry strategy is equivalent to $(\lambda_f.T)/(2.n)$.

5.2 Redundancy Strategy

In the Redundancy strategy, the update operations are performed concurrently. When a controller fails, all states associated with the controller along with the executed transitions on these states are recovered by the Redundancy strategy. To do so, each result of a newly executed transition that becomes available to a controller is updated on its successor before the transition is locally updated. However, since the next controller responsible for sending the result of the executed transition is not required to wait for the transition to be acknowledged before finding a job for the visiting crawler, the delay introduced by the transition update operation is very short and therefore can be ignored.

Finally, a controller noticing a change on its list of successors due to a failed neighbor updates its new successor with all states and transitions the controller maintains and waits for an acknowledgment of reception from the back-up controller before proceeding, resulting in one additional update operation per failure to be performed with a delay of $2c$ units of time, assuming that the size of the message is relatively small. Notice that the update operation delay increases as the size of the data included in the message increases. The overhead of the Redundancy strategy is given by $(2.c)/(t_t)$.

---

[1] http://www.alari.ch/people/derino/apps/bebop/index.php/ (Local version: http://ssrg.eecs.uottawa.ca/bebop/).

5.3 Comparison of the Retry and the Redundancy Strategies When Controllers Are Not Overloaded

Preliminary analysis of experimental results [17] have shown that a controller can support up to 20 crawlers before becoming a bottleneck. In this section, we assume that each controller is associated with at most 20 crawlers so that controllers are not overloaded.

Figure 4 compares the the overhead of the Retry and the Redundancy Strategies with respect to the P2P node failure failure λ_f when controllers are not overloaded. Figure 4 shows that the Redundancy strategy significantly outperforms the Retry strategy as the number of failures increases. However, the Redundancy strategy may not remain efficient compared to the Retry strategy when controllers are overloaded, due to the repetitive back-up update of every executed transition required for redundancy.

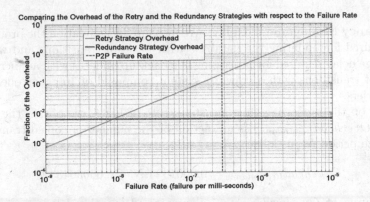

Fig. 4. Comparing the overhead of the Retry and the Redundancy Strategies with respect to the failure rate, assuming that controllers are not overloaded.

5.4 Combined Strategy

The Combined data recovery strategy consists of periodically copying the executed transitions a controller maintains so that, if the controller fails, a portion of the executed transitions remains available in the back-up controller, and the number of lost transitions that have not been copied have to be re-executed again. Let N_t be the number of executed transitions maintained by a given controller per update period. The update period, i.e. the time required for executing N_t transitions, called T_p, is given by:

$$T_p = N_t.t_t \text{ units of time} \tag{1}$$

The overhead introduced for fault handling using the combined data recovery strategy includes two parts: The redundancy management and the retry processing operations. We aim to minimize the sum of the two operations which depends on two parameters: The update period T_p and the failure rate λ_f.

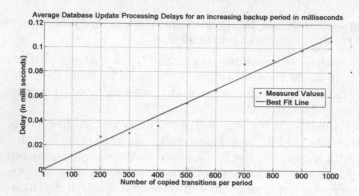

Fig. 5. Measurements of the processing delay p for updating the database for an increasing number of copied transitions.

Redundancy Management Delay: We measure by simulation the processing time required for updating the database with back-up transitions and we plot the average delay required for processing the back-up updates with an increasing number of transitions with a crawling system composed of 100 controllers and 1000 crawlers.

Based on the processing time measurements of Fig. 5, we obtain the linear equation $Overhead_{Redundancy}$ as a function of the number of copied transitions per update period N_t, as follows:

$$Overhead_{Redundancy} = 0.0001094.N_t + 0.00030433 \qquad (2)$$

The curve of $Overhead_{Redundancy}$ corresponds to the delay required for processing the update of backup transitions called p. The delay required for processing one back-up copy is $T_p.p/t_t$ units of time, where p is shown in Fig. 5. Moreover, there is an additional communication delay required for sending the backup copy and receiving the acknowledgment back from the back-up controller of $2.c$ time units. Therefore, the total delay introduced by the redundancy management operation at the end of each period, called T_{bp}, is given by:

$$T_{bp} = \frac{T_p.p}{t_t} + 2.c \qquad (3)$$

Retry Processing Delay: The Retry Processing operation consists of re-executing, after a failure, the lost transitions that were executed after the last redundancy update operation. Assuming that failures occur on average in the middle of an update period, the retry processing delay is given by:

$$T_{rp} = \frac{\lambda_f.T_p^2}{2} \qquad (4)$$

Total Overhead Introduced by the Combined Strategy: The overhead introduced by the Combined strategy is given by:

$$Overhead_{CombinedStrategy} = \frac{T_{bp} + T_{rp}}{T_p} = \frac{\lambda_f.T_p}{2} + \frac{2.c}{T_p} + \frac{p}{t_t} \quad (5)$$

The minimum overhead is obtained when $d(Overhead)/d(T_p) = 0$. We have:

$$T_p = 2\sqrt{\frac{c}{\lambda_f}} \quad (6)$$

The value of T_p with the minimum Combined strategy overhead is shown in Fig. 6. If λ_f is low, T_p is high, i.e. many transitions are executed before the next update operation, allowing for prioritizing the Retry strategy over the Redundancy strategy, hoping that failures are unlikely to occur in the future. In contrast, if λ_f is high, T_p becomes low and a few transitions are executed before the next update operation, allowing for prioritizing the Redundancy strategy over the Retry strategy since failures are likely to occur in the future.

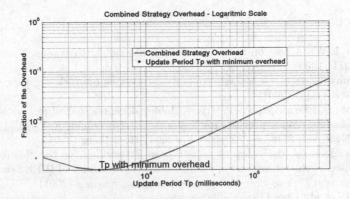

Fig. 6. Minimum overhead of the combined strategy.

Comparison of the Data Recovery Mechanisms: Analytical results show a high delay related to the Retry strategy compared to the Redundancy strategy when controllers are underloaded. Moreover, the Combined strategy outperforms the Redundancy strategy when controllers are overloaded by periodically copying the executed transitions a controller maintains so that if the controller fails, a portion of the executed transitions remains available in the back-up controller, which allows for significantly reducing the number of updates performed compared to the Redundancy strategy.

6   Conclusion

We have presented a resilient P2P RIA crawling system for crawling large-scale RIAs by partitioning the search space among several controllers that share the information about the explored RIA, which allows for fault tolerance, when both crawlers and controllers are vulnerable to crash failures. We defined three different data recovery mechanisms for crawling RIAs in a faulty environment: The Retry, the Redundancy and the Combined strategies. The Redundancy strategy outperformed the Retry strategy when controllers are not overloaded since it allows for reestablishing the situation that was before the failure, while the Retry strategy results in a high delay due to the repetitive execution of lost transitions. However, the Combined strategy outperforms the Redundancy strategy when controllers are overloaded by reducing the number of updates among backup controllers. This makes the Combined strategy the best choice for crawling RIAs in a faulty environment when controllers are overloaded. However, there is still some room for improvement: We plan to evaluate the impact of the data recovery strategies on the crawling performance when controllers are overloaded through simulation studies.

References

1. Dijkstra, E.W.: A note on two problems in connexion with graphs. Numer. Math. **1**, 269–271 (1959)
2. Ratnasamy, S., et al.: A scalable content-addressable network. In: Proceedings of ACM SIGCOMM (2001)
3. Rowstron, A., Druschel, P.: Pastry: scalable, decentralized object location, and routing for large-scale peer-to-peer systems. In: Guerraoui, R. (ed.) Middleware 2001. LNCS, vol. 2218, pp. 329–350. Springer, Heidelberg (2001)
4. Schollmeier, R.: A definition of peer-to-peer networking for the classification of peer-to-peer architectures and applications. In: Proceedings of IEEE International Conference on Peer-to-Peer Computing, Linkping, Sweden (2001)
5. Stoica, I., et al.: Chord: a scalable peer-to-peer look-up service for internet applications. In: Proceedings of ACM SIGCOMM, San Diego, California, USA (2001)
6. Cho, J., Garcia-Molina, H.: Parallel crawlers. In: Proceedings of the 11th International Conference on World Wide Web, WWW, vol. 2 (2002)
7. Fiat, A., Saia, J.: Censorship resistant peer-to-peer content addressable networks. In: Proceedings of the 13th Annual ACM-SIAM Symposium on Discrete Algorithms, Philadelphia, Pennsylvania, USA, pp. 94–103 (2002)
8. Liben-Nowell, D., Balakrishnan, H., Karger, D.: Analysis of the evolution of peer-to-peer systems. In: Proceedings of the 21st ACM Symposium on Principles of Distributed Computing, pp. 233–242 (2002)
9. Shkapenyuk, V., Suel, T.: Design and implementation of a high performance distributed Web crawler. In: Proceedings of the 18th International Conference on Data Engineering (2002)
10. Hwang, S., Kesselman, C.: A flexible framework for fault tolerance in the grid. J. Grid Comput. **1**, 251–272 (2003)
11. Boldi, P., et al.: UbiCrawler: a scalable fully distributed Web crawler. Softw. Pract. Exp. **34**, 711–726 (2004)

12. Zhao, Y., et al.: Tapestry: a resilient global-scale overlay for service deployment. In: IEEE J. Sel. Areas Commun. (2004)

13. Paulson, L.D.: Building rich web applications with Ajax. Computer **38**, 14–17. IEEE Computer Society (2005)

14. Li, X., Misra, J., Plaxton, C.G.: Concurrent maintenance of rings. In: proceedings of the 23rd ACM Symposium on Principles of Distributed Computing, pp. 126–148 (2006)

15. Choudhary, S., Dincturk, M.E., Mirtaheri, S.M., Moosavi, A., Von Bochmann, G., Jourdan, G.V., Onut, I.V.: Crawling rich internet applications: the state of the art. In: Conference of the Center for Advanced Studies on Collaborative Research, Markham, Ontario, Canada, pp. 146–160 (2012)

16. Peng, Z., et al.: Graph-based AJAX crawl: mining data from rich internet applications. In: Proceedings of the International Conference on Computer Science and Electronic Engineering, pp. 590–594 (2012)

17. Mirtaheri, S.M., Von Bochmann, G., Jourdan, G.V., Onut, I.V.: GDist-RIA crawler: a greedy distributed crawler for rich internet applications. In: Noubir, G., Raynal, M. (eds.) NETYS 2014. LNCS, vol. 8593, pp. 200–214. Springer, Heidelberg (2014)

18. Mirtaheri, S.M., Bochmann, G.V., Jourdan, G.-V., Onut, I.V.: PDist-RIA crawler: a peer-to-peer distributed crawler for rich internet applications. In: Benatallah, B., Bestavros, A., Manolopoulos, Y., Vakali, A., Zhang, Y. (eds.) WISE 2014, Part II. LNCS, vol. 8787, pp. 365–380. Springer, Heidelberg (2014)

19. Ben Hafaiedh, K., Von Bochmann, G., Jourdan, G.V., Onut, I.V.: A scalable peer-to-peer RIA crawling system with partial knowledge. In: Noubir, G., Raynal, M. (eds.) NETYS 2014. LNCS, vol. 8593, pp. 185–199. Springer, Heidelberg (2014)

Nearest Neighbors Graph Construction: Peer Sampling to the Rescue

Yahya Benkaouz[1(✉)], Mohammed Erradi[1], and Anne-Marie Kermarrec[2]

[1] Networking and Distributed Systems Research Group,
ENSIAS, Mohammed V University in Rabat, Rabat, Morocco
y.benkaouz@um5s.net.ma, mohamed.erradi@gmail.com
[2] INRIA Rennes, Rennes, France
anne-marie.kermarrec@inria.fr

Abstract. In this paper, we propose an efficient KNN service, called KPS (KNN-Peer-Sampling). The KPS service can be used in various contexts e.g. recommendation systems, information retrieval and data mining. KPS borrows concepts from P2P gossip-based clustering protocols to provide a *localized* and efficient KNN computation in large-scale systems. KPS is a sampling-based iterative approach, combining randomness, to provide serendipity and avoid local minimum, and clustering, to ensure fast convergence. We compare KPS against the state of the art KNN centralized computation algorithm NNDescent, on multiple datasets. The experiments confirm the efficiency of KPS over NNDescent: KPS improves significantly on the computational cost while converging quickly to a close to optimal KNN graph. For instance, the cost, expressed in number of pairwise similarity computations, is reduced by ≈23% and ≈49% to construct high quality KNN graphs for Jester and MovieLens datasets, respectively. In addition, the randomized nature of KPS ensures eventual convergence, not always achieved with NNDescent.

Keywords: K-Nearest Neighbors · Clustering · Sampling · Randomness

1 Introduction

Methods based on nearest neighbors are acknowledged as a basic building block for a wide variety of applications [12]. In an n object system, a K-nearest-neighbors (KNN) service provides each object with its k most similar objects, according to a given similarity metric. This builds a KNN graph where there is an edge between each object and its k most similar objects. Such a graph can be leveraged in the context of many applications such as similarity search [5], machine learning [15], data mining [22] and image processing [8]. For instance, KNN computation is crucial in collaborative filtering based systems, providing users with items matching their interests (e.g. Amazon or Netflix). For instance, in a user-based collaborative filtering approach, the KNN provides each user with her closest ones, i.e. the users which have the most interests in common.

© Springer International Publishing AG 2016
P.A. Abdulla and C. Delporte-Gallet (Eds.): NETYS 2016, LNCS 9944, pp. 48–62, 2016.
DOI: 10.1007/978-3-319-46140-3_4

This neighborhood is leveraged by the recommendation system to provide users with items of interest, e.g. the most popular items among the KNN users.

The most straightforward way to construct the KNN graph is to rely on a brute-force solution computing the similarity between each pair of nodes (in the rest of this paper, we call a node an element of the system and the KNN graph. A node can refer to an object or a user for instance). Obviously the high complexity of such an approach, $O(n^2)$ in a n node system, makes this solution usable only for small datasets. This is clearly incompatible with the current Big Data nature of most applications [4]. For instance, social networks generate a massive amount of data (e.g. on Facebook, 510,000 comments, 293,000 status updates and 136,000 photo uploads are generated every minute). Processing such a huge amount of data to extract meaningful information is simply impossible if an approach were to exhaustively compute the similarity between every pair of nodes in the system. While traditional clustering approaches make use of offline generated KNN graphs [15,20], they are not applicable in highly dynamic settings where the clusters may evolve rapidly over time and the applications relying on the KNN graph expect low latencies. Hence, a periodic recomputation of the KNN graph is mandatory. The main challenge when applying KNN to very large datasets is to drastically reduce the computational cost.

In this paper, we address this challenge by proposing a novel KNN computation algorithm, inspired from fully decentralized (peer-to-peer) clustering systems. More specifically, peer-to-peer systems are characterized by the fact that no peer has the global knowledge of the entire system. Instead, each peer relies on local knowledge of the system, and performs computations using this restricted sample of the system. Yet the aggregated operations of all peers make the system converge towards a global objective. In this paper, we present *KPS (KNN-Peer-Sampling)*, a novel *sampling-based service* for KNN graph construction that combines randomness to provide serendipity and avoid local minimum, and clustering to speed up the convergence therefore reducing the overall cost of the approach. Instead of computing the similarity between a node and all other nodes, our approach relies on narrowing down the number of candidates with which each node should be compared. While a sampling approach has also been proposed in NNDescent [13], acknowledged as one of the most efficient solutions to the KNN problem currently, we show in our experiments that KPS achieves similar results with respect to the quality of the KNN graph while drastically reducing the cost. In addition, KPS avoids the local minimum situation of NNDescent and ensures that the system eventually converges.

To summarize, the contributions of this paper are: (i) the design of a *novel, scalable KNN graph construction* service that relies on sampling, randomness and localized information to quickly achieve, at low cost, a topology close to the ideal one and eventually ensures convergence. Although we focus on a centralized implementation of KPS, it can also be implemented on a decentralized or hybrid architecture, precisely due to its *local* nature; and (ii) *an extensive evaluation* of KPS and a comparison with the state of the art KNN graph construction algorithm NNDescent, on five real datasets. The results show that KPS provides a low-cost alternative to NNDescent.

The remainder of this paper is structured as follows: Sect. 2 presents the suggested KPS. Section 3 describes the experimental setup. Section 4 discusses the results. Section 5 presents related works. Finally, Sect. 6 presents conclusions and expected future work.

2   The KNN Peer Sampling Service

KPS is a novel service that starting from a random graph topology, iteratively converges to a topology where each node is connected to its k nearest neighbors in the system. The scalability of KPS relies on the fact that instead of computing the similarity of a node with every other node in the system, only *local* information is considered at each iteration. This *sample*, referred as the *candidate set*, is based only on the neighborhood information available in the KNN graph. This significantly reduces the number of similarity computations needed to achieve the KNN topology.

We consider a set D of n nodes ($|D| = n$). Each node p is associated with a profile. A profile is a structured representation of a node p, containing multiple features that characterize a node. For instance, in user-based collaborative filtering recommendation systems, a node represents a user u. The user profile in this context is typically a vector of preferences gathering the ratings assigned by the user u to different items (movies, books). In an item-based system, the item profile is generally the feature vector that represents the item, or a vector containing a list of users who liked that item for instance.

We also consider a sampling function $sample(D, k)$, that, given a set of nodes in D, and $k \in \mathbb{N}$, returns a subset of k nodes selected uniformly at random from D. We assume a function $similarity(p_i, p_j)$ that computes the similarity between two nodes, i.e. the similarity between two profiles p_i and p_j. The similarity can be computed using several metrics (e.g. Jaccard, cosine, etc.). KPS is generic and can be applied with any similarity metric.

Let α_p be the number of updates in a given iteration for a node p. In other words, α_p reflects the number of changes that happen in the neighborhood of p over the last iteration. Somehow α_p captures the number of potential new opportunities provided to p to discover new neighbors. KPS constructs the candidate set such that: The candidate set of p contains the neighbors of p, the neighbors of α_p neighbors and $k - \alpha_p$ random nodes. Those α_p neighbors are randomly selected including new and old neighbors. This operation limits the size of the candidate set. KPS does not explore all the nodes two hops away since that can represent a large fraction of the network. This is particularly true for high degree nodes. Instead, KPS limits the exploration to a subset of neighbors. The reason why KPS considers the direct neighbors to be added to the candidate set is to account for potential dynamics. This makes KPS able to dynamically update the KNN graph as nodes profiles change over time.

Algorithm 1 represents the pseudocode of the algorithm used in the KPS service. Initially, each node p starts with a random set of neighbors. This forms

---

Algorithm 1. The KPS Service Algorithm

---

01. **For each** $p \in D$ **do**
02. $KNN_p = sample(D, k)$
03. $\alpha_p = k$
04. **End for**
05. **Do**
06.   **For each** $p \in D$ **do**
07. $oldNN_p = KNN_p$
08. $candidateSet_p.add(KNN_p)$
09. $selectedNeighbors_p = sample(KNN_p, \alpha_p)$
10.   **For each** $q \in selectedNeighbors_p$ **do**
11. $candidateSet_p.add(KNN_q)$
12.   **End for**
13. $candidateSet_p.add(sample(D, k - \alpha_p))$
14.   **For each** $n \in candidateSet_p$ **do**
15. $score[n] = similarity(Profile_n, Profile_p)$
16.   **End for**
17. $KNN_p = subList(k, sort(score))$
18. $\alpha_p = k - sizeOf(OldNN_p \cap KNN_p)$
19.   **End for**
20. **While** $\sum_p \alpha_p > 0$

---

the initial KNN graph (line 02). Therefore, the initial value of α_p is k (line 03). At each iteration, the candidate set of each node includes its current neighbors (line 08), the neighbors of α_p neighbors (lines 09–12) and $k - \alpha_p$ random neighbors (line 13). The $k - \alpha_p$ nodes are randomly selected from the whole set of the system nodes. So, they might contain already-candidate nodes. Finally, the KNN of each node is updated, by selecting the k closest neighbors out of its candidate set (lines 14–17). At each iteration, the value of α_p is re-computed, for each node, based on the number of changes in the node's neighborhood (line 18).

We illustrate several scenarios of KPS operations in Fig. 1. Based on the value of the parameter α_p (number of updates in the KNN list of the node x), the composition of the candidate set of this node can take several forms. In this scenario, we run the KPS protocol for $k = 3$. Therefore, α_p takes values between 0 and 3. In the first iteration (Fig. 1a), the neighbors of x are ($KNN_x = \{A, B, C\}$). As the links in the first KNN graph are randomly built, nodes in the set KNN_x are considered as newly discovered nodes, thus $\alpha_p = k = 3$. The current neighbors present an opportunity to discover relevant new neighbors and considering random nodes is unnecessary. Therefore, the candidate set of x will contain all neighbors and their neighbors. Assuming that, in the second iteration, only the node $A2$ was added to the KNN_x. Thus, $\alpha_p = 1$ (Fig. 1b). In this case, the candidate set contains, the list of neighbors, the neighbors of α_p neighbors and $(k - \alpha_p)$ random nodes. Assuming that, in the third iteration (Fig. 1c), the KNN list of x remains unchanged $KNN_x = \{A, B, A2\}$. This means that $\alpha_p = 0$. In this case, only random nodes are considered in the candidate set. This might

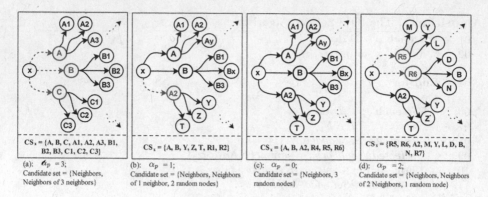

CS_x = {A, B, C, A1, A2, A3, B1, B2, B3, C1, C2, C3}

CS_x = {A, B, Y, Z, T, R1, R2}

CS_x = {A, B, A2, R4, R5, R6}

CS_x = {R5, R6, A2, M, Y, L, D, B, N, R7}

(a): $\alpha_p = 3$;
Candidate set = {Neighbors, Neighbors of 3 neighbors}

(b): $\alpha_p = 1$;
Candidate set = {Neighbors, Neighbors of 1 neighbor, 2 random nodes}

(c): $\alpha_p = 0$;
Candidate set = {Neighbors, 3 random nodes}

(d): $\alpha_p = 2$;
Candidate set = {Neighbors, Neighbors of 2 Neighbors, 1 random node}

Fig. 1. Example scenarios of the KPS service algorithm for $k = 3$. (The black arrows represent old links and the blue dashed ones are new links) (Color figure online)

result in the appearance of nodes with higher similarities such as the random nodes $R5$ and $R6$ (Fig. 1d).

3   Experimental Setup

In this section, we describe the experimental setup that we rely on to evaluate the efficiency of KPS. More specifically, we describe the competitor, NNDescent [13], that we compare KPS against. We also describe the datasets that we used in the evaluation as well as the evaluation metrics.

3.1   NNDescent Algorithm

NNDescent [13] is a recent KNN algorithm which is acknowledged as one of the best generic KNN centralized approach. Similarly to KPS and previous gossip-based protocols [6,7,18,24], NNDescent relies on two principles: (i) the assumption that "The neighbor of a neighbor is also likely to be a neighbor" and (ii) a reduced candidate set to limit the number of similarity computations at each iteration.

The basic algorithm of NNDescent starts by picking a random approximation of KNN for each object, generating a random graph. Then, iteratively, NNDescent iterates to improve the KNN topology by comparing each node against its current neighbors' neighbors, including both KNN and reverse KNN (i.e. in and out degree in the graph). KNN terminates when the number of updates in the graph reaches a given threshold, assuming that no further improvement can be made. Thus, in NNDescent, the candidate set of each node contains the neighbors of neighbors and the reverse neighbors' neighbors, called RNN. The RNNs are defined in such a way that: Given two nodes p and q, if $p \in KNN_q$ then $q \in RNN_p$. Multiple strategies are then proposed to improve the efficiency of the algorithm:

1. A local join operation takes place on a node. It consists of computing the similarity between each pair $p, q \in KNN \cup RNN$, and updating both the KNN lists of p and q based on the computed similarity.
2. A boolean flag is attached to each object in the KNN lists, to avoid computing similarities that have been already computed.
3. A sampling method is used in order to limit the size of the reverse KNN. In order to prepare the list of nodes that will participate to the local join operation, NNDescent differentiate *old* nodes (with a false flag) from *new* nodes (with a true flag). The sampling method works as follows: Firstly, NNDescent samples ρk out of the KNN, where $\rho \in (0, 1]$ is a system parameter. Then, based on the flag of the sampled nodes, it creates two RNN lists: *new'* and *old'*. After that, two sets s_1 and s_2 are created in such a way that: $s_1 = old \cup sample(old', \rho k)$ and $s_2 = new \cup sample(new', \rho k)$. Finally, the local join is conducted on elements of s_1, and between s_1 and s_2 elements.
4. An early termination criterion is used to stop the algorithm when further iterations can no longer bring meaningful improvements to the KNN graph.

Therefore, the main differences between KPS and NNDescent are the following: (i) NNDescent starts from a uniform topology and therefore depending on the initial configuration and the input (dataset), the algorithm might never converge to the ideal KNN graph; (ii) the fact that the candidate set in NNDescent contains nodes from RNN and KNN; (iii) the sampling approach used to define the candidate set is different in both approaches; and (iv) KPS adds some random nodes that turn out to be very useful to explore the graph and later to reduce the risk of being stuck in local minimum.

3.2 Datasets Description

We conducted the evaluation of KPS against five real datasets. Figures are summarized in Table 1: Shape and Audio also used in [13] as well as MovieLens [3], Jester [2] and Flickr. In the following, we detail how node profiles are built for these datasets:

- The Audio dataset contains features extracted from the DARPA TIMIT collection, which contains recordings of 6, 300 English sentences. Each sentence is broken into smaller segments from which the features were extracted. Each segment feature is treated as an individual node.
- The Flickr dataset is constructed based on [17]. This dataset contains 22, 872 image profiles. A Flickr image profile consists of a set of tags associated to the image.
- The MovieLens raw data consists of 1, 000, 209 anonymous ratings of approximately 3, 900 movies made by 6, 040 MovieLens users [3]. Based on the collected data we extracted the users' profiles, such that items in a given user profile contains list of movies that received a rating in the range [3, 5].

Table 1. Datasets characteristics

Dataset	Object	Profile content	Nb. Profiles	Profile size
Audio	Records	Audio features	54387	192
Flickr	Image	Images tags	22872	9 in avg.
Jester	User	Jokes ratings	14116	100
MovieLens	User	Movies	6040	165 in avg.
Shape	3D shape model	Model features	28775	544

– The Jester dataset [1] contains data collected from the Jester Joke Recommender System [2]. We selected only profiles of users that rated all jokes. Therefore, the dataset contains $14,116$ user profiles. Each user profile contains ratings of a set of 100 jokes.
– The Shape dataset contains about $29,000$ 3D shape models. It consists of a mixture of 3D polygonal models gathered from commercial viewpoint models, De Espona Models, Cacheforce models and from the Web. Each model is represented by a feature vector.

3.3   Similarity Metrics

Depending on the nature of nodes profiles, we rely on different similarity metrics: Jaccard similarity and the cosine similarity. Given two sets of attributes, the Jaccard similarity is defined as the cardinality of the intersection divided by the size of the union of the two sets: $Jaccard(s_1, s_2) = |\frac{s_1 \cap s_2}{s_1 \cup s_2}|$. The cosine similarity measure is represented using the dot product and the magnitude of two vectors: $Cosine(v_1, v_2) = \frac{v_1 \cdot v_2}{||v_1|| \cdot ||v_2||}$.

When the node profiles of a given dataset are of different sizes, we use Jaccard similarity, where a node profile is considered as a set. We used the Jaccard similarity metric for MovieLens and Flickr datasets. Otherwise, when the profiles of a dataset are of the same size and when the order of profiles' attributes is important, we use the cosine similarity. Thus, we used the cosine similarity metric for Jester, Shape and Audio datasets.

3.4   Evaluation Metrics

To measure the accuracy of KPS, we consider the *recall* of the KNN lists. This metric tells us to what extent the KNN lists match the ideal ones. The recall for a given node is computed using the following formula: $R = TP/(TP + FN)$, such that: TP (True Positive) is the number of nodes belonging to the nearest neighbors that truly belong to the node's KNN; FN (False Negative) is the number of nodes that belong to the KNN where they should not.

We conducted the following experiments: (i) we evaluate the evolution of the recall against the cost; (ii) we measure the quality of the KNN graph by

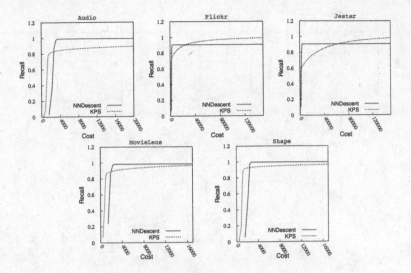

Fig. 2. Recall versus cost in KPS and NNDescent

measuring the average similarity between a node and its k nearest neighbors against the cost; (iii) we compute the *utility* of the algorithm at each cycle; and (iv) as KPS and NNDescent operate in such a way that the size of the samples varies significantly, we artificially increase the size of the sample in KPS so that the same number of similarity computations is achieved for each node at each iteration in the two algorithms. Hence, we provide the recall figures for the two algorithms with similar cost.

4   Experimental Results

We now report on our experimental evaluation comparing KPS and NNDescent. Note that the experiments were run with k set to 20. We start with comparing the cost/recall tradeoff achieved by the two algorithms. We then study the quality of the KNN graph and the utility of each iteration. Finally, for the sake of fairness, we compare the convergence of the algorithms at equal cost.

4.1   Recall Versus Cost

Figure 2 plots the recall as a function of the cost for both KPS and NNDescent. The cost here is measured as the total number of similarity computations. From Fig. 2, we observe that KPS exhibits a lower cost than NNDescent in several datasets i.e. in Audio, MovieLens and Shape, while both approaches provide similar recall. We also observe that NNDescent does not always converge to the maximum recall. This is due to the fact that depending on the initial configuration and the operation of NNDescent, the algorithm may reach a local minimum as shown on the Flickr and Jester datasets. On those two datasets, although

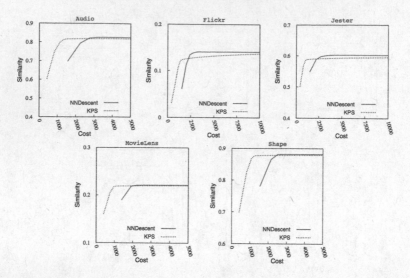

Fig. 3. Quality (Similarity) versus Cost in KPS and NNDescent

slower, KPS converges. This is mainly due to the presence of random nodes in the candidate sets. In NNDescent instead, for some datasets, separated clusters are created during the algorithm operations. For Jester and Flickr, NNDescent does not exceed 90 % of the recall.

In Audio, MovieLens and Shape, we observe that KPS reaches a similar recall than NNDescent at a much lower cost. For instance, for more than 0.8 recall, i.e. 80% of the KNN lists are similar to the ideal ones with a cost for KPS that is 42 %, resp. 50 %, resp. 51 % lower in Audio, resp. MovieLens, resp. Shape. We also observe that in the datasets where NNDescent converges at a lower cost to a high recall, it never converges to the highest (Flickr and Jester). On the other hand, KPS might take too long to converge to an ideal KNN graph (Audio), as it might require comparisons with the whole system nodes.

These results suggest that KPS is an attractive alternative to NNDescent for reaching a high recall at low cost. Although this is out of the scope of this paper, it has been shown in many applications, e.g. collaborative filtering, that an ideal KNN graph is not necessarily required to achieve good performance in the recommendations. For instance, good recommendation quality can be achieved with a close to ideal KNN graph but not necessarily ideal.

4.2   Quality Versus Cost

Regardless of the recall, another important metric is the quality of the KNN graph. For instance, consider a node provided with a non ideal KNN list, if the similarity between that node and its neighbors is high, the KNN data might turn out to be as useful as the exact KNN.

We measure the quality of the KNN graph as the average similarity between a node and its neighbors in the KNN graph for both KPS and NNDescent. Figure 3 displays the quality against the cost for all datasets. We observe that KPS provides almost uniformly across all datasets a better quality at a much lower cost. Based on these results, we can also argue that the differences in recall observed in Fig. 2 are not significant. Effectively in Audio for instance, while NNDescent shows a better recall, the quality is similar in both KPS and NNDescent. This actually suggests that the discrepancy in recall is negligible: KPS provides k nearest neighbors of similar quality (although they are not the ideal neighbors). For instance, to achieve a Jester KNN graph with an average similarity equal to 0.59 (highest similarity), the cost needed in KPS is 2116 while it equals to 2748 for NNDescent. Moreover, KPS requires an average of 956 comparisons to achieve a MovieLens graph with 0.21 similarity, while NNDescent makes an average of 1919 comparisons to construct a graph with the same quality. Therefore, KPS exhibits a cost about ≈23 %, resp. ≈49 % lower for Jester, resp. MovieLens, than NNDescent.

The reason why NNDescent finds the ideal neighbors is due to the very large size of the candidate sets. KPS takes longer to converge because once the almost ideal neighbors are discovered, the graph hardly changes and the ideal neighbors are eventually reached through the presence of random nodes in the candidate set. Other factors related to the characteristics of the dataset, typically sparsity, can also impact the recall and the similarity achieved. We will come back to this issue in Sect. 4.5. This set of experiments shows that KPS achieves almost perfect KNN graph construction at a much lower cost than NNDescent.

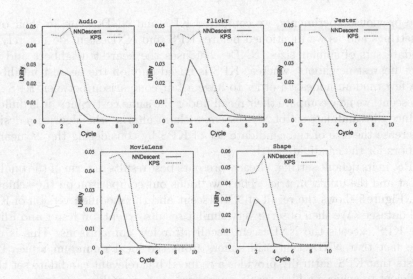

Fig. 4. Utility per cycle

4.3 Utility Study

To understand the impact of the candidate selection strategies used in KPS and NNDescent, we study the impact (utility) of each iteration on the KNN graph. Figure 4 plots the *utility* per cycle for all datasets. The utility tells us how useful similarity comparisons are at each cycle by measuring how many updates were generated (i.e. the number of discovered neighbors that achieves a better similarity). Utility is expressed as the ratio between the number of updates and the number of similarity comparisons. Results depicted in Fig. 4 are consistent over all datasets. Results clearly show that each iteration in KPS is much more useful than a NNDescent iteration. This is partly explained by the fact that NNDescent considers large candidate sets, especially for the first iterations, where its size is twice the size of the KPS candidate set. This also clearly shows that if the candidate set is carefully chosen, there is no need to consider large candidate sets.

After a few iterations, the evaluated utility of both protocols converges to 0. This is due to the usage of the *boolean flag* in NNDescent, and the selection rule in KPS (i.e. the usage of the number of updates to select neighbors of neighbors and random nodes). This also shows that the last steps to converge towards an ideal KNN graph take a very long time. This confirms the results depicted in Figs. 2 and 3: While KPS converges quickly to high quality neighborhoods, reaching the ideal neighborhoods takes much longer. This is a well-known problem in gossip-based sorting protocols [14].

4.4 Recall at Equal Cost

In the previous experiments, we compared KPS and NNDescent, in their original settings and as we mentioned before, KPS and NNDescent do not rely on candidate sets of similar sizes. NNDescent uses the nearest neighbors and the reverse nearest neighbors, whereas KPS is based only on the nearest neighbors and a few random nodes. In order to have a fair comparison between KPS and NNDescent, we now compare their recall under the same cost. Since, it is difficult to reduce the candidate set of NNDescent without altering the algorithm design, we increase the size of the candidate set of KPS by considering the $2k$ nearest neighbors for the candidate set.[1]

KPS, in its default setting, already presents best results in term of the quality, the cost and the utility metrics. Thus, we focus our comparison on the achieved recall. Figure 5 shows the recall of NNDescent and the modified version of KPS for all datasets. We then observe very similar results except for Jester and Flickr where KPS exceeds the NNDescent recall after few comparisons. This is due to the fact that NNDescent still suffers from the local minimum issue. This suggests that KPS naturally provides a reduced but relevant candidate set that is sufficient to achieve a high recall, an almost perfect quality at a low cost.

---

[1] Note that the strength of KPS is to achieve good results with less information so this way of comparing is not in our favor.

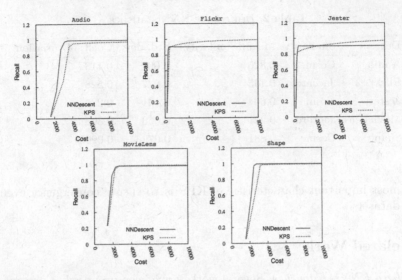

Fig. 5. Recall at equal cost (modified version of KPS with 40 nodes considered in the candidate set)

4.5 Discussion

To understand, in more details, the behavior of KPS, we run the brute force KNN graph construction algorithm for each dataset and study the similarity on the obtained KNN graph. Table 2 shows the similarity characteristics of the ideal KNN graph of the considered datasets.

As shown in Table 2, the best KNN graphs of Shape and Audio have an average similarity respectively equals to 0.88 and 0.82, which represents a higher similarity compared to the average similarity of the other datasets. This means that the profiles in Audio and Shape tend to be very close to each other. Thus, exploring only neighbors of neighbors and the reverse neighbors of neighbors may lead to the comparison of a given node profile with all similar nodes in the system, which is quickly achieved by NNDescent since it relies on both the KNN and RNN lists. This explains the high recall achieved by NNDescent in these datasets. Whereas for datasets with a low average similarity, such as Flickr, the maximum recall achieved by NNDescent does not exceed 90%. In sparser datasets, more exploration of the graph is required to discover the closest nodes since similarity values between nodes have a lower value. KPS precisely provides better exploration capacities due to the use of random nodes. Therefore, KPS eventually ensures the highest possible recall for all datasets.

KPS provides a better quality/cost tradeoff than NNDescent since KPS achieves KNN graphs with higher similarities at a lower cost. Especially, in Audio and Shape (Fig. 3), where the KPS's KNN graph has the same quality as the one generated by NNDescent. For low average similarity datasets (e.g. Flickr), KPS converges rapidly to an approximate high quality KNN graph. Hence, one

Table 2. Brute force KNN statistics

Dataset	Similarity	Mean (Similarity)	Std. dev.	Coeff. of variation
Audio	Cosine	0.825	0.097	0.118
Flickr	Jaccard	0.145	0.077	0.528
Jester	Cosine	0.604	0.141	0.234
MovieLens	Jaccard	0.221	0.068	0.308
Shape	Cosine	0.881	0.079	0.0906

of the most important characteristic of KPS is to ensure convergence even for sparse datasets.

5   Related Work

Centralized KNN Approaches. Several works have been proposed to present efficient KNN graph construction algorithms. In [10], Chen et al. suggest *divide and conquer* methods for computing an approximate KNN graph. They make use of a Lanczos procedure to perform recursive spectral bisection during the divide phase. After each conquer step, an additional refinement step is performed to improve the accuracy of the graph. Moreover, a hash table is used to store the distance calculations during the divide and conquer process. Based on the same strategy (*divide and conquer*), authors of [16] propose an algorithm that engages the locality sensitive hashing technique to divide items into small subsets with equal size, and then the KNN graph is computed on each subset using the brute force method. The divide and conquer principle was used in many other works such as [25]. On the other hand, several KNN graph construction approaches were based on a research index. In this direction, Zhong et al. [26] make use of a balanced search tree index to address the KNN search problem for a specific context in which the objects are locations in a road network. Paredes et al. [23] proposed a KNN graph construction algorithm for general metric space. The suggested algorithm is based on a recursive partition that builds a pre-index by performing a recursive partitioning of the space and on a pivot-based algorithm. Then, the index is used to solve a KNN query for each object. Most of these methods are either based on an additional index, or specific to a given similarity measure [11]. Moreover, they are designed for offline KNN graph construction, while KPS could be also used for online computation.

Gossip-Based Clustering. KPS is inspired from peer-to-peer gossip-based protocols. In such systems, each peer is connected to a subset of other peers in the network and periodically exchanges some information with one of its neighbors. While such protocols have been initially used to build uniform random topologies [19,21], they have also been applied in the context of several applications to cluster peers according to some specific metric (interest, overlap, etc.) to build networks of arbitrary structure [18,24] or to support various applications such as query expansion [7], top-k queries [6] or news recommendation [9]. In such a system, the use of random nodes ensures that connectivity is maintained, each node is responsible to discover its KNN nodes by periodically exchanging neighborhood information with other peers. As opposed to KPS, such algorithms tend to limit the traffic on the network and therefore exchange information with one neighbor at a time, providing different convergence properties.

6   Conclusion

KNN graph computation is a core building block for many applications ranging from collaborative filtering to similarity search. Yet, in the Big Data era where the amount of information to process is growing exponentially, traditional algorithms hit the scalability wall. In this paper, we propose a novel KNN service, called KPS, which can be seen as a centralization of a peer-to-peer clustering service. KPS has been compared to NNDescent. The results show that KPS quickly reaches a close to optimal KNN graph while drastically reducing the complexity of the algorithm. Future works include applying KPS in dynamic settings where the attribute of nodes vary dynamically, inducing some changes in the similarity computation results. Clearly, providing a theoretical analysis of the convergence speed is a natural follow up research avenue.

References

1. Jester dataset. http://grouplens.org/datasets/jester/
2. Jester joke recommender. http://shadow.ieor.berkeley.edu/humor/
3. Movielens dataset. http://grouplens.org/datasets/movielens/
4. Agrawal, D., Das, S., El Abbadi, A.: Big data, cloud computing: current state and future opportunities. In: Proceedings of the 14th International Conference on Extending Database Technology, EDBT/ICDT 2011, pp. 530–533. ACM (2011)
5. Amato, G., Falchi, F.: KNN based image classification relying on local feature similarity. In: Proceedings of the Third International Conference on SImilarity Search and APplications, SISAP 2010, pp. 101–108. ACM (2010)
6. Bai, X., Guerraoui, R., Kermarrec, A.-M., Leroy, V.: Collaborative personalized top-k processing. ACM Trans. Database Syst. **36**(4), 26 (2011)
7. Bertier, M., Frey, D., Guerraoui, R., Kermarrec, A.-M., Leroy, V.: The gossple anonymous social network. In: Gupta, I., Mascolo, C. (eds.) Middleware 2010. LNCS, vol. 6452, pp. 191–211. Springer, Heidelberg (2010)
8. Boiman, O., Shechtman, E., Irani, M.: In defense of nearest-neighbor based image classification. In: Proceedings of the IEEE Conference on Computer Vision and Pattern Recognition, CVPR 2008, pp. 1–8 (2008)
9. Boutet, A., Frey, D., Guerraoui, R., Jegou, A., Kermarrec, A.-M.: WhatsUp: a decentralized instant news recommender. In: Proceedings of the 27th IEEE International Symposium on Parallel Distributed Processing, IPDPS 2013, pp. 741–752 (2013)
10. Chen, J., Fang, H.-R., Saad, Y.: Fast approximate KNN graph construction for high dimensional data via recursive Lanczos bisection. J. Mach. Learn. Res. **10**, 1989–2012 (2009)

11. Connor, M., Kumar, P.: Fast construction of k-nearest neighbor graphs for point clouds. IEEE Trans. Vis. Comput. Graph. **16**(4), 599–608 (2010)
12. Desrosiers, C., Karypis, G.: A comprehensive survey of neighborhood-based recommendation methods. In: Ricci, F., Rokach, L., Shapira, B., Kantor, P.B. (eds.) Recommender Systems Handbook, pp. 107–144. Springer, Heidelberg (2011)
13. Dong, W., Moses, C., Li, K.: Efficient k-nearest neighbor graph construction for generic similarity measures. In: Proceedings of the 20th International Conference on World Wide Web, WWW 2011, pp. 577–586. ACM (2011)
14. Giakkoupis, G., Kermarrec, A.-M., Woelfel, P.: Gossip protocols for renaming and sorting. In: Afek, Y. (ed.) DISC 2013. LNCS, vol. 8205, pp. 194–208. Springer, Heidelberg (2013)
15. Guo, G., Wang, H., Bell, D.J., Bi, Y., Greer, K.: KNN model-based approach in classification. In: Meersman, R., Schmidt, D.C. (eds.) CoopIS 2003, DOA 2003, and ODBASE 2003. LNCS, vol. 2888, pp. 986–996. Springer, Heidelberg (2003)
16. Hajebi, K., Abbasi-Yadkori, Y., Shahbazi, H., Zhang, H.: Fast approximate nearest-neighbor search with k-nearest neighbor graph. In: Proceedings of the 22nd International Joint Conference on Artificial Intelligence, IJCAI 2011, pp. 1312–1317. AAAI Press (2011)
17. Huiskes, M.J., Lew, M.S.: The MIR flickr retrieval evaluation. In: Proceedings of the 1st ACM International Conference on Multimedia Information Retrieval, MIR 2008, pp. 39–43. ACM (2008)
18. Jelasity, M., Montresor, A., Babaoglu, O.: T-Man: gossip-based fast overlay topology construction. Comput. Netw.: Int. J. Comput. Telecommun. Netw. **53**(13), 2321–2339 (2009)
19. Jelasity, M., Voulgaris, S., Guerraoui, R., Kermarrec, A.-M., van Steen, M.: Gossip-based peer sampling. ACM Trans. Comput. Syst. **25**(3) (2007)
20. Olman, V., Mao, F., Wu, H., Xu, Y.: Parallel clustering algorithm for large data sets with applications in bioinformatics. The IEEE/ACM Trans. Comput. Biol. Bioinform. **6**(2), 344–352 (2009)
21. Ormándi, R., Hegedűs, I., Jelasity, M.: Overlay management for fully distributed user-based collaborative filtering. In: D'Ambra, P., Guarracino, M., Talia, D. (eds.) Euro-Par 2010, Part I. LNCS, vol. 6271, pp. 446–457. Springer, Heidelberg (2010)
22. Pan, R., Dolog, P., Xu, G.: KNN-based clustering for improving social recommender systems. In: Cao, L., Zeng, Y., Symeonidis, A.L., Gorodetsky, V.I., Yu, P.S., Singh, M.P. (eds.) ADMI. LNCS, vol. 7607, pp. 115–125. Springer, Heidelberg (2013)
23. Paredes, R., Chávez, E., Figueroa, K., Navarro, G.: Practical construction of k-nearest neighbor graphs in metric spaces. In: Àlvarez, C., Serna, M. (eds.) WEA 2006. LNCS, vol. 4007, pp. 85–97. Springer, Heidelberg (2006)
24. Voulgaris, S., van Steen, M.: VICINITY: a pinch of randomness brings out the structure. In: Eyers, D., Schwan, K. (eds.) Middleware 2013. LNCS, vol. 8275, pp. 21–40. Springer, Heidelberg (2013)
25. Wang, J., Wang, J., Zeng, G., Tu, Z., Gan, R., Li, S.: Scalable k-NN graph construction for visual descriptors. In: Proceedings of the IEEE Conference on Computer Vision and Pattern Recognition, CVPR 2012, pp. 1106–1113 (2012)
26. Zhong, R., Li, G., Tan, K.-L., Zhou, L.: G-tree: an efficient index for knn search on road networks. In: Proceedings of the 22nd ACM International Conference on Information and Knowledge Management, CIKM 2013, pp. 39–48. ACM (2013)

Accurate Optimization Method
for Allocation of Heterogeneous Resources
in Embedded Systems

Aissam Berrahou[✉]

Computer Department, Mohammadia School of Engineering,
Mohamed V University, Rabat, Morocco
aissamberrahou@research.emi.ac.ma

Abstract. In this paper we present a new accurate optimization method to find
an optimal solution for the heterogeneous resources offline allocation problem in
embedded systems. The proposed method is based on Mixed Binary Nonlinear
Programming (MBNLP) using piecewise linear relaxations and uses the fast
branch and bound algorithm for the minimization of a convex nonlinear
objective function over binary variables subject to convex nonlinear constraints.
The produced numerical results show the robustness of the proposed method
compared with conventional method in terms of performance.

Keywords: Offline allocation · Heterogeneous resources · Mixed Binary
Nonlinear Programming · Accurate method

1 Introduction

The mapping and scheduling of tasks to resources in a heterogeneous multi-core
embedded systems that maximizes the robustness of a system performance feature is an
important research problem in resource management [1]. This research focuses
essentially on finding the optimal solutions for the two types of heterogeneous resource
allocation problems: static or off-line allocation and dynamic or on-line allocation. The
problem of resource allocation in the field of heterogeneous multi-core systems is
NP-complete [2]. In this context, some heuristic algorithms are proposed to find a
near-optimal solution, relatively quickly [3], for this problem [2, 4–8]. However,
heuristics are inherently short-sighted and provide no guarantee of optimality. But
besides speed and optimality, another important metric is the extensibility of an
approach: a measure of how easy it is to accommodate practical implementation and
resource constraints. For instance, in a design space exploration framework, the result
of a certain allocation imposes new restrictions on the application and hardware platform to guide exploration. Unfortunately, most heuristic methods are not easily
extensible [9]. They are utilized for a specific problem and will have to be reformulated
each time when new assumptions or constraints are imposed. Constraint optimization
formulations, such as Mixed Integer Linear Programming and Constraint Programming, are accurate method and naturally extensible. In the literature, Thiele [9] is the
only one who used this method to solve an allocation and scheduling problem with

© Springer International Publishing AG 2016
P.A. Abdulla and C. Delporte-Gallet (Eds.): NETYS 2016, LNCS 9944, pp. 63–70, 2016.
DOI: 10.1007/978-3-319-46140-3_5

complex resource constraints on memory size, communication bandwidth and access conflicts to memories and buses. However, this work does not take into account some very important constraints, such as: The heterogeneity of resources, the parallel tasks, and the novel type of interconnection network (e.g. network on chip).

In this paper, we present a new algebraic formulation for static allocation of heterogeneous resource that will find an optimal solution to the problem. The proposed algebraic formulation tries to minimize the multi-core execution cost and inter core communication. The approach will minimize the system cost more than random search algorithm. The remainder of the paper is organized as follows. In Sect. 2, we introduce the preliminary concepts that we will use to model the optimization problem of allocation and scheduling. Section 3 presents the proposed algebraic formulation of allocation problem, by using Mixed Binary Nonlinear Programming (MBNLP) for the minimization of the total execution cost. Section 4 presents experiment results obtained by using the F4MS simulator (Framework for Mixed Systems) [10] which are based on a multi-objective solver named Gurobi [11].

2   Model of Embedded System

This section introduces the notations, hardware platform and application models used throughout the paper.

2.1   Hardware Platform Model

The hardware platform model consists of a set of processing elements. These can be programmable processors of any kind (general purpose, controllers, DSPs, ASIPs, etc.), reconfigurable (FPGA) or specific processors. The hardware platform model is modeled by the graph $GP = (R, L)$, with : R is the nodes of GP, where $R = \{r_1, \ldots, r_k\}$ represent the resources of the platform: switches, routers, memories, processing units or even host. These latter are fitted with the cores (specific or programmable) having its own resources, including a memory of limited size; L: The edges of GP, where $L = \{l_1, \ldots, l_m\}$ represent the communication links of an interconnection network that physically connects the different hosts of the hardware platform model. In addition, each communication link $l_k(r_a, r_b)$ has a bandwidth $Bw(r_a, r_b)$ that is the size of data that can be transferred through a communication link per unit of time.

2.2   Application Model

The application model is modeled by the oriented graph $GA = (T, E)$, where, $T = \{t_1, \ldots, t_n\}$ is a set of n non periodic tasks and $E \subset T \times T$ represent the precedence constraints between the tasks. If a dependence constraint (t_i, t_j) at the level of the application exists between the task t_i and the task t_j it is translated by a sending of a data $e_k \in E$ of the task t_i to the task t_j for that the latter can run.

3 Proposed Formulation

3.1 Notation

For the algebraic formulation of the allocation problem we need the following matrices:

Matrix X: Adjacency matrix of size $t \times r$, such as $X = (x_{ij})$, where $1 \leq i \leq t$, $1 \leq j \leq r$ and x_{ij} a binary decision variable that expresses the assignment of the task i to resource j.

Matrix Y: Adjacency matrix of size $c \times e$, such as $Y = (y_{ij})$, where $1 \leq i \leq c$, $1 \leq j \leq e$ and y_{ij} a binary decision variable that expresses the assignment the data j, provided by a task, to the shortest path i.

Matrix A: Adjacency matrix of size $t \times r$ indicating the task execution costs on resources, such as $A = (a_{ij})$, where $1 \leq i \leq t, 1 \leq j \leq r$ and $a_{ij} = \frac{NI_i}{f_j}$, with NI_i the instructions number of the task i and f_j The clock frequency of the resource j.

Matrix B: Adjacency matrix of size $t \times t$ indicating the parallel tasks, such as $B = (b_{ij})$, where $1 \leq i \leq t, 1 \leq j \leq t$ and

$$b_{ij} = \begin{cases} 1, & \text{if tasks } i \text{ and } j \text{ are parallel.} \\ 0, & \text{else} \end{cases} \tag{1}$$

Matrix D: Adjacency matrix of size $c \times l$ indicating the relation between the shortest paths and links, such as $D = (d_{ij})$, where $1 \leq i \leq c, 1 \leq j \leq l$ and

$$d_{ij} = \begin{cases} 1, & \text{if the link } l_j \text{ belongs to the shortest path } c_i. \\ 0, & \text{else} \end{cases} \tag{2}$$

Matrix F: Adjacency matrix of size $t \times r$ qui indicating incompatibility tasks/resources, such as $F = (f_{ij})$, where $1 \leq i \leq t, 1 \leq j \leq r$ and

$$f_{ij} = \begin{cases} 1, & \text{if the resource } j \text{ is fully compatible with the task } i. \\ 0, & \text{else} \end{cases} \tag{3}$$

Matrix G: Precedence matrix tasks/data of size $t \times e$, such as $G = (g_{ij})$, where $1 \leq i \leq t, 1 \leq j \leq e$ and

$$g_{ij} = \begin{cases} 1, & \text{if the task } i \text{ returns the data } j. \\ -1, & \text{if the task } i \text{ returns the data } j. \\ 0, & \text{else.} \end{cases} \tag{4}$$

Matrix H: Precedence matrix resources/shortest paths of size $r \times c$, such as $H = (h_{ij})$, where $1 \leq i \leq r, 1 \leq j \leq c$ and

$$h_{ij} = \begin{cases} 1, & \text{if the resource } i \text{ is the source of the path } j. \\ -1, & \text{if the resource } i \text{ is the destination of the path } j. \\ 0, & \text{else.} \end{cases} \tag{5}$$

3.2 Quadratic Formulation

The minimization of total execution cost is represented by the following objective function:

$$min : C(X, Y) \tag{6}$$

where, X and Y are tow binary decision variables, such as $C(X, Y) = C_{Ex}(X) + C_{com}(Y)$, with $C_{Ex}(X)$ the execution cost of the application tasks on the hardware platform resources.

$$C_{Ex}(X) = C_S(X) + C_P(X) \tag{7}$$

with $C_S(X)$ is the execution cost of sequential tasks, where

$$C_s(X) = \sum_{i=1}^{t} \sum_{j=1}^{r} a_{ij} \times x_{ij}, \text{ if there is no task } k \text{ parallel to task } i. \tag{8}$$

and $C_P(X)$ represents the execution cost of parallel tasks, where

$$C_P(X) = \sum_{i=1}^{t} \sum_{k=i+1}^{t} \sum_{h=1}^{r} \sum_{=1}^{r} Cost(i, k, h, l) \times x_{ih} x_{kl}, \tag{9}$$

with, $Cost(i, k, h, l) = \begin{cases} a_{ih} + a_{kl}, & \text{if } h = 1. \\ \max(a_{ih}, a_{kl}), & \text{else.} \end{cases}$

$C_{Com}(Y)$ is the communication cost, where

$$C_{Com}(Y) = \sum_{i=1}^{c} \sum_{j=1}^{e} minCostCom(e_j, c_i) \times y_{ij} \tag{10}$$

with, $minCostCom(ej, ci)$ the function that computes the smallest communication cost engendered by transfer of the data e_j on the shortest path c_i.

The objective function $C(X, Y)$ is subject to the following constraints:

Uniqueness constraint of allocation: A task must be assigned to one and only one resource. This constraint is expressed algebraically as follows:

$$\sum_{j=1}^{r} x_{ij} = 1, \quad \text{for any task } i \in \{1, \cdots, t\}. \tag{11}$$

Constraint of incompatibility Tasks/Resources: a task should not be assigned to a resource that is not compatible. For any task $i \in \{1, \cdots, t\}$ and any resource $j \in \{1, \cdots, r\}$, we have

$$x_{ij} = 0 \quad \text{if} \quad b_{ij} = 0. \tag{12}$$

Constraint of task scheduling: it is preferably to assign parallel tasks to different resources instead of assigning them to the same resource, and then only if the overall execution time engendered by latter case is more important than the first case and vice versa. For any task $i \in \{1, \ldots, t\}$ parallel to the task $j \in \{1, \ldots, t\}$, and all resources k et l in $\{1, \cdots, r\}$, such $i \neq j$ and $k \neq l$, we have

$$max(a_{ik}, a_{jl}) x_{ik} x_{jl} < min(a_{ik} + a_{jk}, a_{il} + a_{jl}) \tag{13}$$

Constraint of incompatibility Data/Paths: a data should not be assigned to a path. For shortest path $i \in \{1, \cdots, c\}$ and any data $j \in \{1, \cdots, e\}$, we have

$$y_{ij} = 0 \tag{14}$$

Allocation constraint of the data to the shortest paths: a data can be assigned at most one path. For any data $j \in \{1, \cdots, e\}$, we have

$$\sum_{i=1}^{c} y_{ij} \leq 1 \tag{15}$$

Constraint of coincidence between the allocation of tasks and the allocation of data: the task allocation should be converged (harmony) with the data allocation. For any resource $i \in \{1, \cdots, r\}$ and any data $k \in \{1, \cdots, e\}$, we have

$$\sum_{j=1}^{t} g_{jk} \times x_{ji} = \sum_{h=1}^{c} h_{ih} \times y_{hk} \tag{16}$$

4   Case Study

In this section, the theoretical formulation presented in the previous sections is validated by experiment results. The case study that we propose in this paper is offline mapping of a task graph. The Table 3 shows the resources characteristics of hardware platform model. The Tables 1 and 2 show respectively the tasks characteristics of an application model and the data flow exchanged between these tasks. The application

Table 1. Characteristics of application model.

Tasks	Type	complexity (10^9 s)	Size (MB)
t0	Generic	504	2.5
t1	Reconfigurable	3808	4
t2	Generic	400	1
t3	Generic	280	1
t4	Generic	330	0.5
t5	Generic	440	1.2
t6	Generic	730	1.5
t7	Signal processing	2330	3.2
t8	Signal processing	1250	3
t9	Generic	630	1.3
t10	Physical	7330	4.5
t11	Physical	277	2.5

Table 2. Data flow exchanged between tasks.

Data	Type	Size
e1	t0 $\rightarrow$ t1	1
e2	t1 $\rightarrow$ t2	34
e3	t1 $\rightarrow$ t6	28
e4	t2 $\rightarrow$ t3	58
e5	t2 $\rightarrow$ t4	28
e6	t3 $\rightarrow$ t5	18
e7	t4 $\rightarrow$ t6	65
e8	t5 $\rightarrow$ t10	34
e9	t10 $\rightarrow$ t11	28
e10	t6 $\rightarrow$ t7	38
e11	t6 $\rightarrow$ t8	98
e12	t7 $\rightarrow$ t9	8
e13	t8 $\rightarrow$ t9	65
e14	t9 $\rightarrow$ t10	15

model is composed by 11 heterogeneous tasks, which are to be allocated on 6 heterogeneous resources of the hardware platform model. In order to assist the designer for the decision making in allocation phase, we developed the framework simulator (F4MS: Framework for Mixed Systems) [10] which takes as input the application and hardware platform models to give in output an optimal solution of allocation problem. This framework allows to automatically generate the objective function and the different constraints. After, it uses the Gurobi solver [11] to generate an optimal solution to the problem in question. Table 4, Figs. 1 and 2 illustrate the experiment simulation of this study case, we can observed that the total execution time is 389,984 s compared with 6^{11} s for random search algorithm [12].

Table 3. Characteristics of hardware platform model.

Cores	Frequency	Memory size
CPU1	2.1	30
CPU2	2.3	40
DSP1	3	100
DSP2	3.3	100
ASIC	4	50
FPGA	6	300

Table 4. Total execution cost

Communication cost	Runtime cost	Total
7,171 s	382,813 s	389,984 s

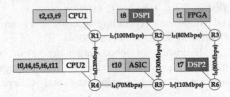

Fig. 1. Mapping diagram

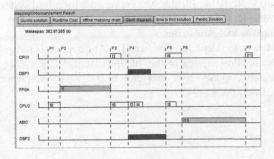

Fig. 2. Gantt diagram

5 Conclusion

In this paper we presented an accurate method of offline mapping an application to an execution platform for heterogeneous cores by minimizing the communication and execution time. After having reviewed the various solutions proposed, we sought to take a new orientation for solving this problem. For that, and according to the research carried, we used no linear programming with Boolean variables as a method of optimizing search for an optimal solution. As perspective, our method must take into account the mapping of composite tasks and non-deterministic tasks.

References

1. Kritikakou, A., Catthoor, F., Goutis, C.: Scalable and Near-Optimal Design Space Exploration for Embedded Systems. Springer International Publishing, Basel (2014)
2. Jiayin, L., Zhong, M., Meikang, Q., Gang, Q., Xiao, Q., Tianzhou, C.: Resource allocation robustness in multi-core embedded systems with inaccurate information. J. Syst. Archit. **57**, 840–849 (2011)
3. Kyle, M.T., Ryan, F., Anthony, A.M., Howard, J.S.: Scalable linear programming based resource allocation for makespan minimization in heterogeneous computing systems. J. Parallel Distrib. Comput. **8**, 76–86 (2015)
4. Braun, T., Siegel, H., Beck, N., Boloni, L., Maheswaran, M., Reuther, A.: A comparison of eleven static heuristics for mapping a class of independent tasks onto heterogeneous distributed computing systems. J. Parallel Distrib. Comput. **61**(6), 810–837 (2001)
5. Tompkins, M.F.: Optimization techniques for task allocation and scheduling in distributed multi-agent operations, Master's thesis, Massachusetts Institute of Technology, Cambridge (2003)
6. Ahmad, I., Kwok, Y.K.: On exploiting task duplication in parallel program scheduling. IEEE Trans. Parallel Distrib. Syst. **9**, 872–892 (1998)
7. Bajaj, R., Agrawal, D.P.: Improving scheduling of tasks in a heterogeneous environment. IEEE Trans. Parallel Distrib. Syst. **15**, 107–118 (2004)
8. Somai R., Mahjoub, Z.: Heuristics for scheduling independent tasks on heterogeneous processors under Limited Makespan Constraint. In: Proceedings of the International Conference on Automation, Control, Engineering and Computer Science, Tunisia, pp. 102–115 (2014)
9. Thiele, L.: Resource constrained scheduling of uniform algorithms. VLSI Signal Process. **10**, 295–310 (1995)
10. Berrahou, A., Raji, Y., Rafi, M., Eleuldj, M.: Framework for mixed systems. In: Proceedings of the 21th International Conference on Microelectronics, Morocco, pp. 330–333 (2009)
11. Gurobi Solver. http://www.gurobi.com
12. Meedeniya, I., Moser, I., Aleti, A., Grunske, L.: Architecture-based reliability evaluation under uncertainty. In: Proceedings of the 7th International Conference on the Quality of Software Architectures, QoSA 2011 and 2nd International Symposium on Architecting Critical Systems, USA, pp. 85–94 (2011)

Understanding the Memory Consumption
of the MiBench Embedded Benchmark

Antoine Blin[1,2]($\boxtimes$), Cédric Courtaud[1], Julien Sopena[1], Julia Lawall[1],
and Gilles Muller[1]

[1] Sorbonne Universités, Inria, UPMC, LIP6, Paris, France
{antoine.blin,cedric.courtaud,julien.sopena,
julia.lawall,gilles.muller}@lip6.fr
[2] Renault S.A.S, Paris, France

Abstract. Complex embedded systems today commonly involve a mix
of real-time and best-effort applications. The recent emergence of small
low-cost commodity multi-core processors raises the possibility of running both kinds of applications on a single machine, with virtualization
ensuring that the best-effort applications cannot steal CPU cycles from
the real-time applications. Nevertheless, memory contention can introduce other sources of delay, that can lead to missed deadlines. In this
paper, we analyze the sources of memory consumption for the real-time
applications found in the MiBench embedded benchmark suite.

1 Introduction

In modern automobiles, computing is characterized by a mixture of real-time
applications, such as management of the dashboard, the engine control, and
best-effort applications, such as multimedia entertainment. Historically, multiple applications are integrated in a vehicle using a *federated architecture*: Every
major function is implemented in a dedicated Electronic Control Unit (ECU)
[23] that ensures fault isolation and error containment. This solution, however,
doesn't scale in terms of costs, power consumption and network congestion when
the number of functions increases. Recently, the AUTOSAR [16] consortium has
been created to develop an *integrated architecture*, in which multiple functions
share a single ECU. The AUTOSAR standard targets applications that control
vehicle electrical systems and that are scheduled on a real-time operating system. Infotainment applications, however, typically target a Unix-like operating
system, and thus still require the use of a federated architecture.

Recent experimental small uniform memory access commodity multicore systems provide a potential path towards a complete low-cost integrated architecture. Systems such as the Freescale SABRE Lite [1] offer sufficient CPU power
to run multiple applications on a single low-cost ECU. Using *virtualized architectures* [12], multiple operating systems can be used without modification. Recent
hypervisors targeting embedded systems, such as SeL4 [2] and PikeOS [5], make
it possible in the context of the automotive domain to dedicate one or several
cores to a class of applications, and thus provide CPU isolation.

© Springer International Publishing AG 2016
P.A. Abdulla and C. Delporte-Gallet (Eds.): NETYS 2016, LNCS 9944, pp. 71–86, 2016.
DOI: 10.1007/978-3-319-46140-3_6

CPU isolation, however, is not sufficient to ensure that real-time applications can meet their performance constraints. Indeed, some resources such as memory buses, memory controllers, and some caches remain shared across all cores. Therefore, it has been observed that the memory usage of applications running on one core may impact the execution time of applications running on the other cores [19, 21]. In recent work [13], we have shown that sharing these resources implies that the operations initiated on a best-effort core can affect the duration of real-time tasks running on other cores. In that work, we have developed an approach to address the memory induced slowdown that uses run-time monitoring to detect when the interference risks causing the real-time task to exceed its deadline beyond a threshold that is considered to be tolerable.

Assessing the benefit of this approach, and others like it that relate to the memory behavior of embedded systems [15, 19, 24, 26], requires appropriate benchmarks. We have used the MiBench benchmark suite [18], that has the goal of representing the spectrum of embedded applications used in industry. This benchmark suite is one of the few that targets the embedded computing domain, and is highly cited. Understanding the memory access behavior of the MiBench applications requires periodic profiling of the application execution. This profiling must be precise without excessively perturbing the application execution. Furthermore, for our experiments with MiBench to be meaningful, it must be the case that the memory access pattern of the MiBench applications is typical of that of embedded applications.

In this paper, we make the following contributions towards better understanding the memory behavior of the MiBench applications and making these applications better represent the memory behavior of embedded applications:

- We present the design of a memory access profiler that has little impact on the behavior of the profiled application, and we assess the various tradeoffs in this design.
- We use the profiler to detect spikes in the memory bandwidth usage of the 13 MiBench applications that we have previously found to be strongly affected by the memory usage of applications running on other cores.
- We use various techniques, including rewriting the application, overloading the C standard library, and changing the size of the file system buffers to isolate the reasons for the observed memory spikes. Based on the results, we classify the memory spikes into those that are derived from the behavior of the C standard library, of the operating system, and of the application.

The rest of this paper is organized as follows. In Sect. 2, we briefly present an overview of our hardware and of our software configuration. In Sect. 3, we present our profiler, evaluate its design decisions, and show the results of profiling the MiBench applications. In Sect. 4, we identify and classify the root causes of the spikes in memory usage observed in the MiBench applications. Finally, in Sect. 5, we present related work, and Sect. 6 concludes.

2   Platform

In this section, we first describe our hardware platform, and then we present MiBench and the software configuration used in our tests.

2.1   Hardware

We focus on embedded systems, as used in the automotive domain, which has strong hardware cost requirements. Therefore, for our tests we use the SABRE Lite board [22], a low-cost development platform designed for multimedia applications on the Android and Linux operating systems. A variant of this platform that has been adapted for the automotive domain is used by a large number of automotive manufacturers and suppliers. The processor of the SABRE Lite is an i.MX 6, which is based on a 1.2 GHz quad-core Cortex A9 MPCore [10]. Each core has a separate Level 1 (L1) 32-KB 4-way set-associative cache for instructions and data [8]. All CPUs are connected to a single 1-MB 16-way set-associative L2 cache [9] that can be partitioned into multiples of the way size. Finally, the Multi Mode DRAM Controller (MMDC) manages access to one gigabyte of DDR3 RAM that can be used by all the cores [22].

The SABRE Lite board provides various hardware performance counters. Each core provides six configurable counters to gather statistics about the operation of the processor (number of cycles) and the memory system (L1 cache hits/misses) [7,8]. The MMDC has a profiling mechanism that gathers statistics (read/write bytes/access) about the global memory traffic on the platform.

2.2   Software Stack

We use the applications of the MiBench [18] benchmark suite as real-time applications because this benchmark suite has been designed to be representative of embedded applications used in industry. This benchmark suite has been referenced almost 2700 times,[1] and thus is a reference benchmark in the academic domain. MiBench is composed of 35 embedded applications, mostly written in C, categorized into six subclasses: industrial control consumer devices, office automation, networking, security and telecommunications. Among these applications we omit 19 that contain x86 assembly code or that represent long-running or office applications. From the remaining applications, we select the 13 that are sensitive to the memory contention, as demonstrated by our previous work [13].

We run the MiBench applications on a Linux 3.0.35 kernel that has been ported by Freescale to the i.MX 6 architecture. All of the MiBench applications are compiled using GCC 4.9.1 with the option -O2. We use the 2.20 GNU C Library as the C standard library. On embedded platforms, the kinds of data inputs used by the Mibench applications are usually provided by external devices such as an on-board camera, network controller, or microphone that interact directly with the CPU, via DMA. To approximate this behavior without modifying the applications, we store the data inputs in an in-memory file system.

---

[1] Google Scholar, January 20, 2016.

3 Memory Profiler

In this section, we present our memory profiler and show the memory profiles of the MiBench applications. We then study the benefits and costs of high resolution profiling.

3.1 Profiler Overview

We have developed a memory profiling module for the Linux kernel that uses counters of the MMDC controller to measure global memory traffic. At the beginning of the profiling process we enable the cycle counter that counts the processor clock cycles. Our profiler then periodically samples several hardware performance counters to obtain information about the memory access behavior. Each sample contains the number of bytes read, the number bytes written and the value of the cycle counter. Samples are stored in memory during profiling and then are written to disk at the end of the application.

A challenge in designing a memory profiler is in how to enforce the sampling interval. One solution would be to use a timer interrupt. Peter et al. [25], however, have shown that timeouts set to a short intervals are frequently delivered a significant fraction of their duration after their expiry time. To allow profiling with intervals down to 1 us, we implement the sampling interval using a busy wait on a dedicated core. This approach allows calibrating the interval fairly precisely, but requires one core to be completely dedicated to profiling.

To prevent the profiler from interfering with the performance of the application, we pin the application to profile on one core (core 0), using the POSIX `sched_setaffinity` function, and pin the profiler to another (core 1). We disable the remaining cores. To avoid any preemption, we schedule the application to profile and the profiling thread using the `SCHED_FIFO` policy with highest priority, and we disable the Real Time throttling mechanism that gives control back to the operating system if a task has been scheduled for a time exceeding a specified delay. We further reduce interference between the application to profile and the profiler by partitioning the L2 cache between their different cores.

After the application execution has completed, the memory bandwidth is computed from the number of bytes read and written in each sample and the corresponding sample duration. The busy-wait delay approach induces small temporal variations between samples. We use the value of the cycle counter to make a temporal readjustment.

Figure 1 shows the resulting memory profiles of the 13 MiBench applications with a sampling interval of 50 us. We observe that the profiling has no impact on the application running time. Based on the memory profiles, we classify the applications into two groups. The applications ADPCM small encode, ADPCM small decode, Patricia small, Rijndael small decode, Rijndael small encode, Sha small and Susan large c have regularly recurring spikes, while the remaining applications have a smoother memory profile.

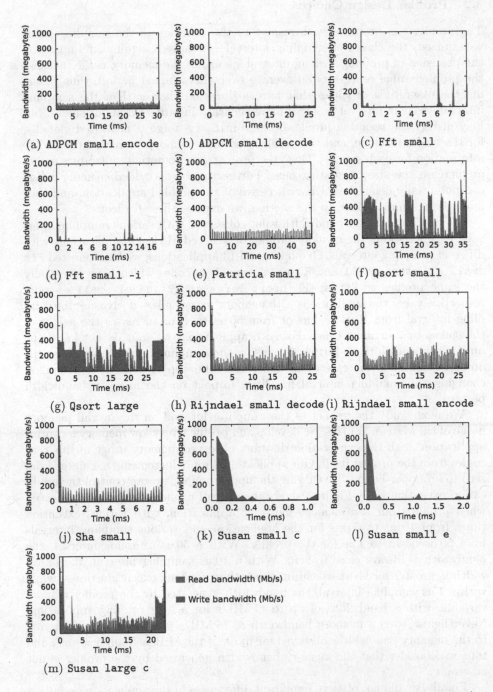

Fig. 1. Memory profiles of selected MiBench applications (sampling interval: 50 us)

3.2   Profiler Design Choices

The profiler can be tuned with respect to the duration of the sampling interval. Indeed, the choice of sampling interval can have a significant impact on the precision of profiling. A long interval smoothes the memory usage, because the profiled value represents an average over the sampled period, thus reducing the magnitude of spikes that have a duration shorter than the sampling interval. A short interval provides more accurate information about spikes, but may distort the resulting profile, because memory usage is measured globally, for the entire machine, and the profiler also uses memory, to record the profile information for each sample. Thus, the profiler can potentially introduce spikes or increase the size of existing ones. Furthermore, this added memory usage can potentially delay the memory accesses of the profiled application, and thus increase its running time. In this section, we explore these tradeoffs.

We first consider the bandwidth values observed with various sampling intervals. Figure 2 shows the memory profiles of selected MiBench applications with different sampling intervals. Of our original 13 applications, we have omitted `Fft small -i`, `qsort small` and `Rijndael small decode`, which have essentially the same profiles as `Fft small`, `qsort large` and `Rijndael small encode`, respectively. For the applications with memory usage spikes, decreasing the sampling interval from 10 us to 1 us or from 50 us to 10 us increases the height of the spikes by 2 or more times. For such applications we thus do not know the maximum bandwidth, as further decreasing the sampling interval may cause the observed spikes to increase even higher. For the applications without spikes, changing the sampling interval has little impact on the memory bandwidth pattern.

We next study the impact of the sampling interval on the overall memory usage of the system. For this, we develop and profile a very low memory footprint application, with the expectation that any observed memory usage in this case comes from the profiler itself. Our application simply increments a counter from zero to an upper bound. By varying the upper bound, we can control the application execution time. Figure 3 shows the overall memory bandwidth observed when profiling our low memory footprint application, with various execution times from 10 ms to 50 ms for the application and various sampling intervals from 50 us down to 1 us for the profiler. With a 50 us sampling interval, the bandwidth is always close to zero. With a 10 us sampling interval, the bandwidth is greater for short execution times than for long execution times, while with a 1 us sampling interval, the bandwidth generated by the profiler is more variable, with a bandwidth of up to 11 MB/s for a long running application. Nevertheless, even a memory bandwidth of 11 MB/s is negligible as compared to the memory bandwidths observed for most of the MiBench applications, and thus we consider that the memory bandwidth generated by the profiler is not an issue.

Finally, we did not observe significant differences in the application execution time with the various sampling intervals.

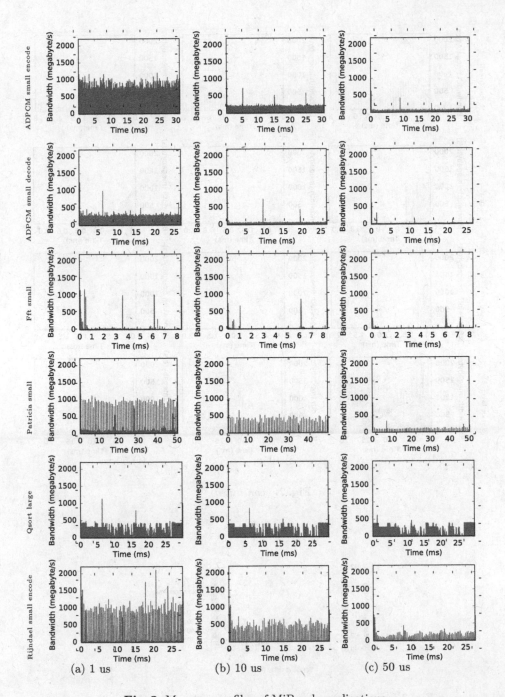

Fig. 2. Memory profiles of MiBench applications

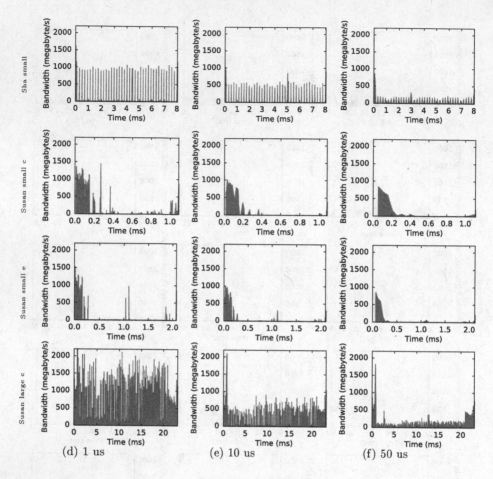

Fig. 2. (*continued*)

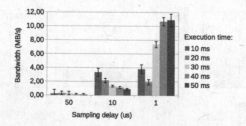

Fig. 3. Approximate memory bandwidth induced by the profiler

4 Origins of the Memory Spikes

For understanding memory behavior, spikes are problematic, because it is difficult to capture their real bandwidth due to their short duration. We now investigate the origins of these spikes. We first present a methodology to localize their origins. We then use various techniques, including rewriting the application, overloading the C standard library, kernel modification, and changing the size of the file system buffers to identify the root causes of the memory spikes.

4.1 Methodology

To identify the origins of the memory spikes, we have developed a tagging mechanism. A tag is basically a set of instructions added in the application source code to obtain and record the value of the cycle counter. Using tags, we can relate a line of source code to the corresponding offset in the application memory profile. Using a large number of tags would substantially increase the application execution time. Therefore, we use tagging only for spike identification.

Our use of tags shows that the main causes of the spikes can be categorized into three groups: I/O functions, the operating system, and the application source code. In the rest of this section, we study each of these sources.

4.2 I/O Functions

For each application that has spikes, Table 1 lists the I/O functions that are the sources of memory spikes. ADPCM uses the low level I/O functions open, read, and close, while the other applications use the buffered I/O functions fopen, fread, fwrite, fgets and fclose, which operate on streams.

Table 1. I/O function call sources of memory spikes

	Open	Read	Close	fopen	fclose	fread	fwrite	fgetc	fgets
ADPCM small encode	x	x	x						
ADPCM small decode	x	x	x						
Patricia small				x	x				x
Rijndael decode				x	x	x	x		
Rijndael encode				x	x	x	x		
Sha small				x	x	x			
Susan small e				x	x	x		x	
Susan small c				x	x	x		x	
Susan large c				x	x	x		x	

Buffered I/O. To understand the impact of the buffered I/O functions we focus on `Rijndael small encode`, which performs both reads and writes. This application performs a computation on 16 byte blocks acquired using `fread`. Each computed block is then written to an output file using `fwrite`. We study the memory behavior of the reads and writes separately.

To study the memory traffic generated by `fread`, we simply comment out the `fwrite` calls, as the application's computation does not depend on them. The resulting memory profile (Fig. 4b) shows a very low memory traffic mixed with regular spikes. Analysis of the tags shows that most of the spikes come from calls to `fread`. On average, there are 79 spikes greater than 600 MB/s per run, out of a total of 19489 calls to `fread`. Thus, on average, we have a memory spike every 246.7 `fread` calls. The size of the input file is 311,824 bytes. Thus, there is a memory spike every time a block of 3947 bytes has been read.

We hypothesize that the memory spikes come from the management of the internal input stream buffer. Using the `__fbufsize` function, we find that the default size of the input stream buffer is 4096 bytes. When `fread` is called, if the requested data are not present in the input stream buffer, `fread` refills the buffer by reading a new block of 4096 bytes from the file. Because the file is stored in a Temporary File System (TMPFS) mounted in memory, refilling the stream buffer involves a copy from the TMPFS to the input stream buffer, which generates a burst of memory traffic. All calls to `fread` also make a copy from the input stream buffer to the application buffer. This copy, however, does not generate any memory traffic, as both buffers are loaded in caches. These observations thus suggest that the memory spikes come from the refilling of the input stream buffer.

To test the hypothesis that the spikes are derived from filling the input stream buffer, we modified the size of this buffer using the `setvbuff` function. Figure 4 shows the memory profiles of `Rijndael small encode` with various input stream buffer sizes. Our hypothesis suggests that increasing the size of the stream buffer should reduce the number of times the buffer needs to be filled and should increase the height and duration of spikes, as filling a bigger buffer generates more memory traffic. Indeed, we see that increasing the size of the stream buffer reduces the number of memory spikes, slightly increases their height when moving from a 2 KB buffer to a 4 KB buffer, and increases their duration, according to the increase in the buffer size.

We next turn to writes. To analyse the memory traffic generated by `fwrite` we first override `fread` by a non-buffered read function, leaving the calls to `fwrite` commented. The resulting memory profile is shown in Fig. 5, in which almost all of the large spikes have disappeared. The remaining spikes are due to operating system effects (Sect. 4.3). Then, we uncomment the call to `fwrite`. As shown in Fig. 6b, the resulting memory profile contains, on average, 83 regular memory spikes per run that are greater than 300 MB/s. The output file size is 311,856 bytes. We thus have a memory spike every time a block of 3757 bytes has been written. We believe that the memory spikes issued from `fread` and `fwrite`

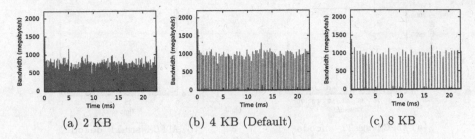

Fig. 4. `Rijndael small encode` without writes and with various input stream buffer sizes

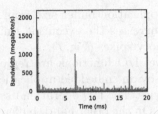

Fig. 5. `Rijndael small encode` without writes and with unbuffered reads

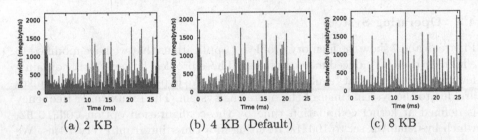

Fig. 6. `Rijndael small encode` with unbuffered reads and with various output stream buffer sizes

functions have the same cause. We modified the size of the output stream buffer and again observe that the number of spikes decreases (Fig. 6).

We performed the same experiments on all of the other applications that use buffered I/O functions and we observed the same behaviour.

Low-Level I/O Functions. ADPCM is a signal encoder/decoder application that performs computation on blocks acquired using `read`. The block size for `ADPCM small encode` is 2 KB and the block size for `ADPCM small decode` is 500 bytes. For both applications, we observe that the number of spikes is exactly the same as the number of calls to `read`, which suggests that the spikes are due to the copy from TMPFS to the application buffer. To see the impact of the

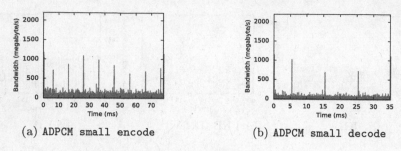

(a) ADPCM `small encode`   (b) ADPCM `small decode`

Fig. 7. ADPCM `small` with a small `read` buffer

`read` calls, we reduce the application buffer size from 2 KB bytes to 100 bytes. This change substantially increases the execution time of the application, but eliminates most of the memory spikes (Fig. 7).

In our view, the low-level I/O functions are representative of the memory accesses that could be done by an embedded application that would access data coming from an external device. The I/O operation itself can be done either by a CPU copy loop or by DMA. On the other hand, buffered I/O functions generate additional spikes that are not suitable in an embedded context. We consider that this is a problem in the design of MiBench.

4.3   Operating System

Figures 5 and 7 show the memory profiles of applications that we have modified to eliminate the I/O induced memory spikes. These profiles, however, still contain a few spikes that occur at regular 10 ms intervals. We hypothesize that these spikes are due to the system timer of the operating system. The Linux timer frequency is defined at kernel compilation time by the configuration option `CONFIG_HZ`, which by default is set to 100 Hz, resulting in a timer interrupt every 10 ms. We generated the memory profile of our low memory footprint application (Sect. 3.2) with the timer frequency at 100 Hz and 50 Hz, and observed that the delays between spikes were around 10 us and 20 us, respectively, thus validating our hypothesis.

4.4   Applications

Most of the applications exhibiting spikes have a continuous behavior across the entire duration of the application. These applications follow the model of `Rijndael` and ADPCM, where the spikes are due to I/O functions and operating system effects. `Susan large c`, an image recognition package, on the other hand, has spikes, but has a more complex overall behavior. Specifically, the graphs for `Susan large c` in Figs. 2d–f show that the heights of the spikes are very variable, and for different spikes, the heights decrease at different rates as the sampling interval increases. To explore the reason for this behavior, we used the tagging mechanism, which revealed three different phases in the execution (Fig. 8a).

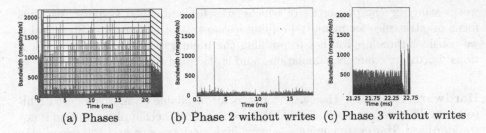

(a) Phases   (b) Phase 2 without writes   (c) Phase 3 without writes

Fig. 8. susan large-c

In the first phase, lasting 0.1 ms, the memory spikes are generated by buffered I/O functions that load the image into a byte array.

In the second phase, lasting around 20 ms, we observe a very low read memory traffic mixed with regularly occurring write spikes of varying magnitudes. We used the tagging mechanism to identify the source code that generates the spikes. Susan uses a for-loop to iterate over the byte array. The loop body contains a complex condition which, when it succeeds, stores values in three integer arrays each having the same size as the image. These array stores are not sequential. Indeed, the average distance between two neighbouring stores is 287.5 bytes, with a standard deviation of 565.8, implying a huge variation. We hypothesize that the read traffic is derived from iterations over the byte array and the write spikes are derived from the stores into the integer arrays.

To test our hypothesis about the origin of the write spikes, we comment out the array writes. The written array values are not read during this phase, and thus removing the writes does not affect this phase's overall computation. Figure 8b shows the resulting memory profile of the second phase. Most of the write spikes disappear, thus validating our hypothesis.

In the third phase, we observe a high memory traffic of around 550 MB/s. Susan uses two nested loops to iterate over an integer array. These read accesses are not sequential. Every 384 iterations the application makes a jump of 288 iterations in the array. The inner loop body contains a complex condition which, when it succeeds, stores values in a structure array. We comment out these writes. Figure 8c shows the resulting memory profile of the third phase, in which the memory traffic is reduced to 500 MB/s. We further modified the code to remove the non-contiguous accesses and observed that the memory traffic decreased dramatically. We conclude that most of the memory traffic comes from the non-contiguous accesses.

5 Related Work

The main focus of our work is on memory profiling and on the behavior of benchmarks for embedded systems. Besides the original paper presenting MiBench [18], which primarily describes the benchmark programs and some aspects of their execution, but does not consider memory bandwidth, we are not aware of other works studying the properties of benchmarks for embedded systems. We thus focus on strategies for memory profiling in the rest of this section. Specifically, we consider three approaches to profiling the memory consumption of applications: hardware counters, simulations, and static analysis.

Hardware Counters. Hardware counters are available on most modern architectures. They require specialized CPU hardware and their implementation is not standardized. Hardware counters achieve high performance and their measures are representative of hardware behaviour. Several projects used hardware counters for profiling multicore systems. Lachaise et al. [20] have developed MemProf, a profiler that allows programmers to choose and implement efficient application-level optimizations for NUMA systems. They rely on an architecture-specific instruction called "ISB" introduced by AMD to perform memory profiling. Traditional profilers, such as Oprofile [3] and Perf [4] are available on ARM architectures, however, they currently do not support our memory controller.

Simulation. Simulators emulate the system architecture in software, allowing performance data to be gathered on any emulated components. To be effective, simulation needs an accurate description of the simulated resources. Another drawback of simulation is the overhead. It is common for a simulator to be 10 to 100 times slower than the native hardware. Valgrind [6] is a widely used instrumentation framework for building dynamic analysis tools. Cachegrind, one of the tools provided by Valgrind, is a cache profiler that provides cache access statistics such as L1/L2 caches misses/hits. The Cachegrind L2 cache implementation uses virtual addresses whereas the SABRE Lite board uses physical addresses.

Static Analysis. Static data-cache analysis techniques rely on the source code and an architecture description. Ghosh et al.'s Cache Miss Equations [17] framework computes tight estimates, but is only applicable to programs that contain regular accesses with predictable patterns. Pellizzoni et al. [24] propose a time-sliced architecture in which applications must be re-structured into phases that have particular memory-access properties. Boniol et al. [14] propose an algorithm relying on a static analyser [11] for restructuring applications automatically to fit the requirements of the time-sliced architecture.

6   Conclusion

In this paper, we have developed a memory access profiler that relies on hardware counters to measure the global memory traffic issued from applications. We have shown that this profiler has little impact on the behaviour of the profiled applications. Using our profiler, we have traced the memory profiles of the 13 MiBench applications that we have previously found to be strongly affected by the memory usage of applications running on other cores. The resulting memory profiles show that the executions of more than half of these applications involve frequent high memory spikes. To identify the origins of these spikes, we have used a methodology that links the application source code to the memory profile. Based on the results, we have classified the memory spikes into those that are derived from the behaviour of the C standard library, the operating system, and the application. We have used various techniques, including rewriting the application, overloading the C standard library, changing the size of the file system buffers, and recompiling the operating system kernel to isolate the reasons for the observed memory spikes. We have established that C standard Library spikes come from buffered I/O functions and from low level I/O functions. Buffered I/O functions generate memory spikes when they refill their internal buffer, while low level I/O functions produce memory spikes on each access to a memory mapped file. We have shown that operating system spikes are due to the system timer. Finally, we explore some reasons for application spikes with a detailed study of Susan large c.

In future work, we plan to develop strategies for recoding the MiBench applications to eliminate the sources of memory bandwidth that derive from the C standard library or the operating system, so that the MiBench applications better mirror the behaviour of embedded applications.

References

1. NXP boards. http://www.nxp.com/
2. OKL4 Microvisor. http://www.ok-labs.com/products/okl4-microvisor
3. OProfile - a system profiler for Linux. http://oprofile.sourceforge.net
4. perf: Linux profiling with performance counters. https://perf.wiki.kernel.org
5. PikeOS. http://www.sysgo.com
6. Valgrind. http://valgrind.org
7. ARM. ARM Architecture Reference Manual ARMv7-A—R, rev C.b, November 2012
8. ARM. Cortex-A9 Technical Reference Manual, rev r4p1, June 2012
9. ARM. Level 2 Cache Controller L2C–310 TRM, rev r3p3, June 2012
10. ARM. Cortex-A9 MPCore Technical Reference Manual, June rev r4p1 (2012)
11. Ballabriga, C., Cassé, H., Rochange, C., Sainrat, P.: OTAWA: an open toolbox for adaptive WCET analysis. In: Min, S.L., Pettit, R., Puschner, P., Ungerer, T. (eds.) SEUS 2010. LNCS, vol. 6399, pp. 35–46. Springer, Heidelberg (2010)
12. Barham, P., Dragovic, B., Fraser, K., Hand, S., Harris, T., Ho, A., Neugebauer, R., Pratt, I., Warfield, A.: Xen and the art of virtualization. In: SOSP (2003)
13. Blin, A., Courtaud, C., Sopena, J., Lawall, J., Muller, G.: Maximizing parallelism without exploding deadlines in a mixed criticality embedded system. Technical report RR-8838, INRIA, January 2016
14. Boniol, F., Cassé, H., Noulard, E., Pagetti, C.: Deterministic execution model on COTS hardware. In: Herkersdorf, A., Römer, K., Brinkschulte, U. (eds.) ARCS 2012. LNCS, vol. 7179, pp. 98–110. Springer, Heidelberg (2012)
15. Fisher, S.: Certifying applications in a multi-core environment: the world's first multi-core certification to SIL 4. In: SYSGO AG (2014)
16. Fürst, S., Mössinger, J., Bunzel, S., Weber, T., Kirschke-Biller, F., Heitkämper, P., Kinkelin, G., Nishikawa, K., Lange, K.: Autosar-a worldwide standard is on the road. In: 14th International VDI Congress Electronic Systems for Vehicles (2009)

17. Ghosh, S., Martonosi, M., Malik, S.: Cache miss equations: a compiler framework for analyzing and tuning memory behavior. TOPLAS **21**(4), 703–746 (1999)
18. Guthaus, M.R., Ringenberg, J.S., Ernst, D., Austin, T.M., Mudge, T., Brown, R.B.: MiBench: a free, commercially representative embedded benchmark suite. In: EEE International Workshop on Workload Characterization, pp. 3–14 (2001)
19. Jean, X., Gatti, M., Faura, D., Pautet, L., Robert, T.: A software approach for managing shared resources in multicore IMA systems. In: DASC, October 2013
20. Lachaize, R., Lepers, B., Quéma, V., et al.: MemProf: a memory profiler for NUMA multicore systems. In: USENIX Annual Technical Conference, pp. 53–64 (2012)
21. Nowotsch, J., Paulitsch, M.: Leveraging multi-core computing architectures in avionics. In: EDCC, pp. 132–143, May
22. S. NXP. i.MX 6Dual/6Quad Processor Reference Manual, rev 1, April 2013
23. Obermaisser, R., El Salloum, C., Huber, B., Kopetz, H.: From a federated to an integrated automotive architecture. IEEE Trans. Comput.-Aided Design Integr. Circ. Syst. **28**(7), 956 (2009)
24. Pellizzoni, R., Betti, E., Bak, S., Yao, G., Criswell, J., Caccamo, M., Kegley, R.: A predictable execution model for COTS-based embedded systems. In: RTAS (2011)
25. Peter, S., Baumann, A., Roscoe, T., Barham, P., Isaacs, R.: 30 seconds is not enough!: a study of operating system timer usage. In: EuroSys (2008)
26. Yun, H., Yao, G., Pellizzoni, R., Caccamo, M., Sha, L.: MemGuard: memory bandwidth reservation system for efficient performance isolation in multi-core platforms. In: IEEE 19th RTAS, pp. 55–64. IEEE (2013)

Benchmarking Energy-Centric Broadcast Protocols in Wireless Sensor Networks

Quentin Bramas[✉] and Sébastien Tixeuil

CNRS, LIP6 UMR 7606, Sorbonne Universités,
UPMC Univ Paris 06, 4 place Jussieu, 75005 Paris, France
quentin.bramas@lip6.fr

Abstract. We consider the problem of broadcasting messages in wireless sensor networks (WSN) in an energy-efficient manner. The problem is central for many application, as WSNs often consist in autonomous battery powered devices that use broadcast for many purposes (*e.g.* synchronization, data collection, etc.). A number of algorithms have been proposed to solve this problem, focusing in particular on node that are able to reduce their communication range, enabling to lower energy consumption.

One of the best known such centralized algorithm is the *Broadcast Incremental Power* (BIP). Then, several distributed algorithms have been proposed, such as *Localized BIP*, *Dynamic Localized BIP*, and *Broadcast Oriented Protocols* (RBOP and LBOP). Those distributed approaches aim to reach the performance of BIP without assuming that the nodes have the knowledge of the whole graph.

In this paper we answer the open question left by those previous work: how do they perform (energy-wise) with *realistic* devices placed in a *realistic* environment? Unlike previous works that consider an ideal MAC layer (with no collisions) and a simple energy consumption model (that assumes that only transmitting messages consumes energy), we use simulated MAC layers (ContikiMac and 802.15.4 MAC layers) that take into account signal propagation and the possibility of collisions, and realistic battery and energy consumption models, that consider all relevant energy aspects of sensor node hardware. It turns out that our findings are significantly different from the aforementioned theoretical studies. Among our findings, we show that the hierarchy of the routing protocols (based on their performance) is not preserved (compared with the theoretical studies), which means that wireless interference impact them in different ways. Also, we found that the MAC layer plays an important role on the performance of the upper layer protocols, and does not impact all routing protocols in the same way.

This work was performed within the Labex SMART supported by French state funds managed by the ANR within the Investissements d'Avenir programme under reference ANR-11-IDEX-0004-02.

© Springer International Publishing AG 2016
P.A. Abdulla and C. Delporte-Gallet (Eds.): NETYS 2016, LNCS 9944, pp. 87–101, 2016.
DOI: 10.1007/978-3-319-46140-3_7

1   Introduction

Wireless Sensor Networks (WSNs) consists of sensor devices deployed in some area that use wireless communication to exchange messages with each other. In the *ad hoc* context, sensor nodes are independent from any architecture, and must cooperate to perform various tasks, such as retrieving sensed data to a sink node, or broadcasting important information (software updates, alerts, etc.) to the whole network. In most WSN applications (*e.g.*, temperature sensors deployed to monitor a forest, heterogeneous sensors deployed in and on the human body, etc.) sensor nodes are battery-powered. In those applications, guaranteeing an extended lifetime for the network is of paramount importance.

In this paper, we focus on the problem of broadcasting a message from a source (that is, a particular sensor node), to the entire network. The source may be unique, or be different for each message. This problem has been extensively studied in the literature (see Sect. 2), and resulted in *energy-centric* algorithms, that target to improving the network lifetime assuming battery-powered sensor nodes. The evaluation of the energy-efficiency may depend on the application: the goal can be to minimize the global energy consumption, to maximize the lifetime of every node, to maximize the lifetime of some given percentage of the nodes, etc.

A significant proportion of the energy consumed by the sensor nodes is related to wireless communications. There exists a number of techniques to reduce the amount of energy consumed for communicating. For instance, a directed antenna uses less power to reach the same distance compared to an omnidirectional antenna, but their ad hoc deployment is problematic as precise adjustments have to hold for two nodes to be able to communicate. A less stringent solution is to consider devices equipped with omnidirectional antennas, but with a radio transceiver that is able to adjust its transmission power (and thus the amount of energy spent on transmissions). In this paper, we consider the latter case.

Existing energy-centric broadcast algorithms for WSNs (see Sect. 2) were all evaluated using a specific simplified energy consumption model. Their model defines a function that maps a communication range to the amount of energy needed to transmit a message within this range. Given this energy consumption model, those solutions were evaluated using simulations to compare their relative efficiency. Those simulations all use an ideal MAC layer, where no collisions ever occurs. This leaves the open question of how those algorithms perform in a more realistic setting.

Our Contribution. In this paper, we consider previously proposed energy-centric broadcasting protocols for WSNs and evaluate them in realistic scenarios. We benchmark them using a simulator that includes a complete communication protocol stack, a realistic physical communication layer, and an accurate energy consumption model. We choose to perform our simulation with ContikiMAC and 802.15.4 MAC, that were both designed for small and energy constrained devices. In particular, in our settings, the MAC layer has to deal with possible collisions, and the energy consumption takes into account all components of the sensor device (including a non-linear battery behavior).

The results of our evaluation is as follows. First, we demonstrate that wireless interference significantly impact the performance of broadcasting protocols in various ways. Indeed, the hierarchy of the broadcasting protocols (based on their performance in an ideal setting) is *not* preserved in the more realistic setting. Also, we show that the MAC layer, also does not impact all broadcast protocols in the same way (some protocols perform better with ContikiMAC than with 802.15.4 MAC, while other do not). Quite surprisingly, it turns out that the very simple *flooding* protocol (used as a theoretical lower bound in previous work), is actually one the best distributed broadcasting protocols in our realistic environment. Our results show that considering only idealized settings in theoretical work does not give accurate performance hierarchies (including relative ones) in practical settings.

Outline. In Sect. 2, we present the broadcasting protocols that we evaluate, and the new interference and energy consumption we consider are delegated to Sect. 3. Section 4 details our experimental protocol. The results of our simulations are presented and discussed in Sect. 5. Concluding remarks are presented in Sect. 6.

2   Related Work

A Wireless Sensor Network (WSN) is modeled as a unit-disk graph $G(V, E)$, where V denotes the set of nodes, and E the set of possible communication links. Two nodes u and v are connected if the Euclidean distance $d(u, v)$ between them is smaller than the transmission range R:

$$E = \{(u, v) \in V^2 \mid u \neq v \wedge d(u, v) \leq R\}$$

We restrict the study to the case where sensor nodes are equipped with omnidirectional antennas: If a node u transmits a message with full power, all its neighbors can receive it. To reduce energy consumption, a node may decrease its transmission power to have a transmission radius $r \leq R$. In this case, only the nodes that are at distance at most r may receive the message. When a given node u wants to broadcast a message to the entire network, the goal of a broadcasting protocol is to assign transmission powers to each node so that the message is received by all the other nodes. The efficiency of a broadcast protocol is based on several criteria we describe hereafter.

Energy-centric broadcasting protocols have received much interest in WSNs for the past ten years [11]. We can distinguish two families of protocols that aim to be energy efficient by adjusting transmitting powers: *topology control oriented protocols*, and *broadcast oriented protocols*.

Topology Control Oriented Protocols. A topology control oriented protocol assigns the transmission power for each node, independently of the source of the broadcast. The goal is to obtain a connected network with minimum total transmission power according to an energy consumption model. Once the radii are assigned, they are used for every broadcast from an arbitrary source. The problem of minimizing the total transmission power that keeps the network connected is known as *min assignment problem* and was considered by Kiroustis et al. [14]. Clementi et al. [8] demonstrated that this problem is NP-hard. Most of these protocols require global knowledge of the entire graph to compute a Minimum Spanning Tree (MST). Recently, localized protocols based on the Relative Neighborhood Graph (RNG) [19], and a Local Minimum Spanning Tree (LMST) construction [15] have been proposed (see [11] for a survey).

Broadcast Oriented Protocols. A broadcast oriented protocol has the same overall goal, but considers that the broadcast starts at a given node. Hence, the induced broadcast network does not have to be strongly connected, leading to possibly more efficient solutions. For instance, the last nodes that receive the message do not need to retransmit it *i.e.*, the algorithm may assign them a null transmission power. However, the source must be able to reach every node of the network. The problem remains difficult, as it has been proved [8] that the minimum-energy broadcast tree construction problem is NP-complete.

In this paper, we consider six broadcast oriented protocol:

Flooding. Flooding is the simplest distributed protocol: when a node has a message to transmit, it transmits it with maximum power. Flooding is typically used for comparison with more elaborate energy-centric protocols, as it tries to maximize reachability without considering energy consumption.

BIP (Broadcast Incremental Power). [20] BIP is the only centralized algorithm we consider in the paper. Although mostly Greedy-based, it is one of the most efficient algorithms, and is commonly used as a reference in the literature. It constructs a tree as follow: Initially, the broadcast tree contains only the source node; then, while there exists a node that is not in the tree, it computes the incremental minimum power needed to add a node to the tree, either by increasing the power transmission of a transmitting node in the tree, or by choosing a non-transmitting node in the tree to transmit.

LBIP (Localized BIP). [12] LBIP is the distributed version of BIP. Since acquiring the knowledge of the full network topology to apply BIP at every node would be to expensive (at least, energy-wise), the goal of the protocol is to discover only the 2-hop neighborhood and use the BIP algorithm on it. Each time a node receives a packet, in addition to the original message, it can contain a list of forwarder nodes. If the node is in this list, it compute the BIP tree on its 2-hop neighbors to choose the right transmission power and transmit the message with a list of nodes that must forward it, according to the BIP tree.

DLBIP (Dynamic Localized BIP). [6] DLBIP is the energy-aware version of LBIP. It is dynamic in the sense that for the same source, two broadcast trees may be different. The broadcast is done in the same way as LBIP, but the BIP tree construct with the 2-hop neighbors take into account the remaining energy of the nodes to promote nodes with higher residual energy.

RBOP (RNG Broadcast Oriented Protocol). [5] RBOP is based on the RNG topology control protocol. A node that has a message sends it with a transmission power such that all its neighbors in the RNG graph receive it. The protocol also contains some optimization to avoid transmission when a node knows that some of its neighbors in the RNG graph already received the message.

LBOP (LMST Broadcast Oriented Protocol). [5] LBOP apply the same scheme as RBOP but the RNG graph is replaced by the LMST one.

There exists other broadcast oriented algorithms that we do not consider in this paper. For instance the INOP (INside-Out Power adaptive approach) defined in [7], is very close to the LBIP algorithm but takes into account only the 1-hop neighborhood. In the same paper, the authors evaluate their algorithm with a realistic network stack but used the 802.11 DCF MAC layer (which does not correspond to sensor network MAC layers), and an ideal per-packet energy consumption model.

Previous Models. All aforementioned works (besides INOP [7]) consider an ideal MAC layer where no interference occurs when two neighboring nodes transmit data within the same timeframe. Such an assumption is unrealistic as further discussed in Sect. 3. INOP [7] does consider a realistic network stack, but the stack is related to full-fledged computer networks, which is not energy-aware. Sensible network stacks for sensor nodes include ContikiMAC and 802.15.4, that we consider in the sequel.

Another oversimplification made by all previous works is even more problematic: the energy consumed by a node is supposed to be equal to the energy consumed by the radio during transmissions. In more details, the energy $E(u)$ consumed by a node u for one transmission is given as a function depending on the radius $r(u)$ of the transmission (1) (which depend on the power transmission of the radio). The energy consumed by the protocol is then the sum E of the energies consumed by all nodes (3). In order to compare several algorithm, we can consider the ratio EER between the energy consumed by a protocol and the energy consumed by the flooding protocol (2–4), which always choose the maximum transmission power.

$$E(u) = \begin{cases} r(u)^\alpha + c & \text{if } r(u) \neq 0 \\ 0 & \text{otherwise} \end{cases} \quad (1) \qquad E = \sum_{u \in V} E(u) \quad (3)$$

$$E_{flooding} = n \times (R^\alpha + c) \quad (2) \qquad EER = \frac{E}{E_{flooding}} \times 100 \quad (4)$$

where $\alpha, c \in \mathbb{R}^+$. Of course, real sensor nodes also consume energy when doing other tasks (reading sensor values, computing, receiving data). Also, low power batteries typically have non-linear behavior (their capacity may vary depending on the intensity of the drained current at a given time).

3　Our Model

In this section, we present the interference, battery, and energy consumption models we use in our evaluation campaign.

Interference Model. The study and development of interference models is an active domain of research in WSNs [2,4,13]. Indeed, in a real environment, any wireless signal is subject to several phenomena, such as attenuation over the distance, and the superposition with other wireless signals, before being received by a receiver. To be properly received, the signal corresponding to the message must be decoded considering the sum of all other incoming signals as noise.

To study an algorithm that is executed by devices communicating through wireless signals, it is necessary to consider an interference model. The survey by Cardieri [4] gives a number of interference models with different levels of detail and their impact on various network layers. Iyer *et al.* [13] show that the interference model has an huge impact on both scheduled transmission networks and random access networks. Their conclusion is that all models used for quantitative evaluation purposes should at least include SINR (signal-to-interference-plus-noise-ratio) considerations. The vast amount of research in this topic highlights the fact that it is not only necessary to have an interference model when analyzing WSN, but it is essential to have a good one. For our study, we use the SINR model incorporated in the WSNet Simulator [2] with a log-distance pathloss propagation model.

Battery and Energy Consumption Models. Independently from the networking context, battery models are an active research domain [3,17,18]. It is known that batteries exhibit non-linear behavior, *e.g.* rate-capacity effect, recovery effect, and non constant voltage. The rate-capacity effect means that the ratio between the load and the capacity may not remain constant. For instance, with the same battery, we can obtain a 100mAh capacity with a 10mA current draw (10 hours before depletion), and a 80mAh capacity with a 20mA current draw (4 hours before depletion). The recovery effect denotes the increase of battery capacity that may occur after a period when the battery is at rest. This effect is not visible with WSN devices since the battery is never at rest (even in deep sleep mode, the CPU and the transceiver have a non-zero current draw). The non constant voltage is an important factor that shortens the lifetime of a device. In more details, the residual capacity of a battery, the internal resistance and the current draw at a given instant impact the output voltage of the battery. Also, any device embedded on a sensor node has a cutoff voltage (that is, the minimum voltage that enables it to work correctly). Therefore, the first time the voltage is below the cutoff, the device stops working and cannot be waken up.

When considering a device composed by multiple piece of hardware, such as a CPU, a transceiver, several sensors, etc., it is important to model their energy consumption. A rough approximation is to consider only the biggest consumer and ignore the other components. Alternatively, we can have a more refined approach and define several states for each component (such as *transmitting*, or *receiving* for the transceiver, *sensing* for the sensor, etc.) and consider that each time a change of state occurs, a predefined amount of energy is consumed by the corresponding component. A recent study [3] shows that the most accurate model is to consider every device component, and to track the current drawn by the whole device at each instant. Then, the battery model can use this information to accurately compute the voltage, and its residual capacity. In more details, using only the number of wireless transmissions by a device to evaluate its lifetime can give estimates that are 27 times greater than the lifetime obtained by measurements on real hardware [3]. Taking into account a proper battery model and a detailed energy consumption tracking permits to obtain between 85 % (in the worst case) and 95 % accuracy on the evaluation of the lifetime of a device, when compared to real device measurements [3]. WiseBat [3] can be configured with the actual data-sheet of the battery and the list of components of the device. It has a low simulation overhead, which allows us to perform simulations campaigns with a reasonable number of nodes. For our study, we use the WiseBat [3] model to evaluate the lifetime of each node.

4   Experimental Setup

We use WSNet simulator [10] to perform our experimental evaluation campaign. We deploy 50 sensor nodes that are located uniformly at random in a square-shaped area. The size of the area varies from 300×300 m to 800×800 m to create various network densities. The protocol stack consists of a broadcast application, a broadcast protocol (whose performance is to be evaluated), a MAC layer (we consider both the 2400 MHz OQPSK 802.15.4 CSMA/CA unslotted [1] and ContikiMAC [9]), a radio transceiver, and an omnidirectional antenna. For the environment, we use OQPSK modulation and the log-distance pathloss propagation model. The log-distance pathloss propagation model is more realistic than the range propagation and is simple enough to be easily predictable. This allow the node to choose the transmission power according to the desired range it wishes to attain.

A simulation setting consists in selecting a broadcasting protocol, a MAC layer, and the size of the area. For each setting, we run 50 simulations with various topologies. All measurements (remaining energy, number of receiving nodes per broadcast, and delay) are averaged over those simulations. Each topology is obtained by randomly deploying the nodes in the square area, and is used for all the simulation settings, so that different protocols are evaluated on the same topology. Table 1 summarizes the properties of the topologies we use (averaged over the 50 topologies we constructed for each size).

For the energy model we used the WiseBat [3] module with a real TMote Sky configuration (see Table 2). The current drawn by the CPU under a voltage

Table 1. Average density, diameter, and connectivity of the topologies, depending on the area size.

Size	Density	Diameter	Connectivity
300	0.60	2.9	13.3
400	0.40	3.8	6.8
500	0.27	4.7	3.9
600	0.20	5.8	2.2
700	0.15	7.7	1.4
800	0.12	9.5	1.1

Table 2. Voltage specification of the TMote Sky Hardware

Radio		CPU	
Chipcon CC2420		Texas Instruments	
Tx 0dB	17.4 mA	MSP430 F1611	
Tx -1dB	16.5 mA	Run 8MHz 3V	4mA
Tx -3dB	15.2 mA	Sleep	2.6μA
Tx -5dB	13.9 mA	voltate cut-off	2.7V
Tx -7dB	12.5 mA		
Tx -10dB	11.2 mA		
Tx -15dB	9.9 mA		
Tx -25dB	8.5 mA		
Rx	19.7mA		
Idle	365μA		
Sleep	1μA		
Volt. Regulator	20μA		

VCC is given by the formula $I[VCC] = I[3V] + 210(VCC - 3)$. We chose to power the device with a rechargeable Lithium Ion battery. Here, we used the data-sheet of the GP Battery 1015L08 model, that is designed for small devices.

Two execution scenarios are considered. In the first scenario (single source broadcast), Node 0 broadcasts a message to the other nodes every ten seconds, until the voltage is not sufficient for the node to work correctly (its cut-off voltage is 2.7 V, see Table 2). In the second scenario(multiple source broadcast), a randomly selected node tries to broadcast its message, until there is no node working correctly and no node can initiate a broadcast.

5   Experimental Results and Discussion

We first present experimental results related to single source broadcast in Sect. 5.1, then multiple source broadcast in Sect. 5.2. Our findings are further discussed in Sect. 5.3

5.1   Single Source Broadcast

When the source of the broadcast does not change, it becomes the first node that stops working. This observation holds for every broadcasting protocol and every MAC layer. The reason is that the CPU of the source consumes some energy to initiate the broadcast, and our simulations shown that no broadcasting protocol take this fact into account when implementing their strategy. However, broadcast protocols exhibit various differences depending on the considered performance metric.

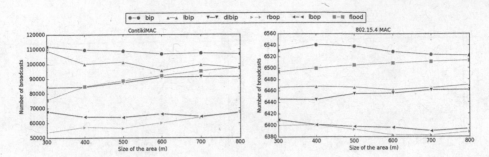

Fig. 1. Average number of broadcasts, depending on the size of the area, for each broadcasting protocol.

Number of Broadcasts. The overall number of broadcasts, which directly depends on the lifetime of the source node, varies depending on the network protocol stack used. Figure 1 presents for each MAC layer the number of broadcasts that could be achieved depending on the size of the area, for each considered broadcasting protocol.

With 802.15.4 MAC, the number of broadcasts are roughly equivalent, and on average, the number of achieved broadcasts lies between 6300 and 6600, and does not depend on the size of the area. BIP has a small advantage, then FLOOD lasts a little longer than the other distributed broadcasting protocols.

With ContikiMAC, the number of broadcasts varies significantly with the considered broadcasting protocol and, to a lesser extent, with the size of the area. For BIP and LBIP protocols, the number of broadcasts is around 110,000 for dense networks. This number decreases to around 100,000 for sparse networks. In contrary, for FLOOD and DLBIP protocols, the number of broadcasts increases with the size of the area from around 80,000 to 95,000. RBOP and LBOP protocols have lower performance with less than 70,000 broadcasts.

We see that LBIP appears to be the best distributed protocol. Surprisingly (considering its energy unawareness) FLOOD exhibits very good performance, similar to DLBIP, and outperforms both RBOP and LBOP.

Number of Receiving Nodes. Contrary to what we expected, all the nodes do not necessarily receive every message. For some broadcasting protocols, the number of receiving nodes can vary a lot. This is due to the fact that when broadcasting a packet, the MAC layer does not request an acknowledgment, so the packet (due to interference) may not be received by its intended destination, and this loss is never notified to the broadcasting protocol. Again, the MAC layer impacts significantly the results (see Fig. 2). In the sequel, the *reachability* metric denotes the percentage of nodes that receive the message.

With ContikiMAC, BIP, DLBIP, and FLOOD protocols offer very good performance regardless of the size of the area. LBIP and RBOP are below, but LBIP performs better as the density of the graph decreases.

With 802.15.4, FLOOD, DLBIP exhibit results that are similar to the previous case. However, BIP has one of the worse performance, with RBOP and

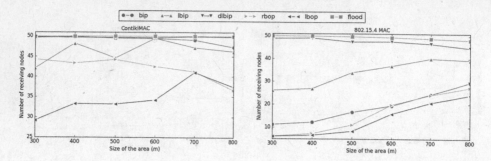

Fig. 2. Average number of receiving nodes, depending on the size of the area, for each broadcasting protocol.

LBOP. Their performance increases with the size of the area but the performance of BIP with 802.15.4 is far below its performance with ContikiMAC. Again, LBIP reachability increases until 80 % as the density of the networks decreases.

In both cases, the improvement observed when density decreases can be explained by the fewer number of message collisions that go unnoticed.

Amount of Remaining Energy. In previous work, the amount of energy in the network upon simulation termination was analyzed. For our purpose, the energy that remains in the rest of the network after that the battery of the source node is depleted is not as relevant as the other metrics we considered. Indeed, for ContikiMAC, the amount of energy remaining is correlated with the two other metrics. In more details, the greater the number of broadcasts and the greater the number of receiving nodes, the fewer the amount of energy remaining will be. So, less remaining energy actually implies better performance of the protocol.

With 802.15.4, the amount of remaining energy is similar for all broadcasting protocols, and cannot be used to differentiate their performance.

5.2   Multiple Source Broadcast (Gossip)

In this scenario, each broadcast is initiated by a randomly chosen source. Each simulation uses the same random order to make sure the differences between two simulations do not depend on this order. The simulation terminates when no nodes are alive (hence, we are not interested either in the amount of energy remaining in the network at the end of the simulation). In this setting, it is interesting to investigate the number of receiving nodes, and the delay over time.

Number of Receiving Nodes. Figure 3 (respectively, Fig. 4) shows the number of nodes that receive the message using ContikiMAC as a MAC layer (respectively, using 802.15.4 MAC), for each considered broadcasting protocol and for various sizes. The x-axis represents the number of broadcasts, and it is proportional to the time (because one broadcast occurs every 10 s). A point of the graph with

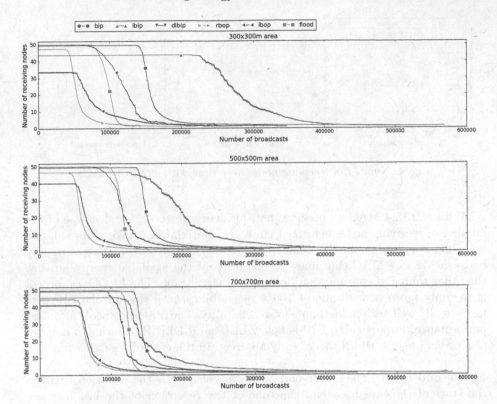

Fig. 3. Number of receiving nodes over time with ContikiMAC.

x-coordinate i is the average number of receiving for the i-th broadcast to the $(i + 100)$-th broadcast, for 50 simulations considering different topologies. Due to the sliding window used to compute the average, the graph is smoother than if we just took the average of the i-th broadcast over all the simulations. We observe that the number of receiving nodes at the beginning is consistent with the case of a unique source (See Sect. 5.1). Also, the number of broadcasts until a decrease starts is slightly more than in the case of a unique source, as the load is more evenly shared among sources.

With ContikiMAC, BIP is the protocol that keeps 100 % reachability for the longest period of time. Then FLOOD and DLBIP are close runner-up. In dense networks, DLBIP is better because the decrease in the number of receiving nodes is slower. However, in sparse networks, FLOOD keeps 100 % reachability for around 10 % more broadcasts. It is interesting to see that LBIP has around 90 % reachability, but performs 50 % more broadcasts compared to BIP and has a really slow decrease. Finally, RBOP and LBOP protocols are outperformed by the other protocols. We can notice that for sparse networks, the performance of BIP, LBIP, DLBIP, and FLOOD appear to converge to about 130,000 broadcasts.

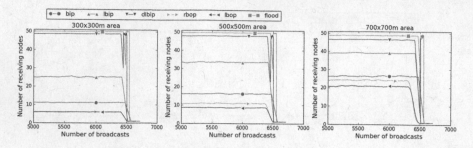

Fig. 4. Number of receiving nodes over time with 802.15.4 MAC.

With 802.15.4 MAC we observe that, for every protocol, the decrease of the number of receiving nodes is faster than with ContikiMAC. Also, all broadcasts are almost equivalent in the number of broadcasts performed. This is mainly because 802.15.4 MAC consumes the majority of the available energy, so that the other source of consumption become less significant. The FLOOD protocol is the only protocol with almost 100 % reachability until the end. DLBIP performs really well with more than 90 % reachability. The other protocols have bad performance. In particular, BIP is below LBIP and DLBIP in terms of number of receiving nodes, which was already observed in the case of a single source.

End-to-End Delay. The end-to-end delay we consider is the duration between the start of the broadcast and the time of the reception of the last message for this broadcast (if not all nodes receives the broadcast message, the time of reception of the last node that receives the message is used).

With ContikiMAC (see Fig. 5), we note that FLOOD, LBIP, and LBIP have really good performance, with a delay from 500 ms for dense networks to 1 s for sparse networks. Also, even if BIP has good performance in terms of number of broadcasts and reachability, it has a high delay of 2.5 s, regardless of the density of the network. LBOP and RBOP have even greater delay.

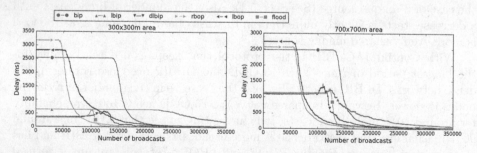

Fig. 5. End-to-end delay (in ms) over time with ContikiMAC.

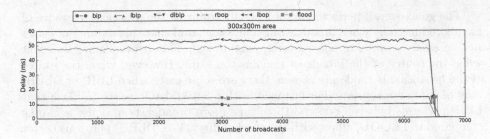

Fig. 6. End-to-end delay (in ms) over time with 802.15.4 MAC.

With 802.15.4 (see Fig. 6), the overall delay is better than with ContikiMAC by two orders of magnitude. BIP, LBIP, DLBIP, and FLOOD have similar performance with a delay around 10 ms. RBOP and LBOP exhibit a delay that is five times greater. The results for the other size of area are not presented because they are equivalent.

In both cases, we can see that the delay decreases when the number of receiving nodes decreases. However, we observe that for FLOOD and DLBIP protocols, the beginning of the decrease is preceded by a small peak, probably because after some nodes have stopped working, the network has a lower density, resulting in a greater delay.

5.3   Discussion

Our results show that the impact of the transmission collisions due to wireless interference is not uniform for each broadcasting protocol. For instance, we saw that the number of receiving nodes with RBOP is low for dense networks and increases as the density of the network decreases. This implies that interference have a huge impact on RBOP. This impact could be: *(i)* direct *i.e.*, the protocols sends only few messages, so that each node often receives the message from only one neighbor, and if this message is lost, a subset of the network does not receives the message, or *(ii)* indirect *i.e.*, the nodes selected for broadcasting the message are chosen in such a way that their transmissions always collide at the receivers, particularly due to the hidden terminal problem (two nodes that are out of range from each other but that have a common destination neighbor). The first point can explain why the FLOOD protocol exhibits such good performance. Indeed, each nodes transmits the message, which causes more interference, but this also increases the probability that a node receives the message and is later able to retransmit it to the rest of the network.

In more details, there is a limit in the amount of interference in the network because if the MAC layer detects that another node is transmitting, it waits until the channel is clear. At some point, increasing the number of nodes that wants to transmit does not increase the number of lost packets. So that the probability that at least one node receives the message for the first time increases.

The good overall performance of FLOOD confirms the practical relevance of having redundancy when broadcasting a message, and that this redundancy *does not necessarily imply a higher overall energy cost*. This is even more stringent when the source of the broadcast remains the same. However, when the source of the broadcast is randomly chosen, there are some cases when LBIP or DLBIP may be more appropriate. For instance, with ContikiMAC, we see in Fig. 3 that LBIP performs between two and three time more broadcasts in dense networks compared to FLOOD, albeit with less reachability. Also, DLBIP performs better than FLOOD in dense networks. So, in general, the overall best candidate is FLOOD, but some specific settings command the use of LBIP or DLBIP.

6 Conclusion

We focused on the problem of broadcasting a message in an energy-efficient manner, in a wireless sensor network where nodes are able to change their transmission power. We studied six broadcasting protocols that are representative of the current state of the art. We answered the question left open by the previous work: how broadcasting protocols performs with realistic devices in a realistic environment? We found that the energy consumption does not depend on the protocols as one could expect from the previous studies. Indeed, it is not realistic to consider only the energy consumed by the radio during the transmission. Also, the collisions prevent many protocols to achieve acceptable coverage, especially when the density of the network is high. Our conclusion is that focusing on power transmission to improve energy-efficiency of broadcast protocols for sensor networks is not the right choice. Future protocols are bound to integrate more realistic interference and energy consumption models to be relevant in practice. A cross-layer approach with the MAC layer and the broadcast layer helping each other is a possible path for future research.

Another interesting open question is the impact of mobility of sensor nodes on the energy efficiency of broadcasts protocols. The six broadcast protocols we considered assume a static topology. Several evaluations of broadcast protocols in WSNs have been done when the nodes are mobile [16,21]. However, protocol schemes and their evaluation are totally different. In the work of S.Medetov et al. [16], the remaining energy is also considered, but with an ideal battery model and full-sized computer network stack (a 802.11 MAC layer is assumed). Energy benchmarking those mobility-aware broadcast protocols in a realistic setting such as that of this paper is a short term research objective.

References

1. 802.15.4   Standard.   https://standards.ieee.org/getieee802/download/802.15. 4-2011.pdf
2. Hamida, E.B., Chelius, G., Gorce, J.: Scalable versus accurate physical layer modeling in wireless network simulations. In: IEEE Computer Society (ed.) 22nd ACM/IEEE/SCS Workshop on Principles of Advanced and Distributed Simulation (PADS 2008), Roma, Italy, pp. 127–134. ACM/IEEE/SCS, June 2008

3. Bramas, Q., Dron, W., Fadhl, M.B., Hachicha, K., Garda, P., Tixeuil, S.: WiSe-Bat: accurate energy benchmarking of wireless sensor networks. In: Proceedings of Forum on Specification and Design Languages (FDL 2015), Barcelona, Spain. IEEE Press, September 2015
4. Cardieri, P.: Modeling interference in wireless ad hoc networks. IEEE Commun. Surv. Tutor. **12**(4), 551–572 (2010)
5. Cartigny, J., Ingelrest, F., Simplot-Ryl, D., Stojmenović, I.: Localized LMST and RNG based minimum-energy broadcast protocols in ad hoc networks. Ad Hoc Netw. **3**(1), 1–16 (2005)
6. Champ, J., Baert, A.-E., Boudet, V.: Dynamic localized broadcast incremental power protocol and lifetime in wireless ad hoc and sensor networks. In: Wozniak, J., Konorski, J., Katulski, R., Pach, A.R. (eds.) WMNC 2009. IFIP AICT, vol. 308, pp. 286–296. Springer, Heidelberg (2009)
7. Chiganmi, A., Baysan, M., Sarac, K., Prakash, R.: Variable power broadcast using local information in ad hoc networks. Ad Hoc Netw. **6**(5), 675–695 (2008)
8. Clementi, A.E.F., Penna, P., Silvestri, R.: The power range assignment problem in radio networks on the plane. In: Reichel, H., Tison, S. (eds.) STACS 2000. LNCS, vol. 1770, pp. 651–660. Springer, Heidelberg (2000)
9. Dunkels, A.: The ContikiMAC radio duty cycling protocol (2011)
10. Fraboulet, A., Chelius, G., Fleury, E.: Worldsens: development and prototyping tools for application specific wireless sensors networks. In: 6th International Symposium on Information Processing in Sensor Networks, IPSN 2007, pp. 176–185. IEEE (2007)
11. Guo, S., Yang, O.W.W.: Energy-aware multicasting in wireless ad hoc networks: a survey and discussion. Comput. Commun. **30**(9), 2129–2148 (2007)
12. Ingelrest, F., Simplot-Ryl, D., et al.: Localized broadcast incremental power protocol for wireless ad hoc networks. Wirel. Netw. **14**(3), 309–319 (2008)
13. Iyer, A., Rosenberg, C., Karnik, A.: What is the right model for wireless channel interference? IEEE Trans. Wirel. Commun. **8**(5), 2662–2671 (2009)
14. Kirousis, L.M., Kranakis, E., Krizanc, D., Pelc, A.: Power consumption in packet radio networks. In: Reischuk, R., Morvan, M. (eds.) STACS 1997. LNCS, vol. 1200, pp. 363–374. Springer, Heidelberg (1997)
15. Li, N., Hou, J.C., Sha, L.: Design, analysis of an MST-based topology control algorithm. IEEE Trans. Wirel. Commun. **4**(3), 1195–1206 (2005)
16. Medetov, S., Bakhouya, M., Gaber, J., Wack, M.: Evaluation of an energy-efficient broadcast protocol in mobile ad hoc networks. In: 20th International Conference on Telecommunications (ICT), pp. 1–5. IEEE (2013)
17. Rakhmatov, D.: Battery voltage modeling for portable systems. ACM Trans. Des. Autom. Electron. Syst. **14**(2), 29:1–29:36 (2009)
18. Rao, R., Vrudhula, S., Rakhmatov, D.N.: Battery modeling for energy aware system design. Computer **36**(12), 77–87 (2003)
19. Toussaint, G.T.: The relative neighbourhood graph of a finite planar set. Pattern Recogn. **12**(4), 261–268 (1980)
20. Wieselthier, J.E., Nguyen, G.D., Ephremides, A.: On the construction of energy-efficient broadcast and multicast trees in wireless networks. In: 19th Annual Joint Conference of IEEE Computer and Communications Societies (INFOCOM 2000), vol. 2, pp. 585–594. IEEE (2000)
21. Williams, B., Camp, T.: Comparison of broadcasting techniques for mobile ad hoc networks. In: Proceedings of 3rd ACM International Symposium on Mobile Ad Hoc Networking and Computing, pp. 194–205. ACM (2002)

Transactional Pointers: Experiences with HTM-Based Reference Counting in C++

Maria Carpen-Amarie[1]([⊠]), Dave Dice[2], Gaël Thomas[3], and Pascal Felber[1]

[1] Université de Neuchâtel, Neuchâtel, Switzerland
{maria.carpen-amarie,pascal.felber}@unine.ch
[2] Oracle Labs, Burlington, USA
dave.dice@oracle.com
[3] Telecom SudParis, Évry, France
gael.thomas@telecom-sudparis.eu

Abstract. The most popular programming languages, such as C++ or Java, have libraries and data structures designed to automatically address concurrency hazards in order to run on multiple threads. In particular, this trend has also been adopted in the memory management domain. However, automatic concurrent memory management also comes at a price, leading sometimes to noticeable overhead. In this paper, we experiment with C++ smart pointers and their automatic memory-management technique based on reference counting. More precisely, we study how we can use hardware transactional memory (HTM) to avoid costly and sometimes unnecessary atomic operations. Our results suggest that replacing the systematic counting strategy with HTM could improve application performance in certain scenarios, such as concurrent linked-list traversal.

1 Introduction

With the increasing degree of concurrency in nowadays hardware, lock-free implementation of applications or data structures gained extensive attention in the last few years. In this context, using classical synchronization mechanisms based on locks (such as mutexes, barriers, etc.) tends to become more and more complex and error-prone. *Transactional memory* (TM) [8] offers an elegant solution for implementing lock-free synchronization. Until recently, TM algorithms were mostly reserved to the research environment, since the considerable overhead generated by software transactional memory (STM) implementations made them unsuitable for real-life applications. However, the emergence of hardware transactional memory (HTM) in mainstream processors overcame the performance pitfall, while conserving the benefits in scalability and correctness.

Automatic memory management mechanisms often suffer from performance drops due to their synchronization strategies. A notable example is represented by the smart pointer implementation in the C++ standard library. This uses *reference counting* to protect a raw pointer from being illegally deallocated and to

© Springer International Publishing AG 2016
P.A. Abdulla and C. Delporte-Gallet (Eds.): NETYS 2016, LNCS 9944, pp. 102–116, 2016.
DOI: 10.1007/978-3-319-46140-3_8

avoid any other memory hazards. Smart pointers are thread-safe and the operations on the shared reference counter are atomic. This provides adequate and safe memory management for multi-threaded programs. Nonetheless, the reference counting strategy is costly and sometimes unnecessary, e.g., when manipulating copies of a smart pointer with a reference count that never drops below 1 and hence never needs to release memory.

In this paper, we explore possible scenarios where HTM could improve the performance of applications that use C++ smart pointers. Specifically, we replace the original reference counting logic based on atomic operations with hardware transactions. The hardware transaction protects the raw pointer against invalid accesses. In this manner, we avoid executing the unnecessary atomic operations required by the reference counting strategy. On the one hand, we expect HTM to improve the performance of smart pointers over the original implementation. On the other hand, by adding this low abort-rate HTM fast-path, we are also addressing some concurrency problems related to smart pointer handling. Gottschlich et al. [7] show that template-based generic structures, such as C++ smart pointers, are deadlock-prone, among other synchronization issues, and they also propose the use of TM in their implementation.

Our contribution consists of an extensive study on the benefits of HTM for C++ smart pointers. We added transactional support for smart pointers, and tested their performance on: (1) *micro-benchmarks*, with mono- and multi-threaded settings, with and without batching multiple pointers in a single transaction, on two different architectures (Intel Haswell and IBM POWER8); and a (2) *concurrent data structure*, with and without batching. The results are generally encouraging and we observe performance improvements in most, but not all scenarios: in some cases there are no or negligible gains (e.g., multi-threaded micro-benchmark with batching enabled), whereas in others the execution time is improved by 50 % (e.g., concurrent lookup operation over a linked-list, with batching enabled).

2   Background and Related Work

Automatic memory management is split into two representative approaches: *reference counting* and *tracing*. Tracing algorithms are most often used in high performance settings, while the reference counting strategy is usually avoided due to its major drawbacks. A critical downside is represented by its considerable overhead over tracing, estimated at 30 % in average [11]. The concept of reference counting is simple: it keeps track of the number of references for each object, updating a counter when references are removed or new ones are added. The object is destroyed only when the count reaches zero. However, this means that each pointer mutation has to be tracked and intercepted, making a naive implementation of reference counting very expensive. Recently, reference counting techniques were reconsidered and optimized, becoming comparable to tracing in terms of performance [1,11,12]. A noteworthy memory management mechanism that depends on reference counting is illustrated by C++ smart pointers.

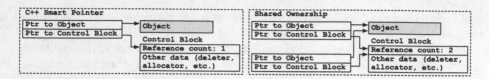

Fig. 1. C++ smart pointer components and reference counting mechanism.

2.1 C++ Smart Pointers

A smart pointer is an abstract data type that encapsulates a pointer while providing additional features, such as automatic memory management or bounds checking. These features were added to classical pointers in order to reduce programming bugs (created by manually managing the memory), while keeping the same efficiency. Smart pointers can prevent most memory leaks and dangling pointers.

In C++, smart pointers are implemented on top of traditional (raw) pointers, but provide additional memory management algorithms. We focus on the `std::shared_ptr` implementation located in the `<memory>` header. A `shared_ptr` represents a container for a raw pointer, for which it maintains reference counted ownership (Fig. 1). The object referenced by this pointer will be destroyed when there are no more copies of the `shared_ptr`.

The smart pointers are implemented as a C++ template that uses a reference counting strategy for memory management. The increments and decrements of the counts are synchronized and thread-safe. The default synchronization mechanism for C++ smart pointers employs atomic operations (increment/decrement).

2.2 Hardware Transactional Memory

Transactional memory (TM) [8] is a synchronization mechanism that can provide lock-freedom by encapsulating blocks of instructions in transactions and executing them atomically. In order to keep track of the changes, TM typically records the write set and applies it to memory atomically if the transaction succeeds; otherwise updates are discarded. There is no moment in time when an intermediate state can be observed. The most common cause for aborting a transaction is upon memory conflict, that is when two threads try to access the same memory areas. An abort can also be deliberately triggered by the application.

Transactional memory was first implemented in software (STM). Even though the benefits of TM over classical synchronization methods are significant, notably in terms of ease of use, STM was the subject of long debates whether it is only a research toy [3,6]. The most important issues are the significant overhead due to the instrumentation of the application, and the limitation to "weak atomicity" (i.e., it identifies conflicts only between two transactional accesses). Starting in 2013, Intel made available for public use its "Haswell" processor with fully integrated hardware transactional memory (HTM) support. HTM overcomes the aforementioned problems of STM. However, it has its own disadvantages: first, the size of the transactions is limited. Careful planning for the contents of the transaction is needed in order to both avoid overflows and amortize the cost of starting and committing the transaction. Moreover, transactions can be aborted at any time by interrupts, faults and other specific instructions, such as debug or I/O. HTM requires a non-transactional fallback path in case of abort, to ensure progress for the transactions that cannot commit. HTM is therefore a very powerful tool in a multi-core environment, although not suitable for all types of applications because of the aforementioned limitations. Nonetheless, it appears to be a suitable solution for tackling specialized concurrency problems, such as concurrent memory management.

2.3   Related Work

Considering the ever increasing interest in transactional memory in the last few years, a reasonable amount of effort has been focused on integrating TM with mainstream programming languages, such as C++. Crowl et al. [4] present a general design that would permit the insertion of transactional constructs into C++. They identify the main issues that need to be addressed and propose a new syntax that could be incrementally adopted in the existing code base. Ni et al. [10] go even further and implement a fully working STM system that adds language constructs for transactional programming in C++. The system includes new C++ language extensions, a compiler and an STM runtime library. They conduct an extensive evaluation on 20 parallel benchmarks ported to use their C++ language extensions. The results show that the STM system performs well on all workloads, especially in terms of scalability. A more focused work is presented by Gottschlich and Boehm [7] regarding the need for transactional memory in generic programming. They give as example C++ shared pointers and similar constructs, and indicate that implementing them with transactions would avoid deadlocks and other synchronization issues. In this case, the authors do not explore the performance of a potential transactional implementation, but the correctness of such a strategy.

In what concerns the synchronization of concurrent data structures with HTM, opinion is divided on the performance benefits of transactions. For example, David et al. [5] report an increase in throughput of at most 5 % when using HTM for concurrent search data structures, considering the improvement as negligible. On the other hand, Bonnichsen et al. [2] present a concurrent ordered map implementation with HTM that performs up to 3.9 times faster than the state of the art.

In this paper, we apply the guidelines that recommend enhancing C++ smart pointers with transactional support, thus avoiding specific concurrency issues, and evaluate the potential performance improvement when using HTM on concurrent data structures.

3   Transactional Pointers

We call *transactional pointer* a C++ smart pointer that protects an object with a hardware transaction and does not modify its reference count. The goal is to avoid the execution of undesired atomic operations on the shared reference counter of an object. The transaction intercepts hazardous accesses to the object (e.g., a non-transactional access trying to release a pointer still in use) and a safe path is chosen.

3.1   Algorithm

The original algorithm for C++ smart pointers is straightforward: when the pointer is created, it contains a raw pointer and a control block for this reference. The reference count is initialized with 1. As seen in Fig. 1, when a new copy of the same pointer is created, they will have in common the reference and the reference count field, which is updated by atomic increment. Every time when a copy of the pointer is destructed, the shared reference count is atomically decreased by one, and the rest of the object destroyed. If there is only one reference left, then the memory is automatically freed. This allows the application to function without any risk of incorrect accesses, dangling pointers or memory leaks.

Our goal was to eliminate the atomic operations on the shared reference count, while keeping the reference protected from memory hazards. In order to do that, we defined a constructor that initializes the reference count with 0 and tries to start a hardware transaction. Inside the transaction, we read a shared field of the transactional pointer, called `state`. In this way, `state` is added to the read-set of the transaction and automatically monitored in hardware. Any other thread that tries to modify this field will cause an abort. If there is no abort, the application will continue its execution, using the transactional pointer protected by the transaction. If a conflict or another event causes the currently running transaction to abort, the transactional pointer will follow a fallback path corresponding to the original implementation of the smart pointers, i.e., the reference count is initialized with the number of references of the smart pointer that we are copying and atomically incremented, or with 1 if it is a new smart pointer. When the transactional pointer is destroyed by the application, we check if there is a transaction running: if yes, the transaction commits; otherwise, the object is destroyed in the same way as a normal smart pointer.

Further on, we modified the algorithm to support batching. More specifically, multiple transactional pointers can be added to an already started transaction, without having their reference count modified and without starting a transaction on their own. In order to achieve this, the constructor exploits an additional parameter indicating whether the transactional pointer in question is the first one in the batch (or a single pointer that needs to be protected) or it needs to be added to an already existing transaction. In the former case, the algorithm follows the steps described above. In the latter, we take advantage of the fact that all initializations happen inside the transaction. Thus, we do not need to specifically read the `state` field anymore. Finally, we add a supplementary

---

Algorithm 1. Transactional pointer implementation

```
 1: function TX_PTR::INIT(boolean add_to_tx, smart_ptr ptr)
 2:     this.ptr ← ptr
 3:     this.refcount ← 0
 4:     this.state ← ptr.state
 5:     this.add_to_tx ← add_to_tx
 6:     if this.add_to_tx ∧ is_fallback then
 7:         FALLBACK(ptr)
 8:     end if
 9:     if ¬this.add_to_tx then
10:         if TX_START() then
11:             READ(this.state)
12:             is_fallback ← false
13:         else
14:             is_fallback ← true
15:             FALLBACK(ptr)
16:         end if
17:     end if
18: end function

19: function TX_PTR::DESTROY()
20:     WRITE(this.state)
21:     if ¬this.add_to_tx ∧ TX_TEST() then
22:         TX_END()
23:     end if
24: end function
```

---

check in the destructor of the transactional pointer: we only try to commit the transaction when the pointer that started it is destroyed. This design assumes a scenario in which:

- either all pointers die at once (e.g., at the end of a function in which they have been created), in which case they are destroyed in the reverse order of creation, thus making the first pointer to be destroyed last and keeping the transaction that protects all pointers running until it is safe to commit; or,
- the pointers added to the transaction are explicitly destroyed before the pointer that started the transaction.

This is particularly convenient for applications using well-delimited groups of pointers, such as some operations on classical data structures.

The above steps are summarized in Algorithm 1. We call **tx_ptr** the data type that enhances C++ smart pointers with hardware transactions. The constructor creates a transactional pointer from an already existing smart pointer, which is passed as a parameter. We use **this** to designate the current transactional pointer being created. We cover in this pseudo-code the extended algorithm suitable both for batching pointers as well as for single transactional pointers. Therefore, the constructor features a boolean parameter **add_to_tx** that indicates whether the current pointer has to be added to a running transaction or start a new one by itself. If it is the first pointer (Line 9), it tries to start a transaction. All subsequent transactional pointers will be monitored by the same transaction and will not attempt to start a new one. If the transaction starts, we read the **state** field, as mentioned; otherwise, the algorithm takes the fallback path. The call to a generic function **READ()** (Line 11) stresses the idea of reading the field inside the transaction, without entering into implementation details.

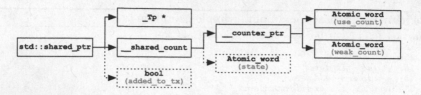

Fig. 2. Class structure of `std::shared_ptr`, with the additional fields for `tx_ptr` in dashed lines.

The variable `is_fallback` is a thread-local variable, set when the first pointer takes the fallback path. When a transaction aborts, all changes are rolled back and the execution is restarted. This means that all the added pointers will run their constructor from the beginning, following the path in Line 6. In other words, all transactional pointers will take a non-transactional path, similar to a classical C++ smart pointer. While the transaction is running correctly, `is_fallback` remains false. We claim that the presented algorithm correctly implements a smart pointer structure, while aiming to reduce the overhead of atomic operations.

3.2   Implementation

We built our transactional pointers on top of the `std::shared_ptr` structure in C++. In particular, we extended the `std::shared_ptr` class with a new constructor and modified several internal methods in order to accommodate the transactional logic. As such, a `tx_ptr` can simulate the normal behaviour of a classical smart pointer and `tx_ptrs` can be created from `std::shared_ptrs`.

The `std::shared_ptr` class is implemented as a C++ template, with the raw pointer (of generic type `_Tp`) and a variable of type `__shared_count` (Fig. 2) as the main fields. The latter is the class that implements the shared reference count object. The reference count object contains a pointer to two counters: `use_count` and `weak_count`. The role of the latter is out of the scope of this work. The former contains the number of references a pointer has throughout the execution. We added in the diagram with dashed lines the necessary fields for implementing `tx_ptr`:

- A boolean variable in the main class, with the aim of indicating which pointers are to be added to the existing transactions or start a new one. This information is critical in the destructor when using batching, since the transaction must be committed only when all pointers in the group have been destroyed.
- The shared `state` field in the reference count class. This field is initialized in the constructor and read inside the transaction, in order to be monitored in hardware. It is further modified in the destructor. Thus, if any other copy of the same pointer tries to destroy the pointer and deallocate the memory, writing the `state` field forces the transaction to abort and the `tx_ptr` to restart as a normal smart pointer.

We implement the transactional memory operations on two different architectures: Intel Haswell and IBM POWER8. While there are several subtle differences in the APIs and the underlying HTM implementations, most of our code is common to both architectures.

4   Evaluation with Micro-Benchmarks

In order to have a preliminary idea of the benefits of our transactional pointer implementation over the original C++ smart pointers, we devised two micro-benchmarks. This enabled us to test both implementations in mono-threaded and multi-threaded scenarios, with or without batching, on two different architectures: Intel Haswell and IBM POWER8.

4.1   Mono-Threaded Scenario

We want to evaluate the possible gains of replacing atomic operations with hardware transactions. We developed a mono-threaded micro-benchmark for studying how many transactional pointers have to be packed in a transaction in order to improve the performance over a pair of atomic operations, when the application runs on a single thread. The micro-benchmark consists of the scenarios presented in Algorithm 2. By *tx shared pointer* we refer to a `tx_ptr` implementation. In the first scenario, starting at Line 1, we measure the time it takes to repeatedly create and destroy a normal C++ shared pointer, for a fixed number of iterations. As previously mentioned, when the pointer is created, an atomic increment is performed on the shared reference count; likewise, an atomic decrement is performed when the pointer is destroyed. This strategy reflects the performance when using a pair of increment/decrement atomic operations for `num_iter` iterations. The second scenario, starting at Line 7 replaces the pair of atomic operations in each iteration with a hardware transaction. The third scenario (Line 15) groups multiple create/destroy operations (i.e., multiple iterations) in a transaction. It behaves identically to the second scenario when $m = 1$.

We implemented and tested the micro-benchmark on two different platforms: a 4-core (2 threads per core) Intel Haswell@3.40 GHz machine with 12 GB RAM and a 10-core (8 threads per core) IBM POWER8@3.42 GHz with 30 GB RAM, both with fully integrated HTM support. For the third scenario at Line 15, we varied m from 2 to 5, since for values greater than 5 the performance was visibly better than the original implementation of shared pointers. We observed that the measured time was varying during the first executions of the benchmark. In order to have accurate results, we first ran the benchmark 50 times until the results were stable (standard error deviation less than 1 %). Subsequently, we considered the average value per iteration over another ten runs for each version of the benchmark. We tested for 10^3, 10^6 and 10^9 iterations. The execution time of one iteration is measured with the system's high resolution clock. Figure 3 shows the performance in all scenarios for the mentioned values of m and number of iterations, both on the Haswell machine and on POWER8. On the Y axis we have the time in nanoseconds per iteration. We made the following observations:

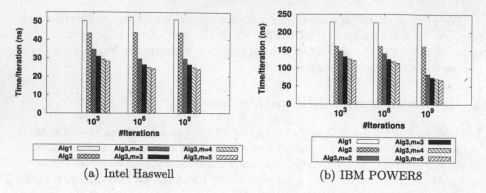

(a) Intel Haswell   (b) IBM POWER8

Fig. 3. Mono-threaded performance (time per iteration) for repeated create/destroy of: original shared pointer (Algorithm 2, Line 1), transactional pointer with one transaction per iteration (Algorithm 2, Line 7) and transactional pointer with one transaction per m iterations (Algorithm 2, Line 15) with $m = 2, 3, 4, 5$.

Algorithm 2. Scenarios for the mono-threaded micro-benchmark

```
 1: function SCENARIO₁              15: function SCENARIO₃
 2:     for i ← 1, num_iter do     16:     for i ← 1, num_iter/m do
 3:         p ← new shared pointer 17:         BEGIN-TX
 4:         delete p               18:         for i ← 1, m do
 5:     end for                    19:             p ← new tx shared pointer
 6: end function                   20:             delete p
                                    21:         end for
 7: function SCENARIO₂              22:         COMMIT-TX
 8:     for i ← 1, num_iter do     23:     end for
 9:         BEGIN-TX               24: end function
10:         p ← new tx shared pointer
11:         delete p
12:         COMMIT-TX
13:     end for
14: end function
```

---

1. When running on a single thread, using a single hardware transaction per iteration results in better performance than a pair of atomic operations. In other words, the second scenario (Line 7) performed better than the first (Line 1) for any number of iterations on both platforms.
2. The performance improves when m increases (up to a certain threshold when the group of instructions becomes too large and the transaction overflows).

In conclusion, according to the presented mono-threaded benchmark, a hardware transaction should be able to replace a single pair of atomic operations without affecting the performance of the application. The application would gain if multiple pairs of atomic operations were replaced by a single hardware transaction.

4.2 Short-Lived Pointers

Consider now the following common scenario where a smart pointer is copied to a local variable inside a function, i.e., the copy of the smart pointer has the lifespan of that function. Generally, when creating such a copy, the reference counter is atomically incremented, while at the end of the function, there is an atomic decrement. If the pointer is not accessed concurrently in the meantime, then the increment/decrement operations are unnecessary. We aim to replace this pair of atomic operations with one transaction spanning the entire function. In order to obtain this behaviour, we use the tx_ptr pointer defined in Sect. 3.

We created a micro-benchmark that starts multiple threads which share an array of smart pointers. Each thread picks a random element from the shared array and calls a function. In the function, the thread creates a tx_ptr copy of the element. Then, it executes several constant-time operations. These operations are meant to simulate a computational workload that accesses the pointer value. If transactional pointers are used, these operations will be executed inside a transaction. Finally, the thread exits the function (which calls the destructor of the transactional pointer, thus committing the transaction). We measure how many iterations of this function are done by each thread in a certain amount of time (customizable by the user). We compare the total number of iterations (i.e., the sum of iterations over all threads) of our tx_ptr implementation with the original implementation of smart pointers. We configured our experiments as follows: shared array of 1,000 smart pointers, run time of 5 s, 100 constant-time operations. The experiments consist of running the micro-benchmark 10 times for an increasing number of threads on both platforms and taking the average over the total number of iterations in each case.

Figure 4(a) shows our first results with this implementation on the Haswell machine. On the X axis we show the number of threads, while on the Y axis we have the number of iterations performed divided by 10^6 (higher values are better). We tested on up to 16 threads. We observe that starting with 4 threads, our implementation performs better than the original. However, the improvement is less than 4 % (on 16 threads). Moreover, on the POWER8 server (Fig. 4(c)) there is almost no performance gain on more than 4 threads, indicating that the transactional implementation on this architecture suffers more from contention than the atomic operations. This result led us to the conclusion that, in a multi-threaded environment where many operations are involved, the creation of a single tx_ptr does not bring an improvement over a pair of atomic operations. As an optimization, we enabled batching in the micro-benchmark, i.e., the creation of multiple pointers in a single transaction. The idea was that, if a pair of atomic operations has almost the same overhead as a transaction, then replacing multiple pairs of atomic increment/decrement with a single transaction would improve the performance.

We modified the benchmark as follows: instead of a single random element, each thread now picks several random elements from the shared array (number defined at runtime). It creates a new array with these elements and calls the specific function having this array as a parameter. The function makes tx_ptr

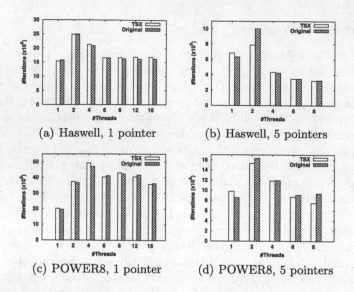

Fig. 4. Number of iterations for one or multiple short-lived `tx_ptr` pointer copies (TSX) and smart pointer copies (Orginal) in a function.

copies of all pointers, using the additional boolean parameter in the constructor in order to indicate which pointers will be added to the running transaction.

Figures 4(b) and (d) show the results of this strategy with a group of 5 pointers per transaction. In this scenario, however, contrary to our expectations, the performance actually suffers. We tested on up to 8 threads, pinned to the cores. We conclude that, by trying to optimize the previous results with batching, we also increased the overhead of the transaction with extra operations. This explains why in this setting we could not observe any improvement over the version with one pointer. Given the negligible performance gain of the latter, we deduce that in this scenario using transactional pointers does not have a significant advantage over the original C++ smart pointers.

5   Evaluation with Shared Data Structures

We implemented a simple data structure to showcase the possible performance improvement of `tx_ptrs` over the original implementation of C++ smart pointers. We chose to build a simply-linked list because of the natural occurrence of pointers with a reference count ≥ 1 (they will always be referenced by at least one other pointer until they are removed or the list is destroyed). That allows us to exploit the design of `tx_ptr` and the benefits of transactions for repeated concurrent traversals of the list.

5.1 Implementation

The shared list was implemented in two steps. First, we designed a concurrent liked-list structure only based on shared pointers and *compare and swap* (CAS) operations. For simplicity and reproducibility of our tests, we only inserted elements at the end of the list and we always removed the first element. Basically, in this experiment the implementation behaved like a concurrent queue, with an additional lookup function.

We implemented the data structure using a classical lock-free queue algorithm [9]. The use of C++ smart pointers for the nodes guarantees the correctness when accessing and manipulating elements. We use CAS operations specifically defined for shared pointers in the C++ standard library libstdc++-v3, included in the GCC5 release.[1] The result of a CAS operation is repeatedly checked in a loop, until it confirms that the desired operation took place. The insert and delete operations are easily implemented with shared pointers and CAS, by changing atomically the first element with the new node, respectively the last element with the next node in the queue. The lookup function iterates over the list sequentially until it finds the requested value or reaches the end of the list. We considered that the list traversal could benefit the most from our implementation of tx_ptrs. The next step was to change the above implementation to use transactional pointers. The only modification needed in the code is replacing the constructor of the pointer that will iterate over the list with the customized constructor defined in Sect. 3.

Our goal was to encapsulate each iteration of the loop in the lookup function in a hardware transaction. In the original implementation, when the pointer iterating over the list passes from a node to the next, it creates and destroys a copy of a smart pointer. As previously mentioned, this is equivalent to a pair of atomic operations. Thus, we replace a pair of atomic increment/decrement with a hardware transaction. In order for the transactional pointers to work transparently in this case, we also extended the overloaded '=' (assignment) operator of C++ smart pointers. More precisely, the first transaction is started when the iterator is initialized in the tx_ptr constructor. Then, each time the iterator moves to the next node, the transaction commits and a new one is started (which will last until the move to the next node and so on). If there is a conflict, the transaction aborts and takes the fallback path described in Sect. 3.

Finally, we implemented support for batching multiple pointers in a single transaction. In the case of list traversal, this means that a hardware transaction will span the traversal of multiple nodes. The size of the group of nodes included in a single transaction is customizable. In order to maintain the transparency of the implementation, we could not reuse in this case the batching strategy described in Sect. 4.2. Rather, we implemented an internal counter for tx_ptr and modified the '=' operator to commit and start a new transaction when the counter indicates the end of a batch. Whenever the transaction aborts due to a

---

[1] In C++11 the operation atomic_compare_exchange_weak(p, expected, desired) checks if p has the same value as expected: if so, the value desired is atomically assigned to p; otherwise, expected becomes equal to p.

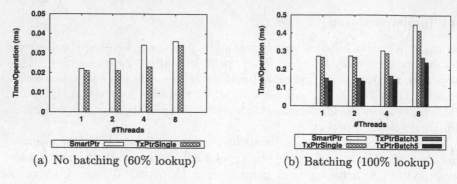

(a) No batching (60% lookup)   (b) Batching (100% lookup)

Fig. 5. Execution time per operation for a concurrent queue implemented with smart pointers and transactional pointers, with (a) a transaction per iteration during lookup and (b) multiple iterations grouped in a single transaction.

conflict, all the changes made to the group of pointers are rolled back and all pointers are recreated as common C++ smart pointers with reference counting.

5.2 Evaluation

We developed a benchmark for comparing the performance of smart and transactional pointer implementations of the concurrent queue. The benchmark works as follows: we initialize the queue and populate it with elements. We start a number of threads that share the queue. Each thread applies insert, delete and lookup operations on the shared queue by a given ratio. We measure the time it takes each thread to finish the associated operations. In order for all threads to have comparable workloads, we generate the workloads before starting the threads. Specifically, we generate a random succession of operations according to the proportions given for each type of operation. Then, we generate a list of elements that will be inserted in the queue, and a list of elements that will be looked up, based on the elements that are inserted. Given the dynamic character of the benchmark (a large number of concurrent insert and delete operations), not all the elements in the lookup list will be found in the queue at the moment when the operation is performed.

First, we experimented with the implementation based on the original C++ smart pointers and our simple transactional version (without batching). We tested on a 4-core Intel Haswell server, on up to 8 threads pinned to the cores. We set the list to be initially populated with 1,000 elements. Each thread had to execute 10^6 operations on the shared list, out of which 20 % insert, 20 % delete and 60 % lookup operations. We measured the time with the `high_resolution_clock` C++ function. We ran each test 10 times, after first observing that the results were stable, with negligible variations from a run to another. For each run we took the maximum between the times reported by each thread, then computed the average over the 10 runs. The results for this test are shown in Fig. 5(a). We observe that our implementation does not perform notably better than the original. However, this result indicates that even if we replace a single pair of atomic operations with a hardware transaction, we already start gaining in performance.

We then tested the transactional version with batching enabled. Since the only difference between the two implementations of the concurrent queue (i.e., with shared_ptr and with tx_ptr) is in the way in which the lookup function works, we focused on stressing and comparing strictly this operation. Thus, we modified the previous configuration to run a workload of 100 % lookup operations, for 10^6 operations per thread, on a 10^4-element shared array. At least half of the elements that will be looked up by the benchmark are found in the initial shared array. Figure 5(b) shows the results in this scenario for the implementation with the original C++ smart pointers, as well as transactional pointers with one transaction per pointer, one transaction for a group of 3 pointers, and one transaction for a group of 5 pointers. We make the following observations: first, when grouping 5 pointers in a transaction, i.e., replacing 10 atomic operations with a hardware transaction, we see an improvement of up to 50 % in the execution time. Second, we observe that the performance increase is more spectacular when passing from no batching to a group of 3 pointers than from a batch of 3 to one of 5 pointers. While the batch size increases, the performance improvement will reach a plateau and start degrading when the batch becomes too large for being handled properly by a hardware transaction. Finally, we remark that the improvement is less noticeable on 8 threads, because of contention.

6   Conclusion and Future Work

Concurrency and automatic memory management are two key components of today's complex multi-core systems. While the number of cores per CPU keeps increasing, the attention of developers seems to turn more and more towards lock-free algorithms and implementations. Transactional memory, and especially its hardware implementation (HTM), represents a suitable non-blocking solution for concurrency hazards. At the same time, reference counting is a useful form of memory management with interesting properties and synchronization features, where each object is protected from invalid accesses by keeping a shared reference counter. Sometimes the atomic increment/decrement operations on the shared counter prove to be unnecessary and expensive. We considered this to be a promising opportunity for improvement with HTM.

We designed a transactional pointer structure on top of the C++ shared_ptr, which uses reference counting for correctly managing the memory. Our goal was to replace the atomic operations needed for the creation/destruction of the smart pointer with a hardware transaction. We experimented with micro-benchmarks, in mono- and multi-threaded settings, on two different architectures and with the possibility of batching multiple pointers in a transaction. We also compared the performance of the original and transactional implementations on a concurrent queue of smart pointers. We believe that the results provide valuable insights into which scenarios would benefit most from using a transactional pointer.

Given the promising results for the concurrent queue (up to 50 % improvement on the execution time for lookup operations), we plan to further pursue this idea and implement more complex data structures with transactional pointers. A future objective could be the implementation of a transactional pointer specialized for concurrent data structure traversal.

References

1. Blackburn, S.M., McKinley, K.S.: Ulterior reference counting: fast garbage collection without a long wait. In: Proceedings of the 18th Annual ACM SIGPLAN Conference on Object-Oriented Programing, Systems, Languages, and Applications, pp. 344–358. ACM, USA (2003)
2. Bonnichsen, L.F., Probst, C.W., Karlsson, S.: Hardware transactional memory optimization guidelines, applied to ordered maps. In: Trustcom/BigDataSE/ISPA, 2015 IEEE, vol. 3, pp. 124–131. IEEE (2015)
3. Cascaval, C., Blundell, C., Michael, M., Cain, H.W., Wu, P., Chiras, S., Chatterjee, S.: Software transactional memory: why is it only a research toy? Queue 6(5), 40:46–40:58 (2008)
4. Crowl, L., Lev, Y., Luchangco, V., Moir, M., Nussbaum, D.: Integrating transactional memory into C++. In: Workshop on Transactional Computing (2007)
5. David, T., Guerraoui, R., Trigonakis, V.: Asynchronized concurrency: the secret to scaling concurrent search data structures. In: Proceedings of the 20th International Conference on Architectural Support for Programming Languages and Operating Systems, pp. 631–644. ACM (2015)
6. Dragojević, A., Felber, P., Gramoli, V., Guerraoui, R.: Why STM can be more than a research toy. Commun. ACM 54(4), 70–77 (2011)
7. Gottschlich, J.E., Boehm, H.J.: Generic programming needs transactional memory. In: The 8th ACM SIGPLAN Workshop on Transactional Computing (2013)
8. Herlihy, M., Moss, J.E.B.: Transactional memory: architectural support for lock-free data structures. In: Proceedings of the 20th Annual International Symposium on Computer Architecture, pp. 289–300. ACM, USA (1993)
9. Herlihy, M., Shavit, N.: The Art of Multiprocessor Programming. Morgan Kaufmann Publishers Inc., Burlington (2008)
10. Ni, Y., Welc, A., Adl-Tabatabai, A.R., Bach, M., Berkowits, S., Cownie, J., Geva, R., Kozhukow, S., Narayanaswamy, R., Olivier, J., Preis, S., Saha, B., Tal, A., Tian, X.: Design and implementation of transactional constructs for C/C++. In: Proceedings of the 23rd ACM SIGPLAN Conference on Object-Oriented Programming Systems Languages and Applications, pp. 195–212. ACM, USA (2008)
11. Shahriyar, R., Blackburn, S.M., Frampton, D.: Down for the count? Getting reference counting back in the ring. In: Proceedings of the 2012 International Symposium on Memory Management, pp. 73–84. ACM, USA (2012)
12. Shahriyar, R., Blackburn, S.M., Yang, X., McKinley, K.S.: Taking off the gloves with reference counting Immix. In: Proceedings of the 2013 ACM SIGPLAN International Conference on Object Oriented Programming Systems Languages and Applications, pp. 93–110. ACM, USA (2013)

A Multi-channel Energy Efficient Cooperative MIMO Routing Protocol for Clustered WSNs

Alami Chaibrassou[✉] and Ahmed Mouhsen

Faculty of Science and Technology Science, Research Laboratory in Mechanical,
Industrial Management and Innovation, Settat, Morocco
alami70@yahoo.fr, mouhsen.ahmed@gmail.com

Abstract. Energy efficiency and quality of service are foremost concerns in Wireless Sensor Networks (WSNs). Among the methods used to achieve these requirements there is Virtual multiple input multiple output (MIMO) technique, where sensors nodes cooperate with each other to form an antenna array. These multiple antennas can be used to improve the performance of the system (lifetime, data rate, bit error rate …) through spatial diversity or spatial multiplexing [1, 2]. In this paper, we propose a distributed multi-channel energy efficient cooperative MIMO routing protocol for cluster based WSNs (MCMIMO) which aims at reducing energy consumption in multi-hop WSNs. In MCMIMO, sensor nodes are organized into clusters and each cluster head utilizes a weighted link function to select some optimal cooperative nodes to forward or receive traffic from other neighboring clusters by utilizing a cooperative MIMO technique, furthermore different channels are assigned to adjacent clusters and cooperative MIMO links in order to reduce collisions. Simulation results indicate that virtual MIMO based routing scheme achieves a significant reduction in energy consumption, compared to SISO one for larger distances.

Keywords: Wireless sensor networks (WSNs) · Cooperative multiple input multiple output (MIMO) · Cooperative communication · Clustering algorithms

1 Introduction

The current progress in the field of wireless technology allows to develop small size sensors called nodes, communicating with each other via a radio link and are characterized by their limited resources (energy supply; processing, memory storage). Their flexibility of use makes them more utilized to form a wireless sensor network (WSN) without returning to a fixed infrastructure. Furthermore, these nodes typically deployed in inaccessible areas to control a definite phenomenon, ensure the transfer of data collected using a multi-hop routing to a base station (BS), which is far from the monitored field. The BS is responsible for the analysis and processing of collected data to be exploited by the end user.

Based on the above observations, for a WSN to accomplish its function without failure of the connection between the nodes, because of a depleting battery of one or more nodes, we need a data routing protocol which gives higher priority to the energy factor compared to other limitations, in order to provide stability of the network. At this

P.A. Abdulla and C. Delporte-Gallet (Eds.): NETYS 2016, LNCS 9944, pp. 117–130, 2016.
DOI: 10.1007/978-3-319-46140-3_9

point, many studies have been made; the most known ones are based on the MIMO technologies. However, the node cannot carry multiple antennas at the same time due to its limited physical size. Therefore, a new transmission technique called "Cooperative MIMO" has been proposed [3]. This technique is based on the cooperation principle where the existence of different nodes in the network is exploited to transmit the information from the source to a specific destination by virtually using the MIMO system [4]. The Cooperative MIMO allows to obtain the space-time diversity gain [5], the reduction of energy consumption [6], and the enhancement of the system capacity [7].

In this paper, we would like to investigate cooperative virtual MIMO and multi-channel for cluster based WSNs, with the objective of maximizing the network lifetime and enhance the network throughput simultaneously. We first introduce a novel approach to grouping sensors into clusters and electing cooperative MIMO links among clusters on such that intra-cluster messages are transmitted over short-range SISO links, while inter-cluster messages are transmitted over long range cooperative MIMO links [8]. Each cluster head selects one or multiple cluster members using a weighted link function to form a MIMO array together with itself. To transmit a message to a neighboring cluster, the cluster head first broadcasts the message to other members in the MIMO array. The MIMO array then negotiates the transmission scheme with the MIMO array in the neighboring cluster, encodes and sends the message over the cooperative MIMO link between them. Second, adjacent clusters and cooperative MIMO links have different channels assignment to avoid collision, that's allows multiple simultaneous transmissions and hence an increase of the network throughput. Theoretical analyses show that, we can achieve high energy efficiency by adapting data rate and transmission made (SISO, SIMO, MISO, MIMO) [9]. Simulation results have proved that the proposed scheme can prolong the sensor network lifetime greatly, especially when the sink is far from the sensor area.

The remainder of the paper is organized as follows. Section 2 describes the related work. Section 3 describes energy efficiency of MIMO Systems. Section 4 describes the proposed network architecture and the total energy consumption of the proposed architecture. Section 5 describes the simulation and results. Finally, Sect. 6 concludes the paper and provides directions for future work.

2 Related Work

In the literature, several studies have been made in this research area; we just cite certain remarkable examples:

In [1] Cui et al., proposed MIMO systems based on Alamouti diversity schemes. They extend this energy-efficiency analysis of MIMO systems to individual single-antenna nodes that cooperate to form multiple antenna transmitters or receivers. By maintaining the proper constellation (bits per symbol) size, MIMO can outperform SISO (Single Input Single Output) after a certain distance.

According to [7] Belmega et al., the Multi-Input Multi-Output (MIMO) systems are more energy efficient than SISO systems if only consumed energy is taken into account. However, when the circuitry energy consumption is also considered, this conclusion is no longer true.

In [2] Cui et al., have investigated the best modulation strategy to minimize the total energy consumption required to send a given number of bits for uncoded systems, by optimizing the transmission time and the modulation parameters they have proved that up to 80 % energy saving is achievable over non-optimized systems. And for coded systems, the benefit of coding varies with the transmission distance and the underlying modulation schemes.

In [9] Sajid et al. have proposed a Virtual (MIMO) routing for WSNs. In which they have investigated virtual MIMO for fixed and variable rates. Their simulation results show that virtual MIMO based routing is more energy efficient as compared to SISO for larger distances.

3 Energy Efficiency of MIMO Systems

3.1 System Model

In our protocol we use the system model proposed in [1], The resulting signal paths on the transmitter and receiver sides are shown in Figs. 1 and 2, respectively, where M_t and M_r are the numbers of transmitter and receiver antennas, respectively, and we assume that the frequency synthesizer (LO) is shared among all the antenna paths. Based on the number of transmitters and receivers, we may get the following combinations: MIMO (multiple input multiple output), SIMO (single input multiple output), MISO (multiple input single output), and in SISO case (single input single output) $M_t = 1$ and $M_r = 1$.

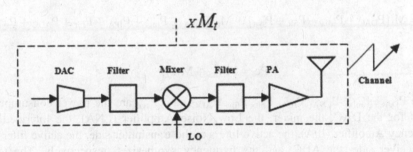

Fig. 1. Transmitter circuit blocks (Analog)

Based on [1], the total average energy consumption of MIMO transmission in WSNs includes two parts: the power consumption of all power amplifiers P_{PA} and the power consumption of other circuit blocks P_C. The transmitted power is given by

$$P_{out} = \bar{E}_b R_b \cdot \frac{(4\pi)^2 d_{i,j}^{k_{i,j}}}{G_t G_r \lambda^2} M_l N_f \qquad (1)$$

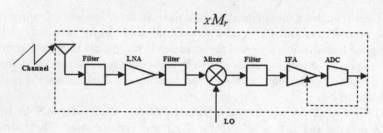

Fig. 2. Receiver circuit blocks (Analog)

where $\bar{E}_b$ is the required energy per bit at the receiver for a given BER requirement, R_b is the bit rate, $d_{i,j}$ is the distance between nodes i and j, $k_{i,j}$ is the path loss factor from node i to j, G_t is the transmitter antenna gain, G_r is the receiver antenna gain, λ is the carrier wavelength, M_l is the link margin and N_f is the receiver noise figure given by $N_f = N_r/N_0$ where N_0 is the single-sided thermal noise power spectral density and N_r is the power spectral density of the total effective noise at the receiver input.

The power consumption of the power amplifiers is dependent on The transmitted power P_{out} and can be approximated as

$$P_{PA} = (1 + \alpha)P_{out} \tag{2}$$

where $\alpha = \left(\frac{\xi}{\eta} - 1\right)$ with η the drain efficiency of the RF power amplifier and ξ the peak-to-average ratio.

The power consumption of the circuit components is given by

$$Pc = M_t\left(P_{DAC} + P_{Mix} + P_{filt} + P_{syn}\right) + M_r\left(P_{LNA} + P_{mix} + P_{IFA} + P_{filr} + P_{ADC} + P_{syn}\right) \tag{3}$$

$$Pc = M_t P_{ct} + M_r P_{cr} \tag{4}$$

where P_{DAC}, P_{mix}, P_{LNA}, P_{IFA}, P_{filt}, P_{filr}, P_{ADC}, and P_{syn} are the power consumption values for the DAC, the mixer, the Low Noise Amplifier (LNA), the Intermediate Frequency Amplifier (IFA), the active filters at the transmitter side, the active filters at the receiver side, the ADC, and the frequency synthesizer, respectively. The total energy consumption per bit according to [1] is given by

$$E_{bt} = \frac{(P_{PA} + P_C)}{R_b} \tag{5}$$

3.2 Variable-Rate Systems

Using MQAM modulation scheme, the constellation size b can be defined as $b = \log_2 M$ Further, we can define constellation size in terms of number of bits L, Bandwidth B, and duration radio transceiver is on T_{on}, and data rate R_b (bits/second) [1].

$$b = \frac{L}{BT_{on}} = \frac{R_b}{B} \tag{6}$$

$$R_b = \frac{L}{T_{on}} \tag{7}$$

The total energy consumption for Variable-rate Systems per bit according to [1] is given by Eq. (8), where $\bar{P}_b$ is the average bit error rate.

$$E_{bt} = \frac{2}{3}(1+\alpha)\left(\frac{\bar{P}_b}{4}\right)^{\frac{-1}{M_t}} \frac{2^b - 1}{b^{\frac{1}{M_t}+1}} M_t N_0 \frac{(4\pi)^2 d_{i,j}^{k_{i,j}}}{G_r G_t \lambda^2} M_l N_f + \frac{P_C}{Bb} \tag{8}$$

Based the Eq. (8) the optimal constellation sizes for different transmission distances are listed in Table 1.

Table 1. Optimized constellation size

Distance(m)	b_{SISO}	b_{MISO}	b_{MIMO}
1	12	14	16
5	6	10	12
10	5	8	10
20	4	6	8
40	4	5	7
70	2	4	5
100	2	3	5

4 The Proposed Protocol

4.1 Clustering Algorithm

The cluster formation and cooperative MIMO link selection state consists of five steps:

(1) 1-hop neighbor discovery step, in which each node broadcasts its residual energy to 1-hop neighbors
(2) 1-hop weight discovery step, in which each node calculates and broadcasts its weight to 1-hop neighbors
(3) cluster formation step, in which clusters are constructed based on the information received in 1-hop weight discovery step
(4) cluster neighbor discovery step, during which each cluster member notifies its cluster head about the cluster information of all its 1-hop neighbors such that the cluster head knows all its neighboring clusters and which nodes are adjacent to them

(5) cooperative MIMO link selection step, in which each pair of neighboring clusters select the optimal cooperative MIMO links for inter-cluster communications;

The details of these steps are discussed in the following subsections.

1. 1-hop neighbor discovery step

In this step, each node broadcasts a message including its residual energy (RE) to its 1-hop neighbors once receiving a RE message from a neighbor, a node adds an entry to its 1-hop neighbor list including the neighbor's residual energy and the estimated distance.

2. 1-hop weight discovery step

In 1-hop weight discovery step, the weight of each node is calculated and broadcast to 1-hop neighbor. Also as part of optimizing the energy resources of a WSN, it will be better to affect the CH role to a node with high residual energy and small average intra-cluster distance. In this regard, the weight for cluster head selection at each node i can be defined by

$$\text{weight}(i) = \frac{E_i}{\frac{\sum_{j=1}^{N(i)} d_{i,j}}{N(i)}} \tag{9}$$

where, $N(i)$ is the 1-hop neighbors number of node i, $d_{i,j}$ denotes the distance between nodes i and j, and E_i is the residual energy of node i.

3. cluster formation step

In this step, sensor nodes with the high weight in their 1-hop neighborhoods elect themselves as cluster heads. The cluster head election procedure is executed on each node as every node is aware of the weights of its 1-hop neighbors. A node broadcasts a Cluster Head Announcement (CHA) message to announce itself to be a cluster head. Once receiving a CHA message from 1-hop neighbors they send out a Cluster Join (CJ) message to join a cluster. After receiving a CJ message, the cluster head replies with an ACK message to confirm the cluster join operation. If a sensor node receives only one CHA message from a neighbor with high weight, the node chooses it as the cluster head and joins its cluster. If a node receives multiple CHA messages from neighbors with high weight, the node joins the closest cluster head. Isolated nodes declare itself as cluster heads. At the end of this step, each sensor node will be either a cluster head or a cluster member [10, 11].

4. cluster neighbor discovery step

In this step, all cluster members send a Cluster Forward (CF) message to their cluster heads, in which the updated 1-hop neighbor list is included. The cluster head acknowledge each CF message with an ACK message. A cluster member retransmits the CF message if it does not receive an ACK message timely. After receiving all the CF messages from its cluster members, a cluster head knows all the neighboring clusters.

5. cooperative MIMO link selection step

In this step, each cluster head negotiates with the cluster heads of neighboring clusters to select the optimal cooperative MIMO links, as more than one such links may exist between two neighboring clusters (see Fig. 3). In general, on one hand, the cooperative MIMO link with high energy efficiency should be selected to save transmission energy; on the other hand, a link with low residual energy should not be selected even if it has high energy efficiency, to avoid exhausting the link. We define E_f (l) as the energy efficiency of a cooperative MIMO link l, which is determined by Eq. (11). We use $E_i(l)$ to represent the residual energy of link l, which is set to the least residual energy of all nodes involved. To balance the effect of both factors, an empirical influence factor β ranging from 0 to 1 is introduced, which can be adjusted according to the type of application. Thus the weight of a cooperative MIMO link is defined as

$$\text{weight(i)} = \beta E_f(l) + (1 - \beta)E_i(l) \qquad (10)$$

$$E_f(l) = \frac{1}{E_{bt}} \qquad (11)$$

The link with the highest weight should be selected as the cooperative MIMO link for inter-cluster communications. The selection of cooperative MIMO links between two clusters can be done at either end of the link, since each cluster head is aware of the information of all neighboring clusters and their adjacent boundary nodes after the cluster discovery step. However, to avoid inconsistency, the cluster with the smaller ID among the two neighboring clusters is designated to select the cooperative link between them. After selecting the cooperative MIMO link, the cluster head with the smaller ID sends out a Cooperative MIMO Link Request (CMIMOLR) message, which is acknowledged by a Cooperative MIMO nodes.

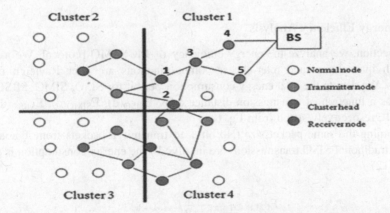

Fig. 3. Example of data collection WSN

4.2   Medium Access Control and Channel Assignment

In the proposed MCMIMO algorithm, there are four types of nodes: normal nodes, transmitter nodes, receiver nodes, and cluster heads. The normal nodes sense and collect data regarding the environment. The Cluster head (CHs) collect data from the normal nodes and use transmitter nodes to transmit their data to the receiver nodes of the neighboring cluster or send data directly to the base station. After, each CH creates a schedule in which time is divided to intervals called slots are assigned for intra cluster communication, data aggregation and communication inter cluster. This management method allows the sensors to remain in sleep state as long time as possible. In order to avoid collision and interference transmission between adjacent clusters and cooperative MIMO nodes, it will be better to assign different channels to each one of them. During the channel assignment and clustering algorithm stages, all communications are on the default channel and all nodes access the channel using a CSMA/CA. As shown in Figs. 3 and 4(a), (b), data forwarding from different nodes (node 1 and node 2) to BS depict the impact of multi channel technique on the throughput. If we use one channel frequency the traffic routing costs 6 timeslots, however when we use two channels frequency, then we have two parallel transmissions the traffic routing cost can reduce to 3 timeslots.

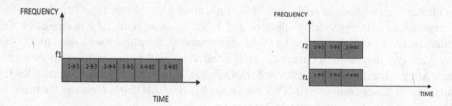

Fig. 4. Data collection using (a) one channel frequency and (b) two channel frequency

4.3   Energy Efficiency Analysis

In this section, we analyze the energy efficiency of MCMIMO protocol. We assume that both intra-cluster and inter-cluster communications are over Rayleigh fading channels. We denote the total energy consumption per bit for SISO, SIMO, MISO and MIMO as a function of transmission distance d by $E_{SISO}(d)$, $E_{SIMO}(d)$, $E_{MISO}(d)$ and $E_{MIMO}(d)$, respectively stated from Eq. (8).

Assuming the same packet size (N_B bits), to transmit T packets from T nodes to CH, the traditional SISO transmissions are involved. The energy consumption is given by Eq. (12)

$$E_{CM \text{ to } CH} = \frac{N_b T}{b_{opt} B} E_{siso}(\bar{d}_{ch})$$

(12)

Cluster head will aggregate the packets and send the aggregated packet to all the transmitter (N_R) nodes, the SIMO transmissions are involved. The energy consumption to transmit the packets from CH to transmitter nodes can be described by Eq. (13)

$$E_{CH\ to\ N_T} = \frac{N_b}{b_{opt}B} E_{simo}(\bar{d}_{ch}) \tag{13}$$

After, the N_T transmitter nodes transmit their data packet to N_R the receiver nodes of the neighboring cluster or send data directly to the base station where the inter-cluster cooperative MIMO transmission is involved. The energy consumption for cluster to cluster communication is given by Eq. (14)

$$E_{N_T\ to\ N_R} = N_b E_{mimo}(\bar{d}_{cc}) \tag{14}$$

Where, $E_{mimo}(\bar{d}_{cc})$ can be stated from Eq. (8) as follow:

$$E_{mimo}(\bar{d}_{cc}) = \frac{2}{3}(1+\alpha)\left(\frac{\bar{P}_b}{4}\right)^{\frac{-1}{M_t}} \frac{2^{b_{opt}}-1}{b_{opt}^{\frac{1}{M_t}+1}} M_t N_0 \frac{(4\pi)^2}{G_r G_t \lambda^2} M_l N_f \sum_{i=1}^{N_T} \bar{d}_{cc}^k + \frac{P_C}{Bb} \tag{15}$$

The energy consumption from the last hop's transmitter nodes to base station is a special condition of from Eq. (15) where $N_R = 1$.

And then, From N_R receivers cooperative MIMO nodes to their corresponding cluster head is assured through MISO transmission and the energy consumption is given by

$$E_{N_R\ to\ CH} = \frac{N_b N_R}{b_{opt}B} E_{miso}(\bar{d}_{ch}) \tag{16}$$

The total energy consumption multi-hop communication model can be described as following:

$$E_{total} = E_{CM\ to\ CH} + (hops + 1).E_{CH\ to\ N_T} + (hops + 1).E_{N_T\ to\ N_R} + hops.E_{N_R\ to\ CH} \tag{17}$$

where hops is the number of intermediate clusters, $\bar{d}_{ch}$ denotes the expected distance between a cluster head and its cluster members that refer to intra cluster communication, and $\bar{d}_{cc}$ denotes the expected distance between the cooperative MIMO transmitters and receivers that refer to inter cluster communication.

5   Simulation Results

5.1   Simulation Environment

To illustrate the value added by our proposed MCMIMO algorithm on network behavior, we evaluated the MCMIMO performances in terms of energy of consumption per bit, stability, lifetime, amount of data sent to the BS and network throughput in three different scenarios (SISO, MISO and MIMO). The stability period and the lifetime are defined respectively according to the following metrics: FND (first node dies) and HND (half node dies). Simulation parameters used for these evaluations are listed in Table 2, where 100 sensor nodes are distributed randomly in a square region of 100×100 m^2, loss of the communication between each pair of nodes is distributed randomly from 2 to 4, each node have random initial energy within the interval [0.5, 1] Joule. The base station is located at the center of the network and in order to illustrate the effect of distance on energy consumption the base station moves in the horizontal direction. The development environment is NS 2.

Table 2. Simulation parameters.

Parameter	Value
σ^2	$N_0/2 = -174$ dBm/Hz
k	$2 \sim 4$
Nodes number (N)	100
Network area	100 m $\times$ 100 m
Round Number	3500
Packet length (N_B)	4000 bit
$G_t G_r$	5 dBi
fc	2.5 GHz
B	10 kHz
N_f	10 dB
M_l	40 dB
η	0.35
$\bar{P}_b$	10^{-3}
P_{ct}	0.0844263 W
P_{cr}	0.112497827 W
N_0	-171 dBm/Hz
λ	0.12 m
ξ	$3 \cdot \dfrac{\sqrt{M}-1}{\sqrt{M}+1}$, $M = 2^b$

5.2   Performance Evaluation Discussion

Firstly, we compare the energy consumption of MCMIMO using different multi-hop transmission MIMO, MISO and SISO with variable data rate according to Table 1. Figure 5 shows the graphs of energy consumption per bit with respect to the distance from the base station. Initially, the base station is placed at the center of the network. Then, the base station is moved away from the center in the horizontal direction. As shown in Fig. 5, the energy consumption of SISO has more advantage in energy saving when the transmission distance is less than 10 m, but the MIMO has more advantage in energy-saving when the distance is more than 10 m, this is because, for small distances circuit block power consumption dominates and for large distances power amplifiers dominates. Further, SISO is still better than MISO until the traversed distance equal

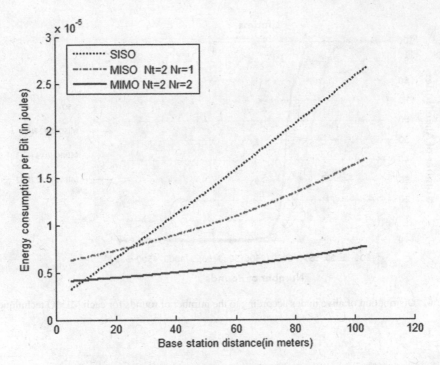

Fig. 5. Energy consumption per bit for MIMO, MISO, SISO networks according to distance

23 m, for distance exceeding this value, the standard deviation of SISO is also higher as compared to the other techniques. MIMO performs better than MISO for all the cases. Then the MCMIMO with MIMO technique and adapted bit rate is more energy efficient routing for large communication distance.

Secondly, we consider a fixe base station initially placed at position (50, 50) and we evaluate our proposed algorithm in terms of stability, lifetime and amount of data sent to the BS. Figures 6 and 7 show the simulation results.

From Figs. 6 and 7, we can see that MIMO 2x2 technique exceeds the other techniques in terms of stability, lifetime and amount of data sent to the BS. Furthermore, the MIMO 2x2 technique has a stability period (FND) considerably larger compared to other algorithms which allows the network to operate without fault for a very long time. Table 3 summarizes the simulation results of this scenario. From the simulation results, 2x2 MIMO is considered as an energy efficient routing technique. In fact the stability period is increased approximately by 82 %, 39 % and 7 % while the network lifetime is increased nearly 25 %, 20 % and 8 % compared with those obtained by SISO, MISO and MIMO 3x3 techniques respectively.

Thirdly, we study the impact of the number of available channels on the system throughput. As shown in Fig. 8, in which the BS is located at the center of the network. We can see that, the network throughput is higher if we assigned more channel resources, which leads to reduce collision between nodes; However, the throughput stops increasing if more than 9 channels are provisioned, as interference no longer exists after that.

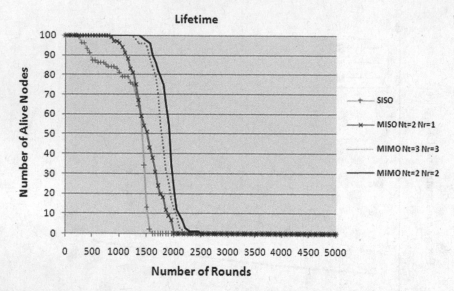

Fig. 6. Distribution of alive nodes according to the number of rounds for each MIMO technique.

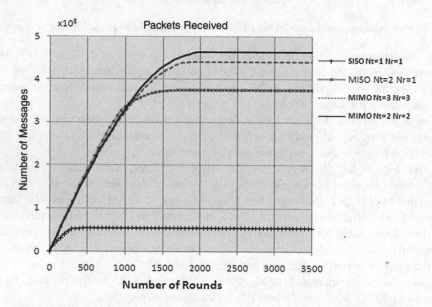

Fig. 7. Received packets by the BS using different transmission MIMO technique.

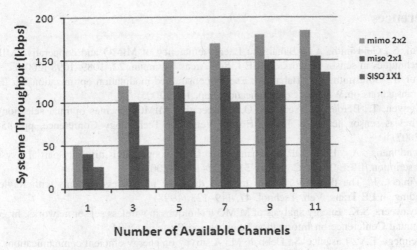

Fig. 8. System throughput vs. number of available channels

Table 3. Simulation results

Protocol	FND	HND	Paquets number
SISO	243	1422	5.4×10^7
MISO 2X1	824	1531	3.8×10^8
MIMO 3X3	1247	1764	4.4×10^8
MIMO 2X2	1350	1908	4.6×10^8

6 Conclusion

In this paper, a multi-channel energy efficient cooperative MIMO routing protocol for cluster based WSNs, called MCMIMO in which, sensor nodes are organized into clusters such that intra-cluster messages are transmitted over short-range SISO links, while inter cluster messages are transmitted over long-range energy-efficient cooperative MIMO links. To reduce energy consumption and prolong the network lifetime, an adaptive cooperative nodes selection strategy is also designed. After that we investigate the use of multiple transmitters and multiple receivers in virtual MIMO. We consider the case of variable data rate. Further, we investigate the impact of distance on the choice of MIMO, MISO and SISO, We demonstrate that in large range applications, by optimizing the constellation size MIMO systems may outperform MISO and SISO systems. Also the MIMO 2X2 technique is more suitable for any application WSN since it exceeds the other techniques tested in terms of stability, lifetime and the number of packets sent to the BS. Finally, multiple channels is exploited to enhance network throughput by avoiding collision between nodes. MCMIMO is designed for stationary WSNs, in future works, our algorithm can be extended to handle the mobile wireless sensor networks under the platform NS2.

References

1. Cui, S., Goldsmith, A.J., Bahai, A.: Energy efficiency of MIMO and cooperative MIMO techniques in sensor networks. IEEE J. Sel. Areas Commun. **22**, 1089–1098 (2004)
2. Cui, S., Goldsmith, A.J., Bahai, A.: Energy-constrained modulation optimization. In: IEEE Transactions on Wireless Communications, pp. 1–7 (2005)
3. Nguyen, T., Berder, O., Sentieys, O.: Cooperative MIMO schemes optimal selection for wireless sensor networks. In: IEEE 65th Vehicular Technology Conference, pp. 85–89 (2007)
4. Sendonaris, A., Erkip, E., Aazhang, B.: User cooperation diversity-part I: system description. IEEE Trans. Commun. **51**, 1927–1938 (2003)
5. Winters, J.: The diversity gain of transmit diversity in wireless systems with Rayleigh fading. IEEE Trans. Veh. Technol. **47**, 119–123 (1998)
6. Jayaweera, S.K.: Energy analysis of MIMO techniques in wireless sensor networks. In: 38th Annual Conference on Information Sciences and Systems (2004)
7. Belmega, E.V., Lasaulce, S., Debbah, M.: A survey on energy-efficient communications. In: International Symposium on Personal, Indoor and Mobile Radio Communications Workshops, Turkey, pp. 289–294 (2010)
8. Dawei, G., Miao, Z., Yuanyuan, Y.: A multi-channel cooperative MIMO MAC protocol for clustered wireless sensor networks. J. Parallel Distrib. Comput. **74**, 3098–3114 (2014)
9. Sajid, H., Anwarul, A., Jong, H.P.: Energy efficient virtual MIMO communication for wireless sensor networks. J. Telecommun. Syst. **42**, 139–149 (2009)
10. Chaibrassou, A., Mouhsen, A.: MGI-LEACH: multi group LEACH improved an efficient routing algorithm for wireless sensor networks. J. Emerg. Technol. Web Intell. **6**, 40–44 (2014)
11. Chaibrassou, A., Mouhsen, A., Lagrat, I.: Efficient and distributed clustering scheme with mobile sink for heterogeneous multi level wireless sensor networks. J. Theor. Appl. Inf. Technol. **63**, 597–604 (2014)

Counting in Practical Anonymous Dynamic Networks is Polynomial

Maitri Chakraborty[1], Alessia Milani[2], and Miguel A. Mosteiro[3(✉)]

[1] Kean University, Union, NJ, USA
chakrabm@kean.edu
[2] LABRI, University of Bordeaux, INP, Talence, France
milani@labri.fr
[3] Pace University, New York, NY, USA
mmosteiro@pace.edu

1 Introduction

Anonymous Dynamic Networks is a harsh computational environment due to changing topology and lack of identifiers. Topology changes are well motivated by mobility and unreliable communication environments of present networks. With respect to node identifiers, in future massive networks it may be necessary or at least convenient to avoid them to facilitate mass production.

Computing the size of the network, a problem known as Counting, is a fundamental problem in distributed computing because the network size is used to decide termination of protocols. An algorithm is said to solve the *Counting* problem if whenever it is executed in a Dynamic Network comprising n nodes, all nodes eventually terminate and output n.

Previous works on Counting in Anonymous Dynamic Networks do not provide enough guarantees to be used in practice. Indeed, they either compute only an upper bound on the network size that may be as bad as exponential [9], or guarantee only double-exponential running time [3], or do not terminate, or guarantee only eventual termination without running-time guarantees [4]. Faster experimental protocols do not guarantee the correct count [5].

Recently, we presented in [10] the first Counting protocol that computes the exact count with exponential running-time guarantees. The protocol, called INCREMENTAL COUNTING, requires the presence of one leader node and knowledge of any upper bound Δ on the maximum number of neighbors that any node will ever have. INCREMENTAL COUNTING achieves a speedup over its predecessors by trying candidate sizes incrementally.

In the present work, we complement the latter theoretical study evaluating the performance of such protocol over a variety of network topologies that may appear in practice, including extremal cases such as trees, paths, and continuously changing topologies. We also tested networks that temporarily are not connected. Our simulations showed that the protocol is polynomial for all the

Partially supported by the Programme IdEx Bordeaux - CPU (ANR-10-IDEX-03-02), the ANR project DISPLEXITY (ANR-11-BS02-014), and Kean Univ. RTR2016.

P.A. Abdulla and C. Delporte-Gallet (Eds.): NETYS 2016, LNCS 9944, pp. 131–136, 2016.
DOI: 10.1007/978-3-319-46140-3_10

inputs tested, paving the way to use it in practical applications where topology changes are predictable. To the best of our knowledge, this is the first experimental study that shows the possibility of computing the exact count in polynomial time in a variety of Anonymous Dynamic Networks that are worse than expected in practice.

2   The Anonymous Dynamic Network Model

We consider a network composed by a set of n nodes. Nodes have no identifiers and are indistinguishable, except for one node ℓ that is called the *leader*. If a given pair of nodes is able to communicate directly, we say that there is a *link* among them, and we say that they are *neighbors*. The communication proceeds in synchronous *rounds* through broadcast in symmetric links. That is, at each round, a node i broadcasts a message to its neighbors and simultaneously receives the messages broadcast in the same round by all its neighbors. Then, each node makes some local computation (if any). To evaluate performance, we count the number of communication rounds to complete the computation.

We assume that there is a value $\Delta \leq n - 1$ that may be used by the protocol such that, for any round r and any node i, i has at most Δ neighbors at round r. The set of links may change from one round to another. In each round a new set of links may be chosen adversarially, as long as the network is connected. Our simulations showed that if a new set of links is chosen uniformly at random for each round, the dissemination of information towards the leader is indeed faster than if changes are less frequent. Hence, for our simulations we generalize the connectivity model assumed in [3,9,10] as follows. We say that the network is T-*stable* if, after a topology change, the set of links does not change for at least T rounds. In contrast, in T-interval connected networks [8] it is assumed that for *any* sequence of T rounds, there is a stable set of links spanning all nodes.

For connected networks both models are the same for $T = 1$, but for $T > 1$ on tree topologies (most of our inputs), T-stable networks restrict less the adversary than T-interval connectivity networks. In this work, we study T-stable networks and we evaluate a range of values for T, from $T = 1$ up to a static network.

3   Incremental Counting Protocol Simulator

The INCREMENTAL COUNTING protocol includes algorithms for the leader and non-leader nodes. Both algorithms are composed by a sequence of synchronous iterations. In each iteration the candidate size is incremented and checked to decide whether it is correct or not. Each of the iterations is divided in three phases: collection, verification, and notification. INCREMENTAL COUNTING runs for a fixed number of rounds for each phase. Given that the upper bound on the number of rounds needed for each phase proved in [10] is exponential, a simulation of INCREMENTAL COUNTING as in [10] would yield exponential time. The purpose of our simulations in the present work is to evaluate whether such upper bound is loose in practice. So, rather than running each phase for a fixed number of communication rounds, we do it until a condition suited for each phase is violated, and we count the number of communication rounds to complete the computation. Consequently, our simulator is necessarily centralized to check such condition, but again, these changes are introduced to obtain experimentally a tighter upper bound on practical inputs, rather than to provide a practical implementation of INCREMENTAL COUNTING. A practical distributed INCREMENTAL COUNTING protocol must be implemented as in [10], that is, executing each phase for a fixed number of rounds, but our simulations provide a polynomial bound on that number. In the following paragraphs, we provide further details on the changes applied to each phase of INCREMENTAL COUNTING, how each phase is implemented in our simulator, and the input networks used. Refer to the full version of this paper in [2] for further details.

During the collection phase of INCREMENTAL COUNTING non-leader nodes are initially assigned a unit of energy, which is later disseminated towards the leader using a gossip-based approach [1,6,7]. That is, each non-leader node repeatedly shares a fraction of its energy with each neighbor. Given that the leader keeps all the energy received, it eventually collects most of the energy in the system. In the original INCREMENTAL COUNTING protocol, for each candidate size k, the number of rounds for sharing energy is fixed to a function $\tau(k)$ that has not be proven to be sub-exponential in the worst case. Thus, to evaluate whether in practice a polynomial number of rounds is enough, in our simulations we iterate the energy transfer until the conditions needed for the verification phase are met. That is, until the leader has collected an amount of energy such that, if its guess is correct, non-leader nodes have transferred almost all their energy, i.e. all non-leader nodes have residual energy smaller than or equal to $1/k^{1.01}$. To simulate the exchange in the collection phase, the energy sharing process is simulated by a multiplication of the vector of energies by a matrix of fractions shared as customary in gossip-based protocols analysis [1,6,7].

During the verification phase of INCREMENTAL COUNTING non-leader nodes disseminate towards the leader the value of the maximum energy held by any non-leader node. If the residual energy of some node is greater than the above threshold, the current candidate size is deemed incorrect by the leader. To guarantee that the leader receives from all nodes, all non-leader nodes iteratively broadcast and update the maximum energy heard, starting from their own. If the candidate size was found to be correct in the verification phase, a halting message is broadcast throughout the network in the notification phase. To synchronize the computation, the notification phase of INCREMENTAL COUNTING runs for a fixed number of rounds, independently of whether the current candidate size is correct or not. The verification and notification phases do not tolerate disconnection of the network, since then some nodes might not be heard or have received by the end of the loop. To evaluate disconnected topologies, in our simulations we continue the iteration of these phases until the leader has received from all nodes (verification) or all nodes receive from the leader (notification).

We have produced different topologies that may appear in practice for all values of $n \in [3, 75]$, and $T \in \{1, 10, 20, 40, 80, 160, 320, 640, 1280, \infty\}$, where $T = \infty$

corresponds to a static network. We evaluate random tree topologies rooted at the leader node. To produce our random rooted unlabeled trees we used the algorithm RANRUT [11], which guarantees uniform distribution on the equivalence classes defined by isomorphisms. These trees may have maximum degree larger than Δ. If that is the case we prune the tree moving subtrees downwards until all nodes have at most Δ neighbors. This procedure may increase the longest path to the leader, which may increase the running time of INCREMENTAL COUNTING. Thus, with respect to a uniform distribution on rooted unlabeled trees of maximum degree Δ, our input distribution is biased "against" INCREMENTAL COUNTING providing stronger guarantees.

As extremal cases of a tree topology, we also evaluated a star rooted at the leader node and a path where the leader is the end point. We also consider Erdos-Renyi random graphs, for which we additionally parameterize the probability p that any given pair of nodes are neighbors. Although graphs have better conductance than the trees underlying them, and consequently graphs achieve convergence faster for gossip-based protocols [12], we evaluate the latter inputs for consistency with previous works.

4   Discussion

All our results where computed as the average over 20 executions of the protocol. For all the topologies and parameter combinations evaluated, INCREMENTAL

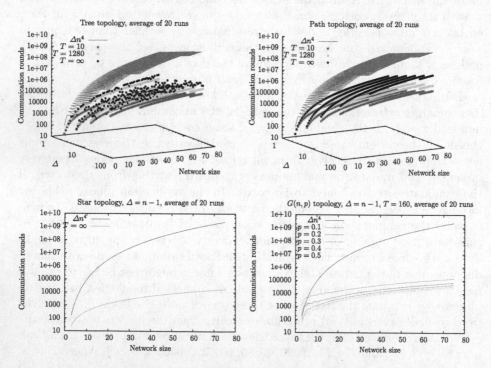

Fig. 1. INCREMENTAL COUNTING time performance compared with a polynomial function.

COUNTING has proved to be polynomial. Consider for instance Fig. 1, where we plot the number of rounds to complete the computation (log scale) as a function of the network size, for various values of degree upper bound Δ, interval of stability T, and probability p of being connected in the random graph. We also plot the function Δn^4 to contrast the growth of such polynomial function with the results obtained. It can be seen that all our results indicate a rate of growth asymptotically smaller than Δn^4. (The upper bound could be tightened but we choose a loose one for clarity.) For small network sizes, random graphs introduce additional delays due to disconnection, but as the network scales the dynamic topology overcomes the effect of disconnections. As a byproduct, our simulations also provided insight on the impact of network dynamics in the dissemination of information by gossip-based protocols. Indeed, our results showed that on average network changes speed-up convergence. That is, as long as the effect is uniform throughout the network, highly dynamic topologies help rather than being a challenge as in a worst-case theoretical analysis. Indeed, our simulations showed the static path to have the worse time performance among all inputs tested. Other observations, such as the impact of Δ or the impact of stability (T) for each topology, are detailed in the full version of this paper in [2].

References

1. Almeida, P.S., Baquero, C., Farach-Colton, M., Jesus, P., Mosteiro, M.A.: Fault-tolerant aggregation: flow-updating meets mass-distribution. In: Fernàndez Anta, A., Lipari, G., Roy, M. (eds.) OPODIS 2011. LNCS, vol. 7109, pp. 513–527. Springer, Heidelberg (2011)
2. Chakraborty, M., Milani, A., Mosteiro, M.A.: Counting in practical anonymous dynamic networks is polynomial. CoRR abs/1603.05459 (2016). http://arxiv.org/abs/1603.05459
3. Di Luna, G.A., Baldoni, R., Bonomi, S., Chatzigiannakis, I.: Conscious and unconscious counting on anonymous dynamic networks. In: Chatterjee, M., Cao, J., Kothapalli, K., Rajsbaum, S. (eds.) ICDCN 2014. LNCS, vol. 8314, pp. 257–271. Springer, Heidelberg (2014)
4. Di Luna, G.A., Baldoni, R., Bonomi, S., Chatzigiannakis, I.: Counting in anonymous dynamic networks under worst-case adversary. In: ICDCS 2014, pp. 338–347. IEEE (2014)
5. Di Luna, G.A., Bonomi, S., Chatzigiannakis, I., Baldoni, R.: Counting in anonymous dynamic networks: an experimental perspective. In: Flocchini, P., Gao, J., Kranakis, E., der Heide, F.M. (eds.) ALGOSENSORS 2013. LNCS, vol. 8243, pp. 139–154. Springer, Heidelberg (2014)
6. Fernández Anta, A., Mosteiro, M.A., Thraves, C.: An early-stopping protocol for computing aggregate functions in sensor networks. J. Parallel Distrib. Comput. 73(2), 111–121 (2013)
7. Kempe, D., Dobra, A., Gehrke, J.: Gossip-based computation of aggregate information. In: FOCS 2003, pp. 482–491. IEEE (2003)
8. Kuhn, F., Lynch, N., Oshman, R.: Distributed computation in dynamic networks. In: STOC 2010, pp. 513–522. ACM (2010)

9. Michail, O., Chatzigiannakis, I., Spirakis, P.G.: Naming and counting in anonymous unknown dynamic networks. In: Higashino, T., Katayama, Y., Masuzawa, T., Potop-Butucaru, M., Yamashita, M. (eds.) SSS 2013. LNCS, vol. 8255, pp. 281–295. Springer, Heidelberg (2013)

10. Milani, A., Mosteiro, M.A.: A faster counting protocol for anonymous dynamic networks. In: OPODIS 2015, LIPIcs (2015, to appear)

11. Nijenhuis, A., Wilf, H.S.: Combinatorial Algorithms for Computers and Calculators, 2nd edn. Academic Press, Cambridge (1978)

12. Sinclair, A., Jerrum, M.: Approximate counting, uniform generation and rapidly mixing Markov chains. Inf. Comput. **82**(1), 93–133 (1989)

Internet Computing: Using Reputation to Select Workers from a Pool

Evgenia Christoforou[1,2]([✉]), Antonio Fernández Anta[1], Chryssis Georgiou[3], and Miguel A. Mosteiro[4]

[1] IMDEA Networks Institute, Madrid, Spain
evgenia.christoforou@imdea.org
[2] Universidad Carlos III de Madrid, Madrid, Spain
[3] University of Cyprus, Nicosia, Cyprus
[4] Pace University, New York, NY, USA
mmosteiro@pace.edu

Abstract. The assignment and execution of tasks over the Internet is an inexpensive solution in contrast with supercomputers. We consider an Internet-based Master-Worker task computing approach, such as SETI@home. A master process sends tasks, across the Internet, to worker processors. Workers execute, and report back a result. Unfortunately, the disadvantage of this approach is the unreliable nature of the worker processes. Through different studies, workers have been categorized as either malicious (always report an incorrect result), altruistic (always report a correct result), or rational (report whatever result maximizes their benefit). We develop a reputation-based mechanism that guarantees that, eventually, the master will always be receiving the correct task result. We model the behavior of the rational workers through reinforcement learning, and we present three different reputation types to choose, for each computational round, the most reputable from a pool of workers. As workers are not always available, we enhance our reputation scheme to select the most responsive workers. We prove sufficient conditions for eventual correctness under the different reputation types. Our analysis is complemented by simulations exploring various scenarios. Our simulation results expose interesting trade-offs among the different reputation types, workers availability, and cost.

Keywords: Volunteer computing · Reinforcement learning · Reputation · Worker reliability · Task computing · Worker unresponsiveness · Pool of workers

1 Introduction

Internet-based computing has emerged as an inexpensive alternative for scientific high-performance computations. The most popular form of Internet-based computing is volunteer computing, where computing resources are volunteered by the public to help solve (mainly) scientific problems. BOINC [4] is a popular platform where volunteer computing projects run, such as SETI@home [20].

© Springer International Publishing AG 2016
P.A. Abdulla and C. Delporte-Gallet (Eds.): NETYS 2016, LNCS 9944, pp. 137–153, 2016.
DOI: 10.1007/978-3-319-46140-3_11

Profit-seeking computation platforms, such as Amazon's Mechanical Turk [3], have also become popular. One of the main challenges for further exploiting the promise of such platforms is the untrustworthiness of the participating entities [4, 5, 16, 18].

In this work we focus on Internet-based master-worker task computing, where a master process sends tasks, across the Internet, to worker processes to compute and return the result. Workers, however, might report incorrect results. Following [9, 11], we consider three types of worker. Malicious[1] workers that always report an incorrect result, altruistic workers that always report a correct result, and rational workers that report a result driven by their self-interest. In addition, a worker (regardless of its type) might be unavailable (e.g., be disconnected, be busy performing other tasks, etc.). Our main contribution is a computing system where the master eventually obtains always the correct task result despite the above shortcomings. Our mechanism is novel in two fronts: (i) it leverages the possibility of changing workers over time, given that the number of workers willing to participate is larger than the number of workers needed, and (ii) it is resilient to some workers being unavailable from time to time.

Worker unreliability in master-worker computing has been studied from both a classical Distributing Computing approach and a Game Theoretic one. The first treats workers as malicious or altruistic. Tasks are redundantly allocated to different workers, and voting protocols that tolerate malicious workers have been designed (e.g., [13, 19, 21]). The Game Theoretic approach views the workers as rational [1, 15, 22], who follow the strategy that would maximize their benefit. In the latter approach, incentive-based mechanisms have been developed (e.g., [14, 27]) that induce workers to act correctly.

Other works (e.g., [9, 11]) have considered the co-existence of all three types of worker. In [9], a "one-shot" interaction between master and workers was implemented. In that work, the master assigns tasks to workers without using knowledge of past interactions (e.g., on the behavior of the workers). In [11], a mechanism was designed taking advantage of the repeated interaction (rounds) of the master with the workers. The mechanism employs reinforcement learning [25] both for the master and for the workers. In each round, the master assigns a task to the same set of workers (which are assumed to be always available). The master may audit (with a cost) the responses of the workers and a reward-punishment scheme is employed. Depending on the answers, the master adjusts its probability of auditing. Rational workers cheat (i.e., respond with an incorrect result to avoid the cost of computing) with some probability, which over the rounds increases or decreases depending on the incentive received (reward or punishment). Rational workers have an aspiration level [8] which determines whether a received payoff was satisfactory or not. To cope with malicious workers (whose behavior is not affected by the above mentioned learning scheme) a reputation scheme [17] was additionally employed. The main objective is to "quickly"

---

[1] We call these workers malicious for compliance with Volunteer Computing [4] literature. This must not be confused with Byzantine malice assumed in classical distributed computing.

reach a round in the computation after which the master always receives the correct task result, with minimal auditing.

Unlike assumed in [11] (and most previous literature), in practice workers are not always available. For instance, Heien et al. [16] have found that in BOINC [4] only around 5 % of the workers are available more than 80 % of the time, and that half of the workers are available less than 40 % of the time. In this work, we extend the work in [11] to cope with worker unavailability.

A feature that has not been leveraged in [11] and previous works is the scale of Internet-based master-worker task computing systems. For example, in BOINC [7] active workers are around a few hundred thousand. In such a large system, replicating the task and sending it to all workers is neither feasible nor practical. On the other hand, randomly selecting a small number of workers to send the task does not guarantee correctness with minimum auditing. For instance, consider a pool of workers where the malicious outnumber those needed for the computation. Then, there is a positive probability that only malicious workers are selected and the master would have to audit always to obtain the correct result. All previous works assume the existence of a fixed/predefined set of workers that the master always contacts. In this work we consider the existence of a pool of N workers out of which the master chooses $n < N$.

Our Contributions

- We present a mechanism (in Sect. 3) where the master chooses the most reputable workers for each round of computation, allowing the system to eventually converge to a state where the correct result will be always obtained, with minimal auditing. Our mechanism does not require workers to be available all the time. To cope with the unavailability of the workers, we introduce a *responsiveness reputation* that conveys the percentage of task assignments to which the worker replies with an answer. The responsiveness reputation is combined with a *truthfulness reputation* that conveys the reliability of the worker. We enrich our study considering three types of truthfulness reputation. Namely, BOINC reputation (inspired in the "adaptive replication" of BOINC), EXPONENTIAL reputation (that we presented in [11]), and LINEAR reputation (inspired on the work of Sonnek et al. [24]).
- We also show formally (in Sect. 4) negative and positive results regarding the feasibility of achieving correctness in the long run in the absence of rational workers. Specifically, we show configurations (worker types, availability, etc.) of the pool of workers such that correctness cannot be achieved unless the master always audits, and the existence of configurations such that eventually correctness is achieved forever with minimal auditing.
- We evaluate experimentally (in Sect. 5) our mechanism with extensive simulations under various conditions. Our simulations complement the analysis taking into account scenarios where rational workers exist. The different reputation types are compared showing trade-offs between reliability and cost.

2   Model

Master-Worker Framework. We consider a master and a pool (set) of workers $\mathcal{N}$, where $|\mathcal{N}| = N$. The computation is broken into *rounds* $r = 1, 2, \ldots$. In each round r, the master selects a set W^r of $n < N$ workers, and sends them a task. The workers in W^r are supposed to compute the task and return the result, but may not do so (e.g., unavailable computing other task). The master, after waiting for a fixed time t, proceeds with the received replies. Based on those replies, the master must decide which answer to take as the correct result for this round. The master employs a reputation mechanism put in place to choose the n most reputable workers in every round. We assume that tasks have a unique solution; although such limitation reduces the scope of application of the presented mechanism [26], there are plenty of computations where the correct solution is unique: e.g., any mathematical function.

Worker Unavailability. In Internet-based master-worker computations, and especially in volunteering computing, workers are not always available to participate in a computation [16] (e.g., they are off-line for a particular period of time). We assume that each worker's availability is stochastic and independent of other workers. Formally, we let $d_i > 0$ be the probability that the master receives the reply from worker i within time t (provided that the worker was chosen by the master to participate in the computation for the given round r, i.e., $i \in W^r$). In other words, this is the probability that the worker is available to compute the task assigned.

Worker Types. We consider three types of workers: *rational, altruistic,* and *malicious.* Rational workers are selfish in a game-theoretic sense and their aim is to maximize their utility (benefit). In the context of this paper, a worker is *honest* in a round, when it truthfully computes and returns the correct result, and it *cheats* when it returns some incorrect value. Altruistic and malicious workers have a predefined behavior: to always be honest and cheat respectively. Instead, a rational worker decides to be honest or cheat depending on which strategy maximizes its utility. We denote by $p_{Ci}(r)$ the probability of a rational worker i cheating in round r, provided that $i \in W^r$. The worker adjusts this probability over the course of the multiround computation using a reinforcement learning approach. The master is not aware of each worker type, neither of the distribution over types. That is, our mechanism does not rely on any statistical information.

While workers make their decision individually and with no coordination, following [13, 21], we assume that all the workers that cheat in a round return the same incorrect value. This yields a worst case scenario for the master to obtain the correct result using a voting mechanism. This assumption subsumes models where cheaters do not necessarily return the same answer, and it can be seen as a weak form of collusion.

Auditing, Payoffs, Rewards and Aspiration. When necessary, the master employs *auditing* and *reward/punish* schemes to induce the rational workers to be honest. In each round, the master may decide to audit the response of the workers, at a cost. In this work, auditing means that the master computes the task by itself, and checks which workers have been honest. We denote by $p_{\mathcal{A}}(r)$ the probability of the master auditing the responses of the workers in round r. The master can change this auditing probability over the course of the computation, but restricted to a minimum value $p_{\mathcal{A}}^{min} > 0$. When the master audits, it can accurately reward and punish workers. When the master does not audit, it rewards only those in the weighted majority (see below) of the replies received and punishes no one.

We consider three worker payoff parameters: (a) $WP_{\mathcal{C}}$: worker's punishment for being caught cheating, (b) $WC_{\mathcal{T}}$: worker's cost for computing a task, and (c) $WB_{\mathcal{Y}}$: worker's benefit (typically payment) from the master's reward. As in [8], we also assume that a worker i has an *aspiration* a_i, which is the minimum benefit that worker i expects to obtain in a round. We assume that the master has the freedom of choosing $WB_{\mathcal{Y}}$ and $WP_{\mathcal{C}}$ with the goal of satisfying *eventual correctness*, defined next. E.g., in order to motivate the worker to participate in the computation, the master ensures that $WB_{\mathcal{Y}} - WC_{\mathcal{T}} \geq a_i$; in other words, the worker has the potential of its aspiration to be covered even if it computes the task.

Eventual Correctness. The goal of the master is to eventually obtain a reliable computational platform: After some finite number of rounds, the system must guarantee that the master obtains the correct task results in every round with probability 1 and audits with probability $p_{\mathcal{A}}^{min}$. We call such property *eventual correctness*. Observe that eventual correctness implies that eventually the master receives at least one (correct) reply in every round.

Reputation. The reputation of each worker is measured and maintained by the master. Reputation is used by the master to cope with the uncertainty about the workers' truthfulness and availability. In fact, the workers are unaware that a reputation scheme is in place, and their interaction with the master does not reveal any information about reputation; i.e., the payoffs do not depend on a worker's reputation. The master wants to assign tasks to workers that are reliable, that is, workers that are both responsive *and* truthful. Hence, we consider the worker's reputation as the product of two factors: responsiveness reputation and truthfulness reputation. Thus, the malicious workers will obtain a low reputation fast due to their low truthfulness reputation, and also the workers that are generally unavailable will get a low reputation due to their low responsiveness reputation. Consequently, these workers will stop being chosen by the master.

More formally, we define the reputation of a worker i as $\rho_i = \rho_{rs_i} \cdot \rho_{tr_i}$, where ρ_{rs_i} represents the responsiveness reputation and ρ_{tr_i} the truthfulness reputation of worker i. We also define the reputation of a set of workers $Y \subseteq W$ as the aggregated reputation of all workers in Y. That is, $\rho_Y(r) = \sum_{i \in Y} \rho_i(r)$.

In this work, we consider three truthfulness reputation types: LINEAR, EXPONENTIAL, and BOINC. In the LINEAR reputation type (introduced in [24]) the reputation changes at a linear rate. The EXPONENTIAL reputation type (introduced in [11]) is "unforgiving", in the sense that the reputation of a worker caught cheating will never increase. The reputation of a worker in this type changes at an exponential rate. The BOINC reputation type is inspired by BOINC [6]. In the

BOINC system this reputation method is used to avoid redundancy if a worker is considered honest[2]. For the responsiveness reputation we use the LINEAR reputation, adjusted for responses. For the worker's availability it is natural to use a "forgiving" reputation, especially when considering volunteer computing. For the detailed description of the reputation types we introduce some necessary notation as follows.

$select_i(r)$: the number of rounds the master selected worker i up to round r.
$reply\_select_i(r)$: the number of rounds up to round r in which worker i was selected and the master received a reply from i.
$audit\_reply\_select_i(r)$: the number of rounds up to round r where the master selected worker i, received its reply and audited.
$correct\_audit_i(r)$: the number of rounds up to round r where the master selected worker i, received its reply, audited and i was truthful.
$streak_i(r)$: the number of rounds $\leq r$ in which worker i was selected, audited, and replied correctly after the latest round in which it was selected, audited, and caught cheating.

Then, the reputation types we consider are as follows.

Responsiveness reputation: $\rho_{rs_i}(r) = \frac{reply\_select_i(r)+1}{select_i(r)+1}$.
Truthfulness reputation:

> LINEAR: $\rho_{tr_i}(r) = \dfrac{correct\_audit_i(r) + 1}{audit\_reply\_select_i(r) + 1}$.
> EXPONENTIAL: $\rho_{tr_i}(r) = \varepsilon^{audit\_reply\_select_i(r)-correct\_audit_i(r)}$, where $\varepsilon \in (0,1)$.
> BOINC: $\rho_{tr}(r) = \begin{cases} 0, & \text{if } streak(r) < 10. \\ 1 - \frac{1}{streak(r)}, & \text{otherwise.} \end{cases}$

All workers are assumed to have the same initial reputation before the master interacts with them. The goal of the above definitions is for workers who are responsive *and* truthful to eventually have high reputation, whereas workers who are not responsive *or* not truthful, to eventually have low reputation.

3   Reputation-Based Mechanism

We now present our reputation-based mechanism. The mechanism is composed by an algorithm run by the master and an algorithm run by each worker.

Master's Algorithm. The algorithm followed by the master, Algorithm 1, begins by choosing the initial probability of auditing and the initial reputation (same for all workers). The initial probability of auditing will be set according to

---

[2] In BOINC, honesty means that the worker's task result agrees with the majority, while in our work this decision is well-founded, since the master audits.

the information the master has about the environment (e.g., workers' initial p_C). For example, if it has no information about the environment, a natural approach would be to initially set $p_A = 0.5$ or $p_A = 1$ (as a more conservative approach). The master also chooses the truthfulness reputation type to use.

At the beginning of each round, the master chooses the n most reputable workers out of the total N workers (breaking ties uniformly at random) and sends them a task T. In the first round, since workers have the same reputation, the choice is uniformly at random. Then, after waiting t time to receive the replies from the selected workers, the master proceeds with the mechanism. The master updates the responsiveness reputation and audits the answers with probability p_A. In the case the answers are not audited, the master accepts the value returned by the weighed majority. In Algorithm 1, m is the value returned by the weighted majority and R_m is the subset of workers that returned m. If the master audits, it updates the truthfulness reputation and the audit probability for the next round. Then, the master rewards/penalizes the workers as follows. If the master audits and a worker i is a cheater (i.e., $i \in F$), then $\Pi_i = -WP_C$; if i is honest, then $\Pi_i = WB_y$. If the master does not audit, and i returns the value of the weighted majority (i.e., $i \in R_m$), then $\Pi_i = WB_y$, otherwise $\Pi_i = 0$.

In the update of the audit probability p_A, we include a threshold, denoted by τ, that represents the master's *tolerance* to cheating (typically, we will assume $\tau = 1/2$ in our simulations). If the ratio of the aggregated reputation of cheaters with respect to the total is larger than τ, p_A is increased, and decreased otherwise. The amount by which p_A changes depends on the difference between these values, modulated by a *learning rate* α_m [25]. This latter value determines to what extent the newly acquired information will override the old information. For example, if $\alpha_m = 0$ the master will never adjust p_A.

Workers' Algorithm. Altruistic and malicious workers have predefined behaviors. When they are selected and receive a task T from the master, if they are available, they compute the task (altruistic) or fabricate an arbitrary solution (malicious), replying accordingly. If they are not available, they do not reply. Rational workers run the algorithm described in Algorithm 2. The execution of the algorithm begins with a rational worker i deciding an initial probability of cheating p_{Ci}. Then, the worker waits to be selected and receive a task T from the master. When so, and if it is available at the time, then with probability $1 - p_{Ci}$, worker i computes the task and replies to the master with the correct answer. Otherwise, it fabricates an answer, and sends the incorrect response to the master. After receiving its payoff, worker i changes its p_{Ci} according to payoff Π_i, the chosen strategy (cheat or not cheat), and its aspiration a_i. Similarly to the master, the workers have a *learning rate* α_w. We assume that all workers have the same learning rate, that is, they learn in the same manner (in [25], the learning rate is called step-size). In a real platform the workers learning rate can slightly vary (since workers in these platforms have similar profiles), making some worker more or less susceptible to reward and punishment. Using the same learning rate for all workers is representative of what happens in a population of different values with small variations around some mean.

Algorithm 1. Master's Algorithm

```
1  p_A ← x, where x ∈ [p_A^{min}, 1]
2  for i ← 0 to N do
3      select_i ← 0; reply_select_i ← 0; audit_reply_select_i ← 0; correct_audit_i ← 0; streak_i ← 0
4      ρ_{rs_i} ← 1; initialize ρ_{tr_i} // initially all workers have the same reputation
5  for r ← 1 to ∞ do
6      W^r ← {i ∈ N : i is chosen as one of the n workers with the highest ρ_i = ρ_{rs_i} · ρ_{tr_i} }
7      ∀i ∈ W^r : select_i ← select_i + 1
8      send a task T to all workers in W^r
9      collect replies from workers in W^r for t time
10     wait for t time collecting replies as received from workers in W^r
11     R ← {i ∈ W^r : a reply from i was received by time t}
12     ∀i ∈ R : reply_select_i ← reply_select_i + 1
13     update responsiveness reputation ρ_{rs_i} of each worker i ∈ W^r
14     audit the received answers with probability p_A
15     if the answers were not audited then
16         accept the value m returned by workers R_m ⊆ R,
17             where ∀m', ρ_{tr_{R_m}} ≥ ρ_{tr_{R_{m'}}} // weighted majority of workers in R
18     else // the master audits
19         foreach i ∈ R do
20             audit_reply_select_i ← audit_reply_select_i + 1
21             if i ∈ F then streak_i ← 0 // F ⊆ R is the set of responsive workers caught cheating
22             else correct_audit_i ← correct_audit_i + 1, streak_i ← streak_i + 1
   // honest responsive workers
23             update truthfulness reputation ρ_{tr_i} // depending on the type used
24         if ρ_{tr_R} = 0 then p_A ← min{1, p_A + α_m}
25         else
26             p'_A ← p_A + α_m(ρ_{tr_F}/ρ_{tr_R} − τ)
27             p_A ← min{1, max{p_A^{min}, p'_A}}
28     ∀i ∈ W^r : return Π_i to worker i // the payoff of workers in W^r \ R is zero
```

Algorithm 2. Algorithm for Rational Worker i

```
1  p_{Ci} ← y, where y ∈ [0, 1]
2  repeat forever
3      wait for a task T from the master
4      if available then
5          decide whether to cheat or not independently with distribution P(cheat) = p_{Ci}
6          if the decision was to cheat then
7              send arbitrary solution to the master
8              get payoff Π_i
9              p_{Ci} ← max{0, min{1, p_{Ci} + α_w(Π_i − a_i)}}
10         else
11             send compute(T) to the master
12             get payoff Π_i
13             p_{Ci} ← max{0, min{1, p_{Ci} − α_w(Π_i − WC_T − a_i)}}
```

4   Analysis

In this section, we prove some properties of the system. We start by observing that, in order to achieve eventual correctness, it is necessary to change workers over time.[3]

---

[3] The omitted proofs can be found at http://arxiv.org/abs/1603.04394.

Observation 1. *If the number of malicious workers is at least n and the master assigns the task to the same workers in all rounds, eventual correctness cannot be guaranteed.*

The intuition behind this observation is that there is always a positive probability that the master will select n malicious workers at the first round and will have to remain with the same workers. This observation justifies that the master has to change its choice of workers if eventual correctness has to be guaranteed. We apply the natural approach of choosing the n workers with the largest reputation among the N workers in the pool (breaking ties randomly). In order to guarantee eventual correctness we need to add one more condition regarding the availability of the workers.

Observation 2. *To guarantee eventual correctness at least one non-malicious worker i must exist with $d_i = 1$. To satisfy eventual correctness at least one worker i that is not malicious must have $d_i = 1$.*

To complement the above observations, we show now that there are sets of workers with which eventual correctness is achievable using the different reputation types (LINEAR and EXPONENTIAL as truthfulness reputations) defined and the master reputation-based mechanism in Algorithm 1.

Theorem 3. *Consider a system in which workers are either altruistic or malicious there are no rational workers and there is at least one altruistic worker i with $d_i = 1$ in the pool. Eventual correctness is satisfied if the mechanism of Algorithm 1 is used with the responsiveness reputation and any of the truthfulness reputations LINEAR or EXPONENTIAL.*

The intuition behind the proof is that thanks to the decremental way in which the reputation of a malicious worker is calculated at some point the altruistic worker i with full responsiveness ($d_i = 1$) will be selected and have a greater reputation than the aggregated reputation of the selected malicious workers. A similar result does not hold if truthfulness reputation of type BOINC is used. In this case, we have found that it is not enough that one altruistic worker with full availability exists, but also the number of altruistic workers with partial availability have to be considered.

Theorem 4. *Consider a system in which workers are either altruistic or malicious there are no rational workers and there is at least one altruistic worker i with $d_i = 1$ in the pool. In this system, the mechanism of Algorithm 1 is used with the responsiveness reputation and the truthfulness reputation BOINC. Then, eventual correctness is satisfied if and only if the number of altruistic workers with $d_j < 1$ is smaller than n.*

Proof. In this system, it holds that every malicious worker k has truthfulness reputation $\rho_{tr_k} = 0$ forever, since the replies that the master receives from it (if any) are always incorrect. Initially, altruistic workers also have zero truthfulness reputation. An altruistic worker j has positive truthfulness reputation after it is selected, and its reply is received and audited by the master 10 times. Observe that, once that happens, the truthfulness reputation of worker j never becomes 0 again. Also note that the reponsiveness reputation never becomes 0. Hence, the first altruistic workers that succeed in raising their truthfulness reputation above zero are always chosen in future rounds. While there are less than n workers with positive reputation, the master selects at random from the zero-reputation workers in every round. Then, eventually (in round r_0) there are n altruistic workers with positive reputation, or there are less than n but all altruistic workers are in that set. After then, no new altruistic worker increase its reputation (in fact, is ever selected), and the set of altruistic selected workers is always the same.

If the number of altruistic workers with $d_j < 1$ is smaller than n, since worker i has $d_i = 1$, after round r_0 among the selected workers there are altruistic workers with $d_j = 1$ and positive reputation. Then, in every round there is going to be a weighted majority of correct replies, and eventual correctness is guaranteed.

If, on the other hand, the number of altruistic workers with $d_j < 1$ is at least n, there is a positive probability that all the n workers with positive reputation are from this set. Since there is a positive probability that n altruistic workers with $d_j < 1$ are selected in round r_0 with probability one the worker i with $d_i = 1$ will never be selected. If this is the case, eventual correctness is not satisfied (since there is a positive probability that the master will not receive a reply in a round). Assume otherwise and consider that after round r_0' it holds that $p_\mathcal{A} = p_\mathcal{A}^{min}$. Then, in every round after r_0' there is a positive probability that the master receives no reply from the selected workers and it does not audit, which implies that it does not obtain the correct result.   □

This result is rather paradoxical, since it implies that a system in which all workers are altruistic (one with $d_i = 1$ and the rest with $d_j < 1$) does not guarantee eventual correctness, while a similar system in which the partially available workers are instead malicious does. This paradox comes to stress the importance of selecting the right truthfulness reputation. Theorem 4 shows a positive correlation among a truthfulness reputation with the availability factor of a worker in the case a large number of altruistic workers.

5   Simulations

Theoretical analysis is complemented with illustrative simulations on a number of different scenarios for the case of full and partial availability. The simulated cases give indications on the values of some parameters (controlled by the master, namely the type of reputation and the initial $p_\mathcal{A}$) under which the mechanism performs better. The rest of the parameters of the mechanism and the scenarios presented are essentially based on the observations extracted from [2,12], and are rather similar to our earlier work [11]. We have developed our own simulation setup by implementing our mechanism (Algorithms 1 and 2, and the reputation types discussed above) using C++. The simulations were executed on a dual-core AMD Opteron 2.5 GHz processor, with 2 GB RAM, running CentOS version 5.3.

For simplicity, we consider that all workers have the same aspiration level $a_i = 0.1$, although we have checked that with random values the results are similar to those presented here, provided their variance is not very large ($a_i \pm 0.1$). We consider the same learning rate for the master and the workers, i.e., $\alpha = \alpha_m = \alpha_w = 0.1$. Note that the learning rate, as discussed for example in [25] (called step-size there), is generally set to a small constant value for practical reasons. We set $\tau = 0.5$ (c.f., Sect. 3; also see [10]), $p_{\mathcal{A}}^{min} = 0.01$, and $\varepsilon = 0.5$ in reputation EXPONENTIAL. We assume that the master does not punish the workers $WP_C = 0$, since depending on the platform used this might not be feasible, and hence more generic results are considered. Also we consider that the cost of computing a task is $WC_T = 0.1$ for all workers and, analogously, the master is rewarding the workers with $WB_y = 1$ when it accepts their result (for simplicity no further correlation among these two values is assumed). The initial cheating probability used by rational workers is $p_{Ci} = 0.5$ and the number of selected workers is set to $n = 5$.

The first batch of simulations consider the case when the workers are fully available (i.e., all workers have $d = 1$), and the behavior of the mechanism under different pool sizes is studied. The second batch considers the case where the workers are partially available.

Full Availability. Assuming full worker availability we attempt to identify the impact of the pool size on different metrics: (1) the number of rounds, (2) number of auditing rounds, and (3) number of incorrect results accepted by the master, all of them measured until the system reaches convergence (the first round in which $p_{\mathcal{A}} = p_{\mathcal{A}}^{min}$)[4]. Additionally, we are able to compare the behavior of the three truthfulness reputation types, showing different trade-off among reliability and cost.

We have tested the mechanism proposed in this paper with different initial $p_{\mathcal{A}}$ values. We present here two interesting cases of initial audit probability, $p_{\mathcal{A}} = 0.5$ and $p_{\mathcal{A}} = 1$. The first row of Fig. 1 (plots (a1) to (c1)) presents the results obtained in the simulations with initial $p_{\mathcal{A}} = 0.5$ and the second row (plots (a2) to (c2)) the case $p_{\mathcal{A}} = 1$. The simulations in this section have been done for systems with only rational and malicious workers, with 3 different ratios between these worker types (ratios 5/4, 4/5, and 1/8), with different pool sizes ($N = \{5, 9, 99\}$), and for the 3 truthfulness reputation types. These ratios consider the three most "critical" cases in which malicious workers can influence the results.

A general conclusion we can extract from the first row of Fig. 1 (plots (a1) to (c1)) is that, independently of the ratio between malicious and rational workers, the trend that each reputation type follows for each of the different pool size scenarios is the same. (When the ratio of rational/malicious is 1/8 this trend

---

[4] As we have seen experimentally, first the system reaches a reliable state and then $p_{\mathcal{A}} = p_{\mathcal{A}}^{min}$.

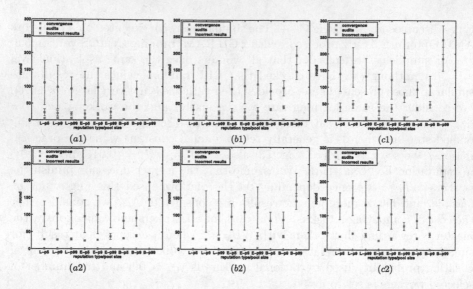

Fig. 1. Simulation results with full availability. First row plots are for initial $p_A = 0.5$. Second row plots are for initial $p_A = 1$. The bottom (red) errorbars present the number of incorrect results accepted until convergence ($p_A = p_A^{min}$), the middle (green) errorbars present the number of audits until convergence; and finally the upper (blue) errorbars present the number of rounds until convergence, in 100 instantiations. In plots (a1) and (a2) the ratio of rational/malicious is 5/4. In plots (b1) and (b2) the ratio of rational/malicious is 4/5. In plots (c1) and (c2) the ratio of rational/malicious is 1/8. The x-axes symbols are as follows, L: LINEAR, E: EXPONENTIAL and B: BOINC reputation; p5: pool size 5, p9: pool size 9 and p99: pool size 99. (Color figure online)

is more noticeable.) Reputation LINEAR does not show a correlation between the pool size and the evaluation metrics. This is somewhat surprising given that other two reputation types are impacted by the pool size.

For reputation EXPONENTIAL and BOINC we can observe that, as the pool size increases, the number of rounds until convergence also increases. It seems like, for these reputation types, many workers from the pool have to be selected and audited before convergence. Hence, with a larger pool it takes more rounds for the mechanism to select and audit these workers, and hence to establish valid reputation for the workers and to reinforce the rational ones to be honest. For both reputation types (EXPONENTIAL and BOINC) this is a costly procedure also in terms of auditing for all rational/malicious ratios. (The effect on the number of audits is more acute for reputation BOINC as the pool size increases.) As for the number of incorrect results accepted until convergence, with reputation EXPONENTIAL they still increase with the pool size. However, reputation BOINC is much more robust with respect to this metric, essentially guaranteeing that no incorrect result is accepted.

Comparing now the performance of the different reputation types based on our evaluation metrics, it seems that reputation LINEAR performs better when the size of the pool is big compared to the other two reputation types. On the other hand reputation types EXPONENTIAL and BOINC perform slightly better when the pool size is small. Comparing reputation types EXPONENTIAL and BOINC, while reputation BOINC shows that has slightly faster convergence, this is traded for at least double auditing than reputation EXPONENTIAL. On the other hand, reputation EXPONENTIAL is accepting a greater number of incorrect results until convergence. This is a clear example of the trade-off between convergence time, number of audits, and number of incorrect results accepted.

Similar conclusions can be drawn when the master decides to audit with $p_A = 1$ initially, see Fig. 1(a2)–(c2). The only difference is that the variance, of the different instantiations on the three metrics is smaller. Hence, choosing $p_A = 1$ initially is a "safer" strategy for the master.

Partial Availability. Assuming now partial worker availability (i.e., workers may have $d < 1$), we attempt to identify the impact of the unavailability of a worker on four different metrics: (1) the number of rounds, (2) number of auditing rounds, and (3) number of incorrect results accepted by the master, all until the system reaches convergence. In addition, we obtain (4) the number of incorrect results accepted by the master *after* the system reaches convergence (which was zero in the previous section). Moreover, we are able to identify how suitable each reputation is, under different workers' ratio and unavailability probabilities.

We keep the pool size fixed to $N = 9$, and the number of selected workers fixed to $n = 5$; and we analyze the behavior of the system in a number of different scenarios where the workers types and availabilities vary. The depicted scenarios present the cases of initial audit probability: $p_A = \{0.5, 1\}$.

Figure 2 (a1)–(b1) compares a base case where all workers are altruistic with $d = 1$ (scenario S1) with scenarios where 1 altruistic worker exists with $d = 1$ and the rest of the workers are either altruistic (scenario S2) or malicious (scenario S3) with a partial availability $d = 0.5$. Our base case S1 is the optimal scenario, and the mechanism should have the best performance with respect to metrics (1)–(3); this is confirmed by the simulations as we can observe. For scenario S2, where the 8 altruistic workers have $d = 0.5$, reputations LINEAR and EXPONENTIAL are performing as good as the base case. While BOINC is performing slightly worse than the base case. Comparing the different reputation types for scenarios S1 and S2, it is clear that, for all metrics, LINEAR and EXPONENTIAL are performing better than BOINC. Moving on to scenario S3, where 8 malicious workers with $d = 0.5$ exist, as expected, the mechanism is performing worse according to our reputation metrics. What is interesting to observe, though, is that reputation BOINC is performing much better than the other two reputation types. It is surprising to observe, for reputation BOINC, how close are the results for scenario S2 and especially scenario S3 to the base case S1. We believe that this is due to the nature of reputation BOINC, which keeps reputation to zero until a reliability threshold is achieved. From the observation of Fig. 2(a1)–(b1), we can conclude that, if there is information on the existence of malicious workers in

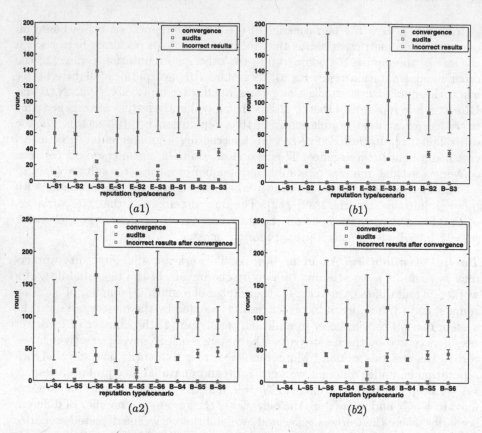

Fig. 2. Simulation results with partial availability: (a1)–(a2) initial $p_A = 0.5$, (b1)–(b2) initial $p_A = 1$. For (a1)–(b1) The bottom (red) errorbars present the number of incorrect results accepted until convergence ($p_A = p_A^{min}$). For (a2)–(b2) the bottom (red) errorbars present the number of incorrect results accepted after convergence. For all plots, the middle (green) errorbars present the number of audits until convergence; and finally the upper (blue) errorbars present the number of rounds until convergence, in 100 instantiations. The x-axes symbols are as follows, L: reputation LINEAR, E: reputation EXPONENTIAL, B: reputation BOINC, S1: 9 altruistic workers with $d = 1$, S2: 1 altruistic with $d = 1$ and 8 altruistic workers with $d = 0.5$, S3: 1 altruistic with $d = 1$ and 8 malicious workers with $d = 0.5$, S4: 9 rational workers with $d = 1$, S5: 1 rational with $d = 1$ and 8 rational workers with $d = 0.5$, S6: 1 rational with $d = 1$ and 8 malicious workers with $d = 0.5$. (Color figure online)

the computation, a "safer" approach would be the use of reputation BOINC. The impact of p_A on the performance of the mechanism, in the particular scenarios, as it is shown on Fig. 2(a1)–(b1), in all cases setting $p_A = 0.5$ initially improves the performance of the mechanism.

The results of Fig. 2(a1)–(b1) are confirmed by Theorem 3. Through the simulation results, we have observed that eventual correctness happens (i.e., no more erroneous results are further accepted) when the system converges, for the depicted scenarios. As for Theorem 4 we have observed that, although the condition of having 5 altruistic with $d = 1$ is not the case for scenarios S2 and S3, in the particular scenarios simulated the system was able to reach eventual correctness. Although from the depicted scenarios reputation BOINC seems like is a good approach, theory tells us that it can only be used when we have info on the workers types.

Figure 2(a2)–(b2), depicts more scenarios with different workers types ratios, in the presence of rational and malicious workers. Following the same methodology as before, we compare a base case (scenario S4) where all workers are rational with $d = 1$, with a scenarios where one rational with $d = 1$ exists and the rest are rational (scenario S5) or malicious (scenario S6) with $d = 0.5$. We can observe that in the base scenario S4, the mechanism is performing better than in the other two scenarios, for reputation metrics (1),(2) and (4), independently of the reputation type. What we observe is that the most difficult scenario for the mechanism to handle is scenario S5, independently of the reputation type, because, although the system converges, eventual correctness has not been reached and the master is accepting incorrect replies for a few more rounds before reaching eventual correctness. This is due to the ratio of the workers' type, and some rational workers that have not been fully reinforced to a correct behavior may have a greater reputation than the rational worker with $d = 1$, while the master has already dropped $p_A = p_A^{min}$. That would mean that the master would accept the result of the majority that might consist of rational workers that cheat. As we can see, EXPONENTIAL is performing worse than the other two types, based on metric (4). As for reputation LINEAR we can see that, for scenarios S4 and S5, although the variation on the convergence round is greater than reputation BOINC, this is traded for half the auditing that reputation BOINC requires. As for scenario S6 (with malicious workers), reputation LINEAR converges much slower, while the number of audits is roughly the same, compared to reputation BOINC. This observation gives a slight advantage to reputation BOINC for scenario S6, while reputation LINEAR has an advantage on S5.

Discussion. One conclusion that is derived by our simulations is that, in the case of full availability, reputation BOINC is not a desirable reputation type if the pool of workers is large. As simulations showed us, convergence is slow, and expensive in terms of auditing. One could select one of the other two reputation types (according to the available information on the ratio of workers' type), since accepting a few more incorrect results is traded for fast eventual correctness and low auditing cost. Additionally, in the scenario with full availability we have noticed that, selecting initially $p_A = 1$ is a "safer" option to have small number of incorrect results accepted, if no information on the system is known and the master is willing to invest a bit more on auditing.

For the case of partial availability, the simulations with only altruistic or with altruistic and malicious converged in all cases. This was expected due to the analysis in all cases except in S2 with reputation BOINC, when we expected to see some rounds after convergence with no replies. The fact is that the altruistic worker with full availability was able to be selected forever in al cases.

Simulations have also shown that, in the presence of malicious and altruistic workers, reputation BOINC has an advantage compared to the other two types. Finally, it is interesting to observe that, in the partial availability case with only rational workers, our mechanism has not reached eventual correctness when the system has converged, but a few rounds later. This means that, although the rational workers are partially available, the mechanism is able to reinforce them to an honest behavior eventually.

Acknowledgments. Supported in part by MINECO grant TEC2014- 55713-R, Regional Government of Madrid (CM) grant Cloud4BigData (S2013/ICE-2894, co-funded by FSE & FEDER), NSF of China grant 61520106005, EC H2020 grants ReCred and NOTRE, U. of Cyprus (ED-CG2015), the MECD grant FPU2013-03792 and Kean University RTR2016.

References

1. Abraham, I., Dolev, D., Gonen, R., Halpern, J.: Distributed computing meets game theory: robust mechanisms for rational secret sharing and multiparty computation. In: Proceedings of ACM PODC 2006, pp. 53–62 (2006)
2. Allen, B.: The Einstein@home Project (2014). http://einstein.phys.uwm.edu
3. Amazon's Mechanical Turk (2014). https://www.mturk.com
4. Anderson, D.P.: BOINC: a system for public-resource computing and storage. In: Proceedings of 5th IEEE/ACM International Workshop on Grid Computing, pp. 4–10 (2004)
5. Anderson, D.P.: Volunteer computing: the ultimate cloud. ACM Crossroads **16**(3), 7–10 (2010)
6. Anderson, D.P.: BOINC reputation (2014). http://boinc.berkeley.edu/trac/wiki/AdaptiveReplication
7. Anderson, D.P.: BOINC (2016). http://boinc.berkeley.edu/
8. Bush, R.R., Mosteller, F.: Stochastic Models for Learning (1955)
9. Christoforou, E., Fernández Anta, A., Georgiou, C., Mosteiro, M.A.: Algorithmic mechanisms for reliable master-worker internet-based computing. IEEE Trans. Comput. **63**(1), 179–195 (2014)
10. Christoforou, E., Fernández Anta, A., Georgiou, C., Mosteiro, M.A., Sánchez, A.: Applying the dynamics of evolution to achieve reliability in master-worker computing. Concurr. Comput.: Pract. Exp. **25**(17), 2363–2380 (2013)
11. Christoforou, E., Anta, A.F., Georgiou, C., Mosteiro, M.A., Sánchez, A.A.: Reputation-based mechanisms for evolutionary master-worker computing. In: Baldoni, R., Nisse, N., van Steen, M. (eds.) OPODIS 2013. LNCS, vol. 8304, pp. 98–113. Springer, Heidelberg (2013)
12. Estrada, T., Taufer, M., Anderson, D.P.: Performance prediction and analysis of BOINC projects: an empirical study with EMBOINC. J. Grid Comput. **7**(4), 537–554 (2009)
13. Fernández Anta, A., Georgiou, C., López, L., Santos, A.: Reliable internet-based master-worker computing in the presence of malicious workers. Parallel Process. Lett. **22**(1) (2012)
14. Fernández Anta, A., Georgiou, C., Mosteiro, M.A.: Designing mechanisms for reliable Internet-based computing. In: Proceedings of IEEE NCA 2008, pp. 315–324 (2008)

15. Golle, P., Mironov, I.: Uncheatable distributed computations. In: Naccache, D. (ed.) CT-RSA 2001. LNCS, vol. 2020, pp. 425–440. Springer, Heidelberg (2001)
16. Heien, E.M., Anderson, D.P., Hagihara, K.: Computing low latency batches with unreliable workers in volunteer computing environments. J. Grid Comput. **7**(4), 501–518 (2009)
17. Jøsang, A., Ismail, R., Boyd, C.: A survey of trust and reputation systems for online service provision. Decis. Support Syst. **43**(2), 618–644 (2007)
18. Kondo, D., Araujo, F., Malecot, P., Domingues, P., Silva, L.M., Fedak, G., Cappello, F.: Characterizing result errors in internet desktop grids. In: Kermarrec, A.-M., Bougé, L., Priol, T. (eds.) Euro-Par 2007. LNCS, vol. 4641, pp. 361–371. Springer, Heidelberg (2007)
19. Konwar, K.M., Rajasekaran, S., Shvartsman, M.M.A.A.: Robust network super-computing with malicious processes. In: Dolev, S. (ed.) DISC 2006. LNCS, vol. 4167, pp. 474–488. Springer, Heidelberg (2006)
20. Korpela, E., Werthimer, D., Anderson, D.P., Cobb, J., Lebofsky, M.: SETI@home: massively distributed computing for SETI. Comput. Sci. Eng. **3**(1), 78–83 (2001)
21. Sarmenta, L.F.: Sabotage-tolerance mechanisms for volunteer computing systems. Future Gener. Comput. Syst. **18**(4), 561–572 (2002)
22. Shneidman, J., Parkes, D.C.: Rationality and self-interest in peer to peer networks. In: Kaashoek, M.F., Stoica, I. (eds.) IPTPS 2003. LNCS, vol. 2735, pp. 139–148. Springer, Heidelberg (2003)
23. Smith, J.M.: Evolution and the Theory of Games. Cambridge University Press, Cambridge (1982)
24. Sonnek, J., Chandra, A., Weissman, J.B.: Adaptive reputation-based scheduling on unreliable distributed infrastructures. IEEE PDS **18**(11), 1551–1564 (2007)
25. Szepesvári, C.: Algorithms for reinforcement learning. Synth. Lect. Artif. Intell. Mach. Learn. **4**(1), 1–103 (2010)
26. Taufer, M., Anderson, D.P., Cicotti, P., Brooks III, C.L.: Homogeneous redundancy: a technique to ensure integrity of molecular simulation results using public computing. In: Proceedings of IEEE IPDPS 2005 (2005)
27. Yurkewych, M., Levine, B.N., Rosenberg, A.L.: On the cost-ineffectiveness of redundancy in commercial P2P computing. In: Proceedings of ACM CCS 2005, pp. 280–288 (2005)

Asynchronous Consensus with Bounded Memory

Carole Delporte-Gallet[(⊠)] and Hugues Fauconnier

IRIF-Université Paris-Diderot, Paris, France
{cd,hf}@liafa.univ-paris-diderot.fr

Abstract. We present here a bounded memory size Obstruction-Free consensus algorithm for the asynchronous shared memory model. More precisely for a set of n processes, this algorithm uses $n + 2$ multi-writer multi-reader registers, each of these registers being of size $O(\log(n))$ bits. From this, we get a bounded memory size space complexity consensus algorithm with single-writer multi-reader registers and a bounded memory size space complexity consensus algorithm in the asynchronous message passing model with a majority of correct processes. As it is easy to ensure the Obstruction-Free assumption with randomization (or with leader election failure detector Ω) we obtain a bounded memory size randomized consensus algorithm and a bounded memory size consensus algorithm with failure detector.

Keywords: Shared memory · Space complexity · Consensus

1 Introduction

Because of its practical impact and for theoretical reasons, the consensus problems are one of the most interesting problem in fault-tolerant computing. Recall that in the consensus problem each process begins with an initial value and has to decide one value (*termination*), this decided value has to be an initial value of some process (*validity*) and all processes have to decide the same value (*agreement*).

But in message passing or shared memory asynchronous systems there is no deterministic solution for the consensus if at least one process may crash [18]. To circumvent this negative result, several ways have been proposed. One of them is to consider *randomized consensus*: with randomization, it is possible to ensure the safety of the consensus (agreement and validity) and the liveness property (termination) with a probability equal to 1 [2,6]. Another way is to add *failure detectors* [10] to the system. Failure detectors are distributed oracles that give processes information about failures. In this way it has been proved [9] that Ω, a failure detector that ensures that eventually all correct processes agree on the id of the same correct process (a leader), is a weakest failure detector to solve the consensus problem (i.e. it solves the consensus and if another failure

Supported by ANR DISPLEXITY.

P.A. Abdulla and C. Delporte-Gallet (Eds.): NETYS 2016, LNCS 9944, pp. 154–168, 2016.
DOI: 10.1007/978-3-319-46140-3_12

detector enables to solve the consensus, then Ω may be implemented from the information given by that failure detector).

In shared memory models, if we limit the concurrency in such a way that each correct process is running alone for an arbitrary long time consensus becomes solvable. An *Obstruction-Free* algorithm [17,23] is an algorithm ensuring safety in all cases and termination under that concurrency property. More precisely it is a deterministic[1] algorithm that guarantees that any process will decide if it performs enough steps alone (i.e. without interference with other processes). Randomization [21] or failure detector Ω enable (with bounded memory size) to ensure that all correct processes are running alone for an arbitrary long time and then an Obstruction-Free algorithm gives directly a randomized algorithm or a deterministic algorithm with failure detector Ω. Hence in the following we consider Obstruction-Free consensus algorithms.

The main result of the paper is to present an Obstruction-Free consensus algorithm tolerating any number of process crashes in the shared memory model using a bounded size of memory and to combine this algorithm with previous results to deduct a comprehensive collection of results on space complexity for consensus algorithms in many classical models in which it can be solved.

For a system of n processes, the Obstruction-Free consensus algorithm uses only $n + 2$ registers that may be written or read by all processes (multi-writer multi-reader (MWMR) registers). Moreover, each of these registers contains at most $O(\log(n))$ bits. In fact our algorithm uses atomic snapshot [1] to access a memory of $n + 1$ registers. In [21], it has been proved that atomic snapshot of registers can be Obstruction-Free implemented with one additional atomic register of size $O(\log n)$-bits. Hence with MWMR registers (and only read-write operations) the space complexity of our algorithm is $O(n \log(n)) - bits$.

Following classical results (e.g. [29,31,34]) one MWMR register shared by n processes may be implemented with $O(n^2)$ single-writer multi-reader (SWMR) registers and bounded timestamps [15,27]. Hence we get a bounded memory size Obstruction-Free consensus algorithm with SWMR registers. In this way, with any number of crashes we obtain a randomized consensus algorithm with bounded memory size and a consensus algorithm with bounded memory size and failure detector Ω.

SWMR registers may be implemented in the message passing model with a majority of correct processes using bounded timestamps [3]. Then if each register to be implemented has a bounded size, the size of the exchanged messages as well as the size of the local memory is bounded. Note that if the size of the local memory is bounded, the size of the messages is bounded too. Our results in the message passing remains written in term of memory. Hence in asynchronous message passing model and a majority of correct processes we obtain a randomized consensus algorithm with bounded memory size and a consensus algorithm with bounded memory size using failure detector Ω. From [14], in message passing system with any number of failure, Σ is the weakest failure detector to implement a SWMR register and $\Sigma \times \Omega$ is the weakest failure detector to solve consensus.

---

[1] Except explicitly specified, our algorithms are deterministic.

Moreover, without a majority of correct processes, registers can be implemented with bounded memory size using failure detector Σ then we obtain also a consensus algorithm with bounded memory size using failure detector $\Sigma \times \Omega$ that tolerates any number of crashes.

In term of number of registers, a lower bound of $\Omega(\sqrt{(n)})$ by Fich et al. [16] appeared a long time ago. Recently a tight lower bound of $\Omega(n)$ appeared in [20, 35]. Moreover, these papers showed that any consensus algorithm requires $n-1$ registers. With unbounded value written in registers, it is possible to achieve any algorithm in shared memory with n SWMR registers and in particular, to achieve consensus algorithm with n registers. It is conjectured that the tight bound is in fact n.

There is no known bound in term of number of bits. In the various models in which consensus can be solved (randomization, failure detector, Obstruction-Free in message passing or in shared memory...) consensus algorithms work with rounds or counters that are unbounded integers (e.g. [8, 10, 26, 28, 33], with the exception of [13]) and sometime use high level abstraction that may use counters too. To the best of our knowledge our results are the first one demonstrating that these unbounded integers are not needed. A starting point could have been the algorithm of [13] that does not use explicit counter and use snapshots of MWMR registers. But we prefer to present a new algorithm that we think interesting by itself. It uses $n + 2$ MWMR registers instead of the $2(n - 1)$ registers needed by [13]. In term of number of registers it is closer to the lower bound. We conjecture that if we require that the size of registers is bounded, we need more than n registers.

We also present similar results concerning the k-set agreement. In this problem processes have to decide on at most k values. Consensus corresponds to 1-set agreement. To get bounded memory size for k-set agreement, we can start from the Obstruction-Free consensus algorithm. In fact, we present a k-set agreement algorithm that use less MWMR registers than the consensus algorithm and we think the algorithm is interesting by itself.

2   Model

The model we consider is the standard asynchronous shared-memory model of computation with $n \geq 2$ processes[2] communicating by reading and writing to a fixed set of shared registers [5, 25]. The processes have unique ids in $\{1, \ldots, n\}$. Processes may take a finite (in this case the process is faulty) or an infinite number of steps (in this case the process is correct) and we assume that at least one process is correct.

Shared Memory. The shared memory consists of a set of atomic multi-writer multi-reader (MWMR) registers. All processes can read and write any MWMR register and these operations are atomic or linearizable [22]. For short, we usually omit the term atomic. A process executes its code by taking three types of atomic

---

[2] The number n of processes is given and is then considered as a constant.

steps: the *read* of a register, the *write* of a register, and the modification of its local state.

Atomic snapshots [1] is another way to access memory. Atomic snapshot is defined by two more powerful operations: *update* and *scan* [1] on an array of m MWMR registers. An update operation takes a register and a data value as arguments and does not return a value. It writes the data value in the register. The scan operation has no argument and returns an array of m elements. The returned array is a *snapshot* of the memory, that is an instantaneous view of the registers.

Space Complexity. We consider here the space complexity of algorithms. By space complexity we mean the maximum over all the runs of the algorithm of the sum of all the sizes in bits of all shared registers. A bounded memory size algorithm is an algorithm such that there exists a constant B, such that in any run of the algorithm the sum over all shared MWMR registers of the size of registers is number of bits is less than B.

Obstruction Freedom. The *Obstruction-Free* [23] progress condition states that eventually one process takes steps alone. In the following we consider deterministic Obstruction-Free implementations.

Giakkoupis et al. give in [21] an Obstruction-Free linearizable implementation of atomic snapshot that uses, in addition to the array of m MWMR registers, say R, one MWMR registers of size $O(\log(n))$, say S. Note that in this implementation, an update operation writes in the register the id of the writer, so if the value written in R does not yet contain the id of the writer, the space complexity is augmented by a multiplicative factor $\log(n)$. In [1], it is observed that if every write leaves a unique indelible mark whenever it is executed in R, then if two consecutive reads of R return identical values then the values returned constitute a snapshot. Using this idea, [21] designed an Obstruction-Free linearizable implementation of scan and update. To perform its j-th update of some value x in register $R[i]$, p first writes its id in S and then it writes the triple $(x, p, j \bmod 2)$ in $R[i]$. To execute a $scan()$, process p first writes its id in S. Then it performs two consecutive reads of all the registers of R: r and r'. Finally, the process reads S. If S does not contain p's id or if the two consecutive views r and r' are not equal then p starts its $scan()$ over; otherwise it returns view r.

Proposition 1 [21]. *Assuming that each written value contains the id of the writer and that the size of the written value is at most w, there is an Obstruction-Free linearizable implementation of scan/update of m MWMR registers with one MWMR register of size $O(\log(n))$ bits and m MWMR registers of size $(w + 1)$ bits.*

We consider the classical consensus decision task [11] in which each process proposes its input value and has to irrevocably decide on one of the proposed inputs, such that there is at most one decided value. We assume that the input values come from a finite set of values *Values*.

Consensus is defined by three requirements:

- *agreement:* at most one value is decided,
- *validity:* if a process decides value v, v is the input value of some process,
- *termination:* if a process takes an infinite number of steps then it decides.

The *wait-free* [22] progress condition states that each process terminates its operations in finite number of its own steps or equivalently with any number of failures. It is well known that consensus is not Wait-Free solvable. Moreover consensus is not solvable as soon as at least one process is faulty [18]. It is also well known that there exits Obstruction-Free consensus implementations (see for example [4,12,13]). So we study the Obstruction-Free solvability of consensus. We are interested here in the space complexity of the implementations and we are going to prove the existence of bounded memory consensus implementations.

3   Algorithm

Algorithm of Fig. 1 solves Obstruction-Free consensus with $n + 2$ MWMR registers.

Shared variables:

R : **array of** $[0, .., n]$ **of pairs** (value, process_ID) **initialized to** $(\bot, \bot)$

CODE FOR PROCESS p:

```
1   r : array of [0,..,n] of pairs (value, process_ID)
2   prop = v_p                                            /*p proposal */
3   pos = 0
4   forever do
5       r[0,..,n]= R.scan()
6       if ∀i r[i] = (prop, p) then decide prop ; exit     /*p decision*/
7       if ∃i, j : (r[i] = r[j] ∧ r[i] ≠ (⊥, ⊥) ∧ r[i].value ≠ prop)
            ∧∄i', j' : (r[i'] = r[j'] ∧ r[i'].value = prop)
8       then          /* two identical values in R different from the current p proposed value */
                                          /*keep the same register to write */
9           let v be r[i].value such that ∃j : r[i] = r[j] ∧ (r[i] ≠ (⊥, ⊥)) ∧ r[i].value ≠ prop
10          prop = v
11      else              /*keep the same proposal, chose another register to write */
12          let k be the smallest index such that r[k] ≠ (prop, p)
13          pos = k
14      R.update(pos, (prop, p))
```

Fig. 1. Consensus with MWMR registers.

In this algorithm the processes share $n+1$ registers and use these registers by snapshots. The implementation of scan/update is the Obstruction-Free implementation described in [21]. As previously mentioned, this implementation uses one additional MWMR register.

Each process p maintains a variable *prop*, its proposal. Initially this variable contains its input value v_p. Each process repeatedly takes a scan of the registers, sets its variable *prop* to v if it finds two registers with the same content (v, q) for some q, and updates some register with a pair formed by *prop* and its id. It decides when it finds in each register this pair. To avoid that a process alternates between two proposals, a process keeps its proposal *prop* if the pair composed with its proposal *prop* and some id appears twice.

Then, in an Obstruction-Free run, the process that takes enough steps alone updates all registers with its proposal and decides.

The agreement property is more intricate. If a process p decides a value d, then (d, p) is written in $n + 1$ registers. We argue that forever at least two registers contain the pair (d, q) for some q and for any (d', q') with $d \neq d', (d', q')$ is contained in at most one register. Intuitively, consider the first scan made after the decision and q the process that made this scan. As processes repeatedly perform a scan and then an update, at most $n - 1$ processes may have written a proposal different from the decided value d. And so at least two registers remain with (d, p) and the other registers contains either (d, p) or the value written by processes since the decision. So after this scan, the value d is adopted by q.

Here we use a trick, when a process changes its proposal it updates the *same* register. So if q writes in register $R[i]$ and q has changed its proposal, the next update of q will be on the same register $R[i]$. After this second update, q performs a scan and this time, it does not modify its proposal. It will update some other register with (d, q). Perhaps it updates one of the two registers that contains (d, p) but in this case we have two registers with the value (d, q). It is also possible that we have (d, p) in at least two registers and (d, q) in two registers. But the main point is that we keep the property that for any (d', x) with $d' \neq d$, the pair (d', x) is contained in at most one register and (d, x) for some x is in two registers. The agreement works in the same way if q does not change its proposal after its first scan (q has already adopted d as proposal).

Now we proceed with the correctness proof of the algorithm Fig. 1.

By definition, scan and update are linearizable and when we say that some scan or update operation *op* occurs at some time τ, the time τ is the linearization time of this operation.

We first prove the termination property of the algorithm:

Proposition 2. *In Obstruction-Free run, if some process p takes steps alone for an arbitrary long time, then p decides.*

Proof. With obstruction freedom, assume that a process, say p, is eventually the only process taking steps. Then there is a time τ after which no other process takes steps. Let *prop* the proposal of p at this time. Notice that in particular, after time τ, only p may modify registers in R.

If p has not already decided, p scans and updates the registers.

If there exists some time $\tau' \geq \tau$ such that (A) after τ', p always finds condition Line 7 false then p never changes its proposal after τ'. Let $prop'$ be this proposal. Each time p updates a register, it writes $(prop', p)$ in it, then in the next loop it writes in another register. After at most $n + 1$ updates every register contains this pair and p decides $prop'$.

We now show that there exists some τ' that satisfies (A). If τ satisfies (A) then we have done else let τ_1 be the first time after τ at which the condition Line 7 is true.

p has found i_1 and j_1 such that $r[i_1] = r[j_1] \wedge r[i_1] \neq (\perp, \perp) \wedge r[i_1].value \neq prop$. Let $prop_1$ be $r[i_1].value$. p changes its proposal Line 8 by $prop_1$ and p writes $(prop_1, p)$ in $R[pos]$ Line 14. If $pos = i_1$ or $pos = j_1$ then in its next scan it is possible that the condition Line 7 is still $true$, There are i_2 and j_2 such that $r[i_2] = r[j_2] \wedge r[i_2] \neq (\perp, \perp) \wedge r[i_2].value \neq prop_1$. Let $prop_1$ be now $r[i_2].value$. But as p updates the same index pos this time $pos \neq i_2$ and $pos \neq j_2$. So in both case we arrive in a situation such that there exist three different indexes i, j and pos such that $r[i] = r[j] \wedge r[i] \neq (\perp, \perp) \wedge r[i].value = prop_1 \wedge r[pos] = (prop_1, p)$ and the proposal of p is $prop_1$.

In its next scan, the second part of the condition Line 7 is now false. p keeps its proposal and updates a register $R[pos']$ for some pos' such that $R[pos'] \neq (prop_1, p)$. In particular we have $pos' \neq pos$.

There are now two registers with $(prop_1, p)$ in R and the current proposal of p is $prop_1$.

We show that this property remains true each time p executes the loop Line 4. Assume it is true at the beginning of the loop, then in the scan as there are two registers with $(prop_1, p)$ in R, the second part of the condition Line 7 is false. Then p keeps its proposal and updates a register with $(prop_1, p)$. And the condition remains true at the end of the loop.

Let $\tau_2 > \tau_1$ be the time at which p has two registers with $(prop_1, p)$ in R and the current proposal of p is $prop_1$. After this time we have just shown that p always finds condition Line 7 false. So τ_2 satisfies the condition (A).

We now proceed to prove the validity and the agreement properties:

Proposition 3. *If a process decides, it decides on the input value of some process.*

Proof. The decided value is the first argument of a pair that is written in all registers. From the algorithm, the proposal of some process, and consequently the value written in registers, is either an input value or an update made in Line 10 i.e. some $r[i].value$ such that $\exists j : r[i] = r[j] \wedge (r[i] \neq (\perp, \perp)) \wedge r[i].value \neq prop$. Then, by induction, the decided value is the input of some process.

Proposition 4. *If two processes decide, they decide the same value.*

Proof. Consider the first process, say p, that is ready to decide d and the time τ at which it has executed Line 5 and found (d, p) written in the $n + 1$ registers.

After time τ, p never writes in the shared memory and so at most $n-1$ processes writes in $n+1$ registers.

We argue that each time after τ a process scans the memory it finds (1) at least two registers with a pair (d,q) for some q, and (2) any pair (d',x) with $d' \neq d$ and some x in at most one register.

At any time $t > \tau$, let X^t let the set of processes that have made at least one write between τ and t. We have $n-1 \geq |X^t|$. Let Y^t be the set of registers that contains (d',x) with $d' \neq d$ and x in X^t.

To decide a process q has to find (a,q) for some a in all registers, so q has to write at least $n+1$ times after τ. So if a process q doesn't write at least third time after τ it can't decide.

Let $\tau' > \tau$ such that some process, say q, makes for the first time a second write since τ. At any time t between τ and τ', we have $|X^t| \geq |Y^t|$.

Until τ', there are at most $n-1$ values in X^t and in Y^t and properties (1) and (2) are satisfied.

If q makes its second write at τ', it has made its scan between τ and τ'. As (1) and (2) are satisfied, the proposal of q after this scan will be d. There are two cases:

1. After this scan, q has modified its proposal. Then q writes (d,q) in the same position. If $|Y^{\tau'}| < |Y^{\tau'-1}|$ then $|X^{\tau'}| \geq |Y^{\tau'}|+1$ and properties (1) and (2) are satisfied. If $|Y^{\tau'}| = |Y^{\tau'-1}|$, this means that another process has already written in the same place then again $|X^{\tau'}| \geq |Y^{\tau'}|+1$ and properties (1) and (2) are satisfied.
2. After this scan, q has not modified its proposal. Then its proposal was already d, q has written (d,q) for its first write in some index i, consequently i is not in $Y^{\tau'}$. Then again $|X^{\tau'}| \geq |Y^{\tau'}|+1$. As $n-1 \geq |X^{\tau'}|$, it remains 3 registers with either (d,p) or (d,q) then one of these pairs is in two registers and (1) is ensured. As q writes (d,q), (2) remains true.

We consider the time τ'' of a next write of a process such that it is its second write or its third write after τ. Between τ' and τ'' it may happen that some process has made its first write but in this case X increases as least as Y and we keep that at any time t, $|X^t| \geq |Y^t|+1$ before this write.

If it is the second write of some process, we have the same argument as previously. (1) and (2) holds and $|X^{\tau''}| \geq |Y^{\tau''}|+2$.

If it is the third write of some process, this process is q. Then before this write, there remains at least 3 registers with either (d,p) or (d,q). If this write is in one of these registers the property (1) is always ensured. If it is in another register then the property (1) trivially holds. As q writes (d,q), (2) remains true.

The proof is made iteratively up to time σ at which all processes that take steps in the run have already made at least two writes. At this time $Y^\sigma = \emptyset$ and every process that takes steps has d as proposal. Note that if a process decides v then at any time: v is the proposal of some process or there is a process z such that (v,z) is the value of some register. Then as at σ d is the proposal of all processes and each register contains a pair (d,z) for some process z then if a process decides it can only decide d.

Theorem 1. *With the Obstruction-Free implementation of snapshot in [21], the algorithm of Fig. 1 solves Obstruction-Free consensus in $O(n \log n)$-bits space complexity. More precisely, it uses $n + 2$ MWMR registers of size $O(\log n)$ bits.*

4   Applications

4.1   Randomized Algorithm

A randomized implementation of consensus that tolerates any number of crashes ensures the agreement and the validity in all runs and the termination (each correct process decides) with probability one.

[21] shows that if there is a deterministic Obstruction-Free algorithm which guarantees that any process finishes after it has executed at most b steps, for some constant b, without interference from other processes then the algorithm can be transformed into a randomized one that has the same space complexity. Observe that in our Obstruction-Free implementation, if a process p takes steps alone, it terminates after $(n+2)$ scan and update operations. It may happen that when it begins to take steps alone it is in a middle of its scan/update. It needs $(n+1)$ complete scan/update alone to terminate. For each $scan()$, p reads twice the array R and the additional register then if p takes steps alone it decides in at most $c(n+2)(n+1)$ atomic steps for some constant c. Then from [21] and Theorem 1:

Corollary 1. *There is a randomized consensus algorithm that tolerates any number of crashes with MWMR in $O(n \log(n))$-bits space complexity. More precisely, it uses $n + 2$ MWMR registers of size $O(\log(n))$ bits.*

4.2   SWMR Registers

As Single-Writer Multi-Reader registers are considered as more primitive than Multi-Writer Multi-Reader registers, we consider the space complexity with SWMR registers. Here, space complexity is again defined as the maximum over all the runs of the algorithms of the sum of the sizes in number of bits of all shared *SWMR* registers.

Following classical results (e.g. [29,31,34]) one MWMR registers may be implemented with $O(n^2)$ SWMR registers and bounded timestamps [15,27]. Hence with these implementations we get again a bounded memory size Obstruction-Free deterministic consensus algorithm and a randomized consensus algorithm that tolerates any number of crashes with SWMR registers. Therefore:

Corollary 2. *There is an Obstruction-Free deterministic consensus algorithm and a randomized consensus algorithm that tolerates any number of crashes with SWMR registers in bounded memory size.*

4.3   Failure Detector

A failure detector [10] outputs at each process some hints about the failure pattern of the processes. Failure detectors enable to solve consensus. In particular, failure detector Ω [9] that eventually outputs to each process the same correct process id, the eventual leader, is the weakest failure detector to achieve consensus in shared memory. That means that if we augment our model (shared memory asynchronous system with any number) with Ω it is possible to get consensus and from the output of any failure detector enabling to solve consensus it is possible to implement Ω.

In asynchronous shared memory model augmented with the leader election failure detector Ω, we also get a bounded memory implementation of consensus.

Indeed assuming a failure detector Ω, if a process takes steps only when it considers itself as the leader, the Ω properties imply that eventually only one process, the eventual correct leader, will take steps. In this way, we get an emulation of the Obstruction-Free property.

Running an Obstruction-Free consensus algorithm in this way with Ω, gives an algorithm with failure detector Ω in which the leader eventually decides. This algorithm is given in Fig. 2. To ensure that the other correct processes decide, when the leader decides it writes the decided value in the register DEC, and the other processes read DEC and adopt this value as their decision value.

If we use the previous consensus algorithm (Fig. 1), we use $n + 3$ MWMR registers of size $O(\log n)$ bits.

Hence contrary to classical consensus algorithms with failure detector Ω that use variables like counters of "rounds" (e.g. [12, 30]) that take unbounded values, we obtain a bounded memory size consensus algorithm with failure detector Ω.

Thus, with Theorem 1:

Shared variables:

$DEC : Values$ **initialized to** $\bot$

CODE FOR PROCESS p:

while *true* **do**
    if $(\Omega = p)$ /* Ω outputs id of the supposed leader*/
    then
        run the next step of an Obstruction-Free consensus algorithm
        if p decides v in this step **then** $DEC = v$; $decide(DEC)$; **exit**
    else
        if $DEC \neq \bot$ **then** $decide(DEC)$; **exit**

Fig. 2. Consensus with Ω.

Corollary 3. *There is a deterministic consensus algorithm in shared memory model MWMR registers augmented with failure detector Ω with $O(n \log(n))$-bits space complexity. There is a deterministic consensus algorithm in shared memory model SWMR registers augmented with failure detector Ω with bounded memory size.*

4.4   Message Passing

Consider now the message passing asynchronous model. In this model processes communicate by messages. We assume here that the communication is reliable (no loss, no corruption, no duplication). SWMR registers may be implemented in message passing system with a majority of correct processes [3] using bounded timestamp and hence with bounded memory size.

Without a majority of correct processes, SWMR registers can be implemented using the failure detector Σ [14]. Moreover in way similar to [3], this implementation can be made with bounded memory size. Failure detector Σ outputs at each process a list of processes that eventually contains only correct processes, such that each output has a non empty intersection with any other output. Note that Σ is the weakest failure detector to implement atomic registers and $\Sigma \times \Omega$ is the weakest failure detector to solve the consensus with any number of crashes [14]. Failure detector $\Sigma \times \Omega$ outputs at each process a couple formed by a list of processes and a process. If we consider only the first member of the couples, it satisfies the properties of Σ and the second member those of Ω.

Thus, with Corollary 3:

Corollary 4. *Assuming a majority of correct processes, there is a consensus algorithm in asynchronous message passing systems with failure detector Ω with bounded memory size.*

Corollary 5. *Assuming any number of crashes, there is a consensus algorithm in asynchronous message passing systems with failure detector $\Sigma \times \Omega$ with bounded memory size.*

And with Corollary 1:

Corollary 6. *Assuming a majority of correct processes, there is a randomized algorithm in asynchronous message passing with bounded memory size.*

5   Extensions

We consider the classical *k-set agreement* decision task [11] in which each process proposes its input value and has to decide on one of the input values, such that there are at most k decided values. We assume that the input values come from a finite set of values *Values*. There are three requirements: at most k values are decided (*k-agreement*), if a process decides v, this value is the input of some process (*validity*), and if a process takes an infinite number of steps then it decides (*termination*). When $k = n - 1$, k-set agreement is also known as set agreement. *Consensus* is nothing else than 1-set agreement.

It is well known that k-set agreement is not wait-free solvable and even, it is not solvable with k faulty processes [7,24,32] in shared memory, so we study the Obstruction-Free solvability of k-set agreement. It is also known that there exits an Obstruction-Free k-set agreement implementation (for example [4,13]), we are interested here on the space complexity of an implementation.

From our algorithm Fig. 1, we can derive an Obstruction-Free implementation of k-set agreement in bounded memory size. More precisely, using scan/update the algorithm uses $n - k + 2$ MWMR registers of size $O(\log(n))$ bits and we need one additional register of size $O(\log(n))$ bits to implement Obstruction-Free the scan/update operations.

The principles of the algorithm is the same as those of the consensus algorithm Fig. 1, but instead of $n + 1$ registers we have only $n - k + 2$ registers. We observe that if we consider the last $n - k + 1$ processes ready to decide, it is possible that the other $k - 1$ processes have decided some value, but these $n - k + 1$ processes share now a set of $(n - k + 1) + 1$ registers and are, roughly speaking, in the condition in which they can achieve consensus as in the consensus algorithm Fig. 1. So there is at most k decided value.

The algorithm is given Fig. 3 and its proof is similar to the proof of the consensus algorithm.

If we combined again the known results we get:

Theorem 2. *There is an Obstruction-Free k-set agreement algorithm and a randomized k-set agreement algorithm that tolerates any number of faults with MWMR registers in $O((n - k)\log(n))$-bits space complexity. More precisely, it uses $n - k + 3$ MWMR registers of size $O(\log(n))$.*

Theorem 3. *There is an Obstruction-Free k-set agreement algorithm and a randomized k-set agreement algorithm that tolerates any number of faults with SWMR registers in bounded memory size.*

vector Ω_k [19] is the weakest failure detector to achieve k-set agreement in shared memory. This failure detector outputs at each process a vector of size k, such that there exists some index i, such that eventually at each process the i-th index of the output is the same correct process. One of the index is eventually the same correct process. A traditional implementation of k-set agreement with this failure detector is the following: Each process runs in parallel k instances of a consensus algorithm with a failure detector such that this algorithm achieves termination with Ω and agreement and validity with any failure detector. Note that our algorithm Fig. 2 satisfies these properties. When a process decides in one of its instances of consensus, it decides for k-set agreement. As one index is an Ω at least one instance decides for all processes. As all instances of consensus algorithm achieve agreement and validity there are at most k decisions and each decision is the initial value of some process.

Shared variables:

> R :**array of** $[0, .., n - k + 1]$ **of pairs** (value, process_ID) **initialized to** $(\perp, \perp)$

CODE FOR PROCESS p

```
1   r : array of  [0,..,n-k+1] of pairs (value,process_ID)
2   prop = v_p                                              /*p proposal */
3   pos = 0
4   forever do
5     r[0,..,n-k+1]= R.scan()
6     if ∀i r[i] = (prop,p) then decide prop ; exit          /*p decision*/
7     if ∃i,j : (r[i] = r[j] ∧ r[i] ≠ (⊥,⊥) ∧ r[i].value ≠ prop)
        ∧∄i',j' : r[i'] = r[j'] ∧ (r[i'].value = prop)
8     then          /* two identical values in R different from the current p proposed value */
                                          /*keep the same register to write */
9       let v be r[i].value such that ∃j : r[i] = r[j] ∧ (r[i] ≠ (⊥,⊥)) ∧ r[i].value ≠ prop
10      prop = v
11    else              /*keep the same proposal, chose another register to write r */
12      let k be the smallest index such that r[k] ≠ (prop,p)
13      pos = k
14    R.update(pos, (prop,p))
```

Fig. 3. k-set agreement with $n - k + 2$ MWMR registers.

Theorem 4. *There is a k-set agreement algorithm in shared memory model MWMR registers augmented with failure detector vector Ω in space complexity $O((n - k) \log(n))$. There is a deterministic k-set agreement algorithm in shared memory model SWMR registers augmented with failure detector vector Ω in bounded memory.*

Finally with the result of [21], we get:

Theorem 5. *There is a randomized k-set agreement algorithm in shared memory model MWMR registers in $O(k \; n \log(n))$-bits space complexity. There is a k-set agreement algorithm in shared memory model SWMR registers in bounded memory size.*

6   Conclusion

We have shown that it is possible to achieve consensus and more generally k-set agreement in various setting with bounded memory. These settings include randomized algorithm, Obstruction-Free deterministic algorithm, deterministic algorithms with failure detectors (we use in each case the weakest failure detector that allows to solve the problem) in shared memory with any number of faults. We get the same kind of results in message passing system.

References

1. Afek, Y., Attiya, H., Dolev, D., Gafni, E., Merritt, M., Shavit, N.: Atomic snapshots of shared memory. J. ACM **40**(4), 873–890 (1993)
2. Aspnes, J.: Randomized protocols for asynchronous consensus. Distrib. Comput. **16**(2–3), 165–175 (2003)
3. Attiya, H., Bar-Noy, A., Dolev, D.: Sharing memory robustly in message passing systems. J. ACM **42**(2), 124–142 (1995)
4. Attiya, H., Guerraoui, R., Hendler, D., Kuznetsov, P.: The complexity of obstruction-free implementations. J. ACM **56**(4), 24:1–24:33 (2009)
5. Attiya, H., Welch, J.: Distributed Computing. Fundamentals, Simulations, and Advanced Topics. Wiley, Hoboken (2004)
6. Ben-Or, M.: Another advantage of free choice: completely asynchronous agreement protocols (extended abstract). In: PODC 1983: Proceedings of the Annual ACM Symposium on Principles of Distributed Computing, pp. 27–30 (1983)
7. Borowsky, E., Gafni, E.: Generalized FLP impossibility result for t-resilient asynchronous computations. In: STOC, pp. 91–100. ACM Press (1993)
8. Bouzid, Z., Raynal, M., Sutra, P.: Anonymous obstruction-free (n, k)-set agreement with n-k+1 atomic read/write registers. In: Proceedings of 19th International Conference on Principles of Distributed Systems, OPODIS 2015, Rennes, France, 14–17 December 2015. LNCS. Springer, Heidelberg (2015, to appear)
9. Chandra, T.D., Hadzilacos, V., Toueg, S.: The weakest failure detector for solving consensus. J. ACM **43**(4), 685–722 (1996)
10. Chandra, T.D., Toueg, S.: Unreliable failure detectors for reliable distributed systems. J. ACM **43**(2), 225–267 (1996)
11. Chaudhuri, S.: More choices allow more faults: set consensus problems in totally asynchronous systems. Inf. Comput. **105**(1), 132–158 (1993)
12. Delporte-Gallet, C., Fauconnier, H.: Two consensus algorithms with atomic registers and failure detector Ω. In: Garg, V., Wattenhofer, R., Kothapalli, K. (eds.) ICDCN 2009. LNCS, vol. 5408, pp. 251–262. Springer, Heidelberg (2008)
13. Delporte-Gallet, C., Fauconnier, H., Gafni, E., Rajsbaum, S.: Black art: obstruction-free k-set agreement with $|MWMR registers| < |proccesses|$. In: Gramoli, V., Guerraoui, R. (eds.) NETYS 2013. LNCS, vol. 7853, pp. 28–41. Springer, Heidelberg (2013)
14. Delporte-Gallet, D., Fauconnier, H., Guerraoui, R.: Tight failure detection bounds on atomic object implementations. J. ACM **57**(4), 22:1–22:32 (2010)
15. Dolev, D., Shavit, N.: Bounded concurrent time-stamping. SIAM J. Comput. **26**(2), 418–455 (1997)
16. Fich, F.E., Herlihy, M., Shavit, N.: On the space complexity of randomized synchronization. J. ACM **45**(5), 843–862 (1998)
17. Fich, F.E., Luchangco, V., Moir, M., Shavit, N.N.: Obstruction-free algorithms can be practically wait-free. In: Fraigniaud, P. (ed.) DISC 2005. LNCS, vol. 3724, pp. 78–92. Springer, Heidelberg (2005)
18. Fischer, M.J., Lynch, N.A., Paterson, M.S.: Impossibility of distributed consensus with one faulty process. J. ACM **32**(2), 374–382 (1985)
19. Gafni, E., Kuznetsov, P.: On set consensus numbers. Distrib. Comput. **24**(3–4), 149–163 (2011)
20. Gelashvili, R.: On the optimal space complexity of consensus for anonymous processes. In: Moses, Y., et al. (eds.) DISC 2015. LNCS, vol. 9363, pp. 452–466. Springer, Heidelberg (2015). doi:10.1007/978-3-662-48653-5_30

21. Giakkoupis, G., Helmi, M., Higham, L., Woelfel, P.: An $O(\sqrt{n})$ space bound for obstruction-free leader election. In: Afek, Y. (ed.) DISC 2013. LNCS, vol. 8205, pp. 46–60. Springer, Heidelberg (2013)
22. Herlihy, M.: Wait-free synchronization. ACM Trans. Program. Lang. Syst. **13**(1), 123–149 (1991)
23. Herlihy, M., Luchangco, V., Moir, M.: Obstruction-free synchronization: double-ended queues as an example. In: ICDCS, pp. 522–529. IEEE Computer Society (2003)
24. Herlihy, M., Shavit, N.: The topological structure of asynchronous computability. J. ACM **46**(2), 858–923 (1999)
25. Herlihy, M., Shavit, N.: The Art of Multiprocessor Programming. Morgan Kaufmann, Burlington (2008)
26. Hurfin, M., Raynal, M.: A simple and fast asynchronous consensus based on a weak failure detector. Distrib. Comput. **12**(4), 209–223 (1999)
27. Israeli, A., Li, M.: Bounded time-stamps. Distrib. Comput. **6**(4), 205–209 (1993)
28. Lamport, L.: The part-time parliament. ACM Trans. Comput. Syst. **16**(2), 133–169 (1998)
29. Li, M., Tromp, J., Vitányi, P.M.B.: How to share concurrent wait-free variables. J. ACM **43**(4), 723–746 (1996)
30. Mostéfaoui, A., Raynal, M.: Leader-based consensus. Parallel Process. Lett. **11**(1), 95–107 (2001)
31. Raynal, M.: Concurrent Programming: Algorithms, Principles, and Foundations. Springer, Heidelberg (2013)
32. Saks, M., Zaharoglou, F.: Wait-free k-set agreement is impossible: the topology of public knowledge. SIAM J. Comput. **29**, 1449–1483 (2000)
33. Schiper, A.: Early consensus in an asynchronous system with a weak failure detector. Distrib. Comput. **10**(3), 149–157 (1997)
34. Singh, A.K., Anderson, J.H., Gouda, M.G.: The elusive atomic register. J. ACM **41**(2), 311–339 (1994)
35. Zhu, L.: A tight space bound for consensus. Technical report, Toronto (2016). http://www.cs.toronto.edu/lezhu/tight-space-bound-for-consensus.pdf

A Fuzzy AHP Approach to Network Selection Improvement in Heterogeneous Wireless Networks

Maroua Drissi[1(✉)], Mohammed Oumsis[1,2], and Driss Aboutajdine[1]

[1] LRIT, Associated Unit to CNRST URAC'29, Faculty of Sciences,
Mohammed V University in Rabat, Rabat, Morocco
drissimaroua@gmail.com, oumsis@yahoo.com, aboutaj@fsr.ac.ma
[2] High School of Technology, Mohammed V University in Rabat, Sale, Morocco

Abstract. One of the most arduous topics for next-generation wireless networks - 4G and beyond - is the operation of vertical handover considering the fact that many wireless communication technologies have been deployed in order to handle mobile users any time, anywhere and anyhow. Furthermore, users are more and more captivated by multimedia applications such as audio, video and voice, which need strict Quality of Service (QoS) support. Thus, keeping the user Always Best Connected (ABC) with such constraints is a challenging task. In this paper, we propose an approach for network selection based on Fuzzy Analytic Hierarchy Process (FAHP), applied to determine the relative weights of the evaluation criteria. Afterwards Simple Additive Weighting (SAW) is used to rank the available networks. Implementation and simulation experiments with Network Simulator NS3 are presented in order to validate our proposed approach. The empirical results show that FAHP, compared with classic AHP, achieves a significant improvement up to 10 % in term of delay and 25 % in term of packet loss.

Keywords: Heterogeneous networks · Vertical handover · Network selection · Always best connected · Fuzzy analytic hierarchy process · Multiple attribute decision making

1 Introduction and Motivation

The next-generation wireless networks involve various wireless technologies. Due to radio resources restraint, coverage problems and user's growing needs, one network may not be able to provide continuous service and required QoS for serving subscriber during an entire session. However, with the coexistence of different network access technologies, moving between different wireless networks seams to be the convenient solutions in today's heterogeneous networks.

The Always Best Connected concept (ABC) was introduced by [1]. The authors assert that a terminal that supports the ABC feature aims to be connected via the best available network and access technology at all times.

© Springer International Publishing AG 2016
P.A. Abdulla and C. Delporte-Gallet (Eds.): NETYS 2016, LNCS 9944, pp. 169–182, 2016.
DOI: 10.1007/978-3-319-46140-3_13

ABC considers user's and operator's benefits. It includes basically all types of access technologies. Meanwhile, the heterogeneous wireless networks require an intelligent network selection algorithm to establish seamless communication in order to provide high QoS for different multimedia applications. To afford pervasive wireless access for users, it is important to choose the best network among the available ones, dynamic network selection algorithms plan is to provide users with the appropriate QoS in terms of metrics and user's preferences since both are acknowledged during the process of network selection. Hence, this technology is a hot research topic in the field of wireless communication.

In this paper, we focus on the real-time selection of always best connected network in heterogeneous environment, while maintaining QoS for multimedia services. We adopt, thereby, a Fuzzy approach to enhance vertical handover decision; it enables a reasonable and intelligent real-time handover decision according to the network parameters. Implementation and simulation with Network Simulator NS3 are presented in order to validate our proposed goals. The results show that our enhancement achieves a significant improvement of the QoS Delay and Packets Loss metrics.

The remainder of this paper is structured as follows. Related works about Network Selection using MADM are summarized in Sect. 2. In Sect. 3, the performance evaluation model is presented and the classic approach to Network Selection problem using AHP and SAW is described. Section 4 addresses the Fuzzy improvement made to AHP and its application in our approach. Section 4 describes simulation parameters and results to illustrate the proposed scheme. Finally, Sect. 5 concludes the work.

2   Related Works

Network Selection is an critical tread to accomplish a smooth vertical handover and reach the best QoS in an heterogeneous environment. It is about gathering the performances of each candidate network, and ranking them in purpose to select the best network. It is a utmost revolution in the internet, by delivering an improved Quality of Experience (QoE) for users of wireless services.

[2] presented an overview of vertical handover techniques, along with the main algorithms, protocols and tools proposed in the literature. In addition, authors suggested the most appropriate vertical handover techniques to efficiently communicate in a such environments considering the particular characteristics of this type of networks. In the same context, [3] proposed an algorithm for network selection based on averaged received signal strength, outage probability and distance. Furthermore, authors enhanced their work in [4], where they proposed a novel network selection algorithm utilizing signal strength, available bit rate, signal to noise ratio, achievable throughput, bit error rate and outage probability metrics as criteria for network selection. They combined selection metrics with Particle Swarm Optimization (PSO) for relative dynamic weight optimization. In the same backdrop, [5] proposed a novel handover scheme that features two operating processes: attributes rating and network ranking. Authors compared

their method with the traditional signal based handover model and they demonstrated a lowest packet drop ratio and Higher average throughput. Moreover, [6] have proposed vertical handover decision which depends on coverage area of the network and the velocity of the mobile user.

Hence, MADM presents many advantages, notably, its implementation simplicity is one of them. But increasing users number make it inefficient since decisional time will be important especially for real-time application. Another loophole of such system is the intervention of humans at the moment of initiation of the performance indicators. Indeed, AHP as an example, needs more objectivity for judgement. In [7], authors explain that a determined collection of weights produces certain quality or merit for each network; these merit values change if we consider another collection of weights. The purpose is to obtain the best merit value, which will correspond to the selected network for the vertical handover decision phase. Accordingly, the more combinations of weights, the more possibilities to get better merit values we will have. In [8], authors investigated in the weights of AHP and proposed a set of weights suitable to Network Selection problem, the outcomes demonstrated a lowest delay but still needs more objectivity.

Fuzzy logic seams to be the best solution to fix the prejudiced indicators. Indeed, [9] explored the use of AHP, Fuzzy AHP in solving a Multi-Criteria Decision Making (MCDM) problem by searching an improved solution to related problems. When the criteria weights and performance ratings are vague and inaccurate, Fuzzy AHP is the effective solution. Such improvements can rather enhance QoS, making it more convenient for all traffic applications.

These constraints have moved us to use fuzzy logic in a performance model for Network Selection presented in section below.

3 AHP-SAW Network Selection

3.1 System Model

For Network Selection, MADM approach consist in choosing the best network from available networks. So as reported in the algorithm block diagram shown in Fig. 1, simulation provides the system with the metrics (Bit Error Rate (Ber), Jitter (J), Delay (D) and Throughput (T)) in real-time and a pairwise comparison is applied according to each QoS class: Conversational (Conv), Streaming (Strea), Interactive (Inter) and Background (Back).

Weight factors are assigned conveniently to each criterion to report its importance which is determined by AHP or Fuzzy AHP. Afterwards, SAW is applied to the weighted matrices to have the ranking of the available networks. The handover decision can be made in real-time and repeatedly, the interval of 5 s.

The vertical handover decision problem can be formulated as a matrix form $Q_{N,M}$, where each row i corresponds to the candidate network and each column j corresponds to an attribute.

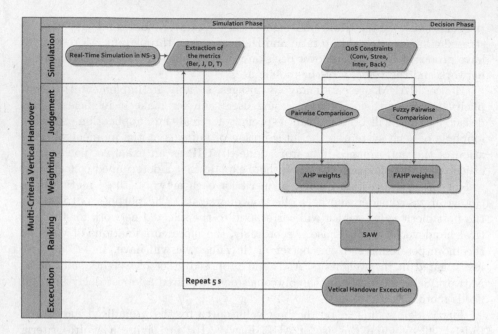

Fig. 1. Algorithm block.

The matrices of alternative networks are established conforming to the attributes.

$$Q_{N,M} = \begin{array}{c} Network_1 \\ Network_2 \\ \vdots \\ Network_N \end{array} \overset{\begin{array}{cccc} Attribute_1 & Attribute_2 & \ldots & Attribute_M \end{array}}{\left(\begin{array}{cccc} q_{11} & q_{12} & \ldots & q_{1M} \\ q_{21} & q_{22} & \ldots & q_{2M} \\ \vdots & \vdots & \ddots & \vdots \\ q_{N1} & q_{N2} & \ldots & q_{NM} \end{array} \right)}$$

Since SAW grants the evaluated criteria to be expressed in different measurement units, it is necessary to normalize the values.

$$n_{ij} = \frac{q_{ij}}{\sqrt{\sum_{i=1}^{i=N} q_{ij}^2}}, j = 1, ..., M \tag{1}$$

3.2 Analytic Hierarchy Process: AHP

The concept of weight associated by SAW, is solved by the use of AHP method. [10] proposed this process for decision-making in multi-criteria problems. They introduced AHP as a method of measurement with ratio scales. AHP allows comparison and a choice of pre-set options. It is based on the comparison of pairs of options and criteria. The AHP decision problem is structured in a hierarchic form with different levels, each level include a fixed number of decision elements. The relative importance of the decision elements (weights of criteria and scores of alternatives) is estimated indirectly through a series of comparative judgements during the decision process. Correspondingly, the decision-makers have to provide their preferences by comparing all criteria, sub-criteria and alternatives with respect to upper level decision elements. However, most of the real users would not have the required technical background to understand parameters such as throughput, delay, jitter or bit error rate. Thus, we suppose that a third-party application translates the preferences of users.

Weight computing needs answering to a sets of comparisons between a pair metrics. The trivial form to ask a question is to consider two element and find out which one satisfies the criterion more. These answers are given by using the fundamental 1–9 AHP scale [10, 11] presented in Table 1 below.

Table 1. AHP scale of importance [10].

Importance	Definition	Explanation
1	*Equal importance*	Two parameters contribute equally
3	*Moderate importance of one over another*	Experience favoured 3 times one than another
5	*Strong importance*	Experience favoured 5 times one than another
7	*Very strong importance*	A parameters is favoured and dominant in practice
9	*Extreme importance*	The evidence favouring one activity over another is of the highest possible order of affirmation
2, 4, 6, 8	*Intermediate values*	When compromise is needed

AHP calculates the weight vector w which represents the importance of each metric with respect to different QoS classes. It provides as results $w_j > 0$ the weight or importance of the jth attribute. Given that $\sum_{j=1}^{j=M} w_j = 1$.

Table 2 presents the relative importance between each pair, for example, in streaming class, the comparison of Jitter and Delay is an answer to the question: How much more is Jitter favoured over Delay in streaming class? Indeed, Jitter is 3 times more important than Delay, so the value in matrix is 1/3, and accordingly 3 is put in the opposite side (symmetrical to the diagonal). The other values can be obtained from Table 1.

In [12] the authors demonstrate that if U is defined as an AHP comparison matrices as in Table 3, then by solving the system: $U.w = n_{max}.w$ where

Table 2. AHP matrices for each traffic class.

Conv	Ber	J	D	T
Ber	1	$\frac{1}{7}$	$\frac{1}{7}$	3
J	7	1	3	7
D	7	$\frac{1}{3}$	1	7
T	$\frac{1}{3}$	$\frac{1}{7}$	$\frac{1}{7}$	1

Inter	Ber	J	D	T
Ber	1	3	7	3
J	$\frac{1}{3}$	1	5	3
D	$\frac{1}{7}$	$\frac{1}{5}$	1	$\frac{1}{7}$
T	$\frac{1}{3}$	$\frac{1}{3}$	7	1

Strea	Ber	J	D	T
Ber	1	$\frac{1}{3}$	$\frac{1}{7}$	$\frac{1}{7}$
J	3	1	$\frac{1}{3}$	$\frac{1}{3}$
D	7	3	1	$\frac{1}{3}$
T	7	3	3	1

Back	Ber	J	D	T
Ber	1	7	7	9
J	$\frac{1}{7}$	1	3	5
D	$\frac{1}{7}$	$\frac{1}{3}$	1	5
T	$\frac{1}{9}$	$\frac{1}{5}$	$\frac{1}{5}$	1

n_{max} is the largest eigenvalue of U, the importance vector w can be obtained. Thus, the weights depend on the QoS prerequisite of the traffic classes. We use the eigenvector method used by the AHP to interpret the weights presented in Table 3.

Table 3. AHP importance weights per class.

Traffic class	Ber	Jitter	Delay	Throughput
Conversational	0.07968	0.55464	0.31956	0.04610
Streaming	0.05104	0.13444	0.29493	0.51957
Interactive	0.50385	0.27509	0.04608	0.17496
Background	0.68037	0.17644	0.10390	0.03926

3.3   Simple Additive Weighting: SAW

SAW, also known as the weighted sum method, is the most generally used MADM method [13]. The basic principle of SAW is to obtain a weighted sum of the performance ratings of each alternative under all attributes. Thus, the overall score of a candidate network is determined by the weighted sum of all attribute values. The score S_{SAW} of each candidate network C_i is obtained by summing the contributions of each n_{ij} normalized metric multiplied by the weight of the importance w_j metric Q_j. The selected network is:

$$S_{SAW} = \sum_{j=1}^{M} w_j \cdot n_{ij} \tag{2}$$

Such that:
w_j is the weight vector. n_{ij} is the value of normalized attribute j of network i. N and M are respectively the number of candidates network and the number of network attributes treated.

The section beneath details the improvement made to this model using fuzzy logic.

4   Fuzzy Approach to Network Selection Improvement

In this paper, in order to solve Multi-Criteria Vertical Handover, we use a fuzzy optimization model of [14] based on a fuzzy enhancement of analytic hierarchy process (FAHP). To deal with the imprecise judgements of decision makers involved by classical AHP, a fuzzy AHP decision-making model aim is to determine the weights of certain Quality of Service indicators that act as the criteria impacting the decision process.

4.1   Fuzzy Logic and Fuzzy Set Theory

The highlight of fuzzy sets theory, introduced by [15] is its capability of representing lax or inconclusive data in a natural form. It has been used as a modelling tool for complex systems that can be managed by humans but are hard to define objectively just as the case for AHP. A fuzzy set is one that assigns grades of membership between 0 and 1 to objects using a particular membership function $\mu_{A(x)}$. This capability is the reason for its success in many applications. Linguistic terms are represented by membership functions, valued in the real unit interval, which translate the vagueness and imprecision of human thought related to the proposed problem.

Triangular Fuzzy Number: In the literature, triangular and trapezoidal fuzzy numbers are commonly used to express the vagueness of the parameters. In this study, the triangular fuzzy numbers (TFN) are used to represent the fuzzy relative importance. The choice of TFN is related to the number of classifications or tunings (Low, Medium, High in case of TFN). A TFN is a special type of fuzzy number whose membership is defined by three real numbers, expressed as (l, m, u) such as: $(l \leq m \leq u)$, where l is the lower limit value, m is the most promising value and u is the upper limit value (see Fig. 2). Particularly, when $l = m = u$, fuzzy numbers become crisp numbers. A TFN can be described as:

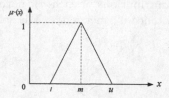

Fig. 2. Triangular Fuzzy Number.

$$\mu_{A(x)} = \begin{cases} \frac{x-l}{m-l}, & l < x < m \\ \frac{u-l}{u-m}, & m < x < u \\ 0, & Otherwise \end{cases} \qquad (3)$$

4.2 Fuzzy Analytic Hierarchy Process: FAHP

Fuzzy AHP uses fuzzy set theory to clear-cut the uncertain comparison judgements as a fuzzy numbers. The main step of fuzzy AHP is to generate the relative fuzzy importance of each pair of factors in the same hierarchy. Using TFN and via pairwise comparison, the fuzzy evaluation matrix $Q = (q_{i,j})_{n*m}$ is constructed, as: $q_{i,j} = (l_{i,j}, m_{i,j}, u_{i,j})$ and $q_{i,j}^{-1} = (1/u_{i,j}, 1/m_{i,j}, 1/l_{i,j})$.

To compare the FAHP with AHP, we translated the weights generated in the previous section (Table 2) regarding the Triangular Fuzzy Conversion Scale of [16], shown in Table 4. Hence, the fuzzy relative importance for each class of traffic namely: Conversational (Conv), Streaming (Strea), Interactive (Inter) and Background (Back) and for each metric Bit Error Rate (Ber), Jitter (J), Delay (D) and Throughput (T) are presented in Table 5.

Table 4. Triangular fuzzy conversion scale [16]

Linguistic scale for importance degrees	Triangular fuzzy scale	Triangular fuzzy reciprocal scale
Just equal (JE)	(1, 1, 1)	(1, 1, 1)
Equally important (EI)	(1/2, 1, 3/2)	(2/3, 1, 2)
Weakly more important (WMI)	(1, 3/2, 2)	(1/2, 2/3, 1)
Strongly more important (SMI)	(3/2, 2, 5/2)	(2/5, 1/2, 2/3)
Very strongly more important (VSMI)	(2, 5/2, 3)	(1/3, 2/5, 1/2)
Absolutely more important (AMI)	(5/2, 3, 7/2)	(2/7, 1/3, 2/5)

Fuzzy AHP of Chang [14]**:** We reviewed the mathematical logic of fuzzy AHP of Chang [14] since it has a wide influence on the theories and applications of fuzzy AHP used in many recent researches as [17–19]. Accordingly, we calculated the fuzzy weighted importance of each class of traffic by translating the values q_{ij} of FAHP matrices presented in Table 5 using the Extent Analysis Method, the value of fuzzy synthetic extent with respect to the i_{th} object is defined in Eq. 4:

$$S_i = \sum_{j=1}^{m} q_{ij} \odot \left[\sum_{i=1}^{n} \sum_{j=1}^{m} q_{ij} \right]^{-1} \qquad (4)$$

The possibility of $S_i \geq S_j$ is defined as:

$$V(S_i \geq S_j) = SUP_{x \geq y}\left[min(S_i(x), S_j(y))\right] \qquad (5)$$

Where x and y are the values on the axis of the membership function of each criterion as shown in Fig. 3.

Table 5. Fuzzy AHP matrices for each traffic class

Conv	Ber	J	D	T		Inter	Ber	J	D	T
Ber	$(1,1,1)$	$(\frac{1}{3},\frac{2}{5},\frac{1}{2})$	$(\frac{1}{3},\frac{2}{5},\frac{1}{2})$	$(1,\frac{3}{2},2)$		Ber	$(1,1,1)$	$(1,\frac{3}{2},2)$	$(2,\frac{5}{2},3)$	$(1,\frac{3}{2},2)$
J	$(2,\frac{5}{2},3)$	$(1,1,1)$	$(1,\frac{3}{2},2)$	$(2,\frac{5}{2},3)$		J	$(\frac{1}{2},\frac{2}{3},1)$	$(1,1,1)$	$(\frac{2}{5},\frac{1}{2},\frac{2}{3})$	$(1,\frac{3}{2},2)$
D	$(2,\frac{5}{2},3)$	$(\frac{1}{2},\frac{2}{3},1)$	$(1,1,1)$	$(2,\frac{5}{2},3)$		D	$(\frac{1}{3},\frac{2}{5},\frac{1}{2})$	$(\frac{3}{2},2,\frac{5}{2})$	$(1,1,1)$	$(\frac{1}{3},\frac{2}{5},\frac{1}{2})$
T	$(\frac{1}{2},\frac{2}{3},1)$	$(\frac{1}{5},\frac{2}{5},\frac{1}{2})$	$(\frac{1}{5},\frac{2}{5},\frac{1}{2})$	$(1,1,1)$		T	$(\frac{1}{2},\frac{2}{3},1)$	$(\frac{1}{2},\frac{2}{3},1)$	$(2,\frac{5}{2},3)$	$(1,1,1)$

Strea	Ber	J	D	T		Back	Ber	J	D	T
Ber	$(1,1,1)$	$(\frac{1}{2},\frac{2}{3},1)$	$(\frac{1}{3},\frac{2}{5},\frac{1}{2})$	$(\frac{1}{3},\frac{2}{5},\frac{1}{2})$		Ber	$(1,1,1)$	$(2,\frac{5}{2},3)$	$(2,\frac{5}{2},3)$	$(\frac{5}{2},3,\frac{7}{2})$
J	$(1,\frac{3}{2},2)$	$(1,1,1)$	$(\frac{1}{2},\frac{2}{3},1)$	$(\frac{1}{2},\frac{2}{3},1)$		J	$(\frac{1}{3},\frac{2}{5},\frac{1}{2})$	$(1,1,1)$	$(1,\frac{3}{2},2)$	$(\frac{3}{2},2,\frac{5}{2})$
D	$(2,\frac{5}{2},3)$	$(1,\frac{3}{2},2)$	$(1,1,1)$	$(\frac{1}{2},\frac{2}{3},1)$		D	$(\frac{1}{3},\frac{2}{5},\frac{1}{2})$	$(\frac{1}{2},\frac{2}{3},1)$	$(1,1,1)$	$(\frac{3}{2},2,\frac{5}{2})$
T	$(2,\frac{5}{2},3)$	$(1,\frac{3}{2},2)$	$(1,\frac{3}{2},2)$	$(1,1,1)$		T	$(\frac{2}{7},\frac{1}{3},\frac{2}{5})$	$(\frac{2}{5},\frac{1}{2},\frac{2}{3})$	$(\frac{2}{5},\frac{1}{2},\frac{2}{3})$	$(1,1,1)$

This expression can be written as:

$$V(S_i \geq S_j) = \begin{cases} 1, & m_i \geq m_j \\ 0, & l_j \geq u_i \\ \frac{l_j - u_i}{(m_i - u_i)(m_j - l_j)}, & Otherwise \end{cases} \qquad (6)$$

The degree possibility for a convex fuzzy number to be greater than k convex fuzzy numbers $S_i(i = 1, 2.....k)$ defined in [14] by:

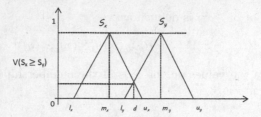

Fig. 3. Membership function of criterion x and y.

$$V(S \geqslant S_1, S_2.....S_k) = V[(S \geqslant S_1,) \cap (S \geqslant S_2) \cap .. \cap (S \geqslant S_k)]$$
$$= min(V(S \geqslant S_i)), i = 1, 2, ..., k. \qquad (7)$$

In this case the weight vector is given by: $W' = (w_1', w_2'...w_m')$ where $A_i(i = 1, 2, ..., m)$ are m attributes. Via normalization, we get the normalized weight vectors, where W is a non-fuzzy number.

$$W = (w_1, w_2...w_m)^T \qquad (8)$$

Finally, the Fuzzy AHP method is applied for the four classes of QoS and the weights are correspondingly generated given in Table 6.

Table 6. FAHP importance weights per class.

Traffic class	Ber	Jitter	Delay	Throughput
Conversational	0.00006	0.45702	0.54286	0.00006
Streaming	0.00005	0.41146	0.17703	0.41146
Interactive	0.41277	0.15101	0.15846	0.27776
Background	0.83725	0.00010	0.16257	0.00008

5   Simulation Model

5.1   Simulation Parameters

To evaluate the fuzzy enhancement proposed, we conducted simulation experiments for both original AHP used in Sect. 3.2 and the enhanced variant FAHP from Sect. 4.2, the obtained results are also compared. As mentioned before, the traffic considered in the evaluation covers all types of application, namely Conversational, Streaming, Interactive and Background. The four traffic classes have different QoS requirements. Thus, they are combined with four QoS parameters: Throughput, end-to-end Delay, Jitter, and Ber. Although the simulation is maintained for 10 min, 100000 packets are supposed to be sent and the decision is made every 5 s in real-time. In all simulations, we use a network consisting of 10 mobile nodes. These nodes follow the same mobility model while roaming between WIFI and WIMAX. The simulations were performed with the Network Simulator NS3.

5.2   Evaluation Criteria

To compare the effectiveness of Fuzzy AHP with classical AHP, we handle the experiments with the network simulator NS3 in order to validate our proposed enhancement, by analysing the impact of the weights given by AHP and those given by FAHP on QoS. To this end, we analyse the Delay and Packet Loss considering that those parameters change within the performance of SAW. They depend on the time taken by each algorithm to be executed which affects the time elapsing from the sending of a packet by the source until it is received by the destination, and rely also on the packets dropped during the vertical handover execution which affects the Packet Loss.

The following section details the development of the network throughout the simulation.

5.3   Simulation Results and Discussion

Figure 4 illustrates the behaviour of delay over time, it compares the performance of AHP and FAHP, both combined with the ranking method SAW. Fuzzy AHP

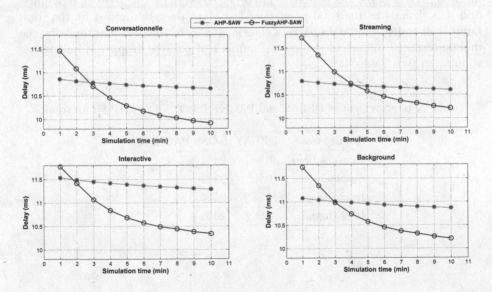

Fig. 4. Behaviour of delay over time.

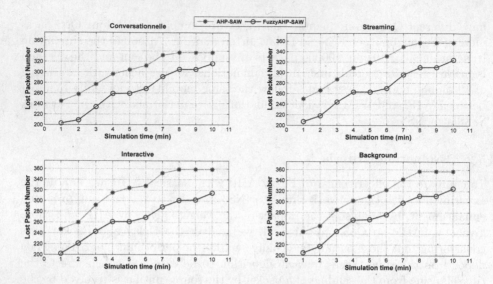

Fig. 5. Behaviour of packet loss over time.

provides weights that enable a fast and intelligent vertical handover considering the time taken by the terminal to calculate the score of each decision, in terms of delay, the proposed approach improve the delay in all types of traffic (see Table 7 below). This is due to the fact that FAHP is tuned better.

As for the delay, Fig. 5 exposes the behaviour of packet loss over time, it contrasts the performance of AHP and FAHP, both combined with the ranking method SAW. Packet loss is analysed in order to evaluate the network reliability, and it is defined as the total number of lost data packets divided by the total number of transmitted data packets. The swiftness of the decisions made by the mobile terminal influences also on the number of packets dropped all along the simulation (see Table 7).

Table 7. Improvement of DELAY and PACKET LOSS by FAHP for all traffics

Traffic class	DELAY	LOSS PACKET
Conversational	8 % ↓	24 % ↓
Streaming	9 % ↓	23 % ↓
Interactive	10 % ↓	25 % ↓
Background	7 % ↓	20 % ↓

6   Conclusion

In this paper, we proposed a system model to enhance network selection by using an improved variant of AHP method called FAHP. The aim is to reach acceptable QoS for all types of traffic. To this end, we used FAHP to generate the weights given afterwards to SAW in order to rank the available networks. The fuzzy logic improvement allows AHP to be tuned better by choosing extra parameters l and u. Thus, FAHP improves QoS in better way against the classical AHP.

Simulation experiments with Network Simulator NS3 show that FAHP achieves a significant improvement of the Quality of Service. The process does not degrade the user quality of experience even with the switching among different networks in view of the fact that FAHP can decrease packet loss and end-to-end delay respectively, up to 25 % and 10 %.

The future work in this direction can be carried out by verifying the effectiveness of FAHP if combined with other MADM method such as TOPSIS or MEW.

References

1. Gustafsson, E., Jonsson, A.: Always best connected. Wirel. Commun. IEEE **10**(1), 49–55 (2003)
2. Mrquez-Barja, J., Calafate, C.T., Cano, J.-C., Manzoni, P.: An overview of vertical handover techniques: algorithms, protocols and tools. Comput. Commun. **34**(8), 985–997 (2011)
3. Ahuja, K., Singh, B., Khanna, R.: Network selection algorithm based on link quality parameters for heterogeneous wireless networks. Optik - Int. J. Light Electron Opt. **125**(14), 3657–3662 (2014)
4. Ahuja, K., Singh, B., Khanna, R.: Particle swarm optimization based network selection in heterogeneous wireless environment. Optik - Int. J. Light Electron Opt. **125**(1), 214–219 (2014)
5. Yang, S.-J., Tseng, W.-C.: Design novel weighted rating of multiple attributes scheme to enhance handoff efficiency in heterogeneous wireless networks. Comput. Commun. **36**(14), 1498–1514 (2013)
6. Jain, A., Tokekar, S.: Application based vertical handoff decision in heterogeneous network. Procedia Comput. Sci. **57**, 782–788 (2015). 3rd International Conference on Recent Trends in Computing (ICRTC-2015)
7. Jaraiz-Simon, M.D., Gomez-Pulido, J.A., Vega-Rodriguez, M.A.: Embedded intelligence for fast QoS-based vertical handoff in heterogeneous wireless access networks. Pervasive Mobile Comput. **19**, 141–155 (2015)
8. Drissi, M., Oumsis, M.: Multi-criteria vertical handover comparison between wimax and wifi. Information **6**(3), 399 (2015)
9. Torfi, F., Farahani, R.Z., Rezapour, S.: Fuzzy AHP to determine the relative weights of evaluation criteria and fuzzy TOPSIS to rank the alternatives. Appl. Soft Comput. **10**(2), 520–528 (2010)
10. Saaty, R.W.: The analytic hierarchy process-what it is and how it is used. Math. Model. **9**(3), 161–176 (1987)
11. Saaty, T.L.: The Analytic Hierarchy Process: Planning, Priority Setting, Resources Allocation. McGraw, New York (1980)

12. Stevens-Navarro, E., Wong, V.W.: Comparison between vertical handoff decision algorithms for heterogeneous wireless networks. In: IEEE 63rd Vehicular Technology Conference, VTC 2006-Spring, vol. 2, pp. 947–951. IEEE (2006)

13. Hwang, C.L., Yoon, K.: Multiple Attribute Decision Making: Methods and Applications: A State-of-the-Art Survey, vol. 13. Springer, New York (1981)

14. Chang, D.-Y.: Applications of the extent analysis method on fuzzy AHP. Eur. J. Oper. Res. **95**(3), 649–655 (1996)

15. Zadeh, L.A.: Fuzzy sets. Inf. Control **8**(3), 338–353 (1965)

16. Bykzkan, G., Feyziolu, O., Nebol, E.: Selection of the strategic alliance partner in logistics value chain. Int. J. Prod. Econ. **113**(1), 148–158 (2008)

17. Mosadeghi, R., Warnken, J., Tomlinson, R., Mirfenderesk, H.: Comparison of fuzzy-AHP and AHP in a spatial multi-criteria decision making model for urban land-use planning. Comput. Environ. Urban Syst. **49**, 54–65 (2015)

18. Zh, K.: Fuzzy analytic hierarchy process: fallacy of the popular methods. Eur. J. Oper. Res. **236**(1), 209–217 (2014)

19. Junior, F.R.L., Osiro, L., Carpinetti, L.C.R.: A comparison between fuzzy AHP and fuzzy TOPSIS methods to supplier selection. Appl. Soft Comput. **21**, 194–209 (2014)

A Fault-Tolerant Sequentially Consistent DSM with a Compositional Correctness Proof

Niklas Ekström$^{(\boxtimes)}$ and Seif Haridi

KTH Royal Institute of Technology, Stockholm, Sweden
{neks,haridi}@kth.se

Abstract. We present the SC-ABD algorithm that implements sequentially consistent distributed shared memory (DSM). The algorithm tolerates that less than half of the processes are faulty (crash-stop). Compared to the multi-writer ABD algorithm, SC-ABD requires one instead of two round-trips of communication to perform a write operation, and an equal number of round-trips (two) to perform a read operation. Although sequential consistency is not a compositional consistency condition, the provided correctness proof is compositional.

1 Introduction

Using fault-tolerant distributed shared memory (DSM) as a building block in the design of a distributed system can simplify the design, as individual process failures are masked through replication. To characterize an implementation of distributed shared memory, we consider the following criteria:

- Consistency: a stronger consistency condition may be easier to program against, but may provide worse performance, and vice versa.
- Multiple writers: an implementation may allow a single process, or multiple processes, to update registers.
- Latency: the number of round-trips of communication required to execute an operation.
- Resilience: the number of processes that can be tolerated to be faulty in an execution, f, in relation to the total number of processes in the system, n.

In this paper, we consider the problem of implementing distributed shared memory that is sequentially consistent, allow multiple writers, can complete a write operation after one round of communication and a read operation after two rounds of communication, and that tolerates $f < n/2$ faulty processes. We present the SC-ABD algorithm as a solution to this problem. In Table 1 in the conclusion section, we present a comparison of SC-ABD to two other DSM algorithms along the mentioned criteria.

This work was supported by the Swedish Foundation for Strategic Research (SSF).

P.A. Abdulla and C. Delporte-Gallet (Eds.): NETYS 2016, LNCS 9944, pp. 183–192, 2016.
DOI: 10.1007/978-3-319-46140-3_14

Proving that a distributed shared memory implementation satisfies sequential consistency can be a difficult task. Unlike some other consistency conditions, sequential consistency is not a *compositional* consistency condition. Never the less, the proof given for the correctness of SC-ABD is compositional, and we therefore present this proof technique as a contribution in itself.

2   Model and Definitions

We consider an asynchronous distributed system composed of n processes, denoted $p_1, \ldots, p_n$, and a communication network with reliable links. We denote by $\Pi = \{1, \ldots, n\}$ the set of process identifiers. In any given system execution, a process is said to be correct if the process never crashes, and otherwise it is said to be faulty. A process that crashes stops taking steps and can never recover. We assume that at most f processes are faulty in any given execution, where $f < n/2$.

2.1   Shared Memory

A distributed shared memory is a distributed implementation of shared memory. We consider a shared memory consisting of read/write registers. Each register holds an integer value, initially zero. The shared memory defines a set of primitive operations, that provide the only means to manipulate the registers. In our case, the operations provided are *read* and *write*. A process invokes an operation and receives a response when the execution of the operation is complete. We will refer to an *operation execution* as an operation, if the distinction is clear from the context. Each process is allowed to have at most one outstanding operation, meaning that a process may not invoke another operation before the process has received the response for the previously invoked operation. Let o refer to a particular operation execution, invoked by process p_i. We denote by $inv(o)$ the *invocation event* that occurs when p_i invokes o, and denote by $res(o)$ the *response event* that occurs when the execution of o completes.

We model an execution using a *history*, which is a sequence of invocation and response events, ordered by the real times when the events occurred. History H is *sequential* if the first event is an invocation event, and every invocation event (except possibly the last) is immediately followed by the matching response event. By $H|p_i$ we denote the subsequence of H where every event occurs in process p_i; we refer to $H|p_i$ as a *process subhistory*. Similarly, by $H|x$ we denote the subsequence of H containing only events related to operations that target register x, and refer to $H|x$ as a *register subhistory*. A history is *well-formed* if each process subhistory is a sequential history, and in the following we only consider well-formed histories. Two histories H and H' are *equivalent*, denoted $H \simeq H'$, if and only if, for each process p_i, $H|p_i = H'|p_i$. For events e_1 and e_2 in history H we write $e_1 <_H e_2$ to denote that e_1 precedes e_2 in H. We say that "operation o is in history H" if $inv(o)$ is in H. For operations o_1 and o_2 in H we write $o_1 <_H o_2$ to denote that $res(o_1) <_H inv(o_2)$.

Operation o is *pending* in history H if the invocation event for o is in H but not the response event. History H is complete if H does not contain any pending operations. For presentational simplicity, we consider only complete histories in the rest of this paper.

The shared memory has a *sequential specification*, which is a set containing all sequential histories such that each read operation of some register returns the value written by the last write to that register (the write closest preceding the read in the sequential history), or the default value if no such write exists. A sequential history is *legal* if it is in the shared memory's sequential specification.

Sequential consistency is a consistency condition that was described by Lamport [7]. We define what it means for a history to be sequentially consistent:

Definition 1. *History H is* sequentially consistent, *denoted $SC(H)$, if and only if there exists a legal sequential history S such that $S \simeq H$.*

The correctness conditions that we require of an algorithm implementing sequentially consistent distributed shared memory are:

- **Termination:** If a correct process invokes an operation, then the operation eventually completes.
- **Sequential Consistency:** Each history corresponding to an execution of the algorithm must be sequentially consistent.

2.2   Causality and Logical Clocks

Causality and logical clocks were described in a paper by Lamport [6]. Event e_1 is said to *causally precede* event e_2, denoted $e_1 \to e_2$, if at least one of the following conditions hold: (1) e_1 and e_2 both occur in the same process and e_1 occurs before e_2, (2) e_1 is the sending of message m and e_2 is the receipt of m, (3) there exists an event e' such that $e_1 \to e'$ and $e' \to e_2$.

A logical clock is a device that assigns integers to events in a manner consistent with the causally precedes relation. More precisely, by letting $lt(e)$ denote the logical time assigned to event e, we require that: $e_1 \to e_2 \Rightarrow lt(e_1) < lt(e_2)$.

3   Algorithm

In this section we present the SC-ABD algorithm, whose pseudo-code is contained in Algorithm 1. The algorithm is given as a set of reactive *handlers*. Each handler has an associated condition that describes when that handler is eligible for execution, e.g., when an operation is invoked, or a message is received.

For each process, the algorithm contains a variable lt that implements a logical clock. Whenever a handler is executed in response to a local condition (i.e., an operation is invoked) the logical clock is incremented by one. When a message is sent from process p_i to process p_j, the current logical time of p_i is included in the message, and when the message is received by p_j and the corresponding handler is executed, p_j's logical clock is updated to a logical time that is one greater than the maximum of p_j's previous logical time and the logical time included in the message.

Each process stores the values that have been written to the registers. In order to determine which value is more recent, a timestamp is associated with each value. A value and its associated timestamp are stored together as a *timestamp-value pair*. The algorithm has a local variable, *tvps*, that maps register identifiers to timestamp-value pairs.

Communication in the algorithm proceeds in *phases*. A phase consists of a round of communication, where the process executing the phase, p_i, sends a request to all processes and waits for responses from a majority of the processes before the phase ends.

A write operation has one phase: the update phase. The process executing the write operation, p_i, creates a timestamp as the pair with p_i's current logical time and p_i's process identifier, i. It then pairs this timestamp together with the value to be written into a timestamp-value pair. p_i sends an update request containing the register identifier and the timestamp-value pair to all processes (lines 16–20 in Algorithm 1). When process p_j receives the update request it updates its *tvps* with the supplied timestamp-value pair if the timestamp is greater than the timestamp of the timestamp-value pair that was previously stored, and then sends an ack response (lines 21–23). After p_i receives acks from a majority of processes, p_i returns OK (lines 24–30).

A read operation has two phases: the query phase and the update phase. The process executing the read operation, p_i, sends a query request to all processes containing the register identifier for the register that is being read (lines 1–5). When process p_j receives the query request, p_j retrieves the timestamp-value pair stored in *tvps* for the register identifier, and sends this timestamp-value pair in a response message to p_i. This timestamp-value pair is the maximal timestamp-value pair that p_j has received so far in an update request, or the initial timestamp-value pair, $((0,0),0)$, if no update request had been received previously (lines 6–7). When p_i has received response messages from a majority of processes, p_i chooses the timestamp-value pair, (ts, v), with the maximum timestamp out of the timestamp-value pairs received. Before returning value v, p_i performs an update phase using the (ts, v) timestamp-value pair, in order to guarantee that a majority of the processes have stored the timestamp-value pair before the read completes (lines 8–15 and 21–30).

4   Correctness Proof

We first prove that SC-ABD satisfies the termination property.

Lemma 1. *Algorithm SC-ABD satisfies the termination property.*

Proof. As links are reliable and a majority of processes are correct according to the assumptions in our model, each communication phase executed by a correct process is guaranteed to eventually complete, and every operation executed by a correct process is therefore guaranteed to complete.   □

In the rest of this section we prove that the algorithm satisfies sequential consistency.

4.1 Linearizability

Linearizability is a consistency condition described by Herlihy and Wing [5].

Algorithm 1. SC-ABD – code for p_i.

Local variables:
lt – logical time; initially 0
rid – current request identifier; initially 0
$tvps$ – map from register ids to timestamp-value pairs; initially maps to $((0,0),0)$
$responses$ – tracking responses/acks; initially $\{\}$
$reading$ – indicating whether currently reading ($true$) or writing ($false$)
$rreg, rval$ – temporary storage for register identifier and return value during reads

Note: bcast $\langle m \rangle$ is an abbreviation for: **for** $j \in \Pi$ **do** send $\langle m \rangle$ to p_j

When READ(r) is invoked:
1: $lt \leftarrow lt + 1$
2: $reading \leftarrow true$
3: $rreg \leftarrow r$
4: $rid \leftarrow rid + 1$
5: bcast $\langle$"query"$, lt, rid, r \rangle$

When WRITE(r, v) is invoked:
16: $lt \leftarrow lt + 1$
17: $reading \leftarrow false$
18: $tsv \leftarrow ((lt, i), v)$
19: $rid \leftarrow rid + 1$
20: bcast $\langle$"update"$, lt, rid, r, tsv \rangle$

When $\langle$"query"$, lt', rid', r \rangle$ is
received from p_j:
6: $lt \leftarrow \max(lt, lt') + 1$
7: send $\langle$"response"$, lt, rid', tvps[r] \rangle$ to p_j

When $\langle$"update"$, lt', rid', r, tsv' \rangle$ is
received from p_j:
21: $lt \leftarrow \max(lt, lt') + 1$
22: $tvps[r] \leftarrow \max(tvps[r], tsv')$
23: send $\langle$"ack"$, lt, rid' \rangle$ to p_j

When $\langle$"response"$, lt', rid', tsv' \rangle$ is
received from p_j with $rid = rid'$:
8: $lt \leftarrow \max(lt, lt') + 1$
9: $responses \leftarrow responses \cup \{(tsv', j)\}$
10: **if** $|responses| = \lfloor |\Pi|/2 \rfloor + 1$ **then**
11: $\quad (tsv, \_) \leftarrow \max(responses)$
12: $\quad (ts, rval) \leftarrow tsv$
13: $\quad responses \leftarrow \{\}$
14: $\quad rid \leftarrow rid + 1$
15: $\quad$ bcast $\langle$"update"$, lt, rid, rreg, tsv \rangle$

When $\langle$"ack"$, lt', rid' \rangle$ is
received from p_j with $rid = rid'$:
24: $lt \leftarrow \max(lt, lt') + 1$
25: $responses \leftarrow responses \cup \{j\}$
26: **if** $|responses| = \lfloor |\Pi|/2 \rfloor + 1$ **then**
27: $\quad responses \leftarrow \{\}$
28: $\quad rid \leftarrow rid + 1$
29: $\quad$ **if** $reading$ **then** RETURN $rval$
30: $\quad$ **else** RETURN OK

Definition 2. *History H is* linearizable, *denoted* LIN(H), *iff there exists a legal sequential history S such that $S \simeq H$, and $\forall o_1, o_2 \in H : o_1 <_H o_2 \Rightarrow o_1 <_S o_2$.* .

Linearizability is *compositional*, in the sense that history H is linearizable if and only if each register subhistory $H|x$ is linearizable:

$$\text{LIN}(H) \Leftrightarrow \forall x : \text{LIN}(H|x) \tag{1}$$

From the definition of sequential consistency and the definition of linearizability, it follows that linearizability is stronger than sequential consistency:

$$LIN(H) \Rightarrow SC(H) \tag{2}$$

4.2   Logical-Time History

We define the *logical-time history* corresponding to history H, denoted H^{lt}, to be the sequence containing the same events as H, but reordered according to the logical times when the events occurred, using the process identifiers of the processes where the events occurred to break ties.

For each process p_i, the relative ordering of events in $H|p_i$ is preserved in $H^{lt}|p_i$, as the logical times of events in $H|p_i$ are monotonically increasing. It follows that the (real-time) history H and its corresponding logical-time history H^{lt} are equivalent, $H \simeq H^{lt}$. Together with the definition of sequentially consistent histories it follows that:

$$SC(H) \Leftrightarrow SC(H^{lt}) \tag{3}$$

4.3   Compositional Reasoning

Combining (1), (2), and (3), we have:

$$\left(\forall x : LIN(H^{lt}|x)\right) \Rightarrow LIN(H^{lt}) \Rightarrow SC(H^{lt}) \Rightarrow SC(H) \tag{4}$$

Equation (4) allows us to reason compositionally, i.e., to reason about, for each register x, the register subhistory $H^{lt}|x$ in isolation.

4.4   Reasoning About the Algorithm

We state a couple of definitions regarding the algorithm:

- The logical time of a handler execution is the value assigned to the lt variable on the handler's first line in the algorithm text.
- The timestamp of operation o, denoted $ts(o)$, is the timestamp used in the operation's update phase.

From the definition of logical-time history H^{lt}, it follows that:

$$o_1 <_{H^{lt}} o_2 \Rightarrow lt(res(o_1)) \leq lt(inv(o_2)) \tag{5}$$

We state and prove the following proposition:

Proposition 1. *Let o_1 and o_2 be operations in $H^{lt}|x$ such that o_1 contains an update phase and o_2 contains a query phase. If $o_1 <_{H^{lt}|x} o_2$ then $ts(o_1) \leq ts(o_2)$.*

Proof. Let p_i be the process that executes the update phase in o_1, and p_j be the process that executes the query phase in o_2. At the time when p_i's update phase completes, p_i will have received response messages from a majority of processes. Let M_u refer to this majority set of processes. Similarly, let M_q refer to the majority set of processes from which p_j received responses before the query phase in operation o_2 completed. As any two majority sets intersect, there must be one process, p_k, that is both in M_u and in M_q.

Let e_1 be the event when p_k processes o_1's update request, and e_2 the event when p_k processes o_2's query request. By causality we have $lt(e_1) < lt(res(o_1))$ and $lt(inv(o_2)) < lt(e_2)$, and together with (5) we get $lt(e_1) < lt(e_2)$. Since e_1 and e_2 are in the same process, this implies that e_1 occurs before e_2.

Since p_k returns the timestamp-value pair with the maximal timestamp that it has received in all previous update requests, the timestamp in the response to o_2's query request is guaranteed to be greater than or equal to the timestamp in o_1's update request. As p_j picks the timestamp-value pair with the maximal timestamp on line 11 of the algorithm, and uses it in its update phase, it follows that $ts(o_1) \leq ts(o_2)$. $\qquad\square$

Lemma 2. *Algorithm SC-ABD satisfies the sequential consistency property.*

Proof. By using Eq. (4), we prove that the algorithm satisfies sequential consistency, by showing, for each execution, and for each register x, that $\mathsf{LIN}(H^{lt}|x)$ holds. From the definition of linearizability, we see that in order to prove that $\mathsf{LIN}(H^{lt}|x)$ holds we are required to show that there exists a legal sequential history S such that $S \simeq H^{lt}|x$, and, for all operations o_1 and o_2 in $H^{lt}|x$, if o_1 precedes o_2 in $H^{lt}|x$ then o_1 also precedes o_2 in S. We proceed by creating a total order on the operations in $H^{lt}|x$ as follows:

1. Order write operations according to their timestamps. Any two write operations have unique timestamps by construction, so this is a total order.
2. Then order each read operation immediately after the write operation that wrote the value that the read operation returned. If there are more than one read operations with the same timestamp then they are internally ordered based on the logical times when they were invoked (breaking ties using process identifiers).

Let S be the sequential history obtained from this total order. As each read operation in S returns the value written by the closest preceding write operation, it follows that S is legal.

We show that $o_1 <_{H^{lt}|x} o_2 \Rightarrow o_1 <_S o_2$ using the following case analysis:

- o_1 is a write, o_2 is a write: By causality we have $lt(inv(o_1)) < lt(res(o_1))$, which together with (5) gives us $lt(inv(o_1)) < lt(inv(o_2))$. Because of how the algorithm constructs timestamps (line 18), this implies that $ts(o_1) < ts(o_2)$, from which $o_1 <_S o_2$ follows.

- o_1 is a read, o_2 is a write: There exists a write w_0 such that $ts(w_0) = ts(o_1)$. Since the invocation event of w_0 causally precedes the response event of o_1, we have $lt(inv(w_0)) < lt(res(o_1))$, and, using (5), we have $lt(inv(w_0)) < lt(inv(o_2))$. From the analysis of the previous case we have $ts(o_1) = ts(w_0) < ts(o_2)$, from which $o_1 <_S o_2$ follows.
- o_1 is a write, o_2 is a read: By the assumption and Proposition 1 it follows that $ts(o_1) \leq ts(o_2)$, from which $o_1 <_S o_2$ immediately follows.
- o_1 is a read, o_2 is a read: Again, by the assumption and Proposition 1 it follows that $ts(o_1) \leq ts(o_2)$. If $ts(o_1) < ts(o_2)$ we directly have $o_1 <_S o_2$. Otherwise, we have $ts(o_1) = ts(o_2)$. By causality and (5) we have $lt(inv(o_1)) < lt(inv(o_2))$, and $o_1 <_S o_2$ follows from the definition of S.

Finally we must show that $S \simeq H^{lt}|x$. For any process p_i, consider the history $(H^{lt}|x)|p_i$, which is sequential. For any pair of operations o_1 and o_2 in $(H^{lt}|x)|p_i$, either $o_1 <_{(H^{lt}|x)|p_i} o_2$ or $o_2 <_{(H^{lt}|x)|p_i} o_1$. The same ordering will be preserved in $S|p_i$, according to the case analysis above. As S and $H^{lt}|x$ contain the same events, we have $S \simeq H^{lt}|x$. □

Theorem 1. *Algorithm SC-ABD is a correct implementation of sequentially consistent distributed shared memory.*

Proof. Follows directly from Lemmas 1 and 2. □

5   Related Work

Research about shared memory has a long history in distributed computing.

5.1   Consistency Conditions

Lamport described sequential consistency [6]. In multiprocessor systems, sequential consistency is widely regarded as the "gold standard", but most multiprocessor systems provide weaker consistency by default, and require that programs use memory fences to achieve sequentially consistent behavior.

Proving that a shared memory implementation satisfies sequential consistency is a well-researched problem. Alur, McMillan, and Peled proved that, in general, the sequential consistency verification problem is undecidable [1].

Bingham, Condon, and Hu suggested that the original formulation of sequential consistency, which is not prefix-closed, may be a reason why the verification problem is hard, and suggested two alternative variants to sequential consistency, Decisive Sequential Consistency (DSC) and Past-Time Sequential Consistency (PTSC) that are prefix-closed [4].

Plakal, Sorin, Condon, and Hill use logical (Lamport) clocks as a tool to reason about correctness of their distributed shared memory protocol [9].

Linearizability was described by Herlihy and Wing [5]. Linearizability has the pleasant property that it is a compositional consistency condition.

The cost of sequential consistency vs. linearizability was analyzed by Attiya and Welch [3]. They proved that the cost of sequential consistency is lower than the cost of linearizability under reasonable assumptions.

5.2   Fault-Tolerant Shared Memory

The ABD algorithm was described by Attiya et al. [2]. ABD was the first algorithm that showed it to be possible to implement fault-tolerant linearizable shared memory in a message passing system, but allowed only a single process to write to the memory. Write operations complete after a single round of communication and read operations complete after two rounds.

The multi-writer ABD (MW-ABD) algorithm was described by Lynch and Shvartsman [8]. MW-ABD extended the ABD algorithm by allowing multiple processes to write to the memory, and in order to do so added a second round of communication to write operations.

6   Conclusion

We presented the SC-ABD algorithm that implements fault-tolerant, sequentially consistent, distributed shared memory, and proved it to be correct using a compositional proof structure.

Table 1 contains a comparison between SC-ABD, ABD, and MW-ABD along the criteria mentioned in the introduction: consistency condition (linearizability (LIN) or sequential consistency (SC)); multiple writers allowed; number of rounds of communication required to complete a write (W)/read (R) operation; and how many faulty processes, f, that the algorithm tolerates.

Table 1. Comparison between three fault-tolerant DSM algorithms.

	ABD	MW-ABD	SC-ABD
Consistency	LIN	LIN	SC
Multiple writers	No	Yes	Yes
Latency	W:1, R:2	W:2, R:2	W:1, R:2
Resilience	$f < n/2$	$f < n/2$	$f < n/2$

In a situation where an application, running on top of distributed shared memory, would satisfy its correctness conditions if the distributed shared memory provides sequential consistency, and the application would benefit from having a lower latency for write operations, we think that SC-ABD is a good choice.

Finally, we showed that, although sequential consistency is not a compositional consistency condition, it was still possible to reason compositionally about the correctness of the algorithm.

Acknowledgements. We would like to thank the Swedish Foundation for Strategic Research for funding this work, and Jingna Zeng for helpful discussions.

References

1. Alur, R., McMillan, K., Peled, D.: Model-checking of correctness conditions for concurrent objects. In: Proceedings of the 11th Annual IEEE Symposium on Logic in Computer Science, LICS 1996, p. 219. IEEE Computer Society, Washington, DC (1996)
2. Attiya, H., Bar-Noy, A., Dolev, D.: Sharing memory robustly in message-passing systems. J. ACM **42**(1), 124–142 (1995)
3. Attiya, H., Welch, J.L.: Sequential consistency versus linearizability. ACM Trans. Comput. Syst. **12**(2), 91–122 (1994)
4. Bingham, J.D., Condon, A., Hu, A.J.: Toward a decidable notion of sequential consistency. In: Proceedings of the Fifteenth Annual ACM Symposium on Parallel Algorithms and Architectures, SPAA 2003, pp. 304–313. ACM, New York (2003)
5. Herlihy, M.P., Wing, J.M.: Linearizability: a correctness condition for concurrent objects. ACM Trans. Program. Lang. Syst. **12**(3), 463–492 (1990)
6. Lamport, L.: Time, clocks, and the ordering of events in a distributed system. Commun. ACM **21**(7), 558–565 (1978)
7. Lamport, L.: How to make a multiprocessor computer that correctly executes multiprocess programs. IEEE Trans. Comput. **28**(9), 690–691 (1979)
8. Lynch, N.A., Shvartsman, A.A.: Robust emulation of shared memory using dynamic quorum-acknowledged broadcasts. In: Proceedings of the 27th International Symposium on Fault-Tolerant Computing (FTCS 1997), p. 272. IEEE Computer Society, Washington, DC (1997)
9. Plakal, M., Sorin, D.J., Condon, A.E., Hill, M.D.: Lamport clocks: verifying a directory cache-coherence protocol. In: Proceedings of the Tenth Annual ACM Symposium on Parallel Algorithms and Architectures, SPAA 1998, pp. 67–76. ACM, New York (1998)

Exploiting Crowd Sourced Reviews to Explain Movie Recommendation

Sara El Aouad[1,2]([✉]), Christophe Dupuy[1,2], Renata Teixeira[2], Francis Bach[2], and Christophe Diot[3]

[1] Technicolor, Issy-les-Moulineaux, France
sara.elaouad@technicolor.com
[2] Inria, Paris, France
[3] Safran, Paris, France

Abstract. Streaming services such as Netflix, M-Go, and Hulu use advanced recommender systems to help their customers identify relevant content quickly and easily. These recommenders display the list of recommended movies organized in sublists labeled with the genre or some more specific labels. Unfortunately, existing methods to extract these labeled sublists require human annotators to manually label movies, which is time-consuming and biased by the views of annotators. In this paper, we design a method that relies on crowd sourced reviews to automatically identify groups of similar movies and label these groups. Our method takes the content of movie reviews available online as input for an algorithm based on Latent Dirichlet Allocation (LDA) that identifies groups of similar movies. We separate the set of similar movies that share the same combination of genre in sublists and personalize the movies to show in each sublist using matrix factorization. The results of a side-by-side comparison of our method against Technicolor's M-Go VoD service are encouraging.

1 Introduction

According to a recent study [10], over 40 % of households in the United States have access to VoD services. With the overwhelming number of videos offered per service, a key challenge is to help users decide which movie to watch. Sophisticated VoD services use recommender systems based on matrix factorization applied to movie ratings [8]. VoD services then display the long list of recommended movies ranked based on the predicted rating per movie. This list is often organized into labeled sublists that help users browse the recommendations. For example, Netflix presents movies in rows according to genres (which go from more traditional, coarse-grained labels such as "Action" or "Comedy" to more specific labels such as "Visually-striking Goofy Action & Adventure") [8]. Existing methods to group movies into sublists and to label sublists require people to manually label each movie [11]. This manual method has two main drawbacks. First, the labels of each sublist are subjective and biased toward the opinion and cultural background of annotators. Second, manual annotation is expensive and

© Springer International Publishing AG 2016
P.A. Abdulla and C. Delporte-Gallet (Eds.): NETYS 2016, LNCS 9944, pp. 193–201, 2016.
DOI: 10.1007/978-3-319-46140-3_15

requires an extensive human effort especially because labels are often specific to a region and movie databases keep growing with new movie releases.

In this paper, we argue that instead of relying on a few people to tag movies, we can use crowd sourced reviews to automatically identify groups of similar movies and label these groups. Many moviegoers enter detailed reviews of movies they have watched on sites such as IMDb and Rotten Tomatoes. The corpus of online reviews represents a source of rich meta-data for each movie. We use a database of 2000 movies and 100 users extracted from IMDb by Diao et al. [7] as a proof of concept in this paper.

The challenge we face is to mine the noisy free-text reviews from a heterogeneous set of people to extract meaningful and personalized sublists of movies. We are tackling this challenge in three steps. First, we design an algorithm based on LDA (Latent Dirichlet Allocation) to estimate the similarity between movies based on the content of reviews (Sect. 2.1). The outcome of this step is a list of the most similar movies to the movie the user selected. Second, we split the list of similar movies into sublists of movies that share common characteristics (Sect. 2.2). Our initial version uses a combination of genres to generate these sublists. For each sublist, we provide a list of words that characterizes this sublist, extracted from the crowd sourced reviews. To give more insight about the recommended movies, users can click on these words to see in which movies of the sublist the word corresponds to. Finally, we personalize each sublist by filtering and ordering the movies using matrix factorization (Sect. 2.3). We only display to the user movies with a predicted rating of at least six (out of ten).

We implement a web service using our method with the same look as Technicolor's VoD service in the United States, M-Go (Sect. 3). This implementation allowed us to perform side-by-side comparisons of M-Go's existing system (which uses manual tagging of movies to extract sublists of similar movies and labels for each sublist) and our sublists. Our initial results are encouraging (Sect. 4).

We do not claim that our method gives better recommendation, but instead that the movies we recommend come with more insight about why they are recommended. Note that this is early results and that we believe that the method can be greatly improved, and extended to many other domains.

2   Method

We envision a scenario where a user will click on a movie, say m, and the recommender will display a list of movies similar to m recommended for the user organized in labeled sublists. We use a database of 2,000 movies and 100 users extracted from IMDb (a subset of the data described in [7]) for our method. Our method works in three steps. First, we identify the list of similar movies. This step uses the content of the IMDb reviews to identify similarities among movies with no personalization. Second, we split the list of similar movies into sub-groups. Finally, we apply matrix factorization to personalize the sublists.

2.1   Movie Similarity

We base our method to identify the list of most similar movies to a given movie on Latent Dirichlet allocation (LDA) [3]. LDA is a probabilistic topic model that extracts K latent topics from a corpus of documents. Each topic is a discrete distribution over the words of the vocabulary. Ideally, in our case, we would like each topic to be consistent around movie features such as genres, actors or directors. To apply LDA, we must define what constitutes a document, an appropriate vocabulary, and a value of K.

We create a corpus where each document is the concatenation of the reviews written for a single movie in the IMDb dataset. This concatenation has the effect of increasing the consistency of each document as users tend to employ the same vocabulary to describe the same movie.

We build the vocabulary by extracting relevant words from the reviews in our dataset. Some words (for example stop words or words such as movie, film, and plot) appear in many reviews, but are not significant. We eliminate such words using a dictionary that we create manually from our dataset. For the remaining words, we apply *term frequency-Inverse document frequency* (TF-IDF) score as a filter. TF-IDF gives a high score for words that are frequent in a document but rare in other documents. We compute TF-IDF for each word of each review in the corpus and select the 10,000 words with the highest score.[1]

We select K empirically. After multiple experiments with values of K between 8 and 260, we observe that for $K \leq 30$, the topics mix several features as there are not enough topics to separate the different aspects expressed in the reviews. For $K \geq 150$, individual features get split over multiple topics. We chose $K = 128$ as a good compromise for movies.

Then we assign a weight to each word in the documents as follows:

$$\hat{f}_w^d = \frac{f_w^d}{\sqrt{N_d}} \tag{1}$$

where f_w^d is the number of occurrences of the word w in the document d, and N_d the number of reviews in the same document. The goal of this normalization is to reduce the imbalance between the most popular movies and the least popular ones.

We apply LDA to this new corpus. The assumption behind the LDA model is that each document d is generated from a mixture of topics denoted θ_d. With LDA, we infer the topic distribution θ_d of each document d and the topics ϕ. To compute similarity between movies, we use their topic distribution θ_d and the *Kullback Leibler divergence* similarity metric (KL). For two topic distributions θ^1 and θ^2 we have:

$$KL(\theta^1 \parallel \theta^2) = \sum_{i=1}^{k} \theta_i^1 log \frac{\theta_i^1}{\theta_i^2} \tag{2}$$

---

[1] After empirical verification, this number of words seems to give the best results for the data bases that we are using.

2.2 Genre-Based Sub-grouping

This section presents the method to split the list of the most similar movies to a movie m (extracted using the method presented in the previous section) into sublists. We also describe our method for extracting a title and a subtitle for each sublist.

We inspire our design on M-Go's interface, which presents four sublists: the first with the most similar movies and the other three grouped around more specific labels. Similarly, we generate four sublists. The first contains the N most similar movies to m. The three remaining sublists groups movies based on a pair of genres. We use the movie genres because they are familiar to users and because genres help create consistent sublists.

First, we generate the list of all the possible pairs of movie genres that appear in our dataset. We repeat the following steps to extract our sublists: for each pair (g1, g2) in our dataset, we will extract the N most similar movies that have at least g1 and g2 as genres. We then compute the average distance between m and the extracted movies. We select the pair of genres and the corresponding sublist that have the smallest average distance to m. For the next sublist, we eliminate the already selected pairs and movies in the previous sublists, in order to avoid redundancy among sublists.

Each sublist has a title and a subtitle. The title corresponds to the pair of movie genres (e.g., Action and Thriller). The subtitle is the set of words that best describes the movies of the sublist. We generate these words with LDA parameters. We define the score of a word as follows:

$$s(w) = \sum_{i=1}^{K} \phi_i[w]\bar{\theta}[i] \tag{3}$$

where K is the number of topics, and $\phi_i[w]$ is the weight of the word w in topic i. We also set:

$$\bar{\theta} = \frac{1}{N} \sum_{j \in currentsublist} \theta_j. \tag{4}$$

where N is the number of movies in each sublist and θ_j is the topic distribution of movie j. We compute the score of each word of the vocabulary. We keep the first twenty words with the highest scores. Figure 1 illustrates our method to generate the subtitle for a sublist with two similar movies.

2.3 Rating Prediction

This section explains how we personalize the movies displayed in each sublist. We order the movies in each sublist according to the predicted ratings of the user on each movie. We predict ratings for movies users have not rated using matrix factorization [2]. We map both the users and the movies to the same space of dimension p. Each user u has a feature vector U_u and each movie i has feature vector V_i. The rating prediction model can be written as follows:

$$r_{u,i} \sim \mathcal{N}(V_i^T U_u, 1) \tag{5}$$

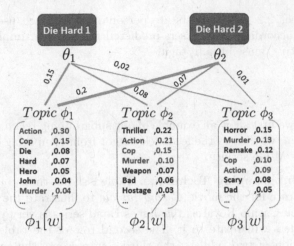

Fig. 1. Example of our technique to extract subtitles for a sublist of recommended movies. The words in red are the selected words (Action, Murder, Cop) as they have the highest scores.

We learn the feature vectors (V_i and U_u) by solving the following regularized minimization problem:

$$\min_{U,V} \sum_{(u,i) \in observations} (r_{u,i} - V_i^T U_u)^2 + \lambda(\|V\|^2 + \|U\|^2) \qquad (6)$$

The goal of the regularization is to avoid over-fitting the observed data. The regularization parameter λ is chosen with cross-validation. We train our algorithm using gradient descent where we loop over all the ratings in our dataset.

3   Prototype

We create a web-based prototype, built using the IMDb dataset to demonstrate our approach. The user interface comes from Technicolor's VoD system, M-Go[2], to easy side-by-side comparisons. We apply the methods described in the previous section to identify groups of similar movies and subgroups. For each user in the IMDb dataset, we compute the predicted ratings using the matrix factorization model. We select pairs of genres to display to each user based on the preferred genres for the user. In our prototype we identify the preferred genres per user based on the most frequent movie genre pairs that the user has already seen. We then organize the recommended movies with a high rating prediction in sublists, according to the user most preferred genre pairs. When a user selects a movie from the sublists of recommended movies, our application suggests the similar movies presented under four sublists with the added list of words as

---

[2] http://www.mgo.com.

described in Sect. 2.2. The sublists are personalized for each user by reordering the movies according to the users predicted ratings. Our implementation is available at: http://muse.inria.fr/tagit.

4   Results

In this section, we first show an example of our subgrouping technique for a popular movie. Then, we discuss the feedback we got from comparing our prototype to Technicolor's M-Go service.

Example of Subgrouping Technique. Table 1 shows the sublists of similar movies we generate for the movie *Casino Royale* to illustrate the results of our method. We pick Casino Royal as the James Bond series is very popular, so we hope most readers will relate to it. The second row of the table presents the genre combination of two sublists; the third row presents the subtitle of each sublist (i.e., the words that describe the movies in each sublist); and the bottom part of the table presents the set of movies in each sublist.

Table 1. Sublists of movies similar to "Casino Royale".

Casino Royale (2006)	
Action and Thriller	Action and Adventure
shoot, blow, rambo, bullet, enemy, bruce, flick, hard, weak, gun, air, machine, pace, bad, kill, escape, impossible, hole, team, pack	cgi, superhero, hero, matrix, rescue, knight, cgus, trilogy, destroy, visual, terminator, batman, battle, earth, comic, blockbuster, super, original, special, superman
Taken 2	Indiana Jones and the Kingdom of the Crystal Skull
From Paris With Love	Captain America: The Winter Soldier
Lethal Weapon	Batman Begins
Mission Impossible III	X-Men Origins: Wolverine
Goldfinger	Transformers: Revenge of the Fallen
Live Free or Die Hard	Pacific Rim
The Dark Knight Rises	Captain America: The First Avenger
Rambo	The Scorpion King
The One	Pirates of the Caribbean: At World's End

We see that using our sub grouping method the movies in each sublist are consistent, which mean that they share common features. For example, in the first sublist, all the movies are action-packed movies. In the second list, almost all movies are sequel adventurous movies.

The words in the subtitle describe the movies in each sublist. These words contain descriptive words such as (visual and battle), and qualitative words for example (super and original), as users tend to use both qualitative and descriptive words while expressing their opinion about a movie. The subtitles help us make a distinction between sublists. For example, the first sublist is about action packed movies: *gun, shoot, kill, blow, escape*, whereas the second is about movies with visual effects (*cgi, visual*) and sequel movies (the fact that it contains *trilogy* movies such as: *Indiana Jones, Captain America, Batman, Transformers* and *The Pirates of the Caribbean*).

User Feedback. During an internal event at Technicolor we demonstrated our prototype service side-by-side with the M-Go website. M-Go groups similar movies using manual labels provided by a third party service. We compare with M-Go because it is the existing service of Technicolor and most of the people attending the event were Technicolor employees. We had feedback from about 50 users who visited our stand; mainly Technicolor's employees expert in the movie domain.

We summarize the lessons learned from their feedback as follows. Almost all users agreed that it is hard to decide quickly on which movie to watch with existing systems. After seeing our sublists users said that they appreciated having the genre pair and the list of words per movies as this information gives them an extra description of the movies in this list; especially when they clicked on a word to see the most related movies to this word. Many users, however, considered the single-word tags hard to interpret because it required extra cognitive effort to combine single words into a meaningful concept; for example to go from *chase* and *car*, to *car chase*. Users also complained because of the presence of some generic words such as *person* or *etc*. These comments indicate that we must improve the method to filter words and that instead of presenting single words we should present short sentences that better capture comments in the reviews. Users also made a number of comments about how they interact with movie recommendation systems. They said that they usually look at the first or second sublist without scrolling down further, also they usually look just at the first displayed movies in each single sublist without looking at the rest of the sublist. This observation implies that we should aim at reducing the number of sublists and the number of movies displayed in each sublist.

5   Related Work

Our work organizes the list of recommended movies into labeled sublists. Prior studies have also focused on organizing items in labeled lists, for example to group query results into labeled categories [12,13]. We can see the title and subtitle of the sublists that our method outputs, as an explanation to movie recommendations. A number of studies have shown that adding explanation to the recommended movies improves the user satisfaction and loyalty to the system [1,4–6]. Herlocker et al. [1] compared between multiple explanation interfaces and showed that using a simple interface outperformed complex explanation interfaces. The types of recommendation explanation include item-based, feature-based, and tag-based explanation. For example item-based explanation has the format: *We Recommend the movie X because you reviewed the movie Y.* Feature-based explanation has the format: *We Recommend the movie X because it contains the features Y and Z.* Finally, in tag-based explanation, the explanatory tags are the tags that characterize both the user profile and the movie profile. Chen et al. [5] showed that using tag-based and feature-based explanation performed better than item-based explanation. Therefore in our study we will combine feature-based and tag-based explanation. Chen et al. [5] also presented a method to explain recommendation using tags. The main difference with our approach is that we extract single-word tags automatically from user reviews rather than using the tags explicitly entered by users. We believe that the full reviews contain rich meta-data that is essential to group and label movies.

6   Conclusion and Future Work

Movie recommenders generally give little insight on why a given movie is recommended. We propose to leverage crowd sourced reviews written by internet users to provide additional information about recommended movies. We use LDA applied to words found in reviews as a novel approach to content similarity that we combine to matrix factorization for personalization of recommendations. We attach to recommended movies a set of single-word tags that best describe these movies using reviewers' own vocabulary. This approach eliminates the manual tagging of movies used in most recommenders. Results are encouraging. We have shown the results of our method to around 50 people (experts in media creation and delivery). Most users found that the insight given by the title and subtitle was helpful as it helped them understand the common characteristics that describe the movies in each sublist. There are several interesting directions to improve this work. First, we plan to use meaningful expressions (e.g. *Complex story* or *Funny action*) rather than single-word tags in labeling the movie sublists. Our next objective is to personalize such vocabulary and use the most likely words a user would use to comment a movie. Last, we intend to evaluate our system with a large panel of real users, using an A/B testing for our system and M-Go in order to understand (1) if users prefer our automatic clustering and explanation over the manual one and (2) if they think our recommendation is more acute.

Acknowledgment. This project is supported by the European Community's Seventh Framework Programme (FP7/2007-2013) no. 611001 (User-Centric Networking).

References

1. Herlocker, J.L., Konstan, J.A., Riedl, J.: Explaining collaborative filtering recommendations. In: Proceedings of the ACM Conference on Computer Supported Cooperative Work. ACM (2000)
2. Koren, Y., Bell, R., Volinsky, C.: Matrix factorization techniques for recommender systems. Computer **42**(8), 30–37 (2009)
3. Blei, D.M., Ng, A.Y., Jordan, M.I.: Latent dirichlet allocation. J. Mach. Learn. Res. **3**, 993–1022 (2003)
4. Tintarev, N., Masthoff, J.: Effective explanations of recommendations: user-centered design. In: Proceedings of the ACM Conference on Recommender Systems. ACM (2007)
5. Chen, W., Hsu, W., Lee, M.L.: Tagcloud-based explanation with feedback for recommender systems. In: Proceedings of the 36th International ACM SIGIR Conference on Research and Development in Information Retrieval. ACM (2013)
6. Symeonidis, P., Nanopoulos, A., Manolopoulos, Y.: MoviExplain: a recommender system with explanations. In: Proceedings of the Third ACM Conference on Recommender Systems. ACM (2009)
7. Diao, Q., et al.: Jointly modeling aspects, ratings and sentiments for movie recommendation (JMARS). In: Proceedings of the 20th ACM SIGKDD International Conference on Knowledge Discovery and Data Mining. ACM (2014)
8. Amatriain, X.: Beyond data: from user information to business value through personalized recommendations and consumer science. In: Proceedings of the 22nd ACM International Conference on Information and Knowledge Management. ACM (2013)
9. Bell, R.M., Koren, Y.: Lessons from the Netflix prize challenge. ACM SIGKDD Explor. Newsl. **9**(2), 75–79 (2007)
10. The Total Audience Report: Q4 2014. http://www.nielsen.com/us/en/insights/reports/2015/the-total-audience-report-q4-2014.html
11. Tom Vanderbilt. The science behind the netflix algorithms that decide what you'll watch next. http://www.wired.com/2013/08/qq_netflix-algorithm
12. Zeng, H.-J., et al.: Learning to cluster web search results. In: Proceedings of the 27th Annual International ACM SIGIR Conference on Research and Development in Information Retrieval. ACM (2004)
13. Zhao, J., He, J.: Learning to generate labels for organizing search results from a domain-specified corpus. In: IEEE/WIC/ACM International Conference on Web Intelligence, WI 2006. IEEE (2006)

A Formal Model for WebRTC Signaling Using SDL

Asma El Hamzaoui[1]([⊠]), Hicham Bensaid[1,2],
and Abdeslam En-Nouaary[1]

[1] Institut National des Postes et Télécommunications, Rabat, Morocco
{elhamzaoui,bensaid,abdeslam}@inpt.ac.ma
[2] Labmia, Faculté des Sciences, Mohammed V University in Rabat, Rabat,
Morocco

Abstract. We present a formal approach to modeling Jingle protocol and the related IETF protocols STUN, TURN and ICE using Specification and Description Language (SDL). The aim is to perform a complete unambiguous model for signaling exchange between two WebRTC communicating entities, and study their behavior in real network conditions like the presence of NAT (Network Address Translation) and firewalls. The main objective is to demonstrate the feasibility of using a formal language, such as SDL to model a system as complex as IETF RTCWeb architecture using Jingle as a signaling mechanism.

1 Introduction

Nowadays, Real Time Communication (RTC) is used daily in our modern society with different forms of rich mobile and desktop applications. This led to the development of new web technologies such as HTML5. Furthermore, innovations on hardware and infrastructure fields increase the available bandwidth. Thus, WebRTC, as an ongoing standardization effort, appears to enhance user experience in RTC via the Web, which is a Peer to Peer (P2P) communication between browsers without any additional installation.

In order to establish a WebRTC session, there is a need for a signaling protocol to allow communicating parties to agree on parameters such as codecs, types of media, transport addresses, etc. Signaling in WebRTC will remain completely abstract, which means that there is no specification that defines how it will be performed. However, it is specified that the session descriptions will be exchanged using Session Description Protocol (SDP); the application is allowed to control the signaling plane of the multimedia session through the interface specified in Javascript Session Establishment Protocol (JSEP) API [1]. In this paper, we focus on Jingle protocol to setup, manage and the teardown multimedia sessions between two peers.

Besides signaling, there are other factors that may cause a session establishment to be denied between peers: NAT traversal and firewall issues. Some technical concepts have been introduced and used in WebRTC to enable connection without having to reveal the IP addresses and to overcome the firewall blocking issues. This is ICE (Interactive Connectivity Establishment) [2], which makes use of two other protocols: Session Traversal Utilities for NAT (STUN) [3] and Traversal Using Relays around NAT (TURN) [4].

© Springer International Publishing AG 2016
P.A. Abdulla and C. Delporte-Gallet (Eds.): NETYS 2016, LNCS 9944, pp. 202–208, 2016.
DOI: 10.1007/978-3-319-46140-3_16

In fact, tests and simulations of implementations are not enough to reach a high level of confidence. It is important to have a formal model in order to asset formal evidence of specifications respect and propose well-founded improvements to this technology. To the best of our knowledge this aspect is not tackled for protocols involved in WebRTC, except the SDL model of SIP protocol that was carried in the context of VoIP [5]. Our contribution to study the signaling part of WebRTC starts by working on Jingle combined with STUN, TURN and ICE for NAT and firewall traversals.

The remainder of this paper is structured as follows: In Sect. 2, we give some clarification about Jingle protocol. Section 3 explains the main features of our Jingle formal model using SDL. Section 4 concludes the paper and presents our future work.

2 Jingle

Jingle is a signaling protocol used for initiating and managing P2P media sessions in a way that is interoperable with existing Internet standards. It was in fact designed to be an open technology that takes into account requirements to inter-operate with SIP-based technologies [6].

In fact, Jingle has many strong points that could be summarized as follows: A conception based on XML; An ability to negotiate each result individually [8]; A good collaboration with NAT traversal mechanisms [10], and a strong authentication, channel encryption, and trusted identities [7].

These considerations have led many software developers to incorporate Jingle into their applications such as Google hangout or iChat for Apple.

Jingle clearly separates the signaling channel from the data channel, and the application formats (e.g., audio) from the transport methods (e.g., RTP). The basic flow to establish a session includes the exchange of Jingle messages such as: "Session-initiate", "ACK" and "Session-Accept". After the exchange of media, one of the peers can close the communication by "Session-terminate" message. Moreover, it is possible to add, modify, and remove both application types and transport methods in an existing session by messages such as: "Transport-Info", "Content-Add" etc.

3 Jingle Signaling Model

In this section, we present our SDL formal model of Jingle protocol collaborating with NAT traversal protocols, such as STUN TURN and ICE, in the context of WebRTC. This work is done by analyzing the protocols (informal) specifications, [2–4], [8–11] and [6]. We describe the various levels of abstraction of our model in terms of architecture, behavior and data. The complete SDL model is available in[1], thus by conciseness only selected diagrams will be presented in this paper.

---

[1] https://sites.google.com/site/jinglesdlmodel/.

3.1   Architectural Design for Jingle Using SDL

SDL is a formal language standardized by ITU, [12], for modeling and developing communication protocols. The SDL architecture represents the division of large systems into more comprehensible structures. Thus, the design of our model starts first by partitioning the system into SDL blocks. Dependencies between blocks are defined by connecting them with channels. A SDL system represents static interactions between WebRTC entities. The channels connected between various block instances specify the signals or Control messages that are sent between Jingle peers and/or ICE servers.

The system level of our SDL model is presented in Fig. 1. The main blocks are the Initiator Browser, the Terminator Browser, which represent the two WebRTC peers and the ICE servers block. The ICE servers block is further divided into two sub-blocks: STUN Server Type, and TURN Server Type. Figure 2 depicts the ICE Servers block.

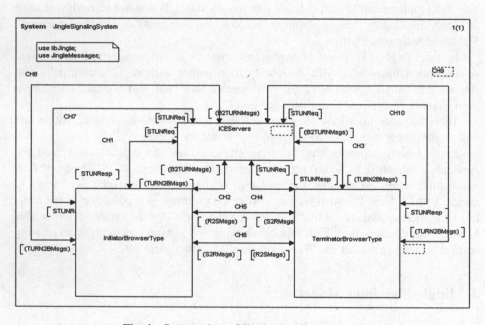

Fig. 1. System view of Jingle signaling protocol.

The Initiator and the Terminator are composed of two sides that represent the bidirectional communication: Sending Browser Type and Responding Browser Type, as shown in Fig. 3. One of the goals of formal modeling is to optimize the structure. From analyzing of the ICE Servers sub-blocks, we notice that there aren't any relations between the two blocks STUN and TURN servers, and that they have mainly the same interfaces with the other blocks with differences in the internal behavior. Thus, in order to optimize the structure, we propose to add to our specification one block named "ICE Proxy" that allows to aggregate all NAT traversal transaction and forward the requests

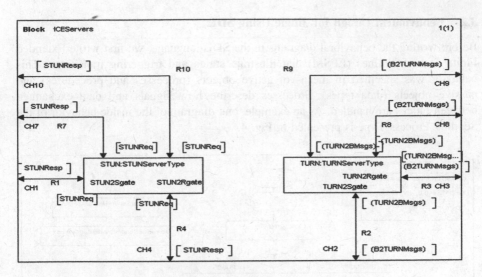

Fig. 2. Block ICE view.

to STUN or TURN server according to the context (the existence of the TURN server or not, the availability of several STUN servers or not in the network…). This addition permits a great flexibility and scalability of the model. However, this proposal can introduce unnecessary latency in the server response. This issue will be investigated in more detail in future work. The next subsection of this paper introduces the behavioral model of Jingle.

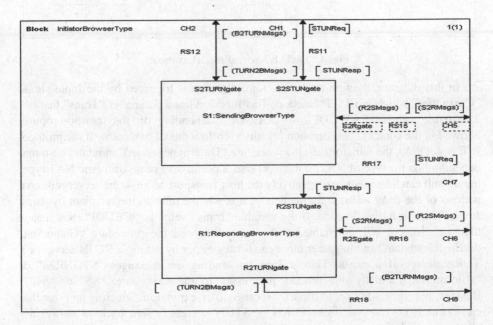

Fig. 3. Block initiator view.

3.2   Behavioural Design for Jingle Using SDL

Before writing the behavioral diagrams in the SDL language, we first wrote Extended Finite State Machines (EFSM) that illustrate states and triggering transitions. This behavior was specified in means of active objects (processes and procedures) and passive objects (data types). Processes describe how signals and data exchanged between blocks are handled. As an example, one diagram of the inside behavior of the Sending Process Type is presented in Fig. 4.

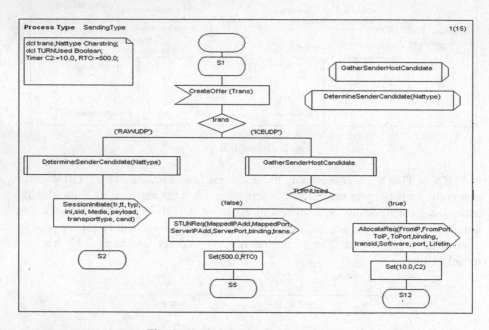

Fig. 4. Jingle behavioral model extracts.

In this diagram, the first transition from idle state is triggered by the Input signal "CreatOffer" which is a JSEP function. This function has a parameter "Trans" that has 2 possible values "RAWUDP" or "ICEUDP" depending on the transport option allowed in the context. This decision permits to follow one of two paths. If the protocol ICE is not used, the initiator calls the procedure "DetermineSenderCandidates". So that depending on the type of NAT, if there is none, a permissive or a symmetric NAT type, the default candidate will be respectively the host transport address, the server reflexive address or the relay address. Subsequently, it sends the offer to the recipient by using Jingle "session-initiate" action. If the variable "trans" value is 'ICEUDP', this means that the protocol ICE is enabled and we need to call the procedure "GatherSenderHostCandidate" and to gather other candidates either by asking a STUN server or a TURN server, if it exists. This is done by sending out messages "STUNReq" or "AllocateReq". Finally, the process progresses to the next state: "S5" or "S12". Besides, two timers are set to model response timer expiration, which is an error that can occur if no response from TURN or STUN servers is sent back to answer the allocate or STUN request in a specific time.

3.3   Data Representation in the Model

Jingle and ICE messages are defined as SDL signals in the "JingleMessages" package. For example, the key header fields in a Jingle message are represented by the corresponding signal parameters. The header fields that we have included in our SDL model are: "From", "To", "Type", "Initiator", "sessionid", "Mediatype", "transporttype", "PayloadTypeList" and "CandidateList". There are many header fields available in Jingle, but we believe these fields are the most important ones. In fact, they convey the state of all the participants in the session. One new data type is named "Jid" (i.e., Jingle id), which is a structure with three Charstring fields: User id, Domain and Resource. This new type describes an address like "ahmed@inpt.ac/office". Overall, we should note that this model can be extensible.

4   Conclusion and Future Work

This paper presents a formal SDL model of a signaling mechanism and NAT traversal utilities used in the context of WebRTC. Those asynchronous communication protocols in the context of a distributed system and manipulating complex data structures are of great interest to be analyzed by formal verification techniques and by performance testing. The first contribution was this unambiguous representation of the WebRTC signaling system that increases the understanding of the behavior by developers, and allows performing a conceptual validation as well as a correct implementation.

In future work, we will proceed to the verification and validation of the model by model checking. Subsequently, a general framework of signaling protocol verification for Web communication will be elaborated. Furthermore, some other WebRTC aspects, such as multiparty communication will be included in the model.

References

1. Javascript Session Establishment Protocol Specification, IETF Internet Draft. V.06 (2015)
2. Interactive Connectivity Establishment: A Protocol for NAT Traversal for Offer/Answer Protocols Specification, IETF Internet Standard track. RFC 5245 (2010)
3. Session Traversal Utilities for NAT (STUN), IETF Internet Standard track. RFC 5389 (2008)
4. Traversal Using Relays around NAT (TURN): Relay Extensions to Session Traversal Utilities for NAT (STUN). IETF Internet Standard track. RFC 5766 (2010)
5. Chan, K.Y., v. Bochmann, G.: Methods for designing SIP services in SDL with fewer feature interactions. University of Ottawa (2003)
6. Jingle Specification, XMPP Standard Foundation, Standard Track. XEP-0166 (2008)
7. Saint-Andre, P., Smith, K., Tronçon, R.: XMPP: The Definitive Guide, Building Real-Time Applications with Jabber, 1st edn., Treseler, M.E. (ed.) O'Reilly Books, New York (2009)
8. Jingle RTP Session Specification. Standard Track. XEP-0167 (2008)

 9. Jingle RAWUDP Transport Specification. Standard Track. XEP-0177, (2009)
10. Jingle ICEUDP Transport Specification. Standard Track. XEP-0176 (2009)
11. RTCWeb JSEP XMPP/Jingle Mapping Specification, IETF Internet Draft. V.02 (2013)
12. ITU-TS Recommendation Z.100: Specification and Description Language (SDL), International Telecommunication Union, ITU-TS, Geneva, Switzerland (1999)

An Incremental Proof-Based Process of the NetBill Electronic Commerce Protocol

Sanae El Mimouni$^{(\boxtimes)}$ and Mohamed Bouhdadi

LMPHE Laboratory, Faculty of Sciences, Mohammed V University, Rabat, Morocco
sanae.elm@gmail.com, bouhdadi@fsr.ac.ma

Abstract. This paper presents an incremental formal modeling of the NetBill protocol using Event-B method. The NetBill protocol is an electronic commerce protocol designed for micropayment systems for selling and delivery of information and goods through the internet. We model the protocol step by step using refinement, which is the key mechanism of the Event-B method. Event-B modeling starts with an abstraction of a system and adds details during refinement levels in order to gain a final model close to the implementation. Moreover mathematical proofs are incorporated into Event-B to verify the correctness of refinement steps. The outcome of this incremental approach was that we achieved a very high degree of automatic proof. In the developed Event-B model of the NetBill protocol described in this paper, all proofs are generated and discharged by the Rodin tool.

Keywords: NetBill protocol · Event-B · Refinement · Formal method · Rodin

1 Introduction

With the growth of the internet community and the endless possibilities the internet offers to the person, it didn't take long before someone realized that the web is a really good place for the commercial business. So, very quickly electronic commerce was born, offering almost all kinds of goods to be purchased and delivered, simply over the internet.

Electronic commerce protocols are security protocols that allow customers and merchants to conduct their business electronically through the internet. In this article we choose to model the NetBill protocol [5, 7].

NetBill is an electronic commerce protocol, which allows customers to purchase information goods from merchants over the internet.

Despite this being a well-known protocol, it is surprisingly difficult to verify the correctness of a design based on this protocol by hand. So it makes very desirable the application of formal methods and techniques to the modeling and design of electronic commerce protocols to gain high assurance about their correctness. Hence, formal methods are needed in order to ensure their correctness and structure their development from specification to implementation. In this paper we presented our approach to modeling NetBill protocol in Event-B [1].

© Springer International Publishing AG 2016
P.A. Abdulla and C. Delporte-Gallet (Eds.): NETYS 2016, LNCS 9944, pp. 209–213, 2016.
DOI: 10.1007/978-3-319-46140-3_17

Event-B [1] is a formal method that uses the concept of refinement [3,6] in modeling. Event-B modeling starts with an abstraction of a system and adds details during refinement levels in order to gain a final model close to the implementation. Moreover mathematical proofs are incorporated into Event-B to verify the correctness of refinement steps. In this approach we liberally used refinements, both of machines and of contexts. We give a great deal of attention to proofs. Consequently, we now have a specification of NetBill protocol where all proof-obligations have been discharged.

The remaining parts are organized as follows. In Sect. 2 we briefly introduce Netbill protocol and Event-B. The main part of this paper, Sect. 3 describes our strategy of refinement, moreover we will specify our protocol using Event-B. Sections 4 and 5 summarize the results and draw a conclusion.

2   Background

Netbill protocol. The NetBill protocol is an electronic commerce protocol optimized for the selling and delivery of low-priced information goods, such as software or journal articles, across the internet. It was developed by Carnegie Mellon University in conjunction with Visa and Mellon Bank to deal with micropayments of the online order. The NetBill transaction model includes three participants: the consumer (C), the merchant (M) and the NetBill server (S). The protocol begins with a customer requesting a quote for some desired goods, followed by the merchant sending the quote. If the customer accepts the quote, then the merchant delivers the goods and waits for an electronic payment order (EPO). The goods delivered at this point are encrypted, that is, not usable. After receiving the EPO, the merchant forwards the EPO and the key to the server, which handles the funds transfer. When the funds transfer completes, the server sends a receipt back to the merchant. The receipt contains the decryption key for the sold goods. As the last step, the merchant forwards the receipt to the customer. After the customer gets the receipt, he can decrypt and use the goods. The server acts as a trusted party between the consumer and the merchant. It ensures that the funds are transferred between the consumers and the merchants banks and holds a copy of the receipt. Hence, if the EPO of the consumer does not clear or if the consumer does not receive a receipt, the server can be contacted.

Event-B Method. Event-B Method models the states and events of a system. Variables present the states. Events transform the system from a state to another state by changing the value of variables. The modeling notation is based on set theory and logic. Event-B uses mathematical proof to ensure consistency of a model. An Event-B model consists of contexts and machines. The contexts describe the static elements(types and constants) of the model, whereas the machines specify the dynamic behavior(variables and events) of the model. Event-B is provided with tool support in the form of a platform for writing and proving specifications called Rodin [2]. A detailed account of the Event-B language can be found in [1].

3   Specifying NetBill Protocol Using Event-B

As we said above, we use the refinement approach to gradually model the protocol. We start with a very abstract model and then we add details, to obtain a correct and concrete model. For our model we consider the transactions from the point of view of the customer and the merchant [4], which is shown in Fig. 1. The development of the Netbill protocol will be done by means of an initial model followed by two refinements: due to a space limit we do not present the complete specifications produced at each refinement. Instead we describe the more interesting aspects of each particular step.

(1) The initial model is a high level of abstraction showing that the customer orders a product and that the transaction terminated. In this initial model, we just formalize what the customer can eventually do which is order a product. First, we define a carrier set Goods: it describes the goods information (PRD, PRICE and KEY). Then we define another carrier set named Transaction. It is made of six distinct elements: idle, ordered, confirmed, delivered, cashing and ended which present the transaction status. We define the dynamics of the system by means of three events: The INIT event makes variable goods empty, agree to false and the status of the transaction to idle, the Order event and the Terminate event which correspond to terminate a transaction.

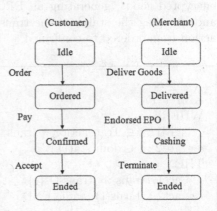

Fig. 1. Customer and merchant view of a transaction

```
      INIT ≙
BEGIN
  act1 : goods := ∅
  act2 : trans := ∅
  act3 : status := ∅ ×
         {idle}
  act4 : agreed :=
         FALSE
END
```

```
      Order ≙
ANY
  g
WHERE
  grd1 : g ∈ goods
  grd2 : goods = ∅
THEN
  act1 : goods := {g}
END
```

```
     Terminate ≙
ANY
  t
WHERE
  grd1 : t ∈ trans
  grd2 : agreed =
         TRUE
THEN
  act1 : status(t) :=
         ended
END
```

(2) The first refinement introduce delivery goods operation along with accepting the encrypted goods by the customer. We are going to refine our abstract model to a more concrete one, by adding more events and more variables to

our model. In this step, event Order from the previous machine will be refined, the (...) indicate the guards and actions of the previous refinement. In addition to refine this latter, we add new events to this refinement which are: Start: corresponding to the start of a transaction where initially all transactions are idle.

Goods_delivery: correspond to sending the encrypted goods to the customer and change the status of the transaction from idle to delivered and event Pay: correspond to accepting the encrypted goods, generating an EPO and changing the status of the transaction from ordered to confirmed.

```
Order ≙
REFINES Order
ANY g, m, t, p
WHERE
...
    grd3 : m ∉ Merchant
    grd4 : t ∈ trans
    grd5 : p ∈ PRICE
THEN
...
    act2 : status(t):=ordered
    act3 : Merchant := Merchant ∪ {m}
    act4 : value(g) := p
    act5 : t_Id := t_Id +1
END
```

```
    Start ≙
ANY t
WHERE
    grd1 : t ∈ Transaction \ trans
    grd2 : t ∈ dom(status)
THEN
    act1 : trans := trans ∪ {t}
    act2 : status(t) :=idle END
```

(3) The second refinement contains the decryption goods along with the operations made in the customer and merchant accounts. Terminate event from previous machine will be refined in form that the NetBill server credits the account of merchant and sends a receipt to the merchant. Then we add new events which are: Endored_EPO: correspond to checking the EPO sent by the customer, then, the status of the transaction will change from delivered to cashing, event accept: getting the decryption key, then, the status of the transaction will change from confirmed to ended and last, event terminate1: NetBill server debits the account of customer.

4 Results and Discussion

In this present paper, NetBill protocol is developed and proved to be correct over a refinement step. The proof of correctness is done concurrently with the development. The stepwise refinement approach allows us to introduce and prove each property at the most appropriate phase in the development, which greatly simplified the task of proving its correctness. The consequence of this incremental approach was that we achieved a very high degree of automatic proof.

Proofs Statistics: The proof statistics for the development of the NetBill protocol is in Table 1. For this specification, most of the proof obligations are automatically discharged by Rodin. The complete development of the NetBill

Table 1. Proof statistics for the NetBill protocol development

Model	Total POs	Automatic proof	Interactive proof
Abstract model	10	10	0
First refinement	48	36	12
Second refinement	37	28	9
Total	95	74	21

protocol results in 95 POs, within which 74 are proved automatically by the
Rodin tool, the remaining 21 POs are proved interactively using the Rodin tool.

5   Conclusion

In this paper we have presented formal modeling of the NetBill protocol using
Event-B. In our approach we have used Event-B as proof-based development
method which integrate formal proof techniques for writing specifications and
building the model systematically using formal refinement, the main idea is to
start with a very abstract model of the system under development. Details are
gradually added to this first model by building a sequence of more concrete ones.
This strategy eases the proof of the correctness of requirements, because only
a small number of proof obligations are generated at each step. An Event-B
model is considered as correct, when each machine, as well as the process of
refinement, are proved by adequate theorems named proof obligations (PO) and
that each event is feasible. The management of proof obligations is a technical
task supported by RODIN, which provides an environment for developing correct
by construction models for software-based systems.

References

1. Abrial, J.R.: Modeling in Event-B: System and Software Engineering. Cambridge
   University Press, Cambridge (2010)
2. Abrial, J.R., Butler, M.J., Hallerstede, S., Hoang, T.S., Mehta, F., Voisin, L.: Rodin:
   an open toolset for modelling and reasoning in Event-B. STTT **12**(6), 447–466
   (2010)
3. Abrial, J.R., Hallerstede, S.: Refinement, decomposition, and instantiation of discrete models: application to Event-B. Fundam. Inform. **77**(1–2), 1–28 (2007)
4. Breitling, M., Philipps, J.: Transitions into black box views -the NetBill protocol
   revisited-. Technical report, Institut fur Informatik Technische Universitat Munchen
   (2000)
5. Cox, B.: NetBill security and transaction protocol. In: USENIX Workshop on Electronic Commerce. USENIX Association (1995)
6. De Roever, W.P., Engelhardt, K.: Data Refinement: Model-oriented Proof Theories
   and their Comparison, Cambridge Tracts in Theoretical Computer Science, vol. 46.
   Cambridge University Press, Cambridge (1998)
7. Sirbu, M.A., Tygar, J.D.: NetBill: an internet commerce system optimized for
   network-delivered services. IEEE Pers. Commun. **2**(4), 34–39 (1995)

Securing NFC Credit Card Payments Against Malicious Retailers

Oliver Jensen$^{(\boxtimes)}$, Tyler O'Meara, and Mohamed Gouda

University of Texas at Austin, Austin, USA
ojensen@cs.utexas.edu

Abstract. The protocol by which "contactless" (NFC) credit cards operate is insecure. Previous work has done much to protect this protocol from malicious third parties, e.g. eavesdroppers, credit card skimmers, etc. However, most of these defenses rely on the retailers being honest, and on their Points of Sale following the credit card protocol faithfully. In this paper, we extend the threat model to include malicious retailers, and remove any restrictions on the operation of their Points of Sale. In particular, we identify two classes of attacks which may be executed by a malicious retailer: Over-charge attacks exploiting victim customers, and Transparent Bridge attacks exploiting victim retailers. We then extend the protocol from previous work in order to defend against these attacks, protecting cardholders and honest retailers from malicious retailers.

1 Introduction

In any credit card purchase, there are two primary parties: the customer and the retailer. Each party controls a device: the customer controls a credit card, and the retailer controls a Point of Sale. It is these devices which communicate on behalf of their controlling parties to coordinate a transaction. The Point of Sale subsequently communicates with the credit card's issuing bank to coordinate the transfer of funds.

Traditional magnetic-stripe credit card readers have been in operation for many years, but they face several important drawbacks: it is easy to accidentally de-magnetize your credit card, and dirty or corroded contacts can make even a well-magnetized card difficult to read. As a result, it is not at all uncommon for a retailer to need to swipe a credit card multiple times before a successful read occurs. Contactless credit card systems solve these problems, using a short-range wireless channel called NFC to communicate with a chip residing within the credit card. This results in more robust credit cards, and less maintenance on credit card readers.

Unfortunately, the protocol used by current NFC credit card payment systems for communication between the Point of Sale and the credit card is insecure. The communications are not encrypted, and the only protection afforded to the customer is the inclusion of a single-use card verification value (called an $iCVV$). This iCVV, freshly generated by the credit card for each transaction, is unpredictable to third parties and thus (in theory) a charge accompanied by a valid

© Springer International Publishing AG 2016

P.A. Abdulla and C. Delporte-Gallet (Eds.): NETYS 2016, LNCS 9944, pp. 214–228, 2016.

DOI: 10.1007/978-3-319-46140-3_18

iCVV must have come from the credit card. However, the only thing a valid iCVV assures is that the credit card was, somehow, involved in the process.

Previous work [8] has focused on securing this protocol against malicious third parties (other than the customer and the retailer). It examines four classes of attackers: eavesdroppers, skimmers, relay attackers, and compromised Points of Sale. In all of these attacks, the attacker gains sensitive cardholder information (i.e. the credit card number and expiration date), since the NFC credit card protocol does nothing to conceal it. Skimmers and relay attackers can easily make fraudulent use of credit card data, since by skimming a credit card they also acquire an unused iCVV (rendering this defence nearly useless). The previous work proposes a modification to the NFC credit card protocol, which prevents the abovementioned attacks, with very little additional computation.

In this paper, we extend this protocol to defend against a new class of attacker: the malicious retailer. Traditionally, systems involving an authentication card (e.g. credit cards, building entry, etc.) focus on protecting a system from unauthorized users, but do little to protect users from a malicious system. This assumption is typically justified when the system is a unified entity such as an office building or communal garage. Credit cards break this mould, wherein every retailer is in control of their own device, and it is to these devices that a credit card holder must authenticate. That is, the credit card model implicitly trusts retailers, and the Point of Sale devices under their control.

We make the case that retailers should not be implicitly trusted. We enumerate two attacks which a malicious retailer may perpetrate: a simple over-charge attack, and a more complex "transparent bridge" attack. These attacks both stem from the lack of involvement of the customer in the protocol, and the ability of the retailer's Point of Sale to display one price to the customer, and then charge a different price to that customer's credit card. We build off of the ideas in the Secure CC Protocol [8] and extend it, preventing these attacks.

2 NFC Credit Card Payments

A credit card payment system has five fundamental principals:

1. A **Customer** who wants to make a purchase.
2. A **Bank** at which the Customer has an account.
3. A **Credit Card** issued by the Bank to the Customer.
4. A **Retailer** from whom the Customer wishes to make the purchase.
5. A **Point of Sale** controlled and initialized by the Retailer. It displays the purchase price to the Customer, and communicates with both the Credit Card and its issuing Bank to coordinate the transaction.

It is increasingly popular for retailers to support credit card payments over NFC. NFC is a very attractive channel for use in payment systems, because it provides the benefits of wireless communication, while simultaneously mitigating many of the drawbacks commonly associated with wireless channels:

- NFC is a wireless channel, and thus is unaffected by card demagnetization or read errors due to dirty or corroded contacts.
- NFC has a very short range, mitigating many privacy concerns associated with wireless channels.
- NFC supports communication with unpowered (termed "passive") devices, meaning that a payment device (e.g. a credit card) need not have its own power source.

In an NFC credit card payment system, the Customer indicates an intention to pay by enabling communication between the Point of Sale and his NFC Credit Card. This is done by bringing the Credit Card within range of the Point of Sale (no more than 4 cm away). Once within range of each other, the Point of Sale may send messages to the Credit Card and receive any resulting responses.

We will refer to the protocol currently used by NFC credit card payment systems to coordinate a transactions as the "Original CC Protocol". The messages involved in this protocol, illustrated in Fig. 1, are as follows:

1. The Point of Sale displays the price of the purchase on its screen, while simultaneously attempting to establish communication over NFC.
2. If the Customer agrees with the displayed price, he brings his Credit Card within 4 cm of the Point of Sale and communication between the Point of Sale and the Credit Card is established.
3. The Point of Sale sends a *solicitation* message to the Credit Card.
4. The Credit Card responds to the solicitation message with a *card information* message, supplying the Point of Sale with the necessary information to issue a charge, and identifying the Credit Card's issuing bank.
5. Then the Point of Sale sends a *charge request* message to the Bank. This message is sent securely over the Internet.
6. The Bank verifies the details of the charge request, and responds to the Point of Sale with a *acceptance* message, indicating whether the charge has been accepted.

The message contents in the Original CC Protocol are as follows:

Solicitation: In practice, the solicitation message actually consists of a number of messages sent in both directions. Its purpose is to exchange information about the Credit Card type (e.g. *Visa Credit*) and the Point of Sale model (e.g. *2PAY.SYS.DDF01*), which defines the format of subsequent messages. It is a choreographed dance with a specific (and constant) set of messages for a given model of Point of Sale and Credit Card, so we abstract this conversation to a single solicitation message.

Card Information: This message contains all information necessary to coordinate an arbitrary charge request to a credit card's issuing bank. It consists of four components:

- The Credit Card number, identical to the number printed on the front of the card.

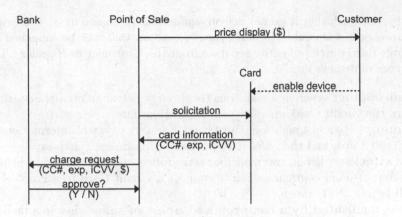

Fig. 1. The original CC protocol

- The Credit Card's expiration date.
- An *iCVV* ("integrated Card Verification Value"). This iCVV is a security code, similar to the 3-digit number printed on the back of a credit card, but is newly generated for each transaction. It is an element in a pseudo-random sequence generated by a secret seed known only to the Credit Card and its issuing Bank, making it unpredictable to third parties.
- The issuing Bank name. This is used for routing purposes, and is not a component of the subsequent charge request. As such, it is not pictured in Fig. 1.

Charge Request: This message is sent to the Bank identified in the card information message, and consists of four components:

- The Credit Card number, identifying the account to be charged.
- The Credit Card's expiration date.
- The Credit Card's iCVV.
- The dollar amount to be charged.

Approval: This message consists of a *response code* determined by the Bank, indicating its decision relating to the charge request. The bank makes this decision after verifying the information supplied in the charge request, and performing additional checks such as matching the purchase to a known location of the Customer. The most common response codes are the result of a simple approval decision (i.e. "Approved" or "Declined"), although a number of different codes (e.g. "Pick up card" if the card was reported lost or stolen, "Waiting for line" to indicate that the issuer's lines are currently busy) are supported. We abstract this message as a single bit: whether or not the Customer's account has been charged.

3   Defending Against Malicious Third Parties

While the iCVV in the Original CC Protocol does offer some protection from fake credit card charges by ensuring that the credit card was involved in some way, there is much that it cannot defend against. As discussed in [8], the Original CC Protocol is vulnerable to four types of attacks that can be launched by a malicious third party (an entity separate from the Customer or Retailer). These four types of attacks are:

Eavesdropping: wherein a malicious third party listens in on a transaction to learn the Credit Card's number and expiration date.

Skimming: wherein a malicious third party harvests payment information from a Credit Card, and then uses it to perform a fraudulent purchase.

Relay attacks: wherein two malicious accomplices use skimming-like behavior and out-of-band communication to connect a Credit Card to a Point of Sale well beyond NFC range.

Attacks facilitated by a compromised point of sale: wherein a malicious third party has actually compromised the Retailer's systems, harvesting credit card information.

To illustrate these attacks, we will discuss the skimming attack, launched by a malicious third party, called the *Skimmer*. The Skimmer controls an NFC-capable smart phone, and approaches an unsuspecting Credit Card to be within NFC range. He then uses his phone to impersonate a Point of Sale to the Credit Card, soliciting the card for its payment information. This impersonation is not difficult as there is no authorization taking place – indeed, an Android application called NFC Proxy [1] exists to make this attack trivial to execute.

This attack is illustrated in Fig. 2.

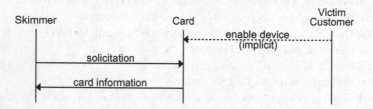

Fig. 2. A skimming attack

Skimming a credit card does not require explicit authorization from the card's owner: an attacker needs only to bring their phone within range of the victim's pocket to communicate with an NFC credit card, as a Credit Card assumes that being able to receive a solicitation message is tantamount to the Customer intending to make a purchase. A fleeting proximity between the Skimmer's device and the Credit Card, perhaps standing in line at a coffee shop or on a crowded subway, is all that is needed. A fraction of a second suffices.

The Original CC Protocol also implicitly trusts the ability of a Retailer to keep its data secure. By allowing persistent sensitive information (e.g. the credit card number and expiration date) to be transmitted to a device under the

Retailer's control, this protocol invites attacks on the Retailer's own systems. This is a very real threat, as evidenced by recent events: over the last three years, a number of high-profile attacks against chains such as Target, Home Depot, Nieman Marcus and P.F. Chang's have delivered *hundreds of millions* of credit card records into the hands of attackers [4, 9, 11, 14, 15]. These records consist of credit card numbers with expiration dates, and in many cases also the cardholder names, billing addresses, and any other information the retailer may have access to.

Previous work in [8] has described simple and inexpensive ways to thwart these attacks and others, proposing a replacement protocol termed the "Secure CC Protocol". When a credit card is solicited under the Secure CC Protocol, the Point of Sale includes a randomly generated challenge value *ch*. Instead of responding with the card's private information (i.e. the credit card number and expiration date), the Credit Card transmits its card *ID* (a unique identifier, not considered private) accompanied with a token *T*, valid for a single purchase. An outline of this protocol is shown in Fig. 3. Its messages consist of the following:

1. The Point of Sale displays a price on its screen as before, prompting the customer to bring his credit card within NFC range of the Point of Sale.
2. The Point of Sale sends a *solicitation* message to the credit card, including a random challenge *ch*.
3. The credit card responds with an (*ID*, *T*) pair accompanied with the issuing bank's name for routing. *ID* is a universally unique identifier (also known as a UUID or GUID) to identify the card. While this value can be used to "track" the card, it is not considered sensitive as it serves no other purpose. *T* is a token which authorizes a single purchase for a given challenge. The function by which it is generated can be thought of as a function which concatenates the challenge *ch*, a card specific secret value known only to the card and the bank, and the iCVV, and then hashing the result.
4. The Point of Sale sends a charge request to the bank consisting of the (*ch, ID, T*) tuple, accompanied with the dollar amount that the retailer wishes to charge.
5. The bank looks up the account associated with *ID* in order to ascertain the card-specific secret value and the next expected iCVV. It then calculates $T_{bank} = Hash(ch, secret, iCVV)$, verifying that $T_{bank} = T$ to authenticate the charge. The token *T* being dependent on the challenge *ch* renders skimming and similar attacks impotent, since the attacker cannot predict the challenge which it will be issued when attempting to use skimmed data.

4   Malicious Retailers

Previous work (including the Secure CC Protocol [8]) has focused primarily on defending the Retailer and Customer from malicious third parties, such as eavesdroppers and credit card skimmers. By contrast, we examine the problems posed

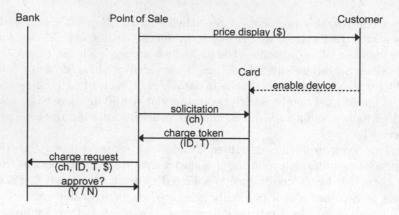

Fig. 3. The secure CC protocol

by malicious retailers, and focus on how to secure NFC credit card payment systems against them. As will be described shortly, attacks by malicious Retailers are particularly pernicious, as they can be less easily identified as fraud. Even when these attacks are detected, the resolutions are not always simple.

Recall that when making a payment, the Customer first views the price about to be charged on the screen of the Retailer's Point of Sale. Using this information, he makes his one and only decision: to allow the payment protocol to occur, or not. The underlying assumption that the customer makes is that the price displayed on the screen is equal to the price which will be charged to his Credit Card. This need not be the case: the information displayed on a screen is merely an assurance in the informal sense: the numbers displayed to the customer *should* reflect the dollar amount which will subsequently be sent with the charge request, but there is no mechanism in place to require this. As a result, two attacks emerge.

4.1 The Over-Charge Attack

An Over-charge attack is characterized by the malicious Point of Sale displaying one price to the customer (in the *price display* message of the CC Protocols shown in Figs. 1 and 3) and then sending a higher price to the Bank (in the *charge request* message of the CC Protocols). As a result, the Customer believes himself to have been charged one amount, but is instead charged an arbitrarily higher amount. Since the Customer is uninvolved in the protocol besides the initial step of allowing it to occur, there is no mechanism ensuring that the price displayed to the Customer matches the price that the (malicious) Point of Sale sends to the Bank.

Should a Customer become aware of an over-charge when reviewing his monthly statement, he may file a charge-back request with his Bank, nullifying the payment as fraudulent. As a result, while the amount by which the Customer may be overcharged is unconstrained by the protocol, it should be

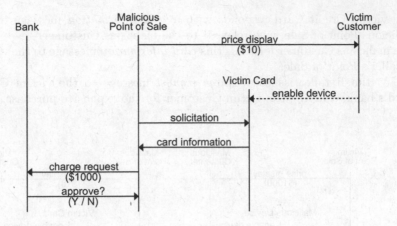

Fig. 4. Over-charge attack

relatively small for the attack to ultimately be successful. For example, it is easy to notice a gas station charge for $500.00 instead of $21.87 on a monthly statement, and the resulting investigation would be uncomplicated. However, should the struggling business choose to increase charges by 5 %, the resulting gas station charge of $22.96 could very easily be overlooked. Even were it to be noticed, the victim Customer may have difficulty proving the discrepancy (Fig. 4).

4.2   The Transparent Bridge Attack

A more interesting attack is described by Drimer and Murdoch [3]. It considers a man-in-the-middle attack, perpetrated by a malicious Retailer and an accomplice with specialized equipment. This attack involves four parties: a victim Customer, a malicious Retailer, a malicious Customer, and a victim Retailer. The malicious retailer and the malicious customer collude to perform this attack.

The malicious Customer is issued with a special card, capable of relaying all messages it receives from a Point of Sale to the malicious Retailer in real time. Similarly, it can relay any responses it receives from the malicious Retailer back to this Point of Sale. As a result, the malicious Customer and malicious Retailer can together form a bridge between the victim Credit Card and the victim Retailer's Point of Sale. The attack is illustrated in Fig. 5 and runs as follows:

1. First, the victim Customer attempts to make a relatively inexpensive purchase from the malicious Retailer. Simultaneously, the malicious Customer prepares to make a relatively expensive purchase from a victim Retailer.
2. The victim Retailer's Point of Sale issues a *solicitation* message to the malicious Customer, who relays it to the malicious Retailer.
3. The malicious Retailer then forwards this *solicitation* to the victim Credit Card.

4. The victim Credit Card responds with a *card information* message to the malicious Point of Sale, who relays it to the malicious Customer.
5. The malicious Customer forwards this *card information* message to the victim Retailer's Point of Sale.
6. The victim Retailer issues a *charge request* message to the victim Credit Card's bank, charging the victim Customer for the expensive purchase.

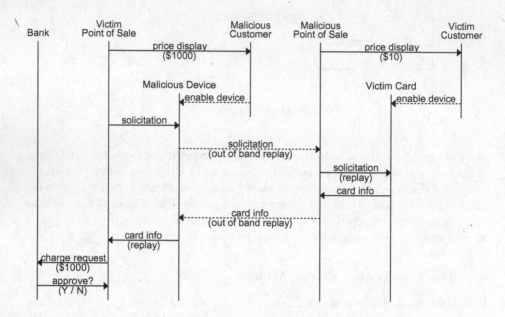

Fig. 5. Transparent bridge attack

In this attack, all messages are transparently relayed between the victim Retailer's Point of Sale and the victim Customer's Credit Card. As a result, the victim Customer believes himself to be making an inexpensive purchase at the malicious Retailer, while he is actually making an expensive purchase at the victim Retailer. The malicious Retailer loses the inexpensive sale, but acquires the merchandise from an expensive purchase in exchange.

The Transparent Bridge attack is particularly interesting, because the malicious parties leave no trace with either of the victims: to the victim Customer there is only a record of an expensive purchase at the victim Retailer, and to the victim Retailer there is only the customer record of the victim Customer. The amount which can be successfully stolen by the malicious Retailer is unconstrained, and needs not evade notice: if the discrepancy is noticed and the victim Customer files a charge-back request, it will be against the victim Retailer (and not the malicious Retailer). As such, detected or not, it is one of the two victims that will be left facing the bill, making the Transparent Bridge attack significantly more dangerous than the Over-charge attack described earlier.

Drimer et al. propose a defense against this attack in the context of EMV credit cards (colloquially known as "chip and pin"). However, this solution is not applicable to contactless credit cards, and as such the problem remains open.

5 Defending Against Malicious Retailers

Passive "smart cards" (such as NFC credit cards) are designed primarily to authenticate the cardholder to the system, and not to provide any assurance to the cardholder *about* the system. As a result, they offer little by way of possibility to defend against malicious retailers. However, it has become increasingly common for the devices engaging in NFC credit card payments to break this mould by not being credit cards at all: smart phones with NFC capabilities have given customers the ability (through applications like Android Pay or Apple Pay) to use their phones to emulate a credit card.

This is particularly attractive to many customers, since it allows for the convenience of carrying a potentially unlimited number of credit cards without a bulky wallet, while also affording additional security against theft (by way of passwords or PINs). In addition, such "virtual credit cards" present a rich interface, allowing for finer-grained control and, as a result, stronger defenses against malicious retailers.

Since the aforementioned attacks allowing a malicious Retailer to exploit a Customer are tied to the Retailer's ability to display one price and charge another, our proposed defense against these attacks is built around removing this ability when possible. When using a virtual Credit Card as implemented on a smart phone, the phone's interface provides an additional communication channel between the Customer and the (virtual) Credit Card. This communication channel can be harnessed to allow the Customer to participate in the payment protocol, beyond simply allowing it to occur.

Previous work in the Secure CC Protocol defines a function H, proves several of its properties and uses it to defend against third party attacks like skimmers and eavesdroppers [8]. We note that each property required of this function H is a property enjoyed by common cryptographic hash functions, such as those in the *SHA* family. As such, using a hash function instead of the derived function H does not reduce the security of the Secure CC Protocol.

We propose an extension to the Secure CC Protocol, while altering it to use a cryptographic hash function for simplicity.

5.1 The Extended Secure CC Protocol

In our description of the Extended Secure CC Protocol, we will use the following notation:

ch: a fresh, randomly generated challenge value, chosen by the Point of Sale.
INFO: the Credit Card's payment information, consisting of the Credit Card number and expiration date.

ID: a UUID, uniquely identifying an individual Credit Card without revealing any information about *INFO*.

iCVV: an unpredictable value freshly generated by the Credit Card for each transaction (the issuing bank can generate the same sequence of values).

B: the name of the issuing Bank, used for the purpose of routing transactions as before.

The Extended Secure CC Protocol, operating between a Point of Sale and a virtual Credit Card, is illustrated in Fig. 6 and proceeds as follows:

1. The Point of Sale displays a price **$d** on its screen, inviting the Customer to bring his Credit Card within NFC range.
2. The Point of Sale sends a solicitation to the Credit Card, including a fresh random challenge **ch** and the price to be charged **$c**. (Recall that if the Point of Sale is honest, **$c = $d**)
3. The virtual Credit Card displays the price **$c** to the Customer, who can choose to accept or reject it. Rejecting the price aborts the protocol here.
4. If granted authorization by the Customer, the Card calculates

$$T = H(\text{INFO}, \text{ch}, \$c, \text{iCVV})$$

and responds to the Point of Sale with a card information message consisting of [**ID, T, B**].
5. The Point of Sale sends a charge request message to the issuing Bank (identified by **B**) consisting of [**ID, T, ch, $r**]. (Again, if the Point of Sale is honest, **$r = $d**)
6. The bank uses **ID** to look up INFO_{bank} and then calculates iCVV_{bank}. It then uses the **ch** and **$r** supplied in the charge request message to determine

$$T_{\text{bank}} = H(\text{INFO}_{\text{bank}}, \text{ch}, \$r, \text{iCVV}_{\text{bank}})$$

If $T \neq T_{\text{bank}}$, the bank will decline the charge, otherwise it approves the charge for **$r**.

When using a physical Credit Card instead of a virtual one, no communication channel exists between the Card and the Customer. As a result, the steps above in which the Card displays the charge price ($c) to the Customer and awaits authorization from the Customer cannot occur. Instead, a physical Credit Card must implicitly assume successful authorization from the Customer, effectively skipping step 3. As a result, while not providing protections from malicious Retailers to physical Credit Cards, the protocol maintains backwards compatibility with no loss of functionality or security against malicious third parties.

We note that a naive implementation of the protocol above might require excessively long timeouts between the Point of Sale sending its solicitation message and receiving the response. Should long timeouts not be desired, a simple solution would be for the Point of Sale to send periodic solicitations (with new challenges). The virtual Credit Card, upon receiving permission from the

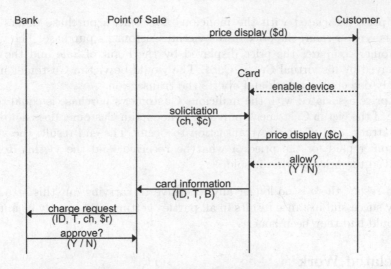

Fig. 6. Extended secure CC protocol

Customer, could then cache this approval and respond immediately to the subsequent solicitation. Besides noting this particular case, we emphasize that issues such as these are implementation details, the decisions for which are best left to those implementing the protocol.

5.2   Defending Against the Over-Charge Attack

The extended protocol prevents the Over-charge attack against Customers using a virtual Credit Card. In step 3, the Customer verifies that $d = $c through visual comparison. Due to theinclusion of $c in the hash when generating token T, we gain the assurance that for any charge accepted by the Bank, $c = $r.

Thus, through a transitive argument, the Customer can be assured that for any successful charge, $d = $r. Should the malicious retailer attempt to issue a charge request with some $r \neq $d, then $T_{bank} \neq T$ and the charge will be declined by the Bank.

5.3   Defending Against the Transparent Bridge Attack

The extended protocol makes no attempt to prevent this attack from occurring. Instead, it removes the economic incentive of performing such an attack against Customers using virtual Credit Cards.

In the Transparent Bridge attack, the malicious Retailer loses the sale paid by the victim Customer, in return for acquiring the purchase made by the malicious Customer. In order for the Transparent Bridge attack to be viable, the malicious actors must have something to gain: the value of the malicious Customer's purchase must be greater than the value of the victim Customer's purchase. When the extended protocol is used, one of two scenarios occurs:

1. The price associated with the malicious Customer's purchase differs from (i.e. is greater than) the price of the victim Customer's purchase. The victim Customer compares the price displayed by the Point of Sale and the price displayed by his virtual Credit Card. The would-be victim Customer immediately detects the attack and aborts the transaction.
2. The price associated with the malicious Customer's purchase is equal to the price of the victim Customer's purchase. The victim Customer does not detect this attack, and allows the transaction to occur. The end result: the victim Customer paid for the price of what he received, and the victim Retailer received the price of what it sold.

As a result, there is no longer any incentive to carrying out this attack, as the only successful instance results in all parties getting paid exactly as much as they would had they been honest.

6   Related Work

Our work builds primarily upon the Secure Credit Card Protocol over NFC [8], extending the protocol to defend against malicious retailers in addition to malicious third parties.

Kortvedt explores the problem of eavesdropping on NFC communications [10], and suggests a symmetric encryption solution with a strong mutual authentication. Madlmayr et al. analyze the state of NFC communication privacy [13], proposing several technical defenses to threats. Both works [10,13] focus on protecting the NFC channel itself, and do not take protocols or applications into account. As a result, while they are effective in defending against channel attacks such eavesdropping, they cannot not affect skimmers, relay attackers, compromised points of sale, or malicious retailers. As such, they fall short of protecting NFC credit card payments.

Haselsteine and Breitfuß provide a broad survey in [7] of several classes of attacks and defenses applicable to the NFC channel. Similarly to [10,13], they focus on securing the channel itself from attackers, suggesting that NFC participants perform a key-exchange protocol such as Diffie-Helmann [2], then use this derived secret key to establish a secure channel. As a result, this approach also falls short of protecting NFC credit card payments, for the same reason.

Drimer and Murdoch [3] present an attack on credit card payment systems, which we described in Sect. 4 as the Transparent Bridge attack. This attack relies on the ability to perform out-of-band real-time proxying and relaying of messages between two parties. Drimer et al. implement this attack against EMV ("chip and pin") credit cards, demonstrating its practicality. They recommend defending against such attacks via distance bounding, essentially measuring round-trip communication timing to detect any delays introduced through the relaying of messages. Such a defense is reasonable when reading responses directly from chip I/O (as in EMV credit card transactions), but does not lend itself well to responses generated by a multitasking computational device such as a smart phone, where delays can be variable depending on unrelated software.

In [6], Francis et al. find that out-of-band real-time proxying and relaying of messages is possible over NFC, constructing a transparent bridge between two NFC devices over Bluetooth. While Drimer et al. only demonstrated the Transparent Bridge attack with EMV credit cards, this result indicates that the attack applies to contactless credit cards as well. Francis et al. propose to use location information such as GPS coordinates in order to detect and defend against this relaying of messages, which in turn would render the Transparent Bridge attack infeasible. However, location information can be unreliable or unavailable in some areas, and as such, one cannot rely on its availability and correctness.

By contrast to [3,6], our approach does not seek to detect or prevent attacks relying on the proxying or relaying of information, choosing instead to render them impotent.

In [12], Lee provides some analysis of relay and skimming attacks on NFC credit card transactions, and presents the Android application *NFCProxy* [1] which implements these attacks. This work focuses on demonstrating how easy it is for any would-be fraudster to perform skimming and relay attacks, but does not discuss or propose any countermeasures.

In [5], Eun et al. explore the issue of privacy in the face of NFC eavesdroppers, considering mobile payments as a case study. Not constraining themselves to supporting physical credit cards, they suggest the creation of an "NFC-SEC" protocol complete with key-exchange and public key cryptography. Their approach includes the concept of "unlinkability" (explicitly excluded by the Secure Credit Card Protocol) wherein a merchant cannot correlate multiple purchases from the same credit card.

7 Concluding Remarks

In this paper, we discussed how to extend the Secure Credit Card Protocol over NFC to defend against Over-charge and Transparent Bridge attacks, protecting honest card-holders using virtual credit cards (such as a smart phone running Android Pay) from malicious retailers. The proposed extension, although effective, is simple and computationally inexpensive. It consists of three components:

1. The Point of Sale includes the price of the transaction in its solicitation message.
2. The virtual Credit Card requests confirmation of the price from its card holder before continuing.
3. The Charge Token generated by the card is bound to the confirmed transaction price.

Note that this defense against malicious retailers is only effective when the customer is using a virtual credit card, since physical cards cannot confirm the transaction price with their card-holders. Customers using physical credit cards can still participate in this extended protocol, and will still enjoy the protections against malicious third parties afforded by the Secure Credit Card Protocol. However, defending against the Over-charge and Transparent Bridge attacks remains an open problem with customers who use physical credit cards rather than smart-devices.

Acknowledgments. Research of Mohamed Gouda is supported in part by the NSF award #1440035.

References

1. BlackwingHQ: Nfcproxy (2012). http://sourceforge.net/projects/nfcproxy/
2. Diffie, W., Hellman, M.: New directions in cryptography. IEEE Trans. Inf. Theory **22**(6), 644–654 (1976)
3. Drimer, S., Murdoch, S.J.: Keep your enemies close: distance bounding against smartcard relay attacks. In: Proceedings of 16th USENIX Security Symposium on USENIX Security Symposium, SS 2007, pp. 7:1–7:16. USENIX Association, Berkeley (2007). http://dl.acm.org/citation.cfm?id=1362903.1362910
4. Harris, E., Perlroth, N., Popper, N.: Neiman marcus data breach worse than first said. http://www.nytimes.com/2014/01/24/business/neiman-marcus-breach-affected-1-1-million-cards.html. Accessed 10 Nov 2014
5. Eun, H., Lee, H., Oh, H.: Conditional privacy preserving security protocol for NFC applications. IEEE Trans. Consum. Electron. **59**(1), 153–160 (2013)
6. Francis, L., Hancke, G., Mayes, K., Markantonakis, K.: Practical NFC peer-to-peer relay attack using mobile phones. In: Ors Yalcin, S.B. (ed.) RFIDSec 2010. LNCS, vol. 6370, pp. 35–49. Springer, Heidelberg (2010)
7. Haselsteiner, E., Breitfuß, K.: Security in near field communication (NFC). In: Workshop on RFID Security, pp. 12–14 (2006)
8. Jensen, O., Gouda, M., Qiu, L.: A secure credit card protocol over NFC. In: Chan, M.C., Pandurangan, G. (eds.) International Conference on Distributed Computing and Networking. ACM, January 2016
9. Kennedy, C.: Millions of card numbers likely stolen during supervalu data breach, security expert says. http://www.bizjournals.com/twincities/news/2014/08/18/supervalu-millions-card-numbers-likely-stolen.html?page=all. Accessed 10 Nov 2014
10. Kortvedt, H.S.: Securing near field communication. Master's thesis, Norwegian University of Science and Technology, Norway (2009)
11. Krebs, B.: P.F. Changs breach likely began in Sept. 2013. http://krebsonsecurity.com/2014/06/p-f-changs-breach-likely-began-in-sept-2013/. Accessed 10 Nov 2014
12. Lee, E.: NFC hacking: the easy way. In: Defcon Hacking Conference, vol. 20 (2012)
13. Madlmayr, G., Langer, J., Kantner, C., Scharinger, J.: NFC devices: security and privacy. In: Third International Conference on Availability, Reliability and Security, 2008. ARES 2008, pp. 642–647. IEEE (2008)
14. Sidel, R., Yadron, D., Germano, S.: Target hit by credit-card breach. http://online.wsj.com/articles/SB10001424052702304773104579266743230242538. Accessed 10 Nov 2014
15. Sidel, R.: Home depot's 56 million card breach bigger than target's. http://online.wsj.com/articles/home-depot-breach-bigger-than-targets-1411073571. Accessed 10 Nov 2014

An Approach to Resolve NP-Hard Problems of Firewalls

Ahmed Khoumsi[1(✉)], Mohamed Erradi[2], Meryeme Ayache[2],
and Wadie Krombi[2]

[1] Department of Electrical and Computer Engineering, University of Sherbrooke,
Sherbrooke, Canada
Ahmed.Khoumsi@USherbrooke.ca
[2] ENSIAS, Mohammed V University, Rabat, Morocco

Abstract. Firewalls are a common solution to protect information systems from intrusions. In this paper, we apply an automata-based methodology to resolve several NP-Hard problems which have been shown in the literature to be fundamental for the study of firewall security policies. We also compute space and time complexities of our resolution methods.

1 Introduction

An essential component of a firewall is its security policy that consists of a table of filtering rules specifying which packets are accepted and which ones are discarded from the network [1]. Designing and analyzing a firewall are not easy tasks when we have thousands of filtering rules as is usually the case. To perform such tasks properly, one requires to solve thousands of instances of known fundamental NP-Hard problems identified in [2]. Recognizing the importance of these problems, their solutions can significantly enhance the ability to design and analyze firewalls. Henceforth, the terms *policy* and *rule* denote "firewall security policy" and "filtering rule", respectively.

In this work, we apply the automata-based methodology of [3] to resolve the 13 NP-Hard problems of [2]. The basic principle of the approach is to describe policies as automata and then to develop analysis methods applicable to automata. We also evaluate time and space complexities of the 13 resolutions.

The paper is organized as follows. Section 2 presents related work on analyzing policies. Section 3 contains preliminaries on policies. Section 4 introduces the methodology of [3]. In Sects. 5 and 6, we resolve the 13 NP-Hard problems of [2] by using the methodology of [3]. Section 7 evaluates the space and time complexities of the 13 resolutions. We conclude in Sect. 8.

2 Related Work

Previous work on firewalls, such as [4–6], provide practical analysis algorithms, while [7–11] provide fundamental analysis algorithms with estimations of their time complexities. [2] proves that many firewall analysis problems are NP-Hard.

© Springer International Publishing AG 2016
P.A. Abdulla and C. Delporte-Gallet (Eds.): NETYS 2016, LNCS 9944, pp. 229–243, 2016.
DOI: 10.1007/978-3-319-46140-3_19

[12,13] present techniques to detect anomalies in a policy. An anomaly is defined in [14] as the existence of several rules that match the same packet. A policy is described by a *Policy tree* in [12] and a *Decision tree* in [13].

[15,16] provide solutions to analyze and handle *stateful* firewall anomalies.

[11] proposes a method to detect discrepancies between implementations of a policy. The policy is modeled by a *Firewall Decision Diagram* (FDD) [17] which maps each packet to the decision taken by the firewall for such a packet.

[18] introduces *Fireman*, which is a toolkit that permits to detect errors such as violation of a policy and inconsistency in a policy. Fireman is implemented using *Binary Decision Diagrams* (BDD) [19].

[20] generates test sequences to validate the conformance of a policy, where the system's behavior is specified by an extended finite state machine [21] and the policy is specified with the model OrBAC [22].

[23] verifies equivalence between two policies by extracting and comparing equivalent policies whose filtering rules are disjoint.

[24] presents a visualization tool to analyze firewall configurations, where the policy is modeled in a specific hierarchical way.

In each of the above works, a specific formalism is used to solve a specific problem. A policy is modeled: by a policy tree to study anomalies, by a FDD to study discrepancies, by a BDD to study policy violation and inconsistency, etc. This observation motivated the work of [3,25], where automata are used to study several aspects of policies. The main contribution of the present article is the resolution of the 13 NP-Hard problems of [2] by using the methodology of [3]. Space and time complexities of the 13 resolutions are provided.

3   Preliminaries

The behavior of a firewall is controlled by its policy which consists of a list of rules defining the actions to take each time a packet tries to cross the firewall. The packets are specified by an n-tuple of headers that are taken into account by the policy. A rule is in the form: *if some conditions are satisfied, then a given action must be taken to authorize or refuse the access.* Therefore, a rule can be specified as (*Condition, Action*), where:

- *Condition* is a set of filtering fields $F^0, \cdots, F^{m-1}$ corresponding to respective headers $H^0, \cdots, H^{m-1}$ of a packet arriving at the firewall. Each F^i defines the set of values that are authorized to H^i. *Condition* is satisfied for a packet P, if for every $i = 0 \cdots m-1$ the value of H^i of P belongs to F^i. We say that P matches a rule R (or R matches P) when the condition of R is satisfied for P. Otherwise, P does not match R (or R does not match P).
- *Action* is Accept or Deny, to authorize or forbid a packet to go through the firewall, respectively.

The rules are denoted $R_1, R_2, \cdots$, and their actions are denoted $a_1, a_2, \cdots$ respectively. The rules are in decreasing priority order, that is, when a packet P arrives at the firewall, matching of P and R_1 is verified: if P matches R_1, then action a_1 is executed; if P does not match R_1, then matching of P and R_2 is verified. And so on, the process is repeated until a rule R_i matching P is found or all the rules are examined.

An *accept-rule* (resp. *deny-rule*) is a rule whose action is Accept (resp. Deny). An *all-rule* is a rule whose condition is TRUE, i.e. it matches all packets. We also combine the definitions to obtain *all-accept-rule* and *all-deny-rule*. A policy is said *complete* if every packet matches at least one of its rules.

Table 1 contains an example of policy. The condition of each rule R_i is defined by four fields: IPsrc, IPdst, Port and Protocol, and its action is in the last column. The term *Any* in the column of a field F^j means any value in the domain of F^j. The term a.b.c.0/x denotes an interval of IP addresses obtained from the 32-bit address a.b.c.0 by keeping constant the first x bits and varying the other bits. A packet P arriving at the firewall matches a rule R_i if: P comes from an address belonging to IPsrc, P is destined to an address belonging to IPdst, P is transmitted through a port belonging to Port, and P is transmitted by a protocol belonging to Protocol.

Table 1. Example of rules

Rule	IPsrc	IPdst	Port	Protocol	Action
R_1	*Any*	212.217.65.201	80	TCP	Accept
R_2	192.168.10.0/24	81.10.10.0/24	*Any*	*Any*	Deny
R_3	194.204.201.0/28	212.217.65.202	21	*Any*	Accept
R_4	192.168.10.0/24	*Any*	*Any*	*Any*	Accept

4 Synthesis Procedure

The basis of the methodology of [3] is a procedure that synthesizes an automaton from a policy. The input of the procedure is a policy $\mathcal{F}$ specified by n rules $R_1, \cdots, R_n$ ordered in decreasing priority. The result is an automaton $\Gamma_{\mathcal{F}}$ implementing $\mathcal{F}$.

The synthesis procedure is presented in detail in [3]. In this section, we illustrate it by the example of policy $\mathcal{F}$ of Table 1, for which the synthesis procedure generates the automaton $\Gamma_{\mathcal{F}}$ of Fig. 1. The states are organized by levels, where the states of level j are reached after j transitions from the initial state (represented with a small incoming arrow). A transition is said of level j if it links a state of level j to a state of level $j + 1$. Transitions of level j are labeled by sets of values of the field F^j. There are two types of final states (represented in bold):

- A *match* state is associated to the action Accept or Deny (noted A or D in the figure). There may be one or several match states in a synthesized automaton. The automaton of Fig. 1 has 5 match states.

– A *no-match* state is indicated by a star $*$. There may be at most one no-match state in a synthesized automaton. The automaton of Fig. 1 has 1 no-match state.

In Fig. 1 and subsequent figures, some transitions are labeled in the form *Any* or *not(X)*, where X is one or more sets of values. A label *Any* in a transition of level j denotes the whole domain of values of the field F^j. A label *not(X)* in a transition of level j denotes the complementary of X in the domain of F^j.

The fundamental characteristics of $\Gamma_{\mathcal{F}}$ is that it implements $\mathcal{F}$ as stated by the following theorem taken from [3]:

Theorem 1. *Consider a packet P arriving at the firewall, and let $H^0, \cdots, H^{m-1}$ be its headers. From the initial state of $\Gamma_{\mathcal{F}}$, we execute the m consecutive transitions labeled by the sets $\sigma_0, \cdots, \sigma_{m-1}$ that contain $H^0, \cdots, H^{m-1}$, respectively. Let r be the (final) reached state of $\Gamma_{\mathcal{F}}$:*

– *r is a match state iff[1] P matches at least one rule of $\mathcal{F}$.*
– *If r is a match state, then the action (Accept or Deny) associated to r is the action of the most priority rule matching P.*

Let us illustrate the fact that $\Gamma_{\mathcal{F}}$ of Fig. 1 implements $\mathcal{F}$ of Table 1. Consider a packet P which arrives at the firewall and assume that its four headers H^0 to H^3 are $(192.168.10.12), (212.217.65.201), (25), (TCP)$, respectively. We start in the initial state $\langle 0 \rangle$. The transition labeled 192.168.10.0/24 (comprising H^0) is executed and leads to state $\langle 1 \rangle$. Then, the transition labeled 212.217.65.201 (comprising H^1) is executed and leads to state $\langle 4 \rangle$. Then, the transition labeled $not(80)$ (comprising H^2) is executed and leads to state $\langle 10 \rangle$. Finally, the transition labeled *Any* (comprising H^3) is executed and leads to the second match state. Since the reached match state is associated to Accept, the packet is accepted.

Consider now a packet whose four headers H^0 to H^3 are $(194.204.201.20)$, $(212.217.65.201), (25), (TCP)$, respectively. We start in the initial state $\langle 0 \rangle$. The transition labeled 194.204.201.0/28 (comprising H^0) is executed and leads to state $\langle 2 \rangle$. Then, the transition labeled 212.217.65.201 (comprising H^1) is executed and leads to state $\langle 8 \rangle$. Then, the transition labeled $not(80)$ (comprising H^2) is executed and leads to the no-match state $\langle * \rangle$. Therefore, no rule of the policy matches such a packet.

5   Resolution of FC, FA and SP

Let us demonstrate the applicability of our synthesis procedure for the resolution of 5 of the 13 problems of [2]: **FC**, **FA-d**, **FA-a**, **SP-d** and **SP-a**.

---

[1] iff means: if and only if.

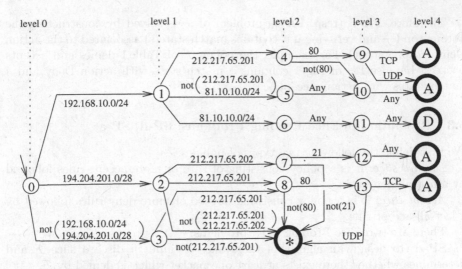

Fig. 1. Automaton synthesized from the policy of Table 1.

5.1 Resolution of Firewall Completeness (FC) Problem

Firewall Completeness (**FC**) problem is to design an algorithm that takes as input a policy $\mathcal{F}$ and determines whether every packet arriving at the firewall matches at least one of the filtering rules of $\mathcal{F}$. From Theorem 1, we obtain:

Proposition 1 (FC). *A policy $\mathcal{F}$ is complete iff its automaton $\Gamma_{\mathcal{F}}$ has no no-match state.*

Therefore, **FC** problem of $\mathcal{F}$ is solved by constructing the automaton $\Gamma_{\mathcal{F}}$ and verifying if it contains the no-match state. For example, the policy $\mathcal{F}$ of Table 1 is incomplete, because $\Gamma_{\mathcal{F}}$ of Fig. 1 contains the no-match state.

5.2 Resolution of Firewall Adequacy Problems: FA-d, FA-a

There are two Firewall Adequacy (**FA**) problems:

FA-d: to design an algorithm that takes as input a policy $\mathcal{F}$ and determines whether there exists at least one packet which is denied by $\mathcal{F}$.

FA-a: to design an algorithm that takes as input a policy $\mathcal{F}$ and determines whether there exists at least one packet which is accepted by $\mathcal{F}$.

From Theorem 1, we obtain:

Proposition 2 (FA-d). *A policy $\mathcal{F}$ denies one or more packets iff its automaton $\Gamma_{\mathcal{F}}$ has one or more match states associated to the action* Deny.

Proposition 3 (FA-a). *A policy $\mathcal{F}$ accepts one or more packets iff its automaton $\Gamma_{\mathcal{F}}$ has one or more match states associated to the action* Accept.

Therefore, **FA-d** (resp. **FA-a**) problem of $\mathcal{F}$ is solved by constructing the automaton $\Gamma_{\mathcal{F}}$ and verifying if it contains match state(s) associated to the action Deny (resp. Accept). For example, the policy $\mathcal{F}$ of Table 1 denies and accepts packets, because $\Gamma_{\mathcal{F}}$ of Fig. 1 contains 1 match state with action Deny and 4 match states with action Accept.

5.3 Resolution of Slice Probing Problems: SP-d, SP-a

We first define the following two types of policies:

Discard slice: it is a policy consisting of zero or more accept rules followed by a last all-deny-rule.

Accept slice: it is a policy consisting of zero or more deny rules followed by a last all-accept-rule.

There are two Slice Probing (**SP**) problems:

SP-d: to design an algorithm that takes as input a discard slice $\mathcal{F}$ and determines whether there exists at least one packet which is denied by $\mathcal{F}$.

SP-a: to design an algorithm that takes as input an accept slice $\mathcal{F}$ and determines whether there exists at least one packet which is accepted by $\mathcal{F}$.

We have two ways to solve **SP**: by using **FC** or **FA**.

Solving SP-d and SP-a by using FC: Consider a discard slice $\mathcal{F}$ consisting of n rules $R_1, \cdots, R_n$, i.e. $R_1, \cdots, R_{n-1}$ are accept rules and R_n is an all-deny-rule. Therefore, $\mathcal{F}$ denies a packet P iff P matches none of the accept-rules of $\mathcal{F}$, and hence matches only the last all-deny-rule of $\mathcal{F}$. Clearly, this situation occurs iff the policy $\mathcal{F} \backslash R_n$ is incomplete, where $\mathcal{F} \backslash R_n$ denotes $\mathcal{F}$ from which R_n is removed. In the same way, we obtain that an accept slice $\mathcal{F}$ accepts at least one packet iff the policy $\mathcal{F} \backslash R_n$ is incomplete. From Proposition 1:

Proposition 4 (SP-d). *A discard slice $\mathcal{F}$ consisting of rules $R_1, \cdots, R_n$ denies one or more packets iff the automaton $\Gamma_{\mathcal{F} \backslash R_n}$ has the no-match state.*

Proposition 5 (SP-a). *An accept slice $\mathcal{F}$ consisting of rules $R_1, \cdots, R_n$ accepts one or more packets iff the automaton $\Gamma_{\mathcal{F} \backslash R_n}$ has the no-match state.*

Therefore, **SP-d** and **SP-a** problems of $\mathcal{F}$ are solved by constructing the automaton $\Gamma_{\mathcal{F} \backslash R_n}$ and verifying if it contains the no-match state.

Solving SP-d (resp. SP-a) by using FA-d (resp. FA-a): **SP-d** is a particular case of **FA-d** which considers only discard slices, instead of any policy. Similarly, **SP-a** is a particular case of **FA-a** which considers only accept slices. Therefore, **SP-d** and **SP-a** can be solved by solving **FA-d** and **FA-a**, respectively. Hence, from Propositions 2 and 3, we obtain:

Proposition 6 (SP-d). *A discard slice $\mathcal{F}$ denies one or more packets iff the automaton $\Gamma_{\mathcal{F}}$ has one or more match states associated to the action Deny.*

Proposition 7 (SP-a). *An accept slice $\mathcal{F}$ accepts one or more packets iff the automaton $\Gamma_{\mathcal{F}}$ has one or more match states associated to the action Accept.*

Example of Accept Slice: Due to the symmetry between **SP-d** and **SP-a**, we will illustrate only the resolution of **SP-a** by the example of the accept slice of Table 2. The symbol # means "same as the field of the preceding rule".

Table 2. Example of accept slice.

Rule	IPsrc	IPdst	Port	Protocol	Action
R_1	192.168.10.0/24	81.10.10.0/24	*Any*	*Any*	Deny
R_2	194.204.201.0/28	212.217.65.202	*not(21)*	*Any*	
R_3	#	212.217.65.201	*not(80)*	*Any*	
R_4	#	#	80	UDP	
R_5	#	*not(212.217.65.201, 212.217.65.202)*	*Any*	*Any*	
R_6	*not(192.168.10.0/24, 194.204.201.0/28)*	212.217.65.201	*not(80)*	*Any*	
R_7	#	#	80	UDP	
R_8	#	*not(212.217.65.201)*	*Any*	*Any*	
R_9	*Any*	*Any*	*Any*	*Any*	Accept

Illustration of SP-a Resolution by Using FC: Figure 2 represents the automaton $\Gamma_{\mathcal{F}\backslash R_9}$ synthesized from the accept slice of Table 2 without R_9. From Proposition 5 and the fact that $\Gamma_{\mathcal{F}\backslash R_9}$ contains the no-match state, we deduce that this accept slice accepts packets.

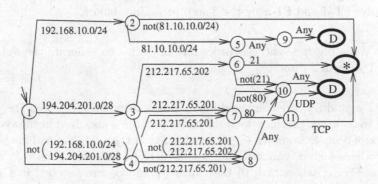

Fig. 2. Automaton $\Gamma_{\mathcal{F}\backslash R_9}$ of the accept slice of Table 2 without R_9.

Illustration of SP-a resolution by using FA-a: Fig. 3 represents the automaton $\Gamma_{\mathcal{F}}$ synthesized from the accept slice $\mathcal{F}$ of Table 2. From Proposition 7 and the fact that $\Gamma_{\mathcal{F}}$ has 4 match states associated to the action Accept, we deduce that this accept slice accepts packets.

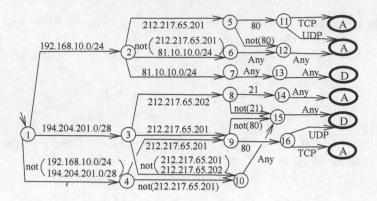

Fig. 3. Automaton $\Gamma_{\mathcal{F}}$ obtained from the accept slice $\mathcal{F}$ of Table 2.

6   Resolution of FI, FV, FE and FR

Let us demonstrate the applicability of our synthesis procedure for the resolution of 8 problems of [2]: **FI-d, FI-a, FV-d, FV-a, FE-d, FE-a, FR-d** and **FR-a**.

6.1   Resolution of Firewall Implication Problems: FI-d, FI-a

There are two Firewall Implication (**FI**) problems:

FI-d: to design an algorithm that takes as input two policies $\mathcal{F}_1$ and $\mathcal{F}_2$ and determines whether $\mathcal{F}_2$ denies all the packets denied by $\mathcal{F}_1$.

FI-a: to design an algorithm that takes as input two policies $\mathcal{F}_1$ and $\mathcal{F}_2$ and determines whether $\mathcal{F}_2$ accepts all the packets accepted by $\mathcal{F}_1$.

We solve **FI-d** and **FI-a** by the 3-step procedure below.

Step 1: We apply the synthesis procedure of Sect. 4 to generate the automata $\Gamma_{\mathcal{F}_1}$ and $\Gamma_{\mathcal{F}_2}$ from $\mathcal{F}_1$ and $\mathcal{F}_2$.

Step 2: $\Gamma_{\mathcal{F}_1}$ and $\Gamma_{\mathcal{F}_1}$ are combined into a single automaton denoted $\Omega_{\mathcal{F}_1,\mathcal{F}_2}$, by applying to them the product operator (this operator is also used in the synthesis procedure of Sect. 4, as shown in [3]). Each state of $\Omega_{\mathcal{F}_1,\mathcal{F}_2}$ is defined in the form $\langle \phi_1, \phi_2 \rangle$, where each ϕ_i is a state of $\Gamma_{\mathcal{F}_i}$. Intuitively, for every packet P, a state $\langle \phi_1, \phi_2 \rangle$ of $\Omega_{\mathcal{F}_1,\mathcal{F}_2}$ is reached, iff the states ϕ_1 and ϕ_2 are reached in $\Gamma_{\mathcal{F}_1}$ and $\Gamma_{\mathcal{F}_1}$, respectively. A state $\langle \phi_1, \phi_2 \rangle$ of $\Omega_{\mathcal{F}_1,\mathcal{F}_2}$ is said final if ϕ_1 and ϕ_2 are final states in Γ_1 and Γ_2, respectively. Hence, a final state of $\Omega_{\mathcal{F}_1,\mathcal{F}_2}$ is in one of the following forms, where q_i is a match state of $\mathcal{F}_i$ and E_i is the no-match state of $\mathcal{F}_i$: $\langle q_1, q_2 \rangle$ associated to two actions a_1 and a_2, $\langle q_1, E_2 \rangle$ associated to a single action a_1, $\langle E_1, q_2 \rangle$ associated to a single action a_2, and $\langle E_1, E_2 \rangle$ associated to no action.

Step 3: From Theorem 1, when a final state r of $\Omega_{\mathcal{F}_1,\mathcal{F}_2}$ is reached for a packet P, the actions a_1 and a_2 associated to r, if any, are dictated by $\mathcal{F}_1$ and $\mathcal{F}_2$, respectively. We obtain:

Proposition 8 (FI-d). $\mathcal{F}_2$ *denies all the packets denied by* $\mathcal{F}_1$ *iff, for every final state* r *of* $\Omega_{\mathcal{F}_1,\mathcal{F}_2}$ *associated to actions* (a_1, a_2): $a_1 = $ Deny *implies* $a_2 = $ Deny.

Proposition 9 (FI-a). $\mathcal{F}_2$ *accepts all the packets accepted by* $\mathcal{F}_1$ *iff, for every final state* r *of* $\Omega_{\mathcal{F}_1,\mathcal{F}_2}$ *associated to* (a_1, a_2): $a_1 = $ Accept *implies* $a_2 = $ Accept.

Therefore, **FI-d** (resp. **FI-a**) problem of $(\mathcal{F}_1, \mathcal{F}_2)$ is solved by constructing the automaton $\Omega_{\mathcal{F}_1,\mathcal{F}_2}$ and verifying if all its final states satisfy the condition of Proposition 8 (resp. Proposition 9).

Due to the symmetry between **FI-d** and **FI-a**, we illustrate only the resolution of **FI-d**. We consider the previous policies $\mathcal{F}_1$ of Table 1 and $\mathcal{F}_2$ of Table 2. The automata $\Gamma_{\mathcal{F}_1}$ and $\Gamma_{\mathcal{F}_2}$ have been previously given in Figs. 1 and 3, respectively. The product automaton $\Omega_{\mathcal{F}_1,\mathcal{F}_2}$ of $\Gamma_{\mathcal{F}_1}$ and $\Gamma_{\mathcal{F}_2}$, is represented in Fig. 4. The notation X-Y associated to the final states means that the actions dictated by $\mathcal{F}_1$ and $\mathcal{F}_2$ are X and Y, respectively. * means the absence of action. For example, *-D means that a_2 is Deny and there is no a_1. Since we have no state with D-A or D-*, we deduce from Proposition 8 that the accept slice of Table 2 denies every packet which is denied by the policy of Table 1.

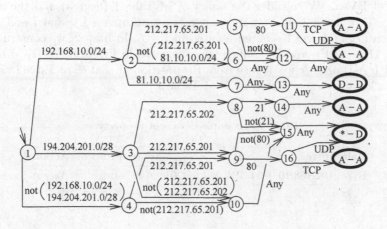

Fig. 4. Product $\Omega_{\mathcal{F}_1,\mathcal{F}_2}$ of $\Gamma_{\mathcal{F}_1}$ and $\Gamma_{\mathcal{F}_2}$ of Figs. 1 and 3.

6.2   Resolution of Firewall Verification Problems: FV-d, FV-a

We first define the following two particular properties:

Discard property: it has exactly the same form and semantics as a filtering rule with the action Deny.

Accept property: it has exactly the same form and semantics as a filtering rule with the action Accept.

There are two Firewall Verification problems (**FV**):

FV-d: to design an algorithm that takes as input a policy $\mathcal{F}$ and a discard property $\mathcal{P}$, and determines whether $\mathcal{F}$ denies all the packets denied by $\mathcal{P}$.

FV-a: to design an algorithm that takes as input a policy $\mathcal{F}$ and an accept property $\mathcal{P}$, and determines whether $\mathcal{F}$ accepts all the packets accepted by $\mathcal{P}$.

FV-d and **FV-a** are particular cases of **FI-d** and **FI-a**, respectively, because a discard property and an accept property are particular policies consisting of a single rule. We can therefore solve **FV-d** and **FV-a** by using exactly the same 3-step method used for solving **FI-d** and **FI-a**. We obtain:

Proposition 10. *$\mathcal{F}$ denies all the packets denied by a discard property $\mathcal{P}$ iff, for every final state r of $\Omega_{\mathcal{P},\mathcal{F}}$ associated to (a_1, a_2): $a_1 = \text{Deny}$ implies $a_2 = \text{Deny}$*

Proposition 11. *$\mathcal{F}$ accepts all the packets accepted by an accept property $\mathcal{P}$ iff, for every final state r of $\Omega_{\mathcal{P},\mathcal{F}}$ associated to (a_1, a_2): $a_1 = \text{Accept}$ implies $a_2 = \text{Accept}$*

Therefore, **FV-d** (resp. **FV-a**) problem of $(\mathcal{P}, \mathcal{F})$ is solved by constructing the automaton $\Omega_{\mathcal{P},\mathcal{F}}$ and verifying if all its final states satisfy the condition of Proposition 10 (resp. Proposition 11).

Due to the symmetry between **FV-d** and **FV-a**, we illustrate only the resolution of **FV-a**. We consider the policy $\mathcal{F}$ of Table 1 (Sect. 3) and the accept property $\mathcal{P}$ of Table 3. In Step 1, we construct automata $\Gamma_{\mathcal{F}}$ and $\Gamma_{\mathcal{P}}$. $\Gamma_{\mathcal{F}}$ has been seen in Fig. 1 and $\Gamma_{\mathcal{P}}$ is represented in Fig. 5. In Step 2, we construct the product $\Omega_{\mathcal{P},\mathcal{F}}$ of $\Gamma_{\mathcal{P}}$ and $\Gamma_{\mathcal{F}}$, which is represented in Fig. 6. Since $\Omega_{\mathcal{P},\mathcal{F}}$ has no state with A-D or A-*, we deduce from Proposition 11 that $\mathcal{F}$ of Table 1 accepts every packet which is accepted by $\mathcal{P}$ of Table 3.

Table 3. Example of accept property

Rule	IPsrc	IPdst	Port	Protocol	Action
R_1	192.168.10.0/24	212.217.65.201	*Any*	*Any*	Accept

Fig. 5. Automaton $\Gamma_{\mathcal{P}}$ obtained from the accept property $\mathcal{P}$ of Table 3.

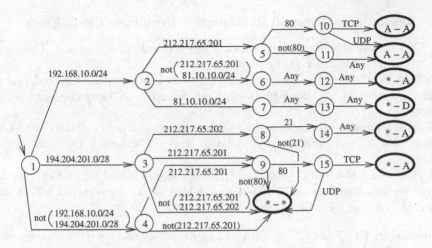

Fig. 6. Product $\Omega_{\mathcal{P},\mathcal{F}}$ of $\Gamma_{\mathcal{P}}$ and $\Gamma_{\mathcal{F}}$ of Figs. 5 and 3.

6.3   Resolution of Firewall Equivalence Problems: FE-d, FE-a

There are two Firewall Equivalence (**FE**) problems:

FE-d: to design an algorithm that takes as input two policies $\mathcal{F}_1$ and $\mathcal{F}_2$ and determines whether $\mathcal{F}_1$ and $\mathcal{F}_2$ deny the same set of packets.

FE-a: to design an algorithm that takes as input two policies $\mathcal{F}_1$ and $\mathcal{F}_2$ and determines whether $\mathcal{F}_1$ and $\mathcal{F}_2$ accept the same set of packets.

FE-d and **FE-a** can be obviously solved by solving **FI-d** and **FI-a**. Indeed, $\mathcal{F}_1$ and $\mathcal{F}_2$ deny the same set of packets is equivalent to: $\mathcal{F}_1$ denies at least all the packets denied by $\mathcal{F}_2$ AND $\mathcal{F}_2$ denies at least all the packets denied by $\mathcal{F}_1$. Similarly, $\mathcal{F}_1$ and $\mathcal{F}_2$ accept the same set of packets is equivalent to: $\mathcal{F}_1$ accepts at least all the packets accepted by $\mathcal{F}_2$ AND $\mathcal{F}_2$ accepts at least all the packets accepted by $\mathcal{F}_1$. We obtain:

Proposition 12. $\mathcal{F}_1$ and $\mathcal{F}_2$ deny the same set of packets iff, for every final state r of $\Omega_{\mathcal{F}_1,\mathcal{F}_2}$ associated to (a_1, a_2): $a_1 = \text{Deny}$ iff $a_2 = \text{Deny}$.

Proposition 13. $\mathcal{F}_1$ and $\mathcal{F}_2$ accept the same set of packets iff, for every final state r of $\Omega_{\mathcal{F}_1,\mathcal{F}_2}$ associated to (a_1, a_2): $a_1 = \text{Accept}$ iff $a_2 = \text{Accept}$.

Therefore, **FE-d** (resp. **FE-a**) problem of $(\mathcal{F}_1, \mathcal{F}_2)$ is solved by constructing the automaton $\Omega_{\mathcal{F}_1,\mathcal{F}_2}$ and verifying if all its final states satisfy the condition of Proposition 12 (resp. Proposition 13).

Due to the symmetry between **FE-d** and **FE-a**, we illustrate only the resolution of **FE-a**. We use the same example used to illustrate the resolution of **FI-d**. We consider therefore the previous policies $\mathcal{F}_1$ of Table 1 and $\mathcal{F}_2$ of Table 2. The automata $\Gamma_{\mathcal{F}_1}$, $\Gamma_{\mathcal{F}_2}$ and $\Omega_{\mathcal{F}_1,\mathcal{F}_2}$ have been represented in Figs. 1, 3 and 4, respectively. Since every final state in Fig. 4 has either two actions Accept or no action Accept, we deduce from Proposition 13 that the accept slice of Table 2 and the policy of Table 1 accept the same set of packets.

6.4   Resolution of Firewall Redundancy Problems: FR-d, FR-a

Let $\mathcal{F} \backslash \mathcal{R}$ denote a policy $\mathcal{F}$ from which a filtering rule $\mathcal{R}$ is removed. There are two Firewall Redundancy (**FR**) problems:

FR-d: to design an algorithm that takes as input a policy $\mathcal{F}$ and one of its discard rules $\mathcal{R}$, and determines whether $\mathcal{F}$ and $\mathcal{F} \backslash \mathcal{R}$ deny the same set of packets.

FR-a: to design an algorithm that takes as input a policy $\mathcal{F}$ and one of its accept rules $\mathcal{R}$, and determines whether $\mathcal{F}$ and $\mathcal{F} \backslash \mathcal{R}$ accept the same set of packets.

FR-d and **FR-a** are obviously particular cases of **FE-d** and **FE-a**, respectively. We can therefore solve **FR-d** and **FR-a** as we have solved **FE-d** and **FE-a**. We obtain: ($\mathcal{R}$ is one of the rules of a policy $\mathcal{F}$)

Proposition 14. $\mathcal{F}$ and $\mathcal{F} \backslash \mathcal{R}$ deny the same set of packets iff, for every final state r of $\Omega_{\mathcal{F}, \mathcal{F} \backslash \mathcal{R}}$ associated to actions (a_1, a_2): $a_1 = $ Deny iff $a_2 = $ Deny.

Proposition 15. $\mathcal{F}$ and $\mathcal{F} \backslash \mathcal{R}$ accept the same set of packets iff, for every final state r of $\Omega_{\mathcal{F}, \mathcal{F} \backslash \mathcal{R}}$ associated to actions (a_1, a_2): $a_1 = $ Accept iff $a_2 = $ Accept.

Therefore, **FR-d** (resp. **FR-a**) problem of $(\mathcal{F}, \mathcal{R})$ is solved by constructing the automaton $\Omega_{\mathcal{F}, \mathcal{F} \backslash \mathcal{R}}$ and verifying if all its final states satisfy the condition of Proposition 14 (resp. Proposition 15).

Due to the symmetry between **FR-d** and **FR-a**, we illustrate only the resolution of **FR-d**. We consider the policy $\mathcal{F}$ of Table 4 which is obtained by adding the rule R_5 to the policy of Table 1. Let us verify that $\mathcal{F}$ and $\mathcal{F} \backslash R_5$ deny the same packets. The automaton $\Gamma_{\mathcal{F} \backslash R_5}$ has been seen in Fig. 1. The automaton $\Gamma_{\mathcal{F}}$ is identical to $\Gamma_{\mathcal{F} \backslash R_5}$, because R_5 is "shadowed" by R_4 and hence never takes effect. The product $\Omega_{\mathcal{F}, \mathcal{F} \backslash \mathcal{R}}$ is represented in Fig. 7. Since every final state in Fig. 7 has either two actions Deny or no action Deny, we deduce from Proposition 14 that $\mathcal{F}$ of Table 4 and $\mathcal{F} \backslash R_5$ deny the same set of packets.

Table 4. Policy to illustrate **FR-d** resolution

Rule	IPsrc	IPdst	Port	Protocol	Action
R_1	*Any*	212.217.65.201	80	TCP	Accept
R_2	192.168.10.0/24	81.10.10.0/24	*Any*	*Any*	Deny
R_3	194.204.201.0/28	212.217.65.202	21	*Any*	Accept
R_4	192.168.10.0/24	*Any*	*Any*	*Any*	Accept
R_5	192.168.10.0/24	*Any*	80	UDP	Deny

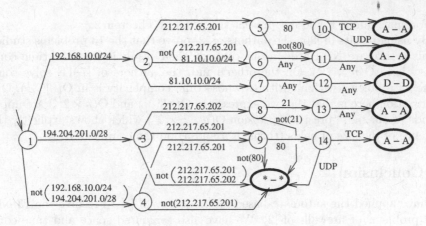

Fig. 7. Product $\Omega_{\mathcal{F},\mathcal{F}\backslash R_5}$ obtained for the policy of Table 4.

7 Evaluation of Space and Time Complexities

We call *great field* a field whose domain contains more than n values, and *small field* a field whose domain contains at most n values. Consider for example the four fields IPsrc, IPdst, Port and Protocol and assume $n = 1000$. IPsrc, IPdst and Port are great fields, because their domains contain 2^{32}, 2^{32} and 2^{16} values, respectively, hence more than 1000 values. Protocol is a small field, because its domain contains much less than 1000 values (the number of considered protocols is negligible to 1000). In addition to n and m, we define:

d_i = number of bits necessary to code the values of field F^i, for $i = 0, \cdots, m-1$.
    Hence, 2^{d_i} is the number of possible values of F^i.
D = sum of the number of bits to code all the fields, i.e. $D = d_0 + \cdots + d_{m-1}$
μ = number of great fields.
δ = sum of the number of bits to code the small fields.

In our computation of complexities, we assume that $d_i \geq 1$ (i.e. several possible values for each field), $n > D$ (hence $n > m$) and $2^n > n^m$ which is realistic when we have hundreds or thousands of filtering rules.

For example, for the $m = 4$ fields IPsrc, IPdst, Port and Protocol, we have used $d_0 = d_1 = 32$ (each IPsrc and IPdst is coded in 32 bits), $d_2 = 16$ (Port is coded in 16 bits), $d_3 = 1$ (Protocol is coded in 1 bit since we consider only TCP and UDP), and $D = 32 + 32 + 16 + 1 = 81$. For $81 < n < 2^{16}$, the above assumptions (all $d_i \geq 1$, $n > 81$ and $2^n > n^4$) are obviously satisfied. Since IPsrc, IPdst and Port are great fields and Protocol is a small field, we obtain $\mu = 3$ (number of great fields) and $\delta = d_3 = 1$ (1 bit is used to code the unique small field protocol).

We have the following result:

Theorem 2. *The space and time complexities for solving each of the 13 problems are in* $O(n^{\mu+1} \times 2^\delta)$*, which is bounded by both* $O(n^{m+1})$ *and* $O(n \times 2^D)$*.*

For space limit, we do not present the proof of Theorem 2.

By using results in [26], the authors of [2] prove that the 13 problems studied in this article are NP-Hard. In our context, their result is that the time complexity is in $O(n \times 2^D)$. On the other hand, the authors of [7–11] solve some of the 13 problems with algorithms whose time complexity is in $O(n^{m+1})$. Our contribution here is that the two expressions $O(n^{m+1})$ and $O(n \times 2^D)$ are upper bounds of our more precise expression $O(n^{\mu+1} \times 2^\delta)$ which shows explicitly the influence of the size of fields (through μ and δ) on the complexity.

8   Conclusion

We have applied the automata-based methodology of [3] to resolve the 13 NP-hard problems of firewalls of [2]. We have also evaluated space and time complexities of the 13 resolutions.

As near future work, we plan to apply our synthesis procedure for the design of efficient security policies that adapt dynamically to the filtered traffic. We also plan to adapt our approach in other areas, such as policies in intelligent health-care (e-health).

References

1. Information Technology Security Evaluation Criteria (ITSEC), v1.2. Office for Official Publications of the European Communities, Luxembourg, June 1991
2. Elmallah, E., Gouda, M.G.: Hardness of firewall analysis. In: International Conference on NETworked sYStems (NETYS), Marrakesh, Morocco, May 2014
3. Khoumsi, A., Krombi, W., Erradi, M.: A formal approach to verify completeness and detect anomalies in firewall security policies. In: Cuppens, F., Garcia-Alfaro, J., Zincir Heywood, N., Fong, P.W.L. (eds.) FPS 2014. LNCS, vol. 8930, pp. 221–236. Springer, Heidelberg (2015)
4. Hoffman, D., Yoo, K.: Blowtorch: a framework for firewall test automation. In: 20th IEEE/ACM International Conference on Automated Software Engineering (ASE), Long Beach, California, USA, pp. 96–103, November 2005
5. Kamara, S., Fahmy, S., Schultz, E., Kerschbaum, F., Frantzen, M.: Analysis of vulnerabilities in internet firewalls. Comput. Secur. **22**(3), 214–232 (2003)
6. Wool, A.: A quantitative study of firewall configuration errors. Computer **37**(6), 62–67 (2004)
7. Acharya, H.B., Gouda, M.G.: Firewall verification and redundancy checking are equivalent. In: 30th IEEE International Conference on Computer Communication (INFOCOM), Shanghai, China, pp. 2123–2128, April 2011
8. Liu, A.X., Gouda, M.G.: Complete redundancy removal for packet classifiers in TCAMs. IEEE Trans. Parallel Distrib. Syst. **21**(4), 424–437 (2010)
9. Acharya, H.B., Gouda, M.G.: Projection, division: linear space verification of firewalls. In: 30th International Conference on Distributed Computing Systems (ICDCS), Genova, Italy, pp. 736–743, June 2010
10. Al-Shaer, E., Marrero, W., El-Atawy, A., Elbadawi, K.: Network configuration in a box: towards end-to-end verification of networks reachability and security. In: 17th IEEE International Conference on Network Protocols (ICNP), Princeton, NJ, USA, pp. 736–743, October 2009

11. Liu, A.X., Gouda, M.G.: Diverse firewall design. IEEE Trans. Parallel Distrib. Syst. **19**(9), 1237–1251 (2008)
12. Al-Shaer, E., Hamed, H.: Modeling and management of firewall policies. IEEE Trans. Netw. Serv. Manag. **1**(1), 2–10 (2004)
13. Karoui, K., Ben Ftima, F., Ben Ghezala, H.: Formal specification, verification, correction of security policies based on the decision tree approach. Int. J. Data Netw. Secur. **3**(3), 92–111 (2013)
14. Madhuri, M., Rajesh, K.: Systematic detection and resolution of firewall policy anomalies. Int. J. Res. Comput. Commun. Technol. (IJRCCT) **2**(12), 1387–1392 (2013)
15. Garcia-Alfaro, J., Cuppens, F., Cuppens-Boulahia, N., Martinez Perez, S., Cabot, J.: Management of stateful firewall misconfiguration. Comput. Secur. **39**, 64–85 (2013)
16. Cuppens, F., Cuppens-Boulahia, N., Garcia-Alfaro, J., Moataz, T., Rimasson, X.: Handling stateful firewall anomalies. In: Gritzalis, D., Furnell, S., Theoharidou, M. (eds.) SEC 2012. IFIP AICT, vol. 376, pp. 174–186. Springer, Heidelberg (2012)
17. Liu, A.X., Gouda, M.G.: Structured firewall design. Comput. Netw.: Int. J. Comput. Telecommun. Netw. **51**(4), 1106–1120 (2007)
18. Yuan, L., Mai, J., Su, Z., Chen, H., Chuah, C.-N., Mohapatra, P.: FIREMAN: a toolkit for FIREwall modeling and analysis. In: IEEE Symposium on Security and Privacy (S&P), Berkeley/Oakland, CA, USA, May 2006
19. Bryant, R.E.: Graph-based algorithms for Boolean function manipulation. IEEE Trans. Comput. **35**(8), 677–691 (1986)
20. Mallouli, W., Orset, J., Cavalli, A., Cuppens, N., Cuppens, F.: A formal approach for testing security rules. In: 12th ACM Symposium on Access Control Models and Technologies (SACMAT), Sophia Antipolis, France, June 2007
21. Lee, D., Yannakakis, M.: Principles and methods of testing finite state machines - a survey. Proc. IEEE **84**, 1090–1126 (1996)
22. El Kalam, A.A., El Baida, R, Balbiani, P., Benferhat, S., Cuppens, F., Deswarte, Y., Miège, A., Saurel, C., Trouessin, G.: Organization based access control. In: IEEE 4th International Workshop on Policies for Distributed Systems and Networks (POLICY), Lake Come, Italy, June 2003
23. Lu, L., Safavi-Naini, R., Horton, J., Susilo, W.: Comparing and debugging firewall rule tables. IET Inf. Secur. **1**(4), 143–151 (2007)
24. Mansmann, F., Göbel, T., Cheswick, W.: Visual analysis of complex firewall configurations. In: 9th International Symposium on Visualization for Cyber Security (VizSec), Seattle, WA, USA, pp. 1–8, October 2012
25. Krombi, W., Erradi, M., Khoumsi, A.: Automata-based approach to design and analyze security policies. In: Internernational Conference on Privacy, Security and Trust (PST), Toronto, Canada (2014)
26. Garey, M.R., Johnson, D.S.: Computers and Intractability: A Guide to the Theory of NP-Completeness. AW.H. Freeman, San Francisco (1979)

Hybrid Encryption Approach Using Dynamic Key Generation and Symmetric Key Algorithm for RFID Systems

Zouheir Labbi$^{(\boxtimes)}$, Ahmed Maarof, Mohamed Senhadji, and Mostafa Belkasmi

TSE Laboratory, ENSIAS, Mohammed V University, Rabat, Morocco
Zouhir.labbi@gmail.com, ahmed.maarof@gmail.com,
{m.senhadji,m.belkasmi}@um5s.net.ma

Abstract. The security of RFID systems become an important subject especially for low cost RFID tags. A lot of Cryptographic algorithms were proposed to insure the security and in the same time meet the resource limitations. In this paper, we proposed a hybrid cryptographic approach as symmetric key encryption technique which generate the key dynamically, together with integrity check parameters. The generation of key stream follows the chained approach, beginning from the initial key pre-shared. As a result, the computational complexity will be reduced as well as increase performance.

Keywords: RFID · Encryption · Integrity · Dynamic key generation

1 Introduction and Literature Review

RFID (Radio Frequency Identification) systems are very useful and convenient to identify objects automatically through wireless communication channel. However, since this channel is not secure from the various security attacks, a security mechanism is needed which necessitating the use of data encryption algorithms [1]. However, the less computational power and storage capabilities of RFID systems restrict and limit to perform sophisticated cryptographic operations [2] like RSA, AES and DES. As a result, a several lightweight encryption algorithms were proposed to the challenging problem of providing security to devices with limited resources (such as Hummingbird [3], RBS (Redundant Bit Security algorithm) [4], etc.).

Engels et al. [3] proposed a symmetric key Encryption (SKE) algorithm called Hummingbird as hybrid encryption approach of the block cipher and key stream. Hummingbird uses the same traditional encryption process of block ciphers as substitution and looping, whereas, the key is derived via the stream cipher principle which remains this encryption process computationally expensive. However, our approach will be compared with Hummingbird without inherit any feature from it.

In our proposed hybrid algorithm, the key stream is generated dynamically as it is derived from previous key block and an Intermediate Cipher Text (ICT) block, which is encrypted block-by-block with a message using the XOR operation. The integrity check is applied using a fixed size final key in each round which is used as the message

© Springer International Publishing AG 2016
P.A. Abdulla and C. Delporte-Gallet (Eds.): NETYS 2016, LNCS 9944, pp. 244–249, 2016.
DOI: 10.1007/978-3-319-46140-3_20

digest (MD) after encryption process. As our algorithm use only the XOR operation during the encryption process and provides an integrity check without using any external hashing algorithm, we can consider that our approach will increase performance as well as reduce the computational complexity.

This paper is organized as follows. In Sect. 2, we explain our proposed algorithm. In Sect. 3, we provide a security analysis of our approach and compare our approach with existing algorithms. Section 4 concludes the paper.

2 Proposed Approach

2.1 Overview

Using cipher text as part of the encryption can lead to some information about the original message being uncovered to an attacker. To avoid this issue, our approach uses an ICT to generate a dynamic key which used on each block of the message encryption, to generate at the end a cipher text bits completely random.

Our hybrid encryption algorithm consists of two parts: key generation part (based on stream ciphers) and two rounds of encryption (or decryption) using a basic XOR operation. The message is encrypted block-by-block with different (block) keys on each message block. The size of the message block is 128-bits in sixteen 8-bit chunks.

Figure 1 illustrates the encryption process. The algorithm needs two initial keys that encrypt the first block in each round. Except the initial keys, every successive key is derived from the bits in the current key block and an ICT block.

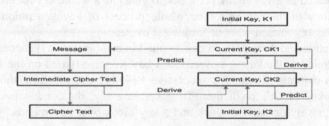

Fig. 1. Overview of the encryption process

2.2 Key Generation

We consider that the initial key used to encrypt the first block of the message in each round is generated by the sender and securely transmitted to the receiver.

The successive keys are generated from the previous keys with the help of an intermediate cipher text (ICT). ICT represents the encrypted message after Round 1, whereas the final cipher text is generated after Round 2. The key generation process uses a different initial key (K_{a0} and K_{b0}) in each round to encrypt the first block in the message. To encrypt each successive block in the message, we introduce a combination of prediction and derivation techniques to generate successive keys ($K_{a1...n}$ for Round 1 and $K_{b1...n}$ for Round 2) from previous key block and ICT block.

In prediction, three bits in every chunk (8 bits) per block are used to choose the i_x^{th} bit within the respective chunk. The value of i_x is based on the three binary bits chosen in the chunk. The value of i_x is a decimal representation of the 3-bit binary. In a chunk, 3-bits are selected in a clock wise direction starting from MSB in the chunk to the LSB to choose one out of eight possible values for i_x, which is repeated 8 times starting from the MSB to the LSB. The value of i represents the position of the binary bit in the chunk. Each value of i_x predicts a new bit that is used to generate chunks per block in every successive key. As shown in Fig. 2, three bits are rotated in a clock wise direction to yield one out of eight possible values for i_x.

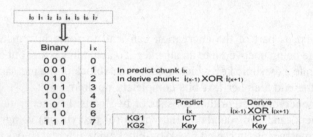

Fig. 2. Key generation process

In derivation, the successive key is generated by XORing the $(i_x - 1)^{th}$ position of the binary bit with the $(i_x + 1)^{th}$ position of the binary bit to form a new bit. The same process is repeated in every chunk per block to generate a whole key for encrypting the successive block in the message. The whole process of key generation offers randomness in the key stream without forming a cycle.

The prediction and derivation process applied in combination to generate a key is as follows. In Round 1, the key is derived from key K_a series based on the ICT block's prediction. In contrast, Round 2's successive keys are derived from the ICT block based on the key block's prediction. To generate a key, the combination process is applied alternatively on an ICT block and a key block over two rounds.

2.3   Encryption or (Decryption)

Initially, in Round 1, four out of eight bits (say 0, 2, 3, 5) in every chunk in a key K_{a0} are inverted. The first chunk in the initial key K_{a0} is XORed with the first chunk in the first block of the message, which produces the first chunk in ICT_0 (which represents the ICT first block). Again, four out of eight bits (say 2, 4, 5, 7) in every chunk in ICT0 are inverted (this process is common throughout the ICT blocks), which is followed by successive key generation operations. The output of the Key generation operation will be the first chunk in the key K_{a1} to encrypt the first chunk of the next message block. The first chunk of key K_{a1} is XORed with the second chunk of key K_{a0} that will be used to encrypt the second chunk in the first block of the message. In conclusion, every first chunk in each block of the message is directly XORed with the first chunk of the respective key, whereas the successive chunks in each block in the message are encrypted with the XORed output of the successive chunk in the present key and the currently derived chunk for the next key. For example, the 4th chunk in message $C_{M2,4}$ will be encrypted with the XORed output of the 4th chunk in the current key $C_{K_{a2},4}$ and the 3th chunk in the next key $C_{K_{a3},3}$.

Round 2 follows the same procedure as Round 1, Except that the message and initial key K_{a0} will be replaced by the ICT and key K_{b0} respectively. In addition, the inversion operation is applied on bits 1, 4, 6, 7 and 0, 1, 3, 6 for the key and the ICT respectively. The output of Round 2 is the final cipher text. Every block in a message is XORed with the key block to generate a cipher text. Figure 3 illustrates the encryption process. A decryption process is symmetric with encryption in reverse manner.

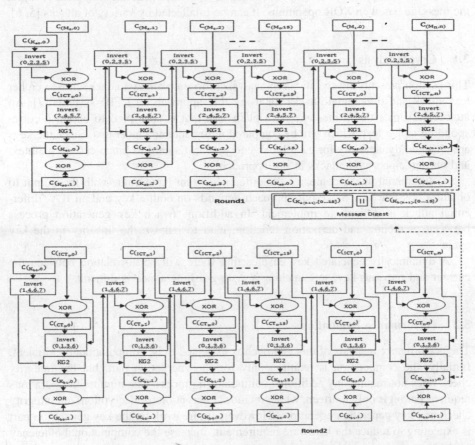

Fig. 3. Encryption process

2.4 Integrity Check

The final keys (say $K_{a(n+1)}$ and $K_{b(n+1)}$) in each round of encryption will act as integrity check parameter. In this approach, the 128-bit key $K_{a(n+1)}$ will be concatenated with the 128-bit key $K_{b(n+1)}$ to form a 256-bit MD, which is used for integrity check.

3 Analysis and Discussion

The successive keys that are generated using both message and key based on prediction or derivation function are completely dynamic. In fact, there is no regular cycle in key bits stream. Our approach is a very simple algorithm which generates keys and encrypts the message based on XOR operations. It can be unaffected by variety of attacks [5, 6].

3.1 Cryptanalysis

This section presents the specific cryptanalysis (chosen-plain text attack, chosen cipher text attack and differential attack) for using this approach on RFID systems [7]. An attacker assumes that a message is in plain text that is encrypted to obtain a corresponding cipher text, which will be compared with captured cipher text. Since the keys are changed dynamically for each block encrypted, it's hard to lunch chosen plaintext and chosen cipher text attacks in our approach.

A differential attack compares the difference in an input value with the output to obtain a possible key. Since our approach depends on both a key and an ICT, differential attack is difficult to implement. In addition, switch key generation process between prediction and derivation function, lead to remove the linearity in the key cycle.

A dynamically generated key ensures that there will be no relation between the current and previous key, so launching a distinguishing attack is difficult.

3.2 Performance Evaluation

The performance analysis of this approach is expected to be computationally efficient. Initially, the computation is required only for the encryption part, but the integrity check does not require any additional computation process. The number of operations required per bit is only fourteen, which includes encryption (or decryption), an integrity check and key generation operations. However, future work on the key generation part is expecting to reduce the hardware requirement, increase the computational efficiency of the proposed approach.

4   Conclusions and Future Work

This paper proposes a novel hybrid symmetric key encryption algorithm that is designed to offer confidentiality, integrity and dynamic key generation. In conclusion, the uniqueness of the algorithms is to achieve more than one security goal without using additional algorithms and this is accomplished with limited resources.

Finally, proposed approaches are not available in real-time environment. For this reason, improved security analysis, study of hardware implementation for our approach, and real-time algorithm deployment will be conducted in the future.

References

1. Molnar, D., Wagner, D.: Privacy and security in library RFID: issues, practices, and architectures. In: Proceedings of the 11th ACM Conference on Computer and Communications Security, pp. 210–219. ACM (2004)
2. Batina, L., Guajardo, J., Kerins, T., Mentens, N., Tuyls, P., Verbauwhede, I.: Public-key cryptography for RFID-tags. In: Fifth Annual IEEE International Conference on Pervasive Computing and Communications Workshops. PerCom Workshops 2007, pp. 217–222. IEEE (2007)
3. Engels, D., Fan, X., Gong, G., Hu, H., Smith, E.M.: Hummingbird: ultra-lightweight cryptography for resource-constrained devices. In: Sion, R., Curtmola, R., Dietrich, S., Kiayias, A., Miret, J.M., Sako, K., Sebé, F. (eds.) RLCPS, WECSR, and WLC 2010. LNCS, vol. 6054, pp. 3–18. Springer, Heidelberg (2010)
4. Jeddi, Z., Amini, E., Bayoumi, M.: RBS: redundant bit security algorithm for RFID systems. In: 21st International Conference on Computer Communications and Networks (ICCCN), pp. 1–5. IEEE (2012)
5. Hell, M., Johansson, T., Brynielsson, L.: An over view of distinguishing attacks on stream ciphers. Crypt. Commun. 1, 71–94 (2009)
6. Zulkifli, M.Z.W.M.: Attack on cryptography (2008)
7. Francois, X., Gilles, P., Jean-Jacques, Q.: Cryptanalysis of block ciphers: a survey. Technical report CG-2003-2 (2003)

Time-Efficient Read/Write Register in Crash-Prone Asynchronous Message-Passing Systems

Achour Mostéfaoui[1] and Michel Raynal[2,3(✉)]

[1] LINA, Université de Nantes, 44322 Nantes, France
[2] Institut Universitaire de France, Paris, France
[3] IRISA, Université de Rennes, 35042 Rennes, France
raynal@irisa.fr

Abstract. The atomic register is certainly the most basic object of computing science. Its implementation on top of an n-process asynchronous message-passing system has received a lot of attention. It has been shown that $t < n/2$ (where t is the maximal number of processes that may crash) is a necessary and sufficient requirement to build an atomic register on top of a crash-prone asynchronous message-passing system. Considering such a context, this paper visits the notion of a fast implementation of an atomic register, and presents a new time-efficient asynchronous algorithm. Its time-efficiency is measured according to two different underlying synchrony assumptions. Whatever this assumption, a write operation always costs a round-trip delay, while a read operation costs always a round-trip delay in favorable circumstances (intuitively, when it is not concurrent with a write). When designing this algorithm, the design spirit was to be as close as possible to the one of the famous ABD algorithm (proposed by Attiya, Bar-Noy, and Dolev).

Keywords: Asynchronous message-passing system · Atomic read/write register · Concurrency · Fast operation · Process crash failure · Synchronous behavior · Time-efficient operation

1 Introduction

Since Sumer time [7], and –much later– Turing's machine tape [13], read/write objects are certainly the most basic memory-based communication objects. Such an object, usually called a *register*, provides its users (processes) with a write operation which defines the new value of the register, and a read operation which returns the value of the register. When considering sequential computing, registers are universal in the sense that they allow to solve any problem that can be solved [13].

Register in Message-Passing Systems. In a message-passing system, the computing entities communicate only by sending and receiving messages transmitted

© Springer International Publishing AG 2016
P.A. Abdulla and C. Delporte-Gallet (Eds.): NETYS 2016, LNCS 9944, pp. 250–265, 2016.
DOI: 10.1007/978-3-319-46140-3_21

through a communication network. Hence, in such a system, a register is not a communication object given for free, but constitutes a communication abstraction which must be built with the help of the communication network and the local memories of the processes.

Several types of registers can be defined according to which processes are allowed to read or write it, and the quality (semantics) of the value returned by each read operation. We consider here registers which are single-writer multi-reader (SWMR), and atomic. Atomicity means that (a) each read or write operation appears as if it had been executed instantaneously at a single point of the time line, between is start event and its end event, (b) no two operations appear at the same point of the time line, and (c) a read returns the value written by the closest preceding write operation (or the initial value of the register if there is no preceding write) [8]. Algorithms building multi-writer multi-reader (MWMR) atomic registers from single-writer single-reader (SWSR) registers with a weaker semantics (safe or regular registers) are described in several textbooks (e.g., [3,9,12]).

Many distributed algorithms have been proposed, which build a register on top of a message-passing system, be it failure-free or failure-prone. In the failure-prone case, the addressed failure models are the process crash failure model, or the Byzantine process failure model (see, the textbooks [3,9–11]). The most famous of these algorithms was proposed by Attiya et al. in [2]. This algorithm, which is usually called ABD according to the names its authors, considers an n-process asynchronous system in which up to $t < n/2$ processes may crash (it is also shown in [2] that $t < n/2$ is an upper bound of the number of process crashes which can be tolerated). This simple and elegant algorithm, relies on (a) quorums [14], and (b) a simple broadcast/reply communication pattern. ABD uses this pattern once in a write operation, and twice in a read operation implementing an SWMR register.

Fast Operation. To our knowledge, the notion of a *fast implementation* of an atomic register operation, in failure-prone asynchronous message-passing systems, was introduced in [5] for process crash failures, and in [6] for Byzantine process failures. These papers consider a three-component model, namely there are three different types of processes: a set of writers W, a set of readers R, and a set of servers S which implements the register. Moreover, a client (a writer or a reader) can communicate only with the servers, and the servers do not communicate among themselves.

In these papers, *fast* means that a read or write operation must entail exactly one communication round-trip delay between a client (the writer or a reader) and the servers. When considering the process crash failure model (the one we are interested in this paper), it is shown in [5] that, when $(|W| = 1) \land (t \geq 1) \land (|R| \geq 2)$, the condition $(|R| < \frac{|S|}{t} - 2)$ is necessary and sufficient to have fast read and write operations (as defined above), which implement an atomic register. It is also shown in [5] that there is no fast implementation of an MWMR atomic register if $\big((|W| \geq 2) \land (|R| \geq 2) \land (t \geq 1) \big)$.

Content of the Paper. The work described in [5,6] is mainly on the limits of the three-component model (writers, readers, and servers constitute three independent sets of processes) in the presence of process crash failures, or Byzantine process failures. These limits are captured by predicates involving the set of writers (W), the set of readers (R), the set of servers (S), and the maximal number of servers that can be faulty (t). Both the underlying model used in this paper and its aim are different from this previous work.

While keeping the spirit (basic principles and simplicity) of ABD, our aim is to design a *time-efficient* implementation of an atomic register in the classical model used in many articles and textbooks (see, e.g., [2,3,9,12]). This model, where any process can communicate with any process, can be seen as a peer-to-peer model in which each process is both a client (it can invoke operations) and a server (it manages a local copy of the register that is built).[1]

Adopting the usual distributed computing assumption that (a) local processing times are negligible and assumed consequently to have zero duration, and (b) only communication takes time, this paper focuses on the communication time needed to complete a read or write operation. For this reason the term *time-efficiency* is defined here in terms on message transfer delays, namely, the cost of a read or write operation is measured by the number of "consecutive" message transfer delays they require to terminate. Let us notice that this includes transfer delays due to causally related messages (for example round trip delays generated by request/acknowledgment messages), but also (as we will see in the proposed algorithm) message transfer delays which occur sequentially without being necessarily causally related. Let us notice that this notion of a time-efficient operation does not involve the model parameter t.

In order to give a precise meaning to the notion of a "time-efficient implementation" of a register operation, this paper considers two distinct ways to measure the duration of read and write operations, each based on a specific additional synchrony assumption. One is the "bounded delay" assumption, the other one the "round-based synchrony" assumption. More precisely, these assumptions and the associated time-efficiency of the proposed algorithm are the following.

- *Bounded delay* assumption. Let us assume that every message takes at most Δ time units to be transmitted from its sender to any of its receivers. In such a context, the algorithm presented in the paper has the following time-efficiency properties.
  - A write operation takes at most 2Δ time units.
  - A read operation which is write-latency-free takes at most 2Δ time units. (The notion of write-latency-freedom is defined in Sect. 3. Intuitively, it captures the fact that the behavior of the read does not depend on a concurrent or faulty write operation, which is the usual case in read-dominated

---

[1] Considering the three-component model where each reader is also a server (i.e., $R = S$), we obtain a two-component model with one writer and reader-server processes. In this model, the necessary and sufficient condition $(|R| < \frac{|S|}{t} - 2)$ can never be satisfied, which means that, it is impossible to design a fast implementation of a SWMR atomic register in such a two-component model.

applications.) Otherwise, it takes at most 3Δ time units, except in the case where the read operation is concurrent with a write operation and the writer crashes during this write, where it can take up to 4Δ time units. (Let us remark that a process can experience at most once the 4Δ read operation scenario.)

– *Round-based synchrony* assumption. Here, the underlying communication system is assumed to be round-based synchronous [3,8,11]. In such a system, the processes progress by executing consecutive synchronous rounds. In every round, according to its code, a process possibly sends a message to a subset of processes, then receives all the messages sent to it during the current round, and finally executes local computation. At the end of a round, all processes are directed to simultaneously progress to the next round. In such a synchronous system, everything appears as if all messages take the very same time to go from their sender to theirs receivers, namely the duration δ associated with a round. When executed in such a context, the proposed algorithm has the following time-efficiency properties.

- The duration of a write operation is 2δ time units.
- The duration of a read operation is 2δ time units, except possibly in the specific scenario where the writer crashes while executing the write operation concurrently with the read, in which case the duration of the read can be 3δ time units (as previously, let us remark that a process can experience at most once the 3δ read operation scenario.)

Hence, while it remains correct in the presence of any asynchronous message pattern (e.g., when each message takes one more time unit than any previous message), the proposed algorithm is particularly time-efficient when "good" scenarios occur. Those are the ones defined by the previous synchrony patterns where the duration of a read or a write operation corresponds to a single round-trip delay. Moreover, in the other synchronous scenarios, where a read operation is concurrent with a write, the maximal duration of the read operation is precisely quantified. A concurrent write adds uncertainty whose resolution by a read operation requires one more message transfer delay (two in the case of the Δ synchrony assumption, if the concurrent write crashes).

Roadmap. The paper consists of 6 sections. Section 2 presents the system model. Section 3 defines the atomic register abstraction, and the notion of a time-efficient implementation. Then, Sect. 4 presents an asynchronous algorithm providing an implementation of an atomic register with time-efficient operations, as previously defined. Section 5 proves its properties. Finally, Sect. 6 concludes the paper.

2   System Model

Processes. The computing model is composed of a set of n sequential processes denoted $p_1, ..., p_n$. Each process is asynchronous which means that it proceeds at its own speed, which can be arbitrary and remains always unknown to the other processes.

A process may halt prematurely (crash failure), but executes correctly its local algorithm until it possibly crashes. The model parameter t denotes the maximal number of processes that may crash in a run. A process that crashes in a run is said to be *faulty*. Otherwise, it is *correct* or *non-faulty*.

Communication. The processes cooperate by sending and receiving messages through bi-directional channels. The communication network is a complete network, which means that any process p_i can directly send a message to any process p_j (including itself). Each channel is reliable (no loss, corruption, nor creation of messages), not necessarily first-in/first-out, and asynchronous (while the transit time of each message is finite, there is no upper bound on message transit times).

A process p_i invokes the operation "send TAG(m) to p_j" to send p_j the message tagged TAG and carrying the value m. It receives a message tagged TAG by invoking the operation "receive TAG$()$". The macro-operation "broadcast TAG(m)" is a shortcut for "**for each** $j \in \{1, \ldots, n\}$ send TAG(m) to p_j **end for**". (The sending order is arbitrary, which means that, if the sender crashes while executing this statement, an arbitrary – possibly empty– subset of processes will receive the message.)

Let us notice that, due to process and message asynchrony, no process can know if an other process crashed or is only very slow.

Notation. In the following, the previous computation model, restricted to the case where $t < n/2$, is denoted $\mathcal{CAMP}_{n,t}[t < n/2]$ (Crash Asynchronous Message-Passing).

It is important to notice that, in this model, all processes are a priori "equal". As we will see, this allows each process to be at the same time a "client" and a "server". In this sense, and as noticed in the Introduction, this model is the "fully connected peer-to-peer" model (whose structure is different from other computing models such as the client/server model, where processes are partitioned into clients and servers, playing different roles).

3 Atomic Register and Time-Efficient Implementation

3.1 Atomic Register

A *concurrent object* is an object that can be accessed by several processes (possibly simultaneously). An SWMR *atomic* register (say REG) is a concurrent object which provides exactly one process (called the writer) with an operation denoted REG.write$()$, and all processes with an operation denoted REG.read$()$. When the writer invokes REG.write(v) it defines v as being the new value of REG. An SWMR atomic register (we also say the register is *linearizable* [4]) is defined by the following set of properties [8].

– Liveness. An invocation of an operation by a correct process terminates.
– Consistency (safety). All the operations invoked by the processes, except possibly –for each faulty process– the last operation it invoked, appear as if they have been executed sequentially and this sequence of operations is such that:
  - each read returns the value written by the closest write that precedes it (or the initial value of REG if there is no preceding write),
  - if an operation $op1$ terminated before an operation $op2$ started, then $op1$ appears before $op2$ in the sequence.

This set of properties states that, from an external observer point of view, the object appears as if it was accessed sequentially by the processes, this sequence (a) respecting the real time access order, and (ii) belonging to the sequential specification of a read/write register.

3.2   Notion of a Time-Efficient Operation

The notion of a time-efficient operation is not related to its correctness, but is a property of its implementation. It is sometimes called *non-functional* property. In the present case, it captures the time efficiency of operations.[2]

As indicated in the introduction, we consider here two synchrony assumptions to define what we mean by time-efficient operation implementation. As we have seen, both are based on the duration of read and write operations, in terms of message transfer delays. Let us remember that, in both cases, it is assumed that the local processing times needed to implement these high level read and write operations are negligible.

Bounded delay-**based definition of a time-efficient implementation.** Let us assume an underlying communication system where message transfer delays are upper bounded by Δ.

Write-Latency-Free Read Operation and Interfering Write. Intuitively, a read operation is *write-latency-free* if its execution does "not interleave" with the execution of a write operation. More precisely, let τ_r be the starting time of a read operation. This read operation is *write-latency-free* if (a) it is not concurrent with a write operation, and (b) the closest preceding write did not crash and started at a time $\tau_w < \tau_r - \Delta$.

Let opr be a read operation, which started at time τ_r. Let opw be the closest write preceding opr. If opw started at time $\tau_w \geq \tau_r - \Delta$, it is said to be *interfering* with opr.

Bounded delay-based definition. An implementation of a read/write register is *time-efficient* (from a bounded delay point of view) if it satisfies the following properties.

---

[2] Another example of a non-functional property is *quiescence*. This property is on algorithms implementing reliable communication on top of unreliable networks [1]. It states that the number of underlying implementation messages generated by an application message must be finite. Hence, if there is a time after which no application process sends messages, there is a time after which the system is quiescent.

– A write operation takes at most 2Δ time units.
– A read operation which is write-latency-free takes at most 2Δ time units.
– A read operation which is not write-latency-free takes at most
   • 3Δ time units if the writer does not crash while executing the interfering write,
   • 4Δ time units if the writer crashes while executing the interfering write (this scenario can appear at most once for each process).

Round synchrony-**based definition of a time-efficient implementation.** Let us assume that the underlying communication system is round-based synchronous, where each message transfer delay is equal to δ. When considering this underlying synchrony assumption, it is assumed that a process sends or broadcasts at most one message per round, and this is done at the beginning of a round.

An implementation of a read/write register is *time-efficient* (from the round-based synchrony point of view) if it satisfies the following properties.

– The duration of a write operation is 2δ time units.
– The duration of a read operation is 2δ time units, except possibly in the "at most once" scenario where the writer crashes while executing the write operation concurrently with the read, in which case the duration of the read can be 3δ time units.

What Does the Proposed Algorithm. As we will see, the proposed algorithm, designed for the asynchronous system model $\mathcal{CAMP}_{n,t}[t < n/2]$, provides an SWMR atomic register implementation which is time-efficient for both its "bounded delay"-based definition, and its "round synchrony"-based definition.

4   An Algorithm with Time-Efficient Operations

The design of the algorithm, described in Fig. 1, is voluntarily formulated to be as close as possible to ABD. For the reader aware of ABD, this will help its understanding.

Local Variables. Each process p_i manages the following local variables.

– reg_i contains the value of the constructed register REG, as currently known by p_i. It is initialized to the initial value of REG (e.g., the default value $\perp$).
– wsn_i is the sequence number associated with the value in reg_i.
– rsn_i is the sequence number of the last read operation invoked by p_i.
– $swsn_i$ is a synchronization local variable. It contains the sequence number of the most recent value of REG that, to p_i's knowledge, is known by at least $(n-t)$ processes. This variable (which is new with respect to other algorithms) is at the heart of the time-efficient implementation of the read operation.
– res_i is the value of REG whose sequence number is $swsn_i$.

---

local variables initialization: $reg_i \leftarrow \perp$; $wsn_i \leftarrow 0$; $swsn_i \leftarrow 0$; $rsn_i \leftarrow 0$.

operation write(v) **is**
(1) $wsn_i \leftarrow wsn_i + 1$; $reg_i \leftarrow v$; broadcast WRITE(wsn_i, v);
(2) **wait** $\big($WRITE($wsn_i, -$) received from $(n - t)$ different processes$\big)$;
(3) return()
end operation.

operation read() **is** % the writer may directly return reg_i %
(4) $rsn_i \leftarrow rsn_i + 1$; broadcast READ($rsn_i$);
(5) **wait** $\big($ (msgs STATE($rsn, -$) rec. from $(n - t)$ different proc.) $\wedge$ ($swsn_i \geq maxwsn$)
          where $maxwsn$ is the greatest seq. nb in the previous STATE($rsn, -$) msgs$\big)$;
(6) return(res_i)
end operation.
%――――――――――――――――――――――――――――――

when WRITE(wsn, v) **is received do**
(7) **if** ($wsn > wsn_i$) **then** $reg_i \leftarrow v$; $wsn_i \leftarrow wsn$ **end if**;
(8) **if** (not yet done) **then** broadcast WRITE(wsn, v) **end if**;
(9) **if** $\big($WRITE($wsn, -$) received from $(n - t)$ different processes$\big)$
(10)   **then if** ($wsn > swsn_i$) $\wedge$ (not already done) **then** $swsn_i \leftarrow wsn$; $res_i \leftarrow v$ **end if**
(11) **end if.**

when READ(rsn) **is received from** p_j **do**
(12) send STATE(rsn, wsn_i) to p_j.

Fig. 1. Time-efficient SWMR atomic register in $\mathcal{AMP}_{n,t}[t < n/2]$

Client Side: Operation write() *invoked by the writer.* Let p_i be the writer. When it invokes REG.write(v), it increases wsn_i, updates reg_i, and broadcasts the message WRITE(wsn_i, v) (line 1). Then, it waits until it has received an acknowledgment message from $(n-t)$ processes (line 2). When this occurs, the operation terminates (line 3). Let us notice that the acknowledgment message is a copy of the very same message as the one it broadcast.

Server Side: Reception of a Message write(wsn, v). when a process p_i receives such a message, and this message carries a more recent value than the one currently stored in reg_i, p_i updates accordingly wsn_i and reg_i (line 7). Moreover, if this message is the first message carrying the sequence number wsn, p_i forwards to all the processes the message WRITE(wsn, v) it has received (line 8). This broadcast has two aims: to be an acknowledgment for the writer, and to inform the other processes that p_i "knows" this value.[3]

Moreover, when p_i has received the message WRITE(wsn, v) from $(n - t)$ different processes, and $swsn_i$ is smaller than wsn, it updates its local synchronization variable $swsn_i$ and accordingly assigns v to res_i (lines 9–11).

---

[3] Let us observe that, due to asynchrony, it is possible that $wsn_i > wsn$ when p_i receives a message WRITE(wsn, v) for the first time.

Server Side: Reception of a Message READ(rsn). When a process p_i receives such a message from a process p_j, it sends by return to p_j the message STATE(rsn, wsn_i), thereby informing it on the freshness of the last value of REG it knows (line 12). The parameter rsn allows the sender p_j to associate the messages STATE($rsn, -$) it will receive with the corresponding request identified by rsn.

Client Side: Operation read(). When a process p_i invokes REG.read(), it first broadcasts the message READ(rsn_i) with a new sequence number. Then, it waits until "some" predicate is satisfied (line 5), and finally returns the current value of res_i. Let us notice that the value res_i that is returned is the one whose sequence number is $swsn_i$.

The waiting predicate is the heart of the algorithm. Its first part states that p_i must have received a message STATE($rsn, -$) from $(n - t)$ processes. Its second part, namely ($swsn_i \geq maxwsn$), states that the value in p_i's local variable res_i is as recent or more recent than the value associated with the greatest write sequence number wsn received by p_i in a message STATE($rsn, -$). Combined with the broadcast of messages WRITE($wsn, -$) issued by each process at line 8, this waiting predicate ensures both the correctness of the returned value (atomicity), and the fact that the read implementation is time-efficient.

5   Proof of the Algorithm

5.1   Termination and Atomicity

The properties proved in this section are independent of the message transfer delays (provided they are finite).

Lemma 1. *If the writer is correct, all its write invocations terminate. If a reader is correct, all its read invocations terminate.*

Proof. Let us first consider the writer process. As by assumption it is correct, it broadcasts the message WRITE($sn, -$) (line 1). Each correct process broadcasts WRITE($sn, -$) when it receives it for the first time (line 8). As there are at least $(n - t)$ correct processes, the writer eventually receives WRITE($sn, -$) from these processes, and stops waiting at line 2.

Let us now consider a correct reader process p_i. It follows from the same reasoning as before that the reader receives the message STATE($rsn, -$) from at least $(n - t)$ processes (lines 5 and 12). Hence, it remains to prove that the second part of the waiting predicate, namely $swsn_i \geq maxwsn$ (line 5) becomes eventually true, where $maxwsn$ is the greatest write sequence number received by p_i in a message STATE($rsn, -$). Let p_j be the sender of this message. The following list of items is such that item $x \implies$ item $(x + 1)$, from which follows that $swsn_i \geq maxwsn$ (line 5) is eventually satisfied.

1. p_j updated wsn_j to $maxwsn$ (line 7) before sending STATE($rsn, maxwsn$) (line 12).
2. Hence, p_j received previously the message WRITE($maxwsn, -$), and broadcast it the first time it received it (line 8).
3. It follows that any correct process receives the message WRITE($maxwsn, -$) (at least from p_j), and broadcasts it the first time it receives it (line 8).
4. Consequently, p_i eventually receives the message WRITE($maxwsn, -$) from $(n - t)$ processes. When this occurs, it updates $swsn_i$ (line 10), which is then $\geq maxwsn$, which concludes the proof of the termination of a read operation. □ $Lemma\,1$

Lemma 2. *The register REG is atomic.*

Proof. Let $read[i, x]$ be a read operation issued by a process p_i which returns the value with sequence number x, and $write[y]$ be the write operation which writes the value with sequence number y. The proof of the lemma is the consequence of the three following claims.

– Claim 1. If $read[i, x]$ terminates before $write[y]$ starts, then $x < y$.
– Claim 2. If $write[x]$ terminates before $read[i, y]$ starts, then $x \leq y$.
– Claim 3. If $read[i, x]$ terminates before $read[j, y]$ starts, then $x \leq y$.

Claim 1 states that no process can read from the future. Claim 2 states that no process can read overwritten values. Claim 3 states that there is no new/old read inversions [3, 11].

Proof of Claim 1.
This claim follows from the following simple observation. When the writer executes $write[y]$, it first increases its local variable wsn which becomes greater than any sequence number associated with its previous write operations (line 1). Hence if $read[i, x]$ terminates before $write[y]$ starts, we necessarily have $x < y$.

Proof of Claim 2.
It follows from line 2 and lines 7–8 that, when $write[x]$ terminates, there is a set Q_w of at least $(n - t)$ processes p_k such that $wsn_k \geq x$. On another side, due to lines 4–5 and line 12, $read[i, y]$ obtains a message STATE() from a set Q_r of at least $(n - t)$ processes.

As $|Q_w| \geq n - t$, $|Q_r| \geq n - t$, and $n > 2t$, it follows that $Q_w \cap Q_r$ is not empty. There is consequently a process $p_k \in Q_w \cap Q_r$, such that $wsn_k \geq x$. Hence, p_k sent to p_i the message STATE($-, z$), where $z \geq x$.

Due to (a) the definition of $maxwsn \geq z$, (b) the predicate $swsn_i \geq maxwsn \geq z$ (line 5), and (c) the value of $swsn_i = y$, it follows that $y = swsn_i \geq z$ when $read[i, y]$ stops waiting at line 5. As, $z \geq x$, it follows $y \geq x$, which proves the claim.

Proof of Claim 3.
When $read[i, x]$ stops waiting at line 5, it returns the value res_i associated with the sequence number $swsn_i = x$. Process p_i previously received the message

WRITE$(x, -)$ from a set Q_{r1} of at least $(n - t)$ processes. The same occurs for p_j, which, before returning, received the message WRITE$(y, -)$ from a set Q_{r2} of at least $(n - t)$ processes.

As $|Q_{r1}| \geq n - t$, $|Q_{r2}| \geq n - t$, and $n > 2t$, it follows that $Q_{r1} \cap Q_{r2}$ is not empty. Hence, there is a process p_k which sent STATE$(, x)$ to p_i, and later sent STATE$(-, y)$ to p_j. As $swsn_k$ never decreases, it follows that $x \leq y$, which completes the proof of the lemma. $\square$ $Lemma\,2$

Theorem 1. *Algorithm 1   implements   an   SWMR   atomic   register   in* $\mathcal{CAMP}_{n,t}[t < n/2]$.

Proof. The proof follows from Lemma 1 (termination) and Lemma 2 (atomicity). $\square$ $Theorem\,1$

5.2   Time-Efficiency: The *Bounded Delay* assumption

As already indicated, this underlying synchrony assumption considers that every message takes at most Δ time units. Moreover, let us remind that a read (which started at time τ_r) is write-latency-free if it is not concurrent with a write, and the last preceding write did not crash and started at time $\tau_w < \tau_r - \Delta$.

Lemma 3. *A write operation takes at most 2Δ time units.*

Proof. The case of the writer is trivial. The message WRITE() broadcast by the writer takes at most Δ time units, as do the acknowledgment messages WRITE() sent by each process to the writer. In this case 2Δ correspond to a causality-related maximal round-trip delay (the reception of a message triggers the sending of an associated acknowledgment). $\square$ $Lemma\,3$

When the Writer Does Not Crash While Executing a Write Operation. The cases where the writer does not crash while executing a write operation are captured by the next two lemmas.

Lemma 4. *A write-latency-free read operation takes at most 2Δ time units.*

Proof. Let p_i be a process that issues a write-latency-free read operation, and τ_r be its starting time. Moreover, Let τ_w the starting time of the last preceding write. As the read is write latency-free, we have $\tau_w + \Delta < \tau_r$. Moreover, as messages take at most Δ time units, and the writer did not crash when executing the write, each non-crashed process p_k received the message WRITE$(x, -)$ (sent by the preceding write at time $\tau_w + \Delta < \tau_r$), broadcast it (line 8), and updated its local variables such that we have $wsn_k = x$ (lines 7–11) at time $\tau_w + \Delta < \tau_r$. Hence, all the messages STATE() received by the reader p_i carry the write sequence number x. Moreover, due to the broadcast of line 8 executed by each correct process, we have $swsn_i = x$ at some time $\tau_w + 2\Delta < \tau_r + \Delta$. It follows that the predicate of line 5 is satisfied at p_i within 2Δ time units after it invoked the read operation. $\square$ $Lemma\,4$

Lemma 5. *A read operation which is not write-latency-free, and during which the writer does not crash during the interfering write operation, takes at most 3Δ.*

Proof. Let us consider a read operation that starts at time τ_r, concurrent with a write operation that starts at time τ_w and during which the writer does not crash. From the read operation point of view, the worst case occurs when the read operation is invoked just after time $\tau_w - \Delta$, let us say at time $\tau_r = \tau_w - \Delta + \epsilon$. As a message STATE$(rsn, -)$ is sent by return when a message READ(rsn) is received, the messages STATE$(rsn, -)$ received by p_i by time $\tau_r + 2\Delta$ can be such that some carry the sequence number x (due to last previous write) while others carry the sequence number $x + 1$ (due to the concurrent write)[4]. Hence, $maxwsn = x$ or $maxwsn = x + 1$ (predicate of line 5). If $maxwsn = x$, we also have $swsn_i = x$ and p_i terminates its read. If $maxwsn = x+1$, p_i must wait until $swsn_i = x + 1$, which occurs at the latest at $\tau_w + 2\Delta$ (when p_i receives the last message of the $(n - t)$ messages WRITE$(y, -)$ which makes true the predicates of lines 9–10, thereby allowing the predicate of line 5 to be satisfied). When this occurs, p_i terminates its read operation. As $\tau_w = \tau_r + \Delta - \epsilon$, p_i returns at the latest $\tau_r + 3\Delta - \epsilon$ time units after it invoked the read operation. $\square$ *Lemma 4*

When the Writer Crashes While Executing a Write Operation. The problem raised by the crash of the writer while executing the write operation is when it crashes while broadcasting the message WRITE$(x, -)$ (line 1): some processes receive this message by Δ time units, while other processes do not. This issue is solved by the propagation of the message WRITE$(x, -)$ by the non-crashed processes that receive it (line 8). This means that, in the worst case (as in synchronous systems), the message WRITE$(x, -)$ must be forwarded by $(t + 1)$ processes before being received by all correct processes. This worst scenario may entail a cost of $(t + 1)\Delta$ time units.

---

when WRITE(wsn, v) or STATE(rsn, wsn, v) **is received do**
(7)   **if** $(wsn > wsn_i)$ **then** $reg_i \leftarrow v$; $wsn_i \leftarrow wsn$; broadcast WRITE(wsn, v) **end if**;
(8)   **if** (not yet done) **then** broadcast WRITE(wsn, v) **end if**;
(9)   **if** $\big($WRITE$(wsn, -)$ received from $(n - t)$ different processes$\big)$
(10)   **then if** $(wsn > swsn_i) \wedge$ (not already done) **then** $swsn_i \leftarrow wsn$; $res_i \leftarrow v$ **end if**
(11) **end if**.

when READ(rsn) **is received from** p_j **do**
(12) send STATE(rsn, wsn_i, reg_i) to p_j.

Fig. 2. Modified algorithm for time-efficient read in case of concurrent writer crash

---

[4]   Messages STATE(rsn, x) are sent by the processes that received READ(rsn) before τ_w, while the messages STATE$(rsn, x + 1)$ are sent by the processes that received READ(rsn) between τ_w and $\tau_r + \Delta = \tau_w + \epsilon$.

Figure 2 presents a simple modification of Algorithm 1, which allows a fast implementation of read operations whose executions are concurrent with a write operation during which the writer crashes. The modifications are underlined.

When a process p_i receives a message READ(), it now returns a message STATE() containing an additional field, namely the current value of reg_i, its local copy of REG (line 12).

When a process p_i receives from a process p_j a message STATE($-, wsn, v$), it uses it in the waiting predicate of line 5, but executes before the lines 7–11, as if this message was WRITE(wsn, v). According to the values of the predicates of lines 7, 9, and 10, this allows p_i to expedite the update of its local variables wsn_i, reg_i, $swsn_i$, and res_i, thereby favoring fast termination.

The reader can check that these modifications do not alter the proofs of Lemma 1 (termination) and Lemma 2 (atomicity). Hence, the proof of Theorem 1 is still correct.

Lemma 6. *A read operation which is not write-latency-free, and during which the writer crashes during the interfering write operation, takes at most 4Δ time units.*

Proof. Let τ_r be the time at which the read operation starts. As in the proof of Lemma 4, the messages STATE($rsn, -, -$) received p_i by time $\tau_r + 2\Delta$ can be such that some carry the sequence number $wsn = x$ (due to last previous write) while some others carry the sequence number $wsn = x + 1$ (due to the concurrent write during which the writer crashes). If all these messages carry $wsn = x$, the read terminates by time $\tau_r + 2\Delta$. If at least one of these messages is STATE($rsn, x + 1, -$), we have $maxwsn = x + 1$, and p_i waits until the predicate $swsn_i \geq maxwsn \ (= x + 1)$ becomes true (line 5).

When it received STATE($rsn, x + 1, -$), if not yet done, p_i broadcast the message WRITE($rsn, x + 1, -$), (line 8 of Fig. 2), which is received by the other processes within Δ time units. If not yet done, this entails the broadcast by each correct process of the same message WRITE($rsn, x + 1, -$). Hence, at most Δ time units later, p_i has received the message WRITE($rsn, x + 1$) from $(n - t)$ processes, which entails the update of $swsn_i$ to $(x + 1)$. Consequently the predicate of line 5 becomes satisfied, and p_i terminates its read operation.

When counting the number of consecutive communication steps, we have: The message READ(rsn) by p_i, followed by a message STATE($rsn, x + 1, -$) sent by some process and received by p_i, followed by the message WRITE($rsn, x + 1$) broadcast by p_i, followed by the message WRITE($rsn, x + 1$) broadcast by each non-crashed process (if not yet done). Hence, when the writer crashes during a concurrent read, the read returns within at most $\tau_r + 4\Delta$ time units. $\quad\square$ *Lemma 6*

Theorem 2. *Algorithm 1 modified as indicated in Figure 2 implements in $\mathcal{CAMP}_{n,t}[t < n/2]$ an SWMR atomic register with time-efficient operations (where the time-efficiency notion is based on the* bounded delay *assumption).*

Proof. The proof follows from Theorem 1 (termination and atomicity), Lemmas 3, 4, 5, and 6 (time-efficiency). $\quad\square$ *Theorem 2*

5.3   Time-Efficient Implementation: The *Round-Based Synchrony* assumption

As already indicated, this notion of a time-efficient implementation assumes an underlying round-based synchronous communication system, where the duration of a round (duration of all message transfer delays) is δ.

Lemma 7. *The duration of write operation is 2δ.*

Proof. The proof follows directly from the observation that the write operation terminates after a round-trip delay, whose duration is 2δ.   □ *Lemma 7*

Lemma 8. *The duration of a read operation is 2δ time units if the writer does not crash while executing a write operation concurrent with the read. Otherwise, it can be 3δ.*

Proof. Considering a read operation that starts at time τ_r, let us assume that the writer does not crash while concurrently executing a write operation. At time $\tau_r+\delta$ all processes receives the message READ(rsn) sent by the reader (line 4), and answer with a message STATE($rsn, -$) (line 12). Due the round-based synchrony assumption, all these messages carry the same sequence number x, which is equal to both their local variable wsn_i and $swsn_i$. It follows that at time $\tau_r + 2\delta$, the predicate of line 5 is satisfied at the reader, which consequently returns from the read operation.

  If the writer crashes while concurrently executing a write operation, it is possible that during some time (a round duration), some processes know the sequence number x, while other processes know only $x - 1$. But this synchrony break in the knowledge of the last sequence number is mended during the next round thanks to the message WRITE(x, v) sent by the processes which are aware of x (See Fig. 2). After this additional round, the read terminates (as previously) in two rounds. Hence, the read returns at the latest at time $\tau_r + 3\delta$. □ *Lemma 8*

Theorem 3. *Algorithm 1 modified as indicated in Figure 2 implements in $\mathcal{CAMP}_{n,t}[t < n/2]$ an SWMR atomic register with time-efficient operations (where the time-efficiency notion is based on the round-based synchrony assumption).*

Proof. The proof follows from Theorem 1 (termination and atomicity), Lemmas 7 and 8 (time-efficiency).   □ *Theorem 3*

6   Conclusion

This work has presented a new distributed algorithm implementing an atomic read/write register on top of an asynchronous n-process message-passing system in which up to $t < n/2$ processes may crash. When designing it, the constraints we imposed on this algorithm were (a) from an efficiency point of view: provide time-efficient implementations for read and write operations, (b) and from a design principle point of view: remain "as close as possible" to the flagship ABD algorithm introduced by Attiya et al. [2].

The "time-efficiency" property of the proposed algorithm has been analyzed according to two synchrony assumptions on the underlying system.

- The first assumption considers an upper bound Δ on message transfer delays. Under such an assumption, any write operation takes then at most 2Δ time units, and a read operation takes at most 2Δ time units when executed in good circumstances (i.e., when there is no write operation concurrent with the read operation). Hence, the inherent cost of an operation is a round-trip delay, always for a write and in favorable circumstances for a read. A read operation concurrent with a write operation during which the writer does not crash, may require an additional cost of Δ, which means that it takes at most 3Δ time units. Finally, if the writer crashes during a write concurrent with a read, the read may take at most 4Δ time units. This shows clearly the incremental cost imposed by the adversaries (concurrency of write operations, and failure of the writer).
- The second assumption investigated for a "time-efficient implementation" is the one provided by a round-based synchronous system, where message transfer delays (denoted δ) are assumed to be the same for all messages. It has been shown that, under this assumption, the duration of a write is 2δ, and the duration of a read is 2δ, or exceptionally 3δ when the writer crashes while concurrently executing a write operation.

It is important to remind that the proposed algorithm remains correct in the presence of any asynchrony pattern. Its time-efficiency features are particularly interesting when the system has long synchrony periods.

Differently from the proposed algorithm, the ABD algorithm does not display different behaviors in different concurrency and failure patterns. In ABD, the duration of all write operations is upper bounded by 2Δ time units (or equal to 2δ), and the duration of all read operations is upper bounded by 4Δ time units (or equal to 4δ). The trade-off between ABD and our algorithm lies the message complexity, which is $O(n)$ in ABD for both read and write operations, while it is $O(n^2)$ for a write operation and $O(n)$ for a read operation in the proposed algorithm. Hence our algorithm is particularly interesting for registers used in read-dominated applications. Moreover, it helps us better understand the impact of the adversary pair "writer concurrency+writer failure" on the efficiency of the read operations.

Acknowledgments. This work has been partially supported by the Franco-German DFG-ANR Project DISCMAT (40300781) devoted to connections between mathematics and distributed computing, and the French ANR project DISPLEXITY devoted to the study of computability and complexity in distributed computing.

References

1. Aguilera, M.K., Chen, W., Toueg, S.: On quiescent reliable communication. SIAM J. Comput. **29**(6), 2040–2073 (2000)
2. Attiya, H., Bar-Noy, A., Dolev, D.: Sharing memory robustly in message passing systems. J. ACM **42**(1), 121–132 (1995)
3. Attiya, H., Welch, J.: Distributed Computing: Fundamentals, Simulations and Advanced Topics, 2nd edn. Wiley, Hoboken (2004). 414 p
4. Herlihy, M.P., Wing, J.M.: Linearizability: a correctness condition for concurrent objects. ACM Trans. Programm. Lang. Syst. **12**(3), 463–492 (1990)
5. Dutta P., Guerraoui R., Levy R., Chakraborty A.: How fast can a distributed atomic read be? In: Proceedings of 23rd ACM Symposium on Principles of Distributed Computing (PODC 2004), pp. 236–245. ACM Press (2004)
6. Dutta, P., Guerraoui, R., Levy, R., Vukolic, M.: Fast access to distributed atomic memory. SIAM J. Comput. **39**(8), 3752–3783 (2010)
7. Kramer, S.N., Begins, H.: History Begins at Sumer: Thirty-Nine Firsts in Man's Recorded History. University of Pennsylvania Press, Philadelphia (1956). 416 p., ISBN 978-0-8122-1276-1
8. Lamport, L.: On interprocess communication part I: basic formalism. Distrib. Comput. **1**(2), 77–85 (1986)
9. Lynch, N.A.: Distributed Algorithms. Morgan Kaufmann Pub., San Francisco (1996). 872 p., ISBN 1-55860-384-4
10. Raynal, M.: Communication and Agreement Abstractions for Fault-tolerant Asynchronous Distributed Systems. Morgan & Claypool Publishers, San Rafael (2010). 251 p., ISBN 978-1-60845-293-4
11. Raynal, M.: Distributed Algorithms for Message-passing Systems. Springer, Heidelberg (2013). 510 p., ISBN 978-3-642-38122-5
12. Raynal, M.: Concurrent Programming: Algorithms, Principles and Foundations. Springer, Heidelberg (2013). 515 p., ISBN 978-3-642-32026-2
13. Turing, A.M.: On computable numbers with an application to the Entscheidungsproblem. Proc. London Math. Soc. **42**, 230–265 (1936)
14. Vukolic, M.: Quorum Systems, with Applications To Storage and Consensus. Morgan & Claypool Publishers, San Rafael (2012). 132 p., ISBN 978-1-60845-683-3

Traffic Lights Optimization with Distributed Ant Colony Optimization Based on Multi-agent System

Mouhcine Elgarej[✉], Mansouri Khalifa, and Mohamed Youssfi

Laboratory SSDIA, ENSET University Hassan II Mohammedia,
Mohammedia, Morocco
mouhcine.elgarej@gmail.com, khamansouri@hotmail.com,
med@youssfi.net

Abstract. Traffic congestion in road networks increase the rate of vehicles at each road and decrease the average of circulation in intersections, this problem can be controlled and managed with some strategies and measures that reduce the number of demand on the road network. Today Traffic signal timing control is a useful technique to control traffic movement to avoid and reduce traffic jam. In industrial cities, the increase of population led to the problem of traffic congestion, where this kind of problem needs intelligence systems to control traffic flow based on artificial intelligence. In this paper, we try to implement a distributed ACO algorithm for optimizing traffic signal timing based on the main objective of self-organization, collective of the ACO algorithm to simulate the traffic road network. The proposed method aim to manage intersections in real time using a decentralized algorithm of ant colony optimization to decrease the traffic flow based on the signal timing and a set of inputs data from the runtime environment.

Keywords: Ant colony system · Ant colony optimization · Swarm intelligence · Multi-agent system · Traffic road · Traffic congestion · Traffic lights system

1 Introduction

In recent years, traffic congestion led us to search for some new methods to control the traffic flow that decrease the wasting time at each intersection in the road. Traffic flow has become a grave problem with the increasing of traffic request in several cities in the world. Today all researchers tried to design an intelligent system to control the traffic flow using intelligent transportation technologies. The main idea is to reduce traffic by avoiding the traffic jam on the intersection in the map of road and optimizing time waiting for each vehicle on this point. Traffic signal operates in different modes, (i) using a loop which the inputs of the control are static, stable and the configuration of the system is done on offline. (ii) Update the traffic signal based on real-time parameters retrieved from the traffic flow environment.

Several systems are deployed to control traffic signal, but each system is based on different parameters that can be a static or dynamic data. To control the traffic signal we

© Springer International Publishing AG 2016
P.A. Abdulla and C. Delporte-Gallet (Eds.): NETYS 2016, LNCS 9944, pp. 266–279, 2016.
DOI: 10.1007/978-3-319-46140-3_22

need to use an intelligent system that can be adaptive with any move occurs on the environment and can show us the state of the road for the following hours.

Traffic signal problems are situated in several researches based on different search methods and algorithms. Some of these systems are based on intelligent system. In this domain, we have systems that are based on the current state of traffic on the road to optimize timing signal, SCOOT (split, cycle and offset optimization technique) [1] and SCATS (Sydney coordinated adaptive traffic system) [2], TRANSYT (traffic network study tool) [3]. Artificial intelligence system are used to control traffic signal, we have fuzzy logic [4] and neural networks [5].

The Ant Colony Optimization methods is one of the meta-heuristic algorithm used to solve combinatorial problems [7, 8, 9]. The Ant colony algorithm can be viewed as a multi-agent system, each ant on the colony can be simulated as an intelligent ant. It is one of the swarm intelligent algorithms and used to find optimal solutions for several problems (Traveling salesman problem, path planning, and vehicle routing problem).

In real world, real ants have the ability to find the shortest paths from their nest to the source of food. Ant deposits some chemical substance called pheromone on their trail toward the nest, this pheromone is used to be a link of communication between ants. A path with a higher amount of pheromone it will be more used by the majority of ants, so it will be more attractive based on the concentration of pheromone on this path.

In this paper, we implement a distributed ant colony optimization to find the shortest green period to decrease the time wasted in a given intersection. With this approach, we propose a new method to optimize traffic signal timing based on a distributed ACO algorithm.

The paper is organized as follows: Sect. 2 presents related approaches. Section 3, describes traffic flow terminology. In Sect. 4, we presents the traffic signal concepts. In Sect. 5, the Ant Colony Optimization behavior is introduced. Section 6 explains the distributed ACO based on multi-agent system for traffic signals control. Section 7 summarizes the simulation results. The conclusion appear in the last section of this work.

2 Related Work

Paper [13] introduces an intelligent system to control traffic lights based on fuzzy logic methods which have the ability to simulate the behavior of human for controlling traffic lights. In the fuzzy logic, we can create an intelligent technology that has the same behavior to the way humans would think. If a junction occurs in a certain direction, the system has the ability to control the traffic lights at this intersection by increasing the duration of the green light until the queue size is reduced.

In this work [14], authors proposed a new hierarchical architecture based on the multi-agent system to design a network urban traffic signal control system. Traffic control strategies can be viewed as traffic control agents using mobile agent technology. The mobile agent has the ability to move between devices in a network of traffic to collect useful data about the state of the traffic flow.

Authors in [10] explain an improved multi-colony algorithm applied to solve the TSP, which all colonies are run on separate machines, the proposed solutions are centrally collected and a local search is performed on the best optimal solution proposed by each intelligent colonies. This solution is not a fully decentralized approach, as it requires a centralized search for the best solutions and all communication are based on a sequential synchronization.

3 Traffic Flow Terminology

Traffic intersection can be view as a set of four streets that are bidirectional and each line has a fixed width (maximum two cars). In the presented Fig. 1, we have eight phases to simulate the different moves inside a direction. For a better vision, we consider only two movement at each intersection (from north to south or from the east to west) and we have two traffic lights green and red light, so, one direction is allowed to move (if direction N/S have the green light so the other direction E/W should have the red light).

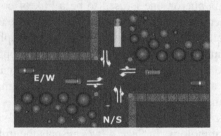

Fig. 1. Traffic intersection

Each movement I (in our case each direction can be viewed as a movement) has a queue size that can be indicated as N^i and i denotes the index of a direction. In addition, to get the number of vehicles at each movement we use a set of sensors that count the number of vehicles at each intersection. Moreover, we need to count the number of waiting vehicle on direction i at a given time t and it will be indicated by $N^i(t)$. The length of the street $N(t)$ is equal to the total of cars at each direction. So, the size of the queue at this intersection can be formulated by:

$$N(t) = [N^1(t) + N^2(t) + N^3(t) + N^4(t)]$$

In period of time (t1, t2), the parameter $N^i_{out}(t2, t1)$ represents the rate of cars leaving the direction i (two by two) and can be represented by the following function:

$$N^i_{out}(t2, t1) = N^i_{out}(t1) - 2;$$

When the intersection receives the green light, it should decrease the length of the queue, where at each departure two cars are allowed to leave the street, because the width of a street is two vehicles and all vehicles are traveling with a static speed.

In the other hand, when the system sends the red signal to a street, the queue size will increase according to the number of new vehicles (ac) at this period (t1,t2), this scenario can be denoted as $N_{in}^i(t2, t1)$:

$$N_{in}^i(t2, t1) = N_{in}^i(t1) + ac;$$

From N_{out}^i and N_{in}^i, the function of traffic at a given intersection can be represented by the following equation:

$$N^i(t) = N^i(t-1) + N_{in}^i(t) - N_{out}^i(t)$$

Where $N^i(t-1)$ is the number of vehicles in the current element, $N_{in}^i(t)$ represents the upstream flow in the given time t and $N_{out}^i(t)$ indicates the total of downstream flow. The Fig. 2 illustrate the network traffic flow in intersection i.

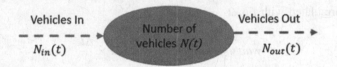

Fig. 2. A traffic network intersection

4 Traffic Signal Concepts

When a direction receives the green light, the queue (a set of waiting cars) will be decreased. A set of cars will leave the queue with a static movement until the expiration of the green duration. In the case when the queue is empty and the green period is still available then the new upstream cars are allowed to pass without waiting.

4.1 Vehicle Waiting Time

We use the Ant Colony Optimization to optimize the waiting time at each intersection. A set of candidate solution (signal time) is used to evaluate the convergence of the algorithm toward the control of the car delay at a given point. To calculate the waiting time for a vehicle, we start with the delay of cars in the initial queue and we add the waiting time for the new arrivals (we are based on a probabilistic rule to get this waiting time because the arrival time for these new cars is unknown).

4.2 Waiting Time of Vehicles Initially in Queue

In the green light, a set of cars will be released. The jth car in the N_{out}^i will have a waiting time equal to $t1 - at_j$ where j is the index of the car on the queue and at_j indicates the hour when the vehicle j arrives. At the end of the green light, a set of seconds are added to each vehicle $(j - 1)hw$ where the hw (headway) represent the distance between two successive cars in seconds. In the Eq. 1 we have the total waiting timing of all cars in the queue.

$$\sum_{j=1}^{N^i_{out}}(WT \text{ of vehicle } j) = \sum_{j=1}^{N^i_{out}}(j-1)hw + (t_1 - at_j) \quad (1)$$

4.3 Waiting Time of Vehicles not Released on the Current Phase

When a vehicle arrive in a long phase (green phase) it will be directly released, in the other case, it will wait until the green phase will occur. In a red cycle or when we meet a congested green cycle, a set of vehicles will be added to the queue and the length of this cycle can be denoted with Δt. The arrival number of new cars is assumed and denoted by $\lambda \Delta t$, λ is the average of upstream per hour, the waiting time for each car is denoted by $\frac{\Delta t}{2}$. The sum of waiting time for the new upstream cars in period $\Delta t = t2 - t1$ is formulated with Eq. 2.

$$wait \text{ time for new cars} = \lambda \Delta t \times \frac{\Delta t}{2} \quad (2)$$

4.4 Total Waiting Time for a Vehicle in a Signal Cycle

The total waiting time for a vehicle in intersection is calculated based on (i) the waiting time of vehicles in the current queue and (ii) new waiting time for cars that are not released on the current signal, (iii) the time used by each vehicle to go out of the queue and finally (iv) the expected duration to release all vehicles in the queue. We consider N be the number of cars on direction i at time t1 [so N can be denoted with $N = N^i(t)$].

To estimate the waiting time for cars under the green signal (green signal with a duration from t1 to t2) several scenarios are studied.

Scenario 1: All Cars are released at the end of the green signal.

If the duration of the green signal (t1, t2) is upper than the time necessary to release all cars in the queue. In this case, all vehicles are able to cross the road without waiting. The required wait time on a green signal can be described by this equation:

$$W_{1\_green}(t1, t2) = \frac{N(N-1)}{2}hw + \frac{hw(N-1)}{2}\frac{(N-1)hw}{1 - \lambda hw} \quad (3)$$

The first term is the wait time for cars in the initial waiting list. The second parameter is the wait time for the new cars and the third term is the time required to release all cars in the queue.

Scenario 2: Only a few cars are released from the initial queue.

In this case, the time required to clear the initial queue is lower than the given period. So, the new expected time in this period will be described as follow:

$$W_{2\_green}(t1, t2) = \frac{N_{out}^i \left(N_{out}^i - 1\right)}{2} hw + \left(N - N_{out}^i\right)(t2 - t1) + \frac{\lambda(t2 - t1)^2}{2} \qquad (4)$$

The first term is the time used for initial cars to leave the waiting list, the second one is the waiting time of the initial cars and the third term is the wait time estimated for the new upstream.

Scenario 3: Red signal, all cars is waiting.

In this signal, more vehicles are added to the waiting list and no car can leave the queue. The waiting time in this phase is denoted as follow:

$$W_{3\_red}(t1, t2) = N(t2 - t1) + \frac{\lambda(t2 - t1)^2}{2} \qquad (5)$$

The first parameter is the wait time for initial cars in the queue and the second parameter is the waiting time for the new upstream cars.

5 The Ant Colony Optimization Behavior

Ant Colony Optimization is a section of swarm intelligence (also known as collective intelligence) which is inspired from the behavior of real ants living in colonies for finding the shortest path between the food source and nest. ACO tries to simulate real ant actions to solve combinatorial optimization problems. When ants took any random path, a kind of chemical substance, known as pheromone is laid on the path, which is detectable and used by other ants. When multiples ants use a path, the pheromone accumulates and evaporates by the time, and the shortest paths are selected when ants tend to choose the path with a higher amount of pheromone.

The first application of ACS (Ant Colony System) algorithm [6] was used to solve the Traveling Salesman Problem (TSP). The main idea of this problem is to find the shortest path between a set of cities, the salesperson should visit all cities and build a tour.

The real ants use pheromone on their edges to mark their paths, other ants try to follow edges with a high amount of pheromone. In the first step, ants build their solution based on a probabilistic decision, the second step, each edge used by an ant should apply a local pheromone update with evaporation, the local pheromone update rule is used to add more amount of pheromone on this edge. The last step is the global pheromone update, in this step only the best ants are allowed to add more pheromone on their tour. For more details, in Fig. 3 we show the algorithm of Ant Colony System.

In the ACOMAS (Ant Colony Optimization based on Multi-Agent System) we propose a distributed architecture based on a multi-agent system to create a distributed ACO algorithm [11], the new approach is based on Ant Colony System. In this version, each ant tries to get the best tour based on a sequential procedure for searching the best solution. For our approach, we design an (i) new distributed system to control the process of communication between agents and (ii) we use a decentralized system to manage the convergence of the system toward the best solution and (iii) implementing a distributed ACO algorithm for finding the optimal solution.

```
Input: Problem_size, SpaceSearch_size, NumberOfAnt, α, β, ρ, Q
Output: S_best
S_best = GenerateBestSolution(Problem_size)
Cost(S_best) = cost(S_hasard)
Ph_0 = ────────1────────
       Problem_size*cost(S_best)
Ph = InitPheromone(Ph_0)
While(!EndCondition()){
  For(i=1 To m)
    S_i = CreateSolution(Ph, Problem_size, α, β)
    If ( cost(S_i) <= cost(S_best))
       Cost(S_best) = cost(S_i)
       S_best = S_i
    End
    RunLocalUpdatePheromone(Ph, S_i, cost(S_i), α)
  End
  RunGlobalUpdatePheromone(Ph, S_best, cost(S_best), ρ, Q)
End
Return S_best
```

Fig. 3. ACS algorithm

In Ant Colony System, ant k tries to move toward node j from node i based on probabilistic transition. In rule (Eq. 6) ant uses heuristic values (the amount of the pheromone and the visibility of the next node) to decide which node will be visited next.

$$p_{ij} = \begin{cases} argmax_{j\in\Omega}(\tau_{ij}^{\alpha}, \eta_{ij}^{\beta}), & if \ q \le q_0 \\ p_{ij}^*, & otherwise \end{cases} \tag{6}$$

The q is a random heuristic variable between [0,1]. q_0 is a parameter that defines which rule is used to move to the next node. Using this parameter, we can choose between a random node or take the amount of pheromone and the visibility of the edge for selecting the next visited node.

An ant at node i will choose to move to next neighbor node j based on the probability p_{ij}^* showing in Eq. (7):

$$p_{ij}^* = \begin{cases} \dfrac{[\tau_{ij}]^{\alpha}[\eta_{ij}]^{\beta}}{\sum_{h\in\Omega}[\tau_{ih}]^{\alpha}[\eta_{ih}]^{\beta}}, & if \ j \in \Omega, \\ 0 & otherwise \end{cases} \tag{7}$$

Parameter η_{ij} is the heuristic visibility of edge (i, j), generally it is a value of $1/d_{ij}$, where d_{ij} is the cost between city i and city j. The collection Ω is a set of cities which remain to be visited when the ant is at city i. τ_{ij} is the amount of pheromone between i and j. The parameters α and β are two adjustable positive parameters used for controlling the relative weights of the heuristic visibility and the pheromone trail.

When ant k visit all nodes on the graph, it will be able to increase the amount of pheromone on each edge visited by this ant. The new amount of pheromone is based on the cost of the proposed solution, the (Eq. 8) explains the evaporation and the local update rule.

$$\tau_{ij}^{new} = (1 - \rho)\tau_{ij}^{old} + \Delta\tau_{ij} \tag{8}$$

In this equation,

$$\Delta\tau_{ij} => \sum_{k=1}^{m}\Delta\tau_{ij}^{k} = \begin{cases} \frac{Q}{L_k}, & if\ ant\ k\ use\ the\ edge\ i,j \\ 0, & else \end{cases}$$

$(1-p)$ is the pheromone reduction parameter $(0 < p < 1)$ where it represents the trail evaporation or the rate of evaporation. The parameter m is the number of ants, L_k is the length of the tour performed by ant k and Q is an arbitrary constant.

The evaporation process is useful for controlling the amount of pheromone on each edge, more edges will have a chance to be visited by other ants. The heuristics values used for the ACS are based on the initial amount of pheromone, the best value for τ0 is to set them to a value equal of τ0 = 1/(nC), C is the cost of a nearest neighbor tour and n is the number of nodes.

Global updating rule is included after all ants have completed their tours. Only the best ants are able to update their solutions and add more pheromone on their trails to be more attractive for the future exploration. The pheromone amount is updated by applying the process of global updating rule of Eq. (9).

$$\tau_{ij}^{new} = (1 - \rho)\tau_{ij}^{old} + \Delta\tau_{ij} + \Delta\tau_{ij}^{best} \tag{9}$$

$$where\Delta\tau_{ij}^{best} => \sum_{k=1}^{m}\Delta\tau_{ij}^{k} = \begin{cases} \frac{Q}{L_k^{best}}, & if\ edge\ ij\ used\ in\ the\ best\ path \\ 0, & else \end{cases}$$

6 Distributed ACO Algorithm Applied to Traffic Signal Optimization

The traffic model contains two directions (N/S, W/E), so in each direction, there is a set of vehicles that should wait until receiving the green signal. The main idea, is found the best signals timing for each intersection. In this presentation, we try to implement a distributed system to control the traffic flow on each intersection, we are based on a set of intelligent agents to create a distributed system, which each one of them is able to share and collaborate in real time with the other agents in the system to provide the best solutions according to the information available on the environment. In Fig. 4, we present a distributed architecture designed for the traffic lights control system, which contain three main agents: Road Supervisor Agent (RSA), Intersection agent (IA), Traffic Cycle Agent (TCA).

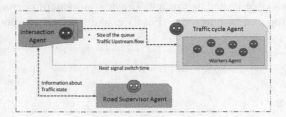

Fig. 4. Distributed traffic lights architecture

Road Supervisor Agent (RSA). The main goal of our solution is to control the state of traffic on each intersection and display the real-time information related to each direction that gives an idea about the estimated waiting time at each intersection and the waiting time of the queue in each point. At each moment, the RSA is able to retrieve a set of information from the IA to be used in the operating process, also these pieces of information are used to help the drivers when they try to select the next intersection to be visited.

Intersection Agent. The main obstacle of traffic road control is the absence of a unit of control able to store all kinds of information about each intersection (number of input and output vehicles, the average of cars per hour, the rate of traffic during a period, etc.). The main objective of the AI is collecting a set of information from sensors, they are able to count the size of upstream and downstream of vehicles in each direction. This information are useful for the RSA to be browsing the condition of intersection for drivers. In addition, IA sends this inputs information to the TCA to calculate the new period of the traffic signal timing according to these parameters.

Traffic Cycle Agent. In our system we have eight traffic signal phase, the possible phases in our case are in two directions (E/W or N/S) are shown in Fig. 5. The possible transitions allowed in our case can be modeled as a graph with a set of nodes (each node represent a period of time that can be an admissible solution) and arcs are represented by time duration between two nodes. At the beginning, ants start in parallel and move toward the next node until creates a signal period (this cycle contains two periods: the green light duration and the red light duration).

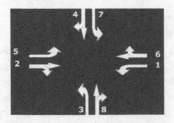

Fig. 5. Traffic signal cycle

The main objective of the TCA is looking for the optimal signal period based on the information which represent the current state of the intersection (number of vehicles at the initial waiting list and the rate of incoming vehicles) using the direct communication with the AI. This information are useful to select the best transitions between the signal phases shown in the Fig. 6. In other words, the TCA will create a set of intelligent workers agents to find the best path between these transitions by using the ACS algorithm rules, those agents are working together in parallel to create the best optimal signal period. Each agent will start his tour through the different movements possible and try to produce a path planning (timeline), which represents the signal cycle movements and the duration of each movement.

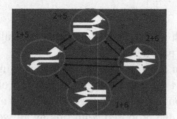

Fig. 6. The traffic lights cycle

Using this model, we have a set of phase sequences based on the eight movements (four movements at each direction) allowed in our system. To better understand the allowed movements on each direction, we take the example of (East/West) direction, if the beginning signal is [2–5], we have only two possible directions which are [2–5] $\rightarrow$ [1 + 5] $\rightarrow$ [1 + 6], or [2 + 5] $\rightarrow$ [2 + 6] $\rightarrow$ [1 + 6]. If we start from [2–6] we have only three possible sequences, which are [2 + 6] $\rightarrow$ [2 + 5] $\rightarrow$ [1 + 5], or [2 + 6] $\rightarrow$ [1 + 6] $\rightarrow$ [1 + 5], or [2 + 6] $\rightarrow$ [1 + 5]. The same behavior is applied on the other direction (Nord/Sud).

To control the green time on each phase, we need to set the $(min_{green}, max_{green})$ value. The goal of this paper is determined the optimal duration that minimize the waiting time on each intersection, two types of waiting time are considered (i) waiting time for the initial queue that contain a set of vehicles and (ii) the waiting time for the cars that just come in this waiting period. A set of workers ants are distributed in each direction, the behavior of each ant is to move toward the next phase depending on the transition rule used in ACS algorithm. Ants need some input data (the number of vehicles that come from several sensors and the size of the upstream flow) to be able to get the optimal green time that is denoted by the amount of pheromone deposit on this street.

In this new approach, a set of distributed ants are used to move toward the best solution depending on the Ant Colony System rules. Each worker agent calculates the waiting time for each signal according to a set of constraints, the amount of pheromone deposit on each direction represents the signal period. The length of the proposed solution or the cost of the solution can be computed by using the new parameters and will be formulated with the new Eq. 10.

$$C^k = \frac{w^k(t1,t2)}{4\lambda(t2-t1) + \sum_{i=1}^{4} N^i(t1)} \tag{10}$$

The first term is the sum of waiting time of all vehicle in the intersection (represents the waiting time needed to release all vehicles on this intersection). The second parameter is the number of the road in the intersection multiplied by the average of upstream vehicles plus the number of cars in each waiting list.

The heuristic value that represent the visibility of t2 to t1 (or the weight of the visibility t1 and t2) can be denoted by the following Eq. 11:

$$\eta_{t1t2} = Exp\left[-\frac{|N^g(t1)-1)hw-(t2-t1)|}{c}\right] \tag{11}$$

$N^g(t1)$ represents the length of the longest queue in the traffic green signal at time t1. The parameter c is a static parameter.

In Fig. 7, we present our algorithm used to find the optimal duration of each phase. At the beginning, we start by calculating the number of vehicles on the current intersection, the rate of incoming vehicles, this information are used by the TCA to find the best transition based on the proposed solutions by all workers agents. TCA is able to select and evaluate the best solutions to generate the best signal cycle. This process is repeated until reaching the final condition (when the maximum number of iterations is met). The IA applies the proposed solution for controlling the traffic light signal at this intersection. In the other hand, the RSA is able to consult the state of the traffic signal cycle on each intersection and share this information with all drivers.

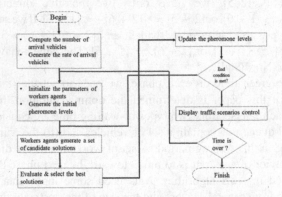

Fig. 7. Distributed ACS for traffic lights control

7 Simulation Results

We created our algorithm using Java-Agent-Development-Environment (JADE) as a distributed and parallel platform [12]. In this architecture, we can run a set of agent situated on a set of computers (we create a network of computers). The main reason of this preparatory setup is to simulate our approach on a real environment. So, the proposed scenario is based on a set of intersections and agents controlled by a set of container agents each group of container are managed by the main container. In Fig. 8, we design our platform based on a distributed ACO.

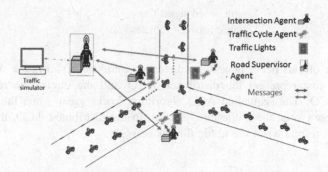

Fig. 8. Multi-agent architecture for traffic signal

To run our solution, we need to set some parameters to control the convergence of our algorithm toward the best solution. At the beginning, we need to fix the number of iterations. The configuration of the distributed architecture for the traffic signal is based on three steps: (i) Creation and initialization of agents and (ii) execution step, (iii) analysis stage.

- In the initialization step, we create a set of containers that contain our agents, the heuristic parameters are initialized according to the traffic information and all agents are ready for computing the next traffic signal cycle. The TCA is able to create and manage a set of workers agents, the life cycle of each worker agent depends on the time elapsed for finding an optimal solution.
- When the TCA receives the information needed to start the search process, a set of workers agents are created to find the best duration for the next phase. These agents work in parallel to generate a set of candidate solutions and the communication process between these agents is based on a set of messages (Agent Communication Language messages).
- At each moment, the RSA is able to ask for the signal cycle duration of each intersection, those states are shared with the drivers to help them in their path traveling toward their destinations.

The new approach is tested to see the convergence of the system and the effectiveness of the proposed solutions, the results of the algorithm are compared with a sequential ACS algorithm to see the difference between the two systems.

In the start of the simulation, the intersection is empty (the length of the queue is zero). The number of cars is known (a set of sensors are able to count the number of cars at each time). The other input parameters are situated in the following Table 1.

The parameter λ (the rate of cars per hours per direction) is set between two values 200 and 800 to see the convergence of the distributed algorithm. In Fig. 9, we show our results proposed by the two algorithms. The x-axis present the average of upstream

Table 1. Traffic signal parameters

Parameters	Value (s)
$min_{timegreen}$	5
$max_{timegreen}$	30
Length of red signal time	2
Distance between vehicles	2

flow (number of cars per hour and per direction) and y-axis shows the waiting time. The squares line represent the distributed ACO and the circle line represent the sequential ACO. The sequential ACO algorithm works great when the size of the problem is low (when the traffic flow is low). In the distributed ACO, the algorithm returns useful results when the traffic flow is massive.

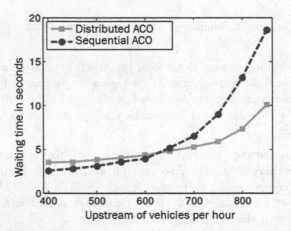

Fig. 9. The average rate of convergence of the distributed and the sequential ACS algorithm

8   Conclusion and Perspectives

In this paper, we introduce a distributed ACO algorithm based on multi-agent system to control the traffic signal time by reducing the cars waiting time at each intersection based on a set of parameters.

In our approach, we are based on the ACS algorithm. There are some modifications made on the ACS: (i) with the new architecture, we avoid the standard iterations used in ACS. The proposed system is based on parallel and asynchronous iterations (we don't need to wait until each ant constructs a tour); (ii) In the classic ACS, after each iteration we need to compare the best tours, so we can allow only the best ants to add more pheromone on their edges. We avoid this (centralized and synchronized behavior) by allowing ant to compare their solutions with the last best tour received from the last visited node. (iii) In the ACS all ants move sequentially, while in our architecture all ants move in parallel.

In the parallel method, we see the convergence of our problem toward a set of useful solutions in a short time period, based on this system, we can reduce the waiting time and the traffic flow at each intersection.

There are few directions that we would like to follow as future works: (a) support the generality of our approach by considering other forms of ACO; (b) investigate new forms of distributed ACO.

References

1. Zhaomeng, C.: Intelligent traffic control central system of Beijing-SCOOT. In: International Conference on Mechanic Automation and Control Engineering (MACE), pp. 5067–5069 (2010)
2. Aydos, J.C., O'Brien, A.: SCATS ramp metering: strategies, arterial integration and results. In: IEEE 17th International Conference on Intelligent Transportation Systems, pp. 2194–2201 (2014)
3. Ceylan, H., Ceylan, H.: A hybrid harmony search and TRANSYT hill climbing algorithm for signalized stochastic equilibrium transportation networks. Transp. Res. Part C Emerg. Technol. 25, 152–167 (2012)
4. Alam, J., Pandey, M.K.: Development of traffic light control system for emergency vehicle using fuzzy logic. In: International Conference on Artificial Intelligence and Soft Computing, IIT- BHU Varanasi, India, 7–9 December 2012
5. Kumar, K., Parida, M., Katiyar, V.K.: Artificial neural network modeling for road traffic noise prediction. In: Third International Conference on Computing Communication & Networking Technologies (ICCCNT), pp. 1–5 (2012)
6. Wang, P., Lin, H.-T., Wang, T.-S.: An improved ant colony system algorithm for solving the IP traceback problem. Inf. Sci. 326, 172–187 (2015)
7. Raval, C., Hegde, S.: Ant-CAMP: ant based congestion adaptive multipath routing protocol for wireless networks. In: International Conference on Emerging Trends in Networks and Computer Communications (ETNCC), pp. 463–468 (2011)
8. Wang, X., Liu, C., Wang, Y., Huang, C.: Application of ant colony optimized routing algorithm based on evolving graph model in VANETs. In: International Symposium on Wireless Personal Multimedia Communications (WPMC), pp. 265–270 (2014)
9. Triay, J., Cervello-Pastor, C.: An ant-based algorithm for distributed routing and wavelength assignment in dynamic optical networks. IEEE J. Sel. Areas Commun. 28(4), 542–552 (2010)
10. Dorigo, M., Manfrin, M., Twomey, C., Birattari, M., Stutzle, T.: An analysis of communication policies for homogeneous multi-colony ACO algorithms. Inf. Sci. 180 (12), 2390–2404 (2010)
11. Hingrajiya, H.K., Gupta, R.K., Chandel, G.S.: An ant colony optimization algorithm for solving travelling salesman problem. Int. J. Sci. Res. Publ. 2(8), 1–6 (2012)
12. Marzougui, B., Hassine, K., Barkaoui, K.: A new formalism for modeling a multi agent systems: agent petri nets. J. Softw. Eng. Appl. 3(12), 1118–1124 (2010)
13. Askerzade Askerbeyli, N., Mahmood, M.: Control the extension time of traffic light in single junction by using fuzzy logic. Int. J. Electr. Comput. Sci. IJECS-IJENS 10(02), 48–55 (2010)
14. Chen, C., Li, Z.: A hierarchical networked urban traffic signal control system based on multi-agent. in accepted, 9th IEEE International Conference on Networking, Sensing and Control, April 2012

A Mechanized Refinement Proof
of the Chase-Lev Deque Using a Proof System

Suha Orhun Mutluergil$^{(\boxtimes)}$ and Serdar Tasiran

Koc University, Istanbul, Turkey
smutluergil@ku.edu.tr

Abstract. We present a linearizability proof for the Chase-Lev work-stealing queue (WSQ) on sequentially consistent (SC) memory. We used the CIVL proof system for verifying refinement of concurrent programs. The lowest-level description of the WSQ is the data structure code described in terms of fine-grained actions whose atomicity is guaranteed by hardware. Higher level descriptions consist of increasingly coarser action blocks obtained using a combination of Owicki-Gries (OG) annotations and reduction and abstraction. We believe that the OG annotations (location invariants) we provided to carry out the refinement proofs at each level provide insight into the correctness of the algorithm. The top-level description for the WSQ consists of a single atomic action for each data structure operation, where the specification of the action is tight enough to show that the WSQ data structure is linearizable.

Keywords: Chase-Lev deque · Owicki-Gries method · Reduction · Abstraction · Refinement · Linearizability · Static verification

1 Introduction

Work stealing is a widely accepted and applied method for scheduling tasks used by many programming languages, run-time systems and frameworks that support distribution of computation into tasks in shared-memory parallel programs. Work stealing queue data structures constitute the core of this method. The queue keeps a pool of tasks to be executed and provides methods to threads for putting and taking tasks from the pool. The WSQ algorithm must provide certain guarantees such as the same task cannot be scheduled twice or given sufficient number of requests, all the tasks in the pool are scheduled. These guarantees are vital for the correct functioning of the system.

In this study, we verify the Chase-Lev WSQ algorithm [2], a widely-used non-blocking algorithm, by providing a linearizability proof for its sequentially consistent (SC) executions. Starting with fine-grained concurrent method bodies, we obtain atomic method abstractions. Those abstractions are tight enough to show that the WSQ algorithm satisfies the desired properties.

P.A. Abdulla and C. Delporte-Gallet (Eds.): NETYS 2016, LNCS 9944, pp. 280–294, 2016.
DOI: 10.1007/978-3-319-46140-3_23

The proof is performed using the CIVL proof system [5] and it has four layers[1]. At the bottom layer, method bodies consist of fine-grained atomic statements supported by most hardware and programming languages. In the following layers, atomic blocks inside the method bodies grow using abstraction, reduction and location annotations until we obtain the desired abstract atomic bodies of the methods at the fourth layer (depicted in the top rows of Figs. 2 and 3).

This study has the following contributions and results:

- We present the first mechanized linearizability proof of the Lev-Chase work stealing queue algorithm for its SC executions using a proof system.
- Obtaining correct location and mover annotations for the fine-grained method bodies require reasoning about all possible interleavings of the program. We believe that the proof annotations at lower layers provide insight about the behavior of SC executions of this program.
- Our proof is based on two important techniques: Owicki-Gries [11] and Lipton's reduction/abstraction [8] method. We show that the combined use of these two techniques is powerful, and each is best suited to carry out certain parts of the reasoning.

Section 2 gives an overview of the Chase-Lev work stealing queue algorithm. In Sect. 3, we give a brief information about the proof techniques we utilized. Details of the mechanized proof are presented in Sect. 4. We compare our work with related studies in Sect. 5 and finish with closing remarks and future work in Sect. 6. Some observations on the WSQ algorithm that will be useful for our proofs are put on Appendix A. Initial abstractions/simplifications on the algorithm applied before the mechanized proof are explained in Appendix B.

2   The Chase-Lev Work Stealing Queue Algorithm

Operations effecting one of the worker thread's queue in the Chase-Lev WSQ algorithm is presented in Fig. 1 using the programming language CIVL.

Shared variables H, T and *items* represent the current head (top), tail (bottom) and the task pool, respectively. Tasks are assumed to be of type *int*. The *items* has an infinite domain. Hence, it is never required to resize it due to an overflow and we do not need to think of it as a circular array.

The put and take methods are executed exclusively by the worker thread (called ptTid in short from now on). The put method adds one more element to the tail of the queue.

The take method first reserves the last element by decrementing T by one (Line 2). If it observes an empty queue, then it increments T back and returns an EMPTY task (if block at Line 4). If it observes more than one elements in the queue, it returns the element at index T (if block at Line 9). If there is a single element in the queue, the ptTid tries to take it by a CAS operation (Line 11).

---

[1] CIVL proof files can be obtained from: http://msrc.ku.edu.tr/projects/chase-lev-wsq/.

```
                          take():(task:int)
                          {
                            var h,t:int;          steal():(task:int)
                            var chk:bool;         {
                                                    var h,t:int;
                          1  t := T-1;             var chk:bool;
                          2  T := t;
                          3  h := H;             1  while(true)
                          4  if(t<h)             {
                             {                   2    h := H;
                          5    T := h;           3    t := T;
H:int;                    6    task := EMPTY;    4    if(h>=t)
T:int;                    7    return;              {
items:[int]int;              }                   5      task := EMPTY;
                          8  task := items[t];   6      return;
put(task:int)             9  if(h<t)                }
{                            {                   7    task := items[h];
  var t:int;              10   return;           8    [if (h==H)
                             }                        {
1  t := T;                11 [if(h==H)                  H := h+1;
2  items[t] := task;         {                          chk := true;
3  T := t+1;                   H := h+1;                }
4  return;                     chk := true;            else
}                            }                          {
                             else                         chk := false;
                             {                          }]
                               chk := false;       9    if(chk)
                             }]                          {
                          12 if(!chk)              10       return;
                             {                           }
                          13   task := EMPTY;          }
                             }                      11 return;
                          14 T := t+1;              }
                          15 return;
                          }
```

Fig. 1. Chase-Lev work stealing queue algorithm

The `steal` method is executed by a stealer thread. If it sees the queue empty, it returns `EMPTY` task (if block at Line 4). Otherwise, it iteratively tries to steal an element by incrementing H by one via a `CAS` statement. If `CAS` is successful, then `steal` returns successfully with the element at index H (If block at Line 9). If `CAS` is not successful, then the current element at index h is stolen or taken. Hence, `steal` tries to steal another element in a new iteration.

The behavior of the methods explained above is easily provable if they execute sequentially. However, we assume SC setting such that execution of methods could be interleaved with operations of other threads but operations of the same thread appear in the sequence of program order to itself and other threads. SC is one of the strongest guarantees that can be given for a concurrent program. Yet it is still more difficult to reason about program correctness in SC then in sequential setting since one needs to consider all possible thread interleavings. We present more detailed observations about the SC executions of the WSQ algorithm in Appendix A.

Our linearizability proof begins with a slightly modified version of the WSQ algorithm presented in Fig. 1 based on valid abstractions/simplifications explained in Appendix B.

3   Overview of Proof Methodology

In this section, we provide some important techniques we utilize in our proof and supported by the proof system CIVL. We only give high-level definitions and explain how we utilized them. Formal definitions of the concepts described here can be found in [3,5].

The language CIVL is specially developed for verification purposes. It allows usual constructs existing in many imperative programming languages and some additional constructs for verification purposes. A CIVL program consists of method bodies and atomic actions. Method bodies contain usual imperative constructs like assignments, sequencing, conditional statements, loops, method calls, thread creation and atomic action calls. Atomic actions consist of single-state location annotations and two-state transition relations.

The method bodies are partitioned into steps. CIVL allows programmers to decide on the granularity of a step in a method body. Hence, a step may contain multiple statements. Atomic actions are single step. We denote steps inside brackets in this paper. A program executes by picking a thread non-deterministically and executing a non-deterministic number of next steps of this thread. An execution is obtained using the SC memory model by interleaving steps from different threads. If the location annotation of an atomic action does not hold in a state of an execution just before executing this action, the program fails. The program is safe if no execution fails the location annotation of an atomic action.

To check safety of a program, CIVL utilizes Owicki-Gries (OG) reasoning [11]. The OG checks two things: (i) a location annotation holds after a thread takes a step (sequential correctness) and (ii) the location annotation is preserved by concurrent threads (non-interference). In addition to the location annotations, CIVL allows programmers to write method pre- and post-conditions. They are also checked via OG reasoning. Moreover, programmers can write conditions to be satisfied inside the atomic blocks as assert statements. Correctness of these statements are checked again by OG reasoning without the non-interference part.

CIVL enables programmers to grow atomic steps inside the procedure bodies using a technique called reduction. To achieve this, each atomic action is annotated with R, L, N or B tags standing for right-, left-, non- and both-movers. A sequence of steps that begins with a sub-sequence of right- or both-movers, followed by an optional non-mover, followed by a sub-sequence of left-movers or both-movers could form a single atomic step. CIVL also performs a check to validate that the atomic action conforms to its mover type. An action A is a right-mover if executing A first and then an action B from another thread in all executions can be simulated by first executing B and then A. A dual definition applies for left-movers. An action is a both-mover (non-mover) if it is both (neither) right-mover and (nor) left-mover.

A layer in CIVL is a program and CIVL performs refinement proofs in a sequence of layers. While moving from one layer to the next layer, CIVL allows programmers to abstract atomic actions so that they have more behavior in the next layer. Hence, they have more relaxed location annotations and they can make actions from other threads mover and grow the steps of method bodies in the next layer. For instance, *havoc* is a keyword in CIVL, used for assigning non-deterministic values to variables. *havoc* x action abstracts $x := t$ action since the former statement allows variable x to have a range of values including the latter value t.

Another option that a programmer can benefit from between layers is the method abstraction. It allows programmers to replace a method body with a single atomic action. This method enables programmers to increase granularity of the program by replacing fine-grained method bodies with a single coarser action block. CIVL also performs a check between layers to validate method abstraction. An atomic action A abstracts a method body B if and only if A abstracts a single step of B in all possible execution paths of B and all the other steps of B in this execution path refines $skip$. Moreover, the return variable must not be modified after the step that refines A. From now on, we call the step that refines A as the action block.

CIVL validates that the program at the bottom layer refines the program at the top-layer if the OG and mover checks pass for all layers and action abstraction and method abstraction checks pass between all layers.

CIVL allows the programmers to use primitive types like boolean or integer and allow users to define their own types. Moreover, it supports linear variables. Difference of a linear variable from a regular variable is that value inside a linear variable cannot be duplicated. Since thread identifiers are unique, we use linear thread identifiers. We modify methods such that each thread gets a linear variable tid as input. For take and put methods, we know that tid must have the value ptTid and for steal method, tid must be different than ptTid. This additional information makes CIVL know that put and take methods cannot be concurrent whereas steal can be concurrent with other methods and itself.

We heavily utilize the techniques above in our proof. In all layers, we provide location annotations that show the relation between the global variables H and T. Those annotations play a crucial role during the method abstractions between layers and mover checks inside the layers. We start with a relatively complicated relation between those global variables in fine-grained method bodies of lower layers. As the methods get coarser at later layers, we establish $H \leq T$ as a global location annotation.

At the end of Layer 0, we abstract some of the atomic actions so that steps inside the method bodies of put and sub-methods of take could grow bigger via reduction. Consequently, method bodies of put and sub-methods of take contain single steps at the end of Layer 1. Then, we can turn them into atomic actions in Layer 2 by applying method abstraction. Since all of the sub-methods of take turn into atomic actions at Layer 2, we can use method abstraction at the end of Layer 2 to obtain the desired atomic action of take at Layer 3. Moreover, $H \leq T$ becomes a global location invariant at Layer 2 and it enables us to use method abstraction at the end of Layer 2 on the steal method to obtain desired atomic action of steal at Layer 3.

4   Mechanized Proof Steps

In this section, we present the mechanized proof of the WSQ algorithm. A schematic of the proof is given in Figs. 2 and 3. Before diving into details of the proof, we provide a brief explanation about the programs in these figures.

Layer	steal(linear tid:Tid):(task:int)	put(linear tid:tid, task:int)

3	<pre>(stTid ∧ H ≤ T ∧ !tics)
	[goto 1A, 1B;
	 1A: assume H<T;
	     task := items[H];
	     H :=H+1;
	     return;
	 1B: assume H<=T;
	     task :=EMPTY;
	     return;]</pre>
		<pre>(ptInv())
		[items[T] := task;
		 T := T+1;]</pre>

2	<pre>pre: (stTid(tid) ∧ ticsCond() ∧ !tics)
	post: (stTid(tid) ∧ ticsCond() ∧ !tics)
	{
	1 (... ∧ !tics)
	  h := H;
	
	2 (... ∧ !tics)
	  [if (h<T)
	     assume h==H ==> H<T;
	   else
	     assume h>=y;]
	
	3 if (h >= t)
	  {
	4 task := EMPTY;
	5 (... ∧ !tics) return;
	  }
	
	6 (... ∧ !tics)
	  [assert !tics && h==H ==> H<T;
	   if (h==H)
	     task := items[h];
	   else
	     havoc(task);]
	
	7 (... ∧ !tics ∧
	   (H=h → task = items[h]))
	  [assume H == h; H := h+1;]
	
	8 (... ∧ !tics) return;
	}</pre>
		<pre>(ptInv())
		[items[T] := task;
		 T := T+1;]</pre>

1	<pre>pre: (stTid(tid) ∧ ticsCond())
	post: (stTid(tid) ∧ ticsCond())
	{
	1 (...)[N] h := H;
	
	2 (...) [N]
	  [if (h<T)
	     assume h==H ==> H<T;
	   else
	     assume h>=y;]
	
	3 if (h >= t)
	  {
	4 [B] task := EMPTY;
	5 (...) return;
	  }
	
	6 (...)[N]
	  [assert !tics && h==H ==> H<T;
	   if (h==H)
	     task := items[h];
	   else
	     havoc task;]
	
	7 (...)[N]
	  [assume H == h; H := h+1;]
	
	8 (...) return;
	}</pre>
		<pre>pre: (ptInv())
		post: (ptInv())
		{
		(ptInv())
		1 [R] t := T;
		2 [R] [assert t==T && !tics;
		       items[t] := task;]
		3 [N] T := t+1;
		
		4 (ptInv()) return;
		}</pre>

0	<pre>pre: (stTid(tid) ∧ ticsCond())
	post: (stTid(tid) ∧ ticsCond())
	{
	1 (ticsCond()) h := H;
	
	2 (H≥h ∧ ticsCond()) t := T;
	
	3 if (h >= t)
	  {
	4 (ticsCond()) task := EMPTY;
	5 return;
	  }
	6 (H≥h ∧ ticsCond()∧ ticsCond2(h))
	  task := items[h];
	
	7 (H≥h ∧ ticsCond() ∧ ticsCond2(h))
	  [assume H == h; H := h+1;]
	
	8 (ticsCond()) return
	}
	ticsCond():
	  (tics ⇒ H ≤ T+1) ∧ (!tics ⇒ H ≤ T)
	ticsCond2(h:int):
	  (tics ∧ h=H ⇒ H ≤ T) ∧
	  (!tics ∧ h=H ⇒ H < T)
	stTid(tid:Tid):
	  tid ≠ NULL ∧ tid ≠ ptTid</pre>
		<pre>pre: (ptInv())
		post: (ptInv())
		{
		1 (ptInv())
		  t := T;
		
		2 (ptInv())
		  items[t] := task;
		
		3 (ptInv())
		  T := t+1;
		
		4 (ptInv()) return;
		}
		ptInv():
		  tid = ptTid ∧ !tics ∧ H ≤ T</pre>

Fig. 2. Proof layers for the mechanized proof of steal and put methods

Layer	take(linear tid:Tid):(task:int)		

3	⟨ptInv()⟩
	[goto 1A, 1B, 1C;
	  1A: assume H==T; task := EMPTY; return;
	  1B: assume H==T−1; task := items[T−1]; H := H+1; return;
	  1C: assume H<T−1; T := T−1; task := items[T]; return;]		

	take1(lnr tid:Tid): (task:int)	take2(lnr tid:Tid): (task:int)	take3(lnr tid:Tid): (task:int)

2	⟨ptInv()⟩
	[assume H==T;
	 task := EMPTY;]
		⟨ptInv()⟩
		[assume H < T−1;
		 T := T−1;
		 task := items[T];]
			⟨ptInv()⟩
			[goto 1A,1B;
			 1A: assume H==T;
			   task := EMPTY;
			   return;
			 1B: assume H==T−1;
			   task := items[T−1];
			   H := H+1;
			   return;]

1	pre: ⟨ptInv()⟩
	post: ⟨ptInv()⟩
	{
	  ⟨ptInv()⟩
	1 [R] t := T−1;
	2 [R] [T := t;
	      tics := true;]
	3 [R] assume h <= H && t<h;
	4 if(t<h)
	  {
	5 [L] [T :=h;
	      tics := false;]
	6 [B] task := EMPTY;
	
	7 ⟨ptInv()⟩ return;
	  }
	  ...
	}
		pre: ⟨ptInv()⟩
		post: ⟨ptInv()⟩
		{
		  ⟨ptInv()⟩
		1 [R] t := T−1;
		2 [R] [T := t;
		      tics := true;]
		3 [N] [h := H;
		      assume h<t;
		      tics := false;]
		4 if(t<h)
		
		8 [B] task := items[t];
		9 if(h<t)
		  {
		10 ⟨ptInv()⟩ return;
		  }
		  ...
		}
			pre: ⟨ptInv()⟩
			post: ⟨ptInv()⟩
			{
			  ⟨ptInv()⟩
			1 [R] t := T−1;
			2 [R] [T := t;
			      tics := true;]
			3 [R] assume h==t && h<=H;
			4 if(t<h)
			  ...
			8 [B] task := items[t];
			9 if(h<t)
			  ...
			11 [N] [if(h==H)
			      H :=h+1;
			      chk := true;
			      else
			      chk := false;]
			12 if(!chk)
			  {
			13 [B] task := EMPTY;
			  }
			14 [L] [T := t+1;
			      tics := false;]
			
			15 ⟨ptInv()⟩ return;
			}

0	pre: ⟨ptInv()⟩
	post: ⟨ptInv()⟩
	{
	1 ⟨ptInv()⟩
	  t := T−1;
	
	2 ⟨ptInv()∧ t=T−1 ⟩
	  [T := t;
	  tics := true;]
	3 ⟨t=T ∧ H≤T+1 ∧ tics⟩
	  [h := H;
	  assume t<h;]
	4 if(t<h)
	  {
	5 ⟨t=T ∧ h≤H ∧ H=T+1 ∧ tics⟩
	  [T :=h;
	   tics := false;]
	6 ⟨ H≤T ∧ !tics⟩
	  task := EMPTY;
	
	7 ⟨ H≤T ∧ !tics⟩
	  return;
	  }
	  ...
	}
		pre: ⟨ptInv()⟩
		post: ⟨ptInv()⟩
		{
		1 ⟨ptInv()⟩
		  t := T−1;
		
		2 ⟨ptInv()∧ t=T−1 ⟩
		  [T := t;
		  tics := true;]
		3 ⟨t=T ∧ H≤T+1 ∧ tics⟩
		  [h := H;
		  assume h<t;
		  tics := false;]
		4 if(t<h)
		  ...
		8 ⟨t=T ∧ H≤T ∧ h<t ∧ !tics⟩
		  task := items[t];
		9 if(h<t)
		  {
		10 ⟨ H≤T ∧ !tics⟩
		  return;
		  }
		  ...
		}
			pre: ⟨ptInv()⟩
			post: ⟨ptInv()⟩
			{
			1 ⟨ptInv()⟩
			  t := T−1;
			
			2 ⟨ptInv()∧ t=T−1⟩
			  [T := t;
			  tics := true;]
			3 ⟨t=T ∧ H≤T+1 ∧ tics⟩
			  [h := H;
			  assume h==t;]
			4 if(t<h)
			  ...
			8 ⟨t=T ∧ h≤H ∧ H≤T+1 ∧ h=t ∧ tics⟩
			  task := items[t];
			9 if(h<t)
			  ...
			11 ⟨t=T ∧ h≤H ∧ H≤T+1 ∧ h=t ∧ tics⟩
			  [if(h==H)
			   H :=h+1;
			   chk := true;
			  else
			   chk := false;]
			12 if(!chk)
			13 ⟨t=T ∧ H=T+1 ∧ tics⟩
			  task := EMPTY;
			  }
			14 ⟨t=T ∧ H=T+1 ∧ tics⟩
			  [T := t+1;
			   tics := false;]
			15 ⟨ptInv()⟩
			  return;
			}

Fig. 3. Proof layers for the mechanized proof of take methods

Numbers inside the method bodies correspond to steps or control points of those methods. Atomic actions are written inside the brackets. We may omit the brackets if the atomic action consists of a single statement. Location annotations of atomic actions are given between $\langle$ and $\rangle$ symbols. If a location annotation has not changed since the previous layer, we denote this as $\langle \ldots \rangle$ or if it is tightened by adding a new constraint ϕ, we denote this as $\langle \ldots \wedge \phi \rangle$.

Mover annotations of the atomic actions are also present in brackets before atomic actions. R, L, B and N denote right-, left-, both- and none-mover, respectively. We may omit the mover tag if the atomic action is labeled as non-mover. Note that we may have labeled an action non-mover although it is a mover, if it is not necessary for our proof.

Atomic actions or statements may contain constructs like `assume`, `assert` and `havoc` which are special for verification. Semantics of `havoc` is explained via an example in Sect. 3. The statements `assume e` or `assert e` cause an execution to block (all threads' next statement to execute becomes not enabled) or fail, respectively, if the boolean expression `e` evaluates to `false` in the state just before executing this statement. Otherwise, they are equivalent to `skip`.

For the `take1`, `take2` and `take3` methods some paths are unreachable due to `assume` statements at Line 3. We omit the program text for the if blocks leading to those paths in Fig. 3 by representing them with three dots as in Line 4 of `take2` at Layer 0.

The programs contain a new boolean ghost variable named `tics`. A ghost variable is similar to a regular variable with only difference that it does not modify the program state i.e., its value is never assigned to a real program variable. Its sole purpose is to guide CIVL during mover and OG checks.

The name `tics` is short for "take in critical section". We know from Observations 3–7 in Appendix A that $H \leq T$ can be temporarily violated inside the `take` method. We say that `take` is in critical section if execution of `take` is in the area that $H \leq T$ invariant can be violated. The `tics` is used to write location annotations considering the current instruction of `ptTid`.

The proof consists of 4 layers. At the bottom layer (Layer 0), we start with the method bodies that we obtained at the end of Appendix B. We decorate the method bodies with location annotations to establish relation between H and T global variables. While going from Layer 0 to Layer 1, we abstract some of the actions of Layer 0 and we use reduction at Layer 1 to make bodies of the `put`, `take1`, `take2` and `take3` methods single step. Between Layer 1 and Layer 2, we use method abstraction on `put`, `take1`, `take2` and `take3` methods and abstract them to single step atomic actions. In Layer 2, $H \leq T$ begins to hold as a global location annotation since `take1`, `take2` and `take3` methods become coarse enough. Finally, we apply method abstraction on `take` and `steal` methods between Layer 2 and Layer 3 to obtain desired atomic actions for these methods. In Layer 3, all the methods of the WSQ algorithm are in the form of atomic actions.

Layer 0. We start with the program obtained after loop-peeling and path-splitting explained in Appendix B. Only difference is the addition of the boolean tics ghost variable. Taking Observations 3–7 into account, we set tics to *true* temporarily inside the bodies of take methods and set it back to *false* at the point where we think the $H \leq T$ condition is restored.

We provide location annotations conforming the value of tics. In the methods, we annotate the locations so that when tics is *true*, $H \leq T + 1$ holds and when tics is *false*, $H \leq T$ holds. This condition is expressed in the sub-formulae called ticsCond provided after steal method. The condition when the tics is *true*, is adjusted in precision. It is tight enough to continue proof in later layers and relaxed enough to be satisfied after non-interference checks. For instance, replacing it with $H == T + 1$ would be too tight and make it unsatisfiable.

$H \leq T$ is not a global invariant at Layer 0, but a relaxed version of it that we call ticsCond is a global invariant. All the location annotations in the method bodies and method pre- post-conditions imply ticsCond.

However, location annotations explained so far does not pass the OG check directly. We need to make location annotations stronger.

First, if $H = T \wedge !tics$ or $H = T+1 \wedge tics$ holds at some state during execution of a ptTid method, a successful CAS operation of a steal could interfere and violate location annotation by incrementing H. We observe that this corner case is not possible in real executions. $H < T$ must hold if $!tics$ or $H < T + 1$ must hold if tics just before the execution of CAS action of steal. For this reason, we introduce ticsCond2 function that reflects our condition and add it to the annotations of Lines 6 and 7 of steal.

Adding ticsCond2 to location annotations of Lines 6 and 7 is still insufficient because two concurrent steals may violate the ticsCond2. If $h = H - 1 \wedge H = T - 1 \wedge !tics$ holds just before a stealer thread t_1 executes Line 6 and another stealer thread t_2 interferes at this point and performs a successful CAS and increments H, we come up with a state satisfying $h = H \wedge H = T \wedge !tics$ for t_2 which violates the ticsCond2. But we know that two successful steals cannot be concurrent by Observation 2. This observation helps us to infer that $H \geq h$ holds during Lines 6 and 7 of the steal method (by Observation 1) which prevents the previous erroneous execution sample. By adding $H \geq h$ on Lines 6 and 7 of steal, we make sure that OG checks for location annotations of steal pass.

Second, methods of the WSQ modify global variables H and T by assigning them local values of h and t. To show that these assignments do not violate the conditions relating H and T, we need to relate local value t to value of T in ptTid methods and h to H in steal, take1, take2 and take3 methods. Since T is only modified by ptTid, adding $t = T$ to location annotations of ptTid methods is correct. By Observation 1, H is always non-decreasing. Hence $H \geq h$ holds for all methods. Adding these two conditions to the location annotations of certain lines is sufficient to show that modifications on global variables does not violate the required conditions.

We omit the mover tags for this layer, since no reduction is performed at Layer 0.

Layer 0 → Layer 1. Our aim for Layer 1 is to grow steps of take1, take2, take3 and put method bodies using reduction. For this reason, we abstract some of the atomic actions between Layer 0 and Layer 1. Lines 2 and 6 of steal method and Line 3 of take1 and take3 methods are abstracted for this purpose. Rationale behind these abstractions are explained in Layer 1 while explaining how the actions satisfy their mover annotations.

Layer 1. We assign mover tags to atomic actions of put, take1, take2 and take3 methods so that we can grow the steps of the action blocks of these methods as large as the ones we need.

First, let us explain how we grow the step of put method. Line 1 becomes right-mover without any abstraction since it reads the global variable T which is not modified by other threads. However, Line 2 of put method is not a right-mover without abstraction since it may be modifying an index of *items* that is read by Line 6 of steal. If h value of steal at Line 6 is equal to t value of put at Line 3, they may be accessing the same index. Since action of put method modifies this index, mover check fails. But, we observe that the actual value of *items*[h] is not needed if $h \neq H$ holds just before execution of Line 7 of steal method. Moreover, we need to read the actual value of *items*[h] if $H = h$ at Line 7 in order to know that steal returns the correct element. Hence, we abstracted Line 6 of steal such that it assigns *items*[h] to *task* if $h = H$ at Line 6 and assigns a non-deterministic value to *task* otherwise.

Next, we enlarge the step of take1 method. Line 1 is a right-mover since it is same as Line 1 of put method and Line 5 is a both-mover since it is a local assignment. However, lines 2 and 6 are not movers in Layer 0. They do not commute with Line 2 of steal method since Line 2 of steal reads the global variable T which is modified by Line 2 (or Line 6) of take1 method. To overcome this problem, let us explore what expect from Line 2 of steal method in our proof. If steal observes $h < t$ after execution of Line 2 and the value of H has not changed yet, then ticsCond2 must hold if it continues execution through Line 6. We may satisfy this condition by assuming only $H < T$ holds after Line 2 if $h = H \wedge h < T$ holds just before Line 2. steal may continue through the if block at Line 3 if it observes $h < t$ before Line 2, since our top-level implementation of steal allows it to return EMPTY even if $H < T$. But, if steal observes $h \geq T$ before Line 2, it must enter the if block at Line 3 since the WSQ is empty. Obtaining only this information after Line 2 would be sufficient for abstracting steal on later layers.

Line 3 of take1 is not a right-mover at Layer 0 since it does not commute with Line 7 of steal method. Instead of reading actual value of H at Line 3 of take1, we abstract to read a non-deterministic value less than or equal to H. This abstract read can commute right of Line 7 of steal since after moving right of Line 7 of steal local value h of take1 can have more distinct values and it is tight enough to infer that $h >= t$. Consequently, we obtain a step for take1 that spans lines through 1 to 6.

Lines 1 and 2 of take2 are right-movers due to reasons explained above. Line 8 becomes a right-mover since steal does not modify the *items* array. Consequently, lines from 1 to 8 of take2 form a step in Layer 1.

Mover annotations for `take3` method also hold and lines from 1 to 14 become a step. Reason for their correctness can be explained with the same arguments above.

Note that location annotations of Layer 1 are same as Layer 0. Abstractions do not violate the conditions established at Layer 0.

Layer 1 → Layer 2. We apply method abstraction on `put`, `take1`, `take2` and `take3` methods between Layer 1 and Layer 2 since action blocks of those methods grow large enough at the end of Layer 1. We obtain the desired atomic action for `put` method.

Layer 2. In this layer, we tighten the location annotations in `steal` method such that they become the old condition and `!tics`. The OG checks pass for these new tighter annotations because no step of the program leaves the `tics` *true* after its execution at Layer 2.

In addition, we add a condition to location annotation of Line 7 of `steal` stating that if the value of H had not changed since `steal` read it, the return variable *task* contains *items*$[H]$. OG check for this condition passes since Line 6 of `steal` is tight enough to assign correct value to *task* if $H = h$. This extra condition on the location invariant is crucial when we apply method abstraction on `steal`.

Layer 2 → Layer 3. Between Layers 2 and 3, we apply method abstraction on `steal` and `take` methods. These methods become atomic actions.

The reason we can not apply method abstraction on `steal` so far is that location annotations of the action blocks of `steal` were not tight enough to obtain the desired atomic action for `steal`. It was possible to perform a successful CAS when $H = T$.

Applying method abstraction on `take` also becomes possible after Layer 2 since we obtained the atomic actions for its sub-methods at Layer 2.

Layer 3. All of the `take`, `put` and `steal` methods are atomic actions.

With these single atomic action bodies of the methods, it is easier to reason about the WSQ algorithm. For instance, one can show that a task pushed into deque cannot be taken or stolen more than once since `take` and `steal` methods' top-level actions atomically increment H or decrement T after taking the first or the last item from the queue.

5   Related Work

Due to its key importance in parallel systems, there are various WSQ algorithms. A notable one is presented in Cilk multi-threaded language [4]. This algorithm is blocking and method bodies are protected by a global lock. Reasoning about correctness of Cilk WSQ algorithm is simpler but it is not efficient due to its blocking nature.

Another WSQ algorithm introduced by Arora et al. [1] is non-blocking, but it requires fixed size queues. This algorithm has been verified in [6] using a model checking approach. Model checking approach validates that the algorithm satisfies desired properties but it does not provide any insight about the behavior of the algorithm. Hence, it is difficult to reason about some side-properties and possible optimizations of the algorithm using this approach. The Chase-Lev WSQ [2] we have studied is an improvement over [1] such that size of the queue can grow without memory leaks.

Since work stealing queues are used in low-level task schedulers, the environment may provide weaker guarantees. It is known that executions of Chase-Lev WSQ under TSO semantics show more behaviour than SC executions [9]. If memory fences are inserted after Line 3 of put and Line 2 of take, non-SC behaviors are prevented [9]. In [7], a pen and pencil proof has been presented that the Chase-Lev WSQ algorithm with previously mentioned memory fences satisfy some desired specifications. A modified version of the Chase-Lev WSQ is presented in [10] such that it is correct under TSO memory-model if we know the size of store buffers.

6   Conclusions and Future Work

In this study, we have performed a linearizability proof of the Chase-Lev WSQ algorithm under SC semantics using proof tool CIVL. Lower layers of the proof provide insight for the behavior of the SC executions and the top layer single atomic block summaries of the methods are simple but tight enough to show the desired properties.

We plan to extend this work to investigate behavior of the WSQ algorithm under weak memory models like TSO by modeling the weak memory semantics explicitly in CIVL. We are particularly interested in the behavior of the executions and the properties satisfied in the absence of memory fences.

A   Observations on the SC Executions of the Program

In this section, we first present some observations on (full or partial) executions of the WSQ algorithm with the finest-grained actions (the algorithm in Fig. 1). They will be helpful for obtaining location annotations and enlarging atomic blocks in upper layers.

Our initial observations are simple and they hold for full executions.

Observation 1: H is non-decreasing throughout an execution.
Observation 2: Let us call a steal operation successful if it returns a value other than EMPTY. Then, last iterations of two successful steals cannot be concurrent.

Next, we want to understand the relation between global variables H and T. For a sequential execution, one expects that $H \leq T$ invariant holds throughout the execution. This is not true for the fine-grained SC execution. We observe that H could exceed T in some special cases. However, this violations occur temporarily if take method follows some paths and they begin to hold again after take method finishes.

We examine execution portions (sub-sequences of executions) in a systematic way to obtain observations showing relation between H and T variables.

Observation 3: If an execution portion consists of only concurrent `steal` operations, we observe that $H \leq T$ is preserved throughout the execution portion.

Observation 4: If an execution portion consists of a single `put` method concurrent with `steal` methods, then $H \leq T$ holds throughout this execution portion.

Next, we consider execution portions that has `take` method concurrent with `steal` operations. The `take` method could follow three different paths by either entering the if block in Line 4 (path 1), by entering the if block in Line 9 (path 2) or by not entering those if blocks and returning by Line 15 (path 3).

Observation 5: If an execution portion consists of path 1 of take method concurrent with steals, then $H \leq T$ holds throughout this execution portion.

Observation 6: If an execution portion consists of path 2 of take method concurrent with steals, then $H \leq T$ holds before Line 2 and after Line 14 of the `take` method and $H = T \vee H = T + 1$ holds between Lines 2 and 14 of `take` method.

Observation 7: If an execution portion consists of path 3 of take method concurrent with steals, then $H \leq T$ holds before Line 2 and after Line 5 of the `take` method and $H = T + 1$ holds between Lines 2 and 5 of `take` method.

B   Path Splitting and Loop Peeling

In this section we present our initial abstractions on `steal` and `take` methods. These abstractions are not performed by CIVL. Rather, they are obtained by applying some proof rules that are not currently supported by CIVL. We explain the rules and their applications in this section. Methods we obtained after initial abstractions constitute the bottom layer of our mechanized proof.

Our first abstraction is performed on `steal` method. If we consider the iterations of the loop at Line 1 of `steal` before the last iteration, they do not modify any global variable and value assigned to return variable is reset by the last iteration. Moreover, value assigned to local variables by reading global variables are also reread by the last iteration before using them. Hence, those iterations has no important effect on OG annotations of other methods and they will not be useful for the refinement proof of `steal`. Our aim is to abstract `steal` method so that we do not need to deal with unsuccessful previous iterations of `steal`.

On the left-side of Fig. 4, we have `steal` method obtained by peeling out the last iteration of the `while` loop. All the unsuccessful iterations are captured by the loop at Line 1. They are guaranteed to be unsuccessful by `assume` statements at lines 4 and 6. The last successful iteration is modeled from Line 7 on.

Lines 2, 3, 5 and 6 could be abstracted by *havoc* $h, t, task, chk$ and line 4 can be abstracted by *skip*. With these abstractions, we obtain the method body in the middle column of Fig. 4. Since h, t, chk and $task$ variables have non-deterministic values at the beginning of `steal`, the whole loop at Line 1 could be removed and we obtain the method at the right-side of Fig. 4 as our basis of `steal` for the mechanized proof.

```
steal(lnr tid:Tid):
     (task:int)
{
  var h,t:int;
  var chk:bool;

1   while(*)
    {
2     h := H;
3     t := T;
4     assume h<t;
5     task := items[h];
6     [assume h != H;
       chk := false;]
    }
7   h := H;
8   t := T;
9   if(h>=t)
    {
10    task := EMPTY;
11    return;
    }
12  task := items[H];
13  [assume h==H;
     H == h;]
14  return;
}
```

```
steal(lnr tid:Tid):
     (task:int)
{
  var h,t:int;
  var chk:bool;

1   while(*)
    {
2     havoc h,t,chk,task;
3     h := H;
4     t := T;
5     if(h>=t)
      {
6       task := EMPTY;
7       return;
      }
8     task := items[H];
9     [assume h==H;
       H == h;]
10    return;
    }
}
```

```
steal(lnr tid:Tid):
     (task:int)
{
  var h,t:int;
  var chk:bool;

1   h := H;
2   t := T;
3   if(h>=t)
    {
4     task := EMPTY;
5     return;
    }
6   task := items[H];
7   [assume h==H;
     H == h;]
8   return;
}
```

Fig. 4. Initial abstractions on `steal` method

For the `take` method, we want to separate `take` in such a way that we can reason about each possible path separately. We use the following rule for this purpose:

Rule 1: Let procedure *foo* has the following body:

`{ s0; s1; s2;}`

```
take(lnr tid:Tid):
     (task:int)
{
  var h,t:int;
  var chk:bool;

1 if(*)
  {
2   task := take1(tid);
  }
  else
  {
3   if(*)
    {
4     task := take2(tid);
    }
    else
    {
5     task := take3(tid);
    }
  }
6 return;
}
```

```
take1(lnr tid:Tid):
      (task:int)
{
  var h,t:int;
  var chk:bool;

1   t := T-1;
2   T := t;
3   [h := H;
4   if(t<h)
    {
5     T := h;
6     task := EMPTY;
7     return;
    }
8   task := items[t];
9   if(h<t)
    {
10    return;
    }
11  [if(h==H)
    {
      H := h+1;
      chk := true;
    }
    else
    {
      chk := false;
    }]
12  if(!chk)
    {
13    task := EMPTY;
    }
14  T := t+1;
15  return;
}
```

```
take(lnr tid:Tid):
     (task:int)
{
  var h,t:int;
  var chk:bool;

1   t := T-1;
2   T := t;
3   [h := H;
    assume t>=h;
    assume t != h;]
4   if(t<h)
    {
5     T := h;
6     task := EMPTY;
7     return;
    }
8   task := items[t];
9   if(h<t)
    {
10    return;
    }
11  [if(h==H)
    {
      H := h+1;
      chk := true;
    }
    else
    {
      chk := false;
    }]
12  if(!chk)
    {
13    task := EMPTY;
    }
14  T := t+1;
15  return;
}
```

```
take(lnr tid:Tid):
     (task:int)
{
  var h,t:int;
  var chk:bool;

1   t := T-1;
2   T := t;
3   [h := H;
    assume t>=h;
    assume t==h;]
4   if(t<h)
    {
5     T := h;
6     task := EMPTY;
7     return;
    }
8   task := items[t];
9   if(h<t)
    {
10    return;
    }
11  [if(h==H)
    {
      H := h+1;
      chk := true;
    }
    else
    {
      chk := false;
    }]
12  if(!chk)
    {
13    task := EMPTY;
    }
14  T := t+1;
15  return;
}
```

Fig. 5. Initial abstractions on `take` method

where s0 and s2 are sequence of statements and s1 is an atomic block. Then, replacing this body with the following one is a valid abstraction of foo:

```
{ if(*){ s0; [s1;assume p;] s2; }
  else { s0;[s1;assume !p;] s2;} }
```

where p is a boolean expression on local variables. The $*$ denotes a non-deterministic value of `true` or `false` To obtain the desired method body in Fig. 5, we apply the following steps:

1. Apply Rule 1 to `take` in Fig. 1 with taking $s0$, $s1$, $s2$ as lines 1, 2; 3 and 4–15 respectively. We also pick p as $h > t$.
2. Collect statements inside the if block in the method `take1` and statements in the else part in the method `take23`.
3. Apply Rule 1 to `take23` with the same line choices in step 1 but taking p as $h = t$.
4. Collect the statements inside the if block of `take23` in `take2` method and statements in the else part in `take3` method.
5. Inline call of `take23` inside the else block of `take` with its body.

References

1. Arora, N.S., Blumofe, R.D., Plaxton, C.G.: Thread scheduling for multipro-grammed multiprocessors. Theor. Comput. Syst. **34**(2), 115–144 (2001)
2. Chase, D., Lev, Y.: Dynamic circular work-stealing deque. In: Proceedings of the Seventeenth Annual ACM Symposium on Parallelism in Algorithms and Architec-tures, pp. 21–28. ACM (2005)
3. Elmas, T., Qadeer, S., Tasiran, S.: A calculus of atomic actions. In: ACM Sympo-sium on Principles of Programming Languages, p. 14. Association for Computing Machinery Inc., January 2009
4. Frigo, M., Leiserson, C.E., Randall, K.H.: The implementation of the Cilk-5 mul-tithreaded language. ACM SIGPLAN Not. **33**, 212–223 (1998). ACM
5. Hawblitzel, C., Petrank, E., Qadeer, S., Tasiran, S.: Automated and modular refine-ment reasoning for concurrent programs. In: Kroening, D., Păsăreanu, C.S. (eds.) CAV 2015. LNCS, vol. 9207, pp. 449–465. Springer, Heidelberg (2015)
6. Aghai, M.K.: Verification of work-stealing deque implementation (2012)
7. Lê, N.M., Pop, A., Cohen, A., Zappa Nardelli, F.: Correct and efficient work-stealing for weak memory models. ACM SIGPLAN Not. **48**, 69–80 (2013). ACM
8. Lipton, R.J.: Reduction: a method of proving properties of parallel programs. Com-mun. ACM **18**(12), 717–721 (1975)
9. Liu, F., Nedev, N., Prisadnikov, N., Vechev, M., Yahav, E.: Dynamic synthesis for relaxed memory models. ACM SIGPLAN Not. **47**, 429–440 (2012). ACM
10. Morrison, A., Afek, Y.: Fence-free work stealing on bounded tso processors. ACM SIGPLAN Not. **49**(4), 413–426 (2014)
11. Owicki, S., Gries, D.: An axiomatic proof technique for parallel programs I. Acta Inf. **6**(4), 319–340 (1976)

The Out-of-core KNN Awakens:
The Light Side of Computation Force on Large Datasets

Nitin Chiluka, Anne-Marie Kermarrec, and Javier Olivares[✉]

Inria, Rennes, France
nitin.chiluka@gmail.com,
{anne-marie.kermarrec,javier.olivares}@inria.fr

Abstract. K-Nearest Neighbors (KNN) is a crucial tool for many applications, e.g. recommender systems, image classification and web-related applications. However, KNN is a resource greedy operation particularly for large datasets. We focus on the challenge of KNN computation over large datasets on a single commodity PC with limited memory. We propose a novel approach to compute KNN on large datasets by leveraging both disk and main memory efficiently. The main rationale of our approach is to minimize random accesses to disk, maximize sequential accesses to data and efficient usage of only the available memory.

We evaluate our approach on large datasets, in terms of performance and memory consumption. The evaluation shows that our approach requires only 7 % of the time needed by an in-memory baseline to compute a KNN graph.

Keywords: K-nearest neighbors · Out-of-core computation · Graph processing

1 Introduction

K-Nearest Neighbors (KNN) is a widely-used algorithm for many applications such as recommender systems [3–5]; information retrieval [8,13,21] in supporting similarity and proximity on stored data; and image classification [2,17,20]: finding similar images among a set of them. Generally, KNN is used for finding similar entities in a large set of candidates, by computing similarity between entities' profiles.

Although the algorithm has been well studied, the computation of KNN on large datasets remains a challenge. Large-scale KNN processing is computationally expensive, requiring a large amount of memory for efficient in-memory computation. The memory requirements of the current datasets (spanning even trillions of edges) is enormous, beyond terabytes. Such memory requirements are often unaffordable. In such scenario, one can think of an *out-of-core* computation as an option. Recent works [11,14,16,19,22] have shown that such approaches perform well on data that cannot be completely stored in memory.

Our first motivation for this work is derived from the fact that processing KNN efficiently on large datasets calls for in-memory solutions, this sort of

© Springer International Publishing AG 2016
P.A. Abdulla and C. Delporte-Gallet (Eds.): NETYS 2016, LNCS 9944, pp. 295–310, 2016.
DOI: 10.1007/978-3-319-46140-3_24

approach intends to store all data into memory for performing better in comparison to disk-based approaches. To do so, current datasets demand large memory, whose cost is not always affordable. Access to powerful machines is often limited, either by lack of resources for all users' needs, or by their complete absence.

The second motivation is that KNN computation has to be often performed offline, because it consumes significant resources. KNN algorithms usually cohabit on a given machine with other applications. Consequently, it is very seldom that it can enjoy the usage of the entire set of machine's resources, be it memory or CPU. For instance, *HyRec* [5], a hybrid recommender system, implements a KNN strategy to search similar users. *HyRec* devotes only a small fraction of its runtime and system resources for KNN computation. The rest is dedicated to recommendation tasks or system maintenance.

Finally, our last motivation comes from the fact that current graph frameworks [11,14,19] can efficiently compute well-known graph algorithms, processing large datasets in a short time. Those systems rely on the static nature of the data, i.e., data remaining the same for the entire period of computation. Unfortunately, to the best of our knowledge, they do not efficiently support some KNN fundamental operations such as neighborhood modification or neighbors' neighbors accesses. Typically they do not support any operation that modifies the graph itself [14,19]. KNN's goal is precisely to change the graph topology.

Summarizing, our work is motivated by the fact that: (i) KNN is computationally expensive, (ii) KNN has to be mainly performed offline, and (iii) Current graph processing frameworks do not support efficiently operations required for KNN computation.

We present *Pons*, an out-of-core algorithm for computing KNN on large datasets that do not completely fit in memory, leveraging efficiently both disk and the available memory. The main rationale of our approach is to minimize random accesses to disk, and to favor, as much as possible, sequential reading of large blocks of data from disk. Our main contributions of the paper are as follows:

- We propose *Pons*, an out-of-core approach for computing KNN on large datasets, using at most the available memory, and not the total amount required for a fully in-memory approach.
- *Pons* is designed to solve the non-trivial challenge of finding neighbors' neighbors of each entity during the KNN computation.
- Our experiments performed on large-scale datasets show that *Pons* computes KNN in only around 7 % of the time required by an in-memory computation.
- *Pons* shows to be also capable of computing online, using only a limited fraction of the system's memory, freeing up resources for other tasks if needed.

2   Preliminaries

Given N entities with their profiles in a D-dimensional space, the *K-Nearest Neighbors* (KNN) algorithm aims to find the K-closest neighbors for each entity. The distance between any two entities is computed based on a given metric (as cosine similarity or Jaccard coefficient) that compares their profiles. A classic application of KNN includes finding the K-most similar users for any given user in a system such as IMDb, where a user's profile comprises of her preferences of various movies.

For computing the exact KNN it can be employed a *brute-force approach*, which has a time complexity of $O(N^2)$ profile comparisons being very inefficient for a large N. To address this concern, *approximate KNN* algorithms (KNN now onwards) adopt an iterative approach. At the first iteration ($t = 0$), each entity v chooses uniformly at random a set of K entities as its neighbors. Each subsequent iteration t proceeds as follows: each entity v selects K-closest neighbors among its candidate set, comprising its K current neighbors, its K^2 neighbors' neighbors, and K random entities [5]. At the end of iteration t, each entity's new K-closest neighbors are used in the computation for the next iteration $t+1$. The algorithm ends when the average distance between each entity and its neighbors does not change considerably over several iterations.

The KNN state at each iteration t can be modeled by a directed graph $G^{(t)} = (V, E^{(t)})$, where V is a set of $N(= |V|)$ entities and $E^{(t)}$ represents edges between each entity and its neighbors. A directed edge $(u, v) \in E^{(t)}$ denotes (i) v is u's out-neighbor and (ii) u is v's in-neighbor. Let B_v denote the set of out-neighbors of the entity v. Furthermore, each entity v has exactly $K(= |B_v|)$ out-neighbors, while having any number (including 0 to $N - 1$) of in-neighbors. Also, we note that the total number of out-edges and in-edges in $G^{(t)}$ is NK.

Let F represent the set of profiles of all entities, and F_v denote the profile of entity v. In many scenarios in the fields of recommender systems and information retrieval, the profiles of entities are typically sparse. For instance, in IMDb, the number of movies an average user rates is significantly less than the total number of movies, D, present in its database. In such a scenario, a user v's profile can be represented by a sparse vector F_v in a D-dimensional space ($|F_v| << D$). For the sake of simplicity, we consider each entity v's profile length to be utmost P ($\geq |F_v|$). In image classification and clustering systems, however, each entity v's profile (e.g., feature vector) is typically of high dimension in the sense that v's profile length is approximately $|F_v| \approx D$. With the above notation, we formally define the *average distance (AD)* for all entities and their respective neighbors at iteration t as:

$$AD^{(t)} = \frac{\sum_{u \in V} \sum_{v \in B_u} Dist(F_u, F_v)}{NK} \tag{1}$$

$Dist(F_u, F_v)$ measures the distance between the profiles of u and v. The KNN computation is considered converged when the difference between the average distances across iterations is minimal: $|AD^{(t+1)} - AD^{(t)}| < \epsilon$, for a small ϵ.

2.1   In-memory Approach

A simple, yet efficient, way to implement KNN is using an *in-memory approach*, where all the data structures required during the entire period of computation are stored in memory. Algorithm 1 shows the pseudo-code for an in-memory implementation. Initially, the graph $G^{(0)}_{(mem)}$ and profiles F are loaded into memory from disk (lines 2-3). At each iteration t, each vertex v selects K-closest neighbors from its candidate set C_v comprising its neighbors (B_v), its neighbors' neighbors $(\bigcup_{u \in B_v} B_u)$, and a set of K random vertices $(Rnd(K))$. Closest neighbors of all vertices put together results in the graph $G_{(mem)}^{(t+1)}$, i.e., KNN graph of the next iteration.

In each iteration, every vertex performs upto $O(2K+K^2)$ profile comparisons. If a distance metric such as cosine similarity or Euclidean distance is used for profile comparisons, the overall time complexity for each iteration is $O(NP(2K+K^2))$. We note that the impact of heap updates (line 14) on overall time is little, since we are often interested in small values of $K(\approx 10-20)$ [5]. In terms of space complexity, this approach requires $O(N(2K+P))$ memory. Each of the KNN graphs of the current and the next iterations $(G_{(mem)}^{(t)}, G_{(mem)}^{(t+1)})$ consume $O(NK)$ memory, while the profiles consume $O(NP)$ memory. Although highly efficient, such an approach is feasible only when all data structures consume less than the memory limit of the machine.

Algorithm 1. In-memory KNN

Data: Graph file: File(G), Profiles file: File(F)
Result: Each vertex $v \in G$ finds its KNN.

1 **begin**
2     $G_{(mem)}^{(0)} \leftarrow$ Read initial graph from File(G)
3     $F_{(mem)} \leftarrow$ Read all profiles from File(F)
4   **foreach** *Iteration t until convergence* **do**
5        $G_{(mem)}^{(t+1)} \leftarrow \phi$
6   **foreach** *Vertex $v \in G_{(mem)}^{(t)}$* **do**
7   Read B_v from $G_{(mem)}^{(t)}$
8           $C_v \leftarrow B_v \cup (\bigcup_{u \in B_v} B_u) \cup Rnd(K)$
9   Initialize heap TopK
10   Read F_v from $F_{(mem)}$
11   **foreach** *Candidate $w \in C_v$* **do**
12   Read F_w from $F_{(mem)}$
13             $distValue \leftarrow Dist(F_v, F_w)$
14   UpdateHeap(TopK, w, $distValue$)
15   Insert($G_{(mem)}^{(t+1)}$, v, TopK)

---

3 Pons

The challenge of KNN computation can be essentially viewed as a trade-off between computational efficiency and memory consumption. Although efficient, an in-memory approach (Sect. 2.1) consumes a significant amount of memory. In this section, we propose *Pons*[1], an out-of-core approach which aims to address this trade-off.

---

[1] The term 'pons' is Latin for 'bridge'.

3.1   Overview

Pons is primarily designed to efficiently compute the KNN algorithm on a large set of vertices' profiles in a stand-alone memory-constrained machine. More specifically, given a large set of vertices' profiles and an upper bound of main-memory X_{limit}, that can be allocated for the KNN computation, *Pons* leverages this limited main memory as well as the machine's disk to perform KNN computation in an efficient manner.

The performance of *Pons* relies on its ability to divide all the data –KNN graph and vertices' profiles– into smaller segments such that the subsequent access to these data segments during the computation is highly efficient, while adhering to the limited memory constraint. *Pons* is designed following two fundamental principles: (i) *write once, read multiple times*, since KNN computation requires multiple lookups of various vertices' neighbors and profiles, and (ii) *make maximum usage of the data loaded into memory*, since disk operations are very expensive in terms of efficiency.

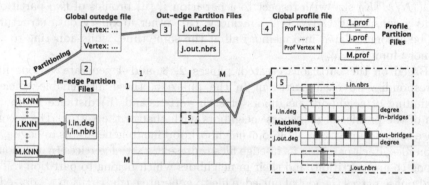

Fig. 1. *Pons* executes 5 phases: (1) Partitioning, (2) In-Edge Partition Files, (3) Out-Edge Partition Files, (4) Profile Partition Files, and (5) Distance Computation

We now present a brief overview of our approach, as illustrated in Algorithm 2, and Fig. 1. *Pons* takes two input files containing vertices, their random out-neighbors, and their profiles. It performs the KNN computation iteratively as follows. The goal of each iteration I is to compute K-closest neighbors for each vertex. To do so, iteration I executes 5 phases (Algorithm 2, lines 2–8). First phase divides the vertices into M partitions such that a single partition is assigned up to $\lceil N/M \rceil$ vertices. This phase parses the global out-edge file containing vertices and their out-neighbors and generates a K-out-neighborhood file for each partition.

Algorithm 2. *Pons*

Data: Graph file: File(G), Profiles file: File(F)
Result: Each vertex $v \in G$ finds its KNN.
1 **begin**
2   **foreach** *Iteration I* **do**
3   1. Partioning($GlobalOutEdges$)
4   2. Create In-edge Partition Files
5   3. Create Out-edge Partition Files
6   4. Write Profile Partition Files
7   5. Compute Distances
8   Update($GlobalOutEdges$)

We note here that the choice of the number of partitions (M) depends on factors such as the memory limit (X_{limit}), the number of nodes (N), the number of neighbors K, the vertices' profile length (P), and other auxiliary data structures that are instantiated. *Pons* is designed such that utmost (i) a heap of O($\lceil N/M \rceil K$) size with respect to a partition i, (ii) profiles of two partitions i and j consuming O($\lceil N/M \rceil P$) memory, (iii) other auxiliary data structures can be accommodated into memory all at the same time, while adhering to the memory limit (X_{limit}).

Based on the partitions created, phases 2, 3, and 4 generate various files corresponding to each partition. In the phase 5, these files enable efficient (i) finding of neighbors' neighbors of each vertex, and (ii) distance computation of the profiles of neighbors' neighbors with that of the vertex. The second phase uses each partition i's K-out-neighborhood file to generate i's in-edge partition files. Each partition i's in-edge files represent a set of vertices (which could belong to any partition) and their in-neighbors which belong to partition i. The third phase parses the global out-edge file to generate each partition j's out-edge partition files. Each partition j's out-edge files represent a set of vertices (which could belong to any partition) and their out-neighbors which belong to partition j. The fourth phase parses the global profile file to generate each partition's profile file.

The fifth phase aims to generate an output of a set of new K-closest neighbors for each vertex for the next iteration $I+1$. We recall that the next iteration's new K-closest neighbors is selected from a candidate set of vertices which includes neighbors, neighbors' neighbors, and a set of random vertices. While accessing each vertex's neighbors in the global out-edge file or generating a set of random vertices is straightforward, finding each vertex's neighbors' neighbors efficiently is non-trivial.

We now describe the main intuition behind *Pons*' mechanism for finding a vertex's neighbors' neighbors. By comparing i's in-edge partition file with j's out-edge partition file, *Pons* identifies the common 'bridge' vertices between these partitions i and j. A bridge vertex b indicates that there exists a source vertex s belonging to partition i having an out-edge (s, b) to the bridge vertex b, and there exists a destination vertex d belonging to partition j having an in-edge (b, d) from the bridge vertex b. Here b is in essence a bridge between s and d, thus enabling s to find its neighbor b's neighbor d. Using this approach for each pair of partitions i and j, the distance of a vertex and each of its neighbors' neighbors can be computed.

As *Pons* is designed to accommodate the profiles of only two partitions at a time in memory, *Pons* adopts the following approach for each partition i. First, it loads into memory i's profile as well as the bridge vertices of i's in-edge partition file. Next, an empty heap is allocated for each vertex which is assigned to partition i. A vertex s' heap is used to accommodate utmost K-closest neighbors. For each partition j, the common bridge vertices with i are identified and subsequently all the relevant pairs (s, d) are generated with s and d belonging to i and j respectively, as discussed above. For each generated pair (s, d), the distance between the source vertex s and the destination vertex d are computed, and then the heap corresponding to the source vertex s is updated with the distance score and the destination vertex d. Once all the partitions $j = [1, M]$ are processed, the heaps of each vertex s belonging to partition i would effectively have the new K-closest neighbors, which are written to the next iteration's global out-edge file. Once all the partitions $i = [1, M]$ are processed, *Pons* moves on to the next iteration $I + 1$.

An illustrative example. Figure 2(a) shows an example graph containing $N = 6$ nodes and $M = 3$ partitions. Let vertices A and T be assigned to partition 1 (red), U and C to partition 2 (blue), and W and I to partition 3 (green). Figure 2(b) shows various in-edge and out-edge partition files corresponding to their respective partitions. For instance, in the 1.in.nbrs file, U and W (denoted by dotted circles) can be considered as bridge vertices with A (bold red), which belongs to partition 1, as the in-neighbor for both of them.

To generate A's neighbors' neighbors, 1.in.nbrs is compared with each partition j's out-edge file j.out.nbrs. For instance, if 1.in.nbrs is compared with 3.out.nbrs, 2 common bridge vertices U and W are found. This implies that U and W can facilitate in finding A's neighbors' neighbors which belong to partition 3. As shown in Fig. 2(c), vertex A finds its neighbors' neighbor I, via bridge vertices U and W.

4   KNN Iteration

At iteration t, *Pons* takes two input files: *global out-edge file* containing the KNN graph $G^{(t)}$, and *global profile file* containing the set of vertices' profiles. Global out-edge file stores contiguously each vertex id v along with its K initial out-neighbors' ids. Vertex ids range from 0 to $N - 1$. The global profile file stores contiguously each vertex id and all the P items of its profile. These files are in binary format which helps in better I/O performance (particularly for random lookups) as well as saves storage space.

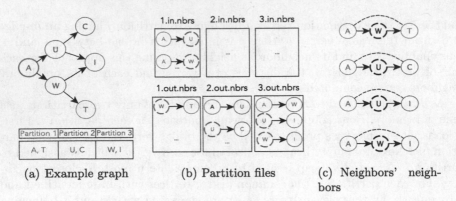

(a) Example graph   (b) Partition files   (c) Neighbors' neigh-
                                                        bors

Fig. 2. [Best viewed in color.] (a) A's out-neighbors and A's neighbors' neighbors. (b) In-edge partition files and out-edge partition files. (c) A's neighbors' neighbors found using bridge vertices

4.1 Phase 1: Partitioning

The memory constraint of the system limits the loading of the whole graph as well as the profiles into memory. To address this issue, we divide these data structures into M partitions, each corresponding to roughly $\lceil N/M \rceil$ distinct vertices, such that the profiles of utmost two partitions ($O(\lceil N/M \rceil P)$) and a K-neighborhood heap of one partition ($O(\lceil N/M \rceil K)$) can be accommodated into memory at any instance.

When a vertex v is assigned to a partition j, the vertex v and its out-neighbors B_v are written to j's K-out-neighborhood file j.knn that contains all vertices assigned to the partition j and their respective out-neighbors.

4.2 Phase 2: In-Edge Partition Files

This phase takes each partition i's K-out-neighborhood file i.knn as input and generates two output files representing bridge vertices and their in-neighbors. For a vertex v assigned to partition i, each of its out-neighbors $w \in B_v$ is regarded as a 'bridge vertex' to its in-neighbor v in this phase. We note here that a bridge vertex $w \in B_v$ could belong to any partition.

The first file i.in.deg stores a list of (i) all bridge vertices b, which could belong to any partition, and (ii) the number of b's in-neighbors that belong to partition i. This list is sorted by the id of each bridge vertex b. The second file i.in.nbrs stores the ids of the in-neighbors of each bridge vertex b stored contiguously according to the bridge vertices' sorted ids in the i.in.deg file.

4.3 Phase 3: Out-Edge Partition Files

This phase takes the global out-edge file as input and generates two output files per partition representing bridge vertices and their out-neighbors, similar to the previous phase. For each partition j, the first file j.out.deg stores a list of (i) all bridge vertices b, which could belong to any partition, and (ii) the number of b's out-neighbors that belong to partition j. This list is sorted by the id of each bridge vertex b. The second file j.out.nbrs stores the ids of the out-neighbors of each bridge vertex b stored contiguously according to the bridge vertices' sorted ids in the j.out.deg file. These files are used in the Phase 5 (in Sect. 4.5) for the KNN computation.

4.4   Phase 4: Profile Partition Files

This phase takes the global profile file and generates M profile partition files as output. Each vertex v's profile is read from the global profile file, and then written to the profile partition file corresponding to the partition that it was assigned. Each profile partition file j.prof consumes upto $O(\lceil N/M \rceil P)$ memory or disk space. Each profile partition file subsequently allows the fast loading of the profiles in the Phase 5, as it facilitates sequential reading of the entire file without any random disk operations.

4.5   Phase 5: Distance Computation

This phase uses each partition's in-edge, out-edge, and partition profile files to compute the distances between each vertex and a collection of its neighbors, neighbors' neighbors, and random vertices, generating the set of new K-closest neighbors for the next iteration.

Algorithm 3 shows the pseudo-code for this phase. Distance computation is performed at the granularity of a partition, processing sequentially each one from 1 to M (line 2–25). Once a partition i is completely processed, each vertex $v \in W_i$ assigned to i has a set of new K-closest neighbors.

The processing of partition i primarily employs four in-memory data structures: $InProf$, $InBrid$, $HeapTopK$, and tuple T. $InProf$ stores the profiles of vertices (W_i) in partition i read from the i.prof file (line 3). $InBrid$ stores the bridge vertices and their corresponding number of in-neighbors in partition i read from the i.in.deg file (line 4). $HeapTopK$ is a heap, which is initially empty (line 5), stores the scores and ids of the K-closest neighbors for each vertex $v \in W_i$, and tuple T stores neighbors, neighbors' neighbors, and random neighbors' tuples for distance computation.

For computing the new KNN for each vertex $s \in W_i$, partitions are parsed one at a time (lines 6–25) as follows. For a partition j, its profile file j.prof and its out-edge bridge file j.out.deg are read into two in-memory data structures $OutProf$ and $OutBrid$, respectively (lines 7–8). Similar to i's in-memory data structures, $OutProf$ stores the profiles of vertices (W_j) in partition j, and $OutBrid$ stores the bridge vertices and their corresponding number of out-neighbors in partition j. By identifying a set of common bridge vertices between $InBrid$ and $OutBrid$, we generate in parallel, all ordered tuples of neighbors' neighbors as follows:

$$(s, d) | s \in W_i, d \in W_j, (s, b) \in E^{(t)}, (b, d) \in E^{(t)}, b \in (InBrid \cap OutBrid) \quad (2)$$

Each ordered tuple (s, d) represents a source vertex $s \in W_i$ and a destination vertex $d \in W_j$, with an out-edge (s, b) from s and an-inedge (b, d) to a bridge vertex b that is common to both $InBrid$ and $OutBrid$. We also generate in parallel, all ordered tuples of each vertex $s \in W_i$ and its immediate neighbors $(w \mid w \in B_v \cap W_j)$ which belong to the partition j. A distance metric such as cosine similarity or euclidean distance is then used to compute the distance score $(Dist(F_s, F_d))$ between each ordered tuple's source vertex s and destination vertex d. The top-K heap $(HeapTopK[s])$ of the source vertex s is updated with d's id and the computed distance score $(Dist(F_s, F_d))$.

Algorithm 3. $NNComputation()$: Neighbors' neighbors computation

---

Data: In-edge partition files, Out-edge partition files, Profiles
Result: New K-nearest neighbors for each vertex

```
 1 begin
 2 │  foreach (In-edge) Partition i do
 3 │  │  Read InProf from File(i.prof)
 4 │  │  Read InBrid from File(i.in.deg)
 5 │  │  HeapTopK[Wᵢ] ← φ
 6 │  │  foreach (Out-edge) Partition j do
 7 │  │  │  Read OutProf from File(j.prof)
 8 │  │  │  Read OutBrid ← from File(j.out.deg)
 9 │  │  │  Initialize tuple T ← φ
10 │  │  │  CndBrid ← (InBrid ∩ OutBrid) ∪ (Wᵢ ∩ OutBrid)
11 │  │  │  foreach Bridge b ∈ CndBrid do
12 │  │  │  │  in parallel
13 │  │  │  │  Src ← ReadInNeig(i.in.nbrs, b)
14 │  │  │  │  Dst ← ReadOutNeig(j.out.nbrs, b)
15 │  │  │  │  AddTuples(T, Src × Dst)
16 │  │  │  foreach (s, d) ∈ T do
17 │  │  │  │  in parallel
18 │  │  │  │  dist ← Dist(Fₛ, F_d)
19 │  │  │  │  UpdateHeap(HeapTopK[s], d, dist)
20 │  │  │  foreach s ∈ Wᵢ do
21 │  │  │  │  in parallel
22 │  │  │  │  Dst ← Rnd(K) ∈ Wⱼ
23 │  │  │  │  Compute tuples s × Dst
24 │  │  │  │  Update HeapTopK[s] as above
25 │  │  File(G^(t+1)).Write(HeapTopK)
```

---

5   Experimental Setup

We perform our experiments on a Apple MacBook Pro laptop, Intel Core i7 processor (Cache 2: 256 KB, Cache 3: 6 MB) of 4 cores, 16 GB of RAM (DDR3, 1600 MHz) and a 500 GB (6 Gb/s) SSD.

Datasets. We evaluate *Pons* on both sparse- and dense- dimensional datasets. For sparse datasets, we use Friendster [15] and Twitter data[2]. Both in Friendster and Twitter, vertices represent users, and profiles are their lists of friends in the social network. For dense datasets, we use a large computer vision dataset (ANN-SIFT-100M) [12] which has vectors of 128 dimensions each. Vertices represent high-dimensional vectors and their profiles represent SIFT descriptors. The SIFT descriptors are typically high dimensional feature vectors used in identifying objects in computer vision (Table 1).

Table 1. Datasets

Dataset	Vertices	P	K	VI[Gb]
ANN-SIFT 30M (30M)	30M	128	10	19.35
ANN-SIFT 50M (50M)	50M	128	10	30.88
Friendster (FRI)	38M	124	10	23.26
Twitter (TWI)	44M	80	10	19.43

Performance. We measure the performance of *Pons* in terms of execution time and memory consumption. Execution time is the (wall clock) time required for completing a defined number of KNN iterations. Memory consumption is measured by the maximum memory footprint observed during the execution of the algorithm. Thus, we use maximum resident set size (RSS) and virtual memory size (VI).

6   Evaluation

We evaluate the performance of *Pons* on large datasets that do not fit in memory. We compare our results with a fully in-memory implementation of the KNN algorithm (INM). We show that our solution is able to compute KNN on large datasets using only the available memory, regardless of the size of the data.

6.1   Performance

We evaluate *Pons* on both sparse and dense datasets. We ran one iteration of KNN both on *Pons* and on INM. We divide the vertex set on M partitions (detailed in Table 2), respecting the maximum available memory of the machine. For this experiment both approaches run on 8 threads.

Execution Time. In Table 2 we present the percentage of execution time consumed by *Pons* compared to INM's execution time for various datasets. *Pons* performs the computation in only a small percentage of the time required by INM for the same computation. For instance, *Pons* computes KNN on the

---

[2] Twitter dataset: http://konect.uni-koblenz.de/networks/twitter_mpi.

Twitter dataset in 8.27% of the time used by INM. Similar values are observed on other datasets. These results are explained by the capacity of *Pons* to use only the available memory of the machine, regardless of the size of the dataset. On the other hand, an in-memory implementation of KNN needs to store the whole dataset in memory for achieving good performance. As the data does not fit in memory, the process often incurs swapping, performing poorly compared to *Pons*.

Table 2. Relative performance comparing *Pons* and INM, and memory footprint

		Exec. Time	RSS[GB]		Virtual[GB]	
Dataset	M	*Pons*/INM %	*Pons*	INM	*Pons*	INM
FRI	5	6.95	11.23	12.79	16.86	23.26
TWI	4	8.27	13.04	13.78	15.55	19.43
50M	9	4.34	12.77	13.16	15.48	30.88

Memory Consumption. As we show in Table 2, our approach allocates at most the available memory of the machine. However, INM runs out of memory, requiring more than 23 GB in the case of Friendster. As a result, an in-memory KNN computation might not be able to efficiently accomplish the task.

6.2 Multithreading Performance

We evaluate the performance of *Pons* and INM, in terms of execution time, on different number of threads. The memory consumption is not presented because the memory footprint is almost not impacted by the number of threads, only few small data structures are created for supporting the parallel processing.

Figure 3 shows the execution time of one KNN iteration on both approaches. The results confirm the capability of *Pons* to leverage multithreading to obtain better performance. Although the values do not show perfect scalability, results clearly show that *Pons*'s performance increases with the number of threads. The fact that is not a linear increase is due to that some phases do not run in parallel, mainly due to the nature of the computation, requiring multiple areas of coordination that would affect the overall performance.

6.3 Performance for different memory availability

One of the motivation of this work is to find an efficient way of computing KNN online, specifically considering contexts where not all resources are available for this task. KNN computation is often just one of the layers of a larger system, therefore online computation might only afford a fraction of the resources. In this regard, we evaluate *Pons'* capacity of performing well when only a fraction of the memory is available for the computation. Figure 4 shows the percentage of

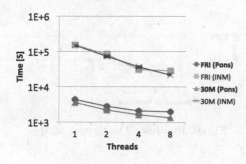
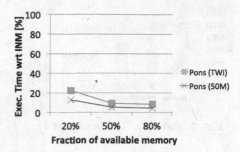

Fig. 3. Impact of multithreading   **Fig. 4.** Impact of the available memory

execution time taken by *Pons* compared to INM, for computing KNN running on a memory-constrained machine.

If only 20 % of the memory is allocated to KNN, *Pons* requires only 12 % of the execution time taken by INM on a dense dataset. In the case of a sparse dataset, *Pons* computes KNN in only 20 % of the time taken by INM, when the memory is constrained to 20 % of the total. On the other hand, when 80 % of the memory is available for KNN, *Pons* requires only 4 %, and 8 % of the INM execution time, on dense and sparse data set, respectively. These results show the ability of *Pons* of leveraging only a fraction of the memory for computing KNN, regardless of the size of data. Therefore, *Pons* lends itself to perform online KNN computation using only available resources, leaving the rest free for other processes.

6.4   Evaluating the Number of Partitions

Pons' capability to compute KNN efficiently only using the available memory relies on the appropriate choice of the number of partitions M. Larger values of M decrease the memory footprint, diminishing likewise algorithm's performance, this is due to the increase in the number of IO operations. On the other hand, smaller values of M increase the memory footprint, but also decrease performance caused by the usage of virtual memory and consequently expensive swapping operations. An appropriate value of M allows *Pons* to achieve better performance.

Execution Time. We evaluate the performance of *Pons* for different number of partitions. Figures 5 and 6 show the runtime for the optimal value, and two suboptimal values of M. The smaller suboptimal value of M causes larger runtimes due to the fact that the machine runs out of memory, allocating virtual memory for completing the task. Although runtime increases, it remains lower than INM runtime (roughly 7 % of INM runtime). Larger suboptimal value of M affects performance as well, by allocating less memory than it is available, thus misspending resources in cases of full availability.

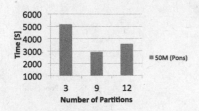

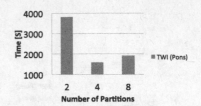

Fig. 5. Runtime: The impact of M   **Fig. 6.** Runtime: The impact of M

Memory Consumption. Figures 7 and 8 show the memory footprint for the optimal value of M, and two suboptimal values. In both cases, smaller values of M increase RSS, reaching the maximum available, unfortunately, virtual memory footprint increase as well, affecting the performance. The optimal value of M increases RSS to almost 16 GB, but virtual memory consumption remains low, allowing much of the task being performed in memory. On the other hand, a larger value of M decreases both RSS and the virtual memory footprint, performing suboptimally. Although, larger values of M affect performance, this fact allows our algorithm to perform KNN computation on machines that do not have all resources available for this task, regardless the size of the data.

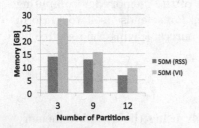

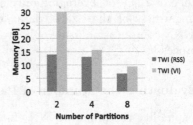

Fig. 7. The impact of M   **Fig. 8.** The impact of M

7   Related Work

The problem of finding K-nearest neighbors has been well studied over last years. Multiple techniques have been proposed to perform this computation efficiently: branch and bound algorithms [10]; trees [1,18]; divide and conquer methods [6]; graph-based algorithms [9]. However, only a few have performed KNN computation in memory-constrained environments [7].

Recently, many studies [11,14,19] have explored 'out-of-core' mechanisms to process large graphs on a single commodity PC. Kyrola et al. in [14] propose *GraphChi*, a disk-based system to compute graph algorithms on large datasets. They present a sliding window computation method for processing a large graph from disk. This system is highly efficient on graphs that remain static during the entire computation. Unfortunately, it does not show same efficiency when the graph changes over time, as the case of KNN computation. *X-Stream* [19] proposes a edge-centric graph processing system on a single shared-memory machine. Graph algorithms are performed leveraging streaming partitions, and processing sequentially edges and vertices from disk. *TurboGraph* [11] consists of a *pin-and-slide*, a parallel execution model for computing on large-scale graphs using a single machine. *Pin-and-slide* model divides the set of vertices in a list of pages, where each vertex could have several pages.

8   Conclusion

We proposed *Pons*, an out-of-core algorithm for computing KNN on large datasets, leveraging efficiently both disk and the available memory. *Pons'* performance relies on its ability to partition a KNN graph and profiles into smaller chunks such that the subsequent accesses to these data segments during the computation is highly efficient, while adhering to the limited memory constraint.

We demonstrated that *Pons* is able to compute KNN on large datasets, using only the memory available. *Pons* outperforms an in-memory baseline, computing KNN on roughly 7 % of the in-memory's time, using efficiently the available memory. Our evaluation showed *Pons'* capability for computing KNN on machines with memory constraints, being also a good solution for computing KNN online, devoting few resources to this specific task.

Acknowledgments. This work was partially funded by Conicyt/Beca Doctorado en el Extranjero Folio 72140173 and Google Focused Award Web Alter-Ego.

References

1. Beygelzimer, A., Kakade, S., Langford, J.: Cover trees for nearest neighbor. In: ICML (2006)
2. Boiman, O., Shechtman, E., Irani, M.: In defense of nearest-neighbor based image classification. In: CVPR (2008)
3. Boutet, A., Frey, D., Guerraoui, R., Jegou, A., Kermarrec, A.M.: WHATSUP: a decentralized instant news recommender. In: IPDPS (2013)
4. Boutet, A., Frey, D., Guerraoui, R., Jegou, A., Kermarrec, A.M.: Privacy-preserving distributed collaborative filtering. In: Noubir, G., Raynal, M. (eds.) Networked Systems. LNCS, vol. 8593, pp. 169–184. Springer, Heidelberg (2014)
5. Boutet, A., Frey, D., Guerraoui, R., Kermarrec, A.M., Patra, R.: HyRec: Leveraging browsers for scalable recommenders. In: Middleware (2014)
6. Chen, J., Fang, H.R., Saad, Y.: Fast approximate KNN graph construction for high dimensional data via recursive Lanczos bisection. J. Mach. Learn. Res. **10**, 1989–2012 (2009)
7. Chiluka, N., Kermarrec, A.M., Olivares, J.: Scaling KNN computation over large graphs on a PC. In: Middleware (2014)
8. Debatty, T., Michiardi, P., Thonnard, O., Mees, W.: Building k-nn graphs from large text data. In: Big Data (2014)

9. Dong, W., Moses, C., Li, K.: Efficient k-nearest neighbor graph construction for generic similarity measures. In: WWW (2011)
10. Fukunaga, K., Narendra, P.M.: A branch and bound algorithm for computing k-nearest neighbors. IEEE Trans. Comput. **C–24**(7), 750–753 (1975)
11. Han, W.S., Lee, S., Park, K., Lee, J.H., Kim, M.S., Kim, J., Yu, H.: TurboGraph: a fast parallel graph engine handling billion-scale graphs in a single PC. In: SIGKDD (2013)
12. Jégou, H., Tavenard, R., Douze, M., Amsaleg, L.: Searching in one billion vectors: re-rank with source coding. In: ICASSP (2011)
13. Katayama, N., Satoh, S.: The SR-tree: An index structure for high-dimensional nearest neighbor queries. In: SIGMOD, vol. 26, pp. 369–380. ACM (1997)
14. Kyrola, A., Blelloch, G.E., Guestrin, C.: GraphChi: Large-scale graph computation on just a PC. In: OSDI (2012)
15. Leskovec, J., Krevl, A.: SNAP Datasets: Stanford large network dataset collection (2014). http://snap.stanford.edu/data
16. Lin, Z., Kahng, M., Sabrin, K., Chau, D., Lee, H., Kang, U.: MMAP: fast billion-scale graph computation on a PC via memory mapping. In: Big Data (2014)
17. McRoberts, R.E., Nelson, M.D., Wendt, D.G.: Stratified estimation of forest area using satellite imagery, inventory data, and the k-nearest neighbors technique. Remote Sens. Environ. **82**(2), 457–468 (2002)
18. Roussopoulos, N., Kelley, S., Vincent, F.: Nearest neighbor queries. In: SIGMOD (1995)
19. Roy, A., Mihailovic, I., Zwaenepoel, W.: X-stream: edge-centric graph processing using streaming partitions. In: SOSP (2013)
20. Wang, J., Yang, J., Yu, K., Lv, F., Huang, T., Gong, Y.: Locality-constrained linear coding for image classification. In: CVPR (2010)
21. Wong, W.K., Cheung, D.W.l., Kao, B., Mamoulis, N.: Secure KNN computation on encrypted databases. In: SIGMOD (2009)
22. Zhu, X., Han, W., Chen, W.: GridGraph: Large-scale graph processing on a single machine using 2-level hierarchical partitioning. In: USENIX ATC (2015)

The 4-Octahedron Abstract Domain

Rachid Oucheikh[1]($\boxtimes$), Ismail Berrada[1], and Outman El Hichami[2]

[1] Laboratoire Informatique, Modélisation et Systèmes (LIMS),
Université Sidi Mohamed Ben Abdellah - Faculté des Sciences Dhar El Mahraz,
Fes, Morocco
cheikh.rachid09@gmail.com, iberrada@univ-lr.fr
[2] National School of Applied Sciences, Tetouan, Morocco
el.hichami.outman@taalim.ma

Abstract. In static analysis, the choice of an adequate abstract domain is an interesting issue. In this paper, we provide a new numerical abstract domain: 4-Octahedron. It is an Octahedra subclass that infers relations of the form: $\{\ x \sim \alpha, x - y \sim \beta, (x - y) - (z - t) \sim \lambda \}$, such that: x, y, z and t are real variables, α, β and λ are real constants and $\sim\ \in \{\leq, \geq\}$. Its precision lies between the octagons and octahedra. We construct a suitable structure for its representation, we provide normalization algorithms for computing its canonical form and we give methods to compute its transfer functions (Union, Intersection, Assignment, Projection, ...). Complexity of the implementation algorithms is proved to be polynomial.

Keywords: 4-Octahedron abstract domain · Static analysis · Real-time systems verification · Canonical form · Galois connection

1 Introduction

Code bugs might provoke a dramatic damages and even human victims. Hence the importance of building correct software using formal methods. The code analysis allows to automatically verify safety of dynamic properties on programs, such as the absence of runtime errors. It aims to compute the set of reachable program states X in order to be sure that are safe, basing on a program semantic function F, such that $F(X) = X$. But unfortunately this is often not computable. So, we define a new abstract semantic function F^*, in order to compute an abstract program invariant X^*, which includes the concrete one X. This technique, so-called abstract interpretation [1], represents an over-approximation of the solution and should include less extra-solutions (false alarms).

Table 1 depicts the commonly used numerical abstract domains in the literature. Analysis using interval domains requires just a linear time and space for its implementation, but it lacks precision of the expressed invariants. On the other side, convex polyhedron is the most rich representation, but its complexity is exponential in the number of program variables. The challenge is to make a trade-off between precision and low-cost. Hence the importance of the weakly relational abstract domains, namely the Difference Bound Matrices [3] and the Octagons [5].

© Springer International Publishing AG 2016
P.A. Abdulla and C. Delporte-Gallet (Eds.): NETYS 2016, LNCS 9944, pp. 311–317, 2016.
DOI: 10.1007/978-3-319-46140-3_25

Table 1. Summary of numerical abstract domains based on inequalities

Abstract domain	Invariants	Example	Reference
Intervals	$k_1 \leq x_i \leq k_2$, $k_1, k_2 \in \mathbb{R}$	$1 \leq x \leq 4$	[1]
Difference Bound Matrices (DBMs)	$k_1 \leq x_i \leq k_2$, $k_1, k_2 \in \mathbb{R}$ $x_i - x_j \leq k$, $k \in \mathbb{R}$	$x \leq 2 \wedge x - y \leq 3$	[4]
Octagons	$\pm x_i \pm x_j \leq k$, $k \in \mathbb{R}$	$x + y \leq 6 \wedge x - y \leq 2$	[5]
4-Octahedra	$x_i \sim k, x_i - x_j \sim$ $k, (x_i - x_j) - (x_p - x_q) \sim k,$ $\sim \in \{\leq, \geq\}, k \in \mathbb{R}$	$x \leq 5 \wedge z \leq$ $6 \wedge x - y + z \leq t + 3$	Our paper
Octahedra	$\sum x_i - \sum x_j \geq k$, $k \in \mathbb{R}$	$x + y - z \leq 7$	[7]
Convex polyhedra	$\sum c_i x_i \geq k\, c_i, k \in \mathbb{R}$	$2x + y - 4z \geq 3$	[8]

In this paper, we introduce a new abstract domain encompassing the invariants of the form: $\{x \sim \alpha, x - y \sim \beta, (x-y) - (z-t) \sim \lambda\}$, such that: $(x, y, z, t) \in \mathbb{R}$, α, β and λ are real constants and $\sim \in \{\leq, \geq\}$. The precision of our domain lies between the octagon domains which encode the relations of the form: $\pm x \pm y \leq k$, for $k \in \mathbb{R}$, and the octahedra domains.

The paper is organized as follows: Sect. 2 highlights some basic definitions. In Sect. 3, we introduce the 4-Octahedron abstract domain and we prove its consistence with the original concrete domain. Then, in Sect. 4, we define its adequate data-structure representation, we elaborate the canonical form computation algorithms and we define the abstract operators. Finally, Sect. 5 concludes and draws some perspectives.

2   4-Octahedron Representation

2.1   Linearly Dependent Vectors

In the rest of this paper, $\mathbb{T}^{\geq 0}$ denotes the set $\{x \,|\, x \geq 0, x \in \mathbb{T}\}$ and $\overline{\mathbb{T}}$ the set $\mathbb{T} \cup \{+\infty, -\infty\}$. $X = \{x_1, x_2, ..., x_n\}$ denotes a set of valued variables over $\mathbb{T}$, x_0 is a special variable that is always equal to zero and $X^0 = X \cup \{x_0\}$. A valuation function ν associates to each variable x_i of X a value ν_i in $\mathbb{T}$. $\mathcal{V}(X)$ denotes the set of valuations over X. The set $\{e_1, e_2, \cdots, e_n\}$ refers to the canonical basis of the n-dimensional vector space $(\mathbb{T}^n, +, \times)$ and e_0 is the zero vector of $\mathbb{T}^n$. A family $f = (V_i)$ of distinct nonzero vectors of $\mathbb{T}^n$ is linearly independent if the only scalars $(\alpha_i) \in \mathbb{N}$ that satisfied the equation $\sum \alpha_i V_i = e_0$ are null. A linearly dependent family f is said to be simple, if every sub-family $f' \subset f$ is linearly independent.

Theorem 1. *Let $f = (V_i)_{i \in [1,r]}$ be a simple dependent family of $\mathbb{T}^n$. Then, for all $p < r$, the only scalars $(\alpha_i)_{i \in [1,p]} \in \mathbb{Z}$ that satisfied the equation $\sum \alpha_i V_i = e_0$, are $\alpha_i = 0$ for $i \in [1,p]$.* $\square$

The corollaries and detailed proofs are available in the link [13].

2.2   4-Octahedra Definition

Let $X \in \mathbb{T}^n$. An **atomic 4-constraint** over X is an inequality of the form: $(\epsilon_i x_i - \epsilon_j x_j) - (\epsilon_p x_p - \epsilon_q x_q) \sim m_{ijpq}$ where $m_{ijpq} \in \mathbb{T}$, $\sim \in \{\leq, \geq\}$, and for all $k \in \{i, j, p, q\}$, $\epsilon_k \in \{0, 1\}$. An atomic 4-constraint is said to be in its **canonical form** iff for all $k \in \{i, j, p, q\}$, $\epsilon_k \neq 0$ and '$\sim$' is '$\leq$'. It is easy to see that, by introducing a special variable x_0, which is always equal to zero, every atomic 4-constraint can be rewritten in its canonical form.

The set of atomic (resp. canonical) 4-constraints over X will be denoted by $\boldsymbol{\Phi(X)}$ (resp. $\boldsymbol{4\text{-}\Phi(X^0)}$). For a canonical 4-constraint $c_{ijpq} = (x_i - x_j) - (x_p - x_q) \leq m_{ijpq}$, we put: $\overline{c_{ijpq}} = c_{jiqp}$ and we get the normal vector of the hyperplane induced by c_{ijpq} by the function F_v that associate to each constraint c_{ijpq} the vector: $e_i - e_j - e_p + e_q$.

A **4-octahedron** O over X, written $O = \bigwedge((x_i - x_j) - (x_p - x_q) \leq m_{ijpq})$, is the solution of m canonical 4-constraints over X^0. Let $C(O)$ be the set of canonical 4-constraints of O. For a valuation $\nu \in \mathcal{V}(X^0)$, $\nu \in O$ iff ν satisfies all constraints of $C(O)$. O is an empty set iff $\nu \notin O$, for all $\nu \in \mathcal{V}(X^0)$.

Next, we define the weight function F_b to be the mapping that associates to a given 4-constraint c_{ijpq} its upper bound m_{ijpq} if $c \in C(O)$ and $+\infty$ otherwise.

2.3   Hyper-paths and Hyper-cycles

Graph-based algorithms has been widely used for checking the satisfiability (or emptiness) of Potential Constraints conjunctions [4] $\bigwedge(x_i - x_j \leq m_{ij})$ and Octagons [5] $\bigwedge(\pm x_i \pm x_j \leq m_{ij})$. Difference Bound Matrices are used to represent the potential constraints. A well known result [6] states that a DBM is empty if and only if there exists, in its associated potential graph, a cycle with a strictly negative total weight. The concept of cycles (simple cycle or closed walk) used in graph theory can catch plan constraints but fails to catch hyperplane constraints of the form $(x_i - x_j) - (x_p - x_q) \leq m_{ijpq}$.

In this paper, we extend the notion of cycles to **hyper cycles** and we use normal vectors to catch hyperplane constraints. Let $C = \{c_1, c_2, \cdots, c_k\}$ be a set of distinct constraints of $4\text{-}\Phi(X^0)$, then C generates a **hyper-cycle** or **h-cycle** (resp. **simple hyper-cycle**) if the normal vectors family $f = (F_v(c_i))$ is linearly (resp. simple linearly) dependent. The set of hyper-cycles over $4\text{-}\Phi(X^0)$ is expressed by: $HCycle(X^0) = \{(C, (\lambda_i)) \mid C = \{c_1, c_2, \cdots, c_k\}$ and $\sum \lambda_i F_v(c_i) = e_0\}$.

The notion of graph paths can be extended to **hyper-paths** as follows: for a set $P = \{c_1, c_2, \cdots, c_k\} \subseteq 4\text{-}\Phi(X^0)$, and $c \in 4\text{-}\Phi(X^0)$, then P generates a **hyper-path** or **h-path** (resp. **simple hyper-path**) of c, if $P \cup \{\overline{c}\}$ generates a hyper-cycle (resp. simple hyper-cycle). The set of hyper-paths is: $HPath(c) = \{(P, (\lambda_i)) \mid P = \{c_1, c_2, \cdots, c_k\}$ and $F_v(\overline{c}) + \sum \lambda_i F_v(c_i) = e_0\}$.

Finally, the weight function F_b^o can be extended to hyper-cycles and hyper-paths in this way:

- For $(P, (\lambda_i)) \in HPath(c)$ such that $P = \{c_1, c_2, \cdots\}$, $F_b^o((P, (\lambda_i))) = \sum \lambda_i F_b^o(c_i)$.

– For $(C, (\lambda_i)) \in HCycle(X^0)$ such that $C = \{c_1, c_2, \cdots\}$, $F_b^o((C, (\lambda_i))) = \sum \lambda_i F_b^o(c_i)$.

Lemma 1. *Let O be a 4-octahedron. If all hyper-cycles of O are positives with the minimal function F_b^o, then for each h-path $P = (p_1, p_2, \cdots, p_k)$ of c, there exists a simple h-path $Q = (q_1, q_2, \cdots, q_l)$ of c such that $F_b^o((P, (\lambda_i))) \leq F_b^o((Q, (\beta_i)))$. And there exists a unique minimal solution (λ_i) such that $F_b^o((P, (\lambda_i))) \leq F_b^o((P, (\beta_i)))$ for all $(P, (\beta_i)) \in HPath(c)$.* □

3   4-Octahedron Abstract Domain

3.1   The Need for 4-Octahedron Abstract Domain

Since its introduction by Cousot and Cousot [1], abstract interpretation has been widely applied to approximate undecidable or very complex problems in computer science. The choice of a suitable abstract domain has then a great impact on the precision of the specification to be proved. We have at least two application fields where the problems can be efficiently approximated by the 4-Octahedra domain: **Static code analysis,** in order to correct programming errors without running the program, and the **Verification of real-time systems** modeled with Parametric Timed Automata (PTA) [9,10], since the 4-Octahedra catches the parametrized clocks of PTA. Furthermore, our abstract domain is very suitable for implementing verification operations (emptiness test, inclusion, post,$\cdots$) for models based on lower/upper bound (L/U) automata, for instance, the Four Phase Handshake Protocol [12] given in [11].

3.2   Emptiness Testing

To check the emptiness of a 4-octahedron, we define the minimum weight function F_{bm}^o that computes the tight upper bound of a constraint c: $F_{bm}^o(c) = min(\{ F_b^o((P, (\lambda_i))) \mid (P, (\lambda_i)) \in HPath(c)\})$.

Theorem 2. *Let $O = \bigwedge c_{ijpq}$ be a 4-octahedron. Then, the next two assertions are equivalents:*

1. *For all hyper-cycles $C = (c_i, c_2, \cdots)$ such that $\sum \lambda_i F_v(c_i) = e_0$ then $\sum \lambda_i F_b^o(c_j) \geq 0$.*
2. *For all hyper-cycles $C = (c_i, c_2, \cdots)$ such that $\sum \lambda_i F_v(c_i) = e_0$ then $\sum \lambda_i F_{bm}^o(c_j) \geq 0$.* □

This theorem states that the minimal weight function preserves positive hyper-cycles of O.

Theorem 3. *A 4-octahedron $O = \bigwedge c_{ijpq}$ is not empty iff all simple hyper-cycles of O are positives.*

3.3   Approximation of the Canonical Form

Finding an efficient algorithm that can compute the minimal weight function, in general case, is an open problem at the time of writing this paper. Note that, computing the minimal weight by finding all $HPath$, is a hard problem since there is an exponential number of $HPath$. Keeping this fact in mind, next, we will introduce some fundamental results that allow us either to compute the canonical form or its upper approximations.

Theorem 4. *Let $(x_i, x_j, x_p, x_q, x_k, x_l) \in (X^0)^6$. If M_{ijpq} denotes the minimal bound of a constraint c_{ijpq}, then the following three equalities are always satisfied: $M_{ijpq} = M_{qpji} = M_{ipjq}$, $M_{ijkk} = M_{ij00}$ and $M_{ijji} = 2M_{ij00}$* $\square$

Theorem 5. *Let $(x_i, x_j, x_p, x_q, x_k, x_l) \in (X^0)^6$ and M_{ijpq} denotes the minimal bound $F^o_{bm}(c_{ijpq})$ of a constraint c_{ijpq}. Then $M_{ijpq} \leq M_{ijkl} + M_{klpq}$ and $M_{ijpq} \leq M_{iklq} + M_{kjpl}$* $\square$

4   4-Octahedra Abstract Domains Implementation

4.1   2D-DBM Data-Structure

For the purpose of implementation and manipulation of the 4-Octahedra abstract domains, we need to create a suitable data structure. So, we extend the Difference Bound Matrices (DBM) in two dimensions, and we obtain what we call "2D-DBM". A DBM is a square matrix M where each coordinate m_{kl} represents the upper bound of the difference $x_l - x_k$. We define the 2-Dimensions Difference Bound Matrix (2D-DBM) to be the square matrix M where m_{kl} is the upper bound M_{ijpq} of the constraints c_{ijpq}, for $1 \leq k, l \leq (n+1)^2$, lines and columns become difference of variables instead of variables.

We note M^c the canonical form of the matrix M. After defining the structure of the 4-Octahedron domain, it is easy to prove its fidelity to the original concrete domain using the Galois Connections.

4.2   Galois Connections

The abstraction allows to easily verify properties satisfaction which was complex or even impossible in the concrete domain. So, it is necessary to prove the Galois Connection between the two domains.

Let $C = (D_C, \sqsubseteq_C)$ and $A = (D_A, \sqsubseteq_A)$ two partially ordered sets. A Galois connection from C to A is a couple $< \alpha, \gamma >$ of functions, where: $\forall c \in C, \forall a \in A, \alpha(c) \sqsubseteq_A a \Leftrightarrow c \sqsubseteq_C \gamma(a)$.

To show these connections, we define firstly the set of concrete valuations:

$$D = \{(x_0, x_1, ..., x_n) \in \mathbb{R}^{n+1} \mid \forall i, j, p, q (x_i - x_j) - (x_p - x_q) \leq M_{ijpq}\}$$

Afterwards, we define the two functions that allow switching from concrete domain to the abstract one. The concretization function returns the set of concrete values framed by a canonical 2D-DBM:

$$\gamma^{2D-DBM}(M^c) = \{(x_0, x_1, ..., x_n) \in \mathbb{R}^{n+1} | (x_i - x_j) - (x_p - x_q) \leq M_{ijpq}\} = D(M^c)$$

And the abstraction function α returns the abstract domain: $\alpha(A) = \bigcap\{m \in \mathcal{M}_\perp | D \subseteq \gamma(m)\}$.

4.3   Computation Canonical Form Algorithm

Here we present the skeleton of the algorithm, its implementation is detailed in [13].

```
Input: non canonical 2D-DBM
Output: Canonical 2D-DBM
Do { for all cell M_ijpq in 2D-DBM representing a 4-Octahedron constraint
M_ijpq := min(M_ijpq, M_ijkl + M_klpq, M_iklq + M_kjpl) }
While 2D-DBM not stationaire yet
```

4.4   Definition of the Abstract Operators

In order to express precisely the whole dynamic behavior of a program, we define the abstract semantics of its primitive operators, namely the transfer functions that model assignment and test statements of the code, the set-theoretic operators such as union (resp. intersection) that interprets the disjunction (resp. conjunction) of many code invariants, and the extrapolation operators, such as widening that computes over-approximations of the variables set in the loops and recursive functions. These abstract operators are defined as manipulations of the associated 2D-DBM.

Intersection: The intersection of two 4-Octahedra represented by their canonical 2D-DBM M_1^c and M_2^c is obtained as follows: $(M_1^c \wedge M_2^c)_{ij} = min((M_1^c)_{ij}, (M_1^c)_{ij})$, $0 \leq i, j \leq (n+1)^2$. The resulting matrix is usually not closed, so we accomplish closure algorithm to obtain its canonical form.

Union: The union of two 4-Octahedra domains described by two 2D-DBM M_1^c and M_2^c is not defined in an exact way, so we get its over-approximation as follows: $(M_1^c \vee M_2^c)_{ij} = max((M_1^c)_{ij}, (M_1^c)_{ij})$, for all $0 \leq i, j \leq (n+1)^2$. The resulting matrix is surely closed.

Linear assignment: We assign to the variable x_k a linear expression over other variables: $x_k \longleftarrow L(x_1, x_2, ..., x_n)$. We perform the assignment in the canonical 2D-DBM (M^c), then we close it applying the previous algorithm. The resulting matrix is canonical.

Projection: A projection of a 4-Octahedron that removes a dimension x_k is accomplished by removing from its canonical associated 2D-DBM (M^c) all columns and lines which concern the variable x_k. Then we perform our algorithm.

5   Conclusion

In this paper, we provided a new abstract domain: the 4-Octahedra, which has an important practical interest in static analysis. It is an Octahedra subclass that infers relations of the form: $\{ x \sim \alpha, x - y \sim \beta, (x - y) - (z - t) \sim \lambda \}$. We proved its consistence with the original concrete domain. In order to represent and manipulate this domain and accomplish the program operators as well, we defined a suitable structure 2D-DBM. Then, we elaborated the algorithm able to obtain the canonical form of this structure. To sum up, in terms of invariants precision, the 4-Octahedron is more rich than Octagons, and regarding the implementation cost, it is less complex than polyhedra.

As perspective of this work, we are using the 4-Octahedron Abstract Domain to formally verify the real-time systems modeled by Parametric Timed Automata. We are elaborating an on-the-fly verification algorithm to analyze the reachability and check the emptiness of PTA parameters set.

References

1. Cousot, P., Cousot, R.: Abstract interpretation: a unified lattice model for static analysis of programs by construction or approximation of fixpoints. In: SPPL, pp. 238–252. ACM Press (1977)
2. Goubault, É., Putot, S.: Static analysis of numerical algorithms. In: Yi, K. (ed.) SAS 2006. LNCS, vol. 4134, pp. 18–34. Springer, Heidelberg (2006)
3. Miné, A.: A new numerical abstract domain based on difference-bound matrices. In: Danvy, O., Filinski, A. (eds.) PADO 2001. LNCS, vol. 2053, pp. 155–172. Springer, Heidelberg (2001)
4. Dill, D.L.: Timing assumptions and verification of finite-state concurrent systems. In: Sifakis, J. (ed.) Timed Specifications: Automatic Verification Methods for Finite State Systems. LNCS, vol. 407, pp. 197–212. Springer, Heidelberg (1989)
5. Miné, A.: The octagon abstract domain. In: Proceedings of Analysis, Slicing and Tranformation, pp. 310–319. IEEE CS Press (2001)
6. Bellman, R.: On a routing problem. Q. Appl. Math. **16**, 87–90 (1958)
7. Clarisò, R., Cortadella, J.: The octahedron abstract domain. Sci. Comput. Program. **64**, 115–139 (2007)
8. Halbwachs, N., Proy, Y.-E., Roumanoff, P.: Verification of real-time systems using linear relation analysis. Form. Methods Syst. Des. **11**, 157–185 (1997)
9. Benes, N., Bezdek, P., Larsen, K.G., Srba, J. Language Emptiness of Continuous-Time Parametric Timed Automata (2015). arXiv preprint arXiv:1504.07838
10. André, É., Markey, N.: Language preservation problems in parametric timed automata. In: Sankaranarayanan, S., Vicario, E. (eds.) FORMATS 2015. LNCS, vol. 9268, pp. 27–43. Springer, Heidelberg (2015)
11. Knapik, M., Penczek, W.: Bounded model checking for parametric timed automata. In: Jensen, K., Donatelli, S., Kleijn, J. (eds.) Transactions on Petri Nets and Other Models of Concurrency V. LNCS, vol. 6900, pp. 141–159. Springer, Heidelberg (2012)
12. Blunno, I., Cortadella, J., Kondratyev, A., Lavagno, L., Lwin, K., Sotiriou, C.: Handshake protocols for de-synchronization. In: The 10th International Symposium on Advanced Research in Asynchronous Circuits and Systems, pp. 149–158 (2004)
13. The detailed proofs and explanations website: http://www.fsdmfes.ac.ma/Octahedron

Reversible Phase Transitions in a Structured Overlay Network with Churn

Ruma R. Paul[1,2]([⊠]), Peter Van Roy[1], and Vladimir Vlassov[2]

[1] Université catholique de Louvain, Louvain-la-neuve, Belgium
{ruma.paul,peter.vanroy}@uclouvain.be
[2] KTH Royal Institute of Technology, Stockholm, Sweden
{rrpaul,vladv}@kth.se

Abstract. Distributed applications break down when the underlying system has too many node or communication failures. In this paper, we propose a general approach to building distributed applications that lets them survive hostile conditions such as these failures. We extend an existing *Structured Overlay Network (SON)* that hosts a transactional replicated key/value store to be *Reversible*, i.e., it is able to regain its original functionality as the environment hostility recedes. For this paper we consider the environment hostility to be measured by the *Churn* parameter, i.e., the rate of node turnover (nodes failing and being replaced by new correct nodes). In order to describe the qualitative behavior of the SON at high churn, we introduce the concept of *Phase* of the SON. All nodes in a phase exhibit the same qualitative properties, which are different for the nodes in different phases. We demonstrate the existence of *Phase Transitions* (i.e., a significant fraction of nodes changes phase) as churn varies and show that our concept of phase is analogous to the macroscopic phase of physical systems. We empirically identify the *Critical Points* (i.e., when there exists more than one phase simultaneously in significant fractions of the system) observed in our experiments. We propose an *API* to allow the application layer to be informed about the current phase of a node. We analyze how the application layer can use this knowledge for self-adaptation, self-optimization and achieve reversibility in the application-level semantics.

Keywords: Phase transition · Maintenance strategies · Churn

1 Introduction

A distributed application breaks down when there are too many node or communication failures, in which case the application can revert to an "offline mode"

This research is partially funded by the SyncFree project in the European Union Seventh Framework Programme under Grant Agreement No. 609551 and by the Erasmus Mundus Doctorate Programme under Grant Agreement No. 2012-0030. Authors would like to thank Manuel Bravo and Zhongmiao Li for their participation to refine the concept of Reversibility.

© Springer International Publishing AG 2016
P.A. Abdulla and C. Delporte-Gallet (Eds.): NETYS 2016, LNCS 9944, pp. 318–333, 2016.
DOI: 10.1007/978-3-319-46140-3_26

with reduced functionality. This can be acceptable for client-server applications, such as mobile applications that depend on a data center that remains a single point of failure. However, this is now changing as the Internet is becoming more and more decentralized: data centers are increasing in number and come in various sizes. Applications running on such an infrastructure need to have a decentralized architecture that is resilient to failure. Ideally, the application should survive with partial functionality during arbitrary system failures and recover its full functionality when the underlying system is restored. This is not just a fringe case: mobile and ad hoc networks, for example, have this kind of failure. Even supposedly stable parts of the Internet have peaks of unstable behavior.

We propose an approach to build applications able to survive arbitrary failures, providing reduced but predictable functionality in that case; and when the failures go away the application recovers its full functionality. We build on the concept of *Structured Overlay Network (SON)*, a known approach to building decentralized systems. We extend a SON to make it *Reversible*, which implies the system is able to regain its original functionality as the stress, e.g., churn or network partitioning, recedes. This paper focuses on one property of the network, namely *Churn*, i.e., nodes failing and being replaced by new correct nodes. We assume that churn varies over time and that the average number of correct nodes at any instant is constant. A SON that provides significant functionality at low churn, e.g., transactions over a key/value store, will no longer be able to do so at high churn. Applications that rely on transactions will no longer be able to use them. We want these applications to continue running nevertheless, with predictable behavior even with reduced functionality. Therefore the SON should inform the application of the provided functionality changes. Ideally, this should be done in a manner that works even for high churn. The SON can therefore not be relied on to do additional computation to determine its level of functionality. Under this constraint, is it possible for the SON to give useful information?

In order to describe the behavior of a SON, we introduce the concept of *Phase* of the system. Phases are well understood in physical systems [25]. We make an analogy for computing systems. A *Phase* is a subset of a system for which the qualitative properties are essentially the same. We consider a system as an aggregate entity composed of a large number of interacting parts, where parts are peers in our case. The phase is not a global property, but is observed separately at each node, and can be different for different nodes. No global synchronization and no extra computation is required to compute the phase; it is a direct consequence of the observed SON structure at each node. The phase of each node has a direct relationship with the available functionalities of the system. In contrast to stress, which is a global condition that cannot easily be measured by individual nodes, the phase is a local property that is directly known at each node. Thus, based on the current phase of a node, the application running on that node can manage its behavior in a stressful environment. As with the constituents of a physical matter, when external conditions change, each node of a SON changes phase independently. If that happens to many nodes, we have a *Phase Transition* at system level. A *Critical Point* occurs when more than one phase exists simultaneously in significant fractions of a system.

Contributions: We define *Reversibility* and design our SON using the principles necessary to make it reversible. To our knowledge, no previous SON provides reversibility for the high values of churn we investigate. We demonstrate reversibility through simulation using realistic network conditions and churn varying over a large range. We present formal definitions of *Phase*, *Phase Transitions* and *Critical Points* in our context. We describe semantics of all the identified phases and sub-phases in our representative system. As a result of having a reversible system, we experimentally demonstrate reversible phase transitions: the nodes of the system change phase as the churn is varied. We present an API so that the application can access the current phase of a node and be notified when a phase transition occurs. Finally, we analyze the applications of these concepts towards the design of *Reversible* and *Predictable* systems. The overall contributions are as follows:

- Definition of *Reversibility*; First demonstration of a reversible SON and conditions to achieve the reversibility, under a wide range of churn values;
- Introduction of the concepts of *Phase*, *Phase Transition* and *Critical Point* in the context of a peer-to-peer network;
- Identification of different phases in a SON; Description of the semantics of all observable phases and sub-phases in the context of that SON;
- First demonstration of reversible phase transitions in a SON;
- An API to expose the current phase of a node, which gives local information about the stress, to the application;
- Analysis of how the application can use the phase concept to manage its behavior in a stressful environment.

The remainder of the paper is as follows. In Sect. 2 we describe a representative class of overlays. Section 3 presents the maintenance strategies of overlays. Section 4 defines and assesses reversibility of the maintenance strategies against churn. In Sect. 5, we study phase transitions in a SON, present an API to expose the current phase of a node to the application, and discuss the use of this knowledge. Section 6 discusses related work, and we conclude in Sect. 7.

2   Representative Overlays

We have chosen ring-based overlays, such as Chord [24], DKS [4], Beernet [20], as our representative systems, because the ring is competitive with other SON structures in terms of routing efficiency and failure resiliency [12]. In this section, we briefly discuss a model of ring overlays as per the reference architecture of [1].

A ring overlay has a virtual identifier space, I, which is a subset of $\mathbb{N}$ of size N. Each peer is associated with a unique id, $p \in I$, mostly using a uniform hash function or some random function. A peer with virtual identifier p is responsible for the interval $(predecessor(p), p]$, i.e., p is responsible for storing data items with keys $k \in (predecessor(p), p]$. Each peer p perceives I to be partitioned into $\log(N)$ partitions, where each partition is k times bigger than the previous one. The routing table of p contains $\log_k(N)$ connections/fingers to some nodes from each partition. The neighborhood of a peer p, $N(p)$, is the set of peers with which p maintains a connection. For a target identifier i, peer p selects the closest preceding link, $d \in N(p)$ to forward the message. Since there are always k intervals, routing converges in $O(\log_k(N))$ hops.

Chord and Beernet: Chord [24] is the canonical ring-based SON. However, studies, e.g. [11], show that churn in Chord can introduce inconsistency. The reason is that the join/leave handling in Chord requires coordination of three peers that is not guaranteed due to non-transitive connectivity (i.e., A can talk to B and B can talk to $C \nRightarrow A$ can talk to C) on the Internet. In contrast to Chord, Beernet [20] does not assume transitive connectivity. This makes Beernet more resilient on Internet-like scenarios. Each step of join/leave handling in Beernet requires the agreement of only two peers, which is guaranteed with a point-to-point communication. Beernet has a correct lock-free three-step join operation, each step involving two peers. Lookup consistency is guaranteed after every step. As a result of such multi-step relaxed join operation, branches

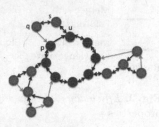

Fig. 1. Branches on a relaxed ring. Peers p and s consider u as successor, but u only considers s as predecessor. Peer q has not established a connection with its predecessor p yet. (Color figure online)

are formed: when a peer is not yet connected to its predecessor it forms a branch from the core ring. Figure 1 shows a Beernet network, where red (dark in B/W) nodes are organized into a ring and green (light in B/W) nodes are on branches. Due to branches, the guarantees about proximity offered by Beernet routing correspond to $O(\log_k(n) + b)$, where b is the distance to the farthest peer on the branch. We have used Beernet for experiments in this work.

3   Overlay Maintenance Strategies

As we consider "Reversible Phase Transitions" due to *Churn*, self-healing is crucial in order to be *Reversible*. This can be achieved by the maintenance strategy of an overlay. A *Maintenance Strategy* maintains the structural integrity of a SON while peers go offline or network connections fail. Several strategies are proposed in existing literature to achieve self-healing; Chord uses *Periodic Stabilization*, whereas DKS and Beernet rely on *Correction-on-Change*. Then there are gossip-based strategies, e.g., T-Man [13], which can construct and maintain a SON. So, why not just use gossip? Correction-on-change is much more efficient than gossip; whereas gossip is much more resilient. Therefore, we organize the maintenance strategies of overlays using *Efficiency* $\leftrightarrow$ *Resiliency* spectrum, as shown in Fig. 2, where maintenance strategies at the top are efficient, but not resilient as churn increases, whereas the strategies at the bottom are resilient,

322   R.R. Paul et al.

Efficiency ↑

Maintenance Strategy	Local/ Global	Reactive/ Proactive	Fast/ Slow	Safety	Bandwidth Consumption
Correction-on-*	Local	Reactive	Fast	Yes	Small
Periodic Stabilization	Local	Proactive	Slow	Lookup inconsistencies and uncorrected false suspicions can be introduced	High
Merger with Passive List	Global	Reactive	Adaptable	Yes	Adaptable
Merger with Knowledge Base	Global	Proactive	Adaptable	Yes	Adaptable

Resiliency ↓

Fig. 2. *Efficiency* ↔ *Resiliency* Spectrum of Overlay Maintenance Strategies with their properties

however lack efficiency. Our goal is to get both efficiency and resiliency, so that a SON can achieve reversibility against extremely high churn. The philosophy behind our work is similar to that used by Plumtree [18].

As already mentioned, correction-on-change and correction-on-use (together referred to as *Correction-on-*), are efficient in terms of bandwidth consumption and rapid response against an event, however they fall short when the stress of the operating environment increases beyond a threshold (due to lack of liveness; without any event no maintenance is done). Correction-on-change handles join/leave/failure of nodes. Whenever a peer detects such events, it updates its neighborhood. Correction-on-use mainly corrects the fingers. Every time messages are routed, information is piggybacked to correct fingers. Thus, correction-on-use provides self-optimization and self-configuration, whereas partial self-healing is achieved through correction-on-change.

Gossip-based strategies are highly resilient against inhospitable environments, but costly in terms of bandwidth consumption and also, react slowly against an event. Using such strategies, each peer maintains a state (local knowledge of the overall system) and uses this knowledge to conduct maintenance. In our work, we have used a simple form of such strategies, *Knowledge Base (KB)* [21], where each peer maintains a best-effort view of the global membership of the system through listening only. The KB at each node can be accessed through an API.

Apart from these extremes, we organize the remaining strategies as per the spectrum: *Periodic Stabilization (PS)* can be seen as a weak form of gossip, where each node exchanges periodic messages with its successor to maintain its immediate vicinity. Such local corrections are able to achieve self-healing; however, might become a slow response while facing an inhospitable environment. As discussed in [10,11], lookup inconsistencies and uncorrected false suspicions can be introduced in real implementations. Also, as per [15], for a low ratio of stabilization frequency to churn, while doing a lookup the longest finger of any peer is always found to be dead, which degrades routing efficiency. To avoid this, it is required to trigger PS often, making an inefficient use of bandwidth. Thus, presenting a trade-off, which is tuned by the period used for this strategy.

A similar bandwidth consumption-convergence time trade-off is added by *ReCircle* [23], in the form of a partition-merger. ReCircle has two parts: a PS algorithm and a *Merger*. The merger is triggered using a *Passive List (PL)*, where each node maintains a list of suspected nodes and whenever a false-suspicion is detected, merger is triggered, thus restricting the gossip messages. The PL approach to trigger the merger is reactive to the operating environment. We have extended this in a proactive manner [21]: instead of PL, the merger is triggered periodically using KB; thus a resilient gossip-based maintenance.

Apart from this spectrum, these strategies can also be classified along two dimensions: local/global and reactive/proactive. Following [2], we classify PS as a proactive and correction-on-* as a reactive mechanism. Using KB, as introduced in [21], the set of strategies covers all points in this two-dimensional space.

4   Reversibility and Its Evaluation

Reversibility. A *Reversible* system is able to regain its original functionality as the external stress recedes. Given a function, $S(t)$, which returns the system stress as a function of time, in some arbitrary but well-defined units. A system is *Reversible* if there exists a function $F_{func}(id, S(t))$ such that the set of available operations of the system, $Op_{set} = F_{func}(id, S(t))$, and when $S(t) = 0$, the system provides full functionality at all nodes. Here, id is a node identifier and an operation is available for a given stress if the operation will eventually succeed. Reversibility is a related, but different property than *Self-Stabilization* [7]. A self-stabilizing system can repair itself from any arbitrary state. Reversibility does not assume anything about the system state. A self-stabilizing system is reversible, but a reversible system is not necessarily self-stabilizing.

Achieving Reversibility Requires Knowledge Base. Reversibility is a nontrivial property. To our knowledge, no existing work demonstrates reversibility for a SON under continuous high churn. Our experimental results, presented in Fig. 3, verify that the knowledge base is essential to ensure reversibility under continuous high churn. We assess reversibility in stepwise fashion, by integrating a new maintenance principle at each step and evaluating the behavior of the resulting system. We achieve reversibility only in the final step, shown in Fig. 3d, which adds the knowledge base. We now explain these experiments in detail.

For our experiments, we have used a SON of 1024 peers. The underlying network is simulated by following the empirical distribution of minimum RTT provided in [3]. We have defined churn as percentage (%) of nodes turnover (nodes failing and being replaced by new correct nodes) per time unit (second in this work). During the steady state of the SON we inject 10 %, 50 % and 100 % churn for 1 min. The churn events are modeled as a *Homogeneous Poisson Process (HPP)* with λ events/sec, where $\lambda = \frac{2*C*1024}{100}$ for $C\%$ churn.

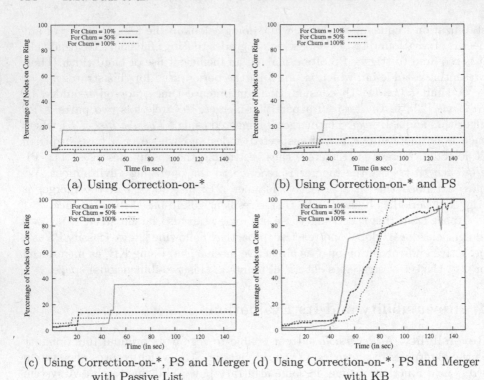

(a) Using Correction-on-*

(b) Using Correction-on-* and PS

(c) Using Correction-on-*, PS and Merger (d) Using Correction-on-*, PS and Merger
   with Passive List   with KB

Fig. 3. % of nodes on the core ring as a function of time (in sec) after withdrawing churn to assess reversibility. Figure 3a, b and c are not reversible (nodes on the core ring never converges to 100 %). Figure 3d using KB is reversible.

After withdrawing churn, we observe the SON's self-healing with time. To quantify self-healing, we have used the metric: % of nodes on the core ring. We find out the maximal ring in the system and report % of nodes on it. The ultimate goal is to have the metric converge to 100 %. A fixed workload is used by injecting transactions, modeled as a HPP with $\lambda = 1$ transaction/s. A transaction reads one key and updates another one. Starting from the withdrawal of churn, for each second we present % of nodes on core ring and an average of 20 independent runs are taken for each second. We remark that the apparent termination time of an experiment in Fig. 3d is the maximum among the samples used.

As Fig. 3a shows correction-on-* fails to achieve reversibility even for the lowest intensity (10 %) of churn used in our experiments. After withdrawing churn, the structure of the system remains almost the same. This is due to the lack of liveness of these principles, thus exhibits very limited reversibility.

In Fig. 3b we can see improvements after integration of PS; however the system is still unable to achieve reversibility. The period used is 3 s.

As Fig. 3c shows, the integration of merger with PL does not show much improvement over the combined local healing. The reason is the existence of isolated nodes in the system (explained below). The nodes on the overlay have no reference to these nodes. So, adding reactive merge does not achieve reversibility.

Why not Reversible Yet? As we can see in Fig. 3c the system is still not reversible. As our investigation shows, there are peers whose joining fails under churn. The first step of joining is to do a *lookup* for successor and after receiving a response a new peer becomes part of the SON. For a join to fail either the lookup request is lost while routing or the successor has failed after receiving the lookup request. If we ignore the processing time at successor, then $P(join\_failure) \propto P(lookup\_failure)$. Figure 4 shows % of incomplete lookups and joins for varying churn. We have used the same experimental setup with lookup requests as a HPP with $\lambda=100$ requests/s. We also present the accumulation of pending join requests with time in Fig. 5, especially for high churn. As is evident, high churn makes the overlay unstable, which does not allow new peers to join.

As shown in Fig. 3d, after the integration of KB the system achieves reversibility. In order to ensure successful joining of new nodes, we have extended nodes with repeated join attempts (until a response is received) with new join references, which are provided by KB. In our experiments, if a node is unable to join with its current join reference within 90 s (a tunable parameter that will be referred to as *Join Timeout*), it requests a new join reference from the application layer. The application layer provides a new join reference by accessing and accumulating the distributed KB, or using a previously cached one. The isolated peer then triggers a new join request with that. We have chosen a conservative value of 90 s for *Join Timeout* to avoid triggering of unnecessary repeated join requests. This parameter can be adapted based on the operating environment and RTT distribution of the underlying network, which is left as future work. Along with this, we have used the proactive merger using KB. In some runs we have observed partition of the system after the isolated nodes complete their join procedures. For these scenarios, the PL approach used in [23] fails to trigger the merging. In order to merge such partitions proactive merger using KB is required. As we can see in Fig. 3d, the system achieves reversibility.

To summarize the outcome of our experiments: *Efficient* maintenance strategies fail to achieve reversibility as churn increases; a *Resilient* maintenance strategy is required to make the system reversible in case of extremely high churn.

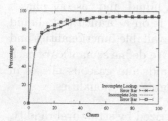

Fig. 4. % of incomplete lookups and joins after 1 min churn injection

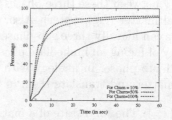

Fig. 5. % of incomplete joins with time during injection of churn for 1 min.

5   Phase, Phase Transitions, API and Application

In this section we formally define *Phase*, *Phase Transition* and *Critical Point* in our context. We describe the semantics of all identified phases and sub-phases in our representative system. We relate our phase concept to Reversibility. We empirically demonstrate reversible phase transitions in a reversible system. We present an API to give useful phase information to the application layer and discuss various applications of this knowledge.

5.1   Definition of Phase, Phase Transition and Critical Point

We present formal definitions of our concepts by drawing an analogy with these terms in physical systems [25]. This analogy is introduced to make it easier to understand intuitively what phase means. We consider a system, $S = \{S_1, \ldots, S_n\}$, where each $S_i : 1 \leq i \leq n$, is an interacting part of S. In our case S is a SON and S_i is a node of the SON. The system is partitioned into k subsets, such that: (1) $P_1 \uplus P_2 \uplus \ldots \uplus P_k = S$, (2) For any $P_i : 1 \leq i \leq k$, qualitative properties are the same $\forall S_x \in P_i$, (3) For $P_i, P_j : i \neq j$, qualitative properties are different, i.e., if F is a function of qualitative property, then $\forall_{i,j:i\neq j} \implies \forall S_x \in P_i, \forall S_y \in P_j : F(S_x) \neq F(S_y)$. We can say each $P_i : 1 \leq i \leq k$ is an observed phase in S. A *Phase Transition* at system level occurs when a significant fraction of a system's parts change phase. This can happen if the local environment changes at many parts. A *Critical Point* occurs when: (1) $k > 1$, (2) at least two, i_1 and i_2, such that $\mid P_i \mid \gg 1$. This paper investigates phases and phase transitions in a SON with varying churn.

Reversibility and Phase: We introduce the concept of phase so that applications can manage their behavior in stressful environments. We have defined the *phase* P_i at each node i to be a well-defined local property of the node. We define the *phase configuration* of the system to be the vector $P_c = (P_1, P_2, P_3, ..., P_n)$. Both phases and phase configurations are functions of time. We can define Op_{set} (See Sect. 4) in terms of them: $Op_{set} = F_{det}(id, P_c(t))$.

In the case of Beernet, we can determine a property that satisfies the formal definition of phase given above. The phase of a node is clearly determinable at that node: there are three mutually exclusive situations depending on neighbor behavior (neighbors on core ring, neighbors on branch, no neighbors). There is an analogy between these three phases and the solid, liquid, and gaseous phases in physical matter (e.g., water). Also, when a node is on a branch (i.e., liquid phase), we can identify three sub-phases in terms of available functionalities and probability of facing an immediate phase transition. We define semantics of each phase and sub-phase, in analogy with the solid, liquid, and gaseous phases in physical matter and translate them in terms of available functionalities.

- **Solid (P_S):** The solid state of a matter is characterized by structural rigidity, where atoms or molecules are bound to each other in a fixed structure. In case of SONs, if a peer has stable predecessor and successor pointers (i.e., the peer is on core ring), along with a stable finger table, then it can be termed to be in solid phase. It can be safely assumed that such a peer can support efficient routing, thus accommodate up-to-date replica sets, thus leading to all the upper layer functionalities, e.g., transactional DHT.

- **Liquid:** A thermodynamic system is in the liquid state where molecules are bound tightly but not rigidly (neighbors can change). In case of SON, if the peer is on a branch, it is less strongly connected than those in P_S; thus in liquid phase. However a peer can be on a branch temporarily, e.g., as part of the join protocol or due to a false suspicion as a result of sudden slow-down of the underlying physical link. We identify three liquid sub-phases.

  - P_{L1}: If the peer is on a branch, but the depth of the peer (distance from the core ring) is ≤ 2. Also, the peer still holds a stable finger table. The justification of depth of 2 for this sub-phase is based on the evaluation of average branch sizes in [20], where it is shown that the average branch size of Beernet is ≤ 2, corresponding to the connectivity among peers on the Internet. So, if a peer's depth on a branch is ≤ 2, the operating environment from a peer's perspective is still the usual one, it might temporarily be pushed on a branch. From an application's perspective, the peer is still able to provide all the higher layer functionalities.

  - P_{L2}: If the peer is on a branch with a depth > 2, but it is not the tail of the branch. Also, the finger table at the peer still holds $> 50\%$ valid fingers. So, the peer is still able to support at least all DHT operations, however successful transactions are not guaranteed anymore.

  - P_{L3}: If the peer is on a branch with a depth > 2 and it is the tail of a branch (farthest node from the core ring). The tail of a branch has higher probability to get isolated during churn, thus introducing unavailability in the key range [20]. Also, most of the fingers in the peer's finger table are invalid or crashed. From a application's perspective, the peer in this sub-phase provides very limited functionality, mostly basic connectivity.

- **Gaseous** (P_G): The gaseous state of matter is made up of individual molecules that are separated from each other. When Beernet experiences high churn, at some point the system is completely dissolved, resulting in isolation, thus gaseous phase, of all nodes. In this work, we have considered only extreme case of partitioning of the system. However, in practice, if there are > 1 nodes per physical machine and the network breaks down, then small ringlets will be formed by the nodes on the same physical machine. For such scenario, the nodes are not completely isolated, however in another form of gaseous phase. The investigation about such gaseous sub-phases is left as future work.

5.2 Observation of Phase Transitions

We show experimentally the existence of phase transitions in our representative reversible system as the churn intensity varies. For this we have used similar experimental setup as described in Sect. 4 with a network of 1024 peers. We have measured the percentages (%) of nodes in different phases and sub-phases.

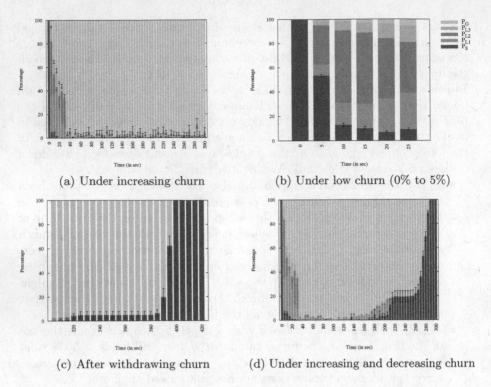

(a) Under increasing churn   (b) Under low churn (0% to 5%)

(c) After withdrawing churn   (d) Under increasing and decreasing churn

Fig. 6. Phase Transitions in Beernet: red, green (different shades corresponds to 3 liquid sub-phases) and blue (dark, gray and light-gray in B/W) areas correspond to % of nodes in solid, liquid and gaseous phases respectively (Color figure online)

Increasing Churn with Time. We study phase transitions under increasing churn and reverse transitions when churn is removed. We start with 5 % churn and increase the intensity by 5 % every 5-second for 5 mins. After that churn is withdrawn; we let the system run until the completion of self-healing (i.e., perfect ring). Every 5-second we take a snapshot of the system, i.e., the percentages of nodes at each phase and sub-phase throughout a run. We have used mean value for 20 independent runs. Figure 6a and c show the states of the system during increasing churn followed by zero churn respectively.

In Fig. 6a (error bars for P_G only) the red area of each bar corresponds to % of nodes which are in phase P_S. At time 0, i.e., starting of the experiment, all nodes are organized into a perfect ring. As churn is increased nodes start moving on branches, the green area of each bar, these are the nodes which are in liquid phase. We have also identified nodes on branches which have different liquid sub-phases, as per the semantics described before. We can figure out some trends apparent in Fig. 6a. For example, 30 % of churn is a critical value, observed at 30 s, as a significant fraction of nodes change from liquid to gaseous phase.

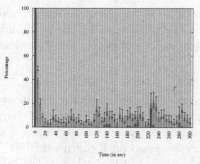

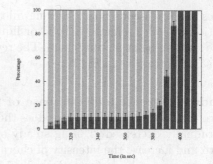

(a) Under continuous churn of 30%   (b) After withdrawal of 30% churn

Fig. 7. Phase Transitions in Beernet: red, green (different shades corresponds to 3 liquid sub-phases) and blue (dark, gray and light-gray in B/W) areas correspond to % of nodes in solid, liquid and gaseous phases respectively (Color figure online)

The solid to liquid transition happens between 0 % and 5 % churn. In Fig. 6a, we can see a sharp fall of % of nodes on core ring from 0 to 5 s. In order to analyze this transition we have zoomed into this area. For this experiment, during steady state of SON, we start with 1 % of churn and every 5-second we increase churn intensity by 1 % till we reach 5 % of churn. Also a snapshot is taken every 5 s as before. Figure 6b shows the result. We have used mean values of 20 samples and only error bars for the P_S are shown. As we can see, as the churn intensity is increased from 1 % to 2 %, during 5 to 10 s, a large fraction of nodes changes phase from solid to liquid.

Figure 6c (error bars for P_S only) shows the recovery of the SON after churn is withdrawn (i.e., 6–9 mins of our experiment). Here starting with all isolated nodes, a small fraction of nodes changes to transient liquid phase. We can see a period of about 90 s, during which the % of isolated nodes remains same. The reason is the *Join Timeout* parameter (see Sect. 4), which is set as 90 s. The transition from gaseous state is controlled by this tunable parameter. Finally all nodes are self-organized into a perfect ring, solid state of SON, within 400 s.

Continuous Moderate Churn. We seek answer to the question: whether a phase transition happens in a SON at continuous moderate churn. For this experiment we have chosen churn equal to 30 %, as we have observed that 30 % of churn is a critical value. During steady state of SON, we start injecting 30 % churn for 5 mins. Then churn is withdrawn and we let the SON do self-healing until all nodes are on the core ring. During our experiment, we take measurements every 5-second and present mean value of 20 independent runs in Fig. 7a (error bars for only P_G) and Fig. 7b (error bars for only P_S). As we can see in Fig. 7a, a significant fraction of nodes change phase during first 10 s, thus justifying our deduction that churn intensity of 30 % to be a critical point. Also, we notice that, as in a thermodynamic system (e.g., water), it takes longer time for the system to reach a gaseous state, in fact there is no clear transition where all nodes are in gaseous phase. During injection of 30 % churn for 5 mins, a small fraction of nodes remains in solid or liquid phase surrounded by the remaining large fraction be in gaseous phase. The reverse transition shown in Fig. 7b follows the same pattern as in Fig. 6c.

Gradual Increase and Decrease of Churn. Till now, we have withdrawn churn completely; what behavior does the system exhibit if the intensity of churn is gradually decreased? During steady state of SON, we start injecting 5 % of churn and increase the intensity of churn every 5-second until churn is of 100 %. Then we gradually decrease churn by 5 % every 5 s until it reaches 0. We take measurements every 5 s throughout the experiment and present mean values of 20 independent runs in Fig. 6d (error bars for only P_S). The behavior follows our previous deductions. Around 30 % of churn a significant fraction of nodes change phase. Between 40 and 100–105 s we see a gaseous system. During gradual decrease of churn intensity, there is increasing connectivity among nodes, followed by organization into ring structure, evidential of reversible phase transitions in our system due to increasing and decreasing churn.

5.3   API for Phases and Phase Transitions

Since phase is a node-specific property, an API exists on each node to expose its phase to the application layer. Next, we describe the use of this knowledge in real application scenarios. In our future work, we intend to empirically demonstrate them. Our API supports push and pull methods to communicate the current phase of a node. A node can be in one of the phases described in Sect. 5.1.

- *getPhase(?P_{cur})* Binds P_{cur} to the current phase of the peer.
- *setPhaseNotify(f)* Sets a user-defined function, *f(?P_{new})* to be executed when the phase changes. P_{new} is bound to the next phase of the peer and *f* is executed. Executions of *f* are serialized in the same thread over a stream of successive phases.

The application running on top of a SON can use the phase information to make the system reversible and predictable. We illustrate the usefulness of the phase concept using a real application scenario. Consider a *Distributed Version Control System* running on top of SON, which is notified that the underlying node changes its phase. The application notifies the user via an indicator, B_{conn}, that changes its color to indicate the phase of the node. B_{conn} can be green or yellow or red, denoting respectively *solid/liquid/gaseous* phase of the node. Suppose the user uses this system on a network having intermittent connectivity (e.g., Wi-Fi on a fast train). As long as B_{conn} is green, the user can continue her work without being concerned. However, as B_{conn} changes to yellow, the user can initiate a *pull* to retrieve the most recent version and *push* her own changes. These allow the user to work productively offline on the up-to-date version and prevent any potential data-loss. Thus, the application itself can achieve reversibility as the connectivity of the underlying network is restored, and the user is able to predict the behavior of the system. For example, the application (e.g., real-time collaborative editing) can adapt the philosophy of exponential back-off as TCP congestion algorithm, which is now brought up to the user level in terms of phase. Further, the underlying node can adapt its maintenance to the current phase. For example, when a node is in P_S phase, an efficient strategy like correction-on-* is sufficient. As the node faces a transition to P_{L1}, it can turn on a more resilient strategy, like PS.

6   Related Work

We briefly summarize the relevant work on self management in SONs and phase transitions. Krishnamurthy et al. in [16] use fluid model approach to analyze the probability of network disconnection and the fraction of incorrect pointers (successor and fingers) in Chord under churn. In their follow-up work [17], they use master-equation of physics to do comparative analysis of periodic stabilization and correction-on-change under churn. Another analytical work [19] establishes a lower bound on the maintenance rate of a SON under churn in order to remain connected. In [8,9], a physics-inspired approach is used to analyze performance of Chord and also investigate about intensive variables (i.e., variables independent of system size) related to self-organization and self-repair. Design decisions such as self-tuning mechanisms are described in [5] for self-organization/self-adaptation of overlay networks. The analytical framework in [14] can be used to characterize the routing performance of SON under churn. Our empirical study can be seen as complementary to these analytical works.

Diligent search has failed to uncover any empirical work on phase transitions in SONs. However, we have found one analytical work [15] carried out for Chord that shows a critical point in the parameter space at which the system with high probability breaks down, i.e., efficient routing becomes impossible. Such phase transitions happen due to high churn and large link delays, resulting in a finite fraction of the connections to be always incorrect. In [6] phase transitions in unstructured P2P network are studied to identify resource-efficient operating points for various global properties. For power-law networks, [22] presents a decentralized monitoring algorithm where each node estimates global statistical parameters and influences them to optimize relevant network characteristics.

7   Conclusion

As *Structured Overlay Networks (SONs)* are a popular choice to implement large-scale distributed software systems, it is important to ensure their reversibility against harsh environments. We have defined *Reversibility* and experimentally demonstrated a reversible system. We have identified the necessary maintenance principles to achieve reversibility against *Churn*. We have proposed the concepts and semantics of *Phase*, *Phase Transition* and *Critical Point* in our context. Also, we show that a reversible system does reversible phase transitions, i.e., it "boils" to the gaseous state (becomes disconnected) when churn increases and "condenses" from gaseous back to solid phase as churn intensity goes down. We also identify the apparent "critical points" from the experiments while doing such transitions. Finally, we have presented an API to make the phase of a node explicit to the application layer and analyze the applications of our concepts of phase and phase transitions toward designing predictable and reversible systems.

This paper is only the first step; we intend to investigate further the analogy between phase in SONs and in physical systems. We will design an application that take advantage of our API to survive in extremely hostile environments. We also intend to gain more insights about the maintenance strategies.

References

1. Aberer, K., Alima, L.O., Ghodsi, A., Girdzijauskas, S., Hauswirth, M., Haridi, S.: The essence of P2P: a reference architecture for overlay networks. In: Proceedings of P2P (2005)
2. Aberer, K., Datta, A., Hauswirth, M.: Route maintenance overheads in DHT overlays. In: Proceedings of WDAS (2004)
3. Aikat, J., Kaur, J., Smith, F.D., Jeffay, K.: Variability in TCP round-trip times. In: Proceedings of ACM SIGCOMM IMC (2003)
4. Alima, L.O., El-Ansary, S., Brand, P., Haridi, S.: DKS (n, k, f): a family of low communication, scalable and fault-tolerant infrastructures for p2p applications. In: Proceedings of CCGrid (2003)
5. Apel, S., Böhm, K.: Self-organization in overlay networks. In: CAiSE Workshop on Adaptive and Self-Managing Enterprise Applications (ASMEA) (2005)
6. Banaei-Kashani, F., Shahabi, C.: Criticality-based analysis and design of unstructured peer-to-peer networks as "complex systems". In: Proceedings of CCGrid (2003)
7. Dijkstra, E.W.: Self-stabilizing systems in spite of distributed control. Commun. ACM 17(11), 643–644 (1974)
8. El-Ansary, S., Aurell, E., Brand, P., Haridi, S.: Experience with a physics-style approach for the study of self properties in structured overlay networks. In: SELF-STAR: International Workshop on Self-* Properties in Complex Information Systems (2004)
9. El-Ansary, S., Aurell, E., Haridi, S.: A physics-inspired performance evaluation of a structured peer-to-peer overlay network. In: Proceedings of PDCN (2005)
10. Freedman, M.J., Lakshminarayanan, K., Rhea, S., Stoica, I.: Non-transitive connectivity and DHTs. In: Proceedings of WORLDS (2005)
11. Ghodsi, A.: Distributed k-ary system: algorithms for distributed hash tables. Ph.D. thesis, KTH, Sweden (2006)
12. Gummadi, K., Gummadi, R., Gribble, S., Ratnasamy, S., Shenker, S., Stoica, I.: The impact of DHT routing geometry on resilience and proximity. In: Proceedings of ACM SIGCOMM (2003)
13. Jelasity, M., Babaoglu, O.: T-Man: gossip-based overlay topology management. In: Brueckner, S.A., Di Marzo Serugendo, G., Hales, D., Zambonelli, F. (eds.) ESOA 2005. LNCS (LNAI), vol. 3910, pp. 1–15. Springer, Heidelberg (2006)
14. Kong, J.S., Bridgewater, J.S.A., Roychowdhury, V.P.: Resilience of structured P2P systems under churn: the reachable component method. Comput. Commun. 31, 2109–2123 (2008)

15. Krishnamurthy, S., Ardelius, J.: An analytical framework for the performance evaluation of proximity-aware structured overlays. Technical report, SICS, Sweden (2008)

16. Krishnamurthy, S., El-Ansary, S., Aurell, E., Haridi, S.: An analytical study of a structured overlay in the presence of dynamic membership. IEEE/ACM TON **16**(4), 814–825 (2008)

17. Krishnamurthy, S., El-Ansary, S., Aurell, E., Haridi, S.: Comparing maintenance strategies for overlays. In: Proceedings of PDP (2008)

18. Leitao, J., Pereira, J., Rodrigues, L.: Epidemic broadcast trees. In: SRDS 2007 (2007)

19. Liben-Nowell, D., Balakrishnan, H., Karger, D.: Analysis of the evolution of peer-to-peer systems. In: Proceedings of PODC (2002)

20. Mejías, B.: Beernet: A relaxed approach to the design of scalable systems with self-managing behaviour and transactional robust storage. Ph.D. thesis, UCL, Belgium (2010)

21. Paul, R.R., Van Roy, P., Vlassov, V.: Interaction between network partitioning and churn in a self-healing structured overlay network. In: Proceedings of ICPADS (2015)

22. Scholtes, I., Botev, J., Höhfeld, A., Schloss, H., Esch, M.: Awareness-driven phase transitions in very large scale distributed systems. In: Proceedings of SASO (2008)

23. Shafaat, T.M.: Partition tolerance and data consistency in structured overlay networks. Ph.D. thesis, KTH, Sweden (2013)

24. Stoica, I., Morris, R., Karger, D., Kaashoek, F., Balakrishnan, H.: Chord: A scalable peer-to-peer lookup service for internet applications. In: Proceedings of ACM SIGCOMM (2001)

25. Wikipedia. Phase (matter) (2016). https://en.wikipedia.org/wiki/Phase_(matter)

Verification of Common Business Rules in BPMN Process Models

Anass Rachdi[✉], Abdeslam En-Nouaary, and Mohamed Dahchour

Institut National des Postes et Télécommunications (INPT), Rabat, Morocco
anass.rach@gmail.com

Abstract. BPMN is an adopted standard used in industry for modeling business processes. However it is not provided with a formal semantics, limiting the possibility of analysis to informal approaches such as observation. In this paper, we present a formal approach that detects business rules violations using the Business Rule Language (BRL) which helps us express many common types of business rules that could be verified by a Depth-First Search algorithm adapted for the BPMN standard.

Keywords: Business process modeling · BPMN · Business rule language · Verification and validation · Depth-first search

1 Introduction

Nowadays Information Systems have become a vital component that contributes to organizations success since they assure automatic execution of several activities that are included in organizations business processes. These processes describe business rules that are intended to constrain some aspect of business and always resolve to either true or false. However, most of the processes that implement these rules are modeled using informal graphical notations such as BPMN (Business Process Management and Notation) which limits business rules verification to informal methods such as inspection. Formal methods help us avoid flow control anomalies, data flow errors as well as Business rules violations. Since many proposals have addressed the control and/or data flow problems [4–7], we will focus in this paper on formal methods that deal with business rules verification issue. In order to formally detect some violations in BPMN diagrams, we have to extract a formal model that respects the specifications on which the initial model was based. The approach we have taken is different from existing ones [3] for it gathers the most important dimensions that have to be found in a functional analysis which are: Resources, Tasks, Agents and Time. Our approach consists of two main steps. Firstly, we extract a formal process schema from the BPMN model, Secondly, we verify that the given Business rules are all respected based on the obtained process schema.

This rest of the paper is organized as follows: In Sect. 2 we provide definitions and notations of BPMN, Common business rules, BRL (Business Rule Language), while Sect. 3 presents our contribution for the analysis of BPMN

© Springer International Publishing AG 2016
P.A. Abdulla and C. Delporte-Gallet (Eds.): NETYS 2016, LNCS 9944, pp. 334–339, 2016.
DOI: 10.1007/978-3-319-46140-3_27

models by proposing an algorithm that detects different violations of common business rules [1]. Finally, Sect. 4 concludes the paper and presents future work.

2 Background

2.1 Business Process Management Notation (BPMN)

In this subsection, we give BPMN a formal definition [2] that takes into consideration most of its components (see Fig. 1).

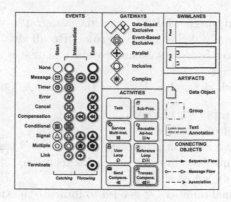

Fig. 1. BPMN elements

Definition 1 (Core BPMN Process): A core BPMN process is a tuple $P = (O_P, SF_P, Data_P, Swi_P, InputSpe_P, DataStates_P)$ where:

- O_P is a set of flow objects which can be partitioned into disjoint sets of activities A_P, events E_P, and gateways G_P, [4]
- $Data_P$ is a set of Data types which can be partitioned into disjoint sets of Data objects DO_P, Messages $Mess_P$ and Flow objects properties PR_P.
- Swi_P is a set of swimlanes which includes Pools Poo_P and lanes within pools Lan_P. Pools Poo_P can be divided into single pools $Poos_P$ (without lanes) and pools with lanes $Poow_P$.
- $SF_P \subseteq O_P \times O_P$ is a set of sequence flows.
- $InputSpe_P \subseteq ((T_P \cup E_P) \times Data_P)$ is the relation between a task and its required data that is defined in the task InputOutputspecification [2] or in the events properties.
- $DataStates_P$ is a set of data states which are related to $Data_P$.
- $Stat_P : InputSpe_P \rightarrow DataStates_P$ is the relation between a pair (task/data) and the data state related to $Data_P$.
- $Tim_P : A_P \rightarrow \mathbb{Q}_{\geq 0}$ is a function assigning a positive rational number which represents the activity's duration. [8].

A core BPMN process P is a directed graph with nodes (objects) O_P and arcs (sequence flows) SF_P. Output nodes of x are given by $out(x) = \{y \in O_P \mid x SF_P y\}$ [4].

2.2 Common Business Rules and Business Rule Language (BRL)

Common Business Rules. Most of the common business rules that we encounter in organizations and enterprises are of the following nature [1]:

- Task-Order Rules: Rules that prohibit or urge a certain Task Order.
- Resources State-Task rules: Rules that urge resources to be in a certain state in order to guarantee a correct execution of tasks.
- Rules that prescribe or prohibit certain task assignments to agents.

Business Rule Language (BRL). In this paragraph, we define the BRL which is used to formally define Business rules. Recall that Business processes description is based on process schema, events and traces of tasks, which are defined in the following:

A process schema is defined as $P_{Sch} = (\text{Ta, Re, } \beta, \text{ A, } \mathbb{Q}, \text{ S})$ where [1]:

- Ta is a finite non-empty set of tasks;
- Re describes the set of resources;
- $\beta \subseteq (\text{Ta} \times \text{Re})$ the relationship between resources and tasks. It indicates the resources that are involved in a certain task execution;
- A is finite non-empty set of agents;
- $\mathbb{Q}$ is the set of rational numbers, it is used to indicate the time the event starts;
- S is a set of all states of resources.

We define EV_{Sch} over a process schema P_{Sch} as a part of the Cartesian product of Ta, A and $\mathbb{Q}$. Event properties are defined as $P_S = \{\text{task, agent, starttime}\} \cup$ Re. Properties values can be defined as $V_S = \text{Ta} \cup \text{A} \cup \mathbb{Q} \cup \text{S}$ [1]. For task order rules, Duration is used to determine the endtime of events (end time = start time + duration). A trace δ over a process schema P_{Sch} is a finite set of events over P_{Sch}.

The syntax of the BRL, the business rule language we present here, is defined by the following abstract grammar

$$E ::= \neg E \mid (E \wedge E) \mid X.P \mid (E = E) \mid (E < E) \mid (X = X) \mid$$
$$\mathbb{Q} \mid A \mid Ta \mid S \mid (E + E) \mid (E.E).$$

Where E represent expressions that return a property value (An expression is called a formula if it returns boolean) and X is a countably finite set of variables that will be used to refer to events. A variable binding is defined as a partial function $\Gamma : X \rightarrow EV_{Sch}$. For expressions $e \in E$ the semantics are defined by the proposition $\delta, \Gamma \vdash e \Rightarrow v$ which states that the value of e is $v \in V_S$ for the trace δ and the variable binding Γ. Let us not that the proposition can involve several events from the trace δ.

3   Our Approach for BPMN Model Analysis

As mentioned so far, BPMN is an adopted standard used for modeling business processes. However, BPMN is informal and leaves room for inconsistencies [9] about the execution of business processes being modeled. Hence, we need to define semantics for BPMN in order to analyze business processes properly. Our analysis will be focused on the common business rules mentioned above. These rules will be expressed using The BRL. Our approach for the analysis of BPMN models basically consists of two main steps which are explained in the following subsections:

3.1   Extracting a Process Schema from BPMN Model

In order to express formally the business rules that are related to the BPMN model, we have to extract a Process schema based on BPMN definition we have given in the previous section. We present, in the following, the process schema extracted from BPMN elements (Table 1):

Table 1. Process Schema extracted from BPMN elements

BPMN	Process schema
$A_P \cup E_P$	Ta: Tasks
$Data_P$	Re: Resources
$InputSpe_P \subseteq ((A_P \cup E_P) \times Data_P)$	$\beta \subseteq (\text{Ta} \times \text{Re})$
$Poos_P \cup Lan_P$	A: Agents
$DataStates_P$	S: Resource states

3.2   Runing Business Rules Analysis Algorithm

The algorithm used to verify business rules violations is shown below. Once we extract a process schema from the BPMN model. We start executing the algorithm by adding the start event (with its properties) to the trace. Then, the algo goes through all the paths by checking for each new event encountered in a path if businessrules are respected. To avoid loops and guarantee the algorithm's termination, a tracehistory variable is created to record all the traces that have taken place during the execution. Therefore the sametrace can not repeated twice. If for some δ and some event ev $\in EV_{Sch}$,

$$\exists \text{ ev } \in EV_{Sch} \text{ such that } \exists \phi \in \Phi : \neg (\delta \cup \{\text{ev}\}) \vdash \phi$$

Then we know that the event ev present a violation of one or many business rules. Consequently, its properties should be reviewed in the model

---

Algorithm 1. Algorithm for the Business rules Analysis of BPMNmodels

---

1: **procedure** BUSINESS RULES ANALYSIS((P,Φ))
  ▷ P is composed of ($A_P \cup E_P \cup G_P$), ($Data_P$), ($Poos_P \cup Lan_P$), ($DataStates_P$) (SF_P) while $\Phi = \{BR_i\}$ i $\in$ 1,....n with n is the number of business rules to be verified.
  ▷ Constitute the schema process $P_{Sch} = $ (Ta, Re, β, A, $\mathbb{Q}$, S) corresponding to the BPMN Process and according to the Table 1
2:    Tracehistory $\leftarrow \emptyset$ ▷ keeps track of all traces,it is used to avoid loops.
3:    Violations $\leftarrow \emptyset$ ▷ Violation=(event ev ,trace δ, business rule ϕ)
4:    Event $\leftarrow$ es,   ▷ Initialize the Variable Event with start event es
5:    Add es to δ and δ to Tracehistory
6:    BrowseBPMNModel(es, δ)   ▷ Main function

7: **function** BROWSEBPMNMODEL(flow object F_O , trace δ)
  ▷ a recursive function That verifies through all paths that common business rules are verified
8:    **for** (i $\in$ Out(F_O)) **do**
9:        δ' = Gettrace (F_O, δ),
10:        **if** (i $\in A_P \cup E_P$) **then**
11:            b = contains (Gettrace(i, δ'$\cup$ i), Tracehistory)
12:            **if** (b) **then**
13:                go to the next iteration in for loop
14:            Event $\leftarrow$ i, Enricheventproperties (Event)
15:            add Event to δ'
16:            VerifyBusinessRules (Φ , δ')
17:        BrowseBPMNModel(i, δ')

18: **function** OUT(flow object F_O)   ▷ returns all output nodes of F_O
19: **function** GETTRACE(flow object F_O , trace δ)   ▷ returns a new trace $\delta \doteq \delta - $ all events (BPMN tasks and events) that came after F_O if the latter exists in the trace, otherwise it returns δ
20: **function** CONTAINS(trace , Tracehistory listr)   ▷ verifies if the trace has taken place in the BPMN model
21: **function** ENRICHEVENTPROPERTIES(event ev)   ▷ enriches the event properties namely starttime, agent,task and duration.
22: **function** VERIFYBUSINESSRULES(List of business rules Φ , trace δ)   ▷ verifies that business rules contained in a list Φ are satisfied for the trace δ, note that last(δ) returns the last event of δ
23:    **for** ($BR_i \in \Phi$) **do**
24:        **if** ($\neg(\delta \vdash BR_i)$) **then**
25:            add (Last(δ), δ, BR_i) to Violations.

4   Conclusion and Future Work

In this paper, we proposed a formal analysis of BPMN models based on Process schema/BRL. The suggested approach allows us to have a more complete analysis that verifies functional aspects of the designed process. In our future work, we intend to include other dimensions such as Task Type, Agent role which can extend the area of covered business rules.

References

1. van Hee, K., Hidders, J., Houben, G.J., Paredaens, J.: Abstracting common business rules to Petri nets. In: Enterprise Information (2010)
2. Object Management Group: Business Process Modeling Notation (BPMN) Specification. Final adopted specification (2011)
3. Sun, W.: Design and implementation of a BPMN to PROMELA translator. M.Sc. dissertation project (2012)
4. Dijkman, R.M., Dumas, M., Ouyang, C.: Formal semantics and analysis of BPMN process models using Petri nets. Technical report, Queensland University of Technology (2007)
5. Awad, A., Decker, G., Lohmann, N.: Diagnosing and repairing data anomalies in process models. In: The 5th International Workshop on Business Process Design (2010)
6. Wong, P.Y.H., Gibbons, J.: A process semantics for BPMN. In: Liu, S., Araki, K. (eds.) ICFEM 2008. LNCS, vol. 5256, pp. 355–374. Springer, Heidelberg (2008)
7. von Stackelberg, S., et al.: Detecting data-flow errors in BPMN 2.0. Open J. Inf. Syst. 1, 1–19 (2014)
8. Rachdi, A., Ennouaary, A., Dahchour, M.: Analysis of BPMN process models using time Petri nets. In: Proceedings of the 2014 INTIS Conference (2014)
9. Aagesen, G., Krogstie, J.: BPMN 2.0 for modeling business processes. In: vom Brocke, J., Rosemann, M., et al. (eds.) Handbook on Business Process Management 1. International Handbooks on Information Systems, pp. 219–250. Springer, Heidelberg (2015)

Is Youtube Popularity Prediction a Good Way to Improve Caching Efficiency?

Nada Sbihi[(✉)] and Mounir Ghogho

Université Internationale de Rabat -
TICLab Technopolis Rabat-Shore Rocade Rabat-Salé, Rabat, Morocco
{nada.sbihi,mounir.ghogho}@uir.ac.ma

Abstract. The use of IP networks is nowadays the de-facto way to telecommunicate information. As IP networks become more and more content-centric, in order to preserve the quality of traffic, operators need not only to continue to invest in infrastructure and bandwidth but also to develop intelligent networking techniques to reduce bandwidth consumption. Caching popular content at the edge of the network is one of such techniques. In this paper, we use YouTube to evaluate the performance of a number of popularity prediction techniques in terms of hit success rate.

1 Introduction

The number of objects in the IP networks continues to increase exponentially[1]. Hence, to reduce bandwidth consumption, it is of paramount importance to invest in caches, especially since the cost of memory is lower than that of bandwidth [5]. With the expanding predictive techniques and machine learning, a new replacement policy emerged: Predicted Least Frequently Used (P-LFU). As the prediction task requires a learning period, it is not clear whether P-LFU can offer better performance than purely reactive caching strategies.

2 Popularity Prediction

The approach to adopt for the prediction of popularity depends on the purpose of the prediction task. If the prediction is intended to measure the suitability of broadcasting an advertisement in a video, next-day popularity prediction is appropriate. If the goal is to develop strategies for caching, hourly popularity prediction may be required, especially for highly popular and dynamic content providers such as Youtube. In November 2014, more than 300 h of video were uploaded on Youtube every minute[2].

---

[1] Cisco Visual Networking Index: Forecast and Methodology, 2014–2019 White Paper.
[2] http://www.webrankinfo.com/dossiers/youtube.

© Springer International Publishing AG 2016
P.A. Abdulla and C. Delporte-Gallet (Eds.): NETYS 2016, LNCS 9944, pp. 340–344, 2016.
DOI: 10.1007/978-3-319-46140-3_28

2.1   The Dataset

Using google Youtube API we collected the viewing statistics for more than 3000 videos. We first retrieved the videos IDs, and then we launched a script that automatically returns the number of views for each video every hour.

2.2   Prediction Methodology

We denote by $N(v,t)$ the number of views for video v at time t. Szabo and Huberman [3] found a linear relationship between the number of views at time t_1 and the number of views at time t_2 ($t_1 < t_2$). Richier et al. [1] assumed that the popularity curves to be functions of time that can be categorized into a small number of classes represented by relatively simple mathematical expressions. The use of P-LFU policy seems more appropriate than P-LRU (Least Recently Used) since it is easier to predict the number of views than the queries order. We aim to predict of the number of views for each video at time t_1 based on the number of corresponding views at time $t_1 - w$. If a window of one day is selected for prediction, the linear regression seems accurate (see Fig. 1). However, as our aim from the popularity prediction task is caching, smaller prediction windows are required. The fitted linear regression model seems less convincing four hourly predictions (i.e. w = 1 h)). It is therefore essential to explore other prediction models.

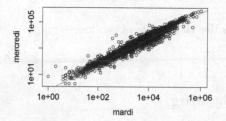
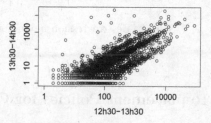

(a) Linear regression between succes-   (b) Linear regression between successive days   sive hours

Fig. 1. Linear regression with different windows

2.3   Mathematical Models for Prediction

To characterize the number of video views, we used five models:

- Logarithmic model: $\hat{N}(v,t) = a * log(t) + b$, this model is the result of our observations of several videos viewcounts.
- Linear model: $\hat{N}(v,t) = a * t + b$, it has been proposed in [2], and corresponds to some observations.
- Power law model: $\hat{N}(v,t) = a * t^\alpha$, this model has been proposed in [6].

- Exponential model: $\hat{N}(v,t) = \alpha * (1 - exp(-\lambda * t))$, this model has been proposed by Famaey et al. [2] and Richier et al. [1].
- Gompertz model: $\hat{N}(v,t) = a * exp(-b * exp(-c * t))$, this model has been proposed by Richier et al. [1]. It is used as a model for some cancerous tumors growth and also as products diffusion model in the market.

For each video, we fit the five models by minimizing the mean squared error (MSE). Figure 2 displays the best fitted regression model for two videos. The best model for the video viewcount may differ from one video to another. It is worth pointing out that the fitted parameters for each model have been obtained using the Levenberg-Marquard algorithm [4].

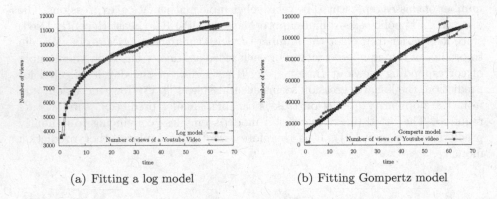

(a) Fitting a log model   (b) Fitting Gompertz model

Fig. 2. Best regression model for the viewcounts of two videos

3   Replacement Policies for Caching

3.1   LFU vs P-LFU

We compare the following predictions methods:

- The predicted number of views at time t_{i+1} is equal to the number of views at the current time, t_i, i.e. $\hat{N}(v, t_{i+1}) = N(v, t_i)$.
- The number of views is predicted using the best mathematical model out of the five models described above, i.e. the model corresponding to the minimum value of the MSE.

Figure 3 shows the MSEs of the two prediction schemes. We notice that the mathematical prediction models do not provide better results than the prediction method which merely assumes $\hat{N}(v, t_{i+1}) = N(v, t_i)$, at least for the first 40 h. These results call into question the relevance of using prediction to implement caching mechanisms. The number of videos arriving every hour is so important that a pending maturity of the video to use the models seems doubtful.

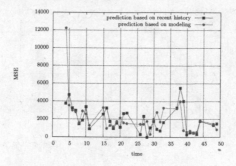

Fig. 3. Mean Squared Error vs time

3.2   Virtual LRU

We use a virtual cache in addition to the actual cache. The virtual cache only stores the IDs of videos whereas the actual cache stores the objects physically. We choose the size of the virtual cache to be equal to the size of the real cache. We describe this new policy next. We first present the algorithm lrucache used in LRU cache. Now we use the function lrucache to define the VLRU policy.

if $i \in C$ then
  | place i at the head of C;
else
  | delete the object least recently used and copy object i at the head of C;
end

Algorithm 1: Lrucache(i,C)

if $i \in C$ OR $i \in VC$ then
  | lrucache(i,C)
end
lrucache(i,VC)

Algorithm 2: VLRU algorithm

3.3   Results and Discussion

We simulate three replacement policies using the real dataset that we have collected. Figure 4 depicts the hit rate of different policies versus the cache size. The VLRU policy produces a better hit rate than LFU.

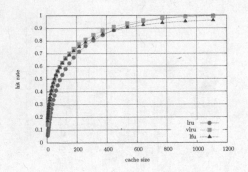

Fig. 4. Hit rate for different replacement policies (LRU, LFU, VLRU) vs cache size

4   Conclusion

The prediction of popularity does not seem to provide an improvement of the performance of caching strategies. This observation was made using Youtube. However, we do not view these results as conclusive, because there may well be better prediction/learning techniques that we have considered in our work.

References

1. Richier, C., Altman, E., Elazouzi, R., Jimenez, T., Linares, G., Portilla, Y.: Bio-inspired models for characterizing YouTube viewcout. In: 2014 IEEE/ACM International Conference on Advances in Social Networks Analysis and Mining (ASONAM), pp. 297–305. IEEE, August 2014
2. Famaey, J., Wauters, T., De Turck, F.: On the merits of popularity prediction in multimedia content caching. In: 2011 IFIP/IEEE International Symposium on Integrated Network Management (IM), pp. 17–24. IEEE, May 2011
3. Szabo, G., Huberman, B.A.: Predicting the popularity of online content. Commun. ACM **53**(8), 80–88 (2010)
4. Levenberg, K.: A method for the solution of certain non linear problems in least squares. Q. Appl. Math. **2**, 164–168 (1944)
5. Roberts, J., Sbihi, N.: Exploring the memory-bandwidth tradeoff in an information-centric network. In: 2013 25th International on Teletraffic Congress (ITC), pp. 1–9. IEEE, September 2013
6. Avramova, Z., Wittevrongel, S., Bruneel, H., De Vleeschauwer, D.: Analysis, modeling of video popularity evolution in various online video content systems: power-law versus exponential decay. In: First International Conference on Evolving Internet, INTERNET 2009, pp. 95–100. IEEE, August 2009

Waiting in Concurrent Algorithms

Gadi Taubenfeld[✉]

The Interdisciplinary Center, P.O. Box 167, 46150 Herzliya, Israel
tgadi@idc.ac.il

Abstract. Between the two extremes, *lock-based* algorithms, which involve "a lot of waiting", and *wait-free* algorithms, which are "free of locking and waiting", there is an interesting spectrum of different levels of waiting. This unexplored spectrum is formally defined and its properties are investigated. New progress conditions, called k-waiting, for $k \geq 0$, which are intended to capture the "amount of waiting" of processes in asynchronous concurrent algorithms, are introduced. To illustrate the utility of the new conditions, they are used to derive new lower and upper bounds, and impossibility results for well-known basic problems such as consensus, election, renaming and mutual exclusion. Furthermore, the relation between waiting and fairness is explored.

Keywords: Synchronization · Wait-freedom · Locks · Enabled process · Enabling step · k-waiting · Consensus · Election · Renaming · Mutual exclusion

1 Introduction

Concurrent access to a data structure shared among several processes must be synchronized in order to avoid interference between conflicting operations. Mutual exclusion locks are the de facto mechanism for concurrency control on concurrent data structures: a process accesses the data structure only inside a critical section code, within which the process is guaranteed exclusive access. However, using locks may degrade the performance of synchronized concurrent applications, as it enforces processes to wait for a lock to be released.

A promising approach, which overcomes some of these difficulties, is the design of concurrent data structures and algorithms which avoid locking. The advantages of such algorithms are that they are not subject to priority inversion, are resilient to failures, and do not suffer significant performance degradation from scheduling preemption, page faults or cache misses. Although desirable, such implementations are often complex, difficult to design, inefficient, memory consuming and require the use of strong synchronization primitives.

Implementations which use locks are usually easier to program than implementations which avoid locking and waiting. Such lock-based implementations usually require "a lot of waiting", compared to implementations which avoid waiting, and may force operations that do not conflict to wait for one another, precluding disjoint-access parallelism.

© Springer International Publishing AG 2016
P.A. Abdulla and C. Delporte-Gallet (Eds.): NETYS 2016, LNCS 9944, pp. 345–360, 2016.
DOI: 10.1007/978-3-319-46140-3_29

In this paper, we show that between these two extremes: "a lot of waiting" (i.e., locks) and "free of locking and waiting", there is an interesting spectrum of different levels of waiting. We identify and formally define this unexplored spectrum, by introducing new progress conditions, called k-waiting, for $k \geq 0$, which are intended to capture the "amount of waiting" of processes in asynchronous concurrent algorithms.

Intuitively, these new progress conditions can be described as follows. A process is *enabled*, if it does not need to wait for an action by any other process in order to complete its operation. A step is an *enabling* step, if after executing that step at least one process which was disabled becomes enabled. For a given $k \geq 0$, the *k-waiting* progress condition guarantees that every process that has a pending operation, will always become enabled once at most k enabling steps have been executed.

To illustrate the utility of the new progress conditions, we use them to derive new lower and upper bounds, and impossibility results for well-known basic problems such as consensus, election, renaming and mutual exclusion. Furthermore, the relation between waiting and fairness is explored.

2   The k-waiting Progress Conditions

In this section, we discuss and formally define the new notion of k-waiting. An implementation of an operation may involve several basic steps. A basic step, like reading, updating or testing, may involve accessing a shared memory location. An implementation of each operation of a concurrent data structure is divided into two continuous sections of code: the *doorway* code and the *body* code. When a process invokes an operation it first executes the doorway code and then executes the body code. The *doorway*, by definition, must be *wait-free*: its execution requires only bounded number of steps and hence always terminates.

A process executes a sequence of steps as defined by its algorithm. A *beginning* process is a process that is about to start executing the first step of some operation. An *active* process, is a process that has already executed the first step of some operation, but has not completed that operation yet. A process has *passed* the doorway of a given operation, if it has finished the doorway code and reached the body code of that operation. The following definitions refer to both beginning and active processes.

A strongly enabled process: A process is *strongly enabled* at the end of a given execution r, if, at the end of any possible extension of r, it does not need to wait for an action by any other process in order to complete its operation, nor can an action by any other process prevent it from doing so. Thus, by executing sufficiently many steps, it will be able to complete its operation, independently of the actions of the other processes.[1]

---

[1] In the case of a beginning process, "its operation" means the operation that the process is about to start executing.

Being strongly enabled is a *stable* property, if a process is strongly enabled at some point then, by definition, it must also be strongly enabled at any later point during the operation.

A weakly enabled process: A process is *weakly enabled* at the end of a given execution r, if, at the end of any possible extension of r, it does not need to wait for an action by any other process in order to complete its operation, however, actions by other processes (while they occur) may prevent it from doing so. Thus, at the end of *any* extension of r, by executing sufficiently many steps, the process will be able to complete its operation, provided it is not interfered (from some point on) by actions of other processes.

Put another way, process p is *weakly enabled* at the end of a given execution r, if at the end of any possible extension of r, when p runs alone it eventually terminates. We notice that once a process becomes weakly enabled, it cannot later become disabled. If a process is weakly enabled at some point then, by definition, it must be weakly or strongly enabled at any later point during the operation. Thus being weakly enabled is also a stable property. A strongly enabled process is, by definition, also weakly enabled. For an execution (run) r and a step s, we denote by $r; s$ the execution obtained by extending r with the step s.

An enabling step: A step is a *strong enabling* (resp. *weak enabling*) step, at the end of a given execution, if after executing that step at least one process which was not strongly (resp. weakly) enabled becomes strongly (resp. weakly) enabled. More formally, s is a strong (resp. weak) enabling step at the end of execution r, if there exists at least one process, say p, such that p is not strongly (resp. weakly) enabled at the end of r and p is strongly (resp. weakly) enabled at the end of $r; s$.

We notice that a strong enabling step is not necessarily also a weak enabling step, and vice versa. A single strong (resp. weak) enabling step may cause several processes, not necessarily just one, to become strongly (resp. weakly) enabled. If s is a strong (resp. weak) enabling step *at* the end of r, and r' is an extension of $r; s$, then we say that s is a strongly (resp. weakly) enabling step *in* r'. For two executions r and r', we use the notation $r \leq r'$ to denote the fact that r' is an extension of r. When $r \leq r'$, we denote by $(r' - r)$ the suffix of r' obtained by removing r from r'. The following definition of a new progress condition is central to our investigation.

k-**waiting:** For $k \geq 0$, the strong (resp. weak) k-*waiting* progress condition guarantees that *every* process, that has *passed* its doorway, will always become strongly (resp. weakly) enabled once at most k strong (resp. weak) enabling steps have been executed. More formally, the strong (resp. weak) k-*waiting* progress condition guarantees that, for every two executions r and r' and for every process p, if (1) p has passed its doorway at the end of r, (2) $r \leq r'$, (3) p has not completed its operation during $(r' - r)$, and (4) at $(r' - r)$ there are (at least) k steps which are strong (resp. weak) enabling steps, *then* p is strongly (resp. weakly) enabled at the end of r'.

We notice that an algorithm that satisfies strong k-waiting, does not necessarily also satisfies weak k-waiting, and vice versa. To simplify the presentation, in the sequel, we will omit the type of a k-waiting progress condition (i.e., strong or weak), the type of an enabling step or the type of an enabling process, when it can be understood from the context or when the statement applies in both cases.

The k-waiting progress conditions capture the time a process may have to wait before it becomes enabled. Consider an implementation of a data structure which is protected by a single lock and assume that n processes access it simultaneously. In such a scenario, each strong enabling step enables exactly one process to acquire the lock, complete its operation and release the lock. The last process captures the lock, after at least, strong $n - 1$ enabling steps have been executed. Thus, such a lock-based data structure at best, satisfies strong $(n - 1)$-waiting.

We point out that k-waiting does *not* guarantee that every process that has passed through its doorway becomes enabled no later than when k other processes have become enabled. The reason for that is that a single enabling step may cause several processes to become enabled. For a given k-waiting algorithm, the lower k is, the higher is the potential that the algorithm, when executed, will exhibit a high concurrency behaviour. However, as in the case of using locks, algorithms which satisfy k-waiting for $k > 0$, may require processes to wait for one another, and thus, in some scenarios slow or stopped processes may prevent other processes from ever completing their operations.

In some scenarios wait-free algorithms (i.e., algorithms in which all the processes are always strongly enabled), preform better than lock-based algorithms and visa versa. For example, in scenarios when a process needs to hold a lock only for very short time, when there are no failures, no scheduling preemption and almost no page faults or cache misses, fine-grained lock-based algorithms might perform better. The decision whether to use a wait-free or a lock-based implementation depends on the assumption regarding the environment (i.e., the expectations regarding, failures, page faults, etc.). Similarly, one should not expect that for $k < k'$, a k-waiting algorithm would always (in all possible scenarios) preform better than the corresponding a k'-waiting algorithm.

As in the case of wait-free or lock-based algorithms, when evaluating a k-waiting algorithm, it is not enough just to identify what progress condition it satisfies, it is also necessary to find out its time (step) complexity. The number of steps before and after enabling events can be arbitrary large, the k-waiting progress condition only gives an indication of how much time a process will have to wait without making progress and does not give any indication of its execution time while not waiting. Put another way, k-waiting is not intended to capture the overall time required for executing an operation, only the waiting time interval during the execution of an operation.

3   Computational Model and Basic Observations

Our model of computation consists of an asynchronous collection of n deterministic processes that communicate via shared objects. Asynchrony means that there is no assumption on the relative speeds of the processes. In most of the cases we considered, the shared objects are registers which supports read and write operations. A register can be atomic or non-atomic. With an *atomic* register, it is assumed that operations on the register occur in some definite order. That is, reading or writing an atomic register is an indivisible action. When reading or writing a non-atomic register, a process may be reading a register while another is writing into it, and in that event, the value returned to the reader is arbitrary. We will consider only atomic registers. In the sequel, by *registers* we mean *atomic* registers.

An event corresponds to an atomic step performed by a process. For example, the events which correspond to accessing registers are classified into two types: read events which may not change the state of the register, and write events which update the state of a register but do not return a value. A (global) state of an algorithm is completely described by the values of the registers and the values of the location counters of all the processes. A run is a sequence of alternating states and events.

A process executes correctly its algorithm until it (possibly) crashes. After it has crashed it executes no more steps. Given a run, a process that crashes is said to be *faulty* in that run, otherwise it is *correct*. In an asynchronous system there is no way to distinguish between a faulty and a very slow process. We will consider both the case where processes never fail and the case where processes may fail by crashing.

Several progress conditions have been proposed for data structures which avoid locking, and in which processes may fail by crashing. *Wait-freedom* guarantees that every active process will always be able to complete its pending operations in a finite number of its own steps [12]. *Non-blocking* (which is sometimes called lock-freedom) guarantees that *some* active process will always be able to complete its pending operations in a finite number of its own steps [15]. *Obstruction-freedom* guarantees that an active process will be able to complete its pending operations in a finite number of its own steps, if all the other processes "hold still" long enough [13].

Observation 1

(1) *An algorithm satisfies strong 0-waiting if and only if it satisfies wait-freedom.*
(2) *An algorithm satisfies weak 0-waiting if and only if it satisfies obstruction-freedom.*

Proof. (1) In a wait-free algorithm, by definition, every beginning process is strongly enabled. Thus, a wait-free algorithm satisfies strong 0-waiting. In a strong 0-waiting algorithm, by definition, every process that has passed its doorway is strongly enabled. Since the doorway is wait free, it follows that also every beginning process is strongly enabled. Thus, a strong 0-waiting algorithm satisfies wait-freedom. (2) In an obstruction-free algorithm, by definition, every beginning process is weakly enabled. Thus, an obstruction-free algorithm satisfies weak 0-waiting. In a weak 0-waiting algorithm, by definition, every process that has passed its doorway is weakly enabled. Since the doorway is wait free, it follows that also every beginning process is weakly enabled. Thus, a weak 0-waiting algorithm satisfies obstruction-freedom. □

Several progress conditions have been proposed for data structures, which may involve waiting in the context where processes never fail. *Livelock-freedom* guarantees that, in the absence of process failures, if a process is active, then *some* process must eventually complete its operation. A stronger property is *starvation-freedom* which guarantees that, in the absence of process failures, *every* active process must eventually complete its operation.

In a model where participation is required, every process must eventually become active and execute its code. A more interesting and practical situation is one in which participation is *not* required, as is usually assumed when solving resource allocation problems or when designing concurrent data structures. We *always* assume that participation is *not* required.

In general, wait-freedom is a strictly stronger progress condition than 0-waiting and starvation-freedom combined. However, this is not the case for $n = 2$.

Observation 2. *Any weak 0-waiting starvation-free algorithm for two processes is wait-free.*

Proof. Assume to the contrary that, there is a 0-waiting starvation-free algorithm for two processes which is not wait-free. Let the names of the two processes be p and q. Since the algorithm is 0-waiting and starvation-free, it follows that,

- By 0-waiting, if only p (resp. q) participates and p (resp. q) does not fail then p (resp. q) will eventually properly terminate.
- By 0-waiting, if both p and q participate and p does not fail but q fails then from some point on p will run alone and will eventually properly terminate.
- By 0-waiting, if both p and q participate and q does not fail but p fails then from some point on q will run alone and will eventually properly terminate.
- By starvation-freedom, if both p and q participate and non of them fails then both will eventually properly terminate.

The fact that in all the above runs, a correct participating process always properly terminates, implies that the implementation also satisfies wait-freedom for two processes. That is, the above runs are exactly the runs in which correct processes are required to terminate when wait-freedom is assumed. A contradiction. □

4 Consensus and Election

The *consensus* problem is to find a solution for n processes, where each process starts with an input value from some domain, and must choose some participating process' input as its output. All n processes together must choose the same output value. In the *election* problem each participating process should eventually output either 0 or 1 and terminate. At most one process may output 1, and in the absence of faults exactly one of the *participating* processes should output 1. The process which outputs 1 is the elected leader.

In [21], an election algorithm is presented, using $\lceil \log n \rceil + 1$ registers, which is correct under the following assumptions: (1) processes never fail, and (2) only the elected leader is required to terminate. A modified version of the election algorithm from [21], is used below for proving the following theorem,

Theorem 1. *There are strong and weak 2-waiting starvation-free consensus algorithms and strong and weak 2-waiting starvation-free election algorithms for $n \geq 2$ processes, using $\lceil \log n \rceil + 2$ registers.*

Proof. The consensus algorithm presented below uses the shared registers *turn* and *decision* and the array of registers $V[1..\lceil \log n \rceil]$. All these registers are initially 0, except for the *decision* register which is initially $\perp$. Also, for each process, the local variables *level* and j are used. The processes have unique identifiers. We will use the statement **await** *condition* as an abbreviation for **while** $\neg condition$ **do** *skip*.

A 2-WAITING STARVATION-FREE CONSENSUS:
process p's program with input value $input_p$.

```
function consensus;
1      turn := p;
2      for level := 1 to ⌈log n⌉ do
3          repeat
4              if decision ≠ ⊥ then return(decision) fi;
5              if turn ≠ p then
6                  for j := 1 to level − 1 do if V[j] = p then V[j] := 0 fi od;
7                  await(decision ≠ ⊥); return(decision) fi
8              until V[level] = 0;
9          V[level] := p;
10         if turn ≠ p then
11             for j := 1 to level do if V[j] = p then V[j] := 0 fi od;
12             await(decision ≠ ⊥); return(decision) fi
13     od;
14     decision := input_p; return(decision)
end_function
```

The process that is last to write to *turn* (line 1) attempts to become the leader and to force all the other processes to decide on its input value. It does so, by waiting for each of the registers $V[j]$ to be 0 (lines 3–8) and then sets the register to its id (line 9). A process becomes the leader if it manages to write its id into all the registers during the period that *turn* equals its id. Any process that notices that *turn* is no longer equals its id, gives up on becoming the leader, and erase any write it has made (lines 6 and 11). The leader writes its input value into *decision*, and all the processes decide on that value.

There are runs of the algorithm in which every process manages to set $\lceil \log n \rceil$ registers before discovering that another process has modified *turn*, and as a result has to set back to 0 some of the registers before terminating. Proving the correctness of the algorithm is rather challenging, due to the existence of such runs.

It is straightforward to use the above consensus algorithm for solving election. Each process uses its identifer as its input. The value that all the processes decide on in the consensus algorithm, identifies the leader.

A Detailed Correctness Proof of the 2-waiting Consensus Algorithm. The proof is an adaptation of the proof for the election algorithm from [21]. The fact that the algorithm uses $\lceil \log n \rceil + 2$ registers is obvious from inspecting the algorithm. In the following, the *leader* is the process that writes its input value in to the *decision* register (line 14). A process is at level k, when the value of its private *level* register is k.

Lemma 1 (Liveness). *In the absence of faults, at least one leader is elected.*

Proof Assume to the contrary that no leader is elected. Let r be an infinite run with no faults where no leader is elected, and let p be the last processes to write to *turn* in run r. Let q be the process with the highest value of *level* when p writes to *turn*. At some point q will notice that $turn \neq q$, and set back to 0, all the entries of the array V which equal to q. Repeat this argument with the new highest process. Thus, any entry of the array V which process p may wait on, will eventually be set back to 0, enabling p to proceed until it is elected. A contradiction.   □

Lemma 2. *For any $k \in \{1, \ldots, \lceil \log n \rceil\}$, out of all the processes that are in level k during a time interval where $V[k]$ continuously holds the value 0, at most one process can: (1) continue level $k+1$ or (2) change any register other than $V[k]$.*

Proof. Assume that a set of processes $p_1, \ldots, p_\ell$ are at level k, and during the time interval where $V[k]$ continuously holds the value 0, they all notice that $V[level] = 0$ when executing the until statement in line 8. One of these processes, say p_1, must be the last to update *turn*. If $k = 1$, each process in $\{p_2, \ldots, p_\ell\}$ will notice that *turn* is different from its id (line 10), possibly write 0 into $V[1]$, wait until a decision is made and return the decision value. Assume $k > 1$. Before p_1 has set *turn* to its id, each of the other processes at level k must have seen in level $k - 1$ that *turn* is equal to its id. This means that before any of the processes $p_2, \ldots, p_\ell$ could execute the assignment at line 9, p_1 has already set $V[1], \ldots, V[k-1]$ to its id. Thus, when each process at level k, other than p_1, executes the if statement in line 10, it finds out that *turn* is different from its id, possibly write 0 into $V[k]$, wait until a decision is made and return the decision value, without a need to write 0 to any of the registers $V[1], \ldots, V[k-1]$ (because it is assumed above that p_1 has already set $V[1], \ldots, V[k-1]$ to its id). Process p_1, may continue to level $k + 1$ or it notices that $turn \neq p_1$ and sets some or all of the registers $V[1], \ldots, V[k-1]$ to 0, but it is the only process, among the processes $p_1, \ldots, p_\ell$, that may set any register other than $V[k]$.   □

Lemma 3 (Safety). *At most one leader is elected.*

Proof. For proving the lemma, an accounting system of credits is used. Initially, the number of credits is $2n - 1$. New credits can not be created during the execution of the algorithm. The credit system ensures that a process acquires exactly 2^{k-1} credits before it can reach level k. Being elected is equivalent to reaching level $\log n + 1$. Thus, the credit system ensures that a process must acquire $2^{\log n + 1 - 1} = n$ credits before it can be elected. Once a process is elected, it may not release any of its credits. Thus, it is not possible for two processes to get elected.

W.l.o.g. it is assumed that n, the number of processes, is a power of 2. Initially, each process holds 1 credit, and each register $V[k]$ where $1 \leq k \leq \log n$ holds 2^{k-1} credits. Thus, the total number of credits is $n + \sum_{k=1}^{\log n} 2^{k-1} = 2n - 1$. As a results of an operation taken by a process credits may be transferred from a register to a process and vice versa. We list below all possible operations by processes and their effect:

- No credits are transferred when a process (1) checks the value of a register, (2) writes into *turn*, or (3) executes a *return* statement.
- When a process writes its id into register $V[k]$, changing $V[k]$'s value from 0 to its id, 2^{k-1} credits are transferred from $V[k]$ to that process. When a process writes 0 into register $V[k]$ which does not already holding 0, 2^{k-1} credits are transferred to $V[k]$ from that process.
- Let one or more processes notice that $V[k] = 0$. By Lemma 2, at most one of them can continue level $k+1$. Assume one of them continues to level $k+1$. By Lemma 2, the processes that do not continue to the next level can only execute $V[k] := 0$, transferring to $V[k]$ the 2^{k-1} credits they have by getting this far. Then 2^{k-1} credits are taken from $V[k]$, and are assigned to the process that continues to the next level, giving it the 2^k credits it needs for level $k+1$.
- Let one or more processes notice that $V[k] = 0$, and assume no one of them continues to level $k+1$. By Lemma 2, at most one of these processes, say process p, changes any register other than $V[k]$. As before, the remaining processes can transfer their credits by setting $V[k]$ to 0. Then, if p is the last to set $V[k]$, 2^{k-1} credits are taken from $V[k]$, and are assigned to p. Thus, p has 2^k credits available, 2^{k-1} credits from reaching level k, plus 2^{k-1} credits from $V[k]$. Setting to 0 every variable from $V[1]$ to $V[k]$ accounts for $2^k - 1$ credits (i.e., $\sum_{i=1}^{k} 2^{i-1} = 2^k - 1$), so p has enough credits and no new credits should be created by p when it sets to 0 multiple registers.

As already mentioned, initially, the number of credits is $2n - 1$. No new credits are created, and a process must acquire n credits before it can be elected. Once a process is elected, it may not release any of its credits. Thus, it is not possible for two processes to get elected. $\qquad\square$

Theorem 2 (Agreement and Validity). *All the participating processes decide on the same value, and this decision value is the input of a participating process.*

Proof. It follows from Lemmas 1 and 3, that exactly one leader is elected. The leader will eventually write its input value into the *decision* register, and all the participating will decide on that value. $\qquad\square$

Theorem 3 (Starvation-Freedom). *In the absence of faults, every partici-pating process eventually terminates.*

Proof. Once a leader is elected and sets the *decision* register to its input value, all correct participating processes will eventually find out that *decision* $\neq \perp$ and properly terminate. In the absence of faults, by Lemma 1, at least one leader is eventually elected, and thus all the participating processes eventually terminate.   □

Theorem 4 (2-waiting). *The consensus algorithm satisfies strong and weak 2-waiting.*

Proof. In every run there are at most two (strong or weak) enabling events. The first is the event after which the leader becomes enabled. (This can happen at most once since being enabled is a stable property.) The second event is when the leader sets the *decision* register to its input value (line 14), after which all the other processes immediately become enabled. In fact, in this particular algorithm in every run in which some process terminates, there are exactly two enabling events. Consider for example a run where process p runs alone until it is elected and terminates. The first enabling event is when the local variable *level* of p equals $\lceil \log n \rceil$ and p reads in Line 10 that $turn = p$. Before that read event all the processes are disabled, and after that read event p becomes (strongly) enabled (and all the other processes are still disabled). Once process p executes line 14, all the processes become enabled even though they haven't started yet. Hence, the consensus algorithm satisfies 2-waiting.

To prevent confusion, we point out that a process does not necessarily become weakly enabled after taking its first step. To see that, recall that being weakly enabled is a stable property. Assume that process p wakes up, runs alone, is elected but is suspended before setting *decision* to its input (in Line 14). At that point all the other processes, regardless of the number of steps they have taken so far, are disabled. Once process p executes line 14 all the other processes become enabled (also those that haven't taken any steps yet).   □

This completes the proof of Theorem 1. In [21], it has been proven that, even in the absence of faults, any election algorithm for n processes must use at least $\lceil \log n \rceil + 1$ registers. This lower bound holds also for consensus. Thus, Theorem 1 provides an almost tight space upper bound. It is known that there are no wait-free consensus or election algorithms, using registers [9,12,18,19]. Below we slightly generalize these known impossibility results for wait-free consensus and election.

Observation 3. *There are no weak 0-waiting starvation-free consensus or election algorithms for $n \geq 2$ processes, using registers.*

Proof. The result follows from Observation 2 and the known impossibility results that there are no *wait-free* consensus and election algorithms for two (or more) processes, using registers [9,12,18,19].   □

5   Adaptive Renaming

The renaming problem allows processes, with distinct initial names from a large name space, to get distinct new names from a small output name space. In the non-adaptive version of the problem, the size of the new name space is a function of n, the total number of processes. Adaptive renaming is more demanding: the size of the new name space must be a function of the actual number of the participating processes.

An *adaptive $f(m)$-renaming* algorithm allows m participating processes with initially distinct names from a large name space to acquire distinct new names from the set $\{1, \ldots, f(m)\}$. A *one-shot* renaming algorithm allows each process to acquire a distinct new name just once. A *long-lived* renaming algorithm allows processes to repeatedly acquire distinct names. We focus below on solving one-shot adaptive renaming. It is known that there is a wait-free adaptive $(2m - 1)$-renaming algorithm using registers, where m is the number of participating processes [6]. Below we extend this result to cover cases where waiting is possible.

Theorem 5. *For any $1 \leq k < n$, there is a strong $(k + 1)$-waiting starvation-free adaptive $(\max\{m, 2m - k - 1\})$-renaming algorithm, where $1 \leq m \leq n$ is the number of participating processes, using registers.*

Proof. For $1 \leq i \leq k$, let E_i be the implementation of a strong 2-waiting election object from registers, from the proof of Theorem 1. Each process, say p, scans the k election objects, $E_1, \ldots, E_k$, in order, starting with E_1. At each step, process p tries to get elected, and either moves to the next election object if the returned value is 0 (i.e., not elected), or stops when the returned value is 1 (i.e., elected). If process p stops on one of the k election objects, then it is assigned the name that equals to the index of the election object on which it is elected. (I.e., if it stopped on E_i then it is assigned name is i.). Otherwise, if all its operations on the election objects have returned 1 (which means that k other processes already got the names 1 through k), process p participates in a wait-free adaptive $(2m - 1)$-renaming algorithm which uses registers only. Let v be the value assigned to p by the optimal renaming algorithm, then process p is assigned the final new name $k + v$. Clearly, only $m - k$ processes will participate in the adaptive wait-free renaming, and thus $v \in \{1, \ldots, 2(m - k) - 1\}$. This proves that the name name space is as stated in the Lemma. Next we prove that the algorithm satisfies $k + 1$-waiting. There are two possible cases:

1. A process, say p, acquires a new name $i \leq k$. This means that p got elected in E_k. So, at some point there was a strong enabling step which made p strongly enabled after which it got elected at E_k. *Before* that strong enabling step, there where at most $k - 1$ other strong enabling steps which strongly enabled $k - 1$ other processes to get elected in objects $E_1, \ldots, E_{k-1}$, a total of k strongly enabling events.
2. A process, say p, acquires a new name $i > k$. This means that p acquired a name while participating in a wait-free adaptive $(2m-1)$-renaming algorithm.

So, at some point there was a strong enabling step which made p strongly enabled after which it acquired a name. *Before* that strongly enabling step, there where at most k other strong enabling steps which strongly enabled k other processes to get elected in objects $E_1, \ldots, E_k$, a total of $k + 1$ strongly enabling events.

We notice that after the k'th enabling step, the step which made the process that got elected in E_k enabled, the next enabling step simultaneously made *all* the remaining processes enabled.   □

The result stated in Theorem 5 holds, with almost the same proof, if we replace the word *strong* with *weak* in the statement of the theorem. A wait-free adaptive $(2m - 1)$-renaming algorithm using registers, where m is the number of participating processes is called an *optimal* adaptive renaming algorithm w.r.t. registers, because it matches the known lower bound on the name space. This known lower bound can be easily derived from the known impossibility result for set-consensus [4,14,20]. Below we slightly generalize this lower bound result.

Observation 4. *There is no weak 0-waiting starvation-free adaptive* $\max\{1, 2m - 2\}$-*renaming algorithm, where m is the number of participating processes, using registers.*

Proof. The result follows from Observation 2 and the known impossibility result that there is no *wait-free* adaptive m-renaming algorithm for two processes, using registers [4,14,20].   □

6   Mutual Exclusion

The mutual exclusion problem is to design an algorithm (i.e., a lock) that guarantees mutually exclusive access to a critical section among n competing processes [7]. It is assumed that each process is executing a sequence of instructions in an infinite loop. The instructions are divided into four continuous sections: the remainder, entry, critical and exit. The entry section consists of two parts: the *doorway* which is *wait-free*, and the waiting part which includes one or more loops. A *waiting* process is a process that has finished its doorway code and reached the waiting part, and a *beginning* process is a process that is about to start executing its entry section. Like in the case of the doorway, the exit section is also required to be wait-free. It is assumed that processes do not fail, and that a process always leaves its critical section.

The *mutual exclusion problem* is to write the code for the entry and the exit sections in such a way that the following *two* basic requirements are satisfied.

Livelock-Freedom: If a process is trying to enter its critical section, then some process, not necessarily the same one, eventually enters its critical section.

Mutual Exclusion: No two processes are in their critical sections at the same time.

Satisfaction of the above two properties is the minimum required for a mutual exclusion algorithm. For an algorithm to be fair, satisfaction of an additional condition is required.

First-in-First-Out (FIFO): A beginning process cannot execute its critical section before a waiting process completes executing its critical section.

Theorem 6. *(1) There is no strong $(n-2)$-waiting livelock-free mutual exclusion algorithm; (2) There are strong $(n-1)$-waiting FIFO mutual exclusion algorithms using strong synchronization primitives; (3) There are strong n-waiting FIFO mutual exclusion algorithms using registers.*

Proof. (1) Let A be an arbitrary mutual exclusion algorithm. Assume that n processes are trying to enter their critical sections of A simultaneously, and they have all passed their doorways. In such a scenario, each strong enabling step enables exactly one process to enter its critical section, complete its operation and release the lock. The last process enters its critical section, after at least strong $n-1$ enabling steps have been executed. Thus, at best, A satisfies strong $(n-1)$-waiting, but it does not satisfy $(n-2)$-waiting. (2) Anderson's queue-based algorithm [1], which uses registers and fetch-and-increment object, is an example of a strong $(n-1)$-waiting FIFO mutual exclusion algorithm. (3) The FIFO mutual exclusion algorithm from [17] use only registers and satisfies strong n-waiting. ▢

In the context of mutual exclusion, it is easy to show that a process is weakly enabled if and only if it is strongly enabled. Thus, the result stated in Theorem 6 holds, if we replace the word *strong* with *weak* in the statement of the theorem.

7 Fairness

Fairness requirements guarantee that a process will not bypass another process "too many times". The problem of implementing a k-*fair* data structure is to write the code of each operation in such a way that the following requirement is satisfied,

> k-**fairness:** No beginning process can complete $k+1$ operations while some other process which has already passed the doorway of some operation has not completed the operation yet.

The term first-in-first-out (FIFO) is used for 0-fairness. For every $k \geq 1$, k-fairness *does not* imply livelock-freedom. We address the following question: When is it possible to transform a non-blocking data structure into the corresponding fair data structure? We show that, when only registers are used, such a transformation *must involve waiting*.

Theorem 7. *For any $k \geq 0$, it is not possible to automatically transform every data structure, which has a non-blocking implementation using registers, into the corresponding k-fair non-blocking data structure, using registers.*

Proof. For any $k \geq 0$, a data structure that satisfies both k-fairness and non-blocking must also satisfy wait-freedom. In [10], it is shown that there exists an object which has a non-blocking implementation using registers, but does not have a wait-free implementation using registers. The existence of such an object implies that it is not possible to automatically transform every non-blocking data structure into the corresponding wait-free data structure using only registers. The result follows.   □

Theorem 8. *It is possible to automatically transform every non-blocking data structure, using only registers, into the corresponding strong 1-waiting data structure which (1) satisfies 1-fairness and starvation-freedom, and (2) guarantees that the execution of the doorway of each operation requires a constant number of steps.*

Proof. It was recently proved in [24] that, using registers, it is possible to automatically transform any non-blocking data structure into the corresponding starvation-free data structure which satisfies the following three properties: (1) no beginning process may complete two operations before another process that has passed its doorway completes its operation; (2) All the processes that have passed their doorways and are not strongly enabled, eventually become strong enabled at the same time; (3) the execution of the doorway requires only three steps, in which only registers are accessed. Property (1) above means that the transformed data structure satisfies 1-fairness; property (2) implies that it satisfies strong 1-waiting. The result follows.   □

8   Related Work

In [8], it is suggested to model contention at a shared object with the help of stall operations. In the case of simultaneous accesses to a single memory location, only one operation succeeds, and other pending operations must stall. The measure of contention is the worst-case number of stalls that can be induced by an adversary scheduler. There is a tradeoff between the strength of the progress condition that an algorithm is required to satisfy and its time complexity. Our study of the new progress conditions complements the study of the complexity measure of [8] which takes contention into account.

As already mentioned, the following important progress conditions have been proposed for data structures which avoid waiting: wait-freedom [12], non-blocking [15], and obstruction-freedom [13]. Symmetric and asymmetric progress conditions are studied in [16,23]. In [11], the authors identify an interesting relationship that unifies six progress conditions ranging from the deadlock-free and starvation-free conditions common to lock-based systems, to the obstruction-free, non-blocking and wait-free conditions common to lock-free systems.

The impossibility result that there is no consensus algorithm that can tolerate even a single crash failure was first proved for the asynchronous message-passing model in [9], and later has been extended for the shared memory model with atomic registers, in [18]. A comprehensive discussion of wait-free synchronization is given in [12].

In [21] it is proved that, in the absence of failures, $\lceil \log n \rceil + 1$ registers are necessary and sufficient for election, assuming that only the elected leader is required to ever terminate. We use the key ideas from [21], in our implementations of the 2-waiting starvation-free consensus and election algorithms. The one-shot renaming problem was first solved for message-passing systems [2], and later for shared memory systems [3]. In [5] a long-lived wait-free renaming algorithm was presented. Many of the results on renaming are discussed in [6].

The mutual exclusion problem was first stated and solved for n processes by Dijkstra in [7]. Numerous solutions for the problem have been proposed since it was first introduced in 1965 [22]. In [24], it is shown that it is possible to automatically transfer any non-blocking or wait-free data structure into a similar data structure which satisfies a strong fairness requirement, without using locks and with limited waiting.

9   Discussion and Open Problems

We have introduced a new set of progress conditions, called k-waiting, for $k \geq 0$. The new conditions are intended to quantitatively capture the "amount of waiting" of processes in asynchronous concurrent algorithms. To illustrate the utility of the new conditions, we have derived lower and upper bounds, and impossibility results for well-known basic problems such as consensus, election, renaming and mutual exclusion. We also presented some results regarding the relation between waiting and fairness. Much, however, remains to be done.

The new progress conditions together with our technical results, indicate that there is an interesting area of concurrent algorithms that deserve further investigation. A few specific interesting open problems are: Are there 1-waiting starvation-free consensus and election algorithms for $n \geq 2$ processes, using registers? Is the upper bound of Theorem 5, on the name space for k-waiting starvation-free adaptive renaming, tight? It would also be interesting to look at various variants of k-waiting.

To conclude, we have focused on identifying some intermediate notion of waiting, and the basic definition of k-waiting appears to make sense as a candidate definition. The various results presented, provide some evidence that this is a good definition. We hope that our conceptual contributions will lead to interesting conversations and further results regarding this unexplored area.

References

1. Anderson, T.E.: The performance of spin lock alternatives for shared-memory multiprocessor. IEEE Trans. Parallel Distrib. Syst. **1**(1), 6–16 (1990)
2. Attiya, H., Bar-Noy, A., Dolev, D., Koller, D., Peleg, D., Reischuk, R.: Renaming in an asynchronous environment. J. Assoc. Comput. Mach. **37**(3), 524–548 (1990)
3. Bar-Noy, A., Dolev, D.: Shared memory versus message-passing in an asynchronous distributed environment. In: Proceedings of 8th ACM Symposium on Principles of Distributed Computing, pp. 307–318 (1989)

4. Borowsky, E., Gafni, E.: Generalizecl FLP impossibility result for t-resilient asynchronous computations. In: Proceedings of 25th ACM Symposium on Theory of Computing, pp. 91–100 (1993)

5. Burns, J.E., Peterson, G.L.: The ambiguity of choosing. In: Proceedings of 8th ACM Symposium on Principles of Distributed Computing, pp. 145–158 (1989)

6. Castaneda, A., Rajsbaum, S., Raynal, M.: The renaming problem in shared memory systems: an introduction. Comput. Sci. Rev. **5**(3), 229–251 (2011)

7. Dijkstra, E.W.: Solution of a problem in concurrent programming control. Commun. ACM **8**(9), 569 (1965)

8. Dwork, C., Herlihy, M.P., Waarts, O.: Contention in shared memory algorithms. J. ACM **44**(6), 779–805 (1997)

9. Fischer, M.J., Lynch, N.A., Paterson, M.S.: Impossibility of distributed consensus with one faulty process. J. ACM **32**(2), 374–382 (1985)

10. Herlihy, M.: Impossibility results for asynchronous PRAM. In: Proceedings of 3rd Annual ACM Symposium on Parallel Algorithms and Architectures, pp. 327–336 (1991)

11. Herlihy, M., Shavit, N.: On the nature of progress. In: Fernàndez Anta, A., Lipari, G., Roy, M. (eds.) OPODIS 2011. LNCS, vol. 7109, pp. 313–328. Springer, Heidelberg (2011)

12. Herlihy, M.P.: Wait-free synchronization. ACM Trans. Program. Lang. Syst. **13**(1), 124–149 (1991)

13. Herlihy, M.P., Luchangco, V., Moir, M.: Obstruction-free synchronization: double-ended queues as an example. In: Proceedings of 23rd International Conference on Distributed Computing Systems, p. 522 (2003)

14. Herlihy, M.P., Shavit, N.: The topological structure of asynchronous computability. J. ACM **46**(6), 858–923 (1999)

15. Herlihy, M.P., Wing, J.M.: Linearizability: a correctness condition for concurrent objects. ACM Trans. Program. Lang. Syst. **12**(3), 463–492 (1990)

16. Imbs, D., Raynal, M., Taubenfeld, G.: On asymmetric progress conditions. In: Proceedings of 29th ACM Symposium on Principles of Distributed Computing, pp. 55–64 (2010)

17. Lamport, L.: A new solution of Dijkstra's concurrent programming problem. Commun. ACM **17**(8), 453–455 (1974)

18. Loui, M.C., Abu-Amara, H.: Memory requirements for agreement among unreliable asynchronous processes. Adv. Comput. Res. **4**, 163–183 (1987)

19. Moran, S., Wolfstahl, Y.: Extended impossibility results for asynchronous complete networks. Inf. Process. Lett. **26**(3), 145–151 (1987)

20. Saks, M., Zaharoglou, F.: Wait-free k-set agreement is impossible: the topology of public knowledge. SIAM J. Comput. **29**, 1449–1483 (2000)

21. Styer, E., Peterson, G.L.: Tight bounds for shared memory symmetric mutual exclusion problems. In: Proceedings of 8th ACM Symposium on Principles of Distributed Computing, pp. 177–191, August 1989

22. Taubenfeld, G.: Synchronization Algorithms and Concurrent Programming, pp. 1–423. Pearson/Prentice-Hall, Upper Saddle River (2006). ISBN 0-131-97259-6

23. Taubenfeld, G.: The computational structure of progress conditions. In: Lynch, N.A., Shvartsman, A.A. (eds.) DISC 2010. LNCS, vol. 6343, pp. 221–235. Springer, Heidelberg (2010)

24. Taubenfeld, G.: Fair synchronization. In: Afek, Y. (ed.) DISC 2013. LNCS, vol. 8205, pp. 179–193. Springer, Heidelberg (2013)

Corona Product Complexity of Planar Graph and S-chain Graph

Fouad Yakoubi$^{(\boxtimes)}$ and Mohamed El Marraki

LRIT Associated Unit the CNRST (URAC29), Faculty of Sciences,
University of Mohammed V, P.O. Box 1014, Rabat, Morocco
fouad.yakoubii@gmail.com, marraki@fsr.ac.ma

Abstract. Since its appearance, the number of spanning trees of a graph has been among the most important problems in graph theory. We aimed to get explicit formula counting this number in the corona product graph of two planar graphs. In this paper, we study the corona product of a planar graph with a linear chain and cycle chain, for which we calculate their number of spanning trees. Our research findings highlight the potential of combinatorial method, which allowed us to count this number for a large graph as corona product graph.

Keywords: Complexity of graph · Spanning tree · Corona product graph · Linear chain · Cycle chain

1 Introduction

The number of spanning trees is a topological invariant in a given graph G, since it appeared, the problem of counting this number is one of the most important studied problems in graph theory. The complexity or the number of spanning trees of the graph G is very useful in many areas of new technologies, namely designing electrical circuits, estimating the reliability of a network [7–9], designing algorithms in cryptography and network security [6], etc. The first way to solve this problem is the matrix tree theorem [1] in which the number of spanning trees that is denoted by $\tau(G)$, can be expressed as the value of the determinant of any co-factor matrix of the Laplacian matrix of the graph G. Although this algebraic method can be used to compute the number of spanning trees for small graphs, it could not be practical for large graphs. For this reason, Many researchers focused on studying this NP-hard problem to provide practical approaches counting the number of spanning trees in some families of undirected graphs [4,5,7].

In this paper, we propose an efficient method to count the number of spanning trees in corona product. Let G_{n_1} be a planar graph and G_{n_2} be an outerplanar graph. We denote by n_1 and n_2 the orders of G_{n_1} and G_{n_2} respectively. The corona product graph of G_{n_1} and G_{n_2} is denoted by $G_{n_1} \diamond G_{n_2}$, defined as the graph obtained by taking one copy of G_{n_1} and n_1 copies of G_{n_2}, then we join each vertex in the ith copy of G_{n_2} by an edge with the ith vertex of G_{n_1} [2].

© Springer International Publishing AG 2016
P.A. Abdulla and C. Delporte-Gallet (Eds.): NETYS 2016, LNCS 9944, pp. 361–366, 2016.
DOI: 10.1007/978-3-319-46140-3_30

Our study is focused on undirected graphs in which we look to investigate the number of spanning trees in the corona product of a planar graph G with s-linear chain and s-cycle chain (See Figs. 1(c) and 2(a)).

2   Preliminary Notes

In this part we give all theorems that we use in our work.

Let G_{n_1} be a planar graph and G_{n_2} an outerplanar graph. Then [3]:

$$\tau(G_{n_1} \diamond G_{n_2}) = \tau(G_1) \times (\tau(G_2 \diamond P_1))^{n_1} \qquad (1)$$

If G is a graph composed of of two subgrpahs G_{n_1} and G_{n_1} as illustrated in Fig. 1(b). Then [5]:

$$\tau(G) = \tau(G_{n_1}) \times \tau(G_{n_2}.uv) + \tau(G_{n_1}.uv) \times \tau(G_{n_2}) \qquad (2)$$

We denote by $G_{n_1}.uv$ and $G_{n_2}.uv$ the graphs obtained from G_{n_1} and G_{n_2} respectively, when we paste the vertex intersection u with v of G_{n_1} and G_{n_2}.

Let G_n is a graph composed of two sub-graphs G_{n_1} and G_{n_2} which have a common edge e as illustrated in Fig. 1(a). Then [5]:

$$\tau(G) = \tau(G_{n_1}) \times \tau(G_{n_2}) - \tau(G_{n_1} - e) \times \tau(G_{n_2} - e) \qquad (3)$$

$G_{n_1} - e$ and $G_{n_2} - e$ are the graphs obtained from G_{n_1} and G_{n_2} respectively after removing the edge e.

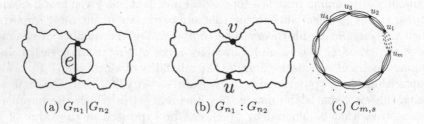

(a) $G_{n_1}|G_{n_2}$ (b) $G_{n_1} : G_{n_2}$ (c) $C_{m,s}$

Fig. 1. Planar graphs type of $G_{n_1}|G_{n_2}$, $G_{n_1} : G_{n_2}$ and S-cycle chain $C_{m,s}$

3   Results and Discussion

To calculate the corona product complexity $\tau(G_n \diamond C_{m,s})$ of a planar graph G_n and a chain map $C_{m,s}$ (S-linear chain or S-cycle chain), which contains m vertex and s edges between each adjacent vertex $\{u_i, u_{i+1}\}$ (See Figs. 1(c) and 2(a)), at the first we must calculate $\tau(C_{m,s} \diamond P_1)$.

3.1   Corona Product Complexity of G_n and S-linear Chain $C_{m,s}$

Lemma 1. *Let $C_{m,s}$ be a S-linear chain. The number of spanning trees in $C_{m,s} \diamond P_1$ is given by:*

$$\tau(C_{m,s} \diamond P_1) = \frac{1}{\sqrt{4s+1}} \left(\left(\frac{2s+1+\sqrt{4s+1}}{2} \right)^m - \left(\frac{2s+1-\sqrt{4s+1}}{2} \right)^m \right), m \geq 2, s \geq 1 \tag{4}$$

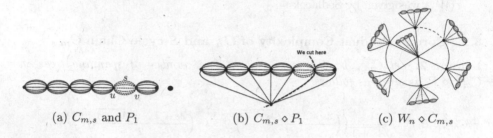

(a) $C_{m,s}$ and P_1 (b) $C_{m,s} \diamond P_1$ (c) $W_n \diamond C_{m,s}$

Fig. 2. S-linear chain $C_{m,s}$, P_1 and $C_{m,s} \diamond P_1$

Proof. Now to simplify notation, $\tau(C_{m,s} \diamond P_1)$ is denoted by $f_{m,s}$. By choosing the edge e as illustrated in Fig. 2(b) and using Eq. (3), we get the sequence of recurrence $f_{m,s} = (2s+1)f_{m-1,s} - s^2 f_{m-2,s}$. By solving its characteristic equation $r^2 - (2s+1)r + s^2 = 0$, we found the roots $r_1 = \frac{2s+1+\sqrt{4s+1}}{2}$ and $r_2 = \frac{2s+1-\sqrt{4s+1}}{2}$, then we use initial values $(f_{1,s} = 1, f_{2,s} = 2s+1)$ we get $f_{m,s}$.   □

Remarks. We treat here some specific cases.
If $s = 1$ then, $C_{m,1}$ is a path P_m which contains m vertex. So, $P_m \diamond P_1$ is a Fan graph F_{m+1}, substituting s by 1 in Eq. (4), we get
$\tau(P_m \diamond P_1) = \tau(F_{m+1}) = \frac{1}{\sqrt{5}} \left(\left(\frac{3+\sqrt{5}}{2} \right)^m - \left(\frac{3-\sqrt{5}}{2} \right)^m \right)$ [4]
If $s = 2$ then, using Eq. (4), we get $\tau(C_{m,2} \diamond P_1) = \frac{1}{3} \left(4^m - 1 \right)$
Now, In order to calculate the complexity of corona product of a planar graph G_n and S-linear chain $C_{m,s}$, we made use of Lemma 1, then applying Eq. (1).

Theorem 1. *The number of spanning tree in $G_n \diamond C_{m,s}$ is given as follow:*

$$\tau(G_n \diamond C_{m,s}) = \tau(G) \times \left(\frac{1}{\sqrt{4s+1}} \left(\left(\frac{2s+1+\sqrt{4s+1}}{2} \right)^m - \left(\frac{2s+1-\sqrt{4s+1}}{2} \right)^m \right) \right)^n, m \geq 2, s \geq 1 \tag{5}$$

Corollary 1. *Let W_n be a Wheel graph which contains n vertex. The number of spanning trees in $W_n \diamond C_{m,s}$ is given as follow:*

$$\tau(W_n \diamond C_{m,s}) = \left(\left(\frac{3+\sqrt{5}}{2}\right)^{n-1} - \left(\frac{3-\sqrt{5}}{2}\right)^{n-1} - 2\right)$$

$$\times \left(\frac{1}{\sqrt{4s+1}}\left(\left(\frac{2s+1+\sqrt{4s+1}}{2}\right)^m - \left(\frac{2s+1-\sqrt{4s+1}}{2}\right)^m\right)\right)^n, n \geqslant 4, m \geqslant 2$$

(6)

$\tau(W_n)$ was given by Sedlacek [4].

3.2   Corona Product Complexity of G_n and S-cycle Chain $C_{m,s}$

Lemma 2. *Let $C_{m,s}$ be a S-cycle chain. The number of spanning trees in $C_{m,s} \diamond P_1$ is given as follows:*

$$\tau(C_{m,s} \diamond P_1) = \frac{1}{\sqrt{4s+1}}\left(\left(\frac{2s+1+\sqrt{4s+1}}{2}\right)^{m+1} - \left(\frac{2s+1-\sqrt{4s+1}}{2}\right)^{m+1} + \right.$$

$$\left. \left(\frac{2s+1-\sqrt{4s+1}}{2}\right)^{m-1} - \left(\frac{2s+1+\sqrt{4s+1}}{2}\right)^{m-1}\right) - 2s^m, m \geqslant 3, s \geqslant 1$$

(7)

Proof. we denoted $C_{m,s} \diamond P_1$ by $N_{m+1,1}$. In $N_{m+1,1}$ We choose the pair of vertex $\{u_1, u_2\}$ as illustrated in Fig. 1(c). Then, we use Eq. (2), we get: $\tau(N_{m+1,1}) = \tau(F_{m+1,1}) + s \times \tau(N_{m,2})$, where $N_{m,2}$ is the graph obtained if we paste the vertex u_1 and u_2, then $N_{m,2}$ has two edges between the central vertex a and u_1, $F_{m+1,1}$ denotes the graph obtained from $N_{m+1,1}$ when we separate the vertex u_1 and u_2, which has one edge between the vertex a and u_1 (See Fig. 3(c)). Now, in the second iteration, we choose the vertex $\{u_2, u_3\}$ in $N_{m,2}$, then repeating the same thing, by using Eq. (2), then we get: $\tau(N_{m,2}) = \tau(F_{m,2}) + s \times \tau(N_{m-1,3})$. So $\tau(N_{m+1,1}) = \tau(F_{m+1,1}) + s(\tau(F_{m,1}) + s \times \tau(N_{m-1,3}))$ We continued doing the same thing until the kth iteration, by choosing the pair of vertex $\{u_k, u_{k+1}\}$ in $N_{m-k+1,k+1}$ (See Fig. 3(b)), we find: $\tau(N_{m+1,1}) = \tau(F_{m+1,1}) + s(\tau(F_{m,2}) + s(\tau(F_{m-1,3}) + s(\tau(F_{m-2,4}) + \cdots s(\tau(F_{m-k+1,k+1}))) + s^{k+1}\tau(N_{m-k,k+2})$. Therefore $\tau(N_{m+1,1}) = \sum_{k=0}^{n-3} S^k \tau(F_{m-k+1,k+1}) + s^{m-2}\tau(N_{3,n-1})$. To calculate the complexity $\tau(F_{m-k+1,k+1})$, which has $k+1$ edges between the vertex a and u_1, we selected the edge e in $F_{m-k+1,k+1}$ as illustrated in Fig. 3(c), then we use Eq. (3), we obtain: $\tau(F_{m-k+1,k+1}) = (k+1)\tau(F_{m-k+1,1}) - sk \times \tau(F_{m-k,1})$. as $F_{m-k+1,1}$ is a corona product of P_1 and s-linear chain which has m-k vertex, then $\tau(F_{m-k+1,1}) = \frac{1}{\sqrt{4s+1}}\left(\left(\frac{2s+1+\sqrt{4s+1}}{2}\right)^{m-k} - \left(\frac{2s+1-\sqrt{4s+1}}{2}\right)^{m-k}\right)$. We put $r_1 = \frac{2s+1+\sqrt{4s+1}}{2}, r_2 = \frac{2s+1-\sqrt{4s+1}}{2}$. Therefore $\tau(F_{m-k+1,k+1}) = \frac{1}{\sqrt{4s+1}}((k+1)(r_1^{m-k} - r_2^{m-k}) - sk(r_1^{m-k-1} - r_2^{m-k-1}))$. Then $\tau(N_{m+1,1}) = \frac{1}{\sqrt{4s+1}}\sum_{k=0}^{n-3} s^k((k+1)(r_1^{m-k} - r_2^{m-k}) - sk(r_1^{m-k-1} - r_2^{m-k-1})) + s^{m-2}\tau(N_{3,n-1}) = \frac{1}{\sqrt{4s+1}}(r_1^m \sum_{k=0}^{n-3}(k+1)(\frac{s}{r_1})^k - r_2^m \sum_{k=0}^{n-3}(k+1)(\frac{s}{r_2})^k) - r_1^m \sum_{k=0}^{n-3} k(\frac{s}{r_1})^{k+1} + r_2^m \sum_{k=0}^{n-3} k(\frac{s}{r_2})^{k+1}) + s^{m-2}(n(2s-1)-1)$. By calculating these series we obtain the result. $\square$

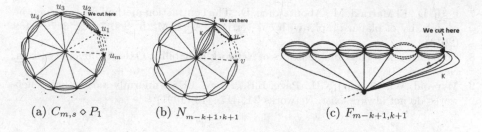

(a) $C_{m,s} \diamond P_1$ (b) $N_{m-k+1,k+1}$ (c) $F_{m-k+1,k+1}$

Fig. 3. $C_{m,s} \diamond P_1$, $N_{m-k+1,k+1}$ and $F_{m-k+1,k+1}$

Theorem 2. *Let G_n be a planar graph and $C_{m,s}$ a s-cycle chain. The number of spanning tree in $G_n \diamond C_{m,s}$ is given as follow:*

$$\tau(G_n \diamond C_{m,s}) = \tau(G_n) \times \left(\frac{1}{\sqrt{4s+1}} \left(\left(\frac{2s+1+\sqrt{4s+1}}{2} \right)^{m+1} - \left(\frac{2s+1-\sqrt{4s+1}}{2} \right)^{m+1} + \right. \right.$$
$$\left. \left. \left(\frac{2s+1-\sqrt{4s+1}}{2} \right)^{m-1} - \left(\frac{2s+1+\sqrt{4s+1}}{2} \right)^{m-1} \right) - 2s^m \right)^n, m \geqslant 3, s \geqslant 3$$

$$(8)$$

4   Conclusion

In graph theory, the number of spanning trees in a small graph, can be given by algebraic methods, such as matrix tree theorem. But these methods practically are not efficient for huge graphs. For that reason we have proposed recursive method providing the explicit formulas to calculate the number of spanning trees in Corona product graph of a planar graph and a chain map.

References

1. Kirchhoff, G.G.: Über die Auflösung der Gleichungen, auf welche man bei der Untersuchung der linearen Verteilung galvanischer Strme gefhrt wird. Ann. Phys. Chem. **72**, 497–508 (1847)
2. West, D.B.: Introduction to Graph Theory, 2nd edn. University of Illinois, Urbana (2002)
3. Yakoubi, F., El Marraki, M.: Enumeration of spanning trees in certain vertex corona product graph. Appl. Math. Sci. **8**(109), 5427–5438 (2014)
4. Sedlacek, J.: On the skeletons of a graph or digraph. In: Proceedings of Calgary International Conference of Combinatorial Structures and Their Applications, Gordon and Breach, pp. 387–391 (1970)
5. Modabish, A., El Marraki, M.: The number of spanning trees of certain families of planar maps. Appl. Math. Sci. **5**(18), 883–898 (2011)
6. Al Etaiwi, clar:ekeW.M.: Encryption algorithm using graph theory. J. Sci. Res. Rep. **3**(19), 2519–2527 (2014). Article No: JSRR.2014.19.004

7. Lotfi, D., El Marraki, M., Aboutajdine, D.: The contraction method for counting the complexity of planar graphs with cut vertices. Appl. Math. Sci. **7**(70), 3479–3488 (2013)
8. Colbourn, C.J.: The Combinatorics of Network Reliability. Oxford University Press, New York (1980)
9. Myrvold, W., Cheung, K.H., Page, L.B., Perry, J.E.: Uniformly-most reliable networks do not always exist. Networks **21**, 417–419 (1991)

Vehicular Ad-Hoc Network: Evaluation of QoS and QoE for Multimedia Application

Imane Zaimi[1]([✉]), Zineb Squalli Houssaini[2], Abdelali Boushaba[3],
Mohammed Oumsis[4], and Driss Aboutajdine[1]

[1] LRIT, Associated Unit to CNRST (URAC 29), Faculty of Sciences,
Mohammed-V University in Rabat, Rabat, Morocco
imanzaimi@gmail.com, aboutaj@fsr.ac.ma

[2] IT Laboratory and Modelling (LIM), Dhar El Mahraz Faculty of Sciences (FSDM),
Sidi Mohammed Ben Abdellah University (USMBA) in Fez, Fez, Morocco
zinebsqualli@gmail.com

[3] Intelligent Systems and Applications Laboratory (LSIA),
Faculty of Sciences and Technology, Sidi Mohamed Ben Abdelah University,
Fez, Morocco
abdelali.boushaba@usmba.ac.ma

[4] LRIT, Associated Unit to CNRST (URAC 29) and Superior school of Technology,
Mohammed-V University, Rabat, Morocco
oumsis@yahoo.com

Abstract. In Vehicular Ad-hoc Networks (VANETs), the most tempting features are usability, availability and service integrity required by the users especially in case of the video streaming. Thus, the concept of quality of experience (QoE) occurred with non-technical aspects which directly influence user's perception. This paper provides a complete performance evaluation of seven ad-hoc routing protocols, for the application of video streaming, considering different number of connections in an urban scenario. Afterwards, since position-based protocols present a major issue of networking for VANETs, we focused our comparative study on the Greedy Perimeter Stateless Routing (GPSR) protocol. The tool-set for this evaluation integrates Evalvid, NS-2 and VanetMobiSim. Besides considering Packet Delivery Ratio (PDR), Throughput and Delay as QoS metrics, we evaluate Peak Signal to Noise Ratio (PSNR), Video Quality Metric (VQM) and Structural Similarity Index (SSIM) as QoE measures. The simulation shows that GPSR offers acceptable results for all metrics except delay, it enables a good improvement of the later though. Therefore, it still needs enhancement for its metrics performances.

Keywords: VANETs · Routing protocols · IEEE 802.11p · QoS · QoE · VanetMobiSim · Evalvid · NS-2

1 Introduction and Motivation

In wireless networks, the most tempting feature is the ability of the user to receive data smoothly over the network regardless of his position. Being a type of wireless

© Springer International Publishing AG 2016
P.A. Abdulla and C. Delporte-Gallet (Eds.): NETYS 2016, LNCS 9944, pp. 367–371, 2016.
DOI: 10.1007/978-3-319-46140-3_31

networks and an application of mobile ad-hoc networks (MANETs), VANETs have emerged as a new powerful technology where many challenges occur [1]. VANET also experiences a critical point that is the supporting inter-vehicle video streaming [2]. In fact, with the growing needs of the users to access various resources during mobility, efficient techniques are required to support their needs from user satisfaction perspectives.

For this purpose, before starting work on VANET, it must be ensured that the selected protocol should have best data delivery, integrity and time delivery, to achieve a safe guard of drivers [3]. Hence, the aim of this paper is to analyse the quality criteria among popular routing protocols, namely, Ad-hoc On Demand Distance Vector (AODV) [4], Destination Sequence Distance Vector(DSDV) [5], Dynamic source routing (DSR) [6], Dynamic Manet On Demand (DYMOUM) [7], Fisheye State Routing (FSR) [8], Greedy Perimeter Stateless Routing (GPSR) [9] and Zone Routing Protocol (ZRP) [10]. The literature has shown that the position-based protocols perform better than traditional protocols of MANETs [11], which led us to give an interest to GPSR during analysis.

The remainder of this paper is organized as follows: The Sect. 2 describes the performance evaluation of our work. Section 3 discusses the experimental results, while Sect. 4 summarizes the main concluding remarks.

2   Performance Evaluation

The main simulation parameters are listed in Table 1.

Table 1. Characteristics of scenario

Parameters used for physical and link layer	
Propagation model	Two ray ground
Bandwidth	100 Mbps
Transmission range	250 m
Parameters used for traffic model	
Type of multimedia	MPEG-4
Real video file	Foreman.yuv (300 frames in YUV CIF (352 x 288) format)
Traffic rate	30 frames/s
Number of background CBR traffic connection	5-10-15-20
Background traffic packets size	512 bytes
Background traffic packets rate	10 packets/second
Simulation time	300s
Parameters used for mobility model	
Ad-hoc network area	670m * 670 m
Number of vehicles	50
Mobility Model	IDM-LC
Parameters used for IDM-LC model	
Traffic light interval	10
Number of lines	2
Velocity of vehicles	18 to 50 (Km/h)

3   Results and Analysis

3.1   QoS Metrics as Function of Data Traffic Load

We note from Table 3 that GPSR decreases delay up to 75 % compared to DSR, which is significant. However, PDR and throughput are decreased by GPSR. Indeed, Fig. 1 illustrates the two metrics in different traffic scenario and shows that, whatever is the number of communication, they still weak. Thus, as shown in Table 3, GPSR decreases PDR up to 67 %, and throughput up to 33 %. In summary, even if GPSR increases the quality level of multimedia transmissions in terms of delay, it remains insufficient since the PDR and throughput are also the keys metrics that influence multimedia quality.

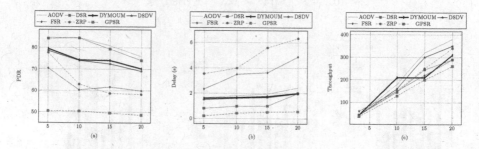

Fig. 1. QoS metrics: (a) Packets delivery ratio (b) End to end delay and (c) Throughput

3.2   QoE Metrics as Function of Data Traffic Load

The Fig. 2 shows the objective metrics (PSNR, VQM and SSIM [12]) considering the aforementioned protocols. It can be seen that the reactive protocols have the best performances. Furthermore, by observing Table 3, GPSR has the lower results even if they are acceptable. It decreases PSNR and SSIM, respectively,

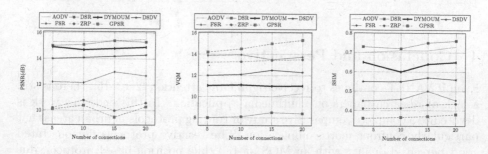

Fig. 2. QoE: PSNR, VQM and SSIM as function of data traffic load

up to 63.36 % and 50.1 %. VQM is also raised up to 87 %. As a subjective metric, the most traditional one is MOS (Mean Opinion Score). The quality level is rated on a scale of 1 to 5 as described in Table 2 (Fig. 3).

Table 2. PSNR, VQM and SSIM mapping to MOS

PSNR (dB)	VQM	SSIM	MOS
> 20	< 3	1	5 (Excellent)
14–20	3–6	0.7–0.9	4 (Good)
12–14	6–10	0.5–0.7	3 (Fair)
10–12	10–14	0.3–0.5	2 (Poor)
< 10	> 14	< 0.3	1 (Bad)

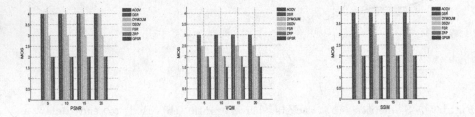

Fig. 3. QoE: PSNR, VQM and SSIM mapping to MOS

Table 3. Performance metrics of GPSR compared with DSR for video traffic

Nbr of Connections	PDR	Delay	Throughput	PSNR	VQM	SSIM
5	↓67 %	↓75.02 %	↓15 %	↓53.20 %	↑87 %	↓47.3 %
10	↓67 %	↓56,12 %	↓28 %	↓62.82 %	↑86.58 %	↓50.1 %
15	↓64 %	↓48,47 %	↓37 %	↓63.36 %	↑80.23 %	↓48.57 %
20	↓56 %	↓71,85 %	↓33 %	↓52.17 %	↑83.64 %	↓46.47 %

4   Conclusion and Perspective

Even if VANET continues to receive significant attention [2,13–15], there is still a lack of research papers on multimedia application. To this end, this work is devoted to a complete comparative study of routing protocols in urban areas that particularly confront more complication. The reactive protocols demonstrated good perceived quality with an MOS of 4. While position-based protocol, due to the location accuracy that represents an essential factor to get a good result, shows some degradation with an average MOS score of 2. The percentages mentioned in section III are calculated by comparing GPSR with DSR since this latter shows the greater performances. In future, we are intended to improve the quality of transmission of video streams through an improved GPSR version.

References

1. Zeadally, S., Hunt, R., Chen, Y.-S., Irwin, A., Hassan, A.: Vehicular ad hoc networks (VANETs): status, results, and challenges. Telecommun. Syst. **50**(4), 217–241 (2012)
2. Xu, S., Guo, P., Xu, B., Zhou, H.: Study on QoS of video communication over VANET. In: Liu, B., Ma, M., Chang, J. (eds.) ICICA 2012. LNCS, vol. 7473, pp. 730–738. Springer, Heidelberg (2012)
3. Mohapatra, S., Kanungo, P.: Performance analysis of AODV, DSR, OLSR and DSDV routing protocols using NS2 simulator. Procedia Eng. **30**, 69–76 (2012)
4. Perkins, C.E., Royer, E.M.: Ad-hoc on-demand distance vector routing. In: Proceedings of the Second IEEE Workshop on Mobile Computer Systems and Applications, p. 90. IEEE Computer Society (1999)
5. Perkins, C.E., Bhagwat, P.: Highly dynamic destination-sequenced distance-vector routing (DSDV) for mobile computers. In: ACM SIGCOMM Computer Communication Review, vol. 24, pp. 234–244. ACM (1994)
6. Johnson, D.B., Maltz, D.A.: Dynamic source routing in ad hoc wireless networks. In: Imielinski, T., Korth, H.F. (eds.) Mobile Computing. The Kluwer International Series in Engineering and Computer Science, vol. 353, pp. 153–181. Springer, New York (1996)
7. Billington, J., Yuan, C.: On modelling and analysing the dynamic MANET on-demand (DYMO) routing protocol. In: Jensen, K., Billington, J., Koutny, M. (eds.) Transactions on Petri Nets and Other Models of Concurrency III. LNCS, vol. 5800, pp. 98–126. Springer, Heidelberg (2009)
8. Pei, G., Gerla, M., Chen, T.-W.: Fisheye state routing: a routing scheme for ad hoc wireless networks. In: IEEE International Conference on Communications, ICC, vol. 1, pp. 70–74. IEEE (2000)
9. Karp, B., Kung, H.-T.: GPSR: Greedy perimeter stateless routing for wireless networks. In: Proceedings of the 6th Annual International Conference on Mobile Computing and Networking, pp. 243–254. ACM (2000)
10. Haas, Z.J., Pearlman, M.R.: ZRP: a hybrid framework for routing in ad hoc networks. In: Ad hoc networking, pp. 221–253. Addison-Wesley Longman Publishing Co. Inc., Boston (2001)
11. Kumar, S., Kumar Verma, A.: Position based routing protocols in VANET: a survey. Wirel. Pers. Commun. **83**(4), 2747–2772 (2015)
12. MSU Graphics: Media lab. MSU video quality measurement tool (2009)
13. Spaho, E., Ikeda, M., Barolli, L., Xhafa, F.: Performance comparison of OLSR and AODV protocols in a VANET crossroad scenario. In: Park, J.J., Barolli, L., Xhafa, F., Jeong, H.-Y. (eds.) Information Technology Convergence. LNEE, vol. 253, pp. 37–45. Springer, Heidelberg (2013)
14. Husain, A., Sharma, S.C.: Simulated analysis of location and distance based routing in VANET with IEEE802. 11p. Procedia Comput. Sci. **57**, 323–331 (2015)
15. Sharef, B.T., Alsaqour, R.A., Ismail, M.: Comparative study of variant position-based vanet routing protocols. Procedia Technol. **11**, 532–539 (2013)

Abstracts of Posters

An Implementation of the Keccak Hash Function

Soufiane El Moumni[1]([✉]), Mohamed Fettach[1],
and Abderrahim Tragha[2]

[1] Information Processing Laboratory, Hassan II University,
Casablanca, Morocco
{soufianeelmoumni, fettachmohamed}@gmail.com
[2] Information Technology and Modeling Laboratory, Hassan II University,
Casablanca, Morocco
atragha@yahoo.fr

Abstract. Cryptographic hash function is one of the most important elements in cryptographic systems. It plays several sensitive roles like generating random numbers, storing passwords, checking data integrity and computing digital signatures. Therefore, it has to be upgraded regularly in order to ensure resistance against recent attacks. For this reason, the National Institute of Standards and Technology (NIST) announced in 2007 a public competition to select a new cryptographic hash function, which is resistant to recent attacks and more efficient in term of hardware implementation. In 2012, NIST announced that the Keccak hash function is the winner in this contest and it will be considered as the SHA-3. In this poster, we are interested to the hardware implementation side of the Keccak hash function, where we applied the unrolling technique to Keccak-512 using Xilinx Virtex-5 FPGA device and we noticed that the throughput increases to 24.72 Gbps. However, It implies an increase on area resources consumption. Our results have been compared to existing FPGA implementations.

© Springer International Publishing AG 2016
P.A. Abdulla and C. Delporte-Gallet (Eds.): NETYS 2016, LNCS 9944, p. 375, 2016.
DOI: 10.1007/978-3-319-46140-3

A Secure Processor
Using Homomorphic Encryption

Bouchra Echandouri[1(✉)], Youssef Gahi[2], Mouhcine Guennoun[2],
and Fouzia Omary[1]

[1] Laboratoire de Recherches Informatique, FSR,
Mohammed V University, Rabat, Morocco
Bouchra.Echandouri@gmail.com, Omary@fsr.ac.ma
[2] School of Electrical Engineering and Computer Science, University of Ottawa,
Ottawa, Canada
Youssef.Gahi@gmail.com, Mguennou@uottawa.ca

Abstract. Outsourcing concepts has interested a number of malicious users. Thus, many strong securing data techniques had been proposed to ensure privacy. Fully homomorphic encryption scheme has been one of the most efficient ways to secure both data storage and computations, whereby it enables performing multiple arithmetic operations over encrypted data, without decryption. Unfortunately, each homomorphic cipher is associated to a small random noise that increases after many operations. In order to refresh the resulting noise and to ensure a successful decryption, a time consuming bootstrapping technique was used. Star gate is a novel homomorphic circuit that helped improving multiple secure applications, namely database systems, location-based services, trust-based routing protocol, video on-demand services etc. To avoid bootstrapping and not reaching the noise threshold, we propose to predict the maximum circuit depth that could be supported by this scheme and make it a leveled-fully homomorphic circuit. In this way, an efficient homomorphic evaluation and a good decryption of Star Gate is guaranteed.

© Springer International Publishing AG 2016
P.A. Abdulla and C. Delporte-Gallet (Eds.): NETYS 2016, LNCS 9944, p. 376, 2016.
DOI: 10.1007/978-3-319-46140-3

An Ontology Based Social Search System

Anas El-ansari[1(✉)], Abderrahim Beni-hssane[1], and Mostafa Saadi[2]

[1] LAROSERI Lab, Computer Science Department Sciences Faculty,
Chouab Doukkali University, El Jadida, Morocco
anas.elansari@gmail.com, abenihssane@yahoo.fr
[2] ENSA Khouribga, University Hassan 1rst – Settat, Settat, Morocco
saadi_mo@yahoo.fr

Abstract. With the tremendous growth of information available on the Web, there is a pressing need for efficient information retrieval systems such as search engines. Nowadays, those systems are based on content matching rather than the meaning and they still suffer from the lack of accuracy. To solve this problem, Ontology and semantic web are becoming centric methodologies to promote the semantic capability of an information retrieval system. The next generation of those systems focus on the meaning of the user query and search data. Our main objective in this poster is to develop ontology based social search system offering the users the possibility to find people, friends and relatives based on multiple search criteria. The system uses a local knowledge base from a social ontology that describes people and social relations. The users do ontology population when they create their profiles and then can search for other users. The initial evaluation result shows the feasibility and benefits of building a semantic social search system based on Ontology.

© Springer International Publishing AG 2016
P.A. Abdulla and C. Delporte-Gallet (Eds.): NETYS 2016, LNCS 9944, p. 377, 2016.
DOI: 10.1007/978-3-319-46140-3

An Adaptive Routing Scheme
in Scale-Free Networks

Nora Ben Haddou[✉], Hamid Ez-zahraouy[✉],
and Abdelilah Benyoussef[✉]

Laboratory of Magnetism and Physics of High Energy Faculty of Sciences,
University Mohammed V, Rabat, Morocco
Nor.Benhaddou@gmail.com, {ezahamid,benyous}@fsr.ac.ma

Abstract. We propose a routing scheme called OTAP (Optimal Traffic Awareness Protocol), which exploits both structural and local dynamic information about the network to determine the path followed by the packets. It is an optimal form of traffic awareness protocol already introduced (TAP). In the present model, the shortest path is replaced with the "efficient path" and a new parameter α is introduced to control the degree of the contribution of queue lengths in the routing process. We find that using the optimal parameters of our model, the capacity of the network reaches more than the double compared to the original model. Moreover, the average travelling time between sources and destinations is minimized.

© Springer International Publishing AG 2016
P.A. Abdulla and C. Delporte-Gallet (Eds.): NETYS 2016, LNCS 9944, p. 378, 2016.
DOI: 10.1007/978-3-319-46140-3

Communication Interface for Distributed SDN

Fouad Benamrane[✉], Mouad Ben Mamoun, and Redouane Benaini

LRI, Faculty of Sciences at Rabat, Mohammed V University,
Rabat, Morocco
benamranefouade@gmail.com,
{ben_mamoun, benaini}@fsr.ac.ma

Abstract. Software Defined Networks (SDN) is a new concept for networking field that allows programmability, automation, agility of services, and innovation using physically or logically centralized controllers. However, there is a lack of scalability and performances in largely distributed SDN domains, where each domain has its own Controller. In this poster, we aim to contribute to the development of logically distributed SDN control planes, by providing an east-west interface that we call Communication Interface for Distributed Control plane (CIDC). Our CIDC provides (i) communication modes such as Notification, Service, or Full to exchange messages between controllers and customize the desired behavior of each controller in the network, and proposes (ii) new mechanism based on policy sharing to support distributed services such as Firewall (FW), and Load Balancer (LB) and secure the communication between controllers using Secure Socket Layer (SSL). Our proposal was evaluated in real wide-area network topologies, and the results show the feasibility of our interface in term of performance and distributed services compared to the previous models based on the cluster.

© Springer International Publishing AG 2016
P.A. Abdulla and C. Delporte-Gallet (Eds.): NETYS 2016, LNCS 9944, p. 379, 2016.
DOI: 10.1007/978-3-319-46140-3

Hybrid Homomorphic Encryption for Cloud Privacy

Yasmina Bensitel[✉] and Romadi Rahal

RIITM Lab, ENSIAS, Mohammed V University, Rabat, Morocco
yasmina_bensitel@um5.ac.ma, romadi@ensias.ma

Abstract. In the age of cloud computing, companies delegate their data processing to third parties. This can be dangerous especially if cloud administrators are malicious. One way to alleviate this problem is to encrypt data before sending them to the cloud and execute calculations on it using the homomorphic encryption. In this poster we propose a hybrid homomorphic encryption (Hy-HE), which consists of the combination of existing partial homomorphic encryption schemes. This hybrid solution secures and preserves data privacy by performing calculations on it in an encrypted form. The goal of our scheme is to analyse the program to be executed in the server and determines for each operation the correspondent homomorphic encryption scheme. This means that each primitive operation f will be evaluated and replaced by the appropriate homomorphic cryptosystem. The program will be executed in the cloud on encrypted data. After the execution, the encrypted result is sent back to the client side, where it is decrypted safely.

© Springer International Publishing AG 2016
P.A. Abdulla and C. Delporte-Gallet (Eds.): NETYS 2016, LNCS 9944, p. 380, 2016.
DOI: 10.1007/978-3-319-46140-3

Static Hand Gesture Recognition Using RGB-D Data

Abdessamad Elboushaki[(⊠)], Rachida Hannane,
Karim Afdel, and Lahcen Koutti

Laboratory of Computer Systems and Vision, Faculty of Science,
Ibn Zohr University, Agadir, Morocco
{abdessamad.elboushaki, rachida.hanane08}@gmail.com,
k.afdel@uiz.ac.ma, lkoutti@yahoo.fr

Abstract. Hand gesture recognition is one of the potential fields of today's research that enables human-computer interaction (HCI) without any physical contact. Despite of many research efforts that have been proposed during the last few years in order to improve the gesture acquisition, processing and classification, static hand gesture recognition is still a challenging problem due to many factors such as: complexity of some gestures, tangled hand articulations, and limited resolution of the sensing devices. In this poster, we propose a novel approach to recognize different static hand gestures. In particular, depth and color information followed by skin filtering is used to segment the hand from image background. In the subsequent step, SIFT-Point Distribution Histogram (SIFT-PDH) is extracted from the segmented hand as a new combination of local and global features. Then, SIFT-PDH feature vector is fed into K-Nearest Neighbors classifier (K-NN) in order to recognize the performed gesture. Finally, Earth Mover's Distance (EMD) is used to compute the dissimilarity between gestures. The extensive experiments on two public datasets show that our method is not only accurate in recognition of the hand gestures, but also robust to scale, illumination and rotation variance, and suitable for real-time applications.

© Springer International Publishing AG 2016
P.A. Abdulla and C. Delporte-Gallet (Eds.): NETYS 2016, LNCS 9944, p. 381, 2016.
DOI: 10.1007/978-3-319-46140-3

Deep Neural Networks for Medical Images

Issam Elaalyani[✉] and Mohammed Erradi

ENSIAS, University Mohammed V, Rabat, Morocco
issam.elaalyani@um5s.net.ma, erradi@ensias.ma

Abstract. Artificial Neural Networks (ANN) are computing systems made up of a number of interconnected units, which process information by their dynamic states in response to their external inputs. In a sense, ANNs use learning by example technique, as do their biological counterparts. We focuses on leveraging deep learning techniques to retrieve visual data from multimedia contents, especially medical scans. Various deep learning architectures such as convolutional neural network have been applied to fields like computer vision and bioinformatics. In this poster, we explore the existing techniques and the state of the art related to convolutional neural networks and their application to medical images. The objective of this poster is to suggest an adaptable technique and algorithm for efficient objects retrieval.

© Springer International Publishing AG 2016
P.A. Abdulla and C. Delporte-Gallet (Eds.): NETYS 2016, LNCS 9944, p. 382, 2016.
DOI: 10.1007/978-3-319-46140-3

IoT for Livestock Monitoring in the Desert

Younes Driouch[1(✉)], Abdellah Boulouz[1], Mohamed. Ben Salah[1],
and Congduc Pham[2]

[1] LabSIV, Faculty of Science, Ibn ZOHR University, Agadir, Morocco
driouch.younes@gmail.com
[2] LIUPPA, UFR Sciences et Techniques, Pau, France

Abstract. The Internet of things is the combination of multiple technologies such as WSN and RFID in order to create smart networks in charge of data collection and decision-making. Wireless Sensor Network (WSN) is a network made of autonomous nodes (sensors) that collects information about its environment and send it back to a central point (base station, or a sink), WSN has so much potentials and possibilities in automation especially data collection. RFID is a technology that allows a variety of items to be automatically identified through small microchips attached to them. The desert presents some very challenging constraints such as long distances, extreme weather conditions and other man made artificial obstacles. This poster tries to present the main challenges facing the process of creation of IoT driven protocol stacks specific to such environment.

© Springer International Publishing AG 2016
P.A. Abdulla and C. Delporte-Gallet (Eds.): NETYS 2016, LNCS 9944, p. 383, 2016.
DOI: 10.1007/978-3-319-46140-3

Dynamic Clustering Algorithm
for Targets Tracking

Mohamed Toumi[✉], Abderrahim Maizate, Mohammed Ouzzif,
and Med said Salah

RITM-ESTC/CED-ENSEM, University Hassan II, Casablanca, Morocco
m_toumy@yahoo.fr, maizate@hotmail.com,
{ouzzif,salahmedsaid}@gmail.com

Abstract. Target tracking with the wireless sensors networks aims to detect
and to locate a target on its entire path within a region of interest. This application arouses interest in multiple research fields. Wireless sensor networks,
thanks to their versatility, can be used in many hostile and inaccessible environments. However, with a limited energy, they cannot remain permanently
active, which can significantly reduce their lifetime. Forming a clustered network seems an effective mechanism to increase the network's lifetime. We
propose to build optimal dynamic clusters on the target trajectory. In order to
increase energy efficiency, our algorithm integrates for the first time, to our
knowledge, strategies to avoid overlapping clusters and a model to re-activate
the sensors, in the context of targets with high and variable speed.

© Springer International Publishing AG 2016
P.A. Abdulla and C. Delporte-Gallet (Eds.): NETYS 2016, LNCS 9944, p. 384, 2016.
DOI: 10.1007/978-3-319-46140-3

ABAC Model for Collaborative Cloud Services

Mohamed Amine Madani[✉] and Mohammed Erradi

Networking and Distributed Systems Research Group, SIME Lab, ENSIAS,
University Mohammed V, Rabat, Morocco
amine.madani@um5s.net.ma, mohammed.erradi@gmail.com

Abstract. Nowadays, tenants in cloud are more open and collaborative by using collaborative applications. They enable collaboration among users from the same or different tenants of a given cloud provider by using a collaborative session. During such collaboration, the users from one tenant need to access and use resources held by other collaborating tenants. In this context, access control is an important issue that should be addressed and well enforced. This poster proposes a Collaborative Session Attribute-Based Access Control CS-ABAC model to ensure access control to the shared resources in a collaborative session with cross-tenant trust. The suggested CS-ABAC model is an extended version of ABAC, in which the collaborative session is added in order to support the collaboration in multi tenant environments. This model is more flexible and more powerful to describe complex, fine-grained access control rules, which is especially suitable for the multi-tenants environments. Finally, we validate this approach by an implementation in the open source cloud-computing platform OpenStack.

© Springer International Publishing AG 2016
P.A. Abdulla and C. Delporte-Gallet (Eds.): NETYS 2016, LNCS 9944, p. 385, 2016.
DOI: 10.1007/978-3-319-46140-3

A Review on Big Data and Hadoop Security

Hayat Khaloufi[1(✉)], Abderrahim Beni-Hssane[1],
Karim Abouelmehdi[1], and Mostafa Saadi[2]

[1] LAROSERI laboratory, Computer Science Department, Sciences Faculty,
Chouaïb Doukkali University, El Jadida, Morocco
{hayat.khaloufi,karim.abouelmehdil}@gmail.com,
abenihssane@yahoo.fr
[2] Département Informatique & Télécoms, ENSA, Université Hassan 1er – Settat,
Khouribga, Morocco
saadi_mo@yahoo.fr

Abstract. Various studies have confirmed that concerns on data security and privacy issues remains the main obstacle for adopting big data technologies by companies. The general public is also increasingly aware and sensitive to these issues. In this poster, we discuss the big data and the Hadoop ecosystem and the difficulty to maintain the Big Data privacy and security. Then, we present the big data privacy and security approaches suggested in the literature in terms of data and Hadoop Architecture. For these reasons, this poster briefs about Hadoop project and presents its security level and threats, and presents the proposed methods to make a Hadoop cluster more secure. Finally, we suggest an approach to increase Hadoop security and privacy.

© Springer International Publishing AG 2016
P.A. Abdulla and C. Delporte-Gallet (Eds.): NETYS 2016, LNCS 9944, p. 386, 2016.
DOI: 10.1007/978-3-319-46140-3

Performance Analysis of Black Hole Attack in VANET

Badreddine Cherkaoui[1]([⊠]), Abderrahim Beni-hssane[1],
and Mohammed Erritali[2]

[1] LAROSERI laboratory, Computer Science Department, Sciences Faculty,
Chouaïb Doukkali University, El Jadida, Morocco
b.cherkaoui@ucd.ac.ma, abenihssane@yahoo.fr
[2] TIAD Laboratory, Computer Sciences Department, Sciences and Technics
Faculty, Sultan Moulay Slimane University, Béni Mellal, Morocco
m.erritali@usms.ma

Abstract. A vehicular ad-hoc network (VANET) basically consists of a group of vehicles that communicate with each other through a wireless transmission, and requires no pre-existing management infrastructure. This communication has as main objective, streamlining and safe traffic for drivers. This exchange of information is not always reliable because of several constraints such as the existence of malicious users who aim to falsify the information for self-interests. These constraints are due to the permanent changing of the topology and the high-speed of vehicles. In our poster, we design a mobility model to simulate continuous road traffic with SUMO and MOVE Tool under NS2 simulator to generate a real world simulation. Then, we implemented a Black Hole attack inside this model to give a real aspect to the attack. Besides, we will analyze simulation results to assess the impact of this attack on the network communications in terms of End-to-End Delay and Packet delivery Ratio Metrics. After this analysis, we find that the quality of service (QOS) decreases at a Black Hole attack on a routed environment by AODV.

© Springer International Publishing AG 2016
P.A. Abdulla and C. Delporte-Gallet (Eds.): NETYS 2016, LNCS 9944, p. 387, 2016.
DOI: 10.1007/978-3-319-46140-3

SNA: Detecting Influencers
over Social Networks

Ali Aghmadi[1]([⊠]), Mohammed Erradi[2], and Abdellatif Kobbane[1]

[1] Mobile Intelligent System Research Group, Rabat, Morocco
ali.aghmadi@um5s.net.ma, kobbane@gmail.com
[2] Networking and Distributed Systems Research Group ENSIAS,
University Mohammed V, Rabat, Morocco
mohamed.erradi@gmail.com

Abstract. This poster describes our ongoing research on Social Network Analysis (SNA) and a presentation about influencers' detection and how it is very useful to detect influencers' communities. Yet, massive amounts of networked data challenge many end users who progressively need to access network datasets, to store them, to apply basic network analysis, and then share findings with others. The important feature of SNA is its concentration on the structure of user relationships. Detecting influencers can be useful in tasks such as planning successful advertising strategies and/or political campaigns. This poster shows is a first attempt to present existing approaches and to suggest a model for influencers' detection in social networks such as twitter. We consider as a basic characteristics: Opinion, claims, argumentation, persuasion, agreement, demographics, dialogue, and patterns over a given period of time from tweets or forums.

© Springer International Publishing AG 2016
P.A. Abdulla and C. Delporte-Gallet (Eds.): NETYS 2016, LNCS 9944, p. 388, 2016.
DOI: 10.1007/978-3-319-46140-3

Performance Evaluation of Smart Grid Infrastructures

Zahid Soufiane[1]([⊠]), En-Nouaary Abdeslam[1], and Bah Slimane[2]

[1] Institut National des Postes et Télécommunications (INPT), Rabat, Morocco
zahidsouftane@gmail.com, abdeslam@inpt.ac.ma
[2] Ecole Mohammadia d'Ingénieurs (EMI), Rabat, Morocco
slimane.bah@emi.ac.ma

Abstract. Smart Grid is the next-generation power grid infrastructure for better efficiency, reliability, with possible integration of renewable and alternate energy sources. It takes advantages of two-way communications and the technologies in sensing, computing, and control to achieve real-time monitoring and self-healing. A scalable and pervasive communication infrastructure is crucial in both construction and operation of a Smart Grid. In this poster, we simulate a radial multi-hop topology using Network Simulator 2. We identify the limitations of this chain in terms of data rate, length and packet size. This showed us the necessity of the optimization of Smart Grid networks. We suggest an architecture based on the conceptual models proposed by international organizations, such as, NIST, IEEE and ITU. These models are insufficient to grab the relation between the network components. Our architecture takes into account all the six functionalities that a Smart Grid network must achieve. For each network, we describe the main and the mandatory components, and finally we synthesize the communication technologies that can be used for interconnecting the components and standards.

© Springer International Publishing AG 2016
P.A. Abdulla and C. Delporte-Gallet (Eds.): NETYS 2016, LNCS 9944, p. 389, 2016.
DOI: 10.1007/978-3-319-46140-3

Communities Detection in Social Networks

Imane Tamimi[(✉)] and Mohamed El Kamili

LIMS, FSDM, Sidi Mohammed Ben Abdellah University, Fez, Morocco
{imane.tamimil,mohamed.elkamili}@usmba.ac.ma

Abstract. The research on communities in social networks takes many paths in the literature, among which: the problematic of accurately detecting communities; modelling the evolution of those communities within the evolving network; and finding the patterns that characterize this evolution over time. In our poster, we focus on the problematic of detecting communities in social networks based on the information disseminated among users of the social network and the type of content shared by these users. The poster presents a brief introduction to the subject and the problem definition, then we move to state the main contribution which consists of a multi-layer model to detect communities of users based on the content shared by users, the lowest layer would detect topics of interest of each user while the upper layer would form communities from generated topics. We conclude the poster stating our perspectives and future works.

© Springer International Publishing AG 2016
P.A. Abdulla and C. Delporte-Gallet (Eds.): NETYS 2016, LNCS 9944, p. 390, 2016.
DOI: 10.1007/978-3-319-46140-3

Keyframe Extraction Using Entropy Singular Values

Rachida Hannane[⊠], Abdessamad Elboushaki, and Karim Afdel

Laboratory of Computer Systems and Vision, Faculty of Science,
Ibn Zohr University, Agadir, Morocco
{rachida.hanane08, abdessamad.elboushaki}@gmail.com,
k.afdel@uiz.ac.ma

Abstract. The long-duration videos resulted from movies, sports and surveillance cameras have made a huge amount of video data available. Owing to the complexity in manipulating this large data, limited memory size, higher transmission rate and long processing time, an abstract of the salient keyframes that could cover the overall content of the video is really required. In this poster, we propose a novel approach for keyframe extraction based on the entropy measurement, computed only for the singular values of each frame within the same shot instead of using the entire information of the frame. The frame holding maximum entropy value is extracted as a keyframe of the shot. To make sure that the extracted keyframe deserves to present the entire shot, an entropy-based verification approach is proposed. Specifically, the amount of added information is extracted by computing the difference of the entropy for each two consecutive frames within the same shot. This total amount of added information should be very tenuous compared to the computed entropy of the selected keyframe. The resulted keyframes show a sufficient representation of the video and summarize it in a concise manner with minimum size and less computationally complexity.

© Springer International Publishing AG 2016
P.A. Abdulla and C. Delporte-Gallet (Eds.): NETYS 2016, LNCS 9944, p. 391, 2016.
DOI: 10.1007/978-3-319-46140-3

Autonomous Vehicular Systems Based on Multi Agents

Najoua Ayache[✉], Ali Yahyaouy, and Sabri My Abdelouahed

Sidi Mohamed Ben Abdellah University, Fes, Morocco
{najouaayache92,abdelouahed.sabri}@gmail.com,
ayahyaouy@yahoo.fr

Abstract. Since the 21st century, vehicles have attracted a great interest due to their potential usage for transportation of people and goods. The initial concerns of industrials and researchers were that radio-equipped vehicles are able to keep the drivers informed about risks and road conditions. However, recent researches focus more on providing the drivers with more comfort and less effort. For instance, air-conditioning, automatic features, GPS, etc., ensure the quality of service for the users. In this poster, we present an overview of existing self-driving vehicles and we propose an autonomous vehicular system based on multi-agents to reduce the complexity of the system. In fact, we aim to delegate each function (communication, specification of goals and execution of actions) to agents that communicate with each other to perform the tasks listed in a pre-defined order.

© Springer International Publishing AG 2016
P.A. Abdulla and C. Delporte-Gallet (Eds.): NETYS 2016, LNCS 9944, p. 392, 2016.
DOI: 10.1007/978-3-319-46140-3

The Integration of Multi-homing in 5G Networks

Salma Ibnalfakih[✉], Essaid Sabir, and Mohammed Sadik

NEST Research Group, ENSEM, Hassan II University of Casablanca,
Casablanca, Morocco
ibnalfakih.salma@gmail.com,
{e.sabir,m.sadik}@ensem.ac.ma

Abstract. The idea of using multiple access links, called multi-homing, to improve the aggregate bandwidth and the availability of Internet connectivity is a key paradigm for the 5G wireless networks. Using multi-homing to spread a user's Internet traffic simultaneously among multiple access links, even via multiple ISPs, can increase the aggregate throughput, and diverts traffic away from non-functional links in a HetNet system. This makes the multi-homing pattern convenient for the 5G standardization since it is expected to undertake the HetNet environment. The 5G paradigm aims to: reach 10 Gbps peak data rate; allow a variety of M2M services and adopt D2D communications. In this poster, we study the multi-homing integration in D2D communications to allow many devices to communicate directly and simultaneously over a D2D instead of the network infrastructure. This situation is valuable from a network and spectral efficiency perspective. In order to integrate this kind of communication in the overall 5G-system design, we focus on the question of how the mode selection between D2D and the device-infrastructure-device communication should ideally be conducted.

© Springer International Publishing AG 2016
P.A. Abdulla and C. Delporte-Gallet (Eds.): NETYS 2016, LNCS 9944, p. 393, 2016.
DOI: 10.1007/978-3-319-46140-3

Author Index